EUROPEAN UNION NON-DISCRIMINATION LAW AND INTERSECTIONALITY

European Union Non-Discrimination Law and Intersectionality

Investigating the Triangle of Racial, Gender and Disability Discrimination

Edited by

DAGMAR SCHIEK
University of Leeds, UK

and

ANNA LAWSON
University of Leeds, UK

ASHGATE

Published by
Ashgate Publishing Limited
Wey Court East
Union Road
Farnham
Surrey, GU9 7PT
England

Ashgate Publishing Company
Suite 420
101 Cherry Street
Burlington
VT 05401-4405
USA

www.ashgate.com

British Library Cataloguing in Publication Data
European Union non-discrimination law and intersectionality :
   investigating the triangle of racial, gender and
   disability discrimination.
   1. Discrimination--Law and legislation--European Union
   countries. 2. Equality before the law--European Union
   countries.
   I. Schiek, Dagmar. II. Lawson, Anna.
   342.2'4087-dc22

Library of Congress Cataloging-in-Publication Data
European Union non-discrimination law and intersectionality : investigating the triangle of racial, gender and disability discrimination / by Dagmar Schiek and Anna Lawson.
      p. cm.
   Includes bibliographical references and index.
   ISBN 978-0-7546-7980-6 (hbk) -- ISBN 978-0-7546-9947-7 (ebk)
1. Discrimination--Law and legislation--European Union countries. 2. Equality before the law--European Union countries. 3. Discrimination--European Union countries. 4. Discrimination--Law and legislation--Europe. 5. Equality before the law--Europe. 6. Discrimination--Europe. I. Schiek, Dagmar. II. Lawson, Anna.
   KJE5142.E839 2011
   342.2408'5--dc22

2010038023

ISBN 9780754679806 (hbk)
ISBN 9780754699477 (ebk)

Reprinted 2012

Printed and bound in Great Britain by the
MPG Books Group, UK

Contents

List of Contributors

Ayse Idil Aybars, Research Fellow at the Center for European Studies of the Middle East Technical University, Ankara.

Susanne Burri, Senior Lecturer in Gender and Law, University of Utrecht, Board Member of Dutch handbooks on equal treatment and European labour law and Co-ordinator of the European Network of Legal Experts in the field of Gender Equality (European Commission).

Isabelle Carles, Researcher at the Interdisciplinary Research Group 'Gender and Migration' of the Free University of Brussels, Coordinator of GendeRace – The Use of Anti-Discrimination Law: Gender and Citizenship in a Multicultural Society.

Theresia Degener, Professor of Law and Disability Studies in the Department of Social Work at the Protestant University of Applied Sciences, Bochum, Germany and Extraordinary Professor of Law in the Faculty of Law at the University of the Western Cape, South Africa.

Stephanie Fehr, PhD candidate in Non-Discrimination and Employment Law, School of Law, University of Manchester.

Suzanne B. Goldberg, Clinical Professor of Law, Director of Sexuality and Gender Law Clinic, and Co-Director of the Programme in Gender and Sexuality Law at the Columbia Law School, USA.

Erica Howard, Senior Lecturer in Law, Middlesex University and Participant in the EU project GendeRace – The Use of Anti-Discrimination Law: Gender and Citizenship in a Multicultural Society.

Stergios Kofinis, PhD candidate in Constitutional Law at the Aristotle University, supported by the Alexander S. Onassis Public Benefit Foundation.

Eleonore Kofman, Professor of Gender, Migration and Citizenship and Co-Director of the Social Policy Research Centre at Middlesex University, London. Participant in the EU project GendeRace – The Use of Anti-Discrimination Laws: Gender and Citizenship in Multicultural Society, and GEMMA: Enhancing Evidence-Based Policy Making in Gender and Migration.

Kristina Koldinská, Lecturer (JUDr.) at the Charles University, Prague, Czech Republic, Assistant Professor, Chair of Labour Law and Social Security.

Anna Lawson, Senior Lecturer at the School of Law, University of Leeds and member of the Centre for European Law and Legal Studies and Centre for International Governance.

Gay Moon, Solicitor and Independent Adviser on equality law policy for the Equality and Diversity Forum, Joseph Rowntree Charitable Trust Fellow, Director and former Chair of the Discrimination Law Association.

Jule Mulder, PhD candidate at School of Law, University of Leeds, member of the Centre for European Law and Legal Studies.

Kevät Nousiainen, LLS, Professor Department of Criminal Law, Procedural Law and Gender, University of Helsinki and Professor, Jurisprudence, Faculty of Law, University of Turku.

Lynn Roseberry, Head of Department, Department of Law at Copenhagen Business School, Associate Professor, Copenhagen Business School, Denmark.

Dagmar Schiek, Professor of European Law, University of Leeds and Director of the Centre for European Law and Legal Studies, Jean Monnet Chair in European Law.

Iyiola Solanke, Senior Lecturer at the School of Law, University of Leeds, and Visiting Lecturer London School of Economics.

Ulrike M. Vieten, Post-doc Researcher in the project 'Inclusive Thinking' at the Faculty of Social Science, Vrije Universiteit Amsterdam.

Preface

This volume emerged from the Second European Conference on Multidimensional Equality Law, held in Leeds on 29 March 2009. That conference was part of a series of European Conferences on Multidimensional Equality Law designed to provide a forum for critical reflection on legislative and jurisprudential developments in EU equality law – a body of law which has been transformed from one focused on gender equality law into a multi-ground affair with a multiplicity of policy aims. The First European Conference on Multidimensional Equality took place in May 2007 and generated the sister-volume of this book (Schiek and Chege 2009).

The European Commission plays a pivotal role in the development and shaping of EU equality law. As well as proposing relevant legislation and policy initiatives, it provides funding for most of the European level non-governmental organizations working in the field and also for a sizeable proportion of the relevant academic work. It has even paid for another 'First European Conference', the First European Conference on Multiple Discrimination held in December 2007 in Denmark, disseminating the results of a Commission study (European Commission 2007a). The European Conferences on Multidimensional Equality Law base themselves mainly on other funding, and therefore provide a valuable space for critical reflection which is entirely independent of the Commission.

The provision of a forum for independent reflection is important and we would like to express our thanks to those who made it possible for us to offer this by supporting the series of European conferences on multidimensional equality law. We are grateful for the participation of speakers at the first conference, the participation of others who joined only at the stage of the second conference and also for the contributions of some authors who provided chapters only after the second conference in order to make this a comprehensive book rather than simply a collection of conference papers.

Further, sincere thanks are due to several institutions and individuals who contributed to this process. These include the main sponsor of the conference, the British Academy. They also include the School of Law at the University of Leeds, which supported this publication through its strategic development funds (which were used to fund a language check of chapters written by non-native speakers of English). Dr Paul Skidmore's contributions to the editing process again went considerably beyond the language check, for which he was commissioned. Jule Mulder also provided invaluable support with the whole editing process in the summer of 2010. We are extremely grateful for their professionalism and their very hard work.

Dagmar Schiek and Anna Lawson

Introduction

Dagmar Schiek and Anna Lawson

The Context of the Book

The First European Conference on Multidimensional Equality Law (FECMEL) and the sister-volume of this book (Schiek and Chege 2009) addressed the heightened complexity of EU non-discrimination law, caused by the multiplication of the 'discrimination grounds' and the expansion of the material scope of the field as well as the agenda pursued by it. The overall conclusion of the conference, which is also mirrored in the book, can be summarized in three points. First, it is necessary to refocus equality law in order to avoid it becoming trivialized by ever more multiplications of grounds and purposes. Second, new manifestations of disadvantage at the intersections of ethnicity, language, religion and gender have emerged, with the consequence that the situation of Muslim and Romani women in Europe has become a seismograph revealing the effectiveness of the response of EU equality law to intersectional discrimination. Third, the multidimensionality of purposes requires the development of a substantive and inclusive concept of equality law, which addresses the question 'equality of what?'. Such a concept might be a good starting point for a specific European approach towards non-discrimination law, rooted in welfarist traditions and collective approaches to enforcement of rights.

This book is based on a collection of chapters initially delivered at the Second European Conference on Multidimensional Equality Law (SECMEL) in May 2009. This conference, as a first step towards further developing this research agenda, addressed legal and policy responses to intersectional disadvantage in the EU and explored ways of refocusing equality law. Between 2007 and 2009, the international and European profile of disability discrimination was heightened by the EU's commitment to concluding the United Nations Convention on the Rights of Persons with Disabilities (CRPD). Our quest for a way of refocusing EU equality law incorporates this heightened profile, being structured around a triangle of 'race', gender and disability.

This introduction will contextualize the substantive chapters by first introducing briefly a number of contributions to the debate on intersectionality and its appearance in international and European legal frameworks under the heading 'multiple discrimination'. This will be followed by an overview of the book's structure which will include brief summaries of the different contributions.

Intersectionality and the Notion of Multiple Discrimination

In the past few years, the issue of discrimination on more than one ground has been widely debated in socio-legal theory under the term of intersectionality (Grabham et al. 2009; Meenan 2007). The term was first used in this context by legal researcher Kimberlé Crenshaw in a 1989 article focusing on the experiences of black women. She used the picture of an intersection of streets:

> Discrimination, like traffic through an intersection, may flow into one direction and it may flow into another. If an accident happens at an intersection, it can be caused by cars travelling from any number of directions, and, sometimes, from all of them. Similarly, if a black woman is

harmed because she is in the intersection, her injury could result from sex discrimination or race discrimination. (Crenshaw 1989: 145)

This image suggests that disadvantage on the intersection between gender and 'race' is likely to be more severe, just as a car accident is likely to cause more damage when vehicles are travelling from all directions. Thus, the term intersectionality was introduced to refer to the specific situation of black women, which can neither be compared to that of black men, nor to that of white women. Crenshaw criticized both feminist and anti-racist politics, the one for neglecting black women's colour, the other for neglecting their gender. Her concern has been understood as a warning of the need to avoid identity politics (Verloo 2006: 212). Even before Crenshaw coined the term intersectionality, similar phenomena had been debated in Europe under different headings (Vieten 2009: 95–7), as well as in the United States (Hancock 2007). Initially, gender, race and class were regarded as the central vectors around which inequalities evolved (Yuval-Davis 2006: 201). Since then, other intersections, such as the intersection between sexualities and ethnicities and between gender and religion, have been explored, particularly in the context of a critical analysis of the notion of 'race'.

Although the intersectionality debate had its origin in legal discourse, it rapidly developed into a notion used more generally within women's studies, an interdisciplinary field integrating sociology, cultural studies, political and economic science and, to a lesser extent, law. Although the notion may originally have been used in order to develop better law and politics, it soon expanded into other dimensions. In the wake of 'post-modern' social theory, it was increasingly used to theorize identities rather than to criticize identity politics. Intersectionality research became dominated by sociological investigations of law, as a practice that was generally ill-suited to achieve change. 'Modern' intersectionality theory has consequently attracted the criticism that it focused on law as a medium of performing identities, instead of exploring law's potential to contribute to overcoming disadvantage. As Conaghan puts it:

> It is largely within the context of such engagements with law – as a performative process of identity formation – that 'modern' Intersectionality theory takes place. (Conaghan 2009: 39)

Twenty years after its official recognition, the concept of intersectionality is increasingly contested, as *inter alia* witnessed by the emergence of a socio-legal edited collection entitled *Intersectionality and Beyond* (Grabham et al. 2009). The concept has been criticized as being too complex to offer guidance in practical matters (Squires 2008: 55) or as being too rooted in the Anglo-Saxon discourse to be of use in Continental contexts (Rey Martinez 2008: IV). From feminist perspectives, especially in the EU context, the critique has focused on the lack of concern for structural inequality (Verloo 2006: 214–16) and on the danger of submerging the aim of achieving gender equality in other aims (Squires 2008: 55). This latter danger, however, does not seem specifically linked to an acknowledgement of intersectional disadvantage as an element of non-discrimination law. Rather, it is said to be inherent in the specific way in which the European Union has embarked upon the agenda of multiplying grounds on which discrimination is prohibited (Holzleithner 2005). The specific strategy of the EU involves pursuing a nominal agenda of equality of grounds with a hidden practice of establishing hierarchies (Verloo 2006).

Although much of this criticism is undoubtedly justified, it is suggested that intersectionality as a concept can be utilized to do justice in cases of disadvantage at the intersections of gender, 'race' and disability. There is, in fact, evidence that cases of multiple discrimination can be adequately dealt with by courts (Gerards 2007: 172–80), although there is certainly scope for further development of judicial practice, as is discussed in the third part of this book. It is therefore necessary to develop appropriate strategies for bringing intersectionality before the courts (Goldberg 2009: 143–6, and the contributions in the third part of this book) and for raising its profile amongst policy-makers (Kantola and Nousiaien 2009).

The practical relevance of intersectionality is also increasingly acknowledged by UN and EU institutions. These typically use the notion of 'multiple discrimination', which is often considered as an umbrella notion for the different forms of discrimination on more than one ground. Guided by an analysis initially commissioned by the Finish Exterior Ministry (Makkonen 2002: 11–13), it has become usual to distinguish between 'additive' or 'compound' discrimination and intersectional discrimination. The former would signify instances of discrimination on more than one ground, where the role of the different grounds can be distinguished. 'Intersectional' discrimination would refer to discrimination on more than one ground where the influence of those grounds cannot be disentangled. Examples of the latter include the denial of the right to bear children for ethnic minority women or disabled women, and harassment specifically directed against disabled women. Prominent examples for the use of 'multiple discrimination' within policy documents include the Beijing platform for Action for Equality, Development and Peace, issued by the United Nations Fourth World Conference on Women. With this platform, the governments affirm their determination:

> to intensify efforts to ensure equal enjoyment of all human rights and fundamental freedoms for all women and girls who face multiple barriers to their empowerment and advancement because of such factors as their race, age, language, ethnicity, culture, religion or disability or because they are indigenous people. (UN 1995)

Similarly, reports by international organizations which increasingly refer to the problems underlying intersectionality usually use the term 'multiple discrimination'. This notion is also preferred by the European Union itself.

This book nevertheless commits itself to intersectional discrimination because the term multiple discrimination conjures up a mathematical notion of adding disadvantage which is at odds with complex social reality (Conaghan 2009: 24) and supports a tendency to assume a separateness of strands of discrimination, which in reality intersect (Yuval-Davis 2007: 565). We aim to contribute to develop strategies for addressing the reality of those affected by intersectional disadvantage by providing a space for reflection on developments to date as well as for deeper conceptual analysis, and the critical notion of 'intersectionality' is better suited to this task. Our focus is the disadvantage which occurs at the intersections of gender, 'race' and disability. The situation of those who lie at the more privileged or advantaged intersections (e.g. white, non-disabled men) is therefore not investigated here.

The Structure and Contents of the Book

The book is divided into four parts. Part I assembles four chapters which reflect on the three central nodes of 'race', gender and disability from social, legal and theoretical perspectives. Part II provides various comparative perspectives on problems of intersectionality by detailing developments in a number of different countries. In Part III, three authors develop proposals which should enable courts to better address disadvantage at the intersection between 'race', gender and disability. In the fourth part three chapters evaluate current development in EU law on intersectionality.

In Chapter 1, Dagmar Schiek opens the debate by proposing a new way of organizing the socio-legal field of EU non-discrimination law and policy. She draws attention to the risks associated with the multiplication of discrimination grounds such as a dilution of non-discrimination law and disproportionate attention being given to some grounds due to their novelty. Schiek identifies three pivotal 'nodes' around which all grounds can be conceptually clustered – the nodes of 'race', gender and disability. The nodes are imagined as being linked through overlapping orbits. The concept thus depicts intersections as a rule rather than the exception in equality law. Schiek also explains that the overlap of several nodes indicates greater severity of the intersectional disadvantage and thus mandates a stronger response. It is the structural cohesion provided by these three nodes that provides the underlying organizing principle of this book. The chapter seeks to demonstrate how the node concept permits a focus on key distinctions and an escape from the hierarchies between grounds which have been created by differences in the political strength of the single-issue social movements that pressed for their inclusion in EU non-discrimination law. The chapter also explicates how the node concept offers an adequate response to intersectional disadvantage.

Chapter 2 investigates how disadvantage at the intersection of all three nodes is addressed by legal frameworks of international (UN), European (Council of Europe and EU) and national level. Theresia Degener points to the scarcity of data about the situation of those at the intersections, and provides narrative accounts of the experiences of intersectional disadvantage by disabled women before highlighting potential difficulties in formulating adequate legal responses. She stresses that disability discrimination was recognized much later than race and sex discrimination and thus still seems underdeveloped. The resulting conceptual inconsistencies (such as the fact that reasonable accommodation is generally confined to disability) and their implications for the three different levels of equality law are then explored. In none of these bodies of legislation have the tensions yet been satisfactorily resolved. UN law seems to be furthest progressed – its bodies have issued a number of recommendations on intersectional discrimination against women, and the recent Convention on the Rights of Persons with Disabilities includes a specific article on disabled women. By contrast, both the Council of Europe and the European Union still focus primarily on single-axis strategies. In conclusion, Degener demands that intersectionality should be included within anti-discrimination law and not be merely left to new governance mechanisms such as positive duties, as the agency of those affected by intersectional disadvantage is of paramount importance.

While Degener argues from a legal action perspective in order to enhance rights for disabled women, Anna Lawson, in Chapter 3, approaches the phenomenon of intersectionality from the perspective of disability studies. She explores the under-researched and under-regulated intersection of disability and 'race'. In the tradition of critical disability studies, she distinguishes between 'impairment' as a physical, psychological and mental individual characteristic potentially restricting functionality, and 'disability' as a form of exclusion rooted in socio-economic factors that operate on people labelled as having 'impairments'. Lawson explores the way in which poverty (to which disproportionate numbers of people from minority ethnic groups are exposed in many countries) increases the likelihood of impairment and the way in which racism sometimes operates to make it more likely that people from such backgrounds will be labelled as having an 'impairment' than would people from the majority ethnic group. The chapter then identifies key forms of disadvantage experienced by people from ethnic minorities who have or are simply labelled as having an impairment. This is followed by a critical analysis of concepts in EU law which are aimed principally at disability and considers their potential to tackle disadvantage at the disability–race intersection. Lawson goes on to criticize the absence of positive duties from

EU non-discrimination law, and demands that such duties should be introduced and used to tackle disadvantage at the intersection between ethnicity and disability.

While Chapters 2 and 3 highlight the neglected corner of the triangle framed by race and gender and disability, Ulrike Vieten in Chapter 4 responds to the challenge to analyse race and gender as fuzzy concepts. Startled by a tendency of officialdom in Continental Europe to prefer the term 'ethnicity' over the term 'race', she traces the genealogy of the two categories from a critical feminist perspective. Vieten criticizes the reluctance to admit the ongoing effects of institutionalized Whiteness in the social fabric of Continental Europe. She argues that there is a strong division between a predominantly Anglo-American critical debate on race and racism on the one hand, and a Continental European one that uses ethnicity, a fundamentally gendered and culturalizing term, on the other. Nonetheless, she exposes the racialization processes underlying the definition of ethnicity, for example when the place of birth or a belonging to one of the Christian religions become decisive for ethnicity. The recurrence of this culturalization discourse also has a sexist dimension in that it reduces all women to a function of markers of boundaries between ethnic or religious minorities and the dominant culture. Culturalization thus underlines the gender dimensions of racialization discourses. Vieten concludes that the different streams of colonial skin colour racism and contemporary culturalized anti-Muslim racism illustrate various forms of racism that have to be understood against the background of a complex archive of European racisms.

Part II offers comparative perspectives. It is opened by Chapter 5 with a comparison between the situations of disabled women in Turkey, not (yet) a Member State of the EU, and France. Ayse Idil Aybars uses the EU non-discrimination acquis and the respective national welfare state arrangements as comparative parameters. Welfare state arrangements are seen to include gender equality regimes as well as regimes for inclusion of vulnerable groups, such as disabled people. France is an atypical representative of the conservative continental welfare model, combining active inclusion policies with high levels of female employment, while Turkey is a representative of the Southern welfare model, relying on familial support networks with corresponding low levels of female employment. As regards equality regimes, both states are similar in their republican tradition. Equality is seen as a general principle, unconnected to groups. While gender equality features more highly in recent years, other equalities are not specifically supported. Only in France has recent impact of EU directives led to the emergence of multidimensional approaches (which is experienced as alien to republican values). Aybars concludes that the different welfare traditions are decisive for higher levels of inclusion of disabled women in France, while intersectional disadvantage is not adequately dealt with in either of the two countries.

Susanne Burri in Chapter 6 offers an analysis of opinions by the Dutch Equal Treatment Commission (ETC) on cases involving discrimination on more than one ground. Her concern, given the recent critique of the concept by Conaghan, is whether an intersectional approach is useful in practice. The practical section offers a wide array of examples of intersectional and multiple discrimination, including intersections between ethnicity and disability, ethnicity and religion, and religion and gender. In her analytical evaluation, Burri takes a pragmatic approach, arguing that 'efforts demanded by intersectional analysis should ... be proportional to the added value ... first'. She concludes that the main added value of using intersectional analysis in practice is to depict accurately the experiences of victims of discrimination, even if their claims are rejected.

In Chapter 7, on reactions in France and Germany to women wearing headscarves in schools, Stephanie Fehr uses different national experiences as illustrations of the stereotypes with which Muslim women wearing headscarves are confronted ('intersectional prejudice'). The stereotypes of the French Stasi Commission are analysed in detail, as are attitudes among German judiciary and policy-makers. Like Burri, Fehr considers headscarf-related discrimination to be situated at the intersection of race/ethnicity, gender and religion. Additional dimensions, consistent with the central 'nodes' framework of this book, can be derived from accounts which capture the 'racialization' of Islam (Schiek, in this volume; Vieten, in this volume). Fehr provides some evidence of such racialization. She further exposes the paternalistic attitudes underlying the headscarf debate and characterizes them as being 'against the interests of women'.

Stergios Kofinis, in Chapter 8, discusses the position of Muslim minority women in Greece, providing another national illustration of the 'race' node: the construction of citizenship in the Greek constitution which results in an intricate web of religious, ethnic and cultural allegiances. The historical account of Greek politics towards the Minority of Thrace reveals an early example of multiculturalism in the most negative sense. Kofinis highlights the tension between individual and group rights, which he considers as insurmountable. The particular status of the Muslim minority in Greece seems not only to smother different cultural traditions within the group, but also to consign women within this minority to a status deprived of the protection of rights, in particular as regards family law and inheritance. Against this negative backdrop, the author also traces some incremental developments towards acknowledging 'Muslim minority women as a social group standing at the intersection of discrimination'.

In Chapter 9, Kevät Nousiainen analyses yet another constellation of disadvantage at the intersection of being female and belonging to a minority ethnic group. She also addresses intersections between non-discrimination rights and social and cultural rights. Her chapter examines the implications for mothers of a lack of provision of children's daycare in minority languages. The underlying problem, which has been reviewed under the CEDAW and under Finnish discrimination legislation, is elaborated against a unique national background. Finland, having joined the Council of Europe only in the late 1980s and the EU only in 1995, had developed a regime for its diverse population based on more 'eastern' traditions. As a consequence, minority protection, including protection of linguistic minorities, has a much longer tradition than anti-discrimination rights. This results in a tendency to preserve the identities of groups, and this can conflict with the women's rights to engage in extra-familial work in the absence of childcare in minority languages. This national problem highlights the position of women as bearers of culture, which was identified as one of the roots of intersectional disadvantage in Chapter 4.

In Chapter 10, Gay Moon evaluates the recent UK Equality Act 2010 as it responds to intersectional discrimination, contextualizing the new provision on this issue with the British legal and political debate from 1965. She shows that the gradual acceptance of multiple and intersectional discrimination as a problem has developed by reference to debates in the United States and Canada, while EU models were given less attention. The new statutory definition of multiple discrimination is restricted to direct discrimination and to combinations of only two grounds. This approach is evaluated as disappointing in comparison with legislation in Canada and in EU countries such as Romania. However Moon acknowledges that the new legislation is an important first step in the right direction.

Part III turns to practical applications of intersectional analysis, in particular in court procedures. Suzanne Goldberg opens this part with Chapter 11, discussing the contrast between wide acceptance of intersectionality in US academia and judicial discourse and the limited extent of successful intersectional litigation strategies. While recognizing the limitations of any political strategy based solely on litigation, she warns against underestimating the potential of judicial rulings, thus echoing a concern expressed by Degener in Part I. Goldberg identifies four factors that have prevented the US courts from ruling in favour of claimants bringing 'complex claims': cognitive preferences for simplicity, as reflected in the comparative framework for discrimination claims; social salience of familiar categories; single-strand identity-based advocacy and judicial institutional legitimacy, which tends to make courts wary of using complex sociological or even anthropological analysis. In conclusion Goldberg advises those bringing intersectional claims to make them easier and attemp to respond to these inhibiting factors.

Lynn Roseberry, in Chapter 12, also devises litigation strategies for intersectional claims. Her focus is on Muslim women who are excluded on grounds of their religious attire, such as headscarves. Using theories developed in relation to sexual orientation discrimination, she proposes to read these women's anti-discrimination claims as assertions of ethnic minority and gender identities in the face of assimilationalist demands. Investigating the discourses of one English and one Danish case in detail, she exposes assimilationalist paradigms. She considers that these paradigms also underlie the hierarchies of equalities: immutable traits eliciting stronger protection against discrimination than traits an individual can overcome, thus suggesting the stronger protection of identity than of behaviour. Based on socio-psychological research, Roseberry concludes by challenging the distinctions between identity and behaviour. She suggests that courts should take into account identity asserting behaviour as part of protecting identity.

In the last of the chapters in Part III, Chapter 13, Iyiola Solanke explores legal responses to the discrimination (in employment and other spheres of life) experienced by 'corpulent women of colour'. This innovative discussion is set against the alarming backdrop of statistical trends about weight gain – trends which demonstrate that obesity is increasing and that discrimination associated with 'fatphobia' is therefore also likely to become more common. Solanke demonstrates how that discrimination has a greater impact on women than on men and presents evidence suggesting that it has a greater impact on black women than on white women. She considers cases in which such discrimination has been challenged as a form of disability discrimination and questions the appropriateness of regarding excess weight as a disability. Solanke draws attention to the link between social factors and excess weight and to the harmful stigmatization experienced particularly by large black women. In line with her previous work on stigma and intersectionality, Solanke proposes an alternative route to the formulation of a legal remedy for corpulent women of colour in EU law and elsewhere – a route based on stigma and context.

Part IV provides conclusions of the foregoing for EU law and policy. Carles, Howard and Kofman initiate this part by presenting results of comparative and socio-legal research on the gender use of race discrimination legislation in Chapter 14. Their comparison between Bulgaria, France, Germany, Spain, Sweden and the UK encounters the difficulty presented by the contestation of the central notion of 'race' in most of the states under enquiry. The authors engage in a comparative assessment of the notion, reflecting and expanding upon Vieten's analysis in Part I. Further, they identify a lack of data, in particular on intersectional identities, and differences in coverage of single-axis legislation for different grounds as barriers for women in using anti-racist legislation. Despite all these difficulties, they also find that the establishment of a multi-ground framework in response to EU directives also encourages social actors and courts to acknowledge the reality of multiple discrimination. They warn that the detail and also the velocity of these developments will differ greatly in line with different national traditions. To ensure a speedier and more consistent process throughout the EU, they suggest providing explicit protection against multiple discrimination, and also implementing adequate methodologies for addressing these claims.

In Chapter 15, Kristina Koldinská considers the effectiveness of legal and policy responses to the situation of Romani women in the central and eastern European countries. Although constituting a regional problem, the situation of the Roma, and in particular of Romani women, has attracted intense attention internationally and at EU level, where a specific directive addressing their situation has been debated. Koldinská provides a legal action perspective on and careful analysis of existing legislation. She concludes that existing EU law can be interpreted to include multiple discrimination in principle, but also notes that there is no practical experience in this direction as yet. Thus, she too proposes the creation of explicit rules on multiple discrimination, though she warns against an overly detailed legislative definition of the concept. She concludes that a combination of law and policy is needed to activate social rights in favour of Romani women. Thus she supports the recently initiated open method of coordination (OMC) on Roma inclusion as the way forward.

In the final chapter, Dagmar Schiek and Jule Mulder provide a critique of EU legal and policy developments with relevance to intersectional discrimination and call for further legislative action. The chapter begins with an overview and analysis of key EU level developments. This is followed by a discussion of ways in which intersectional and other discrimination is tackled by different national legal orders. In a section on comparative socio-legal structures and approaches, attention is then drawn to the pragmatic incremental approach to legal development which characterizes common law systems and to the more systemic approach favoured by civil law countries. The authors explain that, in the field of EU non-discrimination law, the common law approach has been particularly influential and suggest that this helps to explain the current differences in levels of protection afforded to different grounds by the various directives. They call for a systemic legislative EU response to the problem of intersectional disadvantage and argue that attempting to address it in a directive which covers only some of the grounds will only exacerbate the problem. The solution they propose is a new directive dealing with intersectional disadvantage across all the non-discrimination grounds.

PART I
Discrimination Grounds and Intersectionality: A Reappraisal

Chapter 1

Organizing EU Equality Law Around the Nodes of 'Race', Gender and Disability

Dagmar Schiek

Introduction

The closing debate of the First European Conference on Multidimensional Equality Law highlighted a concern that EU non-discrimination and equality law may no longer be sufficiently focused on differences that make a difference (that is, on inequalities that matter). This concern derived from the proliferation of grounds in relation to which discrimination is prohibited.

The proliferation of discrimination grounds may, in itself, have positive effects on the field of equality law, through, *inter alia*, the enhanced potential of cases where several grounds are involved. It will lead to an increase in situations covered by non-discrimination law. Ever more people will believe that they can turn to equality law to right the wrongs which they perceive themselves to suffer. This will enhance public awareness of the field, and its protagonists will be perceived as more important. However, ever greater proliferation of discrimination grounds may also have negative effects. The widely criticized hierarchy of equalities in EU law is but one example. Another less obvious problem is the refocusing of cases closely related to the socio-economic realities of the 'classical' grounds, such as gender or 'race', to grounds such as age and sexual orientation, which may appear more interesting due to their novelty. Above all, a proliferation of discrimination grounds may well result in equality law becoming a more disorganized socio-legal field.

This chapter proposes to restructure the field by organizing discrimination grounds around nodes. First, it will consider the proliferation of discrimination grounds in EU equality law. It will then highlight the opportunities and dangers of proliferation, exposing the risk of unjustified hierarchies and the redefinition of equality cases in line with the most recent ground. As an alternative approach to structure the field, the concept of nodes will be developed. A comprehensive reading of the overlapping grounds of gender, 'race' and disability will be mapped out, which allows also a distinction to be maintained between equality law and policy, on the one hand, and general human rights and welfarist policies, on the other hand.

Proliferation of Grounds in EU Equality Law – from Rome to Lisbon

Is there a Proliferation of Discrimination Grounds?

If we consider only EU law, proliferation seems obvious. Originally, the Treaty founding the European Economic Community prohibited gender discrimination only in the field of equal pay and discrimination on grounds of nationality within the scope of the Treaty's application. In both fields, secondary law was used to expand the scope of application and to specify certain issues.[1] Only in 1997, when the Treaty of Amsterdam entered into force, was the European Community empowered to legislate to combat discrimination on grounds of sex, racial or ethnic origin, religion or belief, disability, age or sexual orientation (Article 13 EC (Treaty of Rome, as amended now: Article 19 Treaty on the Functions of the European Union (TFEU)). Binding secondary legislation followed from 2000.[2] If we consider 'race'/ethnic origin and religion/belief each as one ground, this body of law now encompasses six instead of only two discrimination grounds. In addition, non-discrimination has been used as a regulatory paradigm in directives concerning part-time work,[3] fixed-term contracts[4] and most recently temporary agency work,[5] adding three new discrimination grounds to employment law. Finally, the Treaty of Lisbon has introduced a new dimension to proliferation. Article 21 of the Charter of Fundamental Rights of the European Union, now legally binding (Article 6(1) TEU (Treaty on European Union)), addresses discrimination on grounds 'such as' colour, social origin, genetic features, language, political or any other opinion, membership of a national minority, property and birth in addition to the Treaty grounds. In contrast to the secondary legislation already mentioned, Article 21 is addressed only to public bodies of the EU and those of the Member States when implementing EU law (Article 51 Charter). Thus, there is some variation in the reach of non-discrimination law. Of the 17 grounds, nine apply in the marketplace, of which only three (race, gender and nationality) reach beyond employment, while eight grounds apply only in the public sphere.

---

1   Directives on gender equality were first adopted in the mid-1970s, most importantly: Council Directive 75/117/EEC on the approximation of the laws of the Member States relating to the application of the principle of equal pay for men and women [1975] OJ L45/19 and Council Directive 76/207/EEC on the implementation of the principle of equal treatment for men and women as regards access to employment, vocational training and promotion, and working conditions [1976] OJ L39/40. These have now been consolidated in Directive 2006/54/EC of the European Parliament and of the Council on the implementation of the principle of equal opportunities and equal treatment of women and men in matters of employment and occupation [2006] OJ L204/23, which has recently been complemented by Directive 2010/41/EC of the European Parliament and of the Council on the application of the principle of equal treatment between women and men engaged in an activity in a self-employed capacity and repealing Council Directive 86/613/EEC. Beyond employment law, there is Council Directive 2004/113/EC implementing the principle of equal treatment between men and women in the access to and supply of goods and services [2004] OJ L373/37. Nationality discrimination was first addressed in regulations governing the free movement of workers (in particular Council Regulation 1612/68/EEC on freedom of movement for workers within the Community [1968] OJ English Special Edition (II) 475), and this body of law has now been consolidated in directives concerning rights to recognition of professional qualifications (in particular Directive 2005/36/EC of the European Parliament and the Council on the recognition of professional qualifications [2005] OJ L255/22) and a number of directives on access to specific professions and recognition of diplomas, too numerous to mention here. In both fields, case law concerning primary law continues to play an important practical role.

2   Council Directive 2000/43/EC implementing the principle of equal treatment between persons irrespective of racial or ethnic origin [2000] OJ L180/22 and Council Directive 2000/78/EC establishing a general framework for equal treatment in employment and occupation [2000] OJ L303/16 (covering age, disability, religion and belief and sexual orientation). The implementation deadline for both directives expired in 2003.

3   Council Directive 97/81/EC concerning the Framework Agreement on part-time work concluded by UNICE, CEEP and the ETUC [1998] OJ L14/9, as amended.

4   Council Directive 1999/70/EC concerning the framework agreement on fixed-term work concluded by ETUC, UNICE and CEEP [1999] OJ L175/43.

5   Directive 2008/104/EC of the European Parliament and the Council on temporary agency work [2008] OJ L327/9.

Proliferation is less pronounced in European and international human rights law. The European Convention on Human Rights (ECHR) contains an equality clause addressed to States in Article 14.[6] That provision, although dating from a similar period to the EEC Treaty, contains 11 discrimination grounds (sex, race, colour, language, religion, political or other opinion, national or social origin, association with a national minority, property, birth or other status) instead of only two. While the European Social Charter 1961 only mentioned discrimination in its preamble, the Revised European Social Charter (1996) reiterates Article 14 ECHR (Article G). In both instruments, inclusion of the 'other status' ground means that the list is not closed, and grounds of similar weight can be added if relevant to an individual case. For example, the European Court of Human Rights (ECtHR) has acknowledged sexual orientation as a relevant 'other status' since 1999.[7] The practical relevance of the long list of grounds is diminished by the fact that the ECHR is binding only on signatory states. While there is some scope for judicial development of indirect horizontal effects, the ECtHR only oversees complaints against signatory states and, thus, is unable to create direct horizontal effects (de Witte 2009: 518).

At a global level, the UN is committed by Article 1 of the UN Charter to 'respect for human rights and for fundamental freedoms for all without distinction as to race, sex, language, or religion'. Going beyond these four discrimination grounds, the International Covenant on Civil and Political Rights (ICCPR) and the International Covenant on Economic, Social and Cultural Rights (ICESCR) contain exactly the same list of grounds as the ECHR, including the 'other status' ground. ILO Convention No. 111 lists 'race, colour, sex, religion, political opinion, national extraction or social origin' as non-discrimination grounds relevant to employment, omitting the 'other status' ground.

The UN has extended protection on three grounds by specific conventions: the 1965 UN Convention for the Elimination of all forms of Racial Discrimination (CERD) assembles under the notion of 'racial discrimination' any distinction, exclusion or restriction based on race, colour, descent, national origin or ethnic origin. The 1979 Convention for the Elimination of all Forms of Discrimination Against Women (CEDAW) addresses discrimination of women. The 2007 UN Convention on the Rights of Persons with Disabilities (CRPD), while not restricted to providing cover against discrimination,[8] also targets discrimination on grounds of disability (Article 2), specifying that persons with long-term impairments are included under that notion (Article 1(2)). All three conventions oblige signatory states to extend protection against discrimination from the purely public sphere towards private actors and the marketplace (Article 2(1)(d) CERD, Article 2(e) and Article 14 CEDAW, and Article 4(1)(e) CRPD). This explicit obligation can be understood as an expansion of obligations under the ICCPR and the ICESCR, which also oblige signatory states to grant the rights entailed therein without discrimination and to refrain from discrimination. Without

---

6   This article initially only applied in relation to the substantive rights granted by the ECHR. Following the adoption of Protocol No 12 to the Convention, which entered into force on 1 April 2007, Article 14 ECHR now operates as a free-standing equality clause.

7   In *Salgueiro da Silva Mouta v. Portugal* (ECHR 1999-IX), the ECtHR first acknowledged that distinctions on grounds of sexual orientation are, in principle, unacceptable. In *L. and V. v. Austria* (ECHR 2003-I) the court stressed that only very weighty reasons could justify such distinctions, thus elevating discrimination on grounds of sexual orientation to the same level of scrutiny as sex and birth out of wedlock and, arguably, also 'race'. On sex and birth, see Gerards (2007: 90).

8   According to Article 1, it aims to 'promote, protect and ensure the full and equal enjoyment of all human rights and fundamental freedoms by all persons with disabilities, and to promote respect for their inherent dignity'.

going into the complex issue of horizontal effects of international human rights conventions,[9] it is safe to assume that the possibility for UN conventions to produce horizontal effects is limited as with the ECHR. Even ILO conventions, notwithstanding their focus on employment law, do not go beyond obliging signatory states to act within this sphere. Similarly, the ICESCR, also covering fields governed by market forces in many states, aims to produce changes in the market through state activities, without giving rise to horizontal effects.

Thus, proliferation has differing dimensions. International and European human rights law has always addressed more grounds and in particular also covered class-related discrimination, as evidenced by the grounds of social origin and property. Also, UN conventions such as the ICCPR and ICESCR and at a European level the ECHR have traditionally provided for the subsequent (judicial) development of their discrimination grounds through the existence of an 'other status' ground. Developments such as the CRPD or case law expanding protection to discrimination on grounds of sexual orientation would appear to qualify as intensifying and clarifying protection always inherent in UN or ECHR law. Proliferation is more typical for the EU. Forced to make any expansion of discrimination grounds explicit by the absence of the 'other status' ground, it has expanded from originally only two to the current 17 grounds. Its list encompasses sexual orientation, age and disability, not explicitly embraced by the Council of Europe instruments, and it uses non-discrimination principles also in relation to part-time, fixed-term and agency work. From 2009, the EU Charter of Fundamental Rights reproduces all the grounds found in international human rights law, including 'other status' (with the wording 'grounds such as'), but this wider protection applies only in relation to public actors. This development is atypical for the EU whose equality law focuses on the marketplace, in line with the original economic aims of the organization.

Is Proliferation of Discrimination Grounds Problematic?

Negative consequences of proliferation may result from distinctions between grounds. Also, increased political attention towards 'new' grounds may not always reflect the parameters most relevant to individual cases.

Any system of non-discrimination law addressing more than one ground has to resolve the question whether a difference in treatment on any particular ground always warrants the same legal reaction. Recently, the suggestion has been made that 'the various grounds of discrimination differ substantively, and each demands a tailored response. This is not a question of creating a hierarchy between the various grounds, but of delivering the most appropriate form of protection for each of them' (European Commission 2008a: 5). This statement is correct in so far as no inherent reason exists to treat all grounds identically. However, different treatment of different grounds may also

---

9   In brief, this issue has three dimensions. First, is the question whether international human rights instruments such as the ICCPR and the ICESCR are directly binding on non-state actors such as multinational companies. This is highly disputed (Knox 2008: 28–31 on the current law, 31–43 on draft human rights instruments). Second, is the question whether there can be indirect horizontal effects. Such effects can derive from interpreting national legislation governing parties in horizontal relations in the light of human rights law (Knox 2008: 67). Third, is the question whether signatory states have an obligation under international human rights law to protect individuals against infringements of the actual enjoyment of human rights in horizontal relations. Through the notion of a 'duty to protect', such an obligation has more recently been put forward in official documents in relation to the ICESCR (see UN Doc. E/C.12/2005/3 General Comment No 16 (2005) Article 3 The Equal Right of Men and Women to the Enjoyment of All Economic, Social and Cultural Rights, para. 17). Such obligations have led the committees supervising CERD and CEDAW to hold signatory states to their explicit obligation to enact horizontal non-discrimination law (Vandenhole 2005: 192–6 (CERD). The discussion in the main text focuses on positive obligations to create private law remedies against discrimination in the marketplace.

lead to different levels of protection, in other words, to hierarchies. Critique of hierarchies has partly focused on different treatment of grounds (ibid.: 4), and in particular on a tendency to downgrade of gender equality,[10] without denying the need for some differentiation between different grounds (Pitt 2007: 227–8; Schiek 2002a: 308–11).

Primary EU law still only grants directly effective non-discrimination rights on two grounds, gender and nationality, that is, the nationality of a Member State. In both cases, the prohibition of discrimination has a limited scope of application, extending as regards gender only to employees' remuneration (Article 157 TFEU = ex Article 141 EC) and as regards nationality to activities within the internal market (Articles 45, 49 and 56 TFEU = ex Articles 39, 43 and 49 EC) and concerning citizenship (Article 18 TFEU = ex Article 12 EC). Programmatic Treaty norms continue to grant a prominent position to gender. The EU aims to 'promote equality between women and men', but only to 'combat discrimination' on the other grounds (Article 3(3) TEU). Throughout all its activities, it is committed to eliminate inequalities and to promote equality between women and men (Article 8 TFEU = ex Article 3(2) EC), but only to combating discrimination based on sex and all the other grounds (Article 10 TFEU).

EU non-discrimination directives establish different hierarchies. First, the scope of the non-discrimination prohibition differs between grounds. Directive 2000/43 on race discrimination goes beyond the fields of employment and occupation, in which secondary sex equality law traditionally applied. Its scope extends to include healthcare, social advantages, education and access to and supply with goods and services available to the public. The gap in protection compared with gender equality was partly redressed by Directive 2004/113 on equality between women and men in access to and supply of goods and services. However, the latter directive does not cover education, social advantages and healthcare and has a narrower definition of goods and services available to the public than Directive 2000/43.[11] A clear hierarchy exists also between race discrimination and discrimination on grounds of sexual orientation, religion and belief, disability and age as prohibited by Directive 2000/78 (Employment Framework Directive), with the latter applying only to employment and occupation. The Employment Framework Directive neglects also the important field of social security, where sex discrimination is prohibited by Directive 79/7,[12] and denies protection in the fields of education, social advantages, health care beyond social security and access to and supply with goods and services. The EU Commission's proposal for a new directive (European Commission 2008b) aims to close this gap between 'race' and the other four 'new grounds' (sexual orientation, religion and belief, disability and age). Adoption of this directive would complicate the field further, adding yet another definition of access to and provision of goods and services available to the public. The prohibition on race discrimination would continue to have the widest scope, while gender would be relegated to the bottom of the hierarchy, as

---

10   This has been a theme in writings originating from several Member States. See, for example, from the Netherlands, Veldman (2001) and Holtmaat (2003), from Austria, Holzleithner (2005), from the UK, Bell and Waddington (2001) and from Germany, Schiek (2002a).

11   Contrast Directive 2000/43, Article 3(1) ('this Directive shall apply in relation to: … access to and supply of goods and services which are available to the public, including housing') with Directive 2004/113, Article 3(1) and (2) ('this Directive shall apply to all persons who provide goods and services, which are available to the public irrespective of the person concerned … and which are offered outside the area of private and family life and the transactions carried out in this context. 2. This Directive does not prejudice the individual's freedom to choose a contractual partner').

12   Council Directive 79/7/EEC on the progressive implementation of the principle of equal treatment for men and women in matters of social security [1979] OJ L6/24.

discrimination against women in the fields of education, social advantages and health (outside of social security) would not be addressed by EU law.[13]

Second, hierarchies in levels of protection are established by granting a wider array of justifications and exceptions in relation to some grounds. For example, the Framework Directive includes an unprecedented exception in favour of public security, authorizing Member States to allow discrimination on the grounds, *inter alia*, of religion for those purposes. Furthermore, the Framework Directive establishes a specific regime of exceptions from the prohibitions on discrimination on grounds of religion and belief, disability and age.

Finally, the specific provisions requiring reasonable accommodation to be provided only for persons with disabilities can be read as granting a greater level of protection against this specific form of discrimination.

These divergences have led Mark Bell (2008b) to label the EU's anti-racism policy with a certain irony as the 'leader of the pack', while others question whether the notion of hierarchies is the best conceptual tool for the problem (Holzleithner 2005). Considered reasoning for these different degrees of protection is absent and, thus, the differences or hierarchies lack, at the very least, a convincing rationality.

A less obvious development resulting from the proliferation of grounds is a redefinition of issues. For example, at the time when discrimination on grounds of sexual orientation was not prohibited, claimants argued that discrimination on grounds of the sex of their partner had to be regarded as sex discrimination. The ECJ was unsympathetic to that view in *Grant*,[14] concerning a denial of benefits to same-sex partners, although in an earlier case[15] it had acknowledged that dismissal on grounds of a change of sex fell within the scope of the prohibition on sex discrimination. More recently, it has characterized the denial of a survivor's pension to a transsexual partner on grounds of their change of sex as sex discrimination.[16] One wonders why the claimants in the first case of sexual orientation discrimination following the implementation of the Framework Directive,[17] also concerning survivors' pensions, did not attempt to frame the issue as sex discrimination in the light of that precedent. Was it ideologically or politically more attractive to frame the case as a matter of sexual orientation discrimination? Or was it seen as a risk to highlight the gender dimension? After all, equal pensions irrespective of gender are a costly issue. Following the judgment in *Sievers and Schrage*[18] concerning pensions for female part-time postal service workers, postal duties in Germany had to rise to fund the additional pension costs. Equalizing the pension rights of the estimated 10 per cent of the population who are homosexual will always be less costly and, thus, perhaps less difficult to establish.

Similarly, the major focus on age discrimination in Kücükdeveci[19] arguably ignored the main socio-economic consequences of the national provisions at issue. In that case, following her dismissal as a result of internal reorganization carried out by her employer, before the first instance Labour Court,[20] Ms Kücükdeveci originally claimed that she had suffered ethnic discrimination.

---

13   Not only 'envious feminists' (Guiraudon 2009) criticize this, but also those involved in campaigning for the proposed directive (Bell 2008a: 9). On the prospects of this proposal to be adopted see Schiek and Mulder (in this volume: 259–74).

14   Case C-249/96 *Grant* [1998] ECR I-621.

15   Case C-13/94 *P v. S* [1996] ECR I-2159.

16   Case C-117/01 *K.B.* [2004] ECR I-541.

17   Case C-267/06 *Maruko* [2008] ECR I-1757.

18   Joined Cases C-270/97 and C-271/97 *Sievers and Schrage* [2000] ECR I-929.

19   Case C-555/07 *Kücükdeveci* of 19 January 2010.

20   Proceedings commenced before the Mönchengladbach Labour Court (judgment of 7 June 2007, 7 Ca 84/07 – available from juris and beck online), and proceeded to the Düsseldorf Regional Labour Court,

Her request to transfer to a sales position in another branch in order to avoid redundancy had been rejected, inter alia, because she spoke German with a Turkish accent. However, as the regional labour court dismissed her claim on the substance of her dismissal, the case then focused on the formal aspects of the statutory minimum notice period which increases in line with length of service. Here, it was alleged that German legislation which disregarded service under the age of 25 for the purposes of calculating the seniority-related minimum notice period infringed the prohibition on age discrimination. In Ms Kücükdeveci's case, upon dismissal after 10 years of employment, she was deemed to have accrued only three years of seniority, because she started employment as a semi-skilled worker aged 18. This is rather typical for ethnic minority women due to the de facto limits on their access to formal education and their need to contribute to the family income. In addition, following dismissal at age 28, in relation to obtaining re-employment, her Turkish descent will be equally as problematic as her gender, as she is in the middle of her child-bearing years. However, before the ECJ, age discrimination alone was debated.

In *Coleman*,[21] too, the judgment appears not to cover all the grounds relevant to the case. This case established the principle that detriment imposed on grounds of association with someone who has a disability (or implicitly any other discrimination ground) will be regarded also as discrimination on grounds of disability. The facts of the case, however, were wrought with gender stereotypes. The female claimant worked as a legal secretary, a field clearly gendered female. She took the main responsibility for a child, while a male parent would typically have relied on the female parent to place her career at risk with such an activity. As her child was disabled, she was subjected to additional disadvantage. Unlike mothers of able-bodied children, she was criticized and even harassed for seeking an adjustment to her working time. Only this additional disadvantage was addressed in the strategic litigation, which, as a consequence, lacked the opportunity to consider the gender dimensions of active parenthood.

As regards 'discrimination' on grounds of part-time and other atypical employment forms, the non-discrimination provisions prevent a focus on indirect discrimination on gender or other grounds. For example, in a recent reference from an Italian court, female part-time workers attempted to claim pension rights on the basis of Directive 97/80, and failed to allege, in addition, sex discrimination contrary to Directive 79/7.[22]

At the level of national law, the numerous cases relating to dress codes for women can be cited as a further example of attention misdirected away from the main exclusionary criterion. Frequently, adverse treatment of women who comply with supposedly religious dress codes is categorized as discrimination on grounds of religion, or even as an infringement of religious freedom. Mainly, this arises in relation to what is often known as the 'Muslim headscarf'.[23] This piece of cloth has been considered an issue of religious freedom by the German Constitutional Court (Sacksofsky 2009a) and by UK courts,[24] and as religious discrimination by the Dutch Equal Treatment Commission.[25] This approach denies the fact that such exclusionary policies mainly affect women who are racialized as belonging to the other, thus mirroring the role of women as bearers of cultural symbols and reinforcing their stigma (Ruwanpura 2008: 94). Interestingly,

---

which made the reference to the ECJ (LAG Düsseldorf, 21 November 2007, 12 Sa 1311/07 LAGE § 622 BGB 2002 Nr 3).

21   Case C-303/06 *Coleman* [2008] ECR I-5603, see also Degener (in this volume: 29–46) and Lawson (in this volume: 47–62).

22   ECJ Joined Cases C-395/08 and C-396/08 *Bruno and Pettini* 10 June 2010.

23   To the knowledge of this author, it is rather unlikely that an inanimate object has a religion.

24   See, for example, *R (Begum) v. Governors of Denbigh High School* [2006] UKHL 15.

25   For example, Equal Treatment Commission (Commissie Gelijke Behandeling) Opinion 2004-112.

against this trend, headscarf cases are viewed as multiple discrimination (Roseberry 2009) or even gender discrimination (Skjeie 2009: 303–4) in Scandinavian jurisdictions.

These examples clearly demonstrate that proliferation of non-discrimination grounds has already had an effect on litigation strategies. These no longer focus on the main socio-economic context in which discrimination arises, but on 'new' equalities. Obviously, this arises for reasons of sound advocacy, as claimants are more likely to be successful in these new fields.[26] However, these cases also demonstrate the latent danger of diluting the socio-economic cause of equality law.

Towards a More Consistent and Principled Approach

The proliferation of discrimination grounds in EU law has quite obviously been poorly handled. The EU legislator created differences in protection which seem to clash with the prominent position the Treaties accord to gender equality.[27] In addition to the problem of generating ill-reasoned hierarchies, successive proliferation of discrimination grounds also leads to heightened attention on the grounds most recently added. This may encourage social actors to redefine problems in terms of the latest ground, thus failing to do justice to the underlying issue. In the light of these difficulties, an alternative principle of organizing equality law is needed.

Nodes as an Organizing Principle of EU Equality Law

As the title of this chapter suggests the notion of 'nodes' is proposed as an alternative organizing principle to hierarchies (see Figure 1.1). The notion of organizing is consciously chosen, avoiding

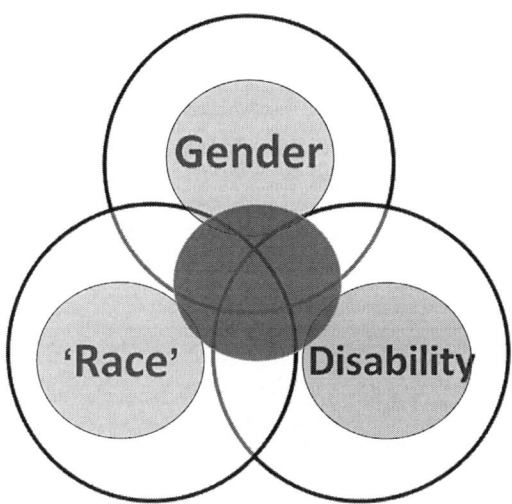

Figure 1.1   Nodes

---

26   This is particularly true in the Member States which acceded in 2004 and 2007 respectively. See Burri and Schiek (2009), in particular reports by Koldinska on the Czech Republic (40) and by Kollonay on Hungary (66–7).

27   This state of affairs is relied upon by feminists in their critique of EU anti-discrimination law (Koukoulis-Spiliotopoulos 2005: 331–4). For a critical perspective see Hepple (2004).

the term 'structuring' which necessarily implies a hierarchy. The idea is to organize the field of non-discrimination law in a heterarchical and not hierarchical manner, around problems solved by this specific body of law and to direct the solution of other problems elsewhere.

Establishing nodes as an organizing principle of EU non-discrimination law aims to regain a certain focus, potentially addressing all the actors involved in shaping the socio-legal field of EU non-discrimination law and policy. The notion of a socio-political field as used in European studies alludes to Bourdieu's notion of a field as a structured social space.[28] This notion is based on social interaction (Fligstein 2008: 8) against the background of power struggles which are rooted in the distribution of social, cultural and monetary capital. Using the notion of a field in relation to a European rights-based policy and its legal emanations requires an adaptation of Bourdieu's notion. First, a European field needs to embrace interrelations between different levels of society and governance. Second, a socio-legal field concerns not only power struggles but also the question how these struggles are influenced and shaped by authoritative legal texts.[29] The European socio-legal field of non-discrimination law and policy comprises, therefore, legislative texts and case law and, in addition, the social field on different levels developing around a certain theme. Accordingly, in proposing a notion such as nodes aimed at refocusing the field, this chapter aims at influencing reasoning in case law, debates around legislation and activities of social actors such as lobby groups and strategic litigators.

The notion of nodes is advanced in order to organize the field of non-discrimination law in a heterarchical and not hierarchical manner. It alludes to an image of overlapping orbits of social inequality which non-discrimination law is to combat. The three nodes proposed each have a centre relating to the main grounds of 'race', gender and disability. However, the nodes also have an orbit. Accordingly, this concept provides an opportunity to organize a multiplicity of grounds around the nodes, thus enabling the law to respond adequately to different degrees of discrimination and exclusion. Grounds related to a node can move closer to the centre, or remain on the periphery. Equally, they can be on the periphery of one ground and at the centre of another. Overlapping orbits imply that overlap and intersections are not the exception but the rule. In this way, nodes as organizing principles will be able also to offer adequate responses to intersectional discrimination.

Why 'Race', Gender and Disability?

The viability of the concept depends on identifying a limited number of nodes, around which other grounds can orbit. The choice of 'race', gender and disability relies both on formal and conceptual grounds.

Formal Arguments: International Law

At a formal level, the argument could rely simply on international law categorizations. As discussed earlier, the UN has established three specific non-discrimination covenants, addressing racial discrimination, discrimination against women (gender discrimination) and discrimination against

---

28   A short definition of the concept reads 'A field is a structured social space, a field of forces, a force field. It contains people, who dominate and people who are dominated. Constant permanent relationships of inequality operate inside this space, which at the same time becomes a space in which various actors struggle for the transformation or the preservation of the field' (Bourdieu 1998: 40–1). In Bourdieu's notion, the law in any nation state is only one field (García Villegas 2004: 57 and 60).

29   For a similar approach in the human rights field, see Nash (2009: 30–4).

persons with disabilities. These instruments define the grounds in a manner which groups the main ground addressed in each covenant together with other, derivative grounds.

In this way, the CERD defines racial discrimination as encompassing distinction on grounds of 'race, colour, descent or national or ethnic origin', thus grouping together a number of grounds separately enumerated under the ICCPR. The CEDAW also groups sex and marital status together under the notion of discrimination against women. The CRPD defines persons with disability to include 'those who have long-term physical, mental, intellectual or sensory impairments which in interaction with various barriers may hinder their full and effective participation in society on an equal basis with others'. Each covenant obliges signatory states to establish legislation outlawing marketplace discrimination. Comparing these obligations with EU non-discrimination law, the relative lack of protection in EU law against disability discrimination appears noteworthy. However, the UN regime is also vulnerable to criticism because its specific hierarchies have not been deliberatively justified beyond the staggered advent of political movements.[30] Thus formal arguments based on its categories need to be complemented by more substantive deliberations.

Purposes of EU Non-Discrimination Law

Such deliberations must reflect the purposes of non-discrimination law. In the EU context, it has become commonplace to describe the development of non-discrimination law as a shift from a merely economic towards a more human-rights based notion (Chalmers et al. 2010: 536–8). This assessment is not wholly precise, given the fact that EU non-discrimination law, in stark contrast to most international human rights law and constitutional law in continental European countries, focuses primarily on marketplace activities. Instead, what can be observed is a two-fold development. In relation to the EU public sphere, that is, Member State and EU institutions, a formal expansion of human rights principles occurred with the Treaty of Lisbon. As a result, the list of discrimination grounds on which public authorities may not rely is extended, bringing EU law into line with international human rights law. Secondary non-discrimination law, as expressed in the directives mentioned above,[31] has ambitions that are much wider and, at the same time, narrower. It aims at reforming society, influencing the interaction of citizens beyond the public sphere. This expansion was originally motivated by concerns about the common market. The oft-quoted French fear of being at a competitive disadvantage should the principle of equal pay for women and men not become a rule of the newly founded EEC (ibid.: 536) was based on a more fundamental concern. The common market should support not only economic efficiency aims but, at the same time, social aims. It is this second dimension which the ECJ acknowledged in 2000, stating that the social aims of the equal pay principle constituted an 'expression of a fundamental human right'.[32] The idea that the non-discrimination directives express fundamental human rights principles has been reiterated in more recent case law.[33] This has acknowledged also that any horizontal effect[34] of this constitutional principle depends on its inclusion in secondary law. In other words, EU non-discrimination law transcends the usual domain of human rights law and aims at the horizontal relationship between market participants, at least to the extent that specific legislation has been adopted.

---

30   The critique of the apartheid regime in the 1960s spurred CERD, the rise of the feminist movement in the 1970s spurred CEDAW, and the emergence of a disability rights movement oriented towards non-discrimination and equality in the 1990s contributed to initiating CRPD.

31   See footnotes 1 to 5.

32   CaseC-50/96 *Schröder* [2000] ECR I-743, paragraph 57.

33   ECJ *Kücükdeveci* (above footnote 19) paragraphs 27, 32 and 51.

34   On the horizontal effects of international human rights law see above footnote 9.

The purposes of discrimination law have been widely debated. For the purpose of its organization, the concept of positional difference, as distinguished from cultural difference, as developed by Iris Marion Young (2009) seems to offer a good starting point.

Young attempts to develop an approach enabling us to recognize 'social groups as constituted through interactions that make categorical distinctions among people in hierarchies of status and privilege' (Young 2009: 275) thus producing what Tilly (1998) refers to as 'durable inequality'. The key to recognizing a durable inequality is a social dynamic in which relations are structured in accordance with external perception of those subject to social disadvantage. The politics of positional difference address injustice arising 'from structural processes of the division of labour, social segregation and a lack of fit between hegemonic norms and interpreted bodies' (Young 2009: 283). They require striving for equality, while acknowledging that these structural processes lead to ingrained differences. These differences need to be taken into account, if any politics to overcome these is to be successful. Young does not restrict her approach to a certain set of grounds, but, interestingly, uses gender, race and disability as illustrations of the categories most relevant in terms of positional difference. Inherent in this approach is the differentiation between structuring and other criteria. At the same time, it criticizes the politics of cultural difference, which, in Young's view, is likely to neglect structural societal disadvantage and liable, thus, to equalize discrimination grounds of differing relevance.

Building on this approach, the purposes of EU non-discrimination law can be reformulated as addressing social disadvantage within social reality. Taking Young's point further, it is suggested that EU non-discrimination law is not intended to address all forms of social disadvantage, only a specific form of disadvantage. Retaining this focus is particularly important in order to prevent the dilution of non-discrimination law. On this view, non-discrimination politics will focus on social disadvantage based on ascription of difference. Ascribed difference in relation to the core categories reinforces ingrained social disadvantage along the axes of the division of labour (both within and outside of the market) and in terms of access to resources (needed for capability building). Non-discrimination law, as the corresponding set of legal rules, aims, thus, to provide legal remedies and positive obligations which correspond to individual disadvantaging acts and establish structures to counteract disadvantage.

These aims are based on two underlying rationales (Schiek 2005: 443–8): individuation as enabling persons to chose beyond stereotypes imposed on them and respecting human dignity despite substantive differences between human beings.

Individuation demands that persons are allowed to move outside the box constructed by expectations based on ascribed difference. In other words, women should become enabled to move beyond traditional expectations for their social role, persons ascribed the status of the 'other' in racial and ethnic terms should become enabled to act as fully accepted members of the community, and persons perceived as disabled should not be subjected to restricting expectations. In today's world, individuation often includes the opportunity to change one's identity. For those who can afford it, there are greater possibilities of accessing medical help to change physically, whether to appear more male or more white, or, more fundamentally, to change one's physical abilities.

Respecting difference, on the other hand, involves avoiding assimilationist pressure. As discussed elsewhere in this book (Roseberry, in this volume), avoiding stereotyping and associated disadvantage is easy for those who are prepared to hide part of their identity or adjust to gendered, 'white' or 'abled' expectations. Pressure to assimilate can have disempowering effects on identities. In this regard, one of the aims of non-discrimination law is to preserve diversity, by respecting difference and protecting those strands of identity a person neither wants nor should be expected to lose. Respecting differences requires also the accommodation of different (cap)abilities (Schiek

2002a: 310) resulting, in part, from physical characteristics. Such differences include the ability to become pregnant, or the different abilities of those considered disabled, as well as abilities which change with increasing age. Without accommodating such differences, non-discrimination law remains an empty promise, as is aptly illustrated by the image of a stork and a fox granted equal rights to drink from a tall vessel.

Homing in on 'Race', Gender and Disability

Both from formal and conceptual perspectives 'race', gender and disability appear to form the core of non-discrimination nodes.

'Race', a notion I prefer to use in inverted commas, is, of course, a cultural construct. Racialization of human beings occurs through a number of processes (Vieten, in this volume) which aim at segregating opportunities and establishing a division of labour. The invidiousness of racialization lies in a naturalization of difference which, at the same time, makes a restriction on the autonomy, access to resources and self-reliance of a certain subsection of humanity (usually more than 50 per cent on a global scale) appear inevitable. Racialization may rely on bodily features such as skin colour or hair texture, but is certainly not restricted to these. The main issue is the ascription of inferiority and 'otherness', which may derive from non-immutable factors such as language and religion.

Gender is a category which refers to biological sex, but naturalizes a social division of labour, access to resources and grant of autonomy over individual reproductive functions. In this regard, the categories of 'women' and 'men' become social categories, with a physical basis in certain respects.

Disability as a concept, again, is a socially constructed category (Degener, in this volume) which refers to notions of bodily autonomy and access to social interaction as well as other resources.

The commonality between these categories is the ascriptive moment, their relevance to individual identity and the inacceptability of politics aiming to equalize such traits. Neglecting differences based on 'race', gender and disability in the name of egalitarian politics will lead to unnecessary and harmful assimilation.

Non-Discrimination Law Aimed at Markets/Society and Other Policies

In order to refocus non-discrimination law, it is necessary to identify the specific driver of this policy field and to distinguish it from other socio-legal fields. The most important 'competing' fields appear to be general human rights law and policy and social policy (including welfarist policies).

As regards human rights law and policy, again, this is a diverse field. From an international human rights perspective, the distinction between civil and liberal rights (as protected by the ICCPR) and socio-economic rights (as protected by the ICESCR) is quite common.[35] Interestingly, in both fields, non-discrimination has a legitimate role, and is mentioned explicitly. Thus, although non-discrimination doubtless constitutes an element of the socio-legal field of human rights, it has also a character of its own. European comparative constitutional lawyers usually distinguish equality rights from liberties and socio-economic rights. A common differentiating moment is the characterization of equality rights as relational rights, as opposed to freedoms as rights relating to a certain field (Alexy 2002: 57–68). By way of distinction to both liberal and socio-economic rights, equality rights require a comparison and, thus, are not necessarily related to a certain field

---

35   For a unifying perspective, based on a human rights approach to non-discrimination law see Fredman (2008a).

of activity (such as uttering an opinion, adhering to a religion or having a family life). Instead, equality law crosscuts all potential fields of human rights law and constitutes a field of its own.

Second, a distinction needs to be drawn between welfare (or social state) policies and equality law and policy. Such policies aim to foster social cohesion at large, mainly through reducing income differentials and disadvantages in acquiring capabilities. This focuses on diminishing stratification along the lines of class and property. These aims are more relevant in Continental and Scandinavian Member States of the EU than in some other regions.[36] Such policies include, but are not restricted to, redistributive measures. Employment protection legislation, consumer law and policy as well as regional policy at EU level all seek to establish a more egalitarian access to resources and capabilities. These policies differ fundamentally from non-discrimination policies as they lack any notion of respecting differences which should persist but no longer constitute the basis for individual or group disadvantage. In other words, addressing class difference within social policy typically aims at overcoming these differences (Verloo 2006: 216–18).

An offshoot of welfarist policies, as witnessed in international human rights documents, is the prohibition on states and their agencies to distinguish according to class and social origin. However, non-discrimination law and policies aimed at societal and market actors would not include these categories as discrimination grounds as, generally, the market is believed to create opportunities to overcome such differences. Social contract law has been developed as a corrective for markets' tendency to entrench differences such as class and social origin (Hesselink 2003; Study Group on Social Justice in European Private Law 2004).

This distinction justifies the elimination of welfarist ideas of social justice from the scope of non-discrimination law and in particular the choice to not establish a node around class and poverty. This is not to negate the relevance of policy aimed at overcoming poverty and societal divisions along the lines of class. However, non-discrimination law is not the socio-legal field in which these aims are best pursued. Likewise, a distinction between freedoms and equality allows us to clarify some of the difficulties in the relation between non-discrimination law and religious freedom.[37] The protection of freedom of religion is not a matter for discrimination law, whereas stereotyping based on a perceived adherence to the 'wrong' religion may constitute a matter of ethnic discrimination.

What Differences Does the Node Concept Make?

The next step is to outline the nodes in more detail, in order to demonstrate how organizing EU non-discrimination law around them will make a difference.

The Gender Node

The gender node is the one with the longest tradition in EU law and, thus, a suitable starting point. This node is meant to capture the social processes which reaffirm and re-establish a higher

---

36   On the divergent European welfare state traditions see Esping-Andersen (1999) and Maydell et al. (2006: 5–27). For Eastern European perspectives see Inglot (2008).

37   This relation is discussed by Vickers (2008) and McColgan (2009). Vickers rejects the possibility to distinguish between freedom and equality and concludes, accordingly, that religious discrimination is a specific category of discrimination law. McColgan argues for protection of religious freedom by instruments other than discrimination law. Both agree with Pitt (2007) that some forms of religious discrimination should be regarded as (in)direct race discrimination.

level of privilege for those categorized as male in relation to access to resources, employment and personal autonomy. Gender discrimination occurs in structuring the division of labour between those perceived as female and those perceived as male along the lines preordained by expectations of heterosexuality as the norm. Naturally, this means different things in different societies (e.g. differences in the gendering – and the pay levels – of medical and judicial professions in Eastern and Western Europe). However, there appears to be little difference in the burdening of women with more unpaid work (and more work in general). Gender discrimination also includes the sexualization and emotionalization of women, and the construction of professional arenas for women and men respectively in line with such stereotypes. It also includes the denial of sex differences by supporting the normality of the male body.[38]

Along the axis featuring the different purposes of equality law, gender equality oscillates between the pursuit of individuation and the right to accommodate physical difference, such as the ability to give birth. If pursued rigorously, gender equality law will also have consequences for the structure of families as the basis for the division of labour and organization of sexuality. Questioning heteronormativity constitutes, thus, an element of gender equality law (Monaghan 2009: 520).

In our model, which other grounds should be grouped around the gender node? Discrimination on grounds of not fulfilling gender role expectations should be included. As a result, discrimination on grounds of sexual orientation, pregnancy and not appearing appropriately male or female form part of the node. At a more conceptual level, the notion of gender departs from the biologist assumption that the world is naturally divided into women and men, acknowledging that gender inequality rests on social constructs related to ascriptions and role expectations (ibid.). This insight will make a difference in cases of discrimination based on dress codes, both for men wearing clothing gendered female and women clothing gendered male.[39] Also, discrimination on grounds of associating with a person of a certain gender should be acknowledged as gender discrimination, where such association contravenes the dominant gender role expectations (McColgan 2007: 78). This implies that cases such as *Maruko*[40] are relevant not only to those openly gay or lesbian but also to the whole spectre of gender role deviants. Considering disadvantage more broadly, the gender dimension in cases such as *Bahl*[41] who, as noted by Solanke (2009b: 744), 'on all accounts, drove too hard', is easier to recognize as based on the assumption that women, and in particular women of colour, should be servile. Focusing on gender not sex permits the recognition as gender discrimination of disadvantage on grounds of child-bearing ability, clearly discrimination based on the expectation that mothers will bear the brunt of caring work, and discrimination against the exceptional fathers who take on their share, resulting, for example, from legislation granting post-maternity advantages to women alone. Both are cases of gender discrimination. Accommodation of the needs of pregnant women in working life, by contrast, constitutes the reasonable accommodation of difference.

The 'Race' Node

While the notion of 'race' has a legitimate space in EU non-discrimination law, this chapter uses inverted commas to signify that there is no objective reason to distinguish different 'races' of

---

38　This section relies on Young (2009). A Spanish trail of discussion proposes defining the social construction of sexuality as the main source of gender discrimination (Platero Mendez 2007; Lombardo 2003: 168).

39　See the Dutch CGB Opinion 1996-108 (male nurse discussing choice of stiletto shoes with colleagues) and for an English law perspective *DWP v. Thompson* [2004] IRLR 348 (EAT).

40　See above footnote 17.

41　*Bahl v. The Law Society* [2004] EWCA Civ 1070.

humankind. 'Race' is a social construct entirely. Nonetheless, the continuing existence of racism necessitates the use of 'race' in discrimination law since the (alternative) concept of ethnicity partly confuses the social structuring process behind race discrimination. Race is ascribed to persons in order to distinguish 'us' from 'them', and is based on a number of superficial traits. These include skin colour, hair texture and bodily stature, but also language, recognizable adherence to a 'foreign' religion, engagement in 'foreign' cultural practices such as using certain spices in cooking or in being more or less hospitable than the 'we' population. Racialization makes use of any notion, not restricting itself to immutable characteristics. Typical starting points for racial ascription are national and ethnic origin and language and religious difference. Being perceived as a stranger and not to belong may lead to a process of racialization. A number of authors cite discrimination against Muslims as the successor (or as additional) to European anti-Semitism, itself a form of racism, complete with stereotyping and exclusion from jobs, housing, etc. (Young 2009: 291; Pitt 2007: 227). Defining racism in socio-constructivist terms permits regional varieties of discrimination to be captured. For example, people of Russian descent are victims of racialization and, thus, race discrimination in some parts of the EU, mainly the Baltic States (Hughes 2005) and also Germany (Schiek 2007b: 77).

Thus, the 'race' node will include, in line with CERD, colour, language, descent, national or ethnic origin. The recent debate on how far religious freedom is adequately protected by means of discrimination law (McColgan 2009; Pitt 2007; Vickers 2008) can be captured within this node. Religion can become a token of racialization, to the extent that being perceived as Muslim (for example) leads to specific detriment (Pitt 2007: 226; Vieten, in this volume: 63–76). In particular visual traits (such as clothing) or specific behaviour will often lead to persons being ascribed minority status, with adverse consequences for market access and social inclusion.

This approach may make a difference in cases currently categorized as religious discrimination against Muslims, in particular Muslim women. The notorious hijab question needs to be recognized as a form of 'race' discrimination, while not neglecting the gender dimensions. However, this applies only where being a Muslim actually leads to racialization. This is not the case in countries such as Turkey, where the hijab issue is purely a matter of religion, as was arguably also the case in *Şahin v. Turkey*.[42] This is not the only consequence of working with the 'race' node. The inclusion of language allows the requirements of speaking the local language without a foreign accent to be recognized as race discrimination as was identified by the first instance labour court in *Kücükdeveci*.[43]

The Disability Node

The disability node is arguably the most difficult one. The notion of a 'person with disabilities' encompasses an enormous degree of diversity, including bodily, psychological and mental differences, which in interaction with social environment may lead to exclusion and discrimination. How can the node concept improve protection and, at the same time, connect to the other nodes of EU non-discrimination law? First, defining the centre of the node can provide some orientation on what needs protection. As is well known, the ECJ began development of the field with a rather

---

42   *Şahin v. Turkey* (ECHR 2005-XI). Accordingly, the judgment could have been based on grounds other than simply the margin of appreciation left to signatory states.

43   Mönchengladbach Labour Court, 15 June 2007 (see footnote 20). In other cases, language requirements have been classified as indirect discrimination (see Swedish Labour Court 4 December 2002 AD 128/2002, partly reprinted in Schiek (2007a: 431–2)).

restrictive definition in *Chacon Navas*.[44] Here, exclusion from the labour market as a result of long-term illness was held not to deserve protection under EU non-discrimination law, because 'the concept of "disability" must be understood as referring to a limitation which results in particular from physical, mental or psychological impairments and which hinders the participation of the person concerned in professional life' (para. 43) only when it is 'probable that it will last for a long time' (para. 45). This has been criticized as a narrow interpretation of the concept of disability, focused on a specific impairment concerning the person deemed to be disabled (Quinn 2008: 254–7). The social notion of disability (Barnes 1990), the base for the CRPD, has been devised to overcome the limits of such a narrow definition. Under the node perspective, the main characteristic, the centre of the discrimination ground, would be any physical, psychological or mental difference resulting in diminished opportunities for participation in social life because those differences are not accommodated. Accordingly, discrimination against people with disabilities is a consequence of 'lack of fit' (Young 2009: 277) between 'structures, practices, norms and aesthetic standards dominant in society' and a certain set of abilities. Implicit in this approach is an acknowledgement of the different abilities which may lead to majority society categorizing a person as disabled. However, the overarching notion of ascription allows persons to be included who are merely considered as having different abilities due to some external appearance. For example, persons who are facially disfigured or have different visual or auditory abilities will often be perceived as lacking in intellectual capability, although such connection is wholly unfounded.

An obvious link for this node is to old age, which often leads to a reduction in bodily functions and associated prejudice. Conversely, age discrimination has been viewed as a more difficult non-discrimination ground, as it does not delimit a distinctive 'group' (Fredman 2003: 21; Manfredi and Vickers 2009). Age affects everyone, and old age is expected to be experienced by each individual sooner or later. Accordingly, under EU non-discrimination law, differentiations on grounds of age are considered less objectionable than those on other grounds. This is reflected in the wide margin of appreciation for Member States in defining justification for such different treatment. Article 6 of Directive 2000/78 does not specify which exceptions are permitted but establishes a general justification. When conditions associated with old age lead to prejudice and over-inclusive assumptions, and the same mechanisms as in cases of disability discrimination are apparent, the same level of protection should apply.

A less obvious case may be found in conditions such as pregnancy, also a gender-related form of discrimination. However, the need to accommodate different physical needs presents a link to the disability node.

Nodes and Intersectionality

The concept of nodes should also allow intersectional forms of discrimination to be conceptualized more easily. In addition to the notorious headscarf issue already mentioned, other examples might include discrimination against older women or disabled persons of ethnic minority origins. These intersectionalities would have to be taken more seriously, as their anchoring is closer to the centre than to the periphery of a node.

To return to some of the earlier examples: discrimination on grounds of wearing religious dress will usually constitute a particularly harsh form of discrimination located between gender and race. Similarly, exclusion from retirement benefits on grounds of the sex of a partner may qualify as sex discrimination rather than 'only' as sexual orientation discrimination and, as such, require a more

---

44   Case C-13/05 *Chacon Navas* [2006] ECR I-8467.

serious legal response. Discrimination on grounds of caring for a disabled child has both a gender and a disability dimension and, consequently, warrants a more robust response than each of those forms of discrimination in isolation.

Also, the nodes model points against single-ground approaches to situations which in reality are clearly intersectional cases. Often, this would require the redefinition of cases of age discrimination as intersected gender and ethnic discrimination. General age bands often reflect stereotyped life-cycles. Compulsory retirement policies, setting de facto upper age limits on remaining in employment, may serve as one example. These rest on the assumption, *inter alia*, that at a certain age a person will have accrued sufficient pension entitlement to allow them comfortably to leave the labour market. Those systematically excluded from labour markets on grounds, for example, of gender or race are more likely to live according to different cycles. For that reason, age barriers very often are indirectly discriminatory on other grounds.

Conclusion

This chapter has demonstrated that organizing EU non-discrimination law around the nodes of gender, 'race' and disability will enable courts, policy-makers and legislators to re-establish focus in this complex socio-legal field, without 'liberating' non-discrimination law from grounds altogether. Refocusing will facilitate an adequate response to all forms of discrimination present in one case, not simply encouraging the disregard of established 'grounds' no longer regarded as current. Organizing the field around nodes also requires giving primary consideration to the centres of the nodes. Cases such as *Kücükdeveci* must be analysed correctly as discrimination at the intersection of the gender and 'race' nodes, with age playing only a supporting role. On the other hand, cases where older employees are excluded generally from tasks such as flying an airplane may have to be re-categorized around the disability node.

These examples demonstrate that the node concept functions as an interpretative device, without need for changes in the written law. It may serve also as a guideline for future legislators. In that regard, it would demand highly compelling reasons for the exclusion of women from equal treatment under EU law in relation to education and health when that protection is offered to homosexuals and religious minorities. Above all, the concept offers an opportunity to identify the differences that make a difference, without imposing less flexible forms of ordering such as a strict hierarchy. In an individual case, it may appear that discrimination on grounds of age is the most pressing issue. This particularly applies when older people are stereotyped as being less able. However, this steers the case towards the centre of the disability node. Similarly, in an individual case, discrimination on grounds of sexual orientation may appear to be the most serious issue. However, it is difficult to imagine how this could not be related to gender stereotypes and, thus, move the case towards the centre of the gender node.

Chapter 2

Intersections between Disability, Race[1] and Gender in Discrimination Law

Theresia Degener

Introduction

Discrimination at the intersection of race, gender and disability is a topic yet to be developed in legal and social science research. Some legal and social science literature on disabled women from various cultural backgrounds now exists (Vernon and Swain 2002; Silvers 1999; Rousso 2001; Duncan and Berman-Bieler 1998; Degener 2001). However, research into disability and discrimination within gender and critical race studies remains limited. Similarly, in the field of disability studies, neither gender nor race has been a prominent research topic (Smith and Hutchison 2004).

There are many parallels between the history and forms of oppression among racism, sexism and ableism, i.e. violence, segregation, institutionalization, denial of citizenship and other rights. While it is important to recognize these parallels and also the differences[2] it is equally important to be aware that these ideologies of oppression have been developed from a mono-dimensional perspective on identity: race, gender or disability. Ayesha Vernon (1998) pointed out more than a decade ago that while there are similarities between ableism and other forms of oppression, such as sexism and racism, drawing parallels does not take into account the experience of disabled women of ethnic minorities.

This chapter seeks to illuminate the issue of discrimination at the intersection of race, gender and disability from a legal point of view. First, data and experiences of disabled women relating to multidimensional discrimination will be presented in order to clarify the concept of multidimensional discrimination at the intersection of race, disability and gender. Second, legal problems will be identified that arise from applying existing anti-discrimination law to cases of intersectional discrimination. Finally, the question will be addressed whether discrimination at the intersection of the three grounds at issue is recognized by international, European and national law.

Data and Discrimination Experiences Regarding the Intersection of Race, Gender and Disability

Data on multidimensional discrimination relating to disability, race and gender is scarce. The World Bank and other international organizations have produced a number of studies on disability and poverty which reveal that disabled persons belong to the poorest of the poor (Braithwaite and Mont

---

1 Using the term 'race' does not mean that I believe humankind can be divided into races, or that races exist from a biological point of view. It is a socially constructed category.

2 For example, barriers in the built environment and in communication constitute a specific form of impairment-based discrimination.

2008). More than two-thirds of the 650 million disabled people in this world live in developing countries. Children and women in this minority group have been identified as being worst off in terms of access to resources, such as food, water, shelter, education and health services. Some data and qualitative research also exist on sexual violence, employment and healthcare (Arnade and Häfner 2005). It reveals that disabled women have a much higher risk of being exposed to sexual abuse and violence than non-disabled women. Similar data exists regarding the employment rate of disabled women compared to disabled men or non-disabled women. With respect to health care and health services, we know that disabled women are at high risk of involuntary sterilization and, at the same time, that they do not have equal access to healthcare services. Research relating to disabled persons from black and ethnic minority backgrounds in the UK indicates that they do not have equal access to social services (Disability Rights Commission 2004). Awareness of multiple discrimination remains underdeveloped. A recent survey on perceptions of (multiple) discrimination within the EU revealed that only 37 per cent of Europeans consider multiple discrimination to be widespread (European Commission 2008c).

This finding is inconsistent with recent discrimination law research which indicates that discrimination cases brought before tribunals, courts or other monitoring bodies, even if not treated as cases of multiple discrimination, often involve more than one ground (European Commission 2007a). Race and gender were found to be the grounds most often involved in multiple discrimination cases and disabled women were described as being at high risk of experiencing multidimensional discrimination (ibid.: 47).

As a disabled self-defence teacher, I listen to stories of disabled women who have experienced violence. They are sometimes unsure whether their violent experience was sexual violence or 'other' violence. One woman told me how she was forced to use a tampon-shoot pistol which was developed by doctors for girls and women with weak arm function. She was told to sit on that device and then pull a trigger so that the tampon would shoot into her. At first, she refused but eventually complied because of the pressure exerted by several male members of medical staff who stood in front of her while she was sitting almost naked on the toilet. 'If you don't do it yourself, we will have to do it for you', they threatened. The woman asked me if what she experienced was sexual violence.

Another woman told me that she was raped and beaten after she asked two men for directions to a nearby cinema. She had lost her way and, because she was blind, she needed guidance. They led her to a remote parking lot where they started to shout at her because she dared, as a blind woman, to go out on the streets alone. It is interesting to note the sexually ambiguous nature of the harassment, which turned out to be the testing phase before a rape.

Another physically impaired woman told me how she was frequently harassed by (male) co-workers who asked her how she could go to the toilet or dress herself as a physically disabled woman. The woman asked herself whether this behaviour fell into the category of sexual harassment or if it was 'just' disability-based harassment. These women's attitudes reflect societal awareness concerning different kinds of oppression. While racism or sexism is strictly condemned in many countries, awareness in relation to ableism is often underdeveloped. Public awareness and opinion on different forms of discrimination correlate with historical developments of social movements and their acknowledgement. The United States is a good example of such historical progression. A strong civil rights movement focused on fighting racial discrimination (Kluger 1975) was followed by the emergence of a women's movement focused on fighting sexism and then by the development of the disability movement, which entered as 'the last civil rights movement' (Shapiro 1993). In Germany, a different sequence applied. After the Second World War, a powerful women's movement was the first to emerge. The issues of racism and ableism were taken up by social movements at a much later stage.

Legal Problems of Intersectional Discrimination

Discrimination at the intersection of race, gender and disability shares many of the problems posed by other types of multidimensional discrimination. First, many anti-discrimination laws are single-ground oriented or cover only a selection of grounds, such as race and gender, but leave out others, such as disability (Schiek et al. 2007; McColgan et al. 2006). Thus, a disabled woman from an ethnic minority might have to have recourse to several laws in order to seek legal protection. This fragmentation in discrimination legislation leads to various legal problems. In addition to having different personal scopes, legislation may vary in its material coverage. Some laws address only the employment area; others include goods and services offered to the general public, or education facilities. For example, in Germany, until recently, legislation prohibited only gender-based employment discrimination. Disability-based employment discrimination was prohibited only in 2001[3] and employment discrimination on grounds of race not until 2006.[4] Thus, prior to those amendments, a disabled woman, a woman from an ethnic minority or a disabled woman from an ethnic minority could file a successful complaint for employment discrimination only if she could establish that the discrimination in question was on grounds of her gender. There is not a single reported case from that period involving a disabled woman.

Discrimination at the intersection of race, gender and disability will rarely be composed of discrete jigsaw pieces corresponding exactly to the three separate grounds. More commonly, it will be based on a mélange of overlapping and undefined prejudices and stigmas. It can also be assumed that often the victims themselves do not know which element of the discrimination in question was triggered by a particular prejudice or devaluation.

The law sometimes creates hierarchies of equality grounds with different levels of legal protection applying to each. The distinction between 'strict', 'intermediate' and 'rational basis' equality standards relating to racial, sex-based and disability-based discrimination is familiar from US constitutional law.[5] In German constitutional law, the standards applicable to race and gender discrimination are stricter than those which apply to disability (Zinsmeister 2007). In addition, the German General Equal Treatment Act of 2006, a cross-cutting anti-discrimination statute covering many different grounds, allows for greater exemptions and justifications for discrimination relating to age, religion or political opinion than for racial discrimination.[6] These hierarchies in the German General Equal Treatment Act correspond to hierarchies present in the underlying EU directives (Baer 2008). Hierarchies in equality standards do not constitute a new problem. Michael Stolleis' analysis (2003) of the equality principle in legal history suggests that equality can be compared to a cake which, ever since the French Revolution, has had to be divided between an increasing number of people and groups. Each new group that receives a share of the equality cake has to demonstrate that it deserves a piece of the same size. Modern human rights law is a manifestation of recent developments in this respect. From the Charter of the United Nations of 1945 to the Charter of

---

3 Book IX of the Social Code (*Sozialgesetzbuch IX* 2001), § 82(2).

4 General Equal Treatment Act 2006 (*Allgemeines Gleichbehandlungsgesetz* 2006 (AGG)).

5 *Korematsu v. United States* 323 U.S. 214 (1944), *Craig v. Boren* 429 U.S. 190 (1976), *City of Cleburne v. Cleburne Living Center* 473 U.S. 432 (1985).

6 AGG, §§ 9 and 10.

Fundamental Rights of the European Union of 2000, the number of acknowledged categories in the relevant anti-discrimination provisions has risen from four to 17.[7]

Because ableism as a form of oppression has been acknowledged relatively recently, disability discrimination law remains underdeveloped when compared to race and gender discrimination law. The main focus of disability discrimination law is on environmental barriers, such as inaccessible workplaces, communication or public transport systems. Other forms of disability-based discrimination, notably harassment (Weber 2007) and bioethical issues (Silvers et al. 1998; Parens and Asch 2000), such as eugenic health laws, have to a lesser extent been the subject of equality discourse.

Further, while the forms of prohibited discrimination are similar in the contexts of race and gender, disability discrimination is often defined in a different fashion. Most European discrimination laws define race or gender discrimination as including direct and indirect forms of discrimination as well as harassment. By contrast, legal definitions of disability discrimination frequently omit harassment but include denial of reasonable accommodation. If harassment is acknowledged in gender discrimination law but not in disability discrimination law, a disabled woman who experiences intersectional harassment might be insufficiently protected by law, because the harassment she experiences might not be recognized under gender discrimination law. To give an example: a blind mother might be repeatedly asked by a colleague how she manages to nurse her child without seeing it and what she thinks about sterilization. Similarly, if denial of reasonable accommodation is acknowledged in disability but not race discrimination law, a Muslim woman who wears a headscarf and uses a wheelchair may demand that a ramp is installed at the workplace but is unable to demand that she be allowed to wear the headscarf. While many national anti-discrimination statutes in Europe provide for reasonable accommodation for persons with disabilities, not all define denial of reasonable accommodation as discrimination (Waddington and Lawson 2009). Furthermore, some countries confine reasonable accommodation provisions to the employment field, whereas others extend those duties to other areas such as social protection, education or goods and services. The 2006 mapping study on national anti-discrimination legislation outside employment and occupation found that Ireland and the UK were the only countries which had reasonable accommodation duties operated in all areas covered by the Race Equality Directive (McColgan et al. 2006: 4). It also found that most countries do not impose these duties beyond disability (ibid.: 29).

Another problem is the issue of enforceability of equality rights. While the planning and transport laws of many countries now include accessibility requirements, they rarely provide for the bringing of individual or collective actions to challenge non-compliance. In relation to education, it is worth noting that although the exclusion of girls and children from black and ethnic minority groups from the general education system is widely condemned, no such consensus exists on the exclusion of children with disabilities. Their segregation in educationally inferior special schools is often considered to be positive action and not unlawful discrimination. Indeed, in 1997, more than 40 years after such a clause was struck down by the US Supreme Court in the context of racial segregation in education in the famous case of *Brown v. Board of Education*,[8] the German Federal Constitutional Court introduced the 'separate but equal clause' in German constitutional law in the context of the education of disabled children.[9]

---

7   UN Charter, Art. 1(3); EU Charter, Art. 21 EU.
8   *Brown v. Board of Education of Topeka* 349 U.S. 294 (1955).
9   Judgment no. 1 BvR 9/97 of 8 October 1997, reported NJW 1998, 131–5.

These legal circumstances could hamper protection against intersectional discrimination. If multiple discrimination is not recognized by law, victims of intersectional discrimination may be forced to present their case as discrimination on a single ground which might reduce their chance of success. If denial of reasonable accommodation is not defined as discrimination, intersectional discrimination which involves access and barrier issues will not be recognized as unlawful treatment. If the law provides for reasonable accommodation duties only in employment, intersectional discrimination related to disability and other grounds in education and other fields may not be prohibited by law. And finally, the fact that very few national laws apply reasonable accommodation duties beyond the sphere of disability may lead to insufficient legal protection against intersectional discrimination.

Discrimination at the Intersection of Race, Gender and Disability in International, European and National Law

UN Law

International human rights law relating to racial, gender and disability discrimination is enshrined in several core human rights conventions, notably, the International Covenant on Civil and Political Rights 1966 (ICCPR); the International Covenant on Economic, Social and Cultural Rights 1966 (ICESCR); the International Convention on the Elimination of all Forms of Racial Discrimination 1965 (ICERD); the Convention on the Elimination of all Forms of Discrimination against Women 1979 (CEDAW); the Convention on the Rights of the Child 1989 (CRC), the International Convention on the Protection of the Rights of All Migrant Workers and Members of their Families 1990 (CMW); and the Convention on the Rights of Persons with Disabilities (CRPD). None of these treaties explicitly mentions discrimination at the intersection of the three categories at stake. However, some treaties mention minorities and sub-groups. For instance, the ICCPR protects the cultural, religious or linguistic identity of minorities.[10] It also explicitly protects the rights of women[11] and children,[12] and accused juveniles.[13] The equal rights of women are also recognized by the ICESCR,[14] which demands special protection for mothers and children.[15] CEDAW recognizes the vulnerable position of rural women[16] and protects children against marriage.[17] The CMW protects specific categories of migrant workers and members of their families, such as frontier workers or seasonal workers.[18] Finally, the CRPD has specific articles on disabled women[19] and children with disabilities.[20] However, except for the CRPD, none of these treaties addresses the concept of multiple discrimination. The CRC has a stand-alone article on disabled children but does not mention the issue of multiple discrimination.

---

10 ICCPR, Art. 27.
11 ICCPR, Arts 3 and 23.
12 ICCPR, Art. 24.
13 ICCPR, Art. 10(2)(b).
14 ICESCR, Art. 3.
15 ICESCR, Art. 10(2) and (3).
16 CEDAW, Art. 14.
17 CEDAW, Art. 16(2).
18 CMW, Art. 57 et seq.
19 CRPD, Art. 6.
20 CRPD, Art. 7.

While most human rights treaties lack a specific reference to multidimensional discrimination, the UN human rights treaty bodies have addressed the issue in their general comments and recommendations, which are authoritative, albeit non-binding, interpretations of the treaties (Makkonen 2002: 37; Vandenhole 2005). While the terminology of 'double discrimination' was initially favoured,[21] more recent general comments and recommendations have tended to refer to multiple or intersectional discrimination. Today, most of the human rights treaty bodies have adopted general comments or general recommendations which include references to multiple or intersectional discrimination. Most notable are those addressing forms of multiple discrimination against girls and women. Some of the recommendations address the difficult 'paradox of multicultural vulnerability' (Makkonen 2002: 52) which arises when ethnic and religious communities support traditional values and practices inconsistent with human rights, such as female genital mutilation, dowry and child marriage. Recognizing and respecting the rights of cultural, religious and ethnic minorities puts the State into the paradoxical situation of not protecting the human rights of those members of the group who are most vulnerable to the harmful consequences of such traditions. At an early stage, the CEDAW Committee made it clear that some of these traditions constitute violence against women and violations of their human rights.[22] In its General Comment on Article 27 of the ICCPR, the Human Rights Committee adopted a similar approach to the rights of minorities – stressing that none of the rights protected by that article may be legitimately exercised in a manner or to an extent inconsistent with the other rights conferred by the Covenant.[23] This approach was affirmed and elaborated upon by the Human Rights Committee in its General Comment on equality rights between men and women. According to this, State Parties have an obligation to actively combat cultural and religious attitudes and values that undermine the equal rights of women.[24]

In addition, the issue of multidimensional discrimination has been addressed in comments and recommendations relating to specific groups such as persons with disabilities,[25] women with disabilities,[26] elderly persons,[27] Roma people,[28] women migrant workers[29] and non-citizens.[30] The CEDAW Committee has recently adopted a general recommendation on temporary special measures permitted under Article 4 of CEDAW.[31] This recommendation emphasizes the importance of special positive measures for the elimination of multiple discrimination.[32] The ICESCR Committee issued a similar general comment in 2005 on non-discrimination.[33] This comment is particularly noteworthy in that it addresses the issue of multiple discrimination and interprets equality as relating to each of the specified and 'other status' categories mentioned in Article 2 of CEDAW.[34] As a result, General Comment No. 20 of the ICESCR Committee acknowledges

---

21   First used by the CEDAW Committee in 1991 in General Recommendation No. 18 on disabled women followed by ICESCR Committee in General Comment No. 5 on persons with disabilities in 1994.

22   CEDAW Committee General Recommendation No. 19, para. 11.

23   Human Rights Committee General Comment No. 23, para. 8.

24   Human Rights Committee General Comment No. 28, paras 5 and 32.

25   ICESCR Committee General Comment No. 5.

26   CEDAW Committee General Recommendation No. 18.

27   ICESCR Committee General Comment No. 6.

28   CERD Committee General Recommendation No. 27.

29   CEDAW Committee General Recommendation No. 26.

30   CERD Committee General Recommendation No. 30.

31   CEDAW Committee General Recommendation No. 25.

32   Ibid., para. 12.

33   ICESCR Committee General Comment No. 20.

34   Ibid., para. 17 and paras 18–35.

the specific types of discrimination faced by various groups. Thus, the human rights monitoring bodies have made significant efforts in the new millennium to address equality issues relating to previously unrecognized groups and minorities. The CEDAW Committee is the treaty body which has most often and most consistently referred to the issue of multidimensional discrimination (Vandenhole 2005: 77; Makkonen 2002: 42). Nevertheless, it should not be forgotten that the CERD Committee was the first treaty body to use multiple discrimination as an analytical device in the review of State reports (Vandenhole 2005: 42).

Despite the fact that disability was among the first categories to be recognized in relation to multidimensional discrimination, the intersection of race/culture and gender has received much more attention and remains the prime focus in the jurisprudence of the treaty bodies. Awareness of harmful traditional or cultural practices and beliefs has led to better human rights protection for women around the world. While female genital circumcision, forced marriage and other harmful practices persist, the UN has clearly condemned them as human rights violations. It is important to note, however, that there are also a great many traditional, religious or superstitious beliefs about impairments – about their causes and their 'treatment', for instance – which are harmful to disabled people. They may lead to detainment (sometimes in isolation), brutal and violent treatment in the name of a 'cure' and to other forms of inhuman and degrading treatment. Disabled women are often the targets of such practices and beliefs, especially when combined with eugenic ideologies. Only the ICESCR Committee has acknowledged the problem of prejudices and superstitious beliefs against persons with disabilities.[35] However, the recognition that such harmful attitudes and practices violate the right to participate in cultural life protected by Article 15 of the ICESCR addresses only one aspect of the problem. Traditional practices and superstitious beliefs infringe a whole set of other rights, including the right to liberty, integrity and equality.

A missed opportunity to address multidimensional discrimination involving disability seems to be General Recommendation No. 31 on the prevention of racial discrimination in the administration and functioning of the criminal justice system adopted by the CERD Committee in 2005.[36] Although multiple discrimination is explicitly mentioned in the context of combating all forms of racial discrimination, disability does not feature in the groups identified as vulnerable to this form of oppression in the criminal justice system.[37] This omission is particularly disappointing given recent jurisprudence of the Human Rights Committee[38] and the European Court of Human Rights (ECtHR)[39] concerning the inhumane and degrading treatment of disabled prisoners. Again, disabled people were not mentioned in the CERD Committee's General Recommendation on Non-Citizens adopted in 2004.[40] This document claims to address multiple discrimination.[41] However, it refers only to certain intersecting grounds, such as gender and age,[42] while ignoring disability. This is regrettable since many countries have immigration laws that blatantly discriminate against persons with disabilities.

---

35 ICESCR Committee General Comment No. 5, para. 38.

36 CERD Committee General Recommendation No. 31.

37 Ibid., 12th recital of the preamble. This identifies as vulnerable: immigrants, refugees, asylum seekers, stateless persons, Roma/Gypsies, indigenous peoples, persons discriminated because of their descent, women and children.

38 *Hamilton v. Jamaica*, Communication No 616/1995 and *Clement Francis v. Jamaica*, Communication No. 606/1994. For an analysis of these cases see Quinn and Degener (2002: 49).

39 *Price v. UK* Application No 33394/96, ECHR 2001-VII.

40 CERD Committee General Recommendation No. 30.

41 Ibid., para. 8.

42 Ibid., paras 8 and 16.

Overall, the jurisprudence of the human rights treaty bodies relating to multiple discrimination is in need of streamlining and further development.[43] The committees most suited for the task of addressing this issue are the ICCPR and the ICESCR Committees. The treaties with which these committees are concerned are non-thematic and cover all grounds of discrimination. However, although the ICESCR Committee has (to some extent at least) begun the task of tackling discrimination against the full range of groups and minorities, the focus of the Human Rights Committee remains on issues of gender and race/culture.

As the youngest treaty, the CRPD is the only convention which explicitly refers to multiple discrimination in the binding text. However, it is only with respect to gender that the treaty poses obligations on States to combat multiple discrimination. While there is also a stand-alone article on disabled children,[44] the CRPD does not explicitly apply the concept of multiple discrimination to disabled children. Only the non-binding preamble mentions any concern for 'multiple or aggravated forms of discrimination on the basis of race, colour, sex, language, religion, political or other opinion, national, ethnic, indigenous or social origin, property, birth, age or other status'.[45] The specific obligation on States to combat multiple discrimination is limited to disabled women and girls.[46]

Age and gender sensitive language is contained also in other provisions of the Convention.[47] Thus, the CRPD imposes explicit duties relating to women with disabilities in the areas of anti-discrimination policies and measures;[48] awareness raising;[49] protection from exploitation, violence and abuse;[50] health policy and programmes;[51] and poverty policy and programmes.[52] Further, because Article 6 is a cross-cutting provision, it must be read together with all other articles of the CRPD with the effect that multiple discrimination against disabled women as an issue must be addressed when implementing the entire convention.

As the first human rights convention of the new millennium, the CRPD is particularly significant for the future development of human rights law. In some respects it has paved the way for a more reform-oriented and effective development of human rights protection (Arnadóttir and Quinn 2009). In relation to the issue of multidimensional discrimination, however, it has only partially fulfilled expectations. Although it addresses discrimination against disabled women, it fails to address also multiple discrimination at the intersections of disability and race and disability and age beyond childhood.

European Law

Gender and race discrimination were addressed relatively early in the Council of Europe and the European Union. Disability as a ground of discrimination, however, was not addressed until the 1990s.

---

43   Detailed recommendations are made by Makkonen (2002: 55–60).

44   CRPD, Art. 7.

45   Recital (p) of the preamble to the CRPD.

46   CRPD, Art. 6(2).

47   See recitals (q) and (s) of the preamble to the CRPD and its Arts 8, 16, 25 and 28. Unlike other human rights treaties, the CRPD also includes an article on data and statistics. It does not refer to women or children but demands that data and statistics are 'disaggregated, as appropriate' (Art. 31).

48   CRPD, Art. 6.

49   CRPD, Art. 8(1)(b).

50   CRPD, Art. 16.

51   CRPD, Art. 25.

52   CRPD, Art. 28(2)(b).

Council of Europe   Among the over 30 human rights treaties of the Council of Europe, the most important are the 1950 Convention for the Protection of Human Rights and Fundamental Freedoms (ECHR), with its various protocols, and the European Social Charter (ESC) in its revised version of 1996. Both treaties contain anti-discrimination provisions relating to race,[53] sex[54] and disability,[55] but none on intersectional discrimination. The Council of Europe has a long history of combating racism, sexism and ableism, although these subjects have been dealt with in different institutional settings.

Prevention of racism, xenophobia and anti-Semitism, principal causes of the Second World War, was the main objective in the establishment of the Council of Europe in 1949. Subsequently, in 1993, alarmed by the resurgence of racism and intolerance, the European Commission against Racism and Intolerance (ECRI) was established (European Commission against Racism and Intolerance 2004: 6). Since then, the ECRI has led the Council of Europe's efforts in combating racism and intolerance. Its main activities are country-by-country monitoring, work on general themes and developing relations with civil society. It has adopted several general policy recommendations on issues such as combating racism and intolerance against Roma/Gypsy communities,[56] and on national legislation[57] but, as yet, none on multiple discrimination.

Equality between men and women has been regarded as a fundamental human right within the Council of Europe for the last three decades (Tavares da Silva 2002). The Steering Committee for Equality between Women and Men (CDEG), an intergovernmental body established in 1992, coordinates a whole range of different measures such as actions against trafficking in human beings, combating violence against women, gender mainstreaming and women in politics and decision-making. A Committee of Ministers (2007a) Recommendation on gender equality standards and mechanisms includes a section on multiple discrimination against women based on a combination of their sex and other grounds such as race, religion and other status (ibid.: paras 59–61). Although disability is not explicitly mentioned in this recommendation as a ground of intersectional discrimination, disabled women are referred to in its explanatory memorandum (Committee of Ministers 2007b: paras 181 and 182).

Disability policy and standard setting within the Council of Europe is evident at the intergovernmental level within the framework of the Partial Agreement in the Social and Public Health Field (Degener et al. 2008: 33; Quinn 1999). This framework was concerned principally with the prevention of disability, rehabilitation and participation. Today, the most important instrument addressing disability is the Council of Europe Action Plan 2006–2015 to promote the rights and full participation of people with disabilities in society (Committee of Ministers 2006). This Action Plan complements the CRPD and aims to provide guidelines for its implementation and monitoring. Multiple discrimination is addressed in a specific section of the action plan entitled 'cross-cutting

---

53   Art. 14 ECHR and Art. 1 of Protocol No. 12 to the ECHR and Art. E ESC prohibit racial discrimination. The ESC also contains a provision for the protection of human rights of migrant workers and their families (Art. 19 ESC).

54   Art. 14 ECHR and Art. 1 of Protocol No. 12 to the ECHR and Art. E ESC prohibit sex-based discrimination. The ESC additionally protects women against employment discrimination (Arts 8 and 20 ESC).

55   Disability-based discrimination is mentioned neither in Art. 14 ECHR nor in Art. 1 of Protocol No. 12 to the ECHR nor in Art. E ESC but falls within the open-ended 'other status' clause in those articles. In addition, Art. 15 ESC protects the rights of persons with disabilities to independence, social integration and participation in community life.

56   ECRI General Policy Recommendation No. 3.

57   ECRI General Policy Recommendation No. 7.

aspects' (ibid.: Appendix, section 4). In particular, the specific circumstances of disabled women, disabled migrants and refugees, disabled children and elderly disabled people with high-level support needs are mentioned. Members of these groups are identified as being the most likely to be subject to multiple discrimination. Policy-makers are called upon to 'acknowledge the barriers and challenges faced by each of these groups and ensure that their policies are equipped to remove those barriers and ensure that individuals can reach their full potential alongside other citizens' (ibid.: Appendix, section 4.1).

The report *Discrimination against Women with Disabilities* (Beleza 2003), prepared for the Second Conference of Ministers responsible for integration policies for people with disabilities (held in Malaga in 2003), addresses the 'two-fold' discrimination experienced by disabled women in European countries. The first high-level European conference on access to training and employment by women with disabilities took place in February 2009 in Spain (Council of Europe 2009).

The European Court of Human Rights and the European Committee of Social Rights have both addressed the issue of discrimination on grounds of race, sex and disability in separate cases. It has been suggested that the case law of the European Court of Human Rights on discrimination reveals three tiers of review standard. The strictest level of review is applied to 'suspect' discrimination grounds such as sex and race. An intermediate level of review is applied to categories which are not suspect grounds but which nevertheless concern personal identity. Disability falls within this intermediate level of review. A more lenient level of review has been identified as applying in cases which involve discrimination unrelated to personal identity factors (Arnadóttir 2009). Multidimensional discrimination has not yet been addressed by either the Court or the Committee, although such opportunities existed.[58]

In sum, while the institutions of the Council of Europe have, to differing extents, tackled racism, sexism and ableism over the past few decades, discrimination at the intersection of race, gender and disability has not yet been addressed.

European Union   Like its sister organization, the Council of Europe, the European Union has developed laws against racism, sexism and ableism. In the primary law of the European Union there are several relevant provisions. The principle of gender mainstreaming is enshrined in Article 8 of the Treaty on the Functioning of the European Union (TFEU). Article 157 TFEU lays down the principal of equal pay between men and women. Article 18 TFEU, as well as other more specific provisions,[59] prohibits discrimination on grounds of nationality. Article 19 TFEU gives the Council a mandate to adopt secondary legislation to combat discrimination based on sex, racial or ethnic origin, religion or belief, disability, age or sexual orientation. The Charter of Fundamental Rights of the European Union prohibits discrimination on 18 grounds (Article 21) including race, sex and disability.

There are now several directives, based on Article 13 EC (Treaty of Rome, as amended now Article 19 TFEU) and other primary law provisions, which prohibit discrimination on the three grounds of interest here. The Article 13 directives include the Employment Framework Directive,[60]

---

58   See, for example, *DH and Others v. The Czech Republic*, ECtHR (Grand Chamber) Application No. 57325/00, 13 November 2007 (on this see also Lawson, in this volume: 47–61).

59   Art. 34 TFEU on free movement of goods, Art. 45 TFEU on workers, Art. 49 TFEU on freedom of establishment, Art. 56 TFEU on services and Art. 63 TFEU on capital.

60   Council Directive 2000/78/EC of 27 November 2000 establishing a general framework for equal treatment in employment and occupation [2000] OJ L303/16.

the Race Equality Directive,[61] and the Gender Goods and Services Directive.[62] There are several gender equality directives (Burri and Prechal 2008) of which the new Recast Gender Directive[63] is the most important. With the exception of the Employment Framework Directive, these directives are all single-ground instruments which do not tackle multiple discrimination. They do, however, contain provisions which could be used to raise awareness of multidimensional discrimination.

The aim of the Race Equality Directive is to eliminate discrimination based on racial or ethnic origin. Its preamble (recital 14) refers to multiple discrimination against women and reminds the EU to have due regard to the gender mainstreaming principle of Article 3(2) EC (now Article 8 TFEU) when implementing that directive. The Commission is also obliged to adhere to the gender mainstreaming principle in its reporting duties under Article 17(2) of the Race Equality Directive. No reference is made in this directive, however, to disabled women or to disability as a ground of multiple discrimination. Nor is the concept of reasonable accommodation included.

The Gender Goods and Services Directive makes no reference to disability or to any other ground of multidimensional discrimination. This single-grounded approach appears unusual, especially as regards harassment. Article 2(c) and (d) defines harassment and sexual harassment as unwanted conduct which violates the dignity of the person and may create an offensive or otherwise unfriendly environment. However, both these forms of harassment relate to the ground of gender alone. But harassment is an example of discrimination which often takes place at the intersection of gender and race or gender and disability[64] (Crenshaw 1991–2; Weber 2007). In addition, this directive lacks the concept of reasonable accommodation.

The Recast Gender Directive, which aims to implement the principle of equal opportunities for and equal treatment of men and women in matters of employment and occupation, contains an explicit reference to disability in its personal[65] and material scope. However, it does not mention the aggravated situation faced by disabled women. Nor does it extend acknowledgement to any other form of multiple discrimination. The concept of reasonable accommodation is absent in this directive, too.

The Employment Framework Directive was adopted to combat discrimination on grounds of sex, religion or belief, disability, age or sexual orientation in the employment area. Its substantive provisions on discrimination include the concept of reasonable accommodation but only in relation to disabled persons.[66] Multiple discrimination against women generally is mentioned in the preamble[67] but not addressed in the provisions on discrimination. The gender mainstreaming principle is acknowledged in the context of the Commission's reporting duties to the European Parliament and the Council on the implementation of this Directive.[68]

The equality directives have different material scopes. Discrimination based on race or ethnic origin is prohibited in non-employment areas such as social protection, healthcare, education and

---

61   Council Directive 2000/43/EC of 29 June 2000 implementing the principle of equal treatment between persons irrespective of racial or ethnic origin [2000] OJ L180/22.

62   Council Directive 2004/113/EC of 13 December 2004 implementing the principle of equal treatment between men and women in the access to and supply of goods and services [2004] OJ L373/37.

63   Directive 2006/54/EC of the European Parliament and of the Council of 5 July 2006 on the implementation of the principle of equal opportunities and equal treatment of men and women in matters of employment and occupation (recast) [2006] OJ L204/23.

64   See the examples given above (29–31).

65   Directive 2006/54, Art. 6.

66   Directive 2000/78, Art. 5.

67   Directive 2000/78, recital 3 of the preamble.

68   Directive 2000/78, Art. 19(2).

access to goods and services (including housing) which are available to the public as well as in employment, occupation and vocational training. Discrimination based on sex, apart from education and media and advertising, is prohibited in the same range of areas. However, discrimination based on age, religion and belief, sexual orientation and disability is prohibited only in employment, occupation and vocational training.

In order to bring European Union law on discrimination up to the standards established in the Race Equality Directive, the Commission in 2008 proposed a draft Council directive on implementing the principle of equal treatment between persons irrespective of religion or belief, disability, age or sexual orientation.[69] The goal of that proposal is to extend the prohibition of discrimination on the relevant grounds to the areas of social protection, including social security and healthcare; social advantages; education; and access to and supply of publicly available goods and services.[70] It also contains provisions intended to clarify the legal workings of the concept of reasonable accommodation as an anti-discrimination measure. In fact, however, these provisions seem merely to add to the widespread confusion on this legal term.[71] Article 4 of the 2008 draft directive proposes the introduction of an anticipatory duty to provide reasonable accommodation. This would require providers of goods and services to anticipate having disabled customers and to take steps to make their goods and services accessible before actually interacting with them. Although the notion of anticipatory reasonable accommodation might make sense in some Member States, such as the UK where it was developed (Lawson 2008), it could lead to confusion in European and international law. The text intertwines two different legal concepts: (1) the principle of accessibility which aims at enabling disabled persons as a group to live independently and participate fully in all aspects of life and (2) the duty to provide reasonable accommodation to an individual with an impairment to ensure equal opportunities for that person with respect to certain aspects of life, such as employment or education. While the principle of accessibility is group-oriented, the concept of reasonable accommodation targets the individual (Degener 2008: 384). Which measure or modification is necessary and appropriate in a given case is a matter of negotiation between the individual entitled and the duty-bearer. In this negotiation process, the principle of proportionality applies. The duty to provide reasonable accommodation is limited to those modifications and measures which do not impose a disproportionate burden. This does not apply to the principle of accessibility. What needs to be done in order to achieve accessibility is a matter of group negotiation (most often between disability organizations and governments) which takes place before the legislative act, regulation or code of conduct is adopted. In combining the two different legal concepts, the 2008 draft directive applies the limitation of disproportionate burden to accessibility. The CRPD, in contrast, draws a clear distinction between the two concepts.[72]

Multiple discrimination is not a key issue in the 2008 draft directive, although this had been recommended in the foregoing consultation process[73] as well as in several studies (European Commission 2007a and 2008d: 22). Some references are made to multiple discrimination against women and the principle of gender mainstreaming in the preamble[74] and in the draft provisions

---

69   COM(2008) 426 final Proposal for a Council Directive on implementing the principle of equal treatment between persons irrespective of religion or belief, disability, age or sexual orientation.

70   Draft directive, Art. 3.

71   I am grateful to Stefan Trömel for pointing this out to me.

72   Accessibility: CRPD, Art. 9 and reasonable accommodation: CRPD, Arts 2 and 5.

73   COM(2008) 426 final, 4.

74   Draft directive, recital 13 of the preamble.

on reporting obligations.[75] However, when tackling intersectional discrimination, the provision of reasonable accommodation, now confined to equal treatment of disabled persons, might lead to the legal problems mentioned above.

In addition to binding primary and secondary legislation, there are numerous soft law instruments which are concerned with combating discrimination. Among these are several gender equality programmes (European Commission 2006a), the PROGRESS[76] programme and the EU Disability Action Plan (2003–2010) (European Commission 2007b) which all include provisions on combating discrimination or creating equality of opportunity. Some of these soft law instruments contain references to multiple discrimination. For instance, the third phase of the EU Disability Action Plan (2008–2009) contains reasonably comprehensive provisions which address the issue of women with disabilities (ibid.). Annex 2 to this Plan provides an overview of the situation of disabled women in the context of various life course stages (European Commission 2007c). The gender equality programmes make some reference to discrimination at the intersection of race and gender (European Commission 2006a: 4). However, disability seems to be almost entirely absent from the EU's gender programme. This is especially true of EU instruments on harassment (European Commission 1991).

Tackling multiple discrimination was the major objective of the European Year of Equal Opportunities for All 2007 (EYEOA).[77] Disability, gender and race were among the categories discussed. Some of the key outcomes of the EYEOA were a report (European Commission 2007a) and a conference on tackling multiple discrimination (European Commission 2007d). Disabled women were identified as one of the groups at high risk of experiencing intersectional discrimination. The report as well as the conference ended with recommendations on how to tackle multiple discrimination in the future through research; legislation; awareness raising; training and education; data collection; and good practice and networking. Conference participants recommended amending existing national and European legislation in order to facilitate efforts to combat multiple discrimination. There were, however, different views as to how this could best be achieved. Representatives of ministries and public authorities noted that framing effective multiple discrimination provisions would be problematic. Representatives of national equality bodies proposed measures such as the extension of equal legal coverage to all grounds, the establishment of single equality bodies and the effective implementation of equality mainstreaming. National equality bodies also recommended that the concept of reasonable accommodation should be extended to all grounds (European Commission 2007d: 6).

Because the prohibition and prevention of gender discrimination was one of the first equality issues on the agenda of the European Communities, it comes as no surprise that there is a rich body of European Court of Justice (ECJ) case law on gender equality (Langenfeld 1990; Schiek and Chege 2009; Bell 2004). Many of these cases involve sub-groups of women (such as single mothers or pregnant women) and allegations of discrimination based on a combination of grounds such as gender and age. To date, however, the ECJ has not analysed these cases from a multiple discrimination perspective but has instead tended to deal with only one of the grounds of the relevant discrimination, typically gender. This tendency to consider only one of the possible grounds is also evident in recent case law on disability discrimination.

---

75   Draft directive, Art. 16.

76   Decision No 1672/2006/EC of the European Parliament and of the Council of 24 October 2006 establishing a Community Programme for Employment and Social Solidarity – Progress [2006] OJ L315/1.

77   Decision No 771/2006/EC of the European Parliament and of the Council of 17 May 2006 establishing the European Year of Equal Opportunities for All (2007) – towards a just society [2006] OJ L146/1.

In *Coleman*,[78] the ECJ held that the prohibition on disability discrimination established in the Employment Framework Directive extends to cases involving non-disabled persons who are associates of individuals with disabilities. In that case, the plaintiff, Mrs Coleman, mother and only carer of a disabled child, brought proceedings for constructive dismissal against her former employer, alleging that it discriminated against her because of her disabled child. In applying the Employment Framework Directive, the ECJ held that the treatment Mrs Coleman received amounted to direct disability-based discrimination and harassment. The facts of *Coleman* provide a good example of intersectional discrimination. Her son's disability was one ground for the discrimination she experienced. The other was her role as sole carer, a role which disproportionately falls on women (European Commission 2009). Accordingly, the unfavourable treatment and harassment she experienced did not occur simply because her child was disabled, but because he was disabled and she needed to take care of him. That caring responsibility gave rise to several disputes between Mrs Coleman and her former employer about her work performance. The ECJ recognized the multidimensional nature of the discrimination in question without naming it. This emerges clearly from paragraph 56 of the judgment:

> Where an employer treats an employee who is not himself disabled less favourably than another employee, has been or would be treated in a comparable situation, and it is established that the less favourable treatment of that employee is based on the disability of his child, whose care is provided primarily by that employee, such treatment is contrary to the prohibition of direct discrimination laid down by Article 2(2)(a) [of Directive 2000/78].

Thus, the court acknowledged indirectly that the discrimination was based on both factors, the impairment of Mrs Coleman's son and her role as sole carer. However, as in many other cases, the court dealt with the case on the basis of only one of these factors.

National Anti-Discrimination Laws – Some Examples

Following the transposition of the various EU equality directives adopted from 2000 onwards, most EU Member States now have anti-discrimination legislation that covers the grounds of disability, race and gender (McColgan et al. 2006; Waddington and Lawson 2009). Racial and gender discrimination were both the subject of much earlier prohibitions in many European countries, i.e. UK, Ireland, the Netherlands, France and, with respect to gender only, the Scandinavian countries (Schiek et al. 2007: 13–24; Degener 2005). National anti-discrimination legislation differs in many ways which, when intersectional discrimination is at stake, may result in the legal problems outlined above. Some countries have specific anti-discrimination statutes on single grounds which have different personal and material scopes and possibilities for justification (McColgan et al. 2006). Others have specific anti-discrimination laws that cover multiple grounds. In some cases, the law on equality results from various sections found in different statutes and from case law, with some countries combining all these approaches. Most countries only apply reasonable accommodation duties in relation to disabled persons and only in certain fields.[79]

Legal responses to multiple discrimination first occurred outside Europe, although not always through the efforts of courts or legislatures. In Australia, the predecessor of the Human Rights Commission took up the issue of intersectional discrimination (European Commission 2007a: 23).

---

78   Case C-303/06 *Coleman* [2008] ECR I-5603.
79   Discussed above (31–3).

Similarly, in the United States, the first legal steps were taken by the public administration. In 2006, the US Equal Employment Opportunity Commission published guidance notes on intersectional discrimination relating to race and other grounds.[80] In Canada, the Ontario Human Rights Commission took a leading role by publishing a discussion paper on intersectional discrimination (Ontario Human Rights Commission 2001a). Some Canadian courts also addressed the issue, the Supreme Court as early as 1993, other courts some years later (European Commission 2007a: 20). In Europe, by 2007, only three countries had legislation explicitly addressing multiple discrimination: Austria, Germany and Spain.[81]

Some of the legal problems regarding protection against discrimination at the intersection of race, gender and disability can be illustrated by reference to German anti-discrimination law. Germany is one of the few countries to have a provision on multiple discrimination in one of its anti-discrimination laws. The General Equal Treatment Act 2006,[82] which covers the grounds of race, ethnic origin, sex, religion, belief, disability, age and sexual orientation[83] in the areas of employment and some civil law contracts offered to the general public, explicitly covers multiple discrimination.[84] Germany is also exceptional in that disabled women are explicitly referred to in several anti-discrimination provisions which require their specific needs to be recognized.[85] Although Germany is ahead of many other European countries in this respect, the protection against intersectional discrimination on the basis of race, gender and disability remains insufficient.

German discrimination law is fragmented with different anti-discrimination laws applying to different grounds with varying material scope. Anti-discrimination provisions can be found in the constitution,[86] the criminal code,[87] labour law,[88] the social code[89] and in laws on other fields. Further, in addition to the General Equal Treatment Act, there are several separate anti-discrimination acts on gender equality and equal opportunities for disabled persons.[90]

---

80   See Section 15.IV.C. headed 'Intersectional Discrimination' in the EEOC Compliance Manual (Equal Employment Opportunity Commission 2006).

81   For more detailed discussion and further development see Moon (in this volume: 157–73) and Schiek and Mulder (in this volume: 259–73).

82   *Allgemeines Gleichbehandlungsgesetz* (AGG).

83   AGG, § 1.

84   AGG, § 4.

85   § 1 Book IX of the Social Code (*Sozialgesetzbuch IX* (SGB IX)); § 2 Disabled Persons Equal Treatment Act (*Behindertengleichstellungsgesetz* (BGG)).

86   Art. 3 Basic Law (*Grundgesetz* (GG)) which prohibits discrimination based on sex, parentage, race, language, homeland and origin, faith, religion, political opinion and disability. It allows for positive actions in favour of women and (to a lesser extent) in favour of disabled persons.

87   E.g. § 130 Criminal Code (*Strafgesetzbuch* (StGB)) on sedition.

88   § 75 Workplace Constitution Act of 1972 (*Betriebsverfassungsgesetz* (BetrVerfG)) provides that the employer and works council are responsible for ensuring that no discrimination occurs on the basis of race, ethnic origin, descent or other origin, nationality, religion, political opinion, disability, age, political or trade union-related activity or opinion, sex or sexual orientation.

89   §§ 17 and 33c Book I of the Social Code (*Sozialgesetzbuch I* (SGB I), § 19a Book IV of the Social Code (*Sozialgesetzbuch IV* (SGB IV), § 81(2) Book IX of the Social Code and § 19 Book X of the Social Code (*Sozialgesetzbuch X* (SGB X)) all prohibit discrimination in the delivery and administration of social security, but address different grounds and have different standards for justification.

90   Legislation on gender: Federal Committee Appointments Act of 1994 (*Bundesgremienbesetzungsgesetz* (BGremBG)) and Federal Equal Treatment Act of 2001 (*Bundesgleichstellungsgesetz* (BGleiG)); on disability: Disabled Persons Equal Treatment Act of 2002.

The General Equal Treatment Act offers protection against multiple discrimination, but its definition of discrimination does not include denial of reasonable accommodation.[91] Thus, a disabled woman from an ethnic or religious minority can challenge intersectional discrimination only in so far as it does not concern accessibility. For example, we might imagine a bar which has three steps leading to the only entrance and which displays a sign saying 'Turks, disabled and women unwelcome'. A Turkish woman who uses a wheelchair would be able to file a lawsuit against the bar owner only in respect of the sign, not the steps. She could obtain a court order requiring the bar owner to remove the sign but not to provide a ramp. It could be argued that the inaccessible entrance constitutes indirect discrimination (on grounds of disability) and thus is prohibited by the General Equal Treatment Act. Indirect discrimination is defined in that act as 'apparently neutral provisions, criteria or practices that could disadvantage persons on the basis of the grounds mentioned in § 1 in comparison with other persons'.[92] Accordingly, it could be said that steps at the entrance to a bar constitute an apparently neutral practice governing entry to the place of service provision. Indeed, several scholars have emphasized the potential entailed in the concept of indirect discrimination for persons facing multidimensional discrimination (Schiek et al. 2007: 475; Waddington and Lawson 2009: 50). As a finding of indirect discrimination may on occasion trigger duties to accommodate differences, in the absence of a duty to make reasonable accommodation, such approach may appear attractive. However, aside from the difficulties involved in proving indirect discrimination in cases of intersectional discrimination, that option is precluded in the context of the General Equal Treatment Act because of its specific legislative history. Whereas in earlier legislation[93] the denial of reasonable accommodation to disabled persons in employment cases was linked to anti-discrimination duties, in replacing that provision, the General Equal Treatment Act omits such link (Degener et al. 2008: 367).

Germany has signed and ratified the CRPD which requires States Parties to 'take all appropriate measures to eliminate discrimination on the basis of disability by any person, organization or private enterprise'.[94] Inserting appropriate amendments to anti-discrimination law is one of the various legislative implementation measures Germany will need to adopt in fulfilment of its CRPD obligations (Degener 2009).

Conclusions

It has been shown that hardly any data exists on the results of discrimination at the intersection of race, gender and disability. Thus, it comes as no surprise to discover that public awareness of multiple discrimination is low. Even the victims of intersectional discrimination – as the three examples I cited above demonstrate – often do not know how to name and classify experiences of intersectional discrimination. While many cases lodged before courts or equality tribunals, in practice, involve discrimination on more than one ground, legal practitioners tend to frame multidimensional discrimination cases as simply concerning a single ground (Fredman 2009). Various legal problems arise when existing anti-discrimination law is applied to discrimination at the intersection of race, gender and disability. The anti-discrimination legislation may be drafted to

---

91   The definition in § 3 AGG covers five forms of discrimination: (1) direct discrimination, (2) indirect discrimination, (3) sexual harassment, (4) harassment, and (5) instructions to discriminate. The definitions used are similar to those found in the Race Equality Directive.

92   AGG, § 3(2).

93   SGB IX of 19 June 2001, § 81, BGBl. I, p. 1046.

94   CRPD, Art. 4(1)(e).

focus on individual grounds and may have a different material scope for each ground. Definitions of discrimination on grounds of race and gender tend to be identical, while discrimination on grounds of disability may be defined differently, either by including denial of reasonable accommodation or by excluding harassment. Differences can also be detected in the justifications considered acceptable and in the degree of enforceability. While discrimination on grounds of race or gender can rarely be justified by law, there is greater scope for justifying discrimination on grounds of disability. And although most building and information technology codes today include accessibility guidelines, they do not come with enforceable rights.

A survey of international law on discrimination has demonstrated that, with the exception of the CRPD, most human rights treaties do not tackle multiple discrimination explicitly. While the CRPD expressly protects disabled women and disabled children against discrimination, the provision which prohibits multiple discrimination relates only to the first group. However, textual gaps in human rights treaties regarding multiple discrimination are increasingly being addressed by the supervising treaty bodies. Disabled women were among the first group experiencing multiple discrimination to be addressed by CEDAW. Meanwhile discrimination at the intersection of race and gender receives the most attention. Today, every treaty body supervising a human rights treaty on discrimination has demonstrated some awareness of multidimensional discrimination issues in general comments or general recommendations. However, as Timo Makkonen (2002) has analysed, general recommendations and comments on multidimensional discrimination need streamlining and further development. In relation to discrimination at the intersection of race, gender and disability, it is recommended that the disability aspect should be included in recommendations and general comments relating to traditional practices and beliefs, the criminal justice system and citizenship.

A review of European non-discrimination law has demonstrated that the existing approach of both the Council of Europe and the European Union has been to focus anti-discrimination legislation, case law and institutional frameworks on single grounds of discrimination. The result is that intersectional discrimination has been insufficiently addressed in both intra-governmental organizations. In the case of the Council of Europe, the first steps towards tackling intersectional discrimination can now be seen in the European Disability Action Plan.

At the European Union level, a major attempt to address the issue of multidimensional discrimination was taken during the European Year of Equal Opportunities for All 2007 (EYEOA). During that year, important studies and recommendations were undertaken and developed on the issue of multidimensional discrimination. Unfortunately, the 2008 draft directive on implementing the principle of equal treatment between persons irrespective of religion or belief, disability, age or sexual orientation misses the opportunity to address multidimensional discrimination. With respect to discrimination at the intersection of gender and disability it is most striking to find that disability issues are almost entirely absent from the EU's gender programme. Finally, in relation to national anti-discrimination laws, it may be observed that a few countries now address multiple discrimination in their legislation. However, as the example of German law illustrates, simply adding a provision on multiple discrimination does not suffice. In order to tackle discrimination at the intersection of race, gender and disability, more comprehensive steps are necessary. These include streamlining both definitions of discrimination and the personal and material scope of the legislation. Further, a consistent approach to reasonable accommodation duties and towards justification is required.

Sandra Fredman (2009) has pointed out that positive measures open up many more possibilities for tackling (intersectional) discrimination than a complaint-led model does. Instead of relying on a disabled woman from an ethnic minority to file a complaint and prove that she has been treated less favourably than a white non-disabled man, a white non-disabled woman, or a white disabled man, positive measures require public or private bodies to identify inequalities and find remedies. However, positive discrimination measures can easily turn into privileges or even charity debates if not accompanied by clear anti-discrimination mandates. Thus, further development of anti-discrimination law is necessary.

Chapter 3

Disadvantage at the Intersection of Race and Disability: Key Challenges for EU Non-Discrimination Law

Anna Lawson

Introduction

The growing body of academic legal and socio-legal literature on multidimensional inequality has been primarily concerned with the intersection of the 'nodes' (Schiek, in this volume) of race and gender (see, for example, Schiek and Chege 2009). Nevertheless, a significant body of work by Disability Studies scholars is now to be found on the intersections of disability and gender (e.g. Fine and Asch 1981, 1988; Boylan 1991; Driedger and Gray 1992; Morris 1993, 1996; Shakespeare 1996; Traustadóttir and Johnson 2000; Robertson 2004; Sheldon 2004); disability and race (e.g. Stuart 1993; Begum et al. 1994; Ahmad 2000; Vernon 2002; Banton and Singh 2004); and disability, gender and race (e.g. Vernon 1996, 1999; Barile 2000; Asch 2001; Hussain 2005; Ostrander 2008). Further, as Theresia Degener explains elsewhere in this book, recent years have witnessed a heightened attention on these disability intersections in international and European political debate.

However, the disability–race intersection has received less attention than the disability–gender intersection – both in the academic literature and also in broader political debate. This appears to provide at least part of the explanation for the appearance, in the United Nations Convention on the Rights of Persons with Disabilities (CRPD), of a specific substantive article on disabled women but not of one on disabled people belonging to minority ethnic or religious groups – a differentiation which itself seems likely to perpetuate and intensify the difference in the levels of attention given to the two types of disability intersection.

The focus of this chapter is the area of the triangle formed by race, gender and disability discrimination which, it is suggested, has received the least scrutiny to date – the disability–race overlap. This overlap covers a multitude of diverse circumstances – the precise manifestations varying according to different impairment types, different cultures, different beliefs and different social, environmental, political and linguistic factors. Despite this diversity, empirical studies on the experiences of people at the disability–race intersection (e.g. Banton and Hirsch 2000; Pierce 2003a) indicate that (at least within the societies in which the studies are conducted) they commonly experience similar types of exclusion and disadvantage.

The first substantive section of this chapter will briefly explore the relationship between race and disability. It will draw attention to a number of factors which are likely to operate so as to disable a disproportionate number of people in minority ethnic groups by increasing the likelihood that they will have, or be labelled as having, a physical or mental impairment or condition. This issue is relevant to the experience of intersectional inequality because, by sucking disproportionate numbers of people from minority ethnic groups into the ranks of disabled people, it disproportionately exposes them to disabling societal forces.

In the second substantive section, an attempt will be made to identify the key types of disadvantage to which disabled people belonging to minority ethnic groups are likely to be exposed. Many of these types of disadvantage will also be experienced by disabled people belonging to the majority ethnic group and by non-disabled people from minority ethnic backgrounds. However, an attempt will be made to identify respects in which people at the disability–race intersection are likely to be at increased risk of the disadvantage and to ways in which they might experience it more intensely than others.

In the third main section, the role of EU law in tackling the types of disadvantage previously identified will be considered. Particular attention will be given to a number of concepts to be found in current or proposed EU non-discrimination law which have particular relevance to disability and which have hitherto received little attention in the intersectionality debate. In addition, an attempt will be made to draw attention to some other dimensions of EU law which also have an important role to play in tackling disadvantage at the disability–race intersection.

Minority Ethnic Status and Impairment

Impairment – Language and Social Factors

The term 'impairment' will be used here in the sense used by proponents of the social model of disability (Oliver 1990, 1996; Campbell and Oliver 1996; Priestley 1998; Barnes 2000; Barnes and Mercer 2003; Finkelstein 2004). Accordingly, it will refer to the existence of some variation from the conventional norm – itself a social construct (Hughes 1998; Linton 1998) – in terms of physical, intellectual, psychosocial or sensory characteristics which is regarded as bringing about a reduced level of functioning. The term 'disability', despite being commonly used in legal instruments to refer to such 'impairments', is generally used by social model theorists to refer to the portion of the marginalization and disadvantage experienced by people with impairments that is caused by the operation of exclusionary or oppressive social forces. Consequently, the term 'disabled people' will be used here in preference to that of 'people with disabilities'.

In this section an attempt will be made to investigate how social, political and economic forces may operate on members of minority ethnic groups so as to result in disproportionate numbers of those groups becoming disabled. Such forces will, for many refugees and asylum seekers, have been at work in countries other than the one in which they now live. The possibility that such experiences will have caused impairments – mental as well as physical – is a very real one which demands recognition in the development and implementation of all transition and resettlement programmes (Forced Migration Review 2010). Socio-economic factors which increase the likelihood of impairment for members of ethnic minority groups (whether they have migrated or not) are, however, also at work within the EU countries in which they currently live and it is these that are of interest here.

The rest of this section will focus on two types of social factor that increase the likelihood of people in minority ethnic groups being classified as disabled. The first is poverty – and the increased risk of impairment which it carries. The second is the process by which people are labelled as having an impairment and the way in which this is likely to affect people in minority ethnic groups.

Poverty

Although comprehensive data on race is not available in all European countries (Simon 2007), there is ample evidence to suggest that minority ethnic groups feature amongst the poorest sections of many European countries. Thus, in the UK, more than two-thirds of Bangladeshis and more than half of Pakistanis live in areas falling into the bottom decile of deprivation (Equalities Review 2007: 42) and there is evidence indicating that members of minority ethnic groups are disadvantaged in many different areas of life (see, for example, Modood et al. 1997; Morris and Clements 2001). In Ireland, the position appears to be similar (Pierce 2003a). Further, in Central and Eastern Europe, international attention has been drawn to the startling levels of poverty and deprivation commonly experienced by Roma people. Thus, in Bulgaria, 10 times as many Roma people as non-Roma people are reported to live in absolute poverty – on the meagre sum of $2.15 a day – and in Hungary, Roma people have been found to be 13 times more likely to do so (Ringold et al. 2005). In Serbia and Montenegro, 9.8 per cent of Roma households have been classified as 'extremely poor' as opposed to only 0.2 per cent of non-Roma households (Bodewig and Sethi 2005). Extremely low levels of income are accompanied by impoverishment in terms of access to educational and employment opportunities, to housing, health and other services.

Life in conditions of poverty and deprivation carries increased risks of illness, injury and impairment. Although there is little data on the numbers of disabled people within different ethnic groups (Morris and Clements 2001; Pierce 2003a), there is some interesting health-related information. This indicates that the life expectancy of Roma people in Central and Eastern Europe is considerably shorter than that of non-Roma people – 10 to 15 years in Hungary (Ringold et al. 2005: 48); that infant mortality rates are much higher for Roma people than non-Roma people – double in Slovakia and the Czech Republic (Ringold et al. 2005: 48); and that Roma women are considerably more likely to experience complications during pregnancy and to give birth prematurely or to have underweight babies than non-Roma women (Purporka and Zádori 1999).

From information such as this, it can be inferred that physical and mental impairment are likely to appear more often in the lives of impoverished minority ethnic communities than in those of the majority ethnic group. The significant underlying factor is poverty – a factor to which evidence demonstrates that (at least in the countries studied) minority ethnic groups are particularly likely to be exposed. Poverty, however, is not the exclusive domain of minority ethnic groups and the increased likelihood of impairment and ill health which it carries will apply to all who live in conditions of deprivation and marginalization.

The existence of a strong link between disability and poverty is now beyond doubt. People living in poverty are more at risk of having impairments and, at the same time, people who have impairments (which may not have been caused by poverty) are likely to be pushed into poverty by a multitude of disabling societal forces (Despouy 1992; Berthoud et al. 1993; UN Economic and Social Council 2008). World Bank studies suggest that a fifth of the world's poorest people are disabled in some way (Elwan 1999, see also Stienstra et al. 2002). In the UK, a quarter of the children living in poverty in 2004–5 had a disabled parent (Department for Work and Pensions 2006) and over half of families with a disabled child live in poverty (Gordon et al. 2000).

Labelling

In many countries, there are indications that people from minority ethnic groups disproportionately appear amongst the ranks of those classified as having learning difficulties or mental health conditions. The former issue was dramatically brought to international consciousness by the case of *DH v. The Czech Republic*.[1] This case concerned the disproportionately high number of Roma children in special schools for pupils with 'mental handicaps'[2] – such schools were attended by 50.8 per cent of Roma children but only by 1.3 per cent of non-Roma children. In a ground-breaking judgement, the European Court of Human Rights (ECtHR) found this to be the result of indirect race discrimination.

An increased likelihood of 'psychosocial' disabilities – the term used by organizations such as the World Network of Users and Survivors of Psychiatry in preference to 'mental health' problems – is almost certainly linked to factors such as living in conditions of deprivation and of encountering hostility and discrimination on a regular basis. However, social factors will often operate to make it more likely that a person from a minority ethnic group will be classified as having some kind of intellectual, cognitive or psychosocial impairment than a person from the majority ethnic group who has exactly the same level of functioning (Gabel et al. 2009).

The tests used to determine on which side of the 'impairment/normal' divide a person should be placed may be culturally insensitive to members of minority ethnic communities. Rigid adherence to the results of such tests would therefore have the effect of classifying people as having impairments of some kind when, in reality, their poor performance was attributable to a difference in cultural or linguistic background rather than to one of intellectual or emotional functioning (Losen and Orfield 2002, see also Solanke 2009a: 125–6). Recognition that this had occurred in the categorization of many Roma children as 'mentally handicapped' formed the basis of the ECtHR's decision in the *DH* case.[3]

Another possible explanation of why people from ethnic minority groups may be classified as disabled when persons with equivalent levels of functioning from the majority ethnic group would not be, concerns the notion of 'normalcy' and the need (albeit generally latent or unconscious) to differentiate between people who fall within the conventional norm and those who do not. People from minority ethnic groups, like people with physical, intellectual or psychosocial impairments, deviate from the norm. However, in many countries it is unacceptable or even illegal to explicitly segregate others on grounds of race whereas segregation on grounds of impairment remains standard practice. Thus, in the words of Reid and Knight (2006: 19):

> In essence, marking students of color as disabled allows their continued segregation under a seemingly natural and justifiable label. Because it makes segregation seem appropriate and even preferable, the enduring belief that impairment and disability are empirical facts is at the center of the disproportionality problem.

That problematic belief, however, is given the power to disadvantage those labelled as having impairments only by virtue of other beliefs – amongst the most disabling of which (particularly in the educational context) are the view that it is desirable to segregate disabled people and the idea that very little should be expected of them. Such beliefs underlie much of the disadvantage which will be considered in the next section.

---

1   App. No. 57325/00 (13 November 2007).
2   This is the term used in the judgement – see, e.g., ibid., para. [41].
3   Ibid.

Disadvantage at the Disability–Race Intersection

Overview

Much has been written of the types of disadvantage and exclusion commonly experienced by disabled people and by people from minority ethnic groups. Space constraints prevent a detailed consideration of these bodies of literature here. Instead, attention will be focused solely on some dimensions of disadvantage which are likely to be distinctive to disabled people from minority ethnic groups and types of disadvantage to which they are particularly likely to be exposed. This task is made challenging by the fact that statistics rarely reveal the situation of people at this intersection (Pierce 2003a: Chapter 3) – a fact which operates to obscure the systemic nature of the disadvantage they experience (Barile 2000: 125–6; Fredman 2009: 84). However, the purpose of this section is not to provide an exhaustive account of the circumstances of disabled people from minority ethnic backgrounds. It is rather to highlight a number of key points designed to assist in the assessment of EU law which is to follow.

Before considering any of these types of disadvantage it should be stressed that, as discussed in the previous section, in many countries people from minority ethnic groups are more likely than others to have impairments and also to be labelled as having them. This means that they are more at risk than people from majority ethnic groups of experiencing all the types of disadvantage commonly experienced by disabled people. Some of these (such as segregated living or segregated education in less good schools) are the product of explicit policies. Many, however, are associated with the absence of policies designed to ensure access, appropriate support and full inclusion.

It should also be noted that, as will become clear, poverty exacerbates many, if not all, of the disadvantages to be discussed. Poverty could itself be identified as a disadvantage but, given the discussion of it in the previous section, it will not be considered separately here.

Institutional Living

In many parts of Central and Eastern Europe, thousands of children – particularly those who are disabled and those who are from minority ethnic groups – live in large residential institutions (Mansell et al. 2007). According to Thomas Hammarberg (the Council of Europe's Commissioner for Human Rights) after a recent visit to Bulgaria (2010: para. 90): 'in Bulgaria, there are approximately 8,000 children living in 138 institutions for children including 26 institutions for children with disabilities'.

Statistics do not reveal what proportion of institutionalized disabled children are from minority ethnic groups, but it is generally assumed to be substantial.

Once in an institution, residents tend to remain in that environment for long periods of time. Indeed, a great many of the disabled people who enter an institution as children remain in institutions for excessively long periods of time (Hammarberg 2010: para. 93). Recent figures suggest that in Romania in 2008, in nearly 70 per cent of cases, the reason a person ceased to be in a residential institution was death as opposed to a move to community living (Institute for Public Policy 2010).

Another serious problem is the lack of nationally applicable standards regulating living conditions in these institutions. This lack, combined with inadequate funding, inevitably results in inadequate food, heating and clothing in some institutions. Assessments of needs and individualized care plans for disabled children are generally impossible due to inadequate resources (Hammarberg 2010: paras 97–100).

The result, for many disabled children from minority ethnic backgrounds (not just in Bulgaria), is thus a life lived apart from the community. It is often a life devoid of education and even of interaction designed to encourage speech and communication skills. It is, moreover, often a life in which physical hardship and deprivation combines with social isolation to produce one of the most seriously disadvantaged sectors of European society.

Education

No education   Disabled children from minority ethnic groups appear to be disproportionately at risk of receiving no formal primary or secondary education. This risk applies particularly to such children in two main types of situation. First, it applies to children living in residential institutions and, second, to children living with their families but in communities in which the levels of school attendance, even for non-disabled children, are low.

First, institutional living has been the fate of thousands of disabled children in Europe and continues to be a feature of disability policy in many Central and Eastern European countries. Roma children, as discussed in the previous section, appear to be disproportionately represented in these institutions. In many countries, including Bulgaria, responsibility for the education of children in these institutions falls to the government department with overall responsibility for the institutions rather than to the government department with responsibility for and expertise in education.

In 2008, the European Committee on Social Rights was faced with a collective complaint centring on the failure of Bulgaria to ensure that disabled children in these institutions (a disproportionate number of whom appear to be Roma) were provided with an education. In *MDAC v. Bulgaria*,[4] it upheld this complaint and ruled that, in failing to provide these children with an education, Bulgaria had violated Article 17(2) of the Revised European Social Charter (on the right to education) and also Article E (on the right to be free from discrimination). Although this case raised the profile of the problem and has initiated some reform, concern remains that thousands of institutionalized children, in Bulgaria alone, are not receiving a meaningful education (Hammarberg 2010).

Outside institutions, there is evidence that school attendance amongst some minority ethnic groups is relatively low. In Scotland, for instance, research indicated that in the mid-1990s 59 per cent of traveller children did not attend primary school and that 80 per cent did not attend secondary school (Morris and Clements 2001: 13). In Bulgaria, only 35 per cent of Roma children were reported to attend primary school and 10 per cent secondary school (Ringold et al. 2005: 42). Research carried out in Serbia and Montenegro (Bodewig and Sethi 2005) indicates that important factors underlying poor school attendance included the costs associated with the purchase of uniforms or other appropriate clothing, books, travel (particularly as there was often a considerable distance between home and school) and with lost working time. Parental lack of interest also appeared to be an important factor – a factor which, according to the interviews conducted by Pierce (2003a) with members of the Irish traveller community, might prove even more important in relation to disabled children. Pierce's research also indicates that, far from having no interest in attending school, many disabled traveller children themselves were keen to do so as they regarded it as a means of enhancing their independence. Nevertheless, doing so was often impossible because of parental opposition or lack of awareness.

Inferior education   For disabled children from minority ethnic groups who do attend school, there appears to be a relatively high risk that the education they receive will be less demanding

---

4   *MDAC v. Bulgaria*, Complaint 41/2007, 3 June 2008.

and fulfilling than that received by others. The whole premise of *DH v. Czech Republic*,[5] accepted by the ECtHR, was that the segregated schools for children with 'mental handicaps' provided an inferior level of education to that provided by mainstream schools. Even where disabled children attend mainstream school, there often remains concern that they have been unable to achieve their full potential due to inadequate support or low teacher expectation (Equalities Review 2007: Chapter 3).

Although there is little data comparing the prospects of disabled children from minority ethnic groups with those of other disabled children, it is likely that the former group will be additionally hampered by race-related factors including the attitudes and expectations of teachers (Rist 1970; Solanke 2009a). This was certainly the experience of many of the disabled people interviewed by Vernon (1996: 58–9).

Culturally insensitive education   Non-disabled children from minority ethnic backgrounds are likely to experience cultural tensions in school and other educational establishments. For disabled children, however, there may well be a higher chance of experiencing such tensions. This is because disabled children are likely to have less choice as to which school to attend – they may be required to attend a special school or a mainstream school with relevant facilities which might be a long distance from home and have little or no relevant cultural awareness. Indeed, they may even be required to board, with the result that all aspects of their lives become subject to regulation by the school. The cultural isolation and confusion which may be caused to children placed in such environments is poignantly illustrated by Vernon's account of her own experience (1996: 50):

> My experience of racism started when I went to my first residential school for the blind which was all white apart from myself and an Asian boy. There I experienced physical and verbal abuse from the children and less favourable treatment from some of the staff. I could hardly speak any English, I wore Indian clothes and as a Muslim I needed a special diet. Gradually and in subtle ways, I was persuaded to wear English clothes and eat English food. The staff promised that they would not tell my father about it. I had to eat the food. If I hadn't I would have starved because the only alternative they would give me was salad. On one occasion they put a plate of sausages in front of me. I knew what it was by its smell. When I asked the housemother why I had sausages on my plate she snatched it from me and said 'Go without then!' That day I didn't eat anything.

Problems have also been identified, particularly for deaf children from minority ethnic groups, in connection with the lack of attention given by the general education system to cultural, historical and religious issues connected with their own culture. Ahmad et al. (2000) demonstrate how this operates to the particular disadvantage of deaf people (and possibly others with communication difficulties). Their work, which focused on ethnic minority families living in the UK, explored the tensions that arose when deaf children were taught British Sign Language in school where they were also familiarized with the culture of the majority ethnic group. Parents often found it impossible to supplement this education with details of their own culture and religion because of communication difficulties. They were often not fluent in British Sign Language, tuition in which is extremely difficult to obtain in languages other than English due to a shortage of sign language interpreters from ethnic minority backgrounds.

---

5   App. No. 57325/00 (13 November 2007).

Employment

In many countries, disabled people and members of minority ethnic groups often experience much lower rates of employment than the average. This is reflected in the findings of the Equalities Review (2007) recently conducted in the UK. There are also indications (at least in the UK and Ireland) that disabled people from minority ethnic groups are considerably more disadvantaged than disabled people from the majority ethnic group or non-disabled people from a minority ethnic group (Berthoud 2003; Pierce 2003a). Unfortunately, however, statistics revealing this information are rarely collected.

The reduced employment prospects of disabled people belonging to ethnic minorities are likely to be caused, not only by discriminatory prejudice, but also by disadvantages in obtaining education (discussed above) and by lack of opportunity to acquire fluency in the dominant language (because, for instance, they have had less access to the school system, less interaction with people outside their ethnic group or because they would have needed additional support to learn a new language). Language barriers were identified by the disabled people from ethnic minorities interviewed by Pierce (2003a) as one potential explanation for their difficulties in finding work.

Another factor that seems likely to disproportionately disadvantage disabled people from minority ethnic groups is the lack of public transport. Minority ethnic groups, such as Roma, often live in areas considerable distances away from where work is likely to be found and beyond the reach of reliable public transport (Goodwin 2009). If there is public transport, accessibility may be a problem – a point which it has not been possible to verify by statistical data.

For some people – disabled or not – a logical solution to transport difficulties would be to move to another location. For many disabled people, however, such a move would be extremely daunting if it involved moving away from established support networks. Given the additional difficulties often encountered by members of minority ethnic groups in becoming aware of and accessing support services and entitlements (discussed in the next section), it seems probable that moving away from family will often seem still more impractical and unsafe to them (Pierce 2003a; Hussain 2005).

Access to Support and Services

A powerful and recurring theme in UK and Irish empirical research on disabled people from minority ethnic groups is the lack of access to information about the availability of health or social services and their entitlement to them (see, for example, Chamba et al. 1999; Banton and Hirsch 2000; Pierce 2003a). The obvious result is that such services are frequently not used by people from minority ethnic groups and that they do not therefore derive the benefits of improved health and independence which those services are designed to afford.

One obvious factor which contributes to this information barrier is the failure of service providers to make information available in minority languages and to offer interpreting services (Chamba et al. 1999). However, it is clear that more subtle communication difficulties, created by cultural difference and associated lack of understanding or mistrust, also constitute a significant barrier. Such communication difficulties may make it difficult for people from minority ethnic groups to make relevant inquiries and to request appropriate support (Keith and Morris 1996: 105). A general lack of awareness of disability issues amongst some ethnic minority groups and a tendency to stigmatize impairment or the need for help have also been identified as relevant barriers (Banton and Hirsch 2000: 22).

Studies have also drawn attention to the difficulties frequently encountered by people from minority ethnic communities when they do attempt to use relevant services. As well as information or communication barriers, other obstacles are often deeply embedded in the structure of the relevant organizations (Banton and Singh 2004). Further, explicit hostility and discrimination are not uncommon experiences (Banton and Hirsch 2000; Pierce 2003a).

Tackling Disadvantage at the Disability–Race Intersection through EU Law

EU Non-Discrimination Law

Narrowing the focus   EU non-discrimination law is structured around a number of discrete and apparently separate grounds, two of which are race and disability. The relatively well-documented difficulties generated by this at the race–gender intersection (Schiek and Chege 2009; Solanke 2009b; Hannett 2003; Crenshaw 1989), which also impact on the disability–race intersection, will not be repeated here. Instead, for reasons of space, the focus here will be on concepts of current and proposed EU non-discrimination law which have particular relevance to disability and which have not therefore as yet received detailed scrutiny in the intersectionality debate. These concepts are reasonable accommodation (which is a current disability-specific feature of that law) and the provision of non-discriminatory access by anticipation (which is a disability-specific proposal for the expansion of that law). Indirect discrimination applies to the disability–race intersection in the same way as it does to other intersections. Nevertheless, it will be considered here because an awareness of its potential and limitations is helpful in assessments of the proposed new duty to provide access through anticipation.

These three concepts will be considered in turn below. Before that, however, a few words will be said about the current key directives and proposal for reform.

Relevant directives and material scope   The key instruments of EU non-discrimination law relating to race and disability are Directive 2000/43/EC (Race Equality Directive) and Directive 2000/78/EC (Employment Framework Directive). The former requires Member States to prohibit various forms of discrimination on grounds of race in a wide range of activities including employment and occupation, education, housing and goods and services. By contrast the latter, which covers a number of grounds one of which is disability, has a much more limited scope and applies only to employment and occupation.

The discrepancy in the extent of protection afforded to different grounds because of differences in relevant laws is a cause of ongoing concern (Schiek, in this volume: 11–27). The European Commission's proposal on 2 July 2008 for a new Equal Treatment Directive[6] represents an attempt to at least partially address such concerns by widening the scope of the protection afforded to disability and the other grounds covered by the Employment Framework Directive. It is also in this proposed directive that the duty to provide access by anticipation (discussed below) is to be found.

Reasonable accommodation   Article 5 of the Employment Framework Directive imposes on employers a duty to provide reasonable accommodation to disabled people (Waddington 2007a). It is an asymmetrical duty, being owed only to disabled people and offering no cause of action

---

6   Proposal for a Council Directive on Implementing the Principle of Equal Treatment Between Persons Irrespective of Religion or Belief, Disability, Age or Sexual Orientation COM (2008) 426.

to non-disabled people. While this has the advantage of sharpening the focus on the removal of disadvantage, it does raise the question of how disability should be defined – a question which has been answered in disturbingly restrictive terms by the Court of Justice[7] (Waddington 2007b). The issue here, however, is the relatively unexplored question of the extent to which the reasonable accommodation duty is capable of addressing disadvantage associated with a combination of characteristics (such as race and impairment) as opposed to disadvantage that can be traced solely to impairment.

The Article 5 reasonable accommodation duty is a duty to take 'appropriate measures, where needed in a particular case' to overcome the disadvantage to which a particular 'person' would otherwise be subjected by the employer's standard mode of operating. According to Recital 20, 'appropriate measures' means 'effective and practical measures to adapt the workplace to the disability' including adaptations to premises and equipment, to work patterns and task distribution, and the provision of training. Measures will therefore be 'appropriate' only if they would effectively tackle the particular disadvantage to which the particular individual would be exposed. It is a reactive or responsive duty which requires sensitivity to the individual's particular circumstances.

This emphasis on tackling the disadvantage encountered by a particular individual, it is suggested, requires attention to be given to all the circumstances relevant to finding an effective solution – including those which might appear to have more relevance to a characteristic other than impairment. A perfect illustration of the type of case in which race or ethnicity might have a bearing on the appropriateness of particular measures potentially required by a reasonable accommodation duty is Opinion 2006-256 of the Dutch Equal Treatment Commission, discussed in detail by Susanne Burri (in this volume: 104–5). That case concerned a blind woman of Turkish origin who was required by her employer to take a test to determine what role she should carry out within the organization. For non-disabled employees, the test was a written one. Because of the claimant's visual impairment, the employer agreed to adjust its standard procedure but refused the claimant's request to take the test in Braille. Instead she was required to take it orally. The claimant successfully argued that this was not an appropriate measure – and therefore not an adequate reasonable accommodation. Her first language was not Dutch and this made the oral examination particularly challenging. The impairment-related disadvantage associated with the written exam had therefore not been effectively removed.

This Dutch example powerfully demonstrates that circumstances related to the ethnicity of the disabled person will sometimes influence the effectiveness of particular measures in tackling the disadvantage which the employer's standard procedures or working methods would otherwise impose on that person because of their impairment. The reasonable accommodation duty, it is suggested, therefore requires regard to be had to these ethnicity-related circumstances in the identification of the appropriate measures to be taken by an employer. Thus, within its sphere of operation, the Article 5 reasonable accommodation duty is well placed to reach into the particularities of disability–race intersectional disadvantage and to require the crafting of appropriate individualized solutions. Its effectiveness in tackling the broad range of disadvantage at the disability–race intersection (considered in the previous section), however, is extremely limited.

The most obvious limitation on the power of the Article 5 duty to tackle disability–race disadvantage is the fact that its reach is confined to the employment context. No equivalent duty applies in other areas of life (such as pre-16 education, public transport, health or other service provision), disadvantage in which will undoubtedly restrict employment opportunities. This serious limitation would be significantly reduced were the proposed Equal Treatment Directive

---

7   Case C-13/05, *Chacón Navas v. Eurest Colectividades SA* [2006] I-6467.

to be enacted. Even if that Directive never acquires the force of law, the EU will be required by its obligations under the CRPD (considered more fully below) to extend, within the limits of its competence, the reasonable accommodation duty to these other areas of life (Waddington 2009).

Another limitation on the power of reasonable accommodation to tackle disadvantage at the disability–race intersection is to be found in its highly individualized, responsive nature. It is this quality which gives reasonable accommodation the power to look beyond impairment to all the relevant circumstances of the individual disabled person (including their ethnicity) and the environment in which they work. The corollary of that very valuable flexibility, however, is that the duty is not forward-looking or group-orientated. It imposes no obligation on employers to anticipate potential barriers or disadvantages for particular groups of people and to take steps to avoid or remove them in advance of the appearance of members of the group in question. It therefore needs to be supplemented by other obligations or prohibitions which are better placed to dismantle structural discrimination or disadvantage. In this regard, the potential contribution of indirect discrimination and the proposed new duty to provide non-discriminatory access by anticipation will be considered below.

Finally, on reasonable accommodation, it should be noted that the Article 5 duty applies only to disabled people and that EU law – unlike that of some EU countries, Canada and (in relation to religion only) the United States (Moon 2006a; Waddington 2007a: 683–5) – imposes no equivalent duty in respect of other grounds. Thus, for people at the disability–race intersection, the Article 5 duty will be triggered only if the employment disadvantage they experience is associated with their impairment – at which point ethnicity-related factors will become relevant in the selection of an appropriate solution. The duty will not be triggered if the initial disadvantage relates to ethnicity or religion and not impairment – even if impairment-related factors might have relevance to the identification of a solution. Thus, there would be no reasonable accommodation duty where the relevant disadvantage arose from a requirement that a Muslim employee should work at the meat counter of a supermarket, even if impairment-related factors (perhaps a back problem) might have been relevant to the identification of a solution – for example, in this case, a reallocation of tasks resulting in additional lifting duties would not seem an appropriate solution. For reasons of consistency, as well as principle, there have been calls for the extension of reasonable accommodation duties to other grounds (e.g. Degener, in this volume: 32–3). However, such an extension may have negative as well as positive consequences and a detailed examination of the different arguments (Lawson 2008: 176–81) is beyond the scope of this chapter.

Indirect discrimination   Indirect discrimination is prohibited by Article 2(1) of both the Race Equality Directive and the Employment Framework Directive (Schiek 2007a) and defined, in virtually identical terms, by Article 2(2)(b) of both. In relation to disability, however, the Employment Framework Directive includes an additional defence based on the provision of reasonable accommodation. The wording of this proviso is ambiguous and consequently its scope is uncertain (Whittle 2002: 310–11).

Thus, the Employment Framework Directive prohibits indirect disability discrimination – albeit somewhat tentatively – in the field of employment and occupation. Many Member States have exceeded the demands of this Directive and prohibited indirect disability discrimination in areas falling outside employment. As yet, however, there is little evidence that such provisions have proved useful in challenging disabling barriers in European countries (Waddington and Lawson 2009). Elsewhere, however, there is evidence of a more creative approach. In Australia, for instance, in *Hurst and Devlin v. Education Queensland*,[8] a challenge was mounted against the practice in schools of communicating with deaf students through British Sign Language and not Auslan (the officially recognized Australian sign language) with which the claimants were more familiar. It was held that this practice indirectly discriminated against the claimants even though they had mitigated the damaging effects of the practice by developing effective coping strategies.

Indirect race discrimination is prohibited by EU law in a much wider range of situations than is indirect disability discrimination. Indirect race discrimination claims therefore seem more likely to emerge from disadvantage at the disability–race intersection than do indirect disability discrimination claims. Although indirect race discrimination might prove a useful means of challenging injustice, there is a danger that in focusing exclusively on the disproportionate impact of a challenged provision, criterion or practice on different racial or ethnic groups, the disadvantage it inflicts on disabled people might be overlooked or even condoned. The high profile ECtHR indirect race discrimination case of *DH v. Czech Republic*[9] may be used to illustrate these potential dangers.

In *DH*, as has already been explained, the disproportionate placement of Roma children in special schools for children with learning difficulties was challenged as a violation of their right to education under Article 2 of Protocol 1 of the ECHR and of their right under Article 14 to be free from discrimination in connection with their enjoyment of that right. The argument proceeded on the basis that the standard of education provided in the special schools was greatly inferior to that provided in the mainstream system – an argument readily accepted by the Court. The adequacy or appropriateness of this inferior education system for disabled children was not addressed. Instead, the argument focused exclusively on the race dimension of the intersectional disadvantage experienced by the claimants – the essence of the claim being that these children were not in fact disabled and it was therefore inappropriate to treat them in the way disabled children were treated.

Exclusively race-based arguments, such as those in *DH*, leave it open to the court to condone the treatment of disabled people at the same time as recognizing the disadvantage which that treatment imposes on non-disabled people. Thus, in *DH* itself, a Chamber of the Second Section of the ECtHR[10] had earlier suggested that decisions as to the establishment of segregated education for disabled children, and as to the curricula to be followed within that system, raised no equality or human rights issues. Such decisions, according to it, 'mainly [involve] questions of expediency on which it is not for the Court to rule'.[11] Fortunately, these views were not reaffirmed by the Grand Chamber.[12] Instead, it indicated that it 'share[d] the disquiet of the other Council of Europe institutions who have expressed concerns about the more basic curriculum followed in these schools and, in particular, the segregation the system causes'.[13] On the facts of the case, however, it was not necessary for the Court to investigate the issue of the reduced educational opportunity afforded to disabled children or, indeed, their educational segregation which therefore continued unchallenged.

Proposed duty to provide effective non-discriminatory access by anticipation   The outline of a new duty of this type is set out in Article 4 of the European Commission's 2008 proposal for a new Equal Treatment Directive. It remains the subject of intense debate and it is unclear how, if

---

8   Full Court Federal Court; 28 July 2006; [2006] FCAFC 100.
9   App. No. 57325/00 (13 November 2007).
10   App. No. 57325/00 (7 February 2006).
11   Ibid., para. [47].
12   App. No. 57325/00 (13 November 2007).
13   Ibid., para. [198].

at all, it will emerge from the discussions of Council about the proposed directive. Nevertheless, it is of sufficient interest to merit some attention here. Given the uncertainty which surrounds its exact shape, the discussion which follows will draw heavily upon the UK anticipatory reasonable adjustment duty which appears to have provided at least some of the inspiration for this proposed new duty.

It should be stressed, at the outset of this discussion, that the UK anticipatory reasonable adjustment duty is distinct and separate from reasonable accommodation in its classic sense – i.e. the individualized, responsive form which it takes in the Employment Framework Directive. For this reason, the use of 'reasonable adjustment' in the name of this anticipatory duty is confusing. Neither the UK anticipatory duty, nor the proposed duty to provide effective non-discriminatory access should therefore be seen as a substitute for reasonable accommodation. Indeed, these anticipatory duties appear to have far more in common with indirect discrimination than with reasonable accommodation (Lawson 2008: Chapter 4).

The UK duty operates by requiring service providers constantly to monitor their provisions, criteria, practices (including equipment and assistance) and physical features for any potential disadvantage to which they might subject broad groups of disabled people (e.g. people with impairments affecting mobility, sight or hearing).[14] If any such disadvantage could be anticipated, then the relevant service provider is required to take reasonable steps to prevent that disadvantage arising or to ensure that the service can be provided in a different way which will circumvent the problem. Failure to anticipate relevant disadvantage or to take reasonable steps to deal with it will render service providers vulnerable to a discrimination claim brought by a disabled person who encounters the relevant disadvantage when attempting to access the service (Lawson 2008: Chapter 3). Questions of intersectionality have not yet arisen in connection with the UK anticipatory reasonable adjustment duty. However, it seems likely that service providers will be expected, when carrying out this duty, to have regard to the multicultural nature of UK society and therefore to anticipate and tackle some of the disadvantages particular to the disability–race intersection.

Anticipatory duties thus have the potential to contribute helpfully to tackling disadvantage at the disability–race intersection. Like reasonable accommodation, they are founded on the removal of disadvantage rather than on insistence on identical treatment. They are more forward-looking and more solution-orientated than indirect discrimination is often interpreted to be. However, they have much in common with indirect discrimination and vigorous development and application of the latter would reduce the need for the former.

Other Relevant Dimensions of EU Law and Policy

Aspects of EU law and policy, falling outside the ambit of the non-discrimination directives, undoubtedly also have an important role to play in tackling disadvantage at the disability–race intersection. A detailed account of these lies well beyond the scope of this chapter. However, some of the relevant mechanisms will be briefly mentioned.

An important dimension of EU activity, relevant to a number of areas in which disability–race disadvantage often exists and not constrained by the strict limits of EU legislative competence, is the Open Method of Co-ordination (OMC) (De Schutter and Deakin 2005). Through this, on a consensual basis with coordination from the Council and the Commission, States set common standards, share information and examples of good practice and receive recommendations from the Commission or other Member States on agreed issues (including employment, education and

---

14   *Roads v. Central Trains* [2004] EWCA Civ. 1540 per Sedley L.J. para. 11.

social inclusion and protection). Fredman (2006) has stressed the importance of underpinning this process with a solid commitment to relevant fundamental rights. Such rights clearly include those contained in the CRPD. That Convention has been signed by all Member States and ratified by many and has also been signed and all but concluded[15] by the EU itself (de Búrca 2010).

The OMC represents a potentially powerful mechanism for the identification and reduction of intersectional and other disadvantage and the CRPD seems destined to raise the profile of intersectional disadvantage within it. As mentioned above, it contains a specific Article requiring States Parties to tackle disadvantage at the disability–gender intersection. In relation to the disability–race intersection, although there is no equivalent provision, the reporting guidelines issued by the Treaty monitoring body (Committee on the Rights of Persons with Disabilities) requires States Parties to address relevant disadvantage in their reports (CRPD 2009). These guidelines ambitiously require States Parties (amongst which the EU will number once it has deposited its concluding documents at the UN)[16] to include:

> A.3.2(h) Statistical data on the realisation of each Convention right, disaggregated by sex, age, type of disability (physical, sensory, intellectual and mental), ethnic origin, urban/rural population and other relevant categories, on an annual comparative basis over the past four years.[17]

An obligation to collect and disseminate appropriately disaggregated statistical and other research data relating to the realization of Convention rights also appears in Article 31 of the Convention itself – though this does not explicitly mention disaggregation by reference to ethnicity. Any attempt to gather statistics relating to ethnicity is likely to meet serious opposition in some EU countries (Carles, Howard and Kofman, in this volume). However, the EU is well placed to encourage and facilitate Member States in their efforts to comply with these obligations. It also has a powerful role (particularly through the Agency for Fundamental Rights)[18] in commissioning and disseminating relevant research.

Another area of EU law and policy which deserves mention here concerns the administration of structural funds – funds which constitute a significant portion of the EU budget and which are granted to Member States to assist in resolving structural economic or social problems. These have great potential to assist States in dismantling some of the disadvantages at the disability–race intersection by, for instance, facilitating community living and inclusion. Indeed, existing regulations specify that they must be used to promote social inclusion.[19] However, a recent report has drawn attention to the fact that, in practice, structural fund money is frequently spent on renovating institutions or even on building new ones rather than being invested in schemes to support community living (Parker with Bulic 2010). This is attributed, in part, to EU level restrictions on the ability of recipients to spend money on land or housing.[20] Given that Article

---

15   Council Decision on the conclusion, by the European Community, of the United Nations Convention on the Rights of Persons with Disabilities, 15540/09. The EU will not become a party to the CRPD, however, until it deposits its concluding documents at the UN.

16   Article 44 of the CRPD makes provision for regional integration organisations, such as the EU, to become party to the Convention and provides that they should have the same obligations as States Parties within the limits of the competence.

17   See note 16 above.

18   www.fra.europa.eu.

19   Council Regulation (EC) No 1083/2006 of 11 July 2006, Art. 3(1).

20   Regulation (EC) No 1080/2006 of the European Parliament and of the Council of 5 July 2006, Arts 7(1)(b) and 7(2)(b).

19 of the CRPD confers on disabled people the right to choose to live in the community (with appropriate support), any tendency of structural funds to perpetuate institutional living will need to be reviewed.

Conclusion

EU non-discrimination law has the potential to play a useful contribution to the reduction of disadvantage at the disability–race intersection. At present, however, its impact is extremely limited both because of the restriction of the material scope of the Employment Framework Directive (and therefore the concept of reasonable accommodation) to employment and because of the absence of proactive duties to tackle disadvantage in either that Directive or the Race Equality Directive. The potential of such proactive duties to tackle intersectional disadvantage has been clearly explained elsewhere (Fredman 2009). It is to be hoped that, in the near future, proposals to introduce such duties will emerge.

The proposed Equal Treatment Directive would remedy some of these deficiencies but by no means does it represent a panacea (Lawson 2008: 56–9). Particularly disappointing are the exclusion of special education from its scope and the absence of any general proactive equality duty. The omission of the latter, at least in the specific context of disability–race disadvantage, however, is somewhat mitigated by the inclusion of the duty to provide non-discriminatory access through anticipation.

Outside the strict confines of EU non-discrimination law, however, there is much that can be done at EU level to promote the tackling of disadvantage at the disability–race intersection. Indeed, the EU's decision to become a party to the CRPD will require it to maintain and intensify its efforts in this regard. Mechanisms such as the OMC (and other forums for the sharing of good practice) and the regulation of structural funds offer the EU a means by which to encourage States to positively engage with issues facing disabled people from minority ethnic groups and with the development of policies for tackling the types of disadvantage to which they (as well as others) are subject. In the absence of positive proactive equality duties, such mechanisms (when coupled with the undergirding support provided by Member State signature and, in many cases, ratification of the CRPD) are likely to prove far more powerful drivers of change for the EU than is its non-discrimination law.

Chapter 4

Tackling the Conceptual Order of Multiple Discrimination: Situating Different and Difficult Genealogies of Race and Ethnicity[1]

Ulrike M. Vieten

Disturbing happiness requires disturbing the technologies through which we make sense; it requires blocking the passages of communication that allows happy messages to be sent out. ... Let's take the figure of the 'kill joy feminist'. Does the feminist kill other people's joy by pointing out moments of sexism? Or does she expose the bad feelings that get hidden, displaced or negated under public signs of joy? (Ahmed 2008: 5)

Introduction

Feminist and critical speech that labels systematic group annihilation of visible minorities as *racism* may potentially create a toxic climate disturbing the seemingly happy consensus of some democratic and liberal societies in Europe.

Strikingly, it is the use of the term rather than the racist situation that is likely to provoke outcry or moral panic. But to take up Ahmed's point, disturbing the *happiness of normality* in this regard may bring to the fore what is otherwise hidden. In an anti-discrimination context, is the use of 'race' and 'ethnicity' as social categories similarly problematic? Do these categories each refer to the same racializing discourses and actions (e.g. hate speech; individual and structural discrimination)? What does each term imply or omit, perhaps, when simply dismissed for comfort-zone purposes?

What need to be sharpened in the overall debate are the notions of race and ethnicity and an awareness of how their analytical use may differ in various European countries. This matters as through the conduit of national anti-discrimination laws EU directives have channelled back the term 'race' to countries such as Germany[2] or France,[3] where, for the purposes of official statistics,

---

1   I would like to thank the book's editors and all the participants, in particular Eleonore Kofman, of the panel 'Conceptual Geographies: Clarifying the Boundaries of Intersectional Terms' at the Second Conference on Multidimensional Equality Law, 29 March 2009, University of Leeds, for their helpful comments enriching the scope of the analysis and, thus, contributing to the development of my argument.

2   Lewis (2009) refers to the debate on 'race' that took place at the conference 'Celebrating Intersectionality', held in Frankfurt in 2009, confirming the hesitation of some participants to use the term race. She sums up that 'it was noted by some speakers that the preferred term in many European countries was that of ethnicity and/or culture, and that much more recently "religion" had entered as a key structural and identity category' (ibid.: 207). As far as Germany is concerned, in the post-Holocaust public debate the term 'race' is rejected (ibid.).

3   This chapter will concentrate on the experience in certain western European countries. However, I fully recognize that the situation in some eastern European countries may differ significantly and deserves separate attention.

measuring populations according to their ascribed race and ethnicity is generally outlawed. Some of the difficulties in comparing reliable information about multiple discrimination on a European level, in particular race and gender, are outlined by Carles et al. (in this volume: 227). As will be argued in this chapter, too, the EU's anti-discrimination policy produces paradoxical consequences. These result from its adoption of a critical discourse on racism and race steeped in the Anglo-American tradition, on the one hand, and the taboo concerning any public debate on race in many parts of continental Europe, on the other. In these countries, discussion tends to focus instead on *culturalized* and gendered notions of ethnic and religious minority identities. Thus, in a European context, it appears necessary to explore the extent to which the placing of a taboo on critical debates on skin colour ignores the post-colonial meaning of race. This chapter aims, first, to follow up some classic approaches developed by scholars seeking to understand notions of race and ethnicity. Both terms contain essentialized meanings of social order. This is not to deny, however, that certain minority groups and individuals who identify politically may act with a liberating intent in attempting to name a historically constructed systematic power hierarchy between different ethnicities and an ascribed race of Blackness. Second, having established some insights into the phenomenology of ethnicity and ascribed race[4] the social power axes of ethnicity, gender and class will be scrutinized in the context of some examples of research into (im-)migration and cultural difference. This will be done while considering how group ascriptions are differently pronounced in some continental European countries when attempting to talk about immigration, national boundary and gender. Contemporary feminist social analysis takes Crenshaw's (1989) analytical model of 'intersectionality'[5] on board while interrogating complex structures of oppression cutting across boundaries and national borders (for example, Yuval-Davis 1997, 2004, 2006) and, at the same time, addressing EU institutional anti-discrimination issues (Verloo 2006). After all, intersecting[6] features of gender and ethnicity; gender and race; and gender, ethnicity and race matter in the anti-discrimination context as they may articulate national integration and equality projects differently. Hence, in a further section, the implications of statistical measurements of populations, minorities in particular, are discussed with a focus on the UK. In a final section, the symbolic salience of racial whiteness will be tackled. Whiteness as a 'contingent hierarchy' (Garner 2006: 264) creates its meaning while constructing Blackness as non-Whiteness in a colonial context. What is particularly evident when looking at 'Mixed-Race' Studies, for example, is the persistence of the *hegemonic white gaze* towards others. Racializing the Other in terms of her identifying and to be identified[7] body unfolds as a '*What are you?* encounter' (Haritaworn 2009: 122). Systems of oppression are characterized by asymmetry and, in this regard, white majorities, who declare 'race' as unspeakable, avoid the deconstruction and problematization of whiteness. Accordingly,

---

4　I am using 'ascribed race' here to highlight its ideological construction and will later on use the term without inverted commas in order to refer to the racialized experience of being black in predominantly white societies.

5　Confronted with concepts unsupportive of a critical understanding of the unfair treatment of black women and, thus, inadequate to grasp different social complexities, black feminist and academic Crenshaw (1989, 1991) initiated a theoretical debate on the intersections of different layers of social identities and group belonging in the United States.

6　I am not going to repeat my critical analysis of feminist methodology, class divisions and the method of intersectional approaches in this contribution, for details see Vieten (2009).

7　This happens frequently when, in asking curious questions regarding place of birth, parents, and nationality, etc., white people intrude on the individual privacy of people who look non-white or 'exotic'. Notwithstanding the likely polite individual reflex to respond to this with a sufficient explanation, the direction of this inquiry is shaped by asymmetric power structures as whites are gazing at the message of the *other* body.

the prominence or lack of attention towards certain dimensions of intersecting social categories and identities poses dilemmas for a comparative approach addressing European patterns of race and ethnicity. This chapter aims to trace the difficult and different genealogies of ethnicity and ascribed race and capture what arguably is characteristic to the ways gendered group difference is targeted in certain European countries. This is intended to encourage further debate on how to undo specific formations of racisms and institutionalized racial discrimination in all EU Member States.

The Taxonomy of 'Race' and 'Ethnicity': Why Make a Fuss about Fuzzy Concepts?

> Races north of the Pyrenees are of cold temperament and never reach maturity; they are of great stature and of white colour. But they lack all sharpness of wit and penetration of Intellect.[8]

Ruth Benedict (1983 [1942]), a US anthropologist, explained race as concerning 'hereditary [traits] and traits transmitted by heredity which characterize all the members of a related group' (1983: 6). She identified certain qualities that could be regarded as 'socially acquired' (ibid.), for example, language, culture, rituals and religion. In her view, all these qualities have to be understood as human expressions and, thus, as *socially learned traits*. These she distinguished from other qualities based on 'skin colour, cephalic index, eyes and hair' (1983: 7), which *we all* inherit from our particular ancestry.

The latter sounds, perhaps, banal, whereas the former presents us with the difficult legacies we have to confront. It is largely *institutionalized racism* that should be of our concern as it is passed on as *normality* through learned patterns of culture and religion, and further framed by social positions within, for example, ethnicity, class, gender and sexuality.

In this context the notion of the human as a 'social animal' (Louis 2002: 670) matters, having regard to the fact that (t)he perception of humanity as 'social' is important because the post-racial search for human sameness re-articulates the foundational anthropocentrism of race thinking and establishes humanity through the abstracted body and the application of disembodied ethical values (ibid.).

Consequently, race as a colonially constructed category of ranking skin colour does not vanish in declaring human relationships as being in equilibrium and ignoring the history of racializing non-whiteness. In this regard the theme of *racial relationships* remains with us.

Further, we could argue that ethnicity merges the two realms of 'hereditary' and 'socially learned' traits as it could be understood as (1) a primordial and fixed state of cultural belonging (heritage) or (2) connoting a more dynamic and *situated* state of symbolic belonging that provides groups with specific resources, which are used flexibly (see Rex 1986: 27). Addressed through gendered patterns, the concrete embodiment of group differences demands a *situating* of the conceptual boundaries between race and ethnicity as the latter is scandalized and targeted, in particular, when articulated in orthodox religious performances. Moreover, the *visibility* (or even *hyper-visibility*) of orthodox ethnic and religious minorities might operate alongside the colonial semiotics of ranking non-white skin colour. Echoing Goldberg (2006: 335), we might ask whether there are specific 'racial arrangements and engagements' that continue to be significant with reference to Europe and, in particular, the European Union. Goldberg argues that whiteness is salient to European nations, assuming that it passes as a relatively unchallenged idiom of power, resources and better

---

8   Eleventh-century remark by Said of Toledo, a Moorish savant, cited in Hogben (1931) and referred to by Benedict (1983 [1942]: 5).

life chances. Thus, despite its framing by intersecting social categories, for example, gender, class, religion, ethnicity, sexuality and ability, this suggests that the power asymmetry of whiteness/non-whiteness structurally inhabits a central place in all configurations.

Beng-Huat (2005: 419), for example, captures profoundly what might disappear from our view when talking about race alone. In his view, 'racial labels homogenize the linguistic and sub-ethnic differences'. In that context, he mentions the prominence of three distinctive 'visible "racial" groups – Chinese, Malays and Indians' in contemporary Singapore, who are not divided for official purposes into further ethnic and lingual groups. However, from the opposite perspective, we might ask what it means for a policy, whether national or European, to ignore colonial racializing discourse and focus only on ethnicity. In addition, it might be significant, too, how the naming of 'visible racial groups' is intertwined with the question of nationality. Whereas race takes and re-inscribes a phenotypic element of the visual impression of an individual body for group distinction, ethnicity links to culture, language, rituals and often religious heritage of people that is expressed in various ways (Omi and Winant 1994). Aspinall argues that '"ethnicity" is increasingly replacing "race" as the preferred term in much official, public and lay discourse, [although] the latter remains in wide use' (2007: 44). The problem of talking about ethnicity and race is not confined to mere semantics but concerns the ways group identities, in particular minority identities, are constructed, maintained or shift in different historical and national settings. In Canada, for example, the terms 'visible minorities' or 'ethnic origin' are used frequently, offering descriptive alternatives to the term 'race'. According to Aspinall (2007: 45 et seq.) categories adopted in official practice vary across nation states and continents and, therefore, deliver perplexing information. Hence, to capture in greater detail the notion of ethnicity in the context of boundary drawing it is helpful to introduce Wimmer's taxonomic differentiation.

Wimmer (2008) proposes four possible taxonomic systems of ethnic boundary marking in order to catch individual and collective dimensions of marking, crossing and passing group differences. One possibility of drawing boundaries is *contraction*; the tendency to draw narrower boundaries. Wimmer gives the example of some British Asians, who do not identify with the category of 'Blackness', but instead identify as Pakistani or even closer to a local ethnic heritage, Punjabi. Second, he characterizes *transvaluation* as a strategy to re-interpret the content of a rather negative ascription (ibid.: 1037). We could, for example, regard the Black Power movement or the political struggle of indigenous populations as examples of this strategy to identify positively with a negative label. As a third option, *positions could be moved* as an individual effort to cross a boundary (assimilation and re-classification) or as a collective endorsement to 'cross', for example, the colour line (ibid.: 1041). Finally, the *blurring* of boundaries delivers the fourth perspective, which in effect might reduce the 'importance of ethnicity as a principle of categorization' (ibid.). *Blurring boundaries* is sometimes linked to cosmopolitanism, fusion of cultures, and the notion of hybridism.

In Wimmer's analytical perspective, *race* is one element of potential or actual group boundary marking, and enclosed in a broader notion of ethnicity. Accordingly, he regards passing as 'white' or 'passing down the stigma of Blackness' (ibid.: 1037) as ethnic strategies of racialized groups. These strategies aim to keep a distance from the most discriminated collective while, perhaps, also creating additional categories of 'darker complexions' (ibid.). Problematically, the racial power asymmetry of whiteness/non-whiteness only gets attention when Wimmer explores the meaning of non-whiteness with reference to variable emanations and black imaginations of group belonging. This perspective keeps alive and does not challenge an internalized *white normativity*. In addition, the positioning of the female as a gendered boundary marker is not considered an issue at all.

This brief critical debate of different approaches to the notion of race and ethnicity should have made clear that the concepts sometimes overlap, but may also pinpoint distinctive social-cultural hierarchies that we need to keep in mind in order to combat adequately group discriminations. In addition, as a matter of historically constructed social stratifications, multiple combinations of ascribed 'race' in terms of skin colour, ethnicity, religion or minority nationality have to be taken on board and understood as an *archive* of *racialized discourses*. In this regard, critical social analysis has to tackle different genealogies of the terms available in different national cultures. This is particularly important in order to be able to situate structural patterns that are encapsulated in discriminatory individual practices and institutionalized racisms of today.

Contemporary debates on immigration and national integration in various European countries epitomize notions of *Occidentalism* vs. *Orientalism*. Indeed, the focus on Muslim communities draws upon prejudiced images of internally homogeneous cultural and religious groups. Whereas some categories (e.g. religion, gender and ethnicity) are singled out and scandalized, other forms of social stratifications (e.g. citizenship, nationality, class origin, physical and cultural capacities, sex and sexuality) are neglected or ignored. Nonetheless, power, education and wealth are accessible mainly through professional positions, which are organized predominantly in a capitalist market manner and, thus, highly dependent on privileged and classed intersecting dimensions (Vieten 2009). In line with the approach taken by the Marxist sociologist Rex (1986), ethnic and racial relations need to be interpreted as a matter of social conflict and, therefore, have to be related to class.[9] In addition, as feminist sociologists Anthias and Yuval-Davis (1983, 1993) argue, they must be analysed also intersectionally with gender and nationalism. It has been suggested that the *female gender* signifies the ethnic boundary in processes of building and maintaining the nation (Yuval-Davis 1997). Hence, culturally-laden notions of (hetero)sexual[10] femininity and masculinity need to be interpreted with reference to the boundary marking of both the majority national collective and its minority groups.

The following section explores current research working along the boundaries of ethnicity and race and at the same time exposing how different notions get blurred. In particular, it will highlight *how* racializing discourses concerning national community, cultural belonging and modern vs. traditional patterns of femininity and masculinity are sustained.

Religion, Ethnicity, Gender and the 'Culturalizing' Discourse in Europe

Although the historical objects of racist labelling and institutionalized racism may shift, hegemonic interests continue to operate through established subject positions when constructing exclusionary and essentialized boundaries in relation to the Other.

In the context of a broader public anxiety that is preoccupied with minority ethnicity, Muslim religion and orthodox forms of anti-modern femininity, the terms *culturalism* (Razack 2004) or *cultural fundamentalism* (Stolcke 1995, 2003) have been introduced, arguably reflecting the prominence of sexism and *Orientalism* (Said 1978) in different (European) countries. As Crowley and Hickman (2008: 1235) emphasize, '(c)ultural fundamentalism is meant as a rhetoric of

---

9 For a neo-socialist feminist reading of current social conflicts which views these as ethnically and 'racially' labelled, see my earlier work (Vieten 2009).

10 The emphasis on heterosexuality should make clear that hegemonic notions of national integration projects are largely framed by hetero-normative female and male gender roles.

exclusion based on cultural segregation rather than hierarchy. It thus legitimates the exclusion of foreigners, strangers'.

However, cultural segregation works in *hierarchical* terms; that is, there is a dominant civil society that proclaims what counts as meaningful national culture while defining collective values and acceptable customs. In that context, following D.T. Goldberg (2002), it is important to recognize that *naturalist racism* (based on a supposed biological 'inferiority' of the Other) moved discursively and structurally to *progressivist* or *historicist racism*. The latter constructs inferiority through a line of progression: an acclaimed and 'advanced' society is contrasted with a 'backward' civil attitude. This entangled asymmetry echoes what Ryan (2002) discusses as the critical potential of 'plurality' and 'alterity' inherent to the interactions of intertwined symbolic positions. The pair of 'master and slave' contains an ideologically sacrosanct, but *enlightened* version of how to overcome colonial pasts. The liberation of 'the slave' ought to *save* the master, too. On this reading, freedom may mean becoming equal. But there is another pair to which we should pay attention. 'The civilized and the savage' are on a different route to 'liberation'. In this case, 'the savage' is thought to progress with his or her domestication. Although supposedly advancing to 'higher stages' of 'civilization', this kind of progress implies, in fact, the perpetuation of processes of subordination and colonialism. In this regard, national histories of colonialism haunt us with their domesticating strategies of categorization.[11]

Work in progress[12] at the VU University Amsterdam, Netherlands, focuses on the specific Dutch binary taxonomy of *autochtoon* (natives) and *allochtoon*[13] (non-natives), while exploring to what degree statistical information gathered in relation to education and health care measures populations according to heritage, nationality and ethno-religious belonging. This binary categorical distinction was established prior to the introduction of statistical recording in the Netherlands. The domestic use of those terms implies the potential for highly problematic consequences on the implementation of EU anti-discrimination law which does not abandon but supplements nationally accepted taxonomies of racializing categories. In that respect, particular 'national', or for that matter, dominant ethno-national traditions in measuring and defining 'who belongs and who does not belong' are of crucial importance.

The research of Alba (2005) specifically examines the construction of national boundaries. In order to understand the impact of different kinds of symbolic margins, and to situate them in particular national-cultural settings, he differentiates 'bright' from 'blurred' boundaries. He compares three countries (United States, Germany and France) with regard to the permeability of their systems and, thus, the extent to which social mobility and boundary crossing is available to specific minorities.

He focuses on the largest significant immigrant groups in the three countries concerned (Mexicans in the United States, Turks in Germany and North Africans in France). Alba established that religion (Christianity) builds the cultural core element to symbolic boundary constructions in the two European countries. Hence, the national cultural boundary is symbolized as a commitment to Christian values and evolves as the central threshold to integration. This 'cultural' perception

---

11   This 'civilization' mission is also an underlying theme as far as dominant perspectives on contemporary discourses of cosmopolitanism are concerned, at least in relation to the UK and Germany, see for details Vieten (2007, 2010).

12   See the research project of Yanow and van der Haar, assisted by Voelke. More information is available online at www.fsw.vu.nl/en/departments/culture-organization-and-management/staff/van-der-haar/index.asp [accessed: 22 February 2010].

13   Geschiere (2009) argues that the terminology of *allochtoon/autochtoon* is prevalent in Belgium, too, in particular in the Flemish part of the country.

of acceptable belonging is prevalent notwithstanding a popular understanding that both of those European states are committed to a strong *secular* public sphere. According to Alba (2005: 39), '[a] bright boundary does not usually eliminate assimilation – even hardened racial boundaries allow for some assimilation, but mostly for minority individuals with a "favoured" appearance'. The 'favoured appearance', however, implies a lighter coloured skin and *secular* behaviour, that is, individuals who to a greater or lesser extent go beyond the boundaries of group orthodoxy (here, minority religion and ethnicity). In addition, a higher degree and, therefore, a good chance of individual success in economic integration generally connote higher social class performances and white normativity. This is likely to be the case, so he argues, in cultural settings where 'the discourse of difference ... rejects the concept of race as inappropriate to their societies' (ibid.). Despite a lack of 'evidence' of *racial discrimination*, Alba concludes that visible difference or phenotypical appearance, 'could serve as a basis of discrimination' (ibid.).

Whereas Alba detects very clearly the influential link between majority religion and ethnic political community, he mentions the category of gender only in the context of the ban on wearing 'headscarves'. As argued above, orthodox femininity signifies a gendered boundary between the dominant secular Christian civil society and the Muslim orthodox minority. But, at the same time, the non-veiled Western and *modern* woman symbolizes 'the positive', in contrast to the 'negative' of the veiled woman, in addition to a gendered boundary; she becomes the signifier of the secular modern nation state. Both directions of claiming the female body, however, indicate how *woman* as a signifier is considered patriarchal property. Collective boundaries are articulated symbolically by female body features and fashions. For example, Korteweg and Yurdakul (2009) tackle the gendered dimensions of religion and ethnicity in an immigration context. Drawing on Alba's distinction and approach they look at the *culturalizing* discourse of 'honour killing' in the Netherlands and Germany. Initially, the researchers assumed that religion, that is, 'belonging' to a Christian church, would be the most important differentiating factor only in the Netherlands.[14] However, they discovered that this is also true for Germany. Hence, there is a common trace of ethno-religious identification that shapes the meaning of community boundary as an essential marker of cultural belonging in both countries. Although the intersections of ethnicity and gender are analysed very clearly with reference to national origin and religion (2009: 235), the meaning of race in terms of a structural power asymmetry of whiteness/non-whiteness remains unchallenged. This appears significant, as both in the Netherlands and Germany, a culturally-connoted symbolic boundary is constructed without regard for the colonial context. The term 'culturalizing' is reminiscent of the approach of Stolcke (2003), who argued that culture is generally regarded as static and primordially rooted and, as a result, social problems are explained in the terminology of inevitable cultural differences between ethnic groups. Clearly, in the aftermath of the public rise and scandalized murder of the gay and right-wing politician Pim Fortuyn[15] and the murder of the film director Theo van Gogh, media and policy preoccupation with 'cultural contrasts or culturalization' (Ghorashi 2007: 129) has gained prominent space in the Netherlands. Meanwhile, in other European countries, for example, Italy and Hungary, and most recently in Northern Ireland,[16] too, Roma have been threatened and are once again hounded as a 'cultural' and ethnic

---

14   Roggeband and Verloo (2007) note how gender emancipation policy of the 1980s became diversity politics in the Netherlands of the 1990s. In their view, however, this responded inadequately to the different social positions of established Dutch faith groups and was over-accommodating to new faith groups. They observe that Moroccans and Turks are addressed, above all, 'culturally' (ibid.: 275).

15   In fact, Fortuyn was murdered by an animal rights activist, which had nothing to do with 'Islamic' fanatics.

16   See online post by McVeigh (2009).

Other. However, the contention that there is something new about this form of racism in the sense that it is 'racism without race' has to be rejected; the history of 'race' is the history of racisms in the plural. In addition, the *colonial* and *pan-European* racializing of black citizens, black refugees and black migrants continues and encompasses the racializing of religious and transnational minority communities. Racism constructs the Other in ascribed embodiments of racialized features that shifted historically and have to be contextualized in relation to different national legacies. Louis argues that the history of race has to be a sociological theory of 'race' (2002: 664). According to Louis, '[w]e have long been aware that "race" has no sustainable biological foundation and, convinced of its socially constructed basis, we instead recognize the *racialization* of different "groups" that are culturally, socially and historically constituted' (ibid.: 652).

To sum up this contention: *racisme différentialiste* (Balibar and Wallerstein 1991) and its emphasis on a presumed homogenous cultural belonging of groups has to be interpreted as *one variation* of racism. What makes this form of racism special in the contemporary European debate is its ideological cross-reference to historical anti-Semitism. In twenty-first century Europe, a religious minority is once again targeted. An active and religious Islamic belief is viewed as the adoption of a coherent and supposedly anti-democratic community ideology. By contrast, Muslims are drawn from considerably diverse, white and non-white, ethnic and national backgrounds. However, notwithstanding this complexity and variety, Muslim individuals become amalgamated into a 'fundamentally' different population group of Others. It is in this context where anti-Muslim racism arises.

This section has discussed primarily the construction of ethno-religious group boundaries and the prominent position of a culturally stigmatized[17] minority female in some continental European countries of the EU. However, it is of relevance to our debate how gender, religion, ethnicity and race are approached in the UK context as in that country ethnic and racial profiling is commonplace and not discouraged by public policy. This may offer an insight on how terminology and discourse could shift and, at the same time, reveal how social science research attempts to grapple with a more cohesive official policy to measure multi-layered or 'hybrid' (Bhabha 1994) identities of citizens.

Race, Religion, Gender and Ethnic Profiling in Britain

In developing legal tools with which to combat forms of racial and ethnic discrimination, European policy confronts academics with contradictory, differently anchored and contested terms of ethnicity and race in various countries. To deal with this problem, Aspinall proposes a method of 'semantic locality' (2007: 60) in which race and ethnicity would have to be interpreted in each country separately and also in comparison with other concepts, for example, citizen/foreigner status or family background. Alternatively, 'input and output harmonization' is suggested, a strategy which concedes that the parameters used in continental Europe avoid the terms of ethnicity and race while asking for 'citizenship, country of birth, language, religious denomination, migrant status and nationality' (ibid.). In this context, it may be productive to consider the extent to which, in the long run, European integration might affect domestic British approaches (and vice versa) to the measurement of populations.

---

17   Solanke (2009a: 121) characterizes stigma as 'being locked out of the norm'. Certain attributes such as skin colour, sexual orientation, physical appearance, disability, etc. might be stigmatized in different places and at different times.

Looking at the contemporary debate in Britain, it would appear that the 'cultural' competence of Asian Sikhs, Hindus and Muslims to accommodate British 'values' is frequently interrogated. Gendered prejudices and ethnic racism become enmeshed, leading to general assumptions on how, for example, Muslim women cope with the English language or Asian girls are victimized in forced marriages (Yuval-Davis et al. 2005). However, research by Brah (1993) and Bhopal (1998) in the 1990s highlighted a high level of diversity when speaking about South Asian British women, making it clear that due to better qualifications and higher degrees of education their proportion in the female workforce was rising steadily.[18] In the final report of the Equalities Review commissioned by the UK Government and published in 2007, we learn that 'the situation of Pakistani and Bangladeshi women merits particular focus and attention because ... [t]he employment penalty associated with this group of women, has remained relatively constant over the 30-year period, in contrast to white women' (2007: 78). The document explicitly emphasizes that women of Pakistani and Bangladeshi background are the most disadvantaged group with respect to the labour market.

In a recent study undertaken by Salway (2008) the focus is on the particularly precarious unemployment situation of young Bangladeshi men. Salway points out, '[o]n virtually every indicator of labour market achievement, a significant gap is found between the white majority and all other *ethnic*[19] groups. That said, diversity is also readily apparent, with Indians and Chinese commonly faring better than other groups' (ibid.: 1127).

Strikingly, Salway refers to a notion of ethnicity that categorizes minorities in contrast to whiteness; a pair of difference employed in public policy.[20] Recalling for a moment Beng-Huat's observations concerning distinctive race groups in Singapore,[21] it is of considerable relevance – certainly to academics interested in international and comparative research perspectives – that the Chinese and Indian groups in that population would be categorized as *ethnicities* in the UK, perhaps even in a wider European context. In addition, on a Singaporean reading, Asian British, Pakistani British and Bangladeshi British would be all regarded as belonging to the 'racial' group of 'Indians'. Accordingly, the British subcategories are constructed as *forming* specific communities. This policy attempts to capture what might characterize the boundaries of a minority community and engages certain aspects of intersecting social groupings, for example, nationality, religion or geographical origin. It offers some insights into the dilemmas and obstacles of national terminology. In this regard, Salway's research illustrates how notions of ethnicity and race as well as the overlap with nationality are entangled and reflected in academic research and national statistics.[22] Further, her work underlines the difficulties for empirical research to negotiate pathways through national data

---

18   According to Bhopal, 'the number of Indian women in employment has shown a gradual increase and is comparable to white women. There has been a rapid increase for Pakistani/Bangladeshi women, however these numbers remain low' (1998: 12).

19   Italics in original.

20   The categories of *ethnic groups* used in the 2001 UK census were as follows: White (British, Irish or any other White background); Mixed (White and Black Caribbean, White and Black African, White and Asian, or any other Mixed background); Asian and Asian British (Indian, Pakistani, Bangladeshi, or any other Asian background); Black or Black British (Caribbean, African, or any other Black background); and Chinese or other ethnic group (Chinese or any other). For further details see European Network Against Racism (ENAR) (2002).

21   See page 66.

22   Clearly, this is not the only case of sociological inquiry reflecting the terminology of public policy as the review of equality statistics by Walby et al. (2008) underscores. These authors note that, although widely used, the concept of ethnicity is contested, with classification 'based on a combination of national identity,

categories if these contradict conceptual considerations, for example, an interpretation of race as a whiteness/non-whiteness power nexus with an intentional distinction from notions of ethnicity.

However, one may question what Salway's research reveals on the correlation between gender and ethnicity and why race and also class are insufficiently analysed. We learn about racial discrimination and the ambivalent positions of young Bangladeshi men torn between close community networks and their social expectations, on the one hand, and difficulties to establish more successful 'income' careers in mainstream society, on the other. As far as the interviewed young men are concerned, the focus, indeed, is on *ethnic belonging*. These young men are 'showing acute ambivalence felt by many towards being a part of this community' (Salway 2008: 1135). In addition, 'street culture' identities and flirtation with Islam are exposed as featuring strongly in their lives, accompanied by highly gendered male life-circle arrangements. Those gendered lifestyle arrangements become entrenched, however, as proper jobs ('English jobs') and, therefore, the economic means to sustain their own family and household are difficult for them to achieve (Salway 2008). Despite the young men's efforts to share their exclusionary experiences with the researchers and, hence, their frustrations in relation to job applications and fear of racial attacks when leaving their local community space the overall impression given to the reader falls back on the narrative of 'tight ethnic kinship identities'. Whereas gender is explicitly taken on board as a subject, the huge cultural impact of lower class status, which might shape attitudes, life expectations and educational chances in conjunction with non-whiteness, is not analysed further.[23] However, it must be recalled that the 2007 Equalities Review concluded that the 'low level of geographical and social mobility ... especially [amongst groups] of Bangladeshi origin, suggests that this concentration of disadvantage will persist into the near future' (2007: 42). On the other hand, social mobility is an effect of education and, ultimately, a matter of class. In practice, there is neither any chance to enter higher education without paying considerable fees nor any clear options to obtain middle-class cultural skills which result in determined self-confidence and systematic career strategies. In structural terms, the possibility of a higher education degree and the capability to enter professional networks and jobs is lacking. As Walby et al. (2008: 33) point out, '[s]ocio-economic status (or social class) is not one of the selected equality strands. Nevertheless, it is an important aspect of inequality and is recommended for inclusion in equality statistics by the ONS in its review'.[24]

McGhee (2003) criticizes New Labour policy for asking individuals to go beyond multiculturalism seeking to 'educate' minorities to *bridge* different communities (e.g. majority community and minority community). At the same time, those individuals identifying in a strong way with their ethnic and religious minority background are asked to leave their thicker community bonds behind. In effect, this flexibility aspect to cultural cosmopolitanization implies that everybody has to obey the rules of a largely individualized middle-class society. Seemingly, this is an ongoing social cohesion project, which also is enmeshed and promoted together with *whiteness*. According to Crowley and Hickman (2008: 1235):

---

national origin and colour' (ibid.: 22). Further, they report considerations to replace the term 'mixed' with 'multiple heritage' for the purposes of the 2011 Census (ibid.: 23).

23   When mentioning that some young men were combining part-time work with college (Salway 2008: 1146) the author unfortunately does not take this as an opportunity to think about loans or extra programmes that might support and, thus, encourage individuals to balance their individual perspectives with community and family-related responsibilities.

24   Anna Lawson reminded me that the Equality Act 2010 includes a clause which might impose a positive duty on public bodies to reduce inequality resulting from socio-economic factors when carrying out their obligations.

Arrival of these migrants[25] in the 1950s stimulated the reconfiguring of a class and ethno-nationally stratified nation as white and homogenous ... leading ultimately to the widespread acceptance of the term 'white', or latterly 'white British', to connote the ethnic majority. In this way class, regional and ethnic differences within 'white' were masked and a homogenous indigenous population was arraigned against 'the other' within.

The struggle for independence by indigenous nations such as the Scots and the Welsh (Colley 1994), and, above all, the situation of the Irish in Ireland and in Britain, highlight the violent and symbolic contestation of the dominance of Englishness. As Kearns remarks, 'Ireland was in some respect a province and in others a colony' (2003: 204). In addition, he makes clear that the particular alliance between Irish nationalism and Catholicism has to be understood as a response to England's attempt to 'extirpate the Catholic religion' (ibid.: 205). Similarly, McVeigh and Rolston argue that the English approach to the colonization of Ireland was framed by an attitude regarding the Irish as 'an "uncivilised" other' (2009: 3).

Thus, in historical terms, an ethno-cultural rift between different Christian faiths and a hegemonic institutional structure for sustaining power also underlie the 'national' conflict. Ultimately, a 'homogenizing' perspective invoking a *white British national community* stands in opposition to historical tensions and various racializing dynamics targeting, initially, indigenous Celtic populations as well as different immigrant minority groups, in particular Jews. Further, this perspective is in stark contrast to the self-ascriptions and distinctive positions of white ethnic and religious minorities in Britain (Anthias 1990, 2001; Anthias and Yuval-Davis 1993; Hickman 1998). The hegemonic narrative of an assimilated cultural melange of 'whiteness' is significant, however, as it illustrates how the meaning of 'foreign' and 'alien' shifted historically to become part of the dominant discourse of *black Otherness* after the Second World War.

In the twenty-first century, a colour of difference[26] continues to be ascribed that conveys the politics of race. In accordance with skin *colour*, access to wider forms of social participation (leisure, education, jobs and the housing market) is more difficult to achieve for non-white men and women. *Ethnicity* and orthodoxy have become gendered symbolic reference points of community belonging and, thus, predominantly women of migrant or newly settled minority communities are addressed as homogenous groups with *special needs*. Notwithstanding its impact on the constitution of hegemony, whiteness often escapes critical analysis, in particular when paired with middle-class subjectivity.

Critical Race Theory, Critical Whiteness Studies and the Perception of Being 'Black', 'White' or 'Mixed/Multiple'

The final issue to be discussed is the cultural pressure to *accommodate individually* to hegemonic whiteness. What are the practical research implications in cases where individuals reject an ascribed or assumed belonging to a black minority?

Maylor's struggle to find 'black' participants for his study on black teachers (2009: 369 et seq.) is a case in point. People on the ground simply did not relate and identify with the research funder's

---

25   That is to say migrants arriving from the Caribbean, the Indian sub-continent and Ireland.

26   The violent conflicts between Catholic Irishness and Protestant Englishness echo ethnic diversity and contradictory religious perspectives within the British nation that predate and are sustained in the current focus on 'cultural' conflicts between Christianity and Islam.

loose definition of 'Black' as 'members of African, African-Caribbean, Asian and other visible minority ethnic communities' (ibid.: 372).

Safran argues that the term 'people of colour' in the United States turned out to be over-inclusive and that it 'conflates race and ethnicity and often also confuses policies of racial identity promotion with cultural pluralism' (2008: 438). Seemingly, the notion of 'blackness' is becoming a fragmented boundary marker that co-exists with the symbolic confines of other identity projects. Remarkably, *neo-nationalizing* discourses prevalent in Europe give way to the revival of smaller nations in Britain, which results in new hyphenated local or regional identities. For example, a Scottish birthplace and the associated cultural belonging and not the meaning implicit in being a black British citizen are accorded centrality in personal narratives of identity (see McCrone and Bechhofer 2008). As those authors conclude, '[b]irthplace is the key identity marker in terms of whether or not someone is thought to be Scottish, and that includes non-whites as well as whites' (ibid.: 1263). Hence, the political identification that used to be an important element to declare solidarity amongst 'black identities' and, thus, enhance minority empowerment, increasingly falls short when 'black', after becoming 'ethnicity' (for the purposes of statistical profiles), runs the risk of being further *whitened*. In fact, the notion of 'black' diffused politically though whiteness is stable in its salient reference to power. That might suggest that an explicit focus on 'black' agents in social fields could fail to appeal to those who, notwithstanding their structural minoritization in specific institutional settings, reject being 'added up' as non-white. Thus, if 'blackness' is diffused and minority ethnicity could be regarded as a social stigma leading to the cultural and religious exclusion of non-white minorities with a recent or parental migration background, we could ask 'Who wants to feel white?' (Essed and Trienekens 2007), in order to understand the normative dimension of hegemonic whiteness.

An examination of the more symbolic allusions of whiteness is helpful to argue for an ongoing need to interrogate systematically the meaning of race in the contemporary moment. Some might suggest that Barack Obama, the first black US President, has become the symbol of post-'race' societies. However, in terms of his professional performance and overall structural position, he acts instead in a 'predominantly white' manner embedded in a hegemonic white culture.

Essed and Trienekens shift the focus of critical race studies[27] to 'white normativity' (2007: 54) in order to grasp the cultural impact of dominant whiteness. The focus on *normativity* enables researchers interested in the 'internalized white' to look for structural patterns that go beyond an individual decision and which in analytical terms exceed Essed's earlier approach of studying 'everyday racism' (1990, 1991). Cultural expressions of whiteness can be observed in taken-for-granted associations, for example, between being European and being white (Essed and Trienekens 2007: 68). These authors conclude (ibid.: 69) that 'whiteness remains a floating concept when European discourse and politics are largely about identifying the cultural and historical criteria of national representation and European-ness. European-ness probably means "white" (whichever way white gets to be defined), "plus" something else'. Consequently, a person could be white, but lack proper social status or the 'correct' religion (Christianity), or one could have a higher social status, identify as Protestant and, nonetheless, be of African descent (ibid.). The latter might suggest that in the hegemonic gaze *non-white* could 'pass' as white, given that the person inhabits or presents a socially valued sample of intersecting profiles. Nonetheless, subjective and positive identification as a citizen might supersede traditional patterns of racial codes opening up space for a new project of European democracy. When it comes to the notion of Englishness, but also to a notion of a supposedly more inclusive Britishness, individuals of ethnic and racial minority

---

27   For details on critical race theory see, for example, Delgado (1995).

background behaved reluctantly to identify with such notions, but did so in terms of their rights as British citizens (Hussain and Bagguley 2005). European heritage, whiteness and the colonial context are largely conveyed through the 'racialised nature' (ibid.: 415) of hegemonic nationality. Therefore, the statement that 'national identity and citizenship identity are not the same thing' (ibid.: 421) expresses certain tensions and contradictions between, on the one hand, a strong civil project of European democracies and, on the other, views that are primordially rooted in whiteness and privilege dominant Christian religions as an indicator of cultural belonging. The latter makes reference to the dominant triad of Christian religion, national belonging and gendered boundary markers in some continental European countries as outlined above, for example, in Germany, the Netherlands or France. In addition, the Dutch classification of *allochtoon*, which addresses mainly non-white others and non-Westerners as non-natives can be regarded as racial-ethnic labelling (Essed and Trienekens 2007: 57).

In Britain, the situation remains slightly different, as more recent critical studies into whiteness and the intersecting dimension of middle-class status reveal. Knowles (2008), for example, analyses the production of whiteness and classed memory of empire in rural South Devon, England; Reay et al. (2007) consider the meaning of whiteness, middle classes and multi-ethnic inner-city schooling; and similarly Byrne (2009: 425) explores the racialized nature of the reproduction of middle-class privilege in school choice in London. Their various research projects focus on an element which Garner (2006) regards as central. He argues that '[w]hiteness however is also mediated by class: we ignore this at the risk of taking the cultural turn away from the material base that I suggested should be adopted' (ibid.: 265).

Concluding Remarks

The question remains how most of the EU Member States, and in particular professionals and lawyers, will tackle discrimination on the grounds of race while not daring to *name* racism. Seemingly, *ethnicity* can be handled more easily, but that concept fails to tackle skin colour racism as a separate and distinctive layer of colonial European history. As I have argued elsewhere (Vieten 2007, 2009), notions of difference are historically and nationally situated and subsequently, *othering difference* as boundary marking unfolds in distinctive ways in the UK and continental Europe.[28]

Most continental European nation states, in contrast to the United States and the UK, have hitherto used neither race nor ethnicity as categories in their compilation of statistical measurements. On the other hand, the terminology of 'race' and 'ethnicity' has been channelled into the anti-discrimination law of EU Member States as a result of EU directives. Correspondingly, Essed and Trienekens remark that 'race is a legal category in European and Dutch law (anti-discrimination legislation) but is not a formal policy category in Dutch political discourse' (2007: 55). Nonetheless, measuring of populations takes place.

As argued above, we find a similar situation in Germany, France and, perhaps, also in other EU Member States in continental Europe. In those circumstances, where does this leave research and anti-discrimination policy with the intention to establish the scale of 'racial and ethnic discrimination'? Public discourses, e.g. media or political speeches, have been critically assessed in terms of their racism and xenophobic content (see, for example, Jäger and Link 1993; Krzyzanowski and Wodak

---

28   It would be interesting to know more in detail how the social and 'legal' categories of ethnicity and 'race' operate in Scandinavian countries, in southern Europe and in eastern Europe and the extent to which 'Western' non-EU states (for example, Switzerland, Norway or Iceland) also adopt a distinctive framework.

2008). European policy, which ambitiously aims to combat multiple discriminations, might fall into the trap of constructing new racialized boundaries while underestimating the consequences of the push to produce statistic material. Hegemonic national traditions may be regarded as an integral element of the global division of power. They encapsulate distinctive pasts whilst also perpetuating the bonding of their dominant ethno-cultural symbolic spaces of belonging at the present time. Currently, some of the 27 EU Member States are introducing statistical measures that reflect, on the one hand, domestic integration policy and, on the other, an unchallenged persistence of racializing categories, which divide and monitor national populations. Thus, the implementation of EU directives in anti-discrimination legislation and policy is initiating a broader agenda of *racializing* ethnicity, national citizenship and religion, when read as signifiers of 'racial'-cultural otherness.

'Orthodox' performance regarding ethnicity and minority religion appear as crucial benchmarks for measuring discriminatory patterns in all countries. That is the locus in which 'visible' difference in terms of an ascribed non-whiteness and claimed *active* ethnicities (or religion) become indicators of vulnerability. Tempting as it is to get rid of the terminology of race, it remains important, nonetheless, to understand that skin colour and cultural heritage undergo and represent distinctive racializing strategies in various colonial contexts. Those strategies are embedded in ideologically situated and nation-state specific discriminatory systems that anchor the notion of ethnicity as a cultural minority reference while often omitting the salience of whiteness for a broader constitutive frame of European nations (Goldberg 2006). Louis (2002) argues that the history of race should be understood as a sociological theory of 'race'; why not go further and declare the European history of race and with it all accounts of racializing groups a *European history of racisms*?

PART II
Tackling Intersectionality
at National Levels

Chapter 5

Women with Disability in Turkey and France

Ayse Idil Aybars

Introduction

The last couple of decades have witnessed an increasing emphasis on intersectionality and multidimensionality in the equality law of the European Union (EU) and its member states. This owes much to the insertion of Article 13 EC (now Article 19 Treaty on the Function of the European Union (TFEU)) in the Treaty of Amsterdam in 1997 (Schiek 2009), which established a legal basis for the EU to combat discrimination based on sex, racial or ethnic origin, religion or belief, disability, age and sexual orientation. Article 13 EC (now Article 19 TFEU) reflects a growing concern with the need to develop an integrated approach to the fight against discrimination (Rorive 2009). The subsequent anti-discrimination directives, namely the Race Equality (2000/43/EC) and Employment Framework Directives (2000/78/EC), reflect this integrated approach. The EU's anti-discrimination law draws much on its long experience in gender equality, particularly in relation to employment issues, which goes back to the inception of the European Economic Community (EEC) in 1957.

The obligation to transpose EU rules into national legislation means that most Member States currently base their anti-discrimination legislation on these. This is also the case for countries aspiring to be EU members, as they need to adapt national legislation to EU standards. At the same time as EU anti-discrimination law is starting to move towards multidimensionality and intersectionality, it also aims to expand its practices and legal rules across the 27 current Member States and the candidate countries. In this respect, concerns have been voiced on 'how to evaluate, balance and generally relate different discriminatory grounds, individual claims and social systems of oppression to each other' (Vieten 2009: 93) across national contexts with diverging and uneven social and cultural divisions, and with different legal frameworks and approaches to discrimination.

This chapter traces the development of anti-discrimination law in two countries, Turkey and France, with a view to questioning the extent to which they have incorporated intersectionality into their legal frameworks. The selection of the two countries rests on their different levels of welfare state development and different perspectives on gender equality, despite similar approaches to equality law. It is assumed that the protection accorded to women with disabilities in France (having a strong welfare state tradition) would be different in scope and extent to Turkey (facing continual challenges, particularly from the EU, regarding its welfare state development). The specific focus is on the intersection between gender and disability so as to investigate the degree of legal protection accorded to women with disabilities, and their integration into social life in line with welfare state provisions. Women with disabilities are therefore discussed as an example of an assessment of intersectionality in anti-discrimination law in two countries. Three particular areas will be emphasized in this respect, namely employment, education and social protection, which are key to understanding the underlying welfare state dynamics and to revealing the patterns of integration of women with disabilities into society. The objective is to understand the implications of, and specific problems posed by, multidimensional equality concepts in different national contexts for people facing specific obstacles on the basis of their gender *and* disability. This gains all the more importance in light of

Article 6 of the Convention on the Rights of Persons with Disabilities (CRPD), which recognizes the multiple discrimination faced by women with disabilities and obliges its State parties to take appropriate measures to ensure the full development, advancement and empowerment of women.

Following Crenshaw (1989), the concept of intersectionality is taken here to refer to situations that occur when two or more discrimination grounds or identities combine to create a unique situation that is more complex and represents more than just the sum of its parts. The chapter approaches intersectionality as a fluid and contextual concept, showing how individual and group identities creating vulnerabilities impact on the social positioning of individuals (Arnardóttir 2009), and the extent to which certain socio-cultural hierarchies, such as gender, nationality, race and disability might intersect while producing social inclusion or exclusion (Vieten 2009). Inequalities at the intersection of gender and disability, although not researched intensively yet (Degener, in this volume: 29–46; Sheldon 2004) seem a good point of departure for comparing France and Turkey, because of their different welfare state conceptions.

The welfare state can be assumed to provide mechanisms promoting the inclusion of vulnerable groups. Following Esping-Andersen (1990, 1999), it is commonly accepted that today's European countries can be clustered into four or more welfare regimes, depending on, among other things, the particular social stratification effects and gender equality outcomes they produce. Although academic interest in the issue has started only recently, the Turkish welfare state has commonly been classified under the Southern European welfare model, which is characterized by low levels of public social expenditure, inconsistency and insufficiency of social services, centrality of the family in welfare provision, and a strong male breadwinner model illustrated by low levels of female employment (Aybars and Tsarouhas 2010; Bugra and Keyder 2006). The position of women vis-à-vis the welfare state, particularly in relation to employment and family responsibilities, is an important aspect of this classification, although gender inequalities are more aggravated in Turkey compared to Southern European countries. While female employment rates have continuously risen in Southern Europe since the 1990s, Turkish female employment rates have been declining continually. Women's labour force participation today remains below 25 per cent, compared to 34 per cent in 1990.[1] The main factor behind this has been a massive rural–urban migration in Turkey since the 1980s, which implies that women previously working in agriculture take recourse to informal jobs or remain unemployed in cities due to lack of skills and education. In terms of educational attainment, around 20 per cent of women in Turkey are illiterate,[2] indicating that Turkey's gender issue is deeply entrenched in socio-economic life (Aybars and Tsarouhas 2010).

France, on the other hand, is commonly discussed under the conservative welfare model together with continental European countries (Esping-Andersen 1990), albeit posing a non-typical example particularly when it comes to gender equality. While its corporatist income maintenance system largely fits in with the conservative model, when examined through the lens of gender France becomes an outlier to the model. Three main factors account for this:

1. The Republican equality, citizenship and solidarity ethos, which replaced the influence of the Catholic Church that was central in the development of the continental welfare regime;
2. The extensive family-friendly public policy approach of the French welfare state; and
3. The relatively high rates of female labour force participation.

---

1 Labour Force Statistics [Online: Turkish Statistical Institute]. Available at: www.turkstat.gov.tr [accessed: 1 March 2010].

2 Ibid.

The influence of social Catholicism has been weaker in France than most other continental European countries. The French Revolution of 1789 set the tradition of a strong and centralized state, inscribed in an 'active Republicanism' based on the premise of pure equality between individuals, which did not differentiate between groups, including women. Although this is, rightly, seen as an important obstacle to the development of equal opportunities in France, the 'Republican' view of motherhood, historically influenced both by the Catholic ideal of the virtuous mother and by the socialist ideal of 'working mothers', meant strong state protection of women's position as both mothers and workers (Reuter and Mazur 2003). This implied highly developed women-friendly policies in the French welfare regime, which were absent in most other exemplars of the conservative model. The relatively high levels of female labour market participation in France (around 65 per cent at the end of 2008)[3] are mainly explained by the progressive nature of French family-friendly policies in content and coverage. Although early employment policies, as established at the end of the Second World War, mainly aimed to protect the male breadwinner as the single earner of a nuclear family, today access to social guarantees founded upon employment is no longer familial, but individual (Fouquet et al. 2000).

While Turkey and France have somewhat similar legal approaches to equality and anti-discrimination matters, their different welfare state structures, and particularly the status of women within them, translate into different frameworks for the protection of the rights of women with disabilities, and into different outcomes regarding the integration of this group in the socio-economic life of their societies. Commonalities in the legal conceptions of equality in Turkey and France offer a fruitful ground for a comparison of the implications of their laws on intersectional inequalities. French legal tradition provided an important influence for the Turkish legal system, particularly during the early phases of the Republic in the 1920s, and the legal reforms dating back to the late nineteenth century were largely modelled on France (Sur 2009). Thus, unsurprisingly, both countries' constitutions rely on a generalized concept of equality, both display reluctance to recognize groups with specific needs, and share a cautious approach to anti-discrimination measures. At the same time, both have faced constant pressure from the EU to adapt to its body of equality law, although to different extents and scopes as a founding member of the EEC and a candidate country respectively. Moreover, while gender equality legislation has developed along different paths and at different paces, both countries adopted specific legislation on disability in the same year, 2005.

The first section of the chapter briefly examines the legal framework for anti-discrimination legislation in the two countries, with a specific focus on gender equality and disability. This will be followed by a discussion of the socio-economic situation of women with disabilities in the fields of employment, education and social protection. The final section will draw conclusions concerning the extent to which (1) the legal protection and social inclusion of women with disabilities differs between the two countries in line with their welfare state patterns, and (2) intersectionality and multidimensionality is incorporated into their anti-discrimination laws.

Legal Framework

In both Turkey and France, anti-discrimination provisions have traditionally been based on a general constitutional equality clause, with specific legislation only developing in response to

---

3   Employment Rate by Gender [Online: Eurostat Online]. Available at: ec.europa.eu/eurostat [accessed: 1 March 2010].

EU requirements – based on membership and the pre-accession process respectively. This section briefly overviews the legal framework for anti-discrimination measures in both countries, focusing specifically on gender and disability.

Anti-Discrimination Legislation

Turkey   Article 10 of the Turkish Constitution provides the basis for equal treatment before the law by establishing that '[a]ll individuals shall be equal before the law without any distinction based on language, race, colour, sex, political opinion, philosophical belief, religion, membership of a religious sect or other similar grounds'. This article does not expressly guarantee equality based on disability. Nevertheless, the expression 'similar grounds' indicates that the list is not exhaustive (Korkut 2003).

In terms of the development of a legal framework for anti-discrimination and equality, a major impetus has been provided by the accession negotiations between Turkey and the EU, which took off in 2005 following the official recognition of Turkey's candidate status at the Helsinki European Council of 1999. The accession process is driven by three main pillars (European Commission 2004a). The first consists of the fulfilment of the Copenhagen political and economic criteria, which, in political terms, require the stability of institutions guaranteeing democracy, the rule of law, human rights and respect for and protection of minorities. They encompass economic and social rights, which include women's rights, labour rights and trade unions, as well as anti-discrimination policies. The second pillar concerns the ability to assume the obligations of membership, referring to the rather technical aspect of the transposition of the EU *acquis communautaire*. Chapter 19 of the *acquis* is specifically concerned with employment, social affairs and equal opportunities. It contains provisions affecting a wide variety of social policies, including social dialogue, trade union activities and full trade union rights, labour market patterns, and equal employment opportunities for men and women. The third pillar concerns civil society development, aiming to enhance social dialogue and inclusion, culture, gender, children and regional issues. Issues of anti-discrimination and equality remain an important concern across all three pillars of the negotiation process. It is, therefore, no surprise that major legislative reforms in this field, particularly in the area of gender equality, have recently taken place in order to comply with the EU entry requirements. This will be discussed in the next section.

France   The French Constitution of 1958, referring to the 1789 Declaration of the Rights of Man and of the Citizen and the Preamble to the 1946 Constitution, rests on the principle that all human beings are born and live equal in rights. This relates to the 'Republican' concept of citizenship and equality, established in the French Revolution of 1789 and based on the premise of pure equality between individuals, not differentiating among groups (Siim 2000; Reuter and Mazur 2003). There is, therefore, no global and specific approach to groups of people with complex needs (Sanchez 2008). The Preamble to the 1946 Constitution, nevertheless, establishes equal rights for women and men in all spheres of life. The French Constitution does not include provisions on the prohibition of discrimination on the basis of disability (nor of age, health or sexual orientation) even though the list of discriminatory grounds has been deemed to be not exhaustive by the Constitutional Council (Latraverse 2008).

While certain principles of anti-discrimination have long been enshrined in French law, discrimination issues, particularly in relation to employment, have only recently become a focus of attention in France. In its Article L122-45, the Labour Code has prohibited discrimination on the grounds of origin, sex, family status, ethnic, national or racial belonging, political opinion, trade union activities and religious belief since 1982;[4] lifestyle, state of health and disability since 1990;[5] sexual orientation, age, physical appearance and name since 2001;[6] genetic features since 2005;[7] and pregnancy since 2006.[8] These additions to the list of prohibited grounds, which originally comprised only trade union membership and pay discrimination, have been made mainly to comply with EU anti-discrimination requirements. The Anti-Discrimination Act of 2001 transposed the Employment Framework Directive and had significant implications for the legal framework for combating discrimination (Laulom 2009).

The High Authority against Discrimination and for Equality (*Haute Autorité de Lutte contre les Discriminations et pour l'Egalité*, HALDE), established in 2004,[9] is an independent administrative body with competence in all forms of discrimination, direct and indirect, forbidden by the laws of the Republic and international agreements ratified by France, and readily adaptable to future legal evolutions. In addition to decision-making powers, HALDE has competence in investigating individual and collective complaints. Its two main tasks are addressing cases of discrimination and promoting equality (Laulom 2009).

It is important to note that the French legislative framework on anti-discrimination is characterized by 'neutrality' towards the grounds mentioned above, meaning that it does not distinguish between different discrimination grounds. Moreover, while the legal framework for anti-discrimination approaches all grounds in the same manner, there is no legal rule addressing multiple grounds of discrimination in France: 'issues of multiple discrimination have been scarcely discussed and French law has up to now not addressed multiple discrimination' (Laulom 2009: 279; Latraverse 2008). Still, this general anti-discrimination framework is complemented by specific provisions for certain groups (Laulom 2009), particularly women but also persons with disabilities, which will be discussed in the following sections.

Gender Equality Legislation

Turkey Gender equality is one of the landmarks in Turkey's accession process to the EU, whose major documents frequently refer to women's rights and gender equality. The process has so far brought about remarkable improvements in legislation, especially the Constitution, Civil Code, Penal Code, Labour Code and other relevant legislation. At the same time, important steps remain to be taken in order to strengthen the principle of gender equality in all areas of social life.

Most importantly, the 2004 amendment to Article 10 of the 1982 Constitution added a specific provision on the equal rights of women and men to the existing grounds of discrimination, accompanied by a positive state obligation to ensure its realization.[10] Article 41 of the Constitution, which stated that 'the family is the essence of Turkish society', was complemented by the suffix 'and it is based on equality between the spouses'. Additionally, Article 90 was amended so as to assign priority to the provisions of international conventions over national legislation in the field of fundamental rights and freedoms, which has significant implications for the implementation of

---

4   Law No. 82-689 of 4 August 1982.
5   Law No. 90-602 of 12 July 1990.
6   *Loi No. 2001-1066 relative a la lutte contre les discriminations.*
7   Law No. 2005-102 of 11 February 2005.
8   Law No. 2006-340 of 23 March 2006 on equal pay between men and women.
9   *Loi No. 2004-1486 du 30 décembre 2004 portant création de la haute autorité de lutte contre les discriminations et pour l'égalité.*
10   Additional provision (7/5/2004-5170/1md.).

the Convention on the Elimination of All Forms of Discrimination against Women (CEDAW) and the CRPD in Turkey.

Alignment of Turkish legislation to Chapter 19 of the EU *acquis* on employment and social policy led to the reform of the Labour Code in 2003,[11] which now contains provisions on the equal treatment of men and women, equal pay for work of equal value, non-discrimination on the basis of gender or pregnancy (Article 5), prohibition of dismissal on the grounds of gender (Article 18), and prohibition of sexual harassment at work (Article 24), alongside a comprehensive prohibition of discrimination at work on the basis of race, sex, language, religion and sect, political opinion, philosophical belief, or any such consideration (Sural 2009). Turkey is also party to ILO Convention No. 100 on Equal Remuneration and No. 111 on Employment and Occupation Discrimination Convention, as well as CEDAW.

Other important legislative reforms include the amendment of the Turkish Penal Code in 2004 to conceptualize crimes against women within the framework of 'crimes against humanity', and to include, for the first time, issues such as sexual harassment at work in legislation. Also, the reform envisages the severest punishment available – life imprisonment – for the perpetrators of honour killings.

Importantly, a gender equality commission was established in the Turkish parliament in February 2009[12] with the aim of monitoring national and international developments on the protection and promotion of women's rights and gender equality, and to issue opinions on draft laws and proposals in the areas that fall under its responsibility. This was a significant development as it signalled that all draft legislation will be inspected, and necessary modifications will be proposed by the commission, which will pave the way for gender mainstreaming.

France   The legal framework for gender equality in France has mainly developed in relation to the principle of equal pay, which had a long-standing tradition going back to the 1950s, when France ratified the ILO Convention No. 100 in 1952. The Preamble to the Constitution of 1958 asserted that '[t]he law guarantees to women, in all domains, equal rights to those of men', consolidating gender equality as a constitutional principle, to be affirmed progressively in the familial, political and economic domains (Laufer 2005). In view of the fact that the equal pay principle was established earlier in France than in other European countries, it comes as no surprise that the equal pay provision (Article 119) was incorporated into the EEC Treaty at French insistence.

A key piece of legislation in terms of gender equality is the *loi Roudy* of 1983,[13] which aimed to promote gender equality in all spheres of life and all areas of employment. The Act incorporated the principles of equal treatment and equal opportunities into the labour law. Apart from enhancing the equal pay provisions, it set out the obligation for companies employing more than 50 employees to prepare an annual report comparing the general employment and training conditions of women and men. It also established a method of negotiating a company-wide agreement or 'positive action plan' for the recruitment, training, promotion and improvement of the working conditions of women, signed by both management and trade unions. On this basis, the *loi Génisson*, adopted in 2001,[14] reinforced the 1983 law in particular by demanding negotiations on gender equality at industry, sector and company levels. A new Law on Equal Pay between Men and Women[15] in 2006 introduced provisions profoundly modernizing the *loi Génisson*, aiming primarily to reduce wage

---

11   Law No. 4857, *Official Gazette*, No. 25134, 10/06/2003.
12   Law No. 5840, 25/02/2009.
13   *Loi du 13 juillet1983 sur l'égalité professionnelle entre les femmes et les hommes.*
14   *Loi no 2001-397 du 9 mai 2001 relative à l'égalité professionnelle entre les femmes et les hommes.*
15   Law No. 2006-340 of 23 March 2006.

disparities between men and women, and to eliminate them by 31 December 2010, entrusting the social partners with the achievement of that aim.

Nonetheless, while France was the main initiator of a Community-level gender equality policy, the national impact of the policy has been limited. Most of the legislation outlined above falls short of EU gender equality standards; and the two major laws promoting gender equality, the *loi Roudy* and *loi Génisson*, did not yield the expected results (Reuter and Mazur 2003; Laufer 2005).

Disability Legislation

Turkey Turkish legislation concerning disability matters addresses persons with disabilities in general. No legislation specifically on disabled women currently exists. Article 61 of the Constitution provides that 'the State shall take all measures to protect disabled people and to ensure their adaptation to social life'. A Disabled People Act[16] (DPA) was adopted in 2005, aiming at preventing disability and enabling people with disabilities to fully participate in society by taking measures regarding their health, education, rehabilitation, employment, care and social security and the removal of the obstacles they face. Article 4 DPA sets out the general principle that 'the State shall develop social policies against all kinds of abuse of disabled people and disability on the basis of the immunity of human honour and dignity', and that '[t]he State shall not discriminate against disabled people; fighting against discrimination shall be the basic principle of the policies towards disabled people'. To ensure the protection of the people with disabilities at all government levels, specific duties for local governments are defined in several Acts[17] on the basis of the DPA. Also, the budgetary allocation for the poor and the needy includes funding for services for people with disabilities and for disability centres. The Labour Code establishes an obligation to employ people with disabilities, under which any private employer with 50 or more employees must ensure that 3 per cent of its employees are persons with disabilities. The quota is 4 per cent for public employers. Moreover, employers exceeding these quotas profit from a 50 per cent reduction of their share to social insurance premiums. Fines for undertakings not fulfilling the quota are used for projects promoting vocational training and rehabilitation for persons with disabilities,[18] enabling them to start up their own enterprises, and supportive technologies to ease finding suitable employment.[19]

Other legal instruments that have been amended include the Turkish Penal Code,[20] which defines discrimination on the basis of language, race, colour, sex, disability, political opinion, philosophical belief, religion, membership of a religious sect and similar grounds as a criminal offence since 2004. 'Disability' as a ground for discrimination was only added by the DPA of 2005 (Article 122). Likewise, the Labour Code contained no separate or general provision on equality

---

16 *Act on Disabled People and on making amendments in some laws and decree laws*, Act No. 5378, *Official Gazette*, 7 July 2005, No. 25868.

17 Act on Municipalities (Act No. 5393, *Official Gazette*, 13 July 2005, No. 25874), Act on Metropolitan Municipalities (Act No. 5216, *Official Gazette*, 23 July 2004, No. 25531), and Act on Special Provincial Administrations (Act No. 5302, *Official Gazette*, 4 March 2005, No. 25745).

18 This article envisages special vocational rehabilitation centres, the functioning of which is the responsibility of the Employment Organization. Administrative fines paid by employers not fulfilling the quota rules contribute to the budget of these. However, the participants of their courses only constitute a small fraction of the totality of people with disabilities in the country (Korkut 2003).

19 Amended Article 30, 15/5/2008-5763/2md.

20 Act No. 5237, *Official Gazette*, 12 October 2004, No. 25611.

and discrimination until recently. The new Labour Code of 2003[21] does not specify 'disability' as a discrimination ground in its non-exhaustive list of grounds.

The Administration for Disabled People (ADP), a specific Turkish government body responsible for the people with disabilities, aims to ensure the regular, efficient and productive provision of services for persons with disabilities; provide coordination and collaboration among national and international institutions and establishments; and assist in the formulation of national policies in this field. It is also responsible for following up international developments on persons with disabilities, and monitoring and evaluating the national implementation of international conventions and agreements. Under its coordination, specific ministries and offices are responsible for the rights under their own remit.

France   The French Law on the Equality of Rights and Opportunities, Participation and Citizenship of Persons with Disabilities[22] (Law on Disability), which was adopted in 2005, establishes that '[a]ll persons with disabilities shall have the right to the solidarity of the nation, which guarantees them access to fundamental rights recognized for all citizens as well as the full exercise of their citizenship'. Article 2 of the Law entrusts the State as the guarantor of the equality of treatment of persons with disabilities on its territories, and provides for specific action to ensure the access of children, adolescents or adults with disabilities to institutions open to the whole population and their support in schooling, employment and life. The same article establishes that 'the State shall guarantee the assistance and support of families and relatives of persons with disabilities'. The Law expounds the following principles: generalized accessibility to all spheres of social life; the right to compensation for the consequences of disability; and participation and proximity realized by the creation of Departmental Houses for Persons with Disabilities (*Maisons départementales des personnes handicapées* – MDPH). It also assigns important functions to MDPHs and CDAPHs (*Commission des droits et de l'autonomie des personnes handicapées*) at the departmental level in relation to various aspects of disability including education, employment, benefits and access to justice.

As there is no specific approach to groups of people with complex needs in France, any person with disability, mild or severe, simple or complex, is covered by the Law on Disability (Sanchez 2008). Article 24 of the Law on Disability adds article L122-45-4 to the Labour Code establishing the principle of equal treatment for disabled workers and prohibiting discrimination against them. The new Law on Disability favours the employment of disabled persons in the mainstream labour market while stressing the importance of sheltered environments and adapted businesses. Adapted companies are considered as mainstream employment and allow people with disabilities to be paid on the basis of the legal minimum income wage. These companies receive fixed financial support from the state for any provision of a job. The disabled worker is considered a full worker with a common right employee status, covered by the Labour Code and subject to the principle of non-discrimination. Currently, around 20,000 disabled workers are employed in adapted companies (Sanchez 2008). People who cannot properly work in mainstream environments because they are severely disabled are guided towards work support services.

Positive action measures targeting persons with disabilities and aiming to favour equality of treatment are defined as not constituting discrimination. In order to guarantee respect for the principle of equal treatment of employees with disabilities, employers shall take appropriate measures allowing these employees to accede to a job or keep a job corresponding to their

---

21   Act No. 4857, *Official Gazette*, 10 June 2003, No. 25134.

22   *Loi No. 2005-102 du 11 février 2005 pour l'égalité des droits et des chances, la participation et la citoyenneté des personnes handicapées*, JORF no. 36 du 12 février 2005, pp. 2353, texte no.1.

qualification, exercise or progress in their jobs, and be offered training adapted to their needs.[23] Refusal to take appropriate measures constitutes discrimination. Employees with disabilities can also benefit from adjusted personalized working hours to facilitate their professional activity or the maintenance of their jobs. The family and relatives of persons with disabilities may benefit under the same conditions from personalized adjustment of their work hours in order to facilitate their accompanying the person with disabilities (Article 24). Disabled workers also enjoy special protection in the event of dismissal and they can take early retirement on advantageous terms.

A quota of 6 per cent was established by the Law on the Employment of Persons with Disabilities[24] of 1987, making it obligatory for any undertaking with at least 20 employees. The Law on Disability creates a fund for the integration of persons with disabilities in both private and public employment as well as sanctions if the employment quota is not respected (Article 36). The same Article maintains the possibility of complying with the quota obligation by making a financial contribution to the AGEFIPH[25] (*Association de Gestion du Fonds pour l'Insertion Professionnel des Personnes Handicapés*), established in 1987, which funds measures to integrate persons with disabilities into private sector employment. It also increases the maximum penalty from 600 to 1,500 times the minimum hourly wage for undertakings that have not employed any disabled worker for more than three years. One of the innovations of the new law is the creation of a public sector fund similar to AGEFIPH. Article 26 of the Law creates an additional reporting obligation on the employer by imposing an annual evaluation of measures taken to integrate the disabled into the workplace.

Summary

Both Turkey and France rely on a generalized concept of equality in their constitutional traditions, display reluctance to recognize groups with specific needs, and share a cautious approach to anti-discrimination measures, which is reflected in a reluctance to issue ground-specific anti-discrimination legislation. Where they have been developed, anti-discrimination measures have mostly been driven by the obligation to transpose EU requirements.

Both countries have generalized guarantees for equal rights in their Constitutions, but neither specifically identifies disability as a ground upon which discrimination should be prohibited. While the Turkish Constitution specifies a non-exhaustive number of grounds upon which discrimination shall be prohibited, the French Constitution provides for the equality of all citizens. Neither Turkey nor, until recently, France has had specific anti-discrimination legislation. Both countries adopted legislation specifically on disability matters in 2005, whereas in neither does there exist specific legislative provisions on women with disabilities. Nevertheless, the Turkish DPA promotes a generalized approach to disabled people without specifying any groups, while the French Law on Disability specifies children, adolescents and adults, as well as their families, as specific groups to focus attention on. While an administrative body specialized in disability exists in Turkey, in France disability is under the remit of HALDE, which has competence in all grounds of discrimination. Unlike the Turkish ADP, HALDE also has investigative powers over claims of discrimination and can refer these claims to courts. The institutional setting of HALDE, as well as the emphasis on specific groups, although not specified on the basis of gender, in the Law on Disability brings

---

23   These aids include the adaptation of machines or equipment, adjustment of workplaces, including individual equipment necessary for employees with disabilities to occupy these posts, and access to workplaces.

24   *Loi No. 87-517 du 10 juillet 1987 en faveur de l'emploi des travailleurs handicapés.*

25   AGEFIPH also campaigns for action by business to promote the employment of people with disabilities and helps finance dedicated job placements structures (Sanchez 2008).

Table 5.1   Legislation in Turkey and France

	Turkey	France
Constitution	1982 Constitution: No mention of disability as discrimination ground but not exhaustive. Equal rights for men and women. State responsibility for adaptation of disabled people to social life.	1958 Constitution: No provision on disability (or age, health or sexual orientation), but not exhaustive. Equal rights for all citizens. Equality between women and men.
Anti-discrimination legislation	No.	No approach to specific groups.
Disability legislation	2005 Disabled People Act.	2005 Law on Disability.
Institutional organization	Administration for Disabled People (ADP) Provision of services. Coordination of institutions. Formulation of policies.	Haute Autorité de Lutte contre les Discriminations et pour l'Egalité (HALDE) Competent for all forms of discrimination. Decision-making. Individual and collective claims.

France closer to a multidimensional approach in anti-discrimination law compared to Turkey. Table 5.1 summarizes the legislative provisions and institutional set-up in Turkey and France.

Integration of Women with Disabilities in Social Life

This section aims at giving an impression of the impact the legal framework described above has on women with disabilities in three specific fields. Some limits derive from the lack of statistical data specific for the situation of women with disabilities, though.

In Turkey, there is no registration system for people with disabilities, and there are major gaps in information as to the disabled population. Relevant data is to be found only in a survey on disabled people[26] conducted in 2002 by the Turkish Statistical Institute (TurkStat) in collaboration with the ADP and the State Planning Organization. In France, as the group of people with complex needs is not defined there no specific statistical data relating to it (Sanchez 2008). National population surveys on disability, incapacity and dependence were held in 1998, 1999, 2000 and 2001 (*Handicap, Incapacité et Dépendance* – HID).

While the results of the Turkish survey on disability are available, those of the French HID are more difficult to obtain. Nonetheless, the data for both countries, albeit limited, are useful to understand the general trends and provide a significant tool for making sense of the differences prevailing between them. In the remaining part, the chapter looks at three important fields which are key to understanding the underlying welfare dynamics and have tremendous implications for the integration of women with disabilities into social life, namely employment, education and training, and social protection.

Employment

Turkey   In the employment field, existing legislation on gender equality and disability in Turkey is quite comprehensive in light of recent reforms. In practice, however, the situation of women in

---

26   *Turkey Disability Survey 2002* [Online: State Institute of Statistics (SIS)]. Available at: www.ozida. gov.tr [accessed: 1 March 2010].

the labour market remains an area of concern. Today, women's labour force participation remains below 25 per cent. This is mainly due to massive rural–urban migration of recent decades. As indicated above, contrary to trends in all EU and OECD countries, the labour force participation of women is actually declining. The official unemployment rate for women was about 12 per cent in 2008, 16 per cent in urban settings, and 4 per cent in rural areas, which is explained by the unpaid family worker status of women in the agricultural sector in rural areas. Moreover, a strong division between 'male' and 'female' jobs is widely accepted as suitable. Accordingly, women are predominantly employed in traditional 'female' sectors, offering lower pay and status and requiring fewer qualifications and skills. Often, these jobs are temporary and precarious, with no social security.

While the female labour force participation rate in Turkey is strikingly low, the same rate for women with disabilities is an alarming 6.7 per cent (especially when compared to the rate for men, which stands at 32 per cent).[27] The unemployment rates for women and men with disabilities are 22 per cent and 15 per cent respectively. The inactivity rate for women is 53 per cent overall, but 93 per cent for those with disabilities, compared with 68 per cent for men.

There has been an emphasis on activation programmes for persons with disabilities in Turkey during recent years. 2005 was declared 'Employment Year for Disabled People',[28] with a view to promoting their participation in social life and to increasing their productivity. On this basis, an Action Plan for the years 2005–2010 was launched by the government in order to formulate an employment policy towards the disabled, particularly indicating women with disabilities as a special group whose employment is to be promoted.

France   In France, in the 15–64 age group, one person in eight declares themselves limited in their work capacity due to a health problem (five million individuals). Of these, 44 per cent are in employment. This ratio significantly decreases with age. Of those working, 80 per cent do not benefit from any assistance at work. This is less common in establishments subject to the obligation to employ persons with disabilities. Women who are subject to limitations in their work capacity have a lower rate of employment compared to men in the same situation (38 per cent against 50 per cent), but this difference is equal to that observed for non-disabled persons. Part-time work is much more common for women with limitations in their work capacity than men in the same condition (40 per cent against 15 per cent), but the scale of difference is the same for rates for persons without disabilities. Only one woman in five obtains the status of employee with disabilities, against one man in three. In total, 1.34 million people benefit from this administrative recognition of disability (DARES 2003).

There is a wide range of activation programmes in France targeting the disabled. The most significant among these is ESAT (*Les établissements ou services d'aide par le travail*), which aims to facilitate the integration of the disabled into the mainstream labour market. The services offered by ESAT include onward referral to vocational training, individual career planning, job matching and placement, post-placement support, advice on workplace reorganization, and guidance for employers. Other initiatives[29] aim to provide guidance for employers, offer psychiatric care, psychological and social support to persons with disabilities, improve their technical and social

---

27   Social Security and Health Statistics, Proportion of disabled population by labour force status, 2002 [Online: TurkStat]. Available at: www.turkstat.gov.tr [accessed: 1 March 2010].

28   Circular on the Employment Year for Disabled People, *Official Gazette*, 3 December 2004, No. 25659.

29   Delta Insertion Project, Isatis, CMRRF (Centre Mutualiste de Rééducation et de Réhabilitation fonctionnelles), Messidor, etc.

skills, and integrate or reintegrate them into the labour market through education and training. Most of these measures observe gender equality in the provision of their services.

To conclude, similar legal frames on preventing discrimination of people with disabilities in employment and establishing quotas for the employment of persons with disabilities are contrasted by a different approach to practical policies in favour of persons with disabilities. France places a remarkable emphasis on the integration of the disabled into mainstream employment. Moreover, in France the range of activation measures and state benefits for persons with disabilities is significantly wider than in Turkey, translating into remarkably higher labour market participation rates for the disabled, including for women, although the quality of this employment is debatable. This relates to the maturity of the French welfare state and a policy-driven approach to anti-discrimination matters. Finally, in neither of the countries do there exist specific legal provisions in the employment field on women with disabilities, while some of the active labour market measures adopted in recent years specifically target this group.

Education and Training

Turkey   In addition to the general legislative framework mentioned above, Article 42 of the Turkish Constitution provides for a 'right to learning and education', and Article 15 DPA repeats this principle particularly for people with disabilities. Disabled children, youngsters and adults are provided with education equal to non-disabled people and in inclusive environments by taking special conditions and differences into consideration. The DPA established a Counselling and Coordination Centre for Disabled People to look after the procurement of tools and equipment and the preparation of special class material, enabling the preparation of educational, research and accommodation environments suitable for disabled people in order to facilitate the educational life of disabled university students. The DPA also provides for procedures for the production of Braille, audio and electronic books, subtitled films and similar material to meet all kinds of educational and cultural needs of persons with disabilities. Other pieces of legislation qualify the right to education for people with disabilities by consigning children with disabilities to special education[30] in specialist educational institutions[31] and providing for special vocational courses for persons with disabilities.[32]

Pre-school education is obligatory for children in need of special education in Turkey and is provided through special educational institutions and other pre-school educational institutions. Preparatory classes can be established for children in need of special education when they reach the age of compulsory primary education in order to develop their capacity to follow the national curriculum. The decree establishes that the necessary measures shall be taken to enable persons in need of special education to benefit from higher education facilities in line with their interests, skills and proficiency. It also provides for the organization of adult education programmes in different subjects and durations for persons in need of special education, with the aim of developing their essential living skills, meeting their need for learning, and preparing them for employment. The decree requires the establishment of special education guidance and psychological counselling units in every city.

---

30   12 Primary Education Act, Act No. 222, *Official Gazette*, 12 January 1961, No. 10705, Articles 1.

31   Act on the Social Services and Child Protection Agency Act No. 2828, *Official Gazette*, 27 May 1983, No. 18059, additional regulation is to be found in the Statutory Decree on Special Education Statutory Decree No. 573, *Official Gazette*, 6 June 1997, No. 23011, Article 25.

32   Vocational Training Act, Act No. 3308, *Official Gazette*, 19 June 1986, No. 19139, Article 39.

In the sphere of education, despite the provisions of the Constitution and other relevant legislation emphasizing equal access to educational opportunities, important disparities remain to the disadvantage of women and girls across different geographical regions as well as between urban and rural contexts. Girls' access to primary education, encouragement of their enrolment in secondary education, and achievement of gender equality in literacy remain significant priorities in this respect. The population census of 2002 found that around 20 per cent of women were illiterate,[33] although, significantly, most of this group consisted of elderly women, pointing to the progress that had been made since the introduction of eight years of compulsory education in 1997. Still, it is remarkable that this rate reaches 46 per cent in the South East Anatolia region, and recedes to 13 per cent in the Marmara region, which is the most industrialized region of Turkey. Nevertheless, important progress has been made in schooling rates and an increase can be observed in the enrolment of girls in primary, secondary and higher education since 1997, also with the help of national campaigns on the issue.

While the literacy rate for women in Turkey was about 80 per cent in 2002, the rate for women with disabilities stood at 49 per cent (compared to that for disabled men of 74 per cent). Eighty-seven per cent of women had completed primary education, whereas this rate was 32 per cent for women with disabilities. While 45 per cent of women had completed high school education, only 4 per cent of women with disabilities had high school education, and only 1.5 per cent had completed higher education.[34]

France Adding to the legal framework referred to above, the French Constitution states that, '[t]he State has the responsibility to organize free and secular public education at all levels'. The Law on Disability underlines the right of disabled students to education and the responsibility of the educational system to guarantee the continuity of their individual schooling routes. In its domains of competence, the State shall put in place the financial and human means necessary for schooling in the ordinary environment of children, adolescents and adults with disabilities. The Law establishes obligations to provide the student, whenever possible, with mainstream school access as close as possible to home; to closely involve parents in the decision process of orienting their child and in all phases of the definition of his personal schooling project (*Projet personalisé de scolarisation* – PPS); to guarantee the continuity of the school career, adapted to the capacities and needs of the student; and to guarantee equality of opportunities for disabled and other candidates by ensuring a legal basis for the adjustment of examination conditions.[35]

There are various options for children with disabilities at the primary and secondary education levels within the adapted general and professional school sections (*Sections d'enseignement general et professionnel adapté* – SEGPA). These include specialized assistance networks; complementary schooling by specialist education and home care services; individual or group schooling alternatives targeting students who cannot follow mainstream education; distance learning alternatives for students who are not able to physically attend mainstream educational institutions; and medico-social facilities for children in this category, offering balanced

---

33   Population and Development Indicators for the year 2002 [Online: TurkStat]. Available at: www. turkstat.gov.tr [accessed: 1 March 2010].

34   Turkey Disability Survey 2002, Table 1.4, p. 11, Ankara; TurkStat, Education Statistics, Schooling ratio by educational year and level of education 2002–3 [Online: State Institute of Statistics (SIS)]. Available at: www.turkstat.gov.tr [accessed: 1 March 2010].

35   France [Online: European Agency for Development in Special Needs Education]. Available at: www. european-agency.org/country-information/france [accessed: 1 March 2010].

educational and therapeutic care.[36] In addition, persons with disabilities have access to the whole range of vocational training programmes offered to workers and job seekers (Sanchez 2008). Financial subsidies and loans allocated to the education and vocational training of persons with disabilities in France include a special education allowance (*l'Allocation d'éducation spéciale* – AES), which is a benefit available to families for the education of young people under 20 with a disability causing permanent incapacity. AES comprises a basic allowance to which complements can be added if the nature or degree of disability requires the assistance of a third person or particularly costly expenses. In 2006 there were 160,000 beneficiaries of the educational allowance (Sanchez 2008).

On the other hand, the effectiveness of these measures has been questioned and it has been argued that statutory instruments relating to the provision of education to persons with disabilities in France are poor in terms of difficulties in accessing special education, long waiting times and structural deficiencies in the programmes in terms of funding, shortages of available places and trained staff.[37]

To sum up, both the Turkish and French constitutions establish the right to education for all citizens. In both countries, special legislation on disability regulates the field of education for the disabled. Once again, neither of the two countries has specific provisions for the education and training of women and girls with disabilities. In this field, too, France favours the involvement of the disabled in mainstream education, and offers a much wider variety of benefits and measures for the integration of persons with disabilities in educational and training activities, despite questions over the success of these programmes.

Social Protection

Turkey   Based on a constitutional right to social security for all citizens (Article 61 Constitution) and adding to statutory rights to old age pensions (Pensions Act)[38] the DPA provides for a monthly salary for those who cannot maintain their lives without the assistance of others, and for those who have a disabled relative younger than 18 whom they are legally liable to look after. In addition, the Act on the Payment of Salaries to the Needy[39] provides for a state salary to persons with disabilities who need the physical support of others to sustain their lives and who do not have a legal carer; to those without an income or with an income less than that envisaged by the law and who do not have a legal carer; and to those under the duty of legal care if their income is less than that which is legally prescribed. The state can also provide care to the disabled either at home or at public or private care centres under certain conditions.

There are no figures concerning the poverty rates of women with disabilities in Turkey. While the Disability Survey 2002 contained questions on the income levels of people with disabilities, the results have not been published.[40] Nevertheless, there are important indicators of the poverty levels of people with disabilities: 57.3 per cent of the disabled state that they cannot benefit

---

36   Ibid.

37   See for instance *Autism Europe v. France*, Complaint No. 13/2002, decision on 4 November 2003, ECSR.

38   Act No. 2022 on Granting Pensions to Dependent, Helpless and Homeless Turkish Citizens over the age of 65, *Official Gazette*, 10 July 1976, No. 15642.

39   Act No. 2022, *Official Gazette*, 10 July 1976, No. 15642.

40   TUBITAK (The Scientific and Technical Research Council of Turkey) 2006, *Turkey Disability Survey 2002: Secondary Analyses* [Online: Ankara: TUBITAK]. Available at: www.ozida.gov.tr [accessed: 1 March 2010].

from services related to their disability due to economic conditions. On the other hand, 51 per cent of women and 45 per cent of men with disabilities are reported as receiving state benefits.[41] Moreover, while 32 per cent of men with disabilities receive this benefit as dependents, this rate reaches 83 per cent for women.

France   In France, the Law on Disability states that a person with disability shall have the right to compensation for the consequences of his/her disability notwithstanding the origins and nature of the deficiency, age or lifestyle. This compensation shall be sufficient to enable him/her to fully exercise citizenship and capacity for autonomy (Article 11). The benefits, calculated according to a personalized plan of compensation, can be paid for costs linked to a need for human or technical aid, the adaptation of accommodation or a vehicle, and transport costs. The law also improves a number of pre-existing rights and creates new ones: invalidity, parking or priority cards for persons with disabilities; support for single parents of children with disabilities; and improvement of the pensions of workers with disabilities benefiting from a lower retirement age. This general rule is complemented by specific statutory benefits, for example the ACTP (*allocation compensatrice pour tierce personne*) provided to persons with disabilities whose conditions necessitate effective help from a third person for the essential acts of life, paid to 77,000 beneficiaries by the end of 2007, the PCH (*prestation de compensation du handicap*) for persons with disabilities to compensate their (human or material) needs for assistance linked to their disability, covering human and technical assistance, as well as assistance for specific or exceptional needs; adaptation of accommodation or a vehicle and animal assistance contributing to autonomy. A household help service and an allowance to employ a person at home are the remaining forms of benefit provided to the disabled and the elderly who have a permanent incapacity rate of at least 80 per cent (Bailleau and Trespeux 2008). In addition, one of the most important measures for children is ASE (*aide sociale à l'enfance*), which has three principal benefits: educational (at home or in institutions), placement, and financial measures.

Another important pillar concerns support for parents of children with disabilities. The Law on Disability establishes a benefit for single parents who have to stop or reduce their professional activity in order to look after a disabled child. The law also contains provisions on early retirement for workers with disabilities. Employees caring for a disabled child can also benefit from the possibility of early retirement. In addition, the admission of disabled children is part of the mission of day-nurseries (for children between two months and three years) and daycare centres (two months to six years), unless the child has health problems which require specialized care. In this last case, the child's admission to a sanitary nursery is possible. Finally, allowances are provided for parents who live with their disabled child to cover the additional costs linked to the disability such as human assistance, technical help, transport and housing adaptations.

To sum up, also in the field of social security for the disabled, France offers a much wider range of benefits and services than Turkey in line with its more developed welfare state tradition and policy-driven approach to anti-discrimination. Still, neither of the two countries provides specific legal measures for the social protection of women with disabilities, while France comes closer to a multidimensional approach with a specific focus on children and families of children with disabilities.

---

41   Social Security and Health Statistics, Proportion of the disabled population having social security and social security registration status, 2002 [Online: TurkStat]. Available at: www.turkstat.gov.tr [accessed: 1 March 2010].

Conclusions

This chapter has examined the development of anti-discrimination legislation in Turkey and France with a view to assessing the way they address intersectionality and multidimensionality in their approach to discrimination issues through the lens of gender and disability. As anti-discrimination legislation is either inexistent or a very recent feature in both countries, discrimination is addressed in a patchy and uneven manner through different legislative provisions in different fields. A generalized concept of equality is reflected in a reluctance to issue ground-specific anti-discrimination legislation in both countries and, particularly in France, a more policy-oriented approach to gender and disability issues. A major impetus in the recent development of anti-discrimination provisions has been provided by the EU. In France, Article 13 and the subsequent anti-discrimination Directives have led to an increase in the number of grounds on which discrimination is prohibited, as well as in the scope of protection offered to specific groups, including women and disabled persons. In Turkey, the accession negotiations with the EU have resulted in modest improvements in the legal framework for anti-discrimination and equality.

When seen through the lens of the intersection of gender and disability, however, neither of the two countries has adequately addressed intersectionality in its respective legal framework for combating discrimination. Neither in Turkey nor in France are disability and gender approached in an integrated manner. While there are specific legal provisions prohibiting discrimination on the grounds of gender and disability, these are formulated at a general level and do not account for women with disabilities, who suffer from multiple grounds for discrimination. This relates to both generalized constitutional provisions and specific disability legislation in both countries.

The analysis of the specific fields of employment, education and social protection in the two countries has also shown that relevant regulations do not contain explicit references to women with disabilities. The importance of these specific fields stems from their potential for promoting the integration of women with disabilities into the social life of their societies. In practice, the lack of an effective multidimensional approach results in particular difficulties for this specific group in accessing employment, education and social protection. Although both countries, particularly recently under EU pressure, have adopted extensive laws on disability matters, the implementation of these laws and the actual outcomes they yield at the practical level are questionable. Particularly in Turkey, the weakness of the welfare state translates into much lower rates of participation in social life for persons with disabilities, and a much wider gap between women and men with disabilities compared to the participation rates of women and men without disabilities. In France, the policy-driven approach to anti-discrimination measures and the maturity of the welfare state result in a much wider variety of policy measures offered to persons with disabilities, and more possibilities for their participation in social life in general.

While intersectionality is not effectively approached by the anti-discriminatory provisions in either country, in a comparative perspective France comes closer to incorporating a more integrated approach to different grounds for discrimination. In Turkey, the lack of a multidimensional perspective is aggravated by the fact that separate institutional arrangements exist in relation to different grounds for discrimination. While an administrative body specialized in disability exists in Turkey, in France disability is under the remit of HALDE, which has competence in all forms of discrimination. The institutional setting and scope of the HALDE's remit brings France closer to a multidimensional approach in anti-discrimination law compared to Turkey. Moreover, contrary to the Turkish DPA, the French Law on Disability places emphasis on specific groups such as children and adolescents, albeit not specified on the basis of gender. In this respect, and in terms of the scope of measures adopted by the government to promote the integration of persons with disabilities, in most of the aspects examined above France is a number of steps ahead of Turkey with regard to promoting a multidimensional approach to discrimination. In Turkey, which faces numerous developmental problems and regional disparities requiring urgent action, extensive financial benefits or services to different groups in need of special protection, including persons with disabilities, cannot be effectively provided, although this situation has improved over recent years under pressure from the EU. It is difficult to deny that Turkey's prospect of EU membership has been a key element in the course of the reform processes in the field of equality and anti-discrimination, and it is 'bound to make a difference in the prevailing attitudes' towards, and debates surrounding, social justice and equality issues (Bugra and Keyder 2006: 225).

While it is clear that remarkable changes have taken place in both countries concerning persons with disabilities, the points outlined above signal different paces and dynamics in terms of the integration of women with disabilities into social life in the two countries, mainly in line with their welfare traditions, as well as the development of intersectionality in anti-discrimination matters. What is clear is that, although the scope of legislation looks promising in terms of promoting a protective environment for persons with disabilities, further efforts are certainly necessary to incorporate an intersectional approach, particularly to enable women with disabilities to fully participate in society.

Chapter 6

Promises of an Intersectional Approach in Practice? The Dutch Equal Treatment Commission's Case Law

Susanne Burri

Introduction

Why is Dutch equal treatment law particularly interesting when addressing the issue of an intersectional approach in practice? In my view, there are several reasons that make it worthwhile to study the Dutch approach. In the first place, the Dutch Equal Treatment Act (ETA) adopted in 1994 covers different discrimination grounds, among which race, gender and religion.[1] There is therefore some 15 years of experience with a single legislative Act covering different grounds of discrimination. The Equal Treatment (Disability and Chronic Illness) Act was adopted in 2003 and the main starting points of the case law of the Dutch Equal Treatment Commission (ETC) regarding discrimination on the ground of disability have now been established (Asscher-Vonk and Hendriks 2005; Koelman 2005; Cremers-Hartman 2004; Gerards and Heringa 2003).[2]

Secondly, the structure of these Acts roughly follows the structure of EU anti-discrimination law. The Dutch law does not have many national-specific features, which would particularly complicate the understanding of the national law for foreign experts.

Thirdly, the Dutch ETC has wide experience in the application of the Equal Treatment Law and high-level experts are members of this Commission. This Equality Body plays an important role as regards the enforcement of all equal treatment legislation applicable in the Netherlands, which is laid down in eight different Acts.[3]

Fourthly, the ETC is willing to adopt an intersectional approach where possible. In a paper presented at a conference in 2006 in Antwerp, *Equality is Not Enough: Dealing with Opportunities in a Diverse Society*, some legal experts working with the ETC concluded: 'So let's just try and

---

1 Dutch legislation can be found (in Dutch) at: www.cgb.nl/artikel/legislation [accessed: 25 November 2010]. The website of the Dutch Equal Treatment Commission provides an overview of the Dutch equal treatment legislation in English: www.cgb.nl/legislation.php [accessed: 10 March 2009].

2 In addition, the ETC publishes an overview of its opinions each year, commented by experts in the field of equal treatment. The electronic versions of these *oordelenbundels* are available at: www.cgb.nl/ publicaties/oordelenbundels [accessed: 17 December 2009].

3 Equal treatment legislation further includes various other Acts, such as the Equal Treatment in Employment (Age Discrimination) Act (*Stb.* 2004, 30) and provisions in the Civil Code (Sections 7: 646 through 7: 649), for example the Equal Treatment (Working Hours) Act (*Stb* 1996, 391), on part-time work and the Equal Treatment Temporary and Permanent Employees Act (*Stb.* 2002, 560).

see whether the promises of an intersectional approach can be realised in everyday practice' (Van den Brink et al. 2006).[4]

Finally, paying attention to the issue of multiple discrimination and intersectionality is a rather recent development. It is therefore rather likely that an Equality Body with wide experience may play an important role regarding the possibilities and difficulties of the application of such concepts in practice.

It therefore seems worth analysing opinions of the Dutch ETC cases in which a person is subjected to discrimination on more than one ground. The aim of this contribution is to analyse when and how the ETC explicitly or implicitly followed an intersectional approach in recent opinions and what the added value is of such an approach in practice. The main questions addressed are: is additional disadvantage caused by a combination of different discrimination grounds recognized as such by the ETC and, if it is, to which consequences does this lead in the opinions of the ETC? What are the specific problems linked to an intersectional approach in practice? Is an intersectional approach really useful for legal practice? This study is limited to the grounds race, religion, gender and disability. As highlighted by Dagmar Schiek (Chapter 1), the grounds race, gender and disability constitute nodes around which other discrimination grounds can be grouped. Discrimination in relation to religion is often linked to discrimination on the ground of race (and/or ethnic origin) and gender.

This chapter is structured along the following lines. The main concepts used in discussions regarding an intersectional approach are explored in the second section. There are many terms in use in literature to describe situations in which more than one discrimination ground is at stake. In the European Union, the term 'multiple discrimination' is used for example by the European Commission (2008a: 9–10) and as a general concept in recent studies (European Commission 2007a; Burri and Schiek 2009). It should therefore be clear what is meant in the relevant literature by different concepts in relation to intersectional approaches. In the third section, some discussions regarding the potentially theoretical added value of an intersectional approach are presented. In order to contribute to a better understanding of the Dutch context, the fourth section offers a short description of the Equal Treatment Law and the role of the ETC. The main part of this chapter provides an analysis of recent opinions of the ETC which might reflect an intersectional approach. Finally, the question whether an intersectional approach has any added value in the opinions of the ETC is addressed.

Multiple, Compound and Intersectional Discrimination

Many terms are used in order to describe situations in which discrimination on more than one discrimination ground is at stake and it remains difficult to give clear definitions of the different concepts used (Makkonen 2002: 3–6). In the report of the Danish Institute for Human Rights, *multiple discrimination* is defined as: a situation where a person can be subjected to discrimination on more than one ground (European Commission 2007a: 16). This concept could be seen as the overreaching notion covering situations in which several grounds of discrimination are at stake (Burri and Schiek 2009: 4). Some authors make a distinction between *additive or compound discrimination* and *intersectional discrimination* (Makkonen 2002: 10).

---

4   See for information about this conference: www.equalisnotenough.org [accessed: 10 March 2009]. The paper presented at the conference is on file with the author and was kindly sent to the author of the present contribution by Dr M. van den Brink, member of the ETC and one of the authors of this paper.

In case of additive or compound discrimination, the role of the different grounds can still be distinguished. In case of intersectional discrimination, the different grounds intersect; their respective roles cannot be disentangled (Burri and Schiek 2009: 3). This concept refers to a situation involving discrimination which is based on several grounds operating and interacting with each other at the same time, and which produces very specific types of discrimination (Makkonen 2002: 10–11). The person confronted with intersectional discrimination is confronted with specific, combined forms of discrimination. This is the case, for example, when minority women are subject to particular types of prejudices and stereotypes. An important feature of intersectional discrimination is the specificity of the types of discrimination and the important role that the context plays (Makkonen 2002: 10–11). It should be noted that even though these proposed definitions seem rather clear, in practice it is not always easy to identify which kind of discrimination is at stake, in particular the difference between additive or compound discrimination on the one hand and intersectional discrimination on the other hand is not easily detected. In addition, the views on the added value in theory of an intersectional approach in law differ.

Added Value of an Intersectional Approach in Law?

It is generally recognized that the first author to develop an intersectionality approach was Crenshaw, who in 1989 pointed out that experiences of discrimination of black women are connected to both racism and sexism. She criticized the fact that discrimination claims could be made on a single ground – race or sex – but not in combination. The particular experiences of discrimination that black women faced at the intersection of race *and* sex could therefore not be addressed by law (Crenshaw 1989, 1991). Since then, quite some literature has been published on approaches which would possibly be useful to address forms of multiple discrimination, in particular in law. Some authors highlight the possibilities of an intersectional approach, even if it is not easy to apply it in practice. Schiek (2005: 465), for example, states that EU non-discrimination legislation does not only prohibit discrimination on single grounds, but also on combined grounds. She stresses that given the fact that women are very likely to face forms of multiple discrimination, in particular intersectional discrimination, they might benefit from such an approach (Burri and Schiek 2009: 5).

Other authors draw attention to the limits of an intersectional approach, in particular in relation to law. This is for example the case for Conaghan (2009: 21–48), who analysed the implications of an intersectional approach for what she calls the feminist project in law. In her view, this approach might on the one hand tackle the complex and diverse manifestations of inequality which women experience and might be useful to provide a better representation of women's experiences and lives. On the other hand, Conaghan argues that the concept of intersectionality has not been adequate to challenge these inequalities effectively; in particular, it does not address the complex multiplicity of inequality. Part of the problem in her view is that intersectionality has its roots in law and that therefore the limits of law and of legal involvement are reflected in this approach. In her view, intersectionality is useful to disentangle experiences of inequality at the local level, but it does not include the wider context in which such experiences are produced and it fails to make the link to relations and processes that are at the roots of such experiences (Conaghan 2009: 29). The diverse experiences of inequality have to be related and connected with the structures, processes, practices and institutions in which they occur (Conaghan 2009: 41). In addition to these theoretical shortcomings of an intersectional approach, some authors – for example Hannett (2003: 65–86) – underline the difficulties that arise when tackling forms of multiple discrimination within an existing anti-discrimination law framework both at the theoretical and practical level. She emphasizes the limits of the legal framework in the UK to address structural forms of discrimination and thus also forms of multiple discrimination. A formal and symmetric approach to equality fails to follow a contextual approach, in which the disadvantage suffered could be acknowledged within a structural, historical and multidimensional perspective. She stresses the advantages of a single equality body for different discrimination grounds. In her view such a body could better identify similarities between types of discrimination and take the appropriate action; in addition, expertise in dealing with discrimination in one area can be shared.

Goldberg (2009: 145–6) brings to light the potential of *amicus* brief in litigation in order to tackle multiple discrimination. She sees a role for barristers to counter the tendency in courts to address cases on a single ground only and instead show how identity categories are interdependent. In her view, cross-identity litigation offers possibilities to transform the law.

The conclusions of Schiek, Hannett and Goldberg would seem promising given the questions addressed in this chapter, in view of the fact that the ETC is a single specialized body in the field of equal treatment law and that Dutch law is very similar to EU non-discrimination law. The added value of an intersectional approach would then be to bring to light inequalities, forms of discrimination which would not be addressed with a single-ground approach. It would thus broaden the scope of anti-discrimination law to situations that would otherwise fall outside this scope by drawing attention to disadvantages suffered by a person (or a group) linked to historical and structural discrimination in a specific case. Before analysing the opinions of the Dutch ETC, it is useful to provide a short overview of the main features of Dutch equal treatment law and the competences of the ETC.

Dutch Equal Treatment Law and the Dutch Equal Treatment Commission

Equal Treatment Law

A short overview of Dutch equal treatment law and the competences of the Equal Treatment Commission is necessary in order to understand the opinions of the ETC discussed below. When the scope of protection is broader for one ground compared to another and/or the possibilities to make exceptions in case of direct discrimination are more restricted, a multiple discrimination approach might have advantages for the petitioner. This is indeed the case when the discrimination ground providing the best protection is addressed specifically as well.

As mentioned in the introduction, the most important piece of legislation is the Equal Treatment Act, adopted in 1994. Another specific law has prohibited discrimination on the ground of disability and chronic illness since 2003.[5] Neither of these Acts contains an explicit prohibition of multiple discrimination. The protection afforded by these two Acts is similar for the four grounds of discrimination studied here: race, gender, disability and religion. The definitions of discrimination are similar, as in the EU gender equality (Burri and Prechal 2008) and EU non-discrimination directives, and the same is true for the provisions regarding the burden of proof, victimization, enforcement, etc. There are, however, some differences regarding the material scope of the prohibition of discrimination between the four grounds and the legal exceptions allowed for direct discrimination.

---

5   *Stb.* 2003, 206.

According to the ETA direct discrimination, indirect discrimination,[6] (sexual) harassment and an instruction to discriminate are prohibited on the grounds of religion, belief, political opinion, race, sex, nationality, heterosexual or homosexual orientation or civil status. Direct discrimination is defined as discrimination between persons on these grounds (Article 1(1)(b)). The concept of discrimination is not defined. Direct discrimination on the grounds of sex includes discrimination on the grounds of pregnancy, childbirth and maternity (Article 1(2)). Indirect discrimination is defined as discrimination on the grounds of characteristics or behaviour other than those referred to above, resulting in direct discrimination. Indirect discrimination which is objectively justified by a legitimate aim and where the means to achieve that aim are appropriate and necessary is not unlawful (Article 1(1)(c)).

As regards direct discrimination, the allowed exceptions differ for each ground and only these written exceptions are not unlawful. Three exceptions apply to direct sex discrimination: when sex is a determining factor; in cases concerning the protection of women, notably in relation to pregnancy and maternity; and when positive action for women is at stake (Article 2(2) and 2(3)). The exceptions to direct race discrimination are similar to those allowed in case of sex discrimination, except the one regarding the protection of women (Article 2(3) and 2(4)).

The exceptions regarding religion are more complicated. First of all, the ETA does not apply to 'legal relations within religious communities, independent sections or associations thereof and within other associations of a spiritual nature' and neither does it apply to the office of minister of religion (Article 3). In the field of (access to) employment, a specific exception is allowed in relation to:

> the freedom of an institution founded on religious or ideological principles to impose requirements which, having regard to the institution's purpose, are necessary for the fulfilment of the duties attached to a post; such requirements may not lead to discrimination on the sole grounds of political opinion, race, sex, nationality, heterosexual or homosexual orientation or civil status (Article 5(2)).

The background of this exception is that, for example, schools based on a Catholic ethos may impose requirements based on the Catholic religion at least for some positions, a teacher of religion for instance, even if this means that a candidate is not hired due to his or her religious expressions (such as a headscarf) or sexual orientation. However, such schools are not allowed to reject a candidate *solely* because of, for example, his or her sexual orientation.[7]

The prohibition on discrimination on the ground of disability and chronic illness also means that the persons on whom this prohibition is imposed are obliged to make effective modifications according to need, unless this would impose a disproportionate burden on them (Article 2). Three exceptions apply to direct (and indirect) discrimination on the ground of disability: if the discrimination is necessary to protect health and safety; if the discrimination relates to a regulation, standard or practice which is aimed at creating or maintaining specific provisions and facilities for the benefit of persons with a disability or chronic illness; and if positive action is at stake.

---

6   In Dutch equal treatment law the term distinction is used, instead of discrimination. However, a proposal is pending to amend the legislation and use the word 'discrimination'. Scholars have submitted that, in practice, both terms offer the same level of protection (Holtmaat 2006b).

7   See *Kamerstukken II* 1990–1991, 22014, no. 3, 19. See for the application of these rules in practice ETC Opinions 1999-38 and 2007-100, in which two schools were not allowed to refuse a job to a homosexual teacher because of the orthodox Christian religious ethos of the school.

The scope of the legislation also differs per discrimination ground. The ETA applies to (access to) employment and professions (Articles 5 and 6); and (the supply of) goods and services (Article 7). The scope is broader in case of race discrimination, which also includes the field of social protection and (access to) social advantages (Article 7a). The prohibition of discrimination on the ground of disability and chronic illness applies to (access to) employment and professions; primary and secondary school education and vocational education; and housing. The provisions on public transport have not entered into force yet.

The Equal Treatment Commission

The ETC plays an important role in the enforcement of all the legal Acts and provisions mentioned above. The ETC is composed of nine members and nine alternating members. The chair and the two assistant chairs have to fulfil the legal requirements governing eligibility for appointment as officers of the court.[8] All the members of the ETC are lawyers and specialized in equal treatment law.

An essential task of the ETC is to answer questions regarding the application of Dutch equal treatment legislation. The ETC issues opinions after a request about an alleged discrimination, in which it investigates whether equal treatment law has been violated. The ETC has an active role and can search information itself. The procedure is short, free of charge and no lawyer is required. The opinions of the ETC are non-binding. This means that in order to get a final decision, petitioners have to bring their case to court. The ETC's opinion might play a role during the proceedings and, in practice, the courts often refer to the opinions and the arguments put forward by the ETC. However courts are not obliged to consider the opinion, let alone come to the same conclusions as the ETC. It is therefore much debated what the effect is of the non-binding opinions of the ETC (Holtmaat 2006b: 55; Moon 2007: 915–21). Follow-up research of the ETC shows that their opinions – even if non-binding – are rather well followed. In the period between September 2007 and August 2008, measures (either individual or structural) were taken by the employers and organizations that had breached equal treatment law in 79 per cent of the cases.[9]

The ETC can also conduct a so-called 'investigation on its own initiative', but has done so only a few times up to now. Much more often, the ETC publishes advice on a specific issue, for example on employment, religion and equal treatment or on niqabs and headscarves in schools.[10]

Multiple Discrimination in Opinions of the Dutch Equal Treatment Commission

Recent opinions of the ETC   In the two most recent annual reports of the ETC on developments in 2007 and 2008, no reference is made to multiple, compound or intersectional discrimination.[11] In 2007, the ETC published 247 opinions. The figures regarding the opinions are categorized according to the different discrimination grounds. The 247 opinions concerned 12 different discrimination grounds: gender (31), race (24), nationality (6), religion (22), sexual orientation (3), civil status (1), political opinion (0), convictions (0), working hours (7), temporary contract (1), disability/chronic

---

8   Equal Treatment Act, Article 16.

9   Commissie Gelijke Behandeling (2008).

10   Some of these recommendations are available in English at: www.cgb.nl/artikel/publications [accessed: 25 November 2010].

11   Commissie Gelijke Behandeling (2007).

illness (29) and age (82). In 39 opinions, more than one discrimination ground was at stake.[12] Three opinions which show an intersectional approach are discussed in the next section. Two recent opinions issued in 2008 reflecting a compound discrimination approach, involving race and sex discrimination in the first case and race, religion and sex discrimination in the second case, are examined later in the chapter (see 106–8).

Intersectional Discrimination

The ETC referred explicitly to the term 'intersection' only once in the above sense in all the opinions issued since the entry into force of the Equal Treatment Act in 1994.[13] This was the case in Opinion 2007-43, about a petitioner of Iranian origin and Muslim who stated that his application for a job had been rejected because of his religion.[14] During the proceedings, he added that discrimination based on race was also at stake. It was an undisputed fact that during the first telephone contact between the petitioner and the contact person of the employer, the latter asked questions regarding the religious convictions of the petitioner in relation to his Iranian origin. In particular the fact that the belief of the petitioner was the reason for leaving Iran was discussed. Both the petitioner and the contact person considered afterwards that it had been a pleasant conversation. Nevertheless, the petitioner was not hired, according to the employer because of the petitioner's lack of extensive and relevant experience. The employer started a second procedure after one of the candidates eventually refused the job. There was still a vacancy and for this reason the Iranian petitioner concluded that he had not been hired because of his religion.

The ETC investigated whether a distinction had been made against the petitioner on the ground of religion *and/or* race. The prohibition of race discrimination in Dutch law also covers colour, origin, national or ethnic origin.[15] The ETC explained why the ground race would be considered as well: both the petitioner and the respondent had acknowledged that due to the Iranian ethnic origin of the petitioner the respondent had asked questions about his religion. The respondent furthermore put forward during the proceedings that the company employed many Muslim migrant workers and that both names like Mohammed or Rachid and the appearance of some Muslim migrant workers indicated Islamic religious convictions. The ETC concluded that the complaint of the petitioner therefore concerned intersection of identity characteristics protected under the ETA and that the petitioner felt disadvantaged on the ground of his Islamic belief that the respondent inferred from his Iranian origin.

The ETC thus clearly linked both grounds and this would indeed indicate intersectional discrimination, because both grounds interact at the same time and might produce additional disadvantage. It is rather likely that a Christian candidate from Switzerland, for example, would not have been confronted with such questions. In the end, no presumption of discrimination was established according to the ETC in this case. It considered that asking questions during an interview about the religious convictions of a candidate can indeed create the impression that belief is one of the applicable criteria, but the mere fact that the contact person had asked such a question was in itself not sufficient for a presumption of discrimination. In this case, the respondent made

---

12   *Jaarverslag 2008*: 36, *supra* note 10. In 2008, the ETC published 155 opinions; in 22 opinions more than one discrimination ground was at stake.

13   This is the result of a search in the opinions of the ETC with the ETC's search engine.

14   All the opinions of the Dutch Equal Treatment Commission are published (in Dutch) on the website of the Commission at: www.cgb.nl.

15   This corresponds to the concept of race in the International Covenant on the Elimination of Race Discrimination.

plausible that the questions were only meant to be part of a general conversation in order to get an impression of how the candidate would fit into the team.[16] Finally, the ETC pointed out that conclusions based on names and/or appearance about the religious convictions of candidates or workers are based on prejudices and stereotypes, which might amount to direct race discrimination. This case makes it clear that the ETC is certainly willing to disentangle the facts at stake in order to find forms of intersectional discrimination. However, the ETC was convinced here that only the lack of experience had been decisive. One may question whether in such a case of intersecting grounds of discrimination in this access to employment context, characterized by a candidate's very weak position, the ETC should not adopt a stronger approach. Undoubtedly, the origin and the religion of the petitioner were discussed in this case and may therefore have played a role during the procedure. The opinion offers insufficient information to conclude that both the origin and the religion of the candidate put him at a disadvantage.

Another case on intersectional discrimination that is worth reporting is that in Opinion 2006-256, in which the disability of a worker and her ethnic origin interact. The petitioner was a blind woman of Turkish origin, who had studied law in Turkey and who was employed by a socially protected subsidized organization. During three years, she was posted in another company. When she came back to the organization originally employing her, she had to undergo a test, in order to define what kind of work she would like to do and would be capable of. Usually, people did a written test in such a situation. However, in this case, the employer decreed an oral test, while she asked for a test in Braille. Taking into account the results of the test, the employer denied her a position as a receptionist or an administrative function, and instead offered her work at the production department. The petitioner complained that the fact that she had to do an oral test, instead of a test in Braille, disadvantaged her. She stated that an oral test is more difficult for a visually disabled person of foreign origin than a written test. During a written test there is a possibility to re-read the questions, derive the meanings of words out of context, there is more time to think about the answers, etc.

The ETC considered that the petitioner convincingly argued that if she had been offered a test in Braille, she could have done the test under the same conditions as people without a visual disability and that she would then have suffered less disadvantage of the fact that Dutch is not her mother tongue. The ETC considered that the petitioner had thus established a presumption of discrimination. It is then for the respondent to refute the presumption. According to the ETC, offering the test in Braille would have been a reasonable accommodation. The respondent did not consider such offer presenting a disproportionate burden. The ETC concluded that the petitioner had been disadvantaged because she had to do an oral test and that the respondent's failure to offer a reasonable accommodation was in breach of the Equal Treatment (Disability/Chronic Illness) Act. As regards the argument that the petitioner suffered additional disadvantage due to the fact that Dutch is not her mother tongue, the ETC stated that there is no direct link between the oral test and her origin. If the petitioner had not been blind, she could have done a written test. However, in this case the coincidence (*samenloop*) of grounds, the disability of the petitioner and her Turkish origin, had the effect that answering the questions became more difficult, and therefore the results of the test less reliable. The employer discriminated both on the ground of disability/chronic illness and race. This case also provides a clear example of intersectional discrimination, because

---

16   According to Article 10 of the ETA, if a person who considers that he or she is a victim of discrimination within the meaning of this Act adduces before a court facts from which it may be presumed that such discrimination has taken place, the other party is required to prove that the action in question was not in breach of this Act.

discrimination based on both these grounds at the same time enhanced the adverse effect of the requirement that the test was to be done orally.

The ETC did not specify whether the race discrimination was direct or indirect and only concluded a breach of race anti-discrimination legislation. In my view, this situation would amount to indirect race discrimination, which eventually could be objectively justified. In this case, however, the respondent did not put forward any argument which could eventually provide a justification, so the ETC did not consider this aspect.

In another case[17] three discrimination grounds intersect: race, gender and age. A Surinamese coloured woman of 60 years of age was entitled to a means-tested welfare benefit. The scheme offered the possibility to start your own company without losing the means-tested benefit for a period of one year and with the help of initial funding. The petitioner started the necessary procedures in order to benefit from this possibility and saw herself confronted with discriminatory behaviour of civil servants who apply the scheme. She complained about discrimination on the grounds of race, gender and age. She provided different examples of discrimination, which in her opinion showed that she had less chance to get the opportunity to start a company under this scheme than, for example, a man of colour, a white woman or a younger coloured woman.

In this case the ETC concluded that due to the scheme at stake, it only had the competence to consider whether race discrimination in the area of social protection had occurred, because Dutch legislation only covers social protection, including social security, and social advantages in relation to race discrimination (Article 7a ETA). The material scope of Dutch anti-discrimination law is thus the broadest for race, as it is in EU law. Very interesting is the consideration of the ETC that when deciding whether race discrimination had occurred, it would do so also from the perspective that the petitioner was a woman and 60 years old. This shows a willingness to examine whether the other two characteristics may also have disadvantaged the petitioner, even if the ETC in this specific case is not competent to look at these forms of discrimination. This 'reading in' of other discrimination grounds in areas which are not (yet) covered by certain discrimination grounds might offer new perspectives and diminish the dangers of a suggested 'hierarchy' between different grounds.

In this opinion, however, the propositions of the petitioner regarding discrimination on the ground of race were all successfully contradicted by the respondent and no presumption of race discrimination was thus established. It became clear, for example, that efforts had been made in order to reach different ethnic groups during various events. The fact that some groups (Turkish and Moroccan people in particular) were overrepresented was due to the population in the areas where the activities were organized. The ETC added that also when race discrimination was considered jointly with gender and age discrimination, the petitioner did not bring forward facts which would establish such presumption. During the proceedings, it became clear, for example, that people between 18 and 65 were entitled to funding in order to start a business and that due to the fact that people from the age of 65 receive a flat-rate pension in the Netherlands, older people would probably be able to guarantee that they could pay back the funding that they had received. Therefore, in this case, taking into account the gender and age of the petitioner seems to have had only little influence on the reasoning of the ETC regarding the issue of race discrimination. The ETC also considered that the petitioner had argued that she was often confronted with discrimination. The ETC recognized that discrimination in relation to ethnic origin is a structural problem, but that in this case no facts were established proving discrimination based on ethnic origin. The petitioner was probably disappointed about the outcome of her case, but at least the ETC showed that it

---

17 Opinion 2008-107.

recognized the different forms of discrimination and its structural characteristics. In that sense, law can play a role in pointing out structural forms of discrimination, even if it cannot offer remedies to combat systemic discrimination.

The approach of the ETC in this opinion is somehow similar to the approach taken by the Norwegian Ombud institution in Muslim headscarf cases. In these cases, the issue was addressed on a single ground (gender) as an issue of indirect sex discrimination. This approach illustrates how intersectionality can be addressed even on the basis of single-ground legislation (Skjeie 2009: 303–5).

Compound Discrimination

A search on the website of the Dutch Equal Treatment Commission regarding opinions published in 2008 addressing both race and sex discrimination shows that one opinion concerns these two grounds.[18] This opinion was requested by a national organization of societal development and concerned their own application procedures. For a welfare project aimed at male migrant workers, the organization launched a procedure to select a project manager/trainer on diversity. The advertisement mentioned that in case of equal qualifications, a man with a migrant or refugee background would be hired. In the end, a man of Palestinian origin got the job. During the proceedings with the ETC, the organization made it clear that they did not consider their policy as a positive action measure, but that instead they invoked the exception on occupational requirements.

In an extensive analysis, taking into account the *actes préparatoires* of the ETA, relevant decrees and previous opinions, the ETC concluded that sex was not a determining factor for this job. The same reasoning was applied to the exception concerning race as a determining factor. Therefore the approach of the ETC was very similar for both grounds in this case and even if this situation can be described as a case of multiple discrimination, no intersectional discrimination was acknowledged. In the end, the ETC applied a single-ground approach twice.

It might be more difficult to follow a multiple discrimination approach when there is no petitioner complaining about discrimination, which was the case here. There was no candidate involved in this case who would have suffered discrimination due to the requirements for this job (for example a non-immigrant woman). In this case, the ETC asked the organization to provide a sex-neutral and race-neutral description of the requirements for this job, which the organization provided. The ETC considered that the list showed that no occupational requirements were at stake. Some requirements might have an indirect discriminatory effect (for example basic knowledge of Turkish, Moroccan or Arabic) but could eventually be objectively justified. Such an approach might prevent direct sex and/or race discrimination in the future.

In another case, two different requirements mentioned in the written conditions for membership of a fitness club were found to be discriminatory.[19] The fitness club offered fitness activities for women only. The first requirement for membership was that no head covering was allowed (like caps, hats, etc.) in the club, except for medical or other reasons. Secondly, during sports, the members were required to speak Dutch as much as possible. Both a Muslim woman wearing a headscarf who was told that she was not allowed to do sports with a headscarf in the women's fitness club and an anti-discrimination organization asked for an opinion of the ETC.

As regards the first requirement, the ETC considered that according to its established case law, the wearing of a headscarf by a woman with Islamic religious convictions forms an expression

---

18   Opinion 2008-48.
19   Opinion 2008-12.

of their belief, and this is thus covered by the ground religion. No direct reference to religion was made in this case; therefore the clothing requirement amounted to indirect discrimination. The ETC stated that it is a fact of general knowledge that Muslim women are disproportionally disadvantaged by such a neutral requirement. The respondent did not offer any arguments that might provide an objective justification, thus the requirement was unlawful. The respondent did amend the written membership conditions, but was not prepared to explicitly mention that a head covering in relation to religious convictions was allowed, because he feared that the number of sportswomen with a headscarf in the club would increase significantly. Such reasoning showed, according to the ETC, that the respondent's objective was to hinder the access to the fitness club for women wearing a headscarf. Furthermore these women ran the risk that they had to explain time and time again that religious reasons were as important as medical reasons. The effect would in fact amount to restrained access to the fitness club for women wearing headscarves because of religious convictions.

As regards the language requirement, the ETC considered that it did not amount to direct race discrimination, but indirectly disadvantaged people whose origin is not Dutch. The ETC considered it probable that in these groups more persons will not express themselves in Dutch. The respondent argued that some, mostly elderly, women, who had been at the club for years, did not feel comfortable or felt outsiders. The communication between the members of this small fitness club was considered important, according to the respondent, and for this reason the language requirement was introduced. The ETC considered that the aim to be met with this requirement was to prevent intimidation. In this case the feeling of being intimidated was not based on verbal or non-verbal expressions of some members of the association, but on assumptions, prejudices and stereotypes regarding people speaking languages other than Dutch. The aim was thus discriminatory in itself and the indirect discrimination not objectively justified. Interestingly, the ETC added that offering the fitness activities to women only amounted to direct sex discrimination, which was not justified. However, it was not clear whether such sex-segregated activities still took place.

The case is interesting in my view because of the single-ground approach the ETC adopted, whereas this could have been construed as a case of compound or even intersectional discrimination. Both the clothing and the language requirement disadvantage the group of women wearing headscarves who want to speak another language than Dutch during fitness. In the Dutch context, it is probable that in the group of women wearing headscarves for religious reasons, more women want to speak another language than Dutch compared to the group of women not wearing headscarves. At the same time, the use of these requirements might have a cumulative negative effect on this group of women in this context. Also interesting is that the ETC always applies the ground religion in headscarf (and similar) cases, without addressing the issue of (indirect) sex discrimination. In this case, the indirect discrimination test is exactly the same for both grounds (gender and religion), and thus the outcome of the case as well. One could say that implicitly indirect sex discrimination is also addressed. If the exclusion had explicitly referred to religion, the ETC would have concluded that direct discrimination based on religion had occurred. This was the case, for example, in a situation very similar to the one described here, where the conditions of the fitness club mentioned that it was not allowed to wear clothes related to religion, such as headscarves.[20] This was therefore a case of direct discrimination on the ground of religion, and no exception was applicable. In such cases, the protection under Dutch law is stronger, due to the closed system of exceptions which was described above, than when the case had been addressed as an indirect sex discrimination case. However, as described above, the written exceptions to

---

20 Opinion 2007-173.

discrimination on the grounds of religion might be applicable and then weaken the protection of women wearing headscarves due to their religious beliefs.

Added Value in Practice?

In practice, the Dutch Equal Treatment Commission often follows a single-ground approach when two or more discrimination grounds are at stake, considering the different grounds separately, as it did in Opinion 2008-48. A multiple-discrimination approach is certainly useful when discrimination based on one ground cannot be established, but another form of discrimination can be proven; or when the scope of the legislation regarding one ground is broader than for others, e.g. the prohibition of discrimination on the ground of race in Dutch law, which also applies to social protection and social advantages, while the other grounds have a more limited scope.[21] It might also be useful when disability is at stake, due to the obligation to provide a reasonable accommodation, which is limited to discrimination on the ground of disability in Dutch equal treatment law.

The fact that the ETC explicitly discusses different discrimination grounds even if the relevant legislation does not cover all grounds at stake in a particular situation shows that the ETC is willing to consider the potential negative impact of different discrimination grounds. The influence of the work of Crenshaw is reflected in such cases, as is illustrated in Opinion 2008-107. This opinion regarding the Surinamese coloured woman of 60 years of age who was denied access to funds in order to set up her own company is one of the examples in which this issue was explicitly addressed, although she was not able to establish facts which would amount to a presumption of discrimination. In such cases, the intersectional approach might contribute to enhancing the awareness of the parties and people interested in the work of the ETC on how exclusion works and to drawing attention to systemic discrimination. This requires a certain 'openness of mind' in order to be able to look at a situation not from one perspective only, i.e. one discrimination ground, but from various perspectives and, last but not least, to examine what the typical negative effects are for the group in question in a certain context. This is certainly not an easy task, in particular when both direct and indirect discrimination are at stake. The cases described above show that in indirect discrimination cases, the ETC often relies on facts of general knowledge to establish a presumption of indirect discrimination. Such an approach might amount to fixed categories which are not true for everyone belonging to a certain group: not all women wearing a headscarf want to speak another language than Dutch; not all elderly black women have difficulties entering the employment market; not all workers working part-time are women who do so in order to take care of their children or relatives, etc. Sociological data should therefore be used as much as possible in order to gain more insight in the cumulative effects of intersecting grounds in a specific context. However, such data are often unavailable and/or the specific facts of the case do not always reflect a situation similar to what the data show. In the everyday practice of an Equality Body like the ETC, it takes a lot of time and energy to establish what exactly happened in a specific situation. It is clear that when different grounds of discrimination have to be examined, the workload will probably rise. It might often be difficult, for example, to establish how many people with various characteristics are disadvantaged by a certain requirement, measure or practice in a specific company or organization compared to people who lack one or more of these characteristics. Often, the data might simply be unavailable and quite some time would be needed to gather such information. The efforts required by intersectional analysis should to a certain extent be proportional to the added value that such an approach offers.

---

21   Opinion 2008-107.

The intersectional approach might, however, show typical cumulative results of different discrimination grounds, which interact in such a way that people with different characteristics suffer particular disadvantages within a specific context. The case of the blind Turkish woman[22] is an especially good example here. Such an intersectional approach can also be helpful to show how prejudices and stereotypes contribute to excluding people with some of the protected characteristics. But actually, Opinion 2006-256 is also the only case in which such an intersectional approach resulted in a successful claim of the petitioner. The effect of applying an intersectional approach is therefore very limited in practice and indeed seems inadequate to challenge inequalities effectively, as pointed out by Conaghan (2009) (see above: 99–100).

As described above (102), the opinions of the Dutch Equal Treatment Commission are non-binding. However, follow-up research of the ETC shows that the party guilty of the discrimination often takes measures to remedy the situation (Commissie Gelijke Behandeling 2008: 35–42).[23] If a person wants compensation, a civil procedure has to be followed. When the ETC has issued an opinion on the case, courts may take the outcome of the opinion into account, but they do not have to. Often, the courts not only consider equal treatment aspects, but also the applicable labour and/or civil law, for example, and eventually reach another decision than the ETC. Mostly, but not always, the courts explain the reasons why they do not agree with the outcome of the ETC's opinion (Asscher-Vonk 2007). The sanctions, including the awarding of damages, will probably therefore depend on different aspects involved and how serious the discrimination is. The fact that different grounds intersect might play a role in determining the amount of compensation, but probably in conjunction with other aspects. When the ETC explicitly pays attention to the typical negative effects of different intersecting grounds in its opinions, this might provide additional relevant information to the courts regarding the specificity and context of the case in a civil procedure. In this sense, the opinions of the ETC could play a role – even if it is a modest one – in drawing attention to more hidden forms of compound or intersectional discrimination within a specific context.

Conclusions

The attention for forms of multiple discrimination is quite recent in the Netherlands and concepts such as intersectionality or compound discrimination are still rather unfamiliar for most practising lawyers and judges. Up to now, there have been no court cases addressing these issues explicitly. Equal treatment cases generally cover only one single ground, at least explicitly, and often the published judgments do not provide enough information about all the facts at stake which would make it possible to identify some forms of multiple discrimination.

Nevertheless, the opinions of the Dutch ETC provide interesting material that allows an assessment of the possibilities and difficulties that a multiple-discrimination approach presents in practice. The ETC has wide experience in examining different grounds of discrimination and shows willingness to follow a multiple-discrimination approach. However, only a few of its opinions reflect an intersectional approach as defined earlier in the chapter (see 99) and the effects of an intersectional approach in practice are quite limited. Still, it is worth noting that sometimes the ETC acknowledges that intersectional discrimination might be at stake, even if the facts of the case do not show such discrimination (105–6). This is certainly positive in at

---

22 Opinion 2006-256.
23 See *supra* note 10.

least two ways: the presumed victim of discrimination might feel that attention has been paid to all the relevant characteristics and circumstances at stake and to some structural forms of discrimination resulting from intersectional discrimination. In addition, this provides a signal function for all those who are interested in the opinions of the ETC and for the courts. The ETC can certainly play an even more important role in this respect in the future.

Chapter 7

Intersectional Discrimination and the Underlying Assumptions in the French and German Headscarf Debates: An Adequate Legal Response?[1]

Stephanie Fehr

Introduction

Prohibitions against the wearing of religious items are a prominent example of laws which disproportionately affect Muslim women who wear the Islamic headscarf and who are often also members of ethnic minorities. The indirect sex or gender (Stoller 1968)[2] and ethnicity or race (Fredman 2002: 53)[3] discrimination caused by such rules has been noted in the literature, as have been the problems faced by intersectionally placed individuals more generally. Attention has been given to the imbalanced scope of the protection afforded to different discrimination grounds by EU law (Loenen 2009; Roseberry 2009; Sacksofsky 2009a; Smith 2007; De Schutter 2005; Bell and Waddington 2003), as well as by the European Convention on Human Rights (Vickers 2008: 227; Vakulenko 2007; Wiles 2007: 669). A number of proposals have been made with the aim of developing a more appropriate response, particularly at the European level, to intersectionality (Pitt 2007: 229; Vakulenko 2007: 195–6; Knights 2005; Modood 1992: 228).[4]

The primary aim of this chapter is to add to the discourse on headscarves and intersectional discrimination (Nielsen 2009: 31–2; Schiek 2009: 13; Verloo 2006; Crenshaw 1989)[5] by analysing the underlying stereotypical (Hall 1996: 103)[6] assumptions and intersectional prejudice underlying two sets of legislation preventing the wearing of headscarves. The secondary aim is to draw attention to the inadequacy of national anti-discrimination law when its formulation has been driven by intersectional prejudice rather than by objective evidence.

Headscarf debates have taken place in many European states. However, in France and Germany the discussion has been particularly intense and full, and for this reason they will form the focus of this chapter. The methodology to be used here is not comparative (Örücü 2007: 44–5). The discourses

1   Many thanks to Anna Lawson and Dagmar Schiek for their very useful and conscientious comments on earlier drafts of this chapter. Any mistakes are solely my own.
2   For the purposes of this chapter, the term gender will be used in a broad sense to encompass social and cultural proscriptions.

3   The term race is increasingly understood as 'a social construct, reflecting ideological attempts to legitimate domination, and heavily based on social and historical context', since racism involves more than mere prejudice due to a person's colour.

4   For instance, it is proposed to bring religious discrimination under the scope of protections against race discrimination, where a high number of adherents to a religion belong to one ethnicity.

5   Intersectional discrimination is said to comprise a concealed interaction of grounds that results in particular disadvantage found and felt only by those at the intersection of more than one ground.

6   Stereotyping understood as reducing people to 'simple, essential characteristics that are presented as fixed by nature'.

in the two jurisdictions will be considered separately. The many differences between the French and German situations – such as those regarding church–state relations (Basdevant-Gaudemet 2005; Robbers 2005),[7] integration policies and concepts of citizenship (Benhabib 2006; Modood et al. 2006; Cesari and McLoughlin 2005; Yazbeck Haddad 2002) – are outside the scope of this chapter.

The French and German headscarf debates reveal much about the assumptions made about ethnic minority women who wear headscarves. In support of the argument that this legislation was grounded on intersectional prejudice, the origin, type and extent of relevant assumptions will be clarified by an analysis of the law and, importantly, the debates which preceded it. For these purposes, the French *Loi no. 2004-228*[8] (the 2004 Act) prohibiting ostentatious religious symbols at school and several of the reformed German Schulgesetze[9] (hereafter the School Acts), which deal with the use of religious objects by teachers, will be considered. In France, the main reflections on which the 2004 Act is based are contained in a governmental report (the Stasi Report), which comprehensively detailed the motives behind the Act and which was written after a period of extensive investigation. By contrast, the German School Acts were introduced after a number of court rulings that prompted a review of the pre-existing legislation. The content of the judgements in question, however, are as revealing of the underlying assumptions as is the French Stasi Report. An analysis of the French and German 'headscarf laws', in conjunction with their underlying assumptions, clearly reveals how those laws inadequately grapple with the situation of the Muslim women in question.

The chapter will begin with an examination of the relevant laws in each jurisdiction. Each of these assessments begins with an outline of the relevant legislation, followed by an examination of the underlying assumptions that led to its enactment. The inadequacy of the legal responses (in terms of effects and reasoning) will then be addressed. This will be followed by a brief consideration of some of the factors which might account for the similarities, differences and nature of intersectional prejudice inherent in the headscarf debates that have taken place in France and Germany.

Intersectional Discrimination and the French Headscarf Debate

The 2004 Act on Religious Symbols

Evaluations of discrimination matters in France must demonstrate sensitivity to two factors which set France apart from many other European jurisdictions. First, discriminators are treated relatively harshly.[10] It is, however, relatively difficult for claimants to prove that discrimination has taken

---

7   Interestingly, the different approaches to church–state relations in France and Germany do not preclude sameness of results in relation to the effects on Muslim women in the two given cases. The links between theoretical and practical church–state relations on the one hand and the scope of religious freedom on the other hand will be the subject of future work, currently conducted jointly with S. Pérez Álvarez.

8   Loi 2004-228 du 15 mars 2004 encadrant, en application du principe de laïcité, le port de signes ou de tenues manifestant une appartenance religieuse dans les écoles, collèges et lycées publics, JO du 17 mars 2004.

9   All translations in this chapter are my own, unless indicated otherwise.

10   In theory, considerable protection from discrimination is afforded to French employees. Resulting from the implementation of Council Directive 2000/78, the *Loi de la modernisation sociale* and the *Loi relative à la lutte contre les discriminations* were issued for the purpose of amending existing law, *inter alia* adding a provision dealing with religious discrimination within the *Code du Travail*. Albeit merely one provision, the new Section L.122-45 is instead considerably comprehensive. It prescribes equal treatment for all aspects of employment, thus taking a holistic stance in this regard, as well as an extensive list of discrimination grounds, including sex, ethnicity, race, appearance and religious beliefs. This provision is

place (Stein and Berthou 2005: 73). Second, the French State does not collect official data on the religious and ethnic composition of its population.[11] This is because of the belief that, for reasons of equality, states ought to be ignorant of such irrelevant issues (Laborde 2008: 37). However, estimates suggest that approximately five million Muslims live in France (McGoldrick 2006: 53; Boyle and Sheen 1997: 294).

For the past six years, the freedom of minors to wear religious items at school has been limited following the most recent French headscarf debate (*affaire du foulard*).[12] By virtue of the changes introduced by the 2004 Act, the wearing of religious symbols that ostentatiously manifest one's religion is prohibited in all state schools.[13] This ban is neutrally worded and as such does not refer explicitly to Islamic manifestations. A government circular accompanying the 2004 Act clarifies the term ostentatious, explaining that it comprises items such as an Islamic headscarf, a kippah and a cross of excessive size, which immediately identify a pupil with a particular religion (Circulaire 2004). It also explains that schools need to transmit the republican values of equal dignity and equality between women and men, as well as a rejection of ethnic and religious discrimination.

French legislation dealing with religious attire in education is limited to the school environment and does not extend to higher education. Unlike in Turkey (*Şahin v. Turkey*),[14] for instance, it is not considered appropriate and necessary to restrict the exercise of religious freedom at universities as an adult is regarded as able to make decisions independently about his or her religious affairs (Stasi Report 2003: 60).

Assumptions Leading to the 2004 Act – Intersectional Discrimination and the Stasi Report

The Stasi Commission and Report   Questions relating to the manifestation of religious symbols at school are part of the ongoing debate (Robert 2003: 655–7) about the meaning and implications of laïcité.[15] Laïcité was officially re-launched in 2003 when Jacques Chirac set up an independent body to study the application of laïcité to 26 aspects of life in contemporary France. The resulting Stasi Commission – named after its chair, Bernard Stasi – was composed of scholars and various officials.[16] The 2004 Act was drafted in response to what were, without a doubt (both within the Stasi Commission and beyond), its most controversial and intensely discussed recommendations. The stereotypical assumptions about Muslim women, which are evident in the Stasi Report and which contributed to its recommendation of the headscarf ban, will now be examined.

---

further underpinned by a twin provision within criminal law, Article L.225-1 of the *Code Pénal*, carrying sanctions of up to two years' imprisonment and a fine of €30,000.

11   Under Loi No. 78-17 of 1978, JO du 6 janvier 1978, Section 8 it is prohibited to collect any information that implies, directly or indirectly, racial origins, political, philosophical or religious opinions, trade union affiliation, or information on a person's health or sex life.

12   An Opinion of the *Conseil d'Etat* of 27 November 1989 marks the actual start of the *affaire du foulard*. The judges found that a general prohibition of headscarves at school would amount to religious discrimination of the relevant pupils. Only in cases where the headscarf pressurizes, provoked or proselytized, disciplinary measures could be taken.

13   L.141-5-1 *Code de l'Education*.

14   Application no. 44774/98 (29 June 2004).

15   Although at times portrayed as a specific form of secularism, laïcité can also be viewed as merely a translation thereof. In this chapter, it solely serves the purpose of highlighting the French context, without any particular importance afforded to the debates surrounding its potential connotations.

16   The number of Commissioners was 19 and these largely comprised scholars in church–state relations, school principals, sociologists, mayors and specialists in immigration and integration.

Views on Muslims and gender equality   The theme of a collision between the demands of Muslims to wear headscarves, on the one hand, and those of gender equality, on the other, runs through large parts of the Report. For instance, it accuses 'certain young girls' of not attending PE lessons (Stasi Report 2003: 41) and observes a rise in sexism demonstrated by female pupils' covering, asexual clothing (Stasi Report 2003: 46). In addition, the Report claims that the headscarf proves that young girls are being blamed for attracting male desire (Stasi Report 2003: 57). Another reason provided in support of a headscarf ban is thus the protection of Muslim girls. According to some, Muslim girls are forced to wear a headscarf, mainly by fellow male pupils, but also by their peer groups or families (Weil 2005: 68). The Report adds that non-complying girls are stigmatized as prostitutes or infidels (Stasi Report 2003: 46–7). The Stasi Commission's stereotyping of Muslims also drew upon other forms of 'violence' against Muslim women, such as female genital mutilation and forced marriages (Haarscher 2004: 43; Stasi Report 2003: 47).

These statements of the Stasi Commission show that the commissioners had a very negative image of gender equality within the Muslim community. The link between practices such as forced marriage and female genital mutilation and Islam and the wearing of headscarves, assumed to exist by the Commission, is in fact not supported by objective evidence. None of the Commission's claims on this issue are based on empirical evidence or on witness statements of Muslim women, despite the fact that the Stasi Commission had the power to call upon such evidence. In reality, Muslim women often claim that headscarves are worn voluntarily (Esposito and Mogahed 2007: 110; Hamdan 2007: 3; Conniff Taber 2004; Gaspard and Khosrokhavar 1995)[17] as an expression of a desire for autonomy, individuality and belonging (Wieviorka 2002: 138). Contrary accounts are rare but appear to be linked to socio-economic disadvantage (Djavann 2006: 95–7; Mernissi 2003). Unfortunately, it seems that the Stasi Commission regarded the coerced adoption of a headscarf as the norm and the ban thereof as the most effective State response.

Views on Muslims and other democratic values   In addition to this gender equality agenda, the Stasi Commissioners also referred to religious manifestations as being racially intolerant and creating disorder in educational institutions. For example, they suggest that the secular state cannot be indifferent towards issues of public order, racist or discriminatory practices carried out under the pretext of religious freedom (Stasi Report 2003: 15). An example of the disorder created by the so-called 'certain young girls', is the refusal to be isolated in a room with a male member of staff during examinations (Stasi Report 2003: 41). The headscarf itself is regarded as a frequent source of conflict and as obstructing the development of a critical awareness (Stasi Report 2003: 57). Again, the Report makes these assumptions without the benefit of any solid proof or explanation.

The unfavourable portrayal of Islam and Muslims is also to be found in the strand of the Stasi Report concerned with laïcité. After observing that all religions need to adapt so as to facilitate coexistence, the Report states that within Islam, the most recently implanted religion in France, the most rational currents of thought agree with the separation of political and spiritual powers (Stasi Report 2003: 16). The reference to 'recent implantation' conspicuously identifies Islam as an immigrant, ethnic minority religion. The implication of diminished rationality for most Muslims associated with the assertion that only 'the most rational' Muslims favour secularism, may well be

---

17   Esposito and Mogahed's study clarifies that the headscarf is not seen as a problem by Muslims and moreover shows that the lack of modesty in 'the West' can be understood by Muslims as women's inferior status in society. Although the study this report is based on considered Muslim opinions worldwide, it can be reasonably expected that European Muslims are at least as likely to wear the headscarf voluntarily, as those from other regions. This has until today been the largest scale and in-depth study conducted, involving more than 50,000 interviews over a period of six years worldwide.

offensive to many. This claim assumes that Muslims of average rationality would prefer the unity of church and state, and at the same time it also suggests that separating the two entities is the only rational approach. In view of the fact that several European jurisdictions still uphold a state–church system, it also seems rather insolent to suggest that such an approach is a specifically Islamic problem. In fact, empirical evidence shows that very few Muslims worldwide would prefer a complete unity of state and religious affairs (Esposito and Mogahed 2007: 48). The Stasi Commission's reference to Muslims' opposition to laïcité thus demonstrates yet another line of prejudice against Muslims. In addition, there is no indication of how the absence of headscarves from state schools would assist in reducing the assumed desire for unified religious and state governance.

Overall, the Stasi Report reflects a negative attitude towards Muslim girls who are portrayed as victims of sexism on the one hand, and as proselytizers and as often irrational creators of public disorder, on the other. The prohibition of headscarves in school appears to reflect a general fear of Islam in France (Ahdar and Leigh 2005: 365). This apparently emotionally charged attitude underlying the Stasi Commission's strategy is revealed, not only in the clear wording of the Report, but also in the fact that anecdotal evidence was readily deemed sufficient for a recommendation of a headscarf ban. Thus, for example, the questions asked of witnesses in preparing the report related not to the headscarf, but to cultural practices such as the stoning of women (Bowen 2006: 118).

Effect and Inadequacy of Response: Banning Pupils' Headscarves in Schools

Effect on ethnic/racial minority female Muslims   Although the prohibition against the wearing of ostentatious religious symbols by the 2004 Act does not directly discriminate against Muslim schoolgirls, it is quite clear that the ostentatious element of this ban presents particular problems for adherents to religions that require outward expressions of beliefs.[18] Accordingly, these problems are particularly likely to affect ethnic minorities: the Circular's interpretation of the prohibition almost exclusively impacts on Muslim, Jewish and Sikh schoolchildren, because large crosses are rarely worn or carried. This rule thus indirectly discriminates against ethnic minorities impacting, as it does, on members of religious groups that are composed largely of non-majority ethnicities (Thorson Plesner 2005b: 13–14). It is reported that in reality, however, orthodox Jewish children often attend faith-based private schools and are thus less likely to be affected (McGoldrick 2006: 92; Gunn 2004). During the Act's first year, nearly 100 Muslim girls who wore headscarves and three Sikh boys who wore turbans were excluded from school (Sintomer 2009: 134; McGoldrick 2006: 92–3; Singh Chowdhary 2004).[19] No pupils have yet been expelled for wearing a cross or kippah (Sintomer 2009: 144). Thus, the vast majority of the pupils required to make difficult choices between school and religious freedom are Muslim, female and members of ethnic minorities (Schofield 2003). Even some of those who oppose the wearing of headscarves regard the exclusionary effect of the 2004 Act on Muslim schoolgirls as a reason for rejecting the law (Mossuz-Lavau 2003), including the suggestion that there is little pedagogic value in requiring minors to lead a schizophrenic, hypocritical life in which they have to betray their religion and their parents (Houziaux 2004: 24).

---

18   This does not presume that any religion per se demands particular manifestations, however, some interpretations of religiously prescribed rules result in the belief that outward signs of these rules are necessary.

19   It is reported that the Sikh families affected had difficulties in finding alternative education. The reaction from the Sikh community parallels the one from the Muslim community in terms of disappointment and counter-arguments. The Muslim pupils are said to have either left education, entered private schools, or moved abroad for schooling.

Most Muslim schoolgirls faced with the prospect of leaving the state education system have opted not to wear a headscarf at school (Laborde 2008: 150). This is likely to have been influenced by a joint statement of French Muslim leadership recommending remaining in state schooling and stressing the importance attached to education by the Qur'an.

Inadequacy of legal response   Imposing a headscarf ban on school pupils is unsatisfactory for a number of reasons. First, the indirect gender and race discrimination to which it gives rise makes it more difficult or impossible for relevant pupils to participate in mainstream education. There is accordingly a tension between the Circular's claim that the 2004 Act pursues the goals of gender, ethnic and religious equality and the directly opposite tendency of that Act in practice. If the empowerment of disadvantaged women is the goal of the 2004 Act, because of its disempowering consequences, state endorsed compulsion against wearing the headscarf does not provide a workable solution (Laborde 2008: 150). Where female pupils are already oppressed by other pupils or by family members, there is a danger that the ban on headscarves at school may increase and intensify concerns, pressure, control or restraint (Knights 2005: 514; Gunn 2004: 18). Consequently, it appears that reliance on intersectional prejudice is likely to have guided legislators in the wrong direction.

The report does not elucidate how the headscarf ban would diminish gender discrimination against Muslim girls. Establishing services to support Muslim girls who experience problems[20] would appear to be a more promising means of tackling such harassment. Simon (2004a: 93) argues that, paradoxically, the 2004 Act treats pupils as if their visible characteristics are causing the discrimination they experience. For these reasons it seems unrealistic to expect the 2004 Act to make a contribution towards any of the aims it allegedly pursues.

Secondly, the 2004 Act was justified by reference to arguments grounded on intersectional prejudice associated with the characteristics of being Muslim, female and from an immigrant background. The gendered, racialized stigmatization of Muslim women evident in the Stasi Report is more likely to increase their perceived alienation from mainstream society than it is to enhance equality and inclusion. Laborde (2008: 149) maintains that the ban is erroneous, 'because it fails to respect the agency of those women it claims to emancipate in the name of a contested conception of secular autonomy and a misguided, neo-orientalist interpretation of Islam'. Further, the assumptions evident in the Stasi Report were not supported by objective evidence. The minimal effort of the Commissioners to ascertain the truth and test their underlying assumptions about headscarves is illustrated by the fact that, of the 140 or so witnesses they heard, only two wore a headscarf (McGoldrick 2006: 84).

Thirdly, the argument that the headscarf as a religious manifestation is irreconcilable with laïcité is also problematic. Crucially in this regard, the 2004 Act was to serve a contemporary implementation of the laïcité concept. Instead, it is suggested, the Act was shaped by the static historical conception of laïcité that it was supposed to overcome (Gunn 2004: 24). Even if the Commissioners' assumptions about Muslims' thoughts on secularism are assumed to be correct, the question as to whether in general the principle of laïcité can justify the prohibition of ostentatious religious symbols arises. This subject is worth investigating as adherence to the

---

20   For example, confidential services within schools, or community centres seem a likely option. In addition, one could think of related support mechanisms and measures, such as improving school curricula accordingly, setting up free telephone helplines, online networks, mediation services and refuges, offering training programmes for imam(ah)s and social workers, facilitating the distribution of relevant information, etc.

principle of laïcité is generally considered to be the main argument in support of banning various religious items in school.

Thus, an eminent supporter of the 2004 Act and member of the Stasi Commission, Weil, argues that the ban is justified because the 1905 Law on the Separation of Church and State prevents religion from interfering in public life (2005: 65–6). On the other hand, several scholars promote a rights-based understanding of laïcité, claiming that neutrality of the state requires non-interference with an individual's right to freedom of religion (Baubérot 2007: 117; Witte 2006: 44; Gunn 2004: 8–15). Similarly, Thorson Plesner (2005a: 585) observes that '[u]sing only or mainly a vague criteria of "neutrality" defined by the majority as a basis for restricting the rights of minorities to freedom of conscience, religion or belief could lead to violations of minority rights' and thus breach the very intentions of the principle of neutrality itself.

This controversy suggests that laïcité neither demands nor forbids the religiously neutral appearance of pupils that the 2004 Act requires. The concept is therefore not capable of justifying the Act's existence. In light of the assumptions that shaped the debate, doubts as to whether the concept of laïcité was abused by the Stasi Commission in order to enforce a religiously intolerant uniformity (Gunn 2004: 24), seem quite plausible. As a consequence, it can be argued that the time is ripe for a review of the 2004 Act.

Intersectional Discrimination and the German Headscarf Debate

The German School Acts

Statistics indicate that there are approximately three million Muslims in Germany (Berghahn 2009: 59; Boyle and Sheen 1997: 304). The pieces of legislation most relevant to the German headscarf debate (*Kopftuchstreit*), which has centred on headscarf-wearing teachers, are the School Acts. Because legislation in the field of education falls under the competence of the 16 states,[21] there are a number of different School Acts. Pupils' ability to wear headscarves is not affected by any of these Acts because their exercise of religious freedom is outside the reach of law.

Eight of the states parliaments[22] have enacted School Acts which do not prescribe, prohibit or mention a particular religious or non-religious appearance for teachers and which are thus religiously neutral. According to the School Acts of the states of Berlin, Bremen and Niedersachsen, however, all teachers are prohibited from displaying any religious affiliation. Arguably, some of the most striking and obscene legal rules that have been created in Germany after 1945 are now found in the remaining School Acts. For instance, Section 38(2) of the School Act of Baden-Württemberg, expressly prohibits teachers from making a religious statement, especially if in so doing they might give the impression that they oppose human dignity, equality and the democratic order. The same subsection also includes an exception for the representation of Christian and other occidental values and traditions.[23] In a similar, slightly less explicit fashion, Section 86(3) of the Hessen School Act prevents teachers from exhibiting clothes or symbols which may create an impression that they do not respect human dignity, equality and democracy. Any decisions in this regard need to take into account the Christian, humanist occidental traditions of the state Hessen.

---

21   This competence is set out under Article 70 of the German Basic Law (*Grundgesetz*).

22   The relevant states are: Brandenburg, Hamburg, Mecklenburg-Vorpommern, Rheinland-Pfalz, Sachsen, Sachsen-Anhalt, Schleswig-Holstein and Thüringen.

23   Since this strongly resembles Section 57 IV of the School Act of Nordrhein-Westfalen, the latter is not analysed separately.

It is again apparent that exceptions are possible for symbols of occidental but not oriental belief systems. Both School Acts thus contain express statements permitting the preferential treatment of Christian and Jewish teachers. Amongst all School Acts, these final two are therefore the most evidently problematic in terms of compliance with public international law,[24] EU legislation[25] and the German constitution.[26]

Assumptions Leading to the School Acts – Intersectional Discrimination and the Ludin Judgement

Headscarf rulings in German courts   The legislation explained above reflects an earlier series of judgements relating to two teachers who attempted to defend the wearing of a headscarf in the classroom. By far the most publicized judgement involved in the *Kopftuchstreit* related to a trainee teacher. Fereshta Ludin was not permitted to become a teacher after completing her training because she wore a headscarf. This case eventually came before the Federal Administrative Court (FAC),[27] which rejected her request to enter the teaching profession.

Ms Ludin then filed a constitutional complaint at the Federal Constitutional Court (FCC). The FCC ruled in her favour, holding that the FAC's ruling was ill-founded because constitutional rights could not be legitimately limited without a legal basis and none existed here. Further, the judges stressed that the Constitution demanded that legally permitted restrictions of constitutional rights must be free from discrimination.[28] It was this FCC judgement that prompted the *states* parliaments to issue amendments to the School Acts. By the time the *Ludin* case returned to the FAC for reconsideration, it was then possible to reject her claim according to the revised Section 38(2) Baden-Württemberg School Act, as she had worn an oriental religious symbol.

Another case concerning a teacher (Iyman Alzayed) came before the courts in the federal state of Lower Saxony. This teacher, who was a white convert to Islam, had worked wearing a headscarf for several years before the case. It is unclear whether her ethnic background influenced the judges but, at the first instance court, she received considerable praise for her attitude at work and it was decided that she presented no threat to the State's neutrality.[29] Pragmatically, the court had thereby considered the actual facts of the case. The school nevertheless won its case on appeal, where the reasoning of the court reflected that in the FAC's judgement in *Ludin*.[30]

Views on Muslims and gender equality   A fundamental issue raised in the *Ludin* case was that only women wear headscarves, and that it therefore signals gender inequality to schoolchildren and thus undermines the State's efforts to promote the constitutional principle of gender equality.[31] This argument was welcomed by commentators who share the view that a headscarf is irreconcilable with equality between the sexes (Pofalla 2004: 1219; Bertrams 2003: 1234; Ipsen 2003: 1212). However, this view is unsatisfactory for several reasons. First, it is culturally biased because it does not take account of the fact that skirts and dresses are also predominantly

---

24   Article 7 UDHR requires equality before the law.

25   Article 2(2)(a) of the Council Directive 2000/78 prohibits direct discrimination on grounds of religion, a principle also implemented in the General Equal Treatment Act (*Allgemeines Gleichbehandlungsgesetz*).

26   Article 3(1) of the *Grundgesetz* guarantees equality before the law and Article 3(3)(1) interdicts discrimination on grounds of *inter alia* religious beliefs.

27   BVerwGE C 21.01, judgement from 4 July 2002, BVerwGE 116, 359.

28   BVerfG judgement from 24 September 2003, BVerfGE 108, 282.

29   VG Lüneburg, judgement from 16 February 2000, NJW 2001, 767.

30   OVG Lüneburg, judgement from 13 March 2002, NVwZ-RR 2002, 658.

31   BVerwG 2 C 45.03, judgement from 24 June 2004, JZ 2004, 1181.

female items of clothing and should therefore also symbolize inequality. Arguably, equality does not logically require women to dress in the same way as men any more than it demands that men should dress in the same way as women. As there is no requirement for teachers to wear unisex clothing, there should be no prohibition against the wearing of particular isolated items such as a headscarf.[32]

To regard a piece of clothing as a symbol of inequality would also risk being paternalistic and running counter to efforts to promote gender equality (Berghahn 2009: 35). A further counter-argument is that a professional woman who wears a headscarf is demonstrating that she cherishes an emancipated life and that this can be reconciled with the wearing of a headscarf (Britz 2003: 99; Debus 2001: 1359). Britz (2003: 99–100) has pointed out that the principle of equality cannot prevent women from choosing traditional roles and that Christian society has not attempted to do this. In any case it ought not to be for constitutional law to determine what amounts to an emancipated life and what does not (Britz 2003: 103). The unsoundness of the headscarf ban is also demonstrated by the fact that a headscarf carries different meanings to different people and can therefore not simply be viewed as a symbol of discrimination or oppression (Czermak 2004: 943). It is noteworthy that in Germany there are currently no Islamic authorities to advise on the meaning of a headscarf or on other religious matters (Muckel 1999: 248).

Views on Muslims and other democratic values   In *Ludin*, the FAC stated that the wearing of a headscarf violated the principle of the religiously neutral state. It also observed that, because of this principle, the state must neither exercise its influence in a religious way nor identify itself with a particular religious community. The judges explained that a headscarf is a symbolic expression of Islamic faith and that, if worn by a teacher during lessons, pupils will be incessantly and inescapably confronted by a clear symbol of a particular religion.[33] However, the judgements included no reference to empirical evidence demonstrating the existence of the types of problems envisaged.

As regards intersectional prejudice, the three dissenting judges in the FCC judgement in Ms Ludin's case claimed that, by contrast with the headscarf, the Christian cross was merely an 'everyday item' and 'a general sign of culture … of a culture that has developed tolerance'.[34] Such observations reveal an assumption that the headscarf symbolizes a culture that has not developed tolerance. Although the term culture is probably used in order to divert attention from the fact that a cross is also a religious symbol. This minority of judges even regarded headscarves as a threat to democratic values.[35] Moreover, in the subsequent parliamentary discussions, members of the CDU (German Christian Democratic Union) argued that headscarves are predominantly political symbols that indicate support for Islamic law, forced marriages and honour killings (Henkes and Kneip 2009: 262–79). Conversely, a major empirical study indicates that the concerns raised in the headscarf controversies as to Muslims' attitudes towards democratic values are largely unfounded (Sintomer 2009: 143; Esposito and Mogahed 2007: 143).[36]

---

32   One could take the argument of cultural bias even further and mention that in many predominantly Muslim countries, headscarves are also worn by men, as are wide dresses.

33   BVerwGE C 21.01, judgement from 4 July 2002, BVerwGE 116, 359.

34   BVerfG judgement from 24 September 2003, BVerfGE 108, 282, 333.

35   Ibid.

36   Esposito and Mogahed's study shows that a majority of Muslims desire improvements to democratic structures, in particular freedom of speech. Although a majority also wish for Sharia to be one of the sources of law, also 46 per cent of US Americans would like to see the Bible as a source of law (2007: 49). In neither

Effect and Inadequacy of Response: Banning Teachers' Headscarves in Schools

Effect on ethnic/racial minority female Muslims   Those School Acts which are silent as to religious attire do not appear to introduce any element of religious or other discrimination against headscarf-wearing teachers. In the three *states* with School Acts which adopt a neutrally phrased prohibition against religious symbols, followers of religions that require outward manifestation cannot teach in mainstream schools. This affects Muslim women who wear headscarves as well as members of other religions (such as Jewish or Sikh men who wear head-coverings). Those School Acts, which are phrased neutrally, constitute a particular detriment to those for whom a particular appearance is a vital part of their religious belief. Indirect religious discrimination thus results. There is a strong argument that laws banning headscarves violate Article 3 of the Constitution in that they amount to indirect sex discrimination because they seriously restrict the opportunities of Muslim women in employment (Britz 2003: 97–8). Considerable scholarship has supported the view that a headscarf ban at work runs counter to the goal of promoting gender equality and potentially exacerbates the social exclusion of Muslim women (Loenen 2009: 315; Roseberry 2009: 344; Sacksofsky 2009a: 361; Vickers 2008; Schiek 2004: 72).

Clearly, such provisions may also limit the employment opportunities of men who express their religious affiliation through items – such as the head-coverings of Jewish and Sikh men and the uniforms of Buddhist monks. Indeed, a Hessian ministerial representative explained, in an interview with Human Rights Watch (2009), that the School Act affects not only women but also men who wear the orange Buddhist dress or the clothing of the Taliban. In reality, however, the resulting indirect discrimination carries particularly serious implications for Muslim women. Since the enactment of these laws, several dozen teachers in the relevant *states have been forced out of mainstream education*, and all of them were Muslim women (Mahrenholz 2009: 193–224).

It is likely that due to the religious composition of the German population, as well as the internal structures of religious groups present in Germany, the vast majority of teachers affected by the neutrally phrased School Acts will be Muslim, belong to a racial minority and be female. For the same reasons, the more explicitly worded rules of the Baden-Württemberg and Hessen School Acts (translated above) disclose an element of intersectional discrimination. These expressly prevent teachers from engaging in expressions of oriental religions but allow Christians and Jews to manifest their religious affiliation as they please. Using the geographical origin of religions as a delineator for acceptability introduces a strong racial bias. Consequently, teachers in Baden-Württemberg can display Christian and Jewish religious symbols but not Islamic or Hindu ones. These two School Acts thus carry an element of indirect race discrimination as almost all followers of oriental religions are also members of an ethnic minority group or, in the case of converts, often perceived as such. The reference to dignity, equality and democracy in the Acts appears to allude to the existence of contrasting Islamic values.

Inadequacy of legal response   The German headscarf rules are unsatisfactory in several respects, not least given the tendency of the provisions of School Acts to cause (in)direct religious and indirect gender and race discrimination. As regards the view that teachers' headscarves portray gender inequality, many arguments have been advanced on both sides. Excluding a disproportionate

---

case does this point towards allocating supreme competence to a religious authority, an idea which a large majority considers undesirable.

number of Muslim women from teaching posts, as is the indirectly discriminatory effect of relevant School Acts, seems unlikely to promote gender equality. On the contrary, a more likely outcome is to increase the economic dependence of such women on men. Such a result would risk having a negative effect on the perceived victims of oppression rather than on the apparent culprits (Sacksofsky 2009b: 291).

A more promising approach to ensuring that teachers do not exercise religious influence over pupils would involve a case-by-case assessment, to take place if and only if there were concerns that the teacher in question might be abusing her or his position in this way. The perceived 'danger' that pupils might regard the headscarf as a symbol of female oppression may, in reality, be negligible. There may be some disquiet about the possibility of parents using the teacher's appearance as a role model in efforts to pressurize their daughter into wearing a headscarf. However, the same argument could be made in relation to any clothing or conduct of a teacher. As in France, the problem of pressure to wear a headscarf needs to be addressed by a more imaginative development of coordinated policy measures.[37]

Secondly, the School Acts are based on intersectional prejudice which particularly relates to Muslim women from an ethnic minority background. Generalizations about Muslims and Islam to be found in the German case law reflect a negative attitude towards Muslims and their religion, especially as regards gender inequality, tolerance and anti-democratic thought. Such views arguably reveal that, amongst parts of the judiciary, there is an unreasoned, emotional approach to the headscarf debate. No empirical evidence or other research was employed to validate the assumptions or to demonstrate the need for legislative action.

Thirdly, the case law demonstrates that the neutrality of the state is the main argument for restrictions on religious manifestations.[38] Several commentators agree with the final FAC judgement in *Ludin* that teachers wearing headscarves is incompatible with state neutrality (Pofalla 2004: 1219; Bertrams 2003: 1234; Ipsen 2003: 1212). Thus, Schavan (2004: 5) argues that neutrality requires refraining from creating the impression that one opposes democratic values. She contends that such abstinence is not required of those wishing to engage in Christian-occidental religious expression because such expression is purely cultural. Nevertheless, considerable criticism has also been voiced, especially since FCC jurisprudence has long promoted a concept of open neutrality.[39] Attention has been drawn to the fact that neutrality in general should not simply be defined as separating the state from church, but as an open concept which leaves space for pluralistic inclusion of the diversity of opinion prevalent in the school sector (Gerstenberg 2005: 98; Czermak 2004: 945; Britz 2003: 96; Debus 2001: 1358). Van Bijsterveld (2001: 303) and Gerstenberg (2005: 98) also argue that the view that occidental traditions and beliefs, unlike those originating outside Europe, do not interfere with the neutrality of the state is a misconception.

Unlike in France, the German concept of neutrality does not explicitly appear in the Constitution (Morlok and Krüper 2003: 1021). As in relation to the French principle of laïcité, there is no fixed interpretation of the German concept of neutrality. There is, moreover, a failure to show how the aim of a religiously neutral teacher is to be fulfilled through the prohibition of outward religious manifestations – a prohibition which cannot prevent teachers expressing their religious affiliation verbally. Absolute neutrality cannot be forced upon an individual without a clear definition of that

---

37   For examples, see footnote 18.

38   The legitimacy of this reasoning based on neutrality remains contested, which is reflected in the differing outcomes of the latest versions of the states' School Acts, as described above.

39   BVerfG, judgement no. 2 BvR 1436/02 from 24 September 2003, BVerfGE 108, 282, 300 and judgement no. I BvR 647/70 and I BvR 7/74 from 16 October 1979, BVerfGE 52, 223.

neutrality. It is crucial to note that even this main rationale for justifying religious discrimination is not generally accepted in legal scholarship.

Given that underlying assumptions remain unsupported, and because it is far from clear that the legal response serves all the relevant aims, the School Acts are based on no more than an unarticulated, debatable concept of neutrality. In conjunction with the intersectional discrimination they cause, as well as the indirect sex and race discrimination, there is sufficient reason to support a review of the legislation.

Magnifying Intersectional Prejudice Occurring in the French and German Headscarf Debates

Intersections of Religious and Racial Prejudice

In Europe, the headscarf is not only a common identifier for women, as well as for adherents of Islam, but also tends to evoke assumptions as to an ethnic minority background (Loenen 2009: 313–28). Cavanaugh (2007: 18) suggests that 'Islam remains the religious identity of immigrants, creating a space between ostensibly "secular", "modern" and "liberal" West and the "otherness" of Islam' (Kumar 2002: 54). Berghahn (2009: 60) adds that forceful de-veiling represents a superiority complex and 'late-colonial' fantasies contrasting the progressive West to the backward, misogynistic Muslim ideology. A survey shows that discrimination on grounds of religion and race are frequently connected, as almost half of relevant experiences are perceived to be based on both religion and ethnic or immigrant background.[40] This link to ethnicity and immigration raises the question of whether racial prejudice was also influential in the headscarf controversies. Some remarks made in the course of the *affaire du foulard* and the *Kopftuchstreit* indeed point in this direction.

Themes of prejudice uncovered in the headscarf debates comprised not only religious tenets, but also cultural practices that generally occur outside Europe and have no standing in Islam. In the French debate, for instance, forced marriage was mentioned. Consequently, conduct and traditions which are cultural and not religious, was ascribed to Muslims (Costa-Lascoux 2004: 90), adding a racist element to the debates. Several authors support this viewpoint. Modood et al. (2007: 353), for instance, describe anti-Muslim prejudice as a form of 'cultural racism'. The French headscarf ban in particular is characterized as not only a manifestation of anti-Muslim tensions, or Islamophobia (Sintomer 2009: 133; Pitt 2007: 204; Ahdar and Leigh 2005: 365; Houziaux 2004: 11), but also as 'an atavistic fear of the "other" … an association of race and religion in the case of Muslims' (McColgan 2009: 24; Pitt 2007: 204). Furthermore the term 'Muslim' in France is even used by some to describe any non-white person (McGoldrick 2006: 53) and converts who wear the headscarf report that they are no longer perceived as white (Franks 2000). Undeniably, these antithetical positions have thereby been used to argue in favour of a headscarf ban in France and Germany. Given the long-standing Muslim presence in Europe, as well as the development of 'Euro-Islam', the deliberate assignation of Islam to another geographical area denotes another facet of racism embedded in the headscarf debates (AlSayyad and Castells 2002). The discourses appear to have been employed by some to vent their racist sentiments.

---

40   See: Fundamental Rights Agency. *Data in Focus Report 2 – Muslims* [Online: EU-MIDIS May 2009]. Available at: http://fra.europa.eu/fraWebsite/eu-midis/eumidis_muslims_en.htm [accessed: 10 May 2010]. According to this Report 11 per cent of Muslims had been victims of racially motivated crime in Europe during the prior year.

The implications of the headscarf debate, and the racist and religious prejudices which it revealed, extend beyond Muslim women to all Muslims. When both Muslims and non-Muslims are made to believe that there are irreconcilable differences and misunderstandings between the two groups, Muslims are likely to encounter increased levels of discrimination and socio-economic disadvantage (McGoldrick 2006: 55). It has also been suggested that the continued marginalization of Muslims might encourage political or other radical forms of behaviour (Bowen 2009: 450–1; Silvestri 2009: 1226). McGoldrick (2006: 57), for instance, links riots in France to the 'fiction of equality' which French Muslims experience. The initial promotion or acceptance of prejudice can thus create a vicious circle. Ultimately, spreading prejudice can even impinge on the non-religious. As Evans (2008: 9) points out, members of ethnic minorities may be subjected to religious discrimination, even if they do not adhere to any or all of a religion's doctrine, simply because they wear clothes or display symbols with cultural or ethnic connections. Headscarf laws therefore have much more serious implications than the exclusion of individual women from education or employment.

Intersections of Religious (and Implicitly Racial) and Gender Prejudice

Reports detailing discrimination experienced by Muslim ethnic minority women can be found in several jurisdictions (Bunglawala 2008; Foroutan 2008). The fact that such discrimination exists is certainly confirmed by the French and German headscarf debates. Although the 2004 Act and the School Acts also apply to Muslim and other ethnic minority men who wear religious dress, these laws came into being as a result of stereotyping linked to the perceived inferiority of women in Islam. Both the *affaire du foulard* and the *Kopftuchstreit* make abundant reference to the headscarf as a symbol of the oppressed woman, endorsed by Islamic tenets, without making any reference to supporting theological texts. Roseberry (2009: 344) fittingly takes this analysis of the prohibition of headscarves further, arguing that it 'perpetuates sexist portrayals of women as being weak-willed and unable to act in their own best interests'. The assumed pattern is also seen as a violation of the liberal right to respect for one's autonomy (Knights 2005: 514) and thereby as oppression exercised by the State (Spinner-Halev 2008: 565–8). Undeniably, justifying a ban by reference to the argument of protecting women's dignity or safeguarding women from male influence, is sexist and potentially insulting to a woman who wears a headscarf for religious reasons.

Proponents of the view that Muslim women who wear the headscarf are dominated by men, submissive and in need of liberation played a powerful role in the French and German debates. Berghahn (2009: 61) convincingly argues that some feminists used the debate to vent anger about their own situation by creating hierarchies amongst disadvantaged women and Bowen (2007: 1013) similarly suggests that responses to Muslim women who wear headscarves are coloured by previous struggles of women to gain control over their bodies. As a result, Muslim women are subjected to 'gendered Islamophobia' (Zine 2003, quoted by Hamdan 2007: 10). The main difference between the discussions in France and in Germany is that, in the former case, claims were made that the pupils wearing headscarves were simultaneously those who were oppressed and those who were safeguarded by the 2004 Act. In the latter, however, it is the teacher wearing a headscarf who is considered oppressed but it is the pupils who are thought to need legal protection. In neither investigation, however, were assumptions tested against empirical evidence or other research. Hence feminist interpretations of the headscarf were conveniently ignored (Baubérot 2004: 49). The ignorance of Islam which was displayed could also be indicative of the absence of personal involvement of decision-makers in the Muslim communities. The resulting defectiveness of information, in conjunction with emotional comments and hearsay evidence, paved the way for laws that are vividly reflective of these shaky underpinnings. As a summary, Skjeie (2007: 145) finds 'largely offhand remarks … made by politicians and judges alike … across Europe, on girls' and women's religious dress symbolizing the clash of antagonistic value systems. Their rhetorical effect is to deprive any "Muslim woman" … of individual choice and autonomy, while maintaining the irreconcilability of "Muslim religious dress" to "European gender equality"'.

Conclusions

The above discussion reveals that current French and German law permit the State to act, consciously or unconsciously, against the interests of women who wear headscarves. Headscarf bans, as found in the 2004 Act and the School Acts, inevitably create a specific disadvantage for Muslim ethnic minority women and result in their further exclusion and alienation (McColgan 2009: 29). It is suggested that, when one reflects on the core assumptions on which the relevant laws are based, the headscarf controversies reveal more than mere coincidental intersectional discrimination. The background history of the two sets of legislation demonstrates that a number of assumptions were made about Muslim women with a minority ethnicity background. These assumptions amount to 'intersectional prejudice' and, because of their influence over the legislation, there are grounds for demanding a review of the relevant laws.

Both in France and in Germany, women who wear headscarves were demeaningly depicted as oppressed and potentially threatening to democratic values. However, none of these assumptions were substantiated. No effort was made to identify or commission empirical studies that would have provided a firm evidence base. Prejudice was thus allowed to play an important role in both jurisdictions. It operated to maintain a one-sided interpretation of laïcité and state neutrality respectively and thus to provide a seemingly objective justification for the legislation. The strict interpretations given to laïcité and neutrality meant that some religions were not regarded as neutral whilst others were, simply because they would not be apparent from a person's clothing. The resulting intersectional discrimination created by the relevant laws is thus an outcome of stereotypes held by the relevant decision-makers.

It is hoped that the inadequacy of legislation based predominantly (or wholly) on prejudice has been demonstrated in this chapter. The exclusionary effects of the resulting headscarf bans in the education and employment spheres increases rather than reduces their disadvantage. Unsurprisingly, given that racist and sexist assumptions about Muslim women who wear headscarves guided the legislation, the reasons provided for the enactment of the 2004 Act and relevant School Acts are generally unconvincing. Because these laws therefore lack a clear justification, the time is ripe for a reassessment.

Chapter 8

The Status of Muslim Minority Women in Greece: Second Class European Citizens?

Stergios Kofinis

Introduction

Kimberlé Crenshaw (2000: 217), in relation to the discrimination suffered by black women, suggests that:

> black women sometimes experience discrimination in ways similar to white women's experiences; sometimes they share very similar experiences with Black men. Yet often they experience double-discrimination – the combined effects of practices which discriminate on the basis of race and on the basis of sex. And sometimes, they experience discrimination as Black women – not the sum of race and sex discrimination, but as Black women.

Following this analytical framework, I suggest in this chapter that women of the Muslim[1] minority in Greece are also subjected to multiple discrimination: first, on grounds of their status as members of a minority, second, on grounds of their sex and, third, on the basis of the interaction between their sex and ethno-religious affiliation. This multidimensional discrimination, that classifies Muslim women as probably the most oppressed[2] social group in Greece, is not properly dealt with by the Greek authorities and no official policy has been adopted to address the issue.

Drawing on the scarce empirical and case-law research conducted by Greek institutions and independent researchers, this chapter will outline the overall situation of Muslim minority women in Greece and subsequently address the issues of multiple discrimination which they suffer. I will argue that Muslim women in Greece experience multidimensional discrimination as a result, first, of the traditional patriarchal structures of their communities and, second, of the Greek State's vision of the minority as a foreign body within the country. The latter in turn stems from the Greek legal order's essentialist understanding of the self as fixed, unitary and immutable and from the historical construction of identities in Greece, both of the Greek individual and the member of

---

1 The term 'Muslim', as used in this chapter, does not refer to all believers of Islam, but to describe the members of the Muslim minority in Greece with its specific traits, as described below, such as the highly conservative and patriarchal structure of their communities along with their physical and cultural isolation from the rest of society. Thus, the terms 'Muslim' and 'member of the minority' will be used interchangeably in the text to describe persons belonging to the minority of Western Thrace. For the purpose of this chapter Muslim women means Muslim minority women in Greece, unless expressed differently.

2 I am using here the concept of oppression as defined by bell hooks (2000: 135): 'Being oppressed means the *absence of choices*'. Muslim women in Greece are subjected to restrictions that leave them with no choice in certain spheres of life; a situation of extreme oppression that majority women in Greece do not face.

the Muslim minority. A brief examination of these issues will permit us to understand the reasons for the exclusion of Muslim women's experience of subordination from the public discourse on minority rights in Greece.

The first part of this chapter explores the identity constructing processes in the Greek legal order, focusing, first, on the principle of formal equality that informs jurisprudential and governmental theory and then on the historical background and current situation of the minority before examining the jurisprudential understanding of minority member identity through an appraisal of the case law. The second part will discuss the status of Muslim women in Greece on the basis of the above analysis, with the first two sections examining the discrimination experienced by members of the minority and by women in Greece. The cumulative discrimination experienced by Muslim women on the basis of the interaction between their minority member status and their sex are then examined in detail. Finally, the last section focuses on the application of Islamic sacred law (the Sharia) as a case of intersectional discrimination faced by Muslim women.

The extent and nature of oppression experienced by Muslim women in Greece practically classifies them as second class citizens of the European Union, since they are *de jure* exempted from the principle of gender equality on the one hand (through the application of the Sharia) and on the other hand they are de facto marginalized in the social, economic and political spheres. This chapter seeks to explore the perspectives that multidimensional equality doctrine offers in addressing the issue.

Constructing Identities in the Greek Legal Order

Conceptualizing the Greek Identity

The Greek legal system leaves little space for the recognition of multidimensional equality as a general legal principle. The general principle of formal equality enacted in Article 4(1) of the Greek Constitution guarantees the similar treatment of situations which are the same and differentiated treatment of situations which are unlike. This Aristotelian formula of equality,[3] however, is not accompanied by a list of prohibited grounds of discrimination like the one established in Article 14 of the European Convention on Human Rights (ECHR). Therefore, under the Greek Constitution, discrimination is dealt with only in terms of violations of the general principle of equality or of one of the specific equality principles (such as gender equality, equality in taxation, and wage equality).

The principle of formal equality of all Greeks, as established in the Constitution, corresponds to a specific understanding of Greek identity in Greek legal and political thought. According to the dominant narrative, language, religion and ethnic origins are considered essential parts of what identifies a person as Greek. This idea can be detected in the Constitution, especially in those provisions establishing the Eastern Orthodox Church of Christ as 'the prevailing religion in Greece' (Article 3(1)), requiring 'Greek descent from the father's or mother's line' as a precondition for election as President (Article 31) and designating the oath that the President

---

3   On the Aristotelian concept of proportional equality, see von Leyden (1985). On the widespread criticism of Aristotle's conception of formal equality, exploration of which would exceed the constraints of this chapter, see Schiek (2002b).

of the Republic must swear before the Parliament ('I do swear in the name of the Holy and consubstantial and Indivisible Trinity', Article 33(2)). It is also visible in the legislation governing compulsory religious instruction in the public education system and the corresponding case law,[4] as well as in the law against proselytism, which is exclusively aimed against the non-Orthodox and non-Christian.[5]

This understanding of Greek identity can be traced back to the building process of the Greek nation-state, which took place during the nineteenth and first half of the twentieth century through assimilation (as in the cases of Vlachs and Arvanites) and expulsion (as in the case of the Jews of Thessaloniki during the Nazi occupation) of the various religious, linguistic and cultural groups that co-existed under the Ottoman Empire on the territory of present-day Greece (Milios 1997; Angelopoulos 1997; Mantzoufas 2000: 1047). This resulted in a high degree of national and religious homogeneity and consequently in a lack of understanding for minority issues, mostly viewed through the lens of national insecurities. Greece's perception of itself as a nation is thus that of a unitary body of people. According to that perspective, categorical distinctions cannot be tolerated because they would traumatize the coherence of the nation.

The Minority of Western Thrace: The 'Foreign' Greeks

Even today in Greece, this vision of Greek society as a monolithic entity overshadows the existence of distinct minorities, the most important being the Muslim minority of Western Thrace. An interesting first insight into the State's understanding of the minority is provided by the tense ongoing debate both between the minority and the State and between Greece and Turkey on the 'correct' term with which to identify the minority. A quick glance at the issue reveals Greece's attitude towards the minority. In a process of abstraction, the State isolates the religious aspect of the identity of the people dwelling in Western Thrace and categorizes its citizens according to their religious affiliation. The internal distinctions and even the conflicts within the minority are thus ignored by the State when regulating the status of its members.

The formulation of the identity of the members of the Western Thrace minority may be better understood through an exploration of the historical background to the minority as well as its present socio-economic status, which will permit us to outline the institutional and social framework of the minority's life.

Historical background of the minority of Western Thrace   The Western Thrace minority was formed as an official minority in Greece when a population of about 86,000 Muslims residing in the area was exempt, as were the Greeks of Istanbul, from the 1923 population exchange

---

4   See, for example, the Council of State (Symvoulion tis Epikrateias) in Decision No. 2176/1998, which held that limiting religious instruction, that is, the teaching of the beliefs of the Greek Orthodox Church, to only one hour per week in the last two years of high school is a violation of the constitutional demand for adequate 'development of the religious consciousness of all Greek children'.

5   See *Kokkinakis v. Greece* Series A No. 260-A. In that case, Mr Kokkinakis, a Jehovah's Witness, was sentenced to imprisonment and a fine for proselytism under section 4 of Law No. 1363/1938, even though there was no evidence of an attempt to convince others with improper means. In fact, under the provisions mentioned above, enacted during the dictatorship of Metaxa (1936–41), any attempt to convert a Greek Orthodox to another religion or dogma is punishable regardless of the means used.

between Greece and Turkey.[6] The minority is mixed on an ethno-linguistic basis,[7] consisting of three distinct groups: individuals of Turkish origin, Roma and Slav-speaking Pomaks. At the time of the population exchange the minority comprised roughly 39,000 Turks (around 45.5 per cent), 35,000 Pomaks (around 40.5 per cent) and 12,000 Roma (around 14 per cent) (Hellenic Ministry of Foreign Affairs 2007).

The Muslim minority of Greece was officially recognized as a religious minority under the provisions of the 1923 Lausanne International Peace Treaty (Articles 37–45). Under the Treaty, civil and political rights of minority members both in Turkey and in Greece were guaranteed and some collective rights were granted, such as the rights to native language education and establishment of places of worship. As far as family law was concerned, the Greek and Turkish Governments undertook to take 'measures permitting the settlement of these questions in accordance with the customs of those minorities' (Article 42).

In fact, the Treaty of Lausanne was the last in a series of treaties and conventions regulating the status of the Muslim populations that remained within Greek territories after the consecutive expansions of the Greek State during the second half of the nineteenth and the first quarter of the twentieth century.[8] The minority protection system established by these bilateral Conventions followed the lines of the Ottoman Empire's millet system according to which the different religious groups of the Empire (the People of the Book, namely Christians and Jews) were recognized as communities ('millet') and granted a certain degree of institutional autonomy. In that context, they were allowed to have their own religious leaders to represent them in front of the Ottoman authorities, keep and exercise their faith, and organize their communal life according to their beliefs and traditions. In fact, individuals gained status and a recognizable identity within the Ottoman society only through their own millet (Aral 2004: 475; Tsitselikis 2007).[9] By virtue of their semi-autonomous status the different millet were exempt from the application of the Sharia and were allowed to enforce their own legal traditions and practices, especially in matters of family law. This multinational, non-assimilative model of state organization was based on the religious affiliation of each community's members rather than ethnicity and facilitated the perpetuation of the given hierarchical social structure of the empire (Ribas Mateos 2000: 136).

---

6   The Convention Concerning the Exchange of Greek and Turkish Populations was signed at Lausanne, Switzerland, on 30 January 1923 by the governments of Greece and Turkey. Some 1.5 million Orthodox Christians living in Turkey and around 400,000 Muslims living in Greece were forced to leave their homelands and migrate to the other State within less than a year in order for the two countries to achieve population homogeneity and inner stability. In fact, more than 1 million of these Christians had already fled from Turkey in the aftermath of the Greco-Turkish war of 1919–22.

7   I am using the term 'ethno-linguistic' in this chapter and not 'ethnic' or 'national' in order to make clear that I am referring to categorizations based on language rather than on common descent. Any reference to ethnicities in the Balkan context is doomed to lead to controversy since no clear lines can be drawn between internal identification and external ascriptions, the case of the Western Thrace minority being a highly typical example of this.

8   These are the Treaty of Constantinople (1881) for the protection of the Muslims of Thessaly and Arta, the Peace Convention of Athens (1913) that confirmed the annexation of Epirus and Macedonia by Greece and the Treaty of Sèvres (1920).

9   The Ottoman concept of minority protection sharply contrasts with the modern approach to minority rights as primarily human rights of the members of the minority (on the issue see further Kymlicka 1995: 156 *passim*). However, it falls beyond the scope of this chapter to explore further the modern theoretical debate on minority rights.

The current status of the minority   Data available today shows that the population of the minority of Thrace has grown to roughly 100,000 people. More accurate figures are impossible to obtain due to large-scale immigration of the members of the minority (Attaóv 1992: 90) and the lack of an official census of the population on the basis of religion and/or ethnic affiliation since 1951 (Asimakopoulou and Hristidou-Lionaraki 2002: 230–2; Anagnostou and Triandafyllidou 2007). NGOs and various authors estimate that the minority's population currently numbers between 80,000 and 120,000, of whom 12,000 reside in Athens and 5,000 in Thessaloniki (Human Rights Watch 1999; Tsitselikis 2004a). The composition of the minority population is poorly documented. However, the Greek Government estimates that 50 per cent are of Turkish origin, 35 per cent Pomaks and 15 per cent Roma (Hellenic Ministry of Foreign Affairs 1999).

During the last 18 years the overall situation of the minority has indisputably improved. The 'legal equality, equal citizenship' (*isonomia – isopoliteia*) policy announced by Prime Minister Konstantinos Mitsotakis on his 1991 visit to Thrace paved the way for an overall liberalization of the official approach towards the minority. The minority was no longer officially considered as the 'internal enemy' and old restrictive measures were reassessed.[10] Hence the practice of forced deprivation of citizenship under the provisions of the infamous Article 19 of the Greek Citizenship Law ceased[11] and the restrictions for entry into zones alongside the Bulgarian border, where Pomaks reside, were abolished for all Greek citizens.

Moreover, under the influence of European Union regional policy the area of Western Thrace has developed both economically (even though it still ranks among the poorest regions in Europe) and socio-politically. Institutional reforms leading to the decentralization of the Greek State favoured the minority's political emancipation and raised awareness among its members concerning the need for active participation in local affairs, while the introduction in 1995 of a university entrance quota of 0.5 per cent for the members of the minority has raised the number of university graduates among that community and has reduced the flow of young Muslims migrating to Turkey for study purposes. At the same time, a more integrative approach of the Greek Government towards the minority in the 1990s allowed for a change of mentality among minority and majority leaders both at local and national level, which has allayed to some degree the intense feelings of hostility and mistrust on both sides (Anagnostou and Triandafyllidou 2007). However, research published in 1995 (Voulgaris et al. 1995) indicated that the majority of Greeks consider the members of the minority to be foreign on grounds of their language, religion and ethnic background. The same research reports a high degree of intolerance towards Muslims, with 52 per cent of the Christian majority members agreeing with the statement that 'they should all go to Turkey' (Asimakopoulou and Hristidou-Lionaraki 2002: 248–9).

In relation to communal rights, the minority's religious leaders, the Muftis, also perform administrative and judicial duties. The autonomous jurisdiction of the Muftis over family law matters concerning Greek Muslims was retained under the provisions of the Treaty of Lausanne and recently reaffirmed by Law No. 1920/1991.

---

10   However, discriminatory practices of the administration against the minority were reported even after the official policy shift. According to Troumpeta's (2001: 195) data gathered in 1996, the authorities were still refusing unofficially but systematically to subsidize industries that employed members of the minority.

11   Article 19 of the Citizenship Law gave the administration arbitrary discretion to revoke the citizenship of the 'non-ethnic (allogeneis)' Greek citizens when they settled abroad with no intent to return. The persons concerned were usually not even informed on the procedures adopted in their case, except after they had already lost their citizenship. The practice of forced deprivations of citizenship, especially of members of the minority of Thrace who had migrated to or simply visited Turkey or other foreign countries, continued almost until the abolition of Article 19 in 1997.

The minority member identity as understood in the context of the Greek legal order   Under the influence of these historical and institutional factors, the Greek legal order perceives the experience of being member of the Muslim minority of Thrace as a stable aspect of the person which has a clear and invariable meaning over time and in relation to different historical, social and political contexts. This essentialism obscures the existence of a multiplicity of distinct groups within the minority on the basis of different characteristics, such as gender, ethno-linguistic affiliation[12] and social status. Not even religion, which is presumed to be the binding, essential characteristic of the group, should be considered as a permanent, immutable and eternal trait: atheism, agnosticism and apostasy are not unheard of among the Muslims of Western Thrace (Hristopoulos 2002: 122). This typification, based on the formulation of the minority in the text of the Treaty of Lausanne, leads to yet another abstraction: the minority is perceived by the Greek State as a united body with common traits and objectives, while the power relations within the minority are considered an internal issue in which – in the name of toleration – the majority should not interfere.

This *neo-millet* approach to the minority issue, according to Tsitselikis' apposite characterization (2007: 372), practised by the modern Greek State is more an institutional remnant of a pre-modern State structure than a sign of commitment to cultural diversity and post-modern legal pluralism (Bano 2007; Merry 1988). Protection of the minority's collective rights appears to serve as sufficient reason to exclude the protection of its members' human rights. This feature can easily be detected in a series of complaints brought before the European Court of Human Rights by members of the Muslim minority and other minorities in Greece. Naturally, in the absence of a minority rights provision in the ECHR (Gilbert 2002), these claims primarily concern the infringement of individual rights protected by the Convention, such as freedom of assembly and association, freedom of religion and prohibition of discrimination on grounds of ethnic origin, and only indirectly invoke the protection of minority rights. Nonetheless, they demonstrate clearly the problems faced by members of minorities in Greece when dealing with the authorities (Psychogiopoulou 2008).[13]

The Status of Muslim Women in Greece

The preceding section indicated that the Greek legal order endorses unidimensional categorizations of the person and, accordingly, that it holds membership of the Muslim minority to be a common experience shared by all the minority members, regardless of their gender, ethno-linguistic background or social class. However, empirical research and case-law analysis demonstrate the contrary. The exclusion and subordination experienced by Muslim women in Greece is quite distinct from that suffered by the male members of the minority, since they face discrimination on

---

12   The ethno-linguistic composition of the minority is important because these groups, notwithstanding their common traits, form distinct communities with different social and economic statuses, different places of residence and different degrees of female emancipation. The Roma communities, for example, are by far the poorest and least-well educated group within the minority (probably in relation to Greek society as a whole), whereas the Pomaks are more attached to their traditions. In the sections below, I wish to stress the differentiated effects that certain discrimination practices have on members of different groups.

13   Some of the most recent cases before the European Court of Human Rights brought against Greece by members of minorities include *Sampanis and Others v. Greece*, Application No. 32526/05, Judgment of 5 June 2008; *Bekir-Ousta and Others v. Greece*, Application No. 35151/05, Judgment of 11 October 2007; *Ouranio Toxo and Others v. Greece*, Application No. 74989/01, ECHR 2005-X; and *Bekos and Koutropoulos v. Greece*, Application No. 15250/02, ECHR 2005-XIII.

three grounds: as Muslim minority members, as women and, finally, as Muslims and women. This section explores each of these grounds and the interaction between them that leads to compound and intersectional discrimination against Muslim women.

Marginalization of the Members of the Muslim Minority of Western Thrace

Notwithstanding the progress that has been achieved since the early 1990s in the field of human rights and equal citizenship for the Muslims of Western Thrace, the situation of the minority is still far from ideal. Marginalization and poverty, illiteracy and unemployment constitute the present situation of the minority. The barriers that restricted access to the villages along the Bulgarian border have been dismantled, but the Pomak villages of the mountainous north of Thrace remain isolated, if not physically, at least culturally and economically. Even in urban areas, the districts of Muslims and Christians are highly segregated and relations between the two communities are rare; inter-community marriages are almost unheard of. The main occupation of the Muslims of Thrace is agriculture and more specifically the cultivation of tobacco in small, household units as well as other manual and low-status jobs (Ribas Mateos 2000).[14]

Politically, the minority is underrepresented at both national and local level. The 1991 introduction of a 3 per cent threshold to enter the Parliament and the formulation in 1994 of two enlarged prefectures in Thrace, prevent – in practical terms – the election to the Parliament or as Prefect of any independent minority candidate and channel all minority political activity through the mainstream Greek parties which are usually reluctant, however, to assume the political cost of advancing minority demands. This marginalization of the minority from the Greek political scene enforces the ties of its members with Turkey and emphasizes the importance of internal political procedures of the minority such as the election of the 'unofficial' Mufti.

In the field of human rights, the situation of the Muslims of Western Thrace has improved in the past few years but violations are still reported by community members and NGOs. First, a significant group remains (estimated to be between 1,000 and 4,000 people) who lost their citizenship under Article 19 of the Citizenship Law and thus have limited access to social services (health, education, etc.) and the labour market (Human Rights Watch 1999), which in any event severely discriminates against Muslims. Second, members of the minority are still denied the right of self-identification and more precisely the right to identify themselves as members of a Turkish minority (Hellenic Ministry of Foreign Affairs 2007).[15] Other reported violations of human rights include disciplinary measures taken against several minority teachers for participating in a strike against the introduction of new books (compiled by the Greek State) for the teaching of the Turkish

---

14   There are, of course, differences between the three ethno-lingustic groups of the minority in terms of their labour market position. The Pomaks, especially those still living in their traditional villages, are occupied mostly in the agricultural sector, whereas there is an active and flourishing commercial class within the Turkish group. The Roma are by far the most marginalized group within the minority and they are occupied mostly in temporary manual work or begging activities (Troumpeta 2001: 106–7 and 169–75).

15   This was at issue in *Turkiki Enosi Xanthis (Turkish Association of Xanthi) and Others v. Greece*, Application No. 26698/05, Judgment of 27 March 2008. In that case, the Strasbourg Court ruled that the dissolution of the association concerned on the ground that its statute ran counter to public policy constituted a violation of Article 11 of the ECHR. The court held that use of the term 'Turkish' in the title of the association could not of itself constitute a danger to public policy. Furthermore, the court observed that even if the real aim of the association had been to promote the idea that there was an ethnic minority in Greece, this, too, could not be said to constitute a threat to a democratic society.

language in minority schools,[16] the refusal of the Pharmaceutical Association of Xanti to register Muslims unless they presented an official document issued by a Greek university proving their excellent command of the Greek language[17] and a refusal to treat degrees awarded by the Special Academy of Primary Education of Thessaloniki as equivalent to those awarded by other Schools of Primary Education of the Greek Universities.[18] In sum, the Muslim minority of Western Thrace suffers from marginalization and low social and economic status as a result of decades of unjust treatment and underdevelopment. Although members of the minority have managed to integrate into Greek society, the overall situation of the members of the minority indicates that they experience severe discrimination both at the hands of the official authorities and the Christian majority.

A Short Overview of the Position of Women in Greece

An extended analysis of gender roles in Greece would exceed the limits of this chapter. However, a short overview of the main features of the social status of women in Greece today is necessary in order to assess both the discrimination experienced by women of the minority when in contact with general Greek society and the gap between minority and majority women in terms of education, employment, political representation and legal status that has tended to broaden over the last two decades as gender inequalities have appeared to diminish or experience a transformation in Greece (Gonzalez et al. 2000). According to research on the political behaviour of Greek women carried out in 2005, 70 per cent of women and 84.2 per cent of men considered the position of women in Greek society as generally satisfactory, whereas in 1988 only 50.5 per cent of women and 58.6 per cent of men gave the same answer in a corresponding survey (Pantelidou-Malouta 2007). Two waves of legislation at national and European level in the early 1980s and in the early 2000s that abolished formal gender inequalities and promoted equality of opportunity ameliorated the formal status of women or at least rendered inequalities less visible.

In fact, gender equality was introduced into the Greek Constitution (Article 4(2)) in 1975 under the influence of International Women's Year. However, that development did not occur without debate, since many members of the Parliament opposed the idea that there was a need for a specific gender equality principle (Yotopoulou-Marangopoulou 1998: 774). Thus, it was not until 1998 that positive action measures for women, such as the introduction of a one-third quota for each of the sexes in public administration councils, were deemed to be constitutional on the basis of promoting factual equality between the sexes. Finally, at the 2001 revision of the Constitution, Article 116(2)

---

16   In accordance with a strike call issued by the Coordination Committee of the Highest Council of the Muslim Turkish Minority of Western Thrace on the ground that the books' content violated the autonomy of the Muslim Turkish minority, the teachers refused to attend a presentation of those books. As a consequence, they were dismissed. In reaching its decision to dismiss, the Disciplinary Board observed that the applicants had alleged that there was no legal equality for members of the minority in Western Thrace and hence it regarded them as the agents foreign powers. See *Molla Houseïn v. Greece*, Application No. 63821/00, Admissibility rejected 12 December 2002.

17   See Symvoulion tis Epikrateias (Council of State) Decision No. 156/1999 and *Tsingour v. Greece*, Application No 40437/98, Judgment of 6 July 2000.

18   In a recent recommendation, the Greek Ombudsman concluded that since members of the minority are indirectly channelled by official policies towards attending the Special Academy of Primary Education, whose graduates are employed as teachers in the minority primary schools of Thrace, the refusal to treat degrees awarded by the Special Academy as equivalent to those awarded by other Schools of Primary Education of the Greek Universities constitutes indirect discrimination against the members of the Muslim minority (Greek Ombudsman 2008).

which permitted certain derogations from gender equality was replaced by a provision allowing for positive measures aimed at promoting equality between men and women. Gender mainstreaming is now being implemented with an expanded jurisdiction for gender equality issues.

Nonetheless, gender roles in domestic life appear to be reproduced as younger women assume the same household tasks (cleaning, cooking, child-raising and caring for elders) as their mothers. The traditional Greek nuclear family is still the dominant model even though there has been a small increase in single-parent families and a much larger increase in divorces (an increase of 50 per cent between 1990 and 2003). The establishment in 1983 of a legal framework ensuring the formal equality of spouses, notwithstanding its undisputable legal and symbolic value, has still to be fully enforced in the daily lives of couples as traditional stereotypes on gender roles and the economic situation of women generally dictate the power relations within families (Stratigaki 2007: 76–82).

In the field of education, although the rate of women acquiring degrees is quite high (more than 50 per cent of all university graduates are women (Eurostat 2006)), their participation in academic jobs is still disproportionately low. Despite the remarkable increase in women's participation in academia since the 1960s (Vosniadou and Vaiou 2006), currently less than one-quarter of all university professors and lecturers in Greece are women (General Secretariat for Gender Equality 2005: 192). Women's participation in the labour market is also problematic: women are generally forced to juggle between traditional household tasks and their newly assumed role of income provider. Moreover, they are more willing to accept a part-time occupation and are thus occupied in less prestigious and demanding jobs, earn less and run a higher risk of unemployment. Many women work in small family businesses or farms, which only increases their dependence on their husbands and makes the distinction between paid and unpaid work for women even less visible. In any event, the unemployment rate for women in Greece is 2.5 times higher than for men and 6 per cent higher than the average European rate of women's unemployment (Eurostat 2006).

Domestic violence and sexual harassment are still not properly dealt with by the Greek State and society. Estimates on the proportion of women in Greece experiencing domestic physical and/or psychological violence vary between around 60 per cent (Artinopoulou et al. 2003) and 83 per cent (OMCT 2002). The recently adopted Law No. 3500/2006 on domestic violence, that criminalizes for the first time intrafamilial abuses such as marital rape, has been heavily criticized for a failure to distinguish between different forms and degrees of violence and its establishment of an out-of-court dispute settlement procedure offering perpetrators the opportunity to obtain an easy way out (Stratigaki 2007: 161–4). Even under this new legal framework women are generally discouraged from pursuing the criminal conviction of perpetrators because of the inadequacy of proper welfare facilities for the support of domestic violence victims and because of social and family pressure (OMCT 2004). In fact, many victims of domestic violence often do not even recognize the violent and illegal nature of the act committed. Estimates suggest that 70.5 per cent of women who define themselves as victims of marital rape and 62.9 per cent of those who have been physically abused by their husbands do not regard this abusive behaviour as violent (Artinopoulou et al. 2003: 103). In addition, Law No. 3488/2006 introducing the concept of sexual harassment in the Greek legal order has also met with criticism, in particular, in relation to the provisions shifting the burden of proof. Even though evidence suggests that about 10 per cent of working women in Greece have some personal experience of sexual harassment (Stratigaki 2007: 165), very few cases of sexual harassment have been brought before the competent authorities (Greek Ombudsman 2006, 2007), mainly because the victims fail to recognize the behaviour of the perpetrators as abusive or fear the career consequences of filing a complaint.

In the public domain, women are heavily underrepresented in all political decision-making bodies. In terms of the parliamentary representation of women, Greece ranks 23 among the 27 EU

Member States, with only 46 out of the 300 seats of the Greek Parliament (15.3 per cent) currently occupied by women (Inter-Parliamentary Union 2009), while only three of the 43 members of Government (ministers, alternate ministers and vice-ministers) are women. Notwithstanding the positive action measures adopted in the early 2000s in order to counter women's underrepresentation in the public realm (a one-third quota for the participation of each sex in candidates' lists for municipal and prefectoral elections, a measure that has recently been extended to parliamentary elections), the proportion of women who considered that they do not have equal opportunities with men in political life was greater in 2005 (67.9 per cent) than in 1988 (65 per cent) (Pantelidou-Malouta 2007).

The relative failure of the legislation and policies adopted during the last three decades to counter the discriminatory effects of the stereotypical gender roles embedded in Greek society may be regarded as a precursor for the inadequacies of the same policies in the case of Muslim women who live in a much more traditional and closed community and are legally excluded from the application of some of the most important aspects of equality law.

The Position of Muslim Women

The United Nations Committee on the Elimination of Discrimination Against Women (CEDAW 2002: 188) in its annual report 'expresses concern at the discrimination against minority women living in Greece … who suffer from double discrimination based on both their sex and ethnic background, in society at large and within their communities'. The disturbing remarks of all the NGOs and independent writers working on minority and/or women's rights issues depict in broad outline and sometimes in detail the inferior status of minority women in Greece today in comparison both to Muslim men and to majority (Christian) women. The discrimination experience of Muslim women is not, however, always simply the sum of the two experiences. The intersection of the traditional structure of Muslim communities and of the marginalization of the minority within Greek society in some cases produces a distinct dimension of disempowerment. Empirical data and legal research show that Muslim women suffer from compound or cumulative discrimination in the fields of employment, education, domestic violence and political representation, while they experience *stricto sensu* intersectional discrimination in matters of family and inheritance law because of the application of Islamic religious law (the Sharia).[19]

Gender roles in domestic life and in the labour market   The Muslim minority communities are structured in a highly traditional and patriarchal manner, even in comparison to general Greek society. Gender roles within both the family and community are fixed and considered an inextricable part of the traditional way of life which ties together the community; thus women who contest the given division of gender roles are thought of as lacking loyalty towards the community, whereas majority women are generally far more emancipated. Gender stereotypes are reproduced through

---

19   I am using here the terminological distinctions proposed by Makkonen (2002) and Hannett (2003), according to which three types of discrimination may be experienced by persons standing at the intersection of subordinated groups: discrimination on the basis of one or other ground at a time, which may be described as *multiple discrimination*, the result of the interaction of discriminatory practices (i.e. *compound* or *additive* or *cumulative discrimination*) and, finally, a unique form of discrimination because of the unique nature of their experience, which we might call *stricto sensu intersectional discrimination*. Even though the lines between the three types are not always clear, these distinctions are a useful tool in order to identify the different discriminatory effects experienced by Muslim women in Greece and thus address more effectively the problems they face.

social patterns of behaviour, such as the traditional headscarf, but also through the Turkish-language reading books taught in minority schools by teachers who are usually graduates of the two Islamic schools (Madrasahs) of the minority (Arabatzi 2008). In terms of personal relations, pre-arranged marriages, underage marriages and marriages by proxy are not rare. Indeed, cases of marriages of 13-year-old girls have been reported (Ktistakis 2006: 53) and marriages by proxy were a common practice under Islamic Law until they were banned by a circular issued by the Ministry of the Interior in 2002 (ibid.: 135).

According to the traditional division of roles, women are mostly confined to the household sphere while men are considered the income earners. Especially in rural communities, women have a dual role: they are care providers for children and elders but also participate in the traditional agricultural process under a strict division of labour governing male and female tasks (Asimakopoulou and Hristidou-Lionaraki 2002: 285–6). However, this model has been challenged by economic and social factors. The financial problems faced by the agrarian economy of Western Thrace over the last two decades caused considerable numbers of Muslim women, especially Pomaks, to enter the mainstream labour market. That entry, however, was accompanied by their proletarianization, since they are mostly employed on manual tasks in the agricultural or industrial sectors or as cleaning personnel. In practice, the majority of Muslim women in Thrace constitute a back-up labour force that is usually underpaid and uninsured (Troumpeta 2001: 104–6). Additionally, the internal migration of the Muslim population towards the cities of Thrace or Athens and Thessaloniki as a result of the economic situation in Western Thrace brought these women in closer contact with Greek society at large, challenging the traditional structure of their communities. Nonetheless, even in Athens, minority Muslims tend to form small, marginalized communities following the patterns of their traditional communities; stereotypical gender roles are still dominant and integration within Greek society is frowned upon (Hountoumadi 1998: 144–5).

Education   According to the terms of the Treaty of Lausanne, the Greek Government is obliged to provide the Muslim minority with primary school education in the Turkish language. The quality of the minority education in terms both of human resources and learning materials is not very high (Greek Ombudsman 2008) and the skills of the students graduating from minority primary schools are on average lower than those of their peers graduating from majority primary schools. In addition, even though there are around 200 secular minority primary schools in Western Thrace and two religious Islamic high schools (*madrasah*), only two secular minority high schools are currently functioning and thus places in secondary minority schools are scarce. The effect of this situation, however, falls disproportionately on women, since families hesitate to allow a female child to attend a majority (i.e. Christian) high school whereas they would be more flexible with a male child (Ribas Mateos 2000: 140; Asimakopoulou and Hristidou-Lionaraki 2002: 312).[20] This stems both from their unwillingness to have their daughters socializing with members of the Greek majority and from their desire to protect them from the experience of exclusion and discrimination that minority students often face in majority schools. Therefore, Muslim women are less likely to benefit from positive action measures aimed at the minority as a whole, such as the 0.5 per cent university entrance quota applied by the Greek Government, since a good command of the Greek language is one of the prerequisites for university entrance. In sum, minority women have been less well-educated than men for decades and thus have had lower skills and fewer opportunities in the

---

20   Roma Muslim women are less likely to attend even primary school and the large majority of them may be considered completely or at least functionally illiterate (Hountoumadi 1998: 96–103).

labour market. However, there appears to have been a shift over the last 10 years with an increase in the number of female Muslim students. Even though the percentage of minority students entering Greek universities remains below the national average, there appears to be an equal representation of both sexes among the minority university students, at least in some faculties (Karafyllis 2006).

Domestic violence and health issues   Although precise data are unavailable (OMCT 2002: 10), it is reported that Muslim women are often victims of domestic violence, in the form of physical or psychological abuse or marital rape, for reasons relating to their pre-arranged or underage marriages. However, the lack of social workers and efficient counselling centres for abused women in the area (Stratigaki 2007: 182–4), as well as the deeply rooted feelings of honour and shame that prevent domestic disputes from being discussed publicly, obscure the real dimensions of the problem and amplify the feelings of isolation experienced by these women.[21]

This contributes to the strikingly high rates of stress-related health problems reported among Muslim women both in rural and urban areas, which are related to the various financial and domestic problems they face, their inability to adapt to the modern way of urban life and the pressure put on them by the authoritative structure of their social environment (Hountoumadi 1998: 63–5; OMCT 2002: 17; Syrigos 2007: 43).

Additionally, according to Hountoumadi's research in the area of Metaxourgio, the average age of first childbirth among the 47 Muslim women interviewed was 16.3 years old, although in one case the first child was born as early as the age of 11. The rate of abortions is also very high (around 77.78 per cent for the minority women) and some women reported as many as 27 abortions (Hountoumadi 1998: 60–3).

Political underrepresentation   As far as the public realm is concerned, women's participation is not satisfactory in Greece in general (Greek Helsinki Monitor and Minority Rights Group 2006: 30–1). However, in the case of Muslim women their underrepresentation is much more pronounced than in the population at large. The exclusion of Muslim women from public life must be attributed to the patriarchal structure of minority society as well as to poor education and their insufficient command of the Greek language. Nevertheless, the latter factor cannot be blamed for the exclusion of women from intra-community political procedures such as elections for the appointment of a new Mufti. Following the pattern established in all the relevant previous elections since 1989, the most recent elections for the (unofficial) Mufti of Xanthi were held on 31 December 2006, the first day of the religious festival Kurban Bayrami during which women are not allowed to enter a mosque and as a result they were de facto excluded from the procedure (Hellenic Ministry of Foreign Affairs 2007; Soltaridis 2006).

In addition, among the 73 members of the unofficial but highly influential Consultative Committee of Western Thrace Turks, which comprises former or current members of Parliament and of local councils, the elected Muftis and the presidents of various minority institutions and associations, not more than five are women.[22] Moreover, nor is the active participation of minority women in the public sphere regularly endorsed by the majority mainstream media and political parties, with only few notable exceptions, such as the nomination by the Socialist Party (PA. SO.K.) of a Muslim Pomak woman, Gulbeyaz Karahasan, to be its candidate for the prefectural

---

21   Kimberlé Crenshaw (1991) offers an insightful approach to the issues of battered women of colour and immigrant women in the United States, demonstrating how different 'patterns of subordination intersect in women's experience of domestic violence'. Even though there is little field research on domestic violence in Greece, direct analogies can be made to the situation suffered by Muslim women of the minority.

22   The list of members is available on the Consultative Committee's website at www.bttadk.org.

elections of 2006 in the enlarged prefecture of Xanthi-Kavala. That choice provoked serious public controversies among majority opinion leaders at local and national level at the time and arguably it contributed more to increasing mutual distrust between the minority and the majority than to the politicization of minority women.

At any rate, Muslim women's underrepresentation in decision-making and political bodies both at minority level and at local or national level amplifies the effects of their marginalization and allows for the preservation of the given hierarchical structure of minority communities.

Application of the Sharia   The application of Islamic Sacred Law to all family and inheritance disputes of Muslim Greek citizens (but in practice even to non-Greek Muslims who reside in Greece (Ktistakis 2006: 42–7)) constitutes a distinct form of discrimination against the women of the minority of Western Thrace. The intersection of the grounds of discrimination against Muslim women in Greece produces a unique form of disempowerment, that is mainly the result but also one of the pillars of the traditional patriarchal structure of the minority communities.

Although the Muftis of Western Thrace follow the most liberal and rationalist of Fiqh (Islamic Law) Schools, the Hanafi School (Munir n.d.), measured against Western standards of human rights, the provisions of Islamic law on family and inheritance matters are highly discriminatory towards women. First, men have an unconditional right to divorce, whereas women may only apply for a divorce in specific cases (e.g. sterility, mental illness). Where a wife files for divorce with her husband's consent (*khul*), she is expected to waive her rights to the three-month period of alimony (*nafaqah*) and to the 'divorce endowment' (*nikāh*). Although the practice of *talaq* (the unilateral right of men to divorce by repudiation) is quite rare among Greek Muslims, it is not totally unheard of. Second, polygamy as well as underage marriages or marriages by proxy are not prohibited. In relation to bigamy, the criminal courts of Thrace considered until recently that Muslims were exempt from the application of the general prohibition of polygamy under the Greek penal code, because Islamic family law does not prohibit that status, as was confirmed by a *fetwa* (opinion issued on the interpretation of the Islamic Law) of the Mufti of Komotini. Nonetheless, polygamy is not considered to be common practice among Greek Muslims and is now regarded as punishable by the criminal courts. Third, the custody of boys until the age of seven and that of girls until the age of nine is given to the mother. From that age on their custody remains with the father (Kotzampasi 2003: 70). Finally, according to Islamic laws of inheritance male descendants are entitled to twice the inheritance of female descendants of the same kinship. In practice, however, the members of the minority tend to avoid the application of the Sharia when it comes to inheritance matters preferring instead to make lifetime transfers of property to their children or to turn to the civil courts (Ktistakis 2006: 82).

It is easy to comprehend that application of the Sharia in the context of the *sui generis* judicial system enjoyed by the Muslim minority results in oppression of minority women. However, with the exception of some lone Greek judges, this view is not endorsed by State officials and mainstream jurisprudence who insist on identifying the interests of the minority with the interests of the privileged group of male Muslims included within that community.[23] The violation of the

---

23   According to recent research, out of a total of 2,679 relevant court decisions issued from 1991 to 2006 only one refused to uphold a Mufti's ruling by reason of a violation of sex equality law and, even in that case, when the Mufti rephrased his ruling in order to render the violation less obvious, ultimately, the Mufti's decision was upheld by the court (Ktistakis 2006: 118–19). This unanimous refusal of the Greek courts in fact to review the constitutionality of Muftis' rulings, despite their obligation to do so, confirms the de facto reluctance of Greek authorities to interfere with the 'internal issues' of the minority and enforce the constitutional rights of its members.

general principle of equality is hailed as a sign of respect for the traditional rights and practices of the minority and the violation of gender equality is ignored or silenced.[24] Strategic litigation (see European Roma Rights Centre 2004) before the European Court of Human Rights, an approach that has proven successful for the promotion of other minority issues in Greece, has not been pursued yet in relation to minority women, even though favourable case law of the Strasbourg Court already exists. For example, in *Refah Partisi (the Welfare Party) and Others v. Turkey*, it held in relation to the dissolution of that political party that 'some of [its] objectives, such as the introduction of Sharia and a theocratic regime, were incompatible with the requirements of a democratic society'.[25] In fact, the only time women from the minority raised a claim before the Court, the complaint concerned a violation of their right to self-identify[26] (Anagnostou and Psychogiopoulou 2008: 8–9), and therefore they acted as class representatives for the entire minority.

The situation of the minority women set out earlier offers an explanation of the complexity of the problem: low education and lack of financial resources limit Muslim women's awareness of their rights and their access to lawyers and courts. In addition, any claim contesting the Sharia would be considered a challenge to the foundations of the community's identity and any woman who dared to bring such a claim before the courts would become an outcast from her community, in practice her only safety net, as Greek society considers all Muslims as foreigners or, worse still, enemies. Finally, Muslim women's exclusion from all intra-community political procedures and their underrepresentation in local and national decision-making bodies lead to the marginalization of all public discourse on the issue and keep women's demands low down on the political agenda of the minority rights movement. The State negotiates with the minority, turning a blind eye to the fact that its counterpart is exclusively the dominant group within the minority and hence reinforces its domination. The authorities accept the preservation of legal institutions, such as the Muftis and the application of the Sharia, and of social structures that would be considered inappropriate for Greek society at large under the pretext of a communitarian approach to the minority issue. At the same time, the conservative establishment of the minority resists the implementation of gender equality agendas that would probably lead to the emancipation of women (Meço 2007).

Concluding Remarks

The compound nature of discrimination experienced by the women of the Muslim minority in Greece is usually not taken into consideration by the authorities when dealing with problems

---

24 During the 37th Session of the Committee on the Elimination of Discrimination against Women, when questioned on the situation of Muslim women the representatives of Greece stated that 'Greece does not have parallel or separate legal orders. The civil code is binding on all citizens. The Government allows minorities to choose traditional legal systems in family and inheritance matters, but only when the outcomes do not contradict fundamental Greek values and the Greek constitutional order and laws. Various practices allowed under Muslim religious law, such as polygamy, underage marriage, marriage by proxy and repudiation of a spouse, are forbidden under Greek law' (CEDAW 2007). In fact, as was mentioned above, Greek courts systematically avoid reviewing the constitutionality of Muftis' rulings and only recently the Areios Pagos confirmed that the Islamic Law of inheritance governs the hereditary relations of Greek Muslims to the exclusion of the provisions of the Greek Civil Code.

25 *Refah Partisi (the Welfare Party) and Others v. Turkey*, Application Nos 41340/98, 41342/98, 41343/98, and 41344/98, ECHR 2003-II.

26 *Emin and Others (Cultural Association of Turkish Women of the Region of Rodopi) v. Greece*, Application No. 34144/05, Judgment of 27 March 2008.

concerning their legal and socio-economic status. For example, the only reference to the distinct problems of Muslim women in any of the gender equality policies and programmes adopted by the General Secretariat for Gender Equality (GSGE) is the fact that implementation of the project 'Comprehensive Interventions in Favour of Women' carried out by GSGE in the country's 13 administrative regions benefited, among others, 'Muslim women in the context of the implementation of the Action Plan in the region of Eastern Macedonia-Thrace' (General Secretariat for Gender Equality 2008). Equally, the only epidemiological research on domestic violence conducted throughout Greece (Artinopoulou et al. 2003) makes no reference to Muslim women as a distinct and perhaps more vulnerable group of the female population of Greece and the methodological data indicates that no particular efforts were made to include Muslim women in the statistical sample.

Trina Grillo (1995: 22) observes that the first lesson that 'the anti-essentialism and intersectionality critiques teach us [is] to look carefully at what is in front of our faces'. What is in front of our faces in this case is the particular situation of Muslim women in Greece, a situation of oppression on grounds of their dual identity. Attempts to dismantle this identity only obscure the real problem, as the two oppressions reinforce each other to produce a unique result. However, Greek authorities tend to see the problems faced by Muslim women through the lens of mutually exclusive grounds of discrimination. The results of this approach are disappointing. Gender equality policies do not reach the minority and minority rights policies lacking gender sensitivity have no effect on the status of women.

Evidently, as there are few chances for a movement to emerge from within the minority, given the political and socio-economic marginalization of Muslim women, the push for change must come from broader society. The essential first step is the recognition of Muslim women's distinct identity as a precondition for the enactment of policies focused on the specific problems of intersectional discrimination which they face. In this context, the recent decision of the Single-Member First Instance Court of Rodopi (Decision No. 9/2008) must be considered a milestone. In that case, the first instance court held, at variance with the case law of the Supreme Court,[27] that where the Islamic Law of inheritance conflicts with fundamental Constitutional rights, the Greek State is obliged to guarantee to its female Muslim citizens the application of their civil rights. The judgment is significant because it goes beyond the typical categorization followed by Greek courts (under which only one-dimensional groups are identified, such as women, disabled persons, members of a minority) and succeeds in identifying Muslim women as a social group that stands at the intersection of discrimination. Even though multidimensional equality was not expressly mentioned, the court applied the principle of gender equality to the case on the ground that application of the Sharia was discriminatory towards the litigant because of her status as a Muslim *and* as a woman. In this manner, the judgment introduced the Muslim minority woman's identity into the Greek legal order and thus managed to offer a new (multidimensional) perspective to the treatment of discrimination experienced by Muslim women in Greece.

In a very recent notable about turn, the Greek Government indicated its willingness to 'study any possible readjustments, such as the abolition of the Sharia law, taking hereby into account the legal obligations as well as the potential changes of the wishes of the Muslim minority' (Hammarberg 2009: Appendix). The abolition of the Sharia will not by itself dramatically change the position of Muslim women, but it will be a strong symbolic move towards the recognition of their equal status within Greek and minority society. This shift of policy, along with court decisions such as the one mentioned above, will help revitalize public debate in Greece in relation to minority rights and the

---

27   See Areios Pagos (Supreme Court of Civil Law) Decision No. 1097/2007.

extent to which the State should intervene in minority affairs, and will hopefully also stimulate discussion concerning the intersectional nature of discrimination suffered by Muslim women and by other multiply subordinated groups, such as immigrant or Roma women.

Chapter 9

Minorities' Right to Day Care: Liberal Tolerance or Identity Maintenance?

Kevät Nousiainen

Prologue

In December 2008, the Finnish Ombudsman for Minorities brought two cases to the National Discrimination Tribunal.[1] In the first case, she claimed that the municipality of Enontekiö had not organized services, including day care for children, in a Sámi language even though the municipality is located in the Sámi Homeland, where the language enjoys special protection as a minority language. In the second case, concerning the city of Rovaniemi, she claimed that the city had discriminated in the organization of day care for Sámi children, who have an equal right with Finnish-speaking children to day care in their mother tongue.

In both cases, the Tribunal found that the municipalities had discriminated against the Sámi population on the grounds of their ethnic origin by failing to provide day care for Sámi children in their native language. Both municipalities claimed that, in practice, it had proved impossible to find professionally qualified day care personnel with the required language skills and, in addition, that the number of children needing the service was extremely small. In Enontekiö, the care of two children in particular was a contested issue, as the municipality had proposed that they attend a 'day home' located almost 70 kilometres away from home. A judicial review of the decisions is now underway.[2]

Introduction

The provision of day care in minority languages involves various types of rights, especially cultural and social ones, which should be enjoyed without discrimination. The starting point of this chapter is that the right to day care, as a social and cultural right, concerns minority women in specific ways which involve intersectional discrimination. Ethnic, national and linguistic discrimination are often closely related. Although children are born to men and women, day care for children is usually considered as of special interest to women. The underlying assumption is that, lacking day care, mothers will care for their children at home and, thus, are prevented from seeking paid employment. Provision of day care is believed to reduce discrimination against women. For example,

---

1 Unfortunately, there are two translations into English of *syrjintälautakunta*, the body in question. The body itself calls itself the Discrimination Tribunal, whereas the translation of the pieces of legislation on which the body is based calls it the Discrimination Board. The body has the authority to prohibit discriminatory practice with the threat of a conditional fine. Its decision is not final but can be challenged before an ordinary court.

2 Decision by the National Discrimination Tribunal of 5 December 2008 concerning the city of Rovaniemi and of 17 December 2008 concerning the municipality of Enontekiö. The decisions are available in Finnish on the website of the Tribunal at www.intermin.fi.

the United Nations (UN) Convention on the Elimination of All Forms of Discrimination against Women (CEDAW Convention) requires that state parties prevent discrimination against women on the grounds of marriage or maternity by encouraging the provision of 'the necessary supporting social services to enable parents to combine family obligations with work responsibilities' through promoting the establishment of child-care facilities (Article 11(2)).

European equality policies emphasize the need to integrate women, including immigrant women, into the labour market. Minority populations meet various obstacles in accessing employment, lack of day care for children being one of them, which disproportionally affects women. The claim that day care must be provided to persons belonging to a minority group without discrimination concerns the right of the parents to paid employment and, thus, is a justice claim of a socially distributive kind.

The main issue in the two cases presented in the Prologue is not merely distribution of resources, but recognition of the right to maintain a minority culture and identity. Politics of recognition require that public institutions assure individuals the right to express their identity, and in so doing ensure the survival of a specific cultural group (Taylor 1992). In this sense, politics of recognition are 'identity politics', which may be problematic for women and gender equality, by burdening women with cultural reproduction of the nation or ethnic group (Yuval-Davis and Anthias 1989) and collapsing their identity into that of the group (Yuval-Davies 2006).

This chapter aims to demonstrate that the provision of day care in minority languages may be regarded as a good evoking both social and cultural rights of minorities. Non-discrimination itself is clearly not sufficient to guarantee provision of day care, especially in a form which is suited to the needs of minorities. However, cultural rights are structured in a hierarchical manner, such that 'old' minorities have a stronger claim to access services aimed at maintaining the culture of the group, whereas the 'new' minorities' right of accommodation is weaker and not intended to nurture multiculturalism. In order to avoid different degrees of disadvantage at the intersection of gender and ethnicity for women of different minorities, a balanced approach to these hierarchies is necessary. The more general aim of the chapter is to draw attention to the fact that prevention of intersectional discrimination on the basis of gender and ethnicity (minority language) requires effective social and cultural rights.

The chapter uses Finland as an example on the grounds of its unique status as a country between East and West and the existence of a statutory right to children's day care. The chapter will first outline the politics of minority protection in Finland, and summarize the different social and legal situation of different linguistic minorities. It will then present the different position with regard to children's day care in those languages against the background of the relevance for minority women. The conclusion will highlight the relevance of this national case for more fundamental issues.

Finnish Minority Protection as a Matter of Human and Constitutional Rights

Ethnic Relations in a Country between East and West

Finland gained independence from the Russian Empire in 1917 and, thus, belongs to the states formed in the reshaping of Eastern Europe after the First World War. Many of these states showed great ethnic diversity, although ethnic unity was an important factor in legitimating their independence. Minority rights were included in treaties with the defeated powers, and the supervision of minority rights was given to the League of Nations. The system failed when the League did (Jackson Preece 1998: 67–94; Fink 2004). Finnish minority policies reflected the trend, as the position of two languages, Finnish and Swedish, was regulated by international treaties on the Åland Islands, and the two 'national' languages gained constitutional protection.

After the Second World War, anti-discrimination policy not minority rights became the main means of combating group-based disadvantage. Only following the end of the Cold War, did minority protection return to the agenda in Eastern Europe (Greer 2006: 30–1). Finland was an exception among the 'new' European states created after the First World War, not being drawn into the Socialist bloc after the Second World War. The main aim of Finnish foreign policy after the war, to remain neutral in relation to the divisions between the Western and Eastern blocs, was regarded as preventing it from joining 'Western' organizations. Thus, Finland joined the Council of Europe only after the collapse of the Soviet Union, and became a member of the EU in 1995. Until then, the main impulse for human rights protection came from the United Nations. Until the 1970s, Finland was a country of emigration, and throughout the Cold War era immigration to Finland remained limited.

In post-Socialist Eastern Europe, mobilization of linguistic minorities led to outbreaks of ethnic conflicts, which in turn led several international organizations to seek standards for linguistic diversity. An interest in language policies became evident in political theory, which had until then concentrated on race and religion (Kymlicka and Patten 2003: 3–4). A further outcome of the political turn was the introduction of new international law instruments for minority protection. Finland also ratified a number of these instruments and, thus, is one of the few EU-15 states with minority rights legislation resulting, in part, from obligations under international or multilateral treaties. Among the European human rights instruments that Finland joined and ratified in the 1990s were two conventions of the Council of Europe: the European Charter of Regional or Minority Languages and the Council of Europe's Framework Convention for the Protection of National Minorities, both ratified in 1998 (SopS (Treaty series of the statute book) 1/1998 and 149/1998). On ratification, Finland did not specify which population groups were to be considered national minorities under these instruments. In practice, Finland has submitted information on the Sámi, the Roma, Jews, Tatars, Old Russians and the Swedish-speaking minority in its reports to monitoring bodies.

International Law Obligations

Since 1990, several international organizations have aimed at better international protection for the cultural rights of minorities, among them the Council of Europe and the Organisation for Security and Cooperation in Europe (OSCE), also known as the 'Helsinki Process'. The parties to the European Charter of Regional or Minority Languages of 1992 commit themselves to protecting languages that are traditionally used by a minority group within a 'given territory' by nationals of the state in question. The languages of migrants are explicitly excluded. The state parties must provide pre-school education 'within the territory in which such languages are used, according to the situation of each of these languages, and without prejudice to the teaching of the official language(s) of the State'. They also undertake to ensure that the regional or minority language is used in providing public services, as far as this is 'reasonably possible' (Article 10(3)).

The Council of Europe's Framework Convention for the Protection of National Minorities of 1995 also protects minorities, especially within the public sphere. Under Article 14 of that convention, the state parties undertake to recognize the right of persons belonging to a minority to 'learn his or her minority language'. Where minority persons inhabit an area 'traditionally or in substantial numbers', provided there is sufficient demand, the parties must 'endeavour to ensure, as far as possible and within the framework of their education systems, that minorities have adequate access to minority language tuition', as well as to learning the official language.

In its Helsinki Decisions of July 1992, the OSCE established a High Commissioner on National Minorities to prevent conflicts. At the Commissioner's request, a group of experts prepared the Hague Recommendations regarding the education rights of national minorities (High Commissioner on National Minorities 1996). The Recommendations stress the importance of acquiring a proper knowledge of the mother tongue in the educational process, whilst noting the responsibility of minorities to integrate into the wider national society and to acquire language skills in the national language. According to the Recommendations, education rights should be used proactively, and a maximum of the available resources allocated to minority language education. Minorities should be able to participate in the implementation of minority education programmes and have the right to establish their own private educational institutions under domestic law. The Recommendations also maintain that the first years of education are of pivotal importance in a child's development, and therefore teaching at pre-school and kindergarten levels should ideally be in the child's language (Recommendation No. 11). The standards of the Hague Recommendations are vague and general 'in view of the delicate nature of this issue'.

On the whole, international human rights norms allow state parties much discretion in establishing what level of accommodating minority culture is reasonable. There are no fixed criteria in international law to determine when language preference is discriminatory. However, the size of the linguistic minority and its territorial concentration will constitute relevant factors. Human rights instruments stress the need to safeguard minorities in encounters with public authorities and not in the provision of everyday services such as day care. The language rights connected to education and day care aim towards the maintenance of minority culture and language but, at the same time, seek to ensure that minority children are not excluded from participation in the political, social and economic life of a nation-state for lack of skills in the dominant language. A distinction exists between the cultural rights of immigrants and those of 'old' minorities, but no definition of what constitutes an 'old' minority is given. Indigenous groups are entitled to more extensive self-determination and protection of traditions than other minorities.

Linguistic rights have concentrated on 'old' minorities and remain unclear on the normative distinction between claims on behalf of immigrant languages and the established minorities within the host society (Patten 2001: 694). Language policies have different aims: language rationalization, through making access to the dominant language easier by relying on the principles of tolerance and equal treatment, or active maintenance of minority languages, which treats speakers of different languages as equals, entitled to similar means of identity formation (ibid.: 699). The former policy aims at integrating minorities and is targeted towards immigrants; the latter policy protects multiculturalism in relation to established old minorities. Language of education may be of crucial importance both to the maintenance of vulnerable languages and to integration or assimilation into the dominant culture. Language used in children's day care is a particularly sensitive issue, because it may operate as a substitute for learning one's 'mother tongue' from one's mother.

Some argue that an emphasis on language rights and identity politics led many East European EU Member States to recognize ethnic minorities and their languages, while few states among the 'old' EU Member States have legal instruments for the protection of the culture, traditions and languages of minority groups. On the other hand, in the 'new' Member States anti-discrimination policy is a relatively new issue, introduced as a condition for EU membership. As immigration in the 'new' states has been low, 'old' ethnic minorities rather than immigrants are the focus of interest. In the 'old' Member States, the most important legal instruments that concern the position of minorities are those that regulate immigration through residence rights. Moreover, differences in the legal status of ethnic minorities are a relevant factor in explaining the access of these groups to social services and the labour market (Corsi et al. 2008: 9–12). Both protection of 'old' minority groups and a growing need for effective policies to integrate new immigrant groups are relevant in the Finnish context, because Finland has become an immigration country since the 1990s.

Constitutional Protection of Minority Rights and Equality

A major reform of the Finnish Constitution undertaken in 1995 and 1999 reflected a changed attitude to human rights. The chapter on fundamental rights was reformulated to protect all persons instead of merely Finnish citizens. The provision on equality was amended from one referring to citizens' formal equality before the law into one that aims at guaranteeing not merely formal but also substantive equality to all. The constitution now includes a new subsection on discrimination, with an open-ended list of prohibited grounds including, amongst others, sex, 'origin' and language. According to the preparatory works, origin covers national and ethnic origin, colour and, thus, race. Another subsection with a provision on the promotion of equality of the sexes was also added.

On the other hand, anti-discrimination law covering grounds other than gender is a late development under Finnish law. Ratification of the CEDAW Convention coincided with the introduction of gender anti-discrimination law in 1986. Although Finland had ratified the UN ICERD Convention (International Convention on the Elimination of All Forms of Racial Discrimination) in 1970 prior to its ratification of the CEDAW Convention, that earlier ratification did not lead to anti-discrimination law proper. Only the need to comply with the minimum requirements set by the EU finally motivated Finland to enact anti-discrimination law covering grounds other than gender.

At present, Finland has a twin-track system of anti-discrimination policy with two different pieces of legislation and different monitoring bodies. Dealing with intersectional discrimination involving gender and some other prohibited ground is complicated by the division of powers between the equality bodies. Discrimination based on gender is prohibited by the Act on Equality between Women and Men (Act 608/1986), monitored by the Ombudsman for Equality. The Non-Discrimination Act (Act 21/2004) prohibits discrimination on the basis of age, ethnic or national origin, nationality, language, religion, belief, opinion, health, disability, sexual orientation or other personal characteristics. Occupational safety and health authorities monitor compliance with the Act in employment matters, while provisions on discrimination based on ethnic origin in situations outside of employment are supervised by the Ombudsman for Minorities and the Discrimination Tribunal. The two cases on Sámi rights described in the Prologue were initiated by the Ombudsman for Minorities. The Ombudsman and the Discrimination Tribunal regarded access to language rights as a matter of ethnic discrimination, and indeed these bodies have no explicit powers to consider discrimination based on language or gender notwithstanding the fact that both the constitutional provision on discrimination and the Non-Discrimination Act explicitly refer to language as a prohibited ground of discrimination.

The Hierarchy of Finnish Language Protection

The Finnish constitutional reform retained the position of the two national languages, Finnish and Swedish, but introduced as a novelty provisions on the cultural rights of certain minority groups: the Sámi, the Romani and persons who use sign language (placing sign language on a par with other 'natural' languages). The status of the Sámi as an indigenous people is mentioned, and the Sámi are guaranteed an individual right of access to authorities in their own language.

A further constitutional novelty was the grant of linguistic and cultural self-government to the Sámi in their 'native region'.

The constitutional reform clearly necessitated amendments to language legislation, which in general is oriented towards provision of public administrative services. The Language Act[3] regulates the use of the two national languages: Swedish and Finnish. The Act on Sámi Language[4] contains provisions on the right to use Sámi mainly before the courts and other public authorities, to ensure a fair trial and good administration in the three northernmost municipalities in Finland (the Sámi Homeland). It aims at enhancing language skills of authorities dealing with those speaking Sámi in one of three varieties of the language (Inari, Skolt and Northern Sámi). The authorities have a duty to offer their services in the language of the client. Specific legislation covers language use in educational, media and cultural institutions, in connection with the rights of patients and social welfare clients, as well as in pre-trial and trial situations. A person's right to use languages other than the national ones in dealings with public authorities whether at trial or in an administrative context is based mainly on a right to interpretation, rather than the ability of officials to speak those languages.

Linguistic rights in education are mainly governed by the Basic Education Act,[5] which provides for basic education and compulsory schooling. Municipalities are required to organize basic education, based on a national core curriculum. In bilingual communities education is to be provided separately for both national language groups, either in Finnish or Swedish, but in the Sámi Homeland pupils who are proficient in Sámi are to be taught primarily in that language. Sámi, Romani or sign language may be used in teaching in addition to Finnish and Swedish. The Act on Day Care[6] decrees that municipalities must arrange day care in Finnish, Swedish and Sámi, but the provision does not specify the obligation further. The Act on State Subsidies to Municipalities[7] provides for a higher level of subsidies to municipalities with bilingual populations where the languages involved are Finnish, Swedish and Sámi, but not on the basis of other languages. An administrative decree on day care of 1995 contains a positive duty on municipalities, in cooperation with representatives of the relevant culture, to take account of Sámi, Romani and immigrant languages and culture in day care. However, the provision is not backed by sanctions.

The legal status of minority languages in Finland varies greatly, therefore, from national minority language (Swedish), to regional minority language in the context of self-government (Sámi in the Sámi Homeland and Swedish in the province of Åland), to 'old' minority languages of Roma and sign language, and further to all other languages protected merely through non-discrimination provisions. The number of speakers of a language does not directly correlate with its status, which is defined instead in terms related to the aims of linguistic policies: bilingualism, maintenance of vulnerable 'old' languages, and tolerance regarding the languages of newcomers.

The strong position of Swedish in Finland is rooted in Finland's history of having been ruled by Sweden for long periods. This also explains the generally high social status of Swedish speakers, and the peculiar autonomous status of the province of Åland, where Swedish is the only official language. Notwithstanding the relatively small number of Swedish speakers (now less than 300,000 in Finland) in comparison to native Finnish speakers (approximately 4.7 million in Finland), traditionally, Finnish language legislation has required that officials have linguistic qualifications in two official languages and that the cultural and economic needs of both language groups are

---

3 Act 423/2003.
4 Act 1086/2003.
5 Act 628/1998.
6 Acr 361/1973.
7 Act 1147/1996.

satisfied on a similar basis. Finnish- and Swedish-speaking populations must receive services in their own language on equal terms. Language education remains a sore point especially due to the requirement that all pupils must learn two other languages besides their native tongue, with one of the two being the 'second national' language. In practice, most native Finnish speakers take the shortest course possible in Swedish, while most Swedish speakers take a much longer course in Finnish. Increased immigration has made it necessary to introduce language tuition in Finnish and Swedish for non-native speakers of both these languages. This strong claim for bilingualism is claimed to complicate the integration of immigrants.

The Sámi are considered an indigenous people, settled since prehistoric times in the Arctic area that is now the territory of three Nordic states and Russia. Originally fishers and hunters, many Sámi later specialized in reindeer herding. Assimilation occurred in all the states mentioned. In Finland, compulsory education in Finnish weakened the Sámi languages. Linguistic assimilation of the Sámi through education occurred also because attending school often involved living away from home in the extremely sparsely populated northern area. The reforms since 1990s have empowered the Sámi identity, but no real change has taken place in the number of officials able to speak the language (Näkkäläjärvi 2006).

In 1999, the number of persons who spoke the three different Sámi languages spoken in Finland (Northern, Inari and Skolt Sámi) was 1,739, 299 and 386, respectively. The majority of those entitled to vote in the Sámi Parliament[8] elections spoke Finnish as their first language (Näkkäläjärvi 2006: 26), and the majority of the registered Sámi live outside the Sámi Homeland.

Of all the minorities residing in Finland, the Sámi have expressed most clearly the wish to develop a transnational (or trans-Nordic) self-determination which surpasses nation-state boundaries. The ideology supporting these claims is tinged with identity politics which refer to the traditional way of life of the Sámi population. The smallness of the group, its dispersal outside the Sámi region and the limited career choices offered by the tradition weaken the impact of identity politics. The emphasis on the traditional values of the community makes women in particular the bearers of cultural values,[9] encumbering them with expectations that may well conflict in many ways with their personal right to self-determination. The demand for public provision of child-care services that respect Sámi traditions and transmit their languages can be seen as an outcome of the tension between cultural aspirations and equality rights.

The Roma, who arrived in Finland from the seventeenth century onwards, are now estimated at 10,000 in Finland, with some 3,000 Finnish Roma who live in Sweden. The Finnish Roma identify as an 'old' Finnish minority and as Finns (Suomen romanit 2004: 3). The Roma are a visible minority, with women in particular wearing traditional dress. Municipalities were given a positive duty to provide the Roma with adequate housing, and state loans for that purpose in the 1970s. The Roma population settled down mainly in the larger cities, but since municipal housing has lately been often outsourced to private companies, the Roma complain of increasing problems in access to housing (ibid.: 9). The use of the Roma language has diminished since 1970s,

---

8   The Sámi Parliament is the self-government body of the Finnish Sámi. It represents the Sámi in international contexts (Act 974/1995) and negotiates with national authorities on issues that have an impact on the position of the Sámi. The statistics reported above have been compiled by that institution.

9   The Declaration from the first Sami Parlamentarian conference issued in Jokkmokk on 24 February 2005 stresses an obligation to recognize Sami indigenous rights and culture, particularly traditional industries such as reindeer herding, hunting and fishing and other nature-based industries (Sami Parliamentarian Conference 1995). Point 8 of the declaration states that Sami women are 'bearers of fundamental values and know-how'. For women's reactions to that culture, see the dialogues with Sámi writers in Helander and Kailo (1998).

and today families often speak a mixture of Roma and Finnish, making it difficult for children to develop adequate language skills in either language (ibid.: 11). Women traditionally have a subordinate position,[10] but since intra-group relations are not readily discussed, complaints are not often heard in public. Discrimination against the Roma is overt and frequent, and the minority is both socially and culturally disadvantaged. In policies on the Roma, an emphasis on cultural rights largely replaced the former stress on social welfare in the 1990s, but neither policy has removed discrimination. A recent report and policy document pays attention to both the social and cultural rights of the Roma and stresses both pre-school and school education (Finnish Ministry of Social Affairs and Health 2009).

As immigrants enjoy no specific cultural rights, the protection of immigrant minorities relies mainly on anti-discrimination policy. Until the 1990s, Finland was a land of emigration not immigration. The first report on Finland by the European Commission against Racism and Intolerance (ECRI) in 1997 paid attention to the change in migration flows. From a country of emigration, Finland had become a destination for immigrants. Since the fall of the Soviet Union, as a result of its geographical position on the border between Eastern and Western Europe, the country had received numerous immigrants from Russia. A high level of intolerance was detected in Finland, a country of relatively few non-citizens, with the authorities having had little training to cope with immigration (ECRI 1997).

Although the number of people of immigrant origin still remains relatively low compared with many Western European states, it is rapidly growing. Between 1994 and 2007, some 190,000 immigrants acquired Finnish citizenship, while around 133,000 residents or 2.5 per cent of the population held foreign citizenship in 2007. The number of children and young people who are native speakers of languages other than the two national languages has risen accordingly. In 2006, the number of such children below school age was estimated at 12,000 with those of compulsory school age numbering some 17,000 (Finnish National Board of Education 2008). Most immigrants come from European and EU countries, with the biggest single country of origin being the Russian Federation.

Russian speakers in Finland are not a homogeneous group, and in Finnish official policies there has been a tendency to separate them into 'old' and 'new' Russians. The 'old' group is quite small, as the number of Russian speakers in the nineteenth century and in the first decades following independence in 1917 was low (Advisory Board for Ethnic Relations 2002: 8). During the Second World War (during which Finland was at war with the Soviet Union), 63,000 Soviet citizens who were ethnic Finns (so-called Ingrians) were transferred from the Leningrad area to Finland, but the majority of them were returned to the Soviet Union at the demand of Soviet authorities after the war. During the decades after the Second World War until the 1990s, Russian immigration to Finland was limited, in practice, to persons marrying a Finn. After the fall of the Soviet Union, a new influx of Russian-speaking immigrants arrived, consisting of three groups: Ingrians and others categorized as Finns by the Soviet authorities and treated in Finland as repatriates, persons of Russian ethnicity emigrating for family or work reasons, and people of other ethnic backgrounds who are Russian native speakers (Hannikainen 2003).

Many Ingrians whose official Soviet ethnicity was Finnish had little or no language skills in Finnish. Arriving in Finland in the midst of the deep economic depression of the early 1990s, they found integration difficult (Nylund-Oja and Pentikäinen 1997). In 2003, the Finnish Parliament

---

10   Miranda Vuolasranta, a Finnish Roma activist and vice-president of the European Platform for the Roma, has at various points referred to the disadvantages met by the Roma women both due 'external' discrimination, but also due to the traditional power structure within the Roma communities.

extended the requirement of a basic knowledge of Finnish or Swedish for a residence permit to the Ingrian immigrants (Advisory Board for Ethnic Relations 2002: 10). In 2006, Russian-speaking immigrants constituted about 40 per cent of the total immigrant population. The number of Russian speakers rose from less than 4,000 in 1990 to over 45,000 in 2007 (Statistics Finland 2007).

A national survey in 2003 showed that Russians were amongst the least welcome of the various immigrant groups in Finland. Russians (or Russian speakers) are not a visible minority in terms of colour or other similar markers of ethnicity. Antagonism and distrust that marked the Finnish–Russian relations in the past are reflected in the negative attitudes of Finns towards Russian immigrants (Jasinskaja-Lahti et al. 2006; Raittila 2004). Estonian and Russian immigration is also linked to crime and prostitution in public discourse (Raittila 2004) which is a cause of stigmatization (Jasinskaja-Lahti et al. 2006). The negative attitudes of the majority seem deeply ingrained, showing little change over time. Lately, the support given by Russian political leaders to Russian-speaking groups in neighbouring states in conflict situations has probably made neighbouring states wary of those groups, regarding them as possible catalysts for future conflict.

A follow-up study of a group of Russian immigrants concerning their identification with their ethnic group and national identity showed that perceived ethnic discrimination led to national disidentification. Perceived discrimination predisposes individuals to perceiving further discrimination, with a vicious circle developing. Therefore, combating racism and prejudice and creating a context which enables positive inter-group encounters between immigrants and host nationals should be a political priority (Jasinskaja-Lahti et al. 2009: 124).

The Right to Minority Language Day Care for Children in Finland

Public Provision of Day Care for Children

Day care for children remains at the margins of recognized linguistic rights, which typically protect public encounters and the integration of various language groups in society. A right to day care in a minority language raises the question of the aims of linguistic policies: maintenance of diversity, integration of diverse ethnic groups, or assimilation of minority groups into the nation as speakers of one majority language.

While European Union policies refer to day care as a social service to be promoted, no clear-cut positive duty has evolved for public authorities as providers of day care. Notwithstanding the role that expanding day care services plays in EU gender equality policies, few Member States fulfil the target for providing day care agreed upon in the Lisbon Strategy. An approach based on the open method of coordination has not proved effective, and the EU lacks the necessary competence to adopt binding legislation. The European provisions against discrimination on grounds of ethnicity and gender apply in the access to and supply of services,[11] but a discrimination-based approach is a viable strategy only where services are already provided. Given that the European level provisions on day care leave much to the discretion of Member States, the issue is best considered at national level.

In that regard, Finland constitutes an interesting case study, as there is a positive public duty to provide day care, facilitating access to day care services. Under Finnish law, a legal basis

---

11   See the provisions in Council Directive 2000/43/EC of 29 June 2000 implementing the principle of equal treatment between persons irrespective of racial or ethnic origin [2000] OJ L180/22 and Council Directive 2004/113/EC of 13 December 2004 implementing the principle of equal treatment between men and women in the access to and supply of goods and services [2004] OJ L373/37.

exists to demand the non-discriminatory implementation of the right to day care for children, as there is a positive public duty to provide day care, and a corresponding right of individuals to receive it. In the absence of such a substantive right, the right to non-discrimination remains relatively toothless.

EU Member States are also free to decide on the extent to which they wish to provide care services especially targeted towards minority groups. Existing interpretation of EU anti-discrimination provisions has not given rise to social rights targeted towards minority groups. However, the entry into force of the Treaty of Lisbon may permit new developments as, under Article 3(3) TEU, the aim of the EU now covers the promotion of social justice and equality between women and men and, in addition, under Articles 8 and 10 of the Treaty on the Functioning of the European Union, the elimination of inequalities between men and women and combating discrimination on various grounds. A stronger emphasis on positive measures for gender equality as well as targeted provision of social services could be brought within the new formulation of the aims of the Union. At the moment, however, day care remains a service to be provided at the discretion of the Member States.

Certain European soft law instruments pay specific attention to minority education. A resolution of the European Parliament on the position of Romani women (European Parliament 2006) stresses the need for Member States to adopt European minimum standards within the open method of coordination to ensure that women and girls have equal access to quality education, and insists on the priority that Romani children must learn to read and write. The Resolution also confirms the need to eradicate segregation and prevent the development of segregated education (ibid.: points 4, 5 and 17). In 2009, a new European platform for Roma inclusion adopted principles which call for the mainstreaming of inclusion politics into all relevant policies, such as education and social policy (European Platform for Roma Inclusion 2009). Day care is not explicitly referred to in that document.

The Finnish public policy of day care for children was a highly contentious issue for two decades after the Second World War (Välimäki 1999). Arguments for public day care provision stressed the economic utility ensuing from easier access to the labour market for women and improving their equality with men in terms of increasing economic independence (Julkunen 1994). The Act on Day Care for Children of 1973 (Act 361/1973) made municipalities responsible for organizing day care. At first, however, the Act did not grant any enforceable rights to service. Supply and demand for day care services tended to be imbalanced. Traditionally, day care was regarded as a social measure of particular benefit to families at risk, whether economically or socially, and an important means of combating social exclusion.

Institutional day care was opposed ideologically and in practice by those who preferred subsidized care at home. In 1985, a national system of subsidizing home care of children was adopted.[12] The home care allowance is a flat-rate benefit paid to parents who do not take advantage of their right to the municipal service. In many municipalities, the allowance is supplemented with an extra subsidy, often calculated to keep supply and demand of municipal care provision in balance. The adoption of the home care allowance coincided with a decline in the labour market participation of women with small children (Kajastie 2000). While public day care in 'day homes' is clearly perceived as a means to provide the mothers of small children with better access to paid work, the home care allowance is promoted as a policy to guarantee 'the family's right to choice'.

---

12   Section 11a of the Act on Daycare establishes the principle by which municipalities are required to offer day care services. The right of children to receive a benefit is established by the Act on subsidy on home care of private care of children, Act 1344/2006.

The subsidized home care of children is seen by some as part of a turn to neo-familism (Niemi 2006: 173–4). Notwithstanding that ideological emphasis, the employment rate of Finnish mothers with small children has remained quite high.[13] As the employment rates of minority women are low, the Finnish system would appear to contain both an incentive for the home care of their children in the form of an allowance and, at the same time, a disincentive in relation to their workforce participation in the form of labour market discrimination.

In 1990, municipally-provided child care services were converted into individual rights of parents. In 1996, entitlement to municipal day care was extended to all children under school age. Thus, the right to day care is a justiciable right, and, correspondingly, the provision of day care for children an obligation on municipalities. During the economic recession of the 1990s, municipalities tended to under-budget their social welfare provision and the quality of day care services has been debated ever since. The cost of introducing the individual right to care was paid for partly through higher service charges to parents and partly in terms of lower quality care (Hiilamo 2005: 75). Political demands to cut the right to day care when a parent is at home due to unemployment, family-related leave or for other reasons have become common during the present recession. Such cuts would hit ethnic minority families more often than those of the majority population, because of their higher levels of unemployment. Seemingly, the former emphasis on prioritizing families at risk and children with special needs has disappeared.

Compulsory basic education starts relatively late in Finland, normally at age seven. Since 1999, municipalities (which are also responsible for organizing basic education) have been required to provide pre-school primary education for children in the year preceding their first school year. In that sense, municipal day homes are involved also in pre-school education.

The output of the Finnish system of basic education is excellent in international comparison. Finland has achieved the highest rank in the international PISA (Programme for International Student Assessment) survey several times. The school reform carried out in the 1970s aimed at equality in education coupled with high levels of achievement, and the outcome of that reform has been excellent. Interestingly, according to some commentators, those good results (obtained within a system of comprehensive schools run by municipalities) can be explained by the relative homogeneity of the Finnish population and the low number of immigrant children among the pupils. Pre-school education has become a factor for subsequent success in the education system, and, thus, the low attendance of minority children may put them at a particular disadvantage later in their lives.

Sámi, Roma and Russian Languages in Day Care

The Finnish Government mentioned provision of day care in its CEDAW report in 1997 as an asset for minority women (CEDAW 1997: 16), but lack of day care in minority languages has since been brought up in the CEDAW hearings at various points as a matter involving multiple discrimination of minority women. The CEDAW Committee has paid attention to the problem repeatedly, making increasingly specific observations over the years. In principle, the national programme for pre-school education of 2000 (Finnish National Board of Education 2000) specifies in relation to various minorities the educational aims. These adopt the division of language maintenance as the aim for 'old' minorities and tolerant integration as the aim for 'new' minorities.

---

13   In 2000, half of the mothers of children aged 1–2 years were in employment, and the employment rate of mothers with children aged six was 84 per cent (Sauli et al. 2002: 50).

The programme for pre-school education mentions teaching in the three Sámi languages, as well as empowering the Sámi identity of the children, and their belonging to an indigenous group which transcends national borders. Traditional cultural arts are to be promoted in coordination with the local community (ibid.: 16–17). Since all Sámi language groups in Finland are small, revitalizing measures are considered necessary, if the languages are to survive. However, the positive duty to arrange day care in Sámi has not led to the provision of sufficient services.

The Finnish Government admitted to the CEDAW Committee in 2001 that Sámi mothers, whose role 'includes the transmission and strengthening of Sámi identity and the Sámi language and culture to her child' have problems in getting the service, which affects their participation in working life. According to the Sámi Parliament, where day care is not available, a Sámi woman may have to choose between economic factors and Sámi identity. The municipalities in the Sámi area were criticized by the Sámi Parliament for not providing services to children and the young, with the consequence that the responsibility for building up their Sámi identity rests with the parents (CEDAW 2004: 29).[14]

Language rights and politics concerning the Sámi languages under Finnish law are 'promotion oriented', and based on the protection of endangered languages, an orientation often assumed in relation to indigenous languages, seen as a symbol of a more general crisis of biodiversity (Kymlicka and Patten 2003: 7). Typically, the policy is vulnerable where the population disperses. All schools in the Finnish Sámi Homeland now offer teaching in Sámi, either as the language of instruction, or as the first or second language. Outside the region, the language is hardly taught, although the majority of the Sámi population now lives there. Language tuition in Sámi in the Homeland is subsidized by the State, but elsewhere state subsidies follow the same rules both for Sámi and immigrant languages. The Sámi Parliament has proposed that special funding should be provided in the whole country, not merely in the Homeland (Näkkäläjärvi 2006).

The cases concerning day care in Sámi, referred to in the Prologue, constitute the outcome of a longer series of actions by Sámi activists, supported by international human rights monitoring bodies. The cases were no doubt chosen by the Ombudsman on their legal merits; the Sámi have clearly the strongest claim among Finnish minorities to receive services in their own language, at least in their Homeland. Rovaniemi, the most important city in Finnish Lapland, does not, however, belong to the Sámi region. Both the Ombudsman for Minorities and the Discrimination Tribunal based their decisions on the Non-Discrimination Act. The Ombudsman considered the case important for the fact that although there was no identified victim of discrimination, nonetheless the municipality of Rovaniemi was held to have acted in a discriminatory manner by failing to arrange day care (Ombudsman for Minorities 2009: 6). The municipality of Enontekiö belongs to the Sámi region, where the authorities have a special obligation to provide public services in the Sámi language.

The Ombud and the Discrimination Tribunal both held that the Sámi children have a right to day care in their own language in the same way as children speaking Finnish. The municipality had not taken appropriate measures to provide the service. Thus, the Discrimination Tribunal considered that the Sámi population had been discriminated against on the ground of ethnic origin. It is obvious that ethnicity and language are inherently intertwined in these cases. It remains to be seen whether courts will accept the argument that Sámi children are entitled to specific linguistic rights, or revert to the principle of equal treatment and non-discrimination in terms of services in national languages. It remains also to be seen to what extent the issue is discussed as one involving

---

14   For the response of the CEDAW Committee to the Fifth and Sixth Periodic Reports of Finland see CEDAW (2008: 125–33).

intersectional discrimination of Sámi women. The fact that the Minority Ombud has no competence to assist victims of gender discrimination may weaken effective recognition of intersectionality in these cases.

The national programme and recommendations on early education for municipalities also stress taking into account special needs arising from the Romani culture, and 'as far as possible' teaching in the Roma language. The aim of teaching is to empower the identity and cultural consciousness of Roma children, as well as their bilingual cultural identity. The aim is to encourage the use of the language among the Romani community, and the teaching is intended to help maintain oral linguistic tradition and the Romani way of life (Finnish National Board of Education 2000: 17).

The Roma, a minority group protected in Finland by constitutional and other legal provisions, nonetheless suffers discrimination of a type known elsewhere in Europe. In response to the first reporting by Finland, the monitoring body under the National Minorities Convention noted in 2000 the relatively high proportion of Roma children in special and adapted education in the public school system. Bearing in mind the fact that experiences at the day care and pre-school level are often important, the body regretted that support for Roma language and culture as one of the educational objectives of the legislation on day care had not had a real impact on practice at the local level (Council of Europe 2000: 38), and that Roma language classes were available only in eight municipalities (ibid.: 40). While the status of Swedish in the educational system was noted with approval, the status of Russian and Roma languages was considered problematic (ibid.: 42–4). Schools, not day care, were mentioned as a problem for the Roma in Finland's third CEDAW report (CEDAW 2007: 16).

In 2003, the Finnish Government cited to the CEDAW Committee the opinion of the Advisory Board for Romani Affairs, claiming that while the educational background of the Roma was weak, younger Roma women had sought adult education, especially in the social sector. It noted that adult students had problems in finding child-care and maintenance during their studies and that child-care was essential also in regard to working. Roma children attend day homes less frequently than other children, with the National Board of Education noting in 2002 that only about 2 per cent of Roma children attend pre-school education. The explanation given by the Finnish Government was a lack of awareness of the service among Roma women (CEDAW 2004: 31). In addition, Roma parents were unwilling to avail themselves of existing services, as they did not believe them to be adapted to their cultural needs and feared that Roma children would experience discrimination when in care.

The positive note of the 1997 Finnish Government report to CEDAW identifying the availability of day care to immigrants as an opportunity for immigrant women (CEDAW 1997: 15) was modified later, when problems in the use of the service started to appear. Experts working with migrants noted that measures aimed at immigrants, such as language courses, were more often used by men than women. The reason behind the pattern was that fathers usually appeared as job seekers who were entitled to language classes and other integration measures, which were targeted at helping immigrants to find jobs. Mothers tended to remain at home with children. Single mothers were seen to be at particular risk of not integrating into society, as they lacked the necessary language skills (CEDAW 2004: 25–6).

Russian speakers are considered as a group of immigrants in the national programme for pre-school education. According to that programme, different immigrant backgrounds are to be taken into account within the limits of local resources. The aim of teaching is to promote language skills in Finnish or Swedish. While cultural traditions are said to be important for the growth of a child's identity, the main objective is to impart a functional knowledge of the majority language through the teaching of Finnish or Swedish as a second language. Immigrant children should learn to be proud of their culture and transmit it to future generations, while, at the same time, they integrate into the majority culture. Education is given in the child's native language only when this is possible (Finnish National Board of Education 2000: 18–19). The experts interviewed in 2008 on the problems of being a Russian in Finland supported day care in bilingual day homes (Tanttu 2008). In their view, day care provision in accordance with those principles would allow positive encounters between children belonging to the majority and immigrant populations.

Bilingual integration of immigrants in day care, unsupported as it is by mandatory provisions, has not prospered. In its comments on the first country report submitted by Finland in 1999, the Expert Committee which monitors the implementation of the European Charter of Regional or Minority Languages drew attention to the limited provision of education and day care services in the Russian language (Council of Europe 2001a). In its comments on the latest available country report on Finland under the National Minorities Convention, the Committee of Ministers was concerned that Russian speakers reported obstacles in access to social services (Council of Europe 2007). A specific consultation body for the Russian-speaking population had not progressed. Finland was recommended to address the shortcomings of its language laws, and take into account Russian speakers in the provision of public services. In addition, it was recommended to expand the availability of minority language education, including Russian.

Positive duties, administratively established and not backed up by sanctions, do not appear to give the policy on bilingual day care strong enough backing to overcome the obstacles of inadequate funding and widespread prejudice. Where day care is not provided by authorities on a bilingual basis, Russian speakers, numerous as they are, may establish and maintain their own day care institutions. In terms of a tolerance-based language policy, that approach is legitimate. However, the aim of pre-school integration may suffer and problems caused by segregation in pre-school education may surface later during compulsory schooling.

In practice, children with immigrant backgrounds are mostly offered a special course at school in Finnish as a second language. In 2006, the National Discrimination Tribunal prohibited a school in the city of Helsinki from using the native language of pupils as a criterion for allocating children to classes. The school and the city of Helsinki argued that children with an immigrant background would learn Finnish as a second language and putting them together in the same group made it easier to provide them with adequate teaching. The decision of the Tribunal was referred to Helsinki Administrative Court, which upheld it. According to the Administrative Court, segregation of pupils on the basis of being native or non-native speakers of Finnish could be considered neither positive action nor justified on educational or practical grounds.[15] Therefore, schools are prevented from giving way to pressures from majority parents to segregate immigrants from native speakers. However, it is difficult to prevent majority population parents from shunning residential areas with large immigrant populations to ensure that their children are admitted to more mono-cultural schools. Thus, a more profound segregation of society takes place in the wake of the choice of school. The decision on whether actively to accommodate teaching to the needs of the immigrant groups rests with schools which face budget cuts as a result of the present economic recession.

Conclusion

The aim of this chapter was to consider how cultural, social and equality rights have an impact on the access to day care for minority children. Increasing availability of day care services is

---

15 Decision by the National Discrimination Tribunal of 31 January 2006, Case No. 2732/66/2004. The decision was upheld by Helsinki Administrative Court, judgment of 15 June 2007, Case No. 02464/06/1205.

seen as an important part of the Lisbon Strategy, both as a means to economic growth through increasing labour market participation of mothers and as a measure for enhancing gender equality. The progress of policies concerning day care depends on the EU Member States. Community law has not granted minorities any specific rights to access these services, although equality rights provide some grounds for claiming equal access. In Finland, the right to day care services is a strong entitlement. Minorities and their languages are protected by international and constitutional obligations. Finland shows features that are typical for Eastern Europe, where ethnic and linguistic minorities already achieved protection in the era in which nation-states arose, and protection of minority identities gained ground in the post-Socialist period. On the other hand, Finland has received an increasing number of immigrants since 1990, similar to the experience of many Western European states. In those countries, immigrant cultures and languages are mainly protected simply through a prohibition on ethnic discrimination. For Finland, however, protection of ethnic minorities through anti-discrimination law constitutes a recent innovation.

Finnish minorities do not benefit from the day care services for children to the extent that the majority does. Cultural reasons for this disparity were discussed by considering three minority groups and their access to day care services which take into account their linguistic needs. Cultural rights protecting the provision of child care in minority languages were shown to be at the margin of minority rights and dependent on a hierarchy of more and less privileged languages. As a result, access to day care services in different languages is protected by legislation with differing degrees of intensity. The aims of the linguistic arrangements vary. In relation to indigenous groups and 'old' minorities, empowering traditional identities is stressed. Language maintenance policies go together with identity politics which present conflicting claims on women belonging to the minority in question.

The strongest rights considered, those of the indigenous Sámi, suffer from acute problems arising from the notion of reasonable accommodation. The protected group is small and dispersed, and thus those under a duty to provide services can claim insurmountable difficulties in providing such. Social marginalization in the case of the Roma continues during a period of stronger identity politics and weakening social welfare regime. In the case of immigrant children, bilingual pre-school education is considered ideal, but the legal provisions guaranteeing such education are weak. The linguistic rights of the immigrant group considered here, Russian speakers, are protected merely by administrative recommendations and anti-discrimination policy. Where prejudice against a group is prevalent, the relatively large number of people belonging to that group is inadequate to ensure the efficient implementation of vaguely formulated positive public duties.

The right to subsidized home care of children in Finland constitutes an incentive for minority women to stay at home with their children. The solution may help to sustain cultural traditions but does not strengthen the bilingual language skills of the children. The social integration of home-making mothers remains weak, as integration policies concentrate on the working population. In a society with a strong tradition of dual breadwinner families, minority women risk both social and cultural marginalization, if they rely on subsidies that keep mothers at home.

Chapter 10

Justice for the Whole Person:
The UK's Partial Success Story

Gay Moon

Introduction

Multiple discrimination has been widely recognized for some time by those working in the equality field as a problem that must be addressed. Yet creating appropriate legal and policy responses to disadvantage based on a variety of grounds has proved difficult. This chapter explores the development of the distinctive UK perspective on problems of multiple disadvantage and multiple discrimination. It covers a 45-year period culminating in the Equality Act 2010. It will examine the recognition of multiple discrimination in both policy and practice. It will discuss how the case for specific provisions to counter such discrimination has been developed and explain why 2004 marked a significant transition in thinking. It will trace how these developments culminated in a new statutory provision in the Equality Act 2010 that will, when brought into force,[1] prohibit 'combined' direct discrimination (sometimes referred to as 'dual' discrimination).

Recognition of the need to address multiple discrimination specifically forms an important part of a much wider equality discourse. The proposals for a new Equality Act, comprehensively addressing all the main grounds of discrimination, arose from recognition of the fact that different approaches to different grounds had developed in an ad hoc way without the consistency and coherence that ought to underpin an effective equality law.

In the UK, discussion of multiple disadvantage initially centred on the intersection of only two grounds – race and sex. One reason for this starting point was that race and sex were covered by the only two Acts to provide protection from discrimination in most of the UK.[2] In addition, there were indeed many problems experienced by black and ethnic minority women (Fredman and Szyszczak 1992; Mirza 1992).[3] However as this chapter will explain, the discussion has widened as the number of protected grounds has expanded. Now, for instance, the public discourse is interested in such complex cases as older women newsreaders who suddenly find that their contracts are not renewed;[4] or ethnic minority people with disabilities (Pierce 2003b: 7–23; Bhavnani et al. 2005: 61–2; Bignall and Butt 2000); or lesbian school teachers whose schools fail

---

1 Though the precise date for implementation has not yet been given, the author has been informed by the Government Equalities Office that this was expected to be in April 2011, however, the new Coalition Government is currently reviewing these statements and may take a different view.

2 As discussed below, in Northern Ireland only, the Fair Employment Acts of 1976 and 1989 provided protection against discrimination on grounds of religious or political opinion.

3 As explained below the intersection of religion and ethnicity in the Jewish community led to different outcomes.

4 See, for example, report on the dismissal of Moira Stewart (Thynne 2007). Later reports covered further examples. The Equalities Minister Harriet Harman referred to this problem in January 2010 (*Guardian* 2010).

to protect them from pupils' abusive behaviour;[5] or female soldiers of Caribbean origin needing child care.[6] These examples show how this discussion has deepened the public awareness of the specific, complex and multi-layered identities of every human being.

This chapter will examine these developments by focusing on three different periods of time, which, despite not being rigidly demarcated, represent discrete stages in the development of the discourse. The first period is from about 1965 to 2003, the second from 2004 to 2009, and the final from 2009 onwards.

From 1965 to 2003

Limits of the UK Law

It was in this period that all the current grounds for protection, apart from age,[7] were first established in broadly their current form. Modern legislation really began with the provision made for race discrimination in the Race Relations Act 1965 whose key aims were set out in its long title as being 'to prohibit discrimination on racial grounds in places of public resort; to prevent the enforcement or imposition on racial grounds of restrictions on the transfer of tenancies; to penalize incitement to racial hatred'. Following riots in Bristol and consideration of the limited range of the 1965 Act it was extended to employment in 1968 (Lester and Bindman 1972). However neither of these Acts gave a right of individual action to victims of discrimination, and neither directly contemplated multiple identities.[8]

In relation to sex, only in 1970 – spurred on by ILO Convention 100 – was the Equal Pay Act 1970 enacted. At this stage the UK was not a signatory to the Treaty of Rome and so had no obligations to transpose Article 119 EEC (now: Article 157 TFEU). The Equal Pay Act 1970 is jurisprudentially anomalous in the canon of discrimination law because it works in contract rather than tort by implying an equality clause into a contract of employment. It makes no direct provision for multiple discrimination.

After the UK's accession to the European Communities in 1972, the incoming Labour Government of 1974 recognized the need to make more extensive provision for sex equality going beyond implied contractual terms. Influenced by new European obligations, and also by equality law developments in the United States (particularly the Supreme Court ruling in *Griggs v. Duke Power Co*)[9] the Sex Discrimination Act 1975 was passed (Pannick 1985). This anticipated obligations resulting from the EEC's Equal Pay and Equal Treatment Directives, which became due for implementation in 1976 and 1978 respectively.[10]

The Race Relations Act 1976 was passed the following year to give similar individual rights in the field of race equality. Meanwhile in response to the worsening disagreements between Catholics

---

5   See, for example, *Pearce v. Governing Body of Mayfield Secondary School* [2003] IRLR 215.

6   See *Tilern De Bique v. Ministry of Justice* [2010] IRLR 471. Case discussed at the BBC Caribbean (2010).

7   Which came in 2006, see below.

8   However as discussed below the religious component of ethnicity was a significant consideration.

9   401 U.S. 424 (1971).

10   Respectively, the Council Directive 75/117/EEC on the approximation of the laws of the Member States relating to the application of the principle of equal pay for men and women and Council Directive 76/207/EEC on the implementation of the principle of equal treatment for men and women as regards access to employment, vocational training and promotion, and working conditions.

and Protestants, and Unionists and Republicans in Northern Ireland, the Fair Employment Act 1976 was passed. This prohibited religious and political discrimination in Northern Ireland, but not in Great Britain.

The Race Relations Act 1965 conferred protection against discrimination 'on the ground of colour, race, or ethnic or national origins'.[11] This concept of direct discrimination as being 'on the ground of' a single basis was to be the model for subsequent anti-discrimination law right up to 2010.

This approach is essentially comparative. A complainant in a direct discrimination case has to show that they have received 'less favourable treatment' than an actual or hypothetical comparator. In an indirect discrimination case the approach is also comparative, since a complainant has to show that a provision, criterion or practice was applied to her which applies, or would apply, equally to others but which puts, or would put, her at a disadvantage compared to people who do not share the protected characteristic. Further, it has to be shown that the provision, criterion or practice disadvantages her and is not justifiable. In making this comparison the relevant circumstances of the one case must be the same or not materially different from those of the other.[12] This comparative approach required the identification of the claimant on a specific unitary ground so that a comparator (real or hypothetical) with a different specificity can be identified.

The problems of this approach for multiple identities are now obvious, but in this early period the only consideration of whether there was adequate protection of multiple identities took place in relation to Jews (and similarly, though to a lesser extent, Sikhs). The nature of this dialogue is of some interest as it demonstrates the lack of appreciation of the importance of intersectional effects.

Being Jewish may be classified as an ethnic as well as a religious identity. This was recognized early in the consideration of race legislation. Thus the Race Relations Board,[13] as early as 1967, considered the question whether Jews were adequately protected by the legislation. It noted as among the deficiencies of the Act which should be considered in the preparation of any amending legislation its view that:

> [t]he limitation of the Act to discrimination on the ground of 'colour race or ethnic or national origins' may exclude certain groups such as the Jews, Sikhs and the Gypsies which may not be primarily ethnic or racial but which are so regarded by those who discriminate against them. The position of such groups should be clarified.[14]

As a result the Board commissioned a report from Professor Harry Street, Geoffrey Howe QC and Geoffrey Bindman (1967) to examine anti-discrimination legislation in other countries, to assess its effectiveness and to consider what type of legislation Parliament might consider suitable should it decide that the Act requires amendment or extension. *The Street Report* considered in very great depth the steps taken elsewhere, in particular in the United States and Canada, to protect against discrimination. It made numerous recommendations as to the extension of the legislation then in place and these helped shape the Race Relations Act 1968.

It noted that discrimination on grounds of 'creed' was prohibited elsewhere and proposed that new legislation in the UK might also prohibit religious discrimination. It also noted the

---

11   See section 1.

12   See, for example, SDA s5(3), RRA s3(4).

13   This was set up by the Race Relations Act 1965 and its initial members of the Board were Sir Learie Constantine, Mr Mark Bonham Carter, and Alderman B.S. Langton, CBE, JP.

14   See paragraph 38(v) of the Report of the Race Relations Board for 1966–7 presented to Parliament pursuant to section 2 of the 1965 Act and printed by the House of Commons on 26 April 1967.

then undecided question of whether Jews were protected from discrimination and urged that this must be resolved. It was, however, much more confident than the Race Relations Board, that Jews were protected by existing legislation; though it was not clear as to the exact basis for this view.

This left open the policy question whether a distinction should be made as between discrimination by or against Jews on religious grounds that might also be discrimination on grounds of racial or ethnic origin. It also did not specifically address what we would now consider to be multiple discrimination. Though it must be added that *The Street Report* noted that religious discrimination might also be a cover for racial discrimination:

> Our concern is with discrimination on account primarily of race, and not religion, age or sex. None of the last three grounds is covered by the 1965 Act. Without considering whether as a matter of policy religious discrimination should be brought within the scope of the legislation, we have considered the possibility that racial discrimination might be concealed under the guise of religious discrimination. There might be a temptation for a racial discriminator to conceal his prejudice on the pretence that his discrimination was purely religious.

Whether Jewishness was a racial, religious or national characteristic was more fully discussed later by Lester and Bindman (1972: 156–8). However, in the event, the Race Relations Act 1976 made no specific provision for religious discrimination, though in Parliament it was stated that Jews were fully protected.[15] In retrospect it is remarkable that the interplay between religious and ethnic identities of Jews was not fully unpicked in litigation until 2009.[16] In the event religious discrimination was only specifically covered for Northern Ireland in the Fair Employment Act of the same year, and that Act surprisingly did not cover discrimination where religion and political opinion were joint causes of disadvantage.

Nevertheless, the intersection of religion and ethnicity did provide the first example of significant litigation about the intersection of different identities. In 1979, the New Zealand Court of Appeal in *King-Ansell v. Police*[17] held that Jews had a common ethnic origin and noted the role of religion. This judgment was applied in the UK in 1983 when in *Mandla v. Dowell Lee*[18] the House of Lords confirmed that a Sikh boy, whose religious practice required him to wear a turban, was protected by the Race Relations Act 1976. The boy had been barred from access to a school which required pupils to wear a cap because he would not remove his turban. *Mandla* is thus interesting as showing how the concept of ethnicity could be used to protect aspects of ethnic identity that are linked to religion. It may be seen as the first reported UK case to contain a key issue of multiple discrimination.

In the 1990s the failings of the Disabled Persons (Employment) Act 1944 became ever more evident. Disabled activists pressurized for new legislation which would take the positive action provisions of the 1944 Act and marry them with equal treatment provisions of the type to be found in the field of UK race and sex law, as well as reasonable adjustment provisions of the type to be found in the Americans with Disabilities Act 1990 (Doyle 2008). No thought was given to multiple discrimination in this legislation, though the different ways in

---

15   See the notes to section 2 of the Race Relations Act 1976 in Current Law 1976.

16   See *R (on the application of E) v. Governing Body of JFS & Anor* [2009] UKSC 15, [2010] 2 WLR 153.

17   [1979] 2 N.Z.L.R. 531.

18   [1983] 2 AC 548.

which a person can be disabled was undoubtedly significant in opening the debate about more complex identities.[19]

In *P v. S*[20] the European Court of Justice made it clear that the Equal Treatment Directive (and thus also the Sex Discrimination Act 1976) had to be interpreted to include discrimination on grounds of gender re-assignment. Domestic legislation thereafter extended protection to those having transgendered status.[21] The simple fact that this case concerned changed gender identity certainly increased awareness of the complexity of human individuality.

Council Directive 2000/43/EC implementing the principle of equal treatment between persons irrespective of racial or ethnic origin (Race Equality Directive) and Council Directive 2000/78/EC establishing a general framework for equal treatment in employment and occupation (Employment Framework Directive) extended the reach of EC secondary legislation to grounds other than gender (Bell 2002; Meenan 2007). These two Directives, in turn, led to domestic legislation in 2003 on sexual orientation,[22] religion or belief[23] and later in 2006 (in the second period considered in this chapter) on age.[24] These Directives acknowledged the existence of multiple discrimination in relation to gender and race, but they did not require Member States to address it.

It can thus be seen that there were different drivers for each of these particular pieces of domestic legislation so that, while conceptually linked, each piece of legislation has reflected the campaigns of different 'and often single' interest groups. While there have been common themes in the resulting body of single-issue legislation, there has been a lack of overall coherence. There has also been a failure (except, as noted above, in the case of religion and ethnicity) to consider the intersection of protected characteristics. The net effect is a complex web of, at times, inconsistent provisions.

The content of these provisions demonstrates that almost no express consideration was given to the possibility that a person might experience discrimination on more than one ground. This absence reflected a similar silence in the research base. Although particular categories of people were seen to be vulnerable to discrimination, there were very few studies in this period that drew together and highlighted the consequences of a combination of these particular disadvantages (Mirza 1992; Bhavnani 1994; Owen 1994). It was simply assumed that such problems could be adequately dealt with by seeking a single-ground remedy. The law and the collection of statistical information mirrored one another in their emphasis on single-issue characteristics. This materially inhibited the preparation of a more sophisticated, realistic and thorough analysis of the operation of discrimination in society.

The Deeper Analysis of the Nature of Disadvantage in the United States of America

In contrast to the UK, at this time academics in the United States began to identify and analyse the cumulative disadvantage suffered by some groups, or indeed groups within groups. Most notably

---

19   Thus a person may be disabled within the concept used in that Act by reason of a mental or physical impairment, which is long-term and has a significant effect on day to day activities: see section 1 of, and schedule 1 to, the Disability Discrimination Act 1995.

20   Case C-13/94 [1996] ECR I-2143.

21   The Sex Discrimination Act was formally amended by the Sex Discrimination (Gender Re-assignment) Regulations 1999 as from 1 May 1999 to include gender re-assignment protection in the field of employment.

22   Employment Equality (Sexual Orientation) Regulations 2003 in respect of employment and occupation.

23   Employment Equality (Religion or Belief) Regulations 2003 in respect of employment. Equality Act 2006 in respect of access to facilities, goods and services.

24   Employment Equality (Age) Regulations 2006 in respect of employment only.

the problems arising from such intersectional discrimination were identified and discussed by Kimberlé Crenshaw (1989) who looked at the position of African American women. She argued that a single-ground approach to discrimination law ensured that comparisons were only made with the privileged members of the class in question:

> in race discrimination cases, discrimination tends to be viewed in terms of sex or class-privileged Blacks; in sex discrimination cases, the focus is on race- or class-privileged women. This focus on the most privileged group members marginalizes those who are multiply burdened and obscures claims that cannot be understood as resulting from discrete sources of discrimination. I suggest further that this focus on otherwise-privileged group members creates a distorted analysis of racism and sexism because the operative conceptions of race and sex become grounded in experiences that actually represent only a subset of a much more complex phenomenon ... Because the intersectional experience is greater than the sum of racism and sexism, any analysis that does not take intersectionality into account cannot sufficiently address the particular manner in which Black women are subordinated. (Crenshaw 1989: 150)

Crenshaw made a further important step in the analysis by pointing out that this way of thinking about discrimination influenced the way that the politics of equality were presented: if struggles against prejudice are posed as arising only from singular issues, remedies will tend to be crafted in the same way.

It was also important for UK developments that US Courts began to develop a ground-plus jurisprudence.[25] However, this approach was limited because the complainant could only raise two grounds of discrimination. Further, a victim had to elect which was the primary and which the secondary cause of action despite the fact that, in cases of complex intersectional discrimination, such distinctions would be inappropriate and ineffective as they would be difficult, if not impossible, to make.

Canada's Holistic Approach

Another important contribution to the debate came from Canada where relevant law and policy has developed differently (Small and Grant 2005: 25–63; Grabham 2002: 641–61). It has long had the same provisions for each prohibited ground of discrimination. It has also, and from much earlier than in the UK, had an increasing awareness of the need for an intersectional approach to discrimination – an awareness facilitated by the legal system.

The Canadian Charter of Human Rights has been critical. It has an open list of equality grounds and, because of this, Canadian Courts have found it easier to adapt the law to encompass multiple grounds of discrimination. The Charter permitted a combined ground to be treated as simply a new possible ground. It was important that the Charter, following international texts such as Article 26 of the International Covenant on Civil and Political Rights, permitted claims to be brought on the basis of 'other status'.[26]

---

25   *Jeffries v. Harris County Community Action Association* 615 F 2d 1025 (5th Circuit 1980) and *Judge v. Marsh* 649 F 2d 1025 (5th Circuit 1980).

26   Article 26 states 'All persons are equal before the law and are entitled without any discrimination to the equal protection of the law. In this respect, the law shall prohibit any discrimination and guarantee to all persons equal and effective protection against discrimination on any ground such as race, colour, sex, language, religion, political or other opinion, national or social origin, property, birth or other status'.

Initially, discrimination under the Canadian Human Rights Act 1998, which had a closed list of grounds, was not so flexibly addressed. However the benefit of the Charter approach was recognized and, as a result of the increasing recognition of the complexity of discriminatory events, a clause was added to make it clear that a discriminatory practice included one that is based on more than one ground – 'for greater certainty, a discriminatory practice includes a practice based on one or more prohibited grounds of discrimination or on the effect of a combination of prohibited grounds'.[27]

The effect of this legislation was to liberate a new way of thinking which was more closely aligned to peoples' experiences.

The Ontario Human Rights Commission has estimated that between April 1997 and December 2000, 48 per cent of the complaints that it received included more than one ground. It has noted that in cases of discrimination on multiple grounds the discrimination experienced is different from that experienced on any of the individual grounds. So, for example, it has concluded that the experience of discrimination suffered by a black woman is intrinsically different from that suffered by a black man, or a white woman. This has been described by the Commission as 'intersectional oppression [that] arises out of the combination of various oppressions which, together, produce something unique and distinct from any one form of discrimination standing alone' (Eaton 1994: 229).

The Canadian experience has been highly progressive. The great merit of this approach is that it has permitted the particular experience of an individual to be acknowledged and so remedied. The Ontario Human Rights Commission has noted that taking an intersectional approach leads to a greater focus on society's response to the individual and a lesser focus on the category into which the person may fit. This enables a Court to make a more person-specific analysis of the effect of the treatment in question:

> within the Commission, there is a growing recognition that we can improve our understanding of the impact when grounds of discrimination intersect and that tools for applying an intersectional analysis will be very helpful in the handling of complaints, from inquiries through to litigation, and in our policy work. (Human Rights Commission 2001)

The Effect of the Canadian and US Experience on the UK

Equality rights discourse knows no national boundaries, and these different approaches to multiple discrimination were discussed between jurists at international events.[28] These discussions did take some time to filter through to mainstream political thought in the UK. In the early 1990s, for reasons considered above, the first discussions of what we would now call multiple or intersectional discrimination centred on the colour-blindness of much feminist research and the over-simplification of the analysis which focussed too single-mindedly on the position of white women (Fredman and Szyszczak 1992: 215). This was paralleled by a criticism of the assumption

---

27 Canadian Human Rights Act 1998, section 3(1).

28 See, for example, UN General Assembly Report of the World Conference against Racism, Racial Discrimination, Xenophobia and Related Intolerance: 'We recognize that racism, racial discrimination, xenophobia and related intolerance occur on the grounds of race, colour, descent or national or ethnic origin and that victims can suffer multiple or aggravated forms of discrimination based on other related grounds such as sex, language, religion, political or other opinion, social origin, property, birth or other status' (UN 2000: no. 2).

of homogeneity within racial groups. In what was possibly the most significant discussion at the time, Reena Bhavnani (1994) noted that:

> Empirical evidence demonstrates that whilst black women do have a specific experience in the labour market, this is mediated by factors such as 'race', gender, age, class and disability. These categories cross cut with each other to produce both similar and different experiences between white and black women. (Bhavnani 1994: xvi)

She and others returned to this problem in the ensuing years, so that by 2000 the argument for recognition of multiple discrimination took place alongside the increasingly vociferous debate about the need for substantial reform and simplification of our equality laws.

However, whilst there was some limited acknowledgement of the incidence of multiple discrimination, it was still not at first recognized that a specific provision to permit multiple discrimination claims was needed. For instance, a major study in 2000 (Hepple et al. 2000), that made no less than 53 extensive recommendations for the amendment of UK anti-discrimination law, contained no specific recommendation for protection against multiple discrimination.

In contrast with the relative shortage of information about multiple disadvantage in this early period, by 2010 a significant amount of detailed information became available through reports such as the National Equality Panel Report, *An Anatomy of Economic Inequality in the UK* (National Equality Panel Report 2010). This noted, for example, that:

> Pakistani and Bangladeshi Muslim men and Black African Christian men have pay penalty 13–21 per cent lower than White Christian men ... Women from nearly all ethno-religious backgrounds have pay between a quarter and a third less than a White British Christian man with the same qualifications, age and occupation. (National Equality Panel Report 2010: 390)

Overall then this pre-2003 period is characterized by an initial period of activity in which single-ground legislation was proposed and enacted and a later growing realization of the inadequacy of this approach, driven particularly by an increasingly probing domestic analysis promoted by an awareness of developments elsewhere.

From 2004 to 2009

2004: The Watershed Year

It was inevitable that as information was gathered the debate about policy should alter. A dramatic shift in the UK debate took place in 2004 when a new synthesis about the possibilities of addressing this kind of discrimination began to emerge.

Thus, in May 2004, the then Secretary for Trade and Industry (Patricia Hewitt) stated: 'as individuals, our identities are diverse, complex and multi layered. People don't see themselves as solely a woman, or black, or gay and neither should our equality organisations' (Hewitt 2004).

This statement was made to justify combining three existing single-ground Commissions[29] into a new overarching Commission for Equality and Human Rights. This new Commission was finally established by the Equality Act 2006.

---

29   For race, sex and disability.

Although the 2006 Act did not expressly refer to multiple or intersectional discrimination, it did focus specifically on the diversity of identities. Thus section 10 set out the Commission's duties to promote understanding of the importance of good relations between members of different groups and others, and this includes a smaller group within a group.

In July 2004, and in stark contrast with the Minister's vision, the Court of Appeal (upholding the ruling of the Employment Appeal Tribunal) rejected the possibility of interpreting the statutory provisions on discrimination to encompass multiple discrimination in *Bahl v. the Law Society*[30] (Malik 2007: 73–94; Clarke 2007: 79–105; O'Cinneide 2008). Lord Justice Peter Gibson stated:

> In our judgment, it was necessary for the ET to find the primary facts in relation to each type of discrimination against each alleged discriminator and then to explain why it was making the inference which it did in favour of Dr Bahl on whom lay the burden of proving her case. It failed to do so, and thereby, as the EAT correctly found, erred in law.[31]

Thus the Court of Appeal made it clear that each ground had to be separately considered, and a ruling made in respect of each, even if the claimant had experienced them as inextricably linked. The mismatch between law and reality was palpable.

The importance of the case in this story justifies a more detailed discussion of the facts. Ms Bahl was a black Asian woman. She claimed sex and race discrimination in her treatment as deputy vice-president of the Law Society. She said she was treated the way that she was because she was a black woman. The Employment Tribunal (ET) found that the Law Society's President and its Secretary General had committed unconscious direct sex and race discrimination. The Employment Tribunal held:

> We do not distinguish between the race or sex of the applicant in reaching this conclusion … Kamlesh Bahl was the first office holder that the Law Society ever had who was not both white and male … It is sufficient for our purposes to find, where appropriate, that in each case they would not have treated a white person or a man less favourably.

It was this finding that prompted the Law Society to appeal. The Employment Appeal Tribunal held that:

> if the evidence does not satisfy the tribunal that there is discrimination on grounds of race or on grounds of sex, considered independently, then it is not open to a tribunal to find either claim satisfied on the basis that there is nonetheless discrimination on grounds of race and sex when both are taken together … Nor can the tribunal properly conclude, if it is uncertain about whether it is race or sex, that it will find both.[32]

Ms Bahl then appealed against this ruling to the Court of Appeal. The main basis on which that Court rejected Ms Bahl's appeal was that, while the employer might have behaved unreasonably, there was no evidence of any race or sex discrimination. Quite apart from this, the Court of Appeal ruled that the Employment Tribunal had made a legal mistake in failing to distinguish between the elements of the alleged race and sex discrimination. It held that the Employment Tribunal should:

---

30 [2004] IRLR 799.

31 Ibid., para. 137.

32 [2003] IRLR 640, para. 158.

identify what evidence goes to support a finding of race discrimination and what evidence goes to support a finding of sex discrimination. It would be surprising if the evidence for each form of discrimination was the same.[33]

Thus the Court of Appeal held that the fact-finding tribunal should have found the primary facts in relation to each type of discrimination and then explained why it was making the inference which it did.

While this ruling was interpreted to mean that an Employment Tribunal must look at race and sex discrimination separately and not make a combined finding of multiple discrimination, it did not deter the Equal Opportunities Commission from publishing a guidance leaflet in November 2004, *Advising Ethnic Minority Women about Discrimination at Work*. This set out to assist ethnic minority women in bringing discrimination claims. However, the Court of Appeal's judgment did affect the advice given which, in retrospect, seems very timid. The leaflet merely advised that:

> If your client appears to have been discriminated against for more than one reason, for example race and sex, a balance will need to be struck between pursuing all the claims. Don't ignore the other elements, but concentrate on the one with the strongest evidence. (Equal Opportunities Commission 2004: 5)

The leaflet went on to describe a series of Employment Tribunal cases in which ethnic minority women were found to have been discriminated against on multiple grounds – their race and their sex.

Further Case Law Developments

Two years later, in *Network Rail Infrastructure Ltd v. Griffiths-Henry*,[34] an increase in judicial awareness of multiple discrimination was evident. Following a redundancy exercise, nine employees competed for five positions. All except Ms Griffiths-Henry were white and male. She was black and female and, despite being equally qualified for the vacant posts, was unsuccessful. She claimed race and sex discrimination, although it is unclear from the report whether she claimed race and/or sex discrimination (in the alternative) or whether she claimed race and sex discrimination operating in conjunction, intersectionally.

The Employment Appeal Tribunal upheld the tribunal's finding that the facts were sufficient to shift the burden of explaining the treatment of Ms Griffiths-Henry to Network Rail under both the Race Relations Act 1976 and the Sex Discrimination Act 1975. However, it overturned the tribunal's finding on the facts, ruling that Network Rail had not discharged the burden of showing no discrimination. The employer had also appealed on the basis that the tribunal did not separately consider the question of race and sex. The Employment Appeal Tribunal agreed that the effect of the ruling in *Bahl* was that it was not legitimate for a tribunal to treat both race and sex discrimination together, but held that the tribunal had not made this mistake in *Network Rail*.

The Employment Appeal Tribunal also addressed another question connected with the transfer of the burden of proof. The question was: what happens if, as here, the facts were sufficient to raise a prima facie case that race or sex discrimination or both are present, but do not indicate which? The

---

33   Ibid., para. 137.
34   [2006] IRLR 865, EAT.

answer it gave was that, if the employer cannot provide a satisfactory non-discriminatory reason for the treatment, and cannot identify any features which distinguish race from sex discrimination, then a tribunal would be obliged to find discrimination with regard to each. In *Network Rail*, however, the employer had provided a non-discriminatory explanation, so the question of whether it was race or sex discrimination did not arise.

The question of damages payable when discrimination has been established on more than one ground was considered in *Al Jumard v. Clywd Leisure Ltd.*[35] In this case, discrimination on grounds of race and separately on grounds of disability, was found to have arisen from the same set of facts. It is interesting that, contrary to the approach taken in *Bahl*, the Employment Appeal Tribunal agreed with the Employment Tribunal that it was artificial and unrealistic to ask to what extent each discrete head of discrimination had contributed to the injured feelings experienced by the claimant – although it would not necessarily be wrong for a tribunal to do that in an appropriate case.

Recently, the Employment Appeal Tribunal held in *Ministry of Defence v. Tilern De Bique*,[36] that indirect discrimination arising from the intersection of race and sex could be considered by the Employment Tribunal. Ms De Bique was a British soldier of Caribbean origin. She was also a single parent with a young daughter. The Tribunal found that two provisions, criteria or practices were applied to her by the MOD, namely that she be a soldier available for deployment on a 24/7 basis; and also that she could not have a member of her extended family (a half-sister) to stay with her in the Service Families Accommodation because she was a foreign national who was only entitled to stay in the UK for a short period. The Employment Appeal Tribunal considered that discrimination is often a 'multifaceted experience ... The Tribunal recognized that this double disadvantage reflected the factual reality of her situation and found that indirect discrimination had occured'.[37]

Research and Policy Contributions to the Debate

As the arguments in the Courts and Tribunals progressed, a greater awareness of the issue was also emerging from research. In seeking to persuade the Government of the case for multiple discrimination protection, concerned UK NGOs pointed to some of the research studies that highlighted the reality of multiple discrimination in the day-to-day experience of a variety of different categories of people. In 2003 a significant study commissioned by the Joint Equality and Human Rights Forum of the UK and Ireland, *Re-thinking Identity: The Challenge of Diversity*, examined the position of people belonging to a number of multiple disadvantaged groups – from disabled minority ethnic groups to young gay people. This study concluded that 'people with multiple identities ... are not adequately protected by current legislation ... Even with harmonized legislation, people with multiple identities that increase their social vulnerability and marginalisation may require an "intersectional approach" to equality and human rights claims' (Zappone 2003: 148–9).

In 2004 the National AIDS Trust produced a report that examined the position of gay men and African people with HIV. This report observed that when discrimination against people living with HIV was combined with another ground for discrimination, the disadvantage experienced often became more acute. For instance, it found that 'all African people with HIV suffer racism and xenophobia in a heightened form' (Dodds et al. 2004: 25).

---

35   [2008] IRLR 345, EAT.
36   [2010] IRLR 471.
37   Ibid., para. 165.

In 2005 the Fawcett Society produced a report on *Black Minority Ethnic Women in the UK*. It reviewed their employment and financial security, their representation and participation in public life and their experiences of the criminal justice system. It observed that 'thinking continues to be hampered by lack of data which takes into account both ethnicity and gender: it is enormously frustrating that this remains the case' (Brittain et al. 2005: 2).

This study found that Pakistani and Bangladeshi women experienced 'a pattern of disadvantage that is so consistent, and extreme in parts, that it merits special attention' (Brittain et al. 2005: 48). Overall it observed that 'in some areas, sexism and racism combine to create an intensity of discrimination that far exceeds the impact of any single strand' (Brittain et al. 2005: 1).

Accordingly it concluded: 'put simply, the experience of racism can be quite different for women and men and equally the experience of sexism can be different for women of different ethnic groups and neither gender nor race alone fully capture the experience of BME women' (Brittain et al. 2005: 50).

These findings were echoed in *Moving on Up* (Equal Opportunities Commission 2007), which examined the position of Bangladeshi, Pakistani and Black Caribbean women at work. It concluded that racism, sexism and anti-Muslim prejudice based on widespread stereotypes made it harder for ethnic minority women to integrate in the workplace and to be promoted. It found that the workplace culture, or the practices and procedures in an organization, might put anyone who was not from the majority group at a disadvantage. It noted that, whilst not intentional, this could still have a very damaging effect. It concluded that although these young women had left school with good qualifications they were still more likely to be unemployed than white women and less likely to have senior roles within the workplace.

Academic Contributions to the Debate

During the first decade of 2000 the problems posed by multiple discrimination came increasingly to interest academic writers within the United Kingdom (Hannett 2003: 65–86; McColgan 2007: 74–94; Conaghan 2009: 21–48). The model for discrimination law that some favoured was the Canadian jurisprudence as set out in the Canadian Charter of Human Rights. It was, for instance, recommended that there should be an open-ended approach, adding 'other status' to the list of prohibited grounds. This, it was argued, would allow for the combination of two or more recognized grounds to be considered (Conaghan 2009: 21–48).

Whilst superficially appearing to be a neat solution, there was a problem with this approach which rendered it fatally unattractive to the Government Equalities Office when it was proposing new legislation. An 'other status' provision, it was feared, would be too wide and encompass more than was acceptable to law makers. An 'other status' clause would therefore have to be accompanied by a justification defence for direct discrimination. This was not acceptable as it would have conflicted with a cardinal principle of UK equality law – the idea that direct discrimination should never be capable of being justified.[38]

---

38   The sole exception to this in European Law is that Member States may enact provisions providing for direct age discrimination to be justified: see Article 6 of the Framework Directive 2000/78/EC. The contrary has been argued as being desirable by some (Bowers and Moran 2002), but rejected emphatically by others (Gill and Monaghan 2003). The courts hold fast to the view that direct discrimination cannot be justified save in relation to age, though this has been described as a possible defect per Lord Phillips PSC at para. 9 of his judgment in *R (on the application of E) v. Governing Body of JFS & Anor*, op. cit.

A second, and perhaps more powerful criticism of the 'other status' approach, was that this approach would be inconsistent with legal certainty. There was concern that uncertainty as to what was within the concept of 'other status' would provoke voluminous litigation and be opposed by the business community.

The Government Equality Office therefore never even considered 'other status' as a practical way forward.[39]

Government Responses

In February 2005, in response to the now overwhelming demand for new streamlined equality legislation, two extensive reviews of equality in Britain were announced – the Equalities Review and the Discrimination Law Review. The Equalities Review was set up to provide an understanding of the long-term and underlying causes of disadvantage that needed to be addressed by public policy, to make practical recommendations on key policy priorities and to inform the modernization of equality legislation. The Discrimination Law Review was asked to consider the fundamental principles of discrimination legislation, to investigate and assess different approaches to enforcing discrimination law and to consider ways of creating a simpler, fairer and more streamlined legislative framework in an Equality Act. Both these reviews took two years to produce their reports. During this time a number of equality agencies and non-governmental organizations made representations setting out the need for explicit multiple discrimination provisions.

The Equalities Review final report (2007) reviewed the numerous markers of discrimination and, significantly, noted that where people had multiple markers of disadvantage this could drastically reduce the probability of their being employed. For example, the employment penalties suffered by Pakistani and Bangladeshi women were found to be greater than those of women as a group or than those of Pakistani or Bangladeshi men.

Meanwhile many NGOs and practitioners who submitted responses to the Discrimination Law Review raised the question of the need for a multiple discrimination provision within any new Equality Act. Surprisingly, and incorrectly, in its response to the Discrimination Law Review (the consultation paper on the Single Equality Bill), the Government suggested that it was only 'academics' who had argued for multiple discrimination provisions (Discrimination Law Review 2007). It rejected these arguments, observing that to allow 'fully combined multiple claims … would significantly complicate the law and place additional burdens on business and the public sector' (Discrimination Law Review 2007).

No explanation was given as to why there would be such problems. The Government justified its decision not to legislate on the issue by stating that it had no evidence that people were failing to bring cases in practice because they involved more than one protected ground. It requested further evidence and examples of problems and indicated that it would reconsider its position if it was supplied with relevant evidence (Discrimination Law Review 2007).

This led the House of Commons Communities and Local Government Committee, in its report on Equality, to comment aptly:

> The Government's hesitancy towards permitting combined multiple discrimination claims rests upon the additional complexity this might add to any legislation and the consequent additional burden it would place on employers. These are not insignificant concerns but we urge the

---

39   The author was intimately involved in the discussions on this concept with the Government Equalities Office in the run up to the Equality Act 2010 and this was made quite plain on several occasions.

> Government to recognise the inherent difficulty in amassing evidence of actions that have not been taken. (House of Commons Communities and Local Government Committee 2006/7: 15)

Yet there was now plenty of evidence that multiple discrimination was really occurring as an important social phenomenon. It was of course impossible to measure how many legal cases had *not* been brought on a multiple discrimination basis because advisers were afraid of legal problems. This request from the Government for evidence of cases not brought also ignored the greatly increased potential for intersectional cases resulting from the recent addition of new discrimination grounds.

The Government was roundly criticized for its hesitancy by jurists, academics and practitioners alike. In November 2007 the Equality and Diversity Forum, an important network of all the major national equality NGOs, held a conference, 'Multi-dimensional discrimination: justice for the whole person', which focused on multiple discrimination provisions. It was attended by both government and non-government representatives and helped to stimulate a wider national debate. Simultaneously a new information leaflet was issued and widely distributed (Equality and Diversity Forum 2008). Ultimately both the Parliamentary Joint Committee on Human Rights and the House of Commons Work and Pensions Committee (2009: paras 62–8) noted the need to include multiple discrimination provisions in the forthcoming Equality Bill.

Notwithstanding all this pressure, when the Equality Bill was finally published in the House of Commons on 24 April 2009, no provision for multiple discrimination claims was included. Instead the Government announced that it was going to initiate yet another short consultation exercise on a proposed multiple discrimination clause (Government Equalities Office 2009c). It was proposed that this clause would prohibit direct discrimination and only on a combination of two protected characteristics. The Government Equalities Office received a number of written responses from businesses, trade unions, public service providers, equality representatives and lawyers, the majority of whom agreed that there was a need for protection from discrimination because of a combination of protected characteristics. Whilst businesses welcomed the proposed restriction of protection to direct discrimination on a combination of only two grounds, equality representatives considered that it should extend to indirect discrimination and harassment as well as combinations involving more than two grounds (Government Equalities Office 2009a: 2).

After this consultation, a direct discrimination clause based on a maximum of two grounds was added to the Bill in July 2009. It is now Section 14 of the Equality Act 2010, the content of which is discussed below.

Overall this period shows how the increased awareness of multiple identities has produced its own inexorable logic and drive for specific legislative provision, notwithstanding a governmental reluctance to address such complexity and the opposition of some parts of the business community to what has been seen as a further regulatory burden.

From 2009

The British Solution – Combined Discrimination in the Equality Act 2010

The new section 14 of the Equality Act 2010 states:

Combined discrimination: Combined characteristics

1. A person (A) discriminates against another (B) if, because of a combination of two relevant protected characteristics, A treats B less favourably than A treats or would treat a person who does not share either of those characteristics.

2. The relevant protected characteristics are:
   a. age;
   b. disability;
   c. gender reassignment;
   d. race
   e. religion or belief;
   f. sex;
   g. sexual orientation.

3. For the purposes of establishing a contravention of this Act by virtue of subsection (1), B need not show that A's treatment of B is direct discrimination because of each of the characteristics in the combination (taken separately).

4. But B cannot establish a contravention of this Act by virtue of subsection (1) if, in reliance on another provision of this Act or any other enactment, A shows that A's treatment of B is not direct discrimination because of either or both of the characteristics in the combination.

5. Subsection (1) does not apply to a combination of characteristics that includes disability in circumstances where, if a claim of direct discrimination because of disability were to be brought, it would come within section 116 (special educational needs).

6. A Minister of the Crown may by order amend this section so as to:
   a. make further provision about circumstances in which B can, or in which B cannot, establish a contravention of this Act by virtue of subsection (1);
   b. specify other circumstances in which subsection (1) does not apply.

7. The references to direct discrimination are to a contravention of this Act by virtue of section 13 [direct discrimination].

It will thus prohibit direct discrimination on a combination of two of any of the specified grounds.[40] It prohibits discrimination if, because of a combination of two relevant protected characteristics, a person treats another less favourably than they treat, or would treat, a person who does not share either of those characteristics. Thus the comparison must be with a real or hypothetical comparator who does not possess either of the characteristics in question.

The Labour Government responded to criticism related to the limitation of the new provision to only two characteristics, by asserting that claims involving a combination of more than two grounds are rare. It suggested that 90 per cent of cases involve only two grounds. This argument is based mainly on information gained from a short survey it commissioned from Citizens Advice

---

40   Equality Act 2010, section 14(2), the grounds of pregnancy and maternity and marriage and civil partnership are not included as relevant grounds.

(Government Equalities Office 2009b). It is certainly true that the majority of cases are likely to involve only two grounds but whether the numbers involving three or more grounds combined are as small as 10 per cent of all multiple discrimination cases must be uncertain.

In order to establish that there has been combined discrimination the new section makes it clear that it is not necessary to show that there was sufficient proof to establish discrimination on a single ground. This is important since it ensures for protection in cases in which the disadvantage is not merely aggravated by reason of the combination of protected grounds but is caused solely by the combination.

Furthermore, bringing a claim on combined grounds does not prevent a claimant bringing a claim on one or both of the single grounds and no doubt many claimants will claim in the alternative.

The new section provides that a combined discrimination claim will not succeed where an exception or justification applies to the treatment in respect of either of the protected characteristics in question. Hence, for example, where a genuine occupational requirement for one of the characteristics is established, the direct discrimination would be lawful.

This prohibition on discrimination will cover both the employment and non-employment fields[41] and will even extend to the operation of the public sector equality duty so that public authorities will be under a duty to eliminate unlawful combined discrimination.

However, the section does not extend to indirect discrimination or to harassment, because, according to the Government, it received little evidence of a need for such provisions (Government Equalities Office 2009c: 16). There are organizations that have submitted evidence of multiple indirect discrimination cases or multiple harassment cases that would challenge this assertion (Discrimination Law Association 2009). Yet concerns about unacceptable levels of complexity merit some consideration. In respect of indirect discrimination, the Government has argued that:

> Extending the law to enable claims of intersectional indirect discrimination would require businesses and organisations to actively consider the impact of their provisions, criteria and practices on all 21 possible combinations of protected characteristics to ensure that they do not have an unlawfully disproportionate impact. We consider this to be disproportionate burden, given that there is no evidence of a need. (Government Equalities Office 2009b: 3)

This concern about excessive complexity certainly reflects the concerns expressed by a number of employer's organizations (Government Equalities Office 2009a: 2). However, the recent *De Bique* case[42] demonstrates that intersectional discrimination can very well occur in the context of indirect discrimination.

Section 14 also includes a specific power enabling a Minister of the Crown to make orders further specifying what a claimant does or does not need to show in order to establish a combined discrimination claim or to restrict the circumstances in which such claims can be brought. The Government indicated that this power had been included because combined discrimination is still a new and untested concept and it was therefore 'prudent to provide flexibility to address any undesirable results and accommodate future changes' (Government Equalities Office 2009b: 4).

The section does not deal with the assessment of damages for combined discrimination. The Government Equalities Office observed that nothing in the Act 'requires the award of additional

---

41   Except for combined discrimination involving disability in the field of education which is specifically excluded because disability discrimination in schools is subject to adjudication by a specialist tribunal.

42   See above footnote 36.

compensation or increased damages for dual discrimination. Therefore we would not expect a person who was successful in a dual discrimination claim to receive twice the damages of a single strand claim' (Government Equalities Office 2009b: 4).

However, awards of damages are essentially in the discretion of the judge hearing the case so s/he will assess the facts and, if the duality of the discrimination has substantially exacerbated the discrimination experienced, this will presumably be reflected in the quantification of damages.

Conclusions

The former Government claimed that this new UK combined discrimination clause was a 'world leading provision' and that 'we are the first country in the world to develop such a provision' (Government Equalities Office 2009b: 1 and 4). While it is certainly a provision to be welcomed, which does create some protection against multiple discrimination, it is not world leading. As noted above, Canada established a much better provision to deal with multiple discrimination some time ago. Further, other European countries also have protection against multiple discrimination which in some cases is more wide reaching than that of the Equality Act 2010 (Burri and Schiek 2009).

Section 14 is not a comprehensive provision, as it only deals with direct discrimination on a maximum of two grounds. Nonetheless overall it is a helpful addition to our range of discrimination protection and is definitely a step in the right direction. Perhaps once it has come into operation and employers and service providers have discovered that it does not create a plethora of further problems it will be possible to extend its operation to indirect discrimination and harassment.

Whatever happens in the courts and tribunals as this new section is applied, it will certainly provoke a deeper interest in the complexity of the causes of discrimination. This is a positive trend away from an atomized approach that can only be beneficial in the long run.

PART III
Convincing the Judiciary to Entertain Intersectional Analysis

Chapter 11

Identity-based Discrimination and the Barriers to Complexity

Suzanne B. Goldberg

Introduction

In recent decades, both scholars and advocates have pressed a variety of thoughtful arguments through the frame of intersectionality theory to foster more textured treatment of identity categories in anti-discrimination law.[1] The theory, which has been elaborated extensively since its introduction in the legal literature in the early 1990s,[2] illuminates the ways in which discrimination is often based on the junction of multiple identity axes rather than on a single category designated for protection within an anti-discrimination law. The theory addresses, too, the ways in which an individual's experience of discrimination may vary as a result of these intersections. So, for example, black women, held out in the early literature as paradigmatic examples of the experience of intersectional discrimination, may experience qualitatively different discrimination than either white women or black men because they are targeted simultaneously at two points of subordination.

It is rare today to find a court, much less a scholar, who disagrees fundamentally with intersectionality's major premise and insists, instead, on the unitary and monolithic nature of identity categories.[3] Yet despite the acceptance of intersectionality theory at a general level, efforts to advance and expand upon the theory have been met, in the scholarship, with serious critiques. Moreover, to the limited extent advocates have embraced these efforts by bringing claims for discrimination based on intersecting identity categories, adjudicators have been largely unresponsive and litigants lose their cases at disproportionately high rates.[4]

---

1 By identity categories, I mean the designations that are listed as prohibited grounds in anti-discrimination laws. For example, one of the most expansive employment anti-discrimination laws in the United States, 42 U.S.C. § 2000e et seq. (known as Title VII), covers race, colour, religion, sex and national origin. Other similar statutes at the federal and local level in the United States (and elsewhere) cover age, disability, sexual orientation and gender identity.

2 *See infra* note 21.

3 Earlier on, a number of courts were explicitly resistant to recognizing intersectionality theory's insights in the course of adjudicating discrimination claims. See, e.g., *Rogers v. American Airlines, Inc.*, 527 F. Supp. 329 (E.D. Mich. 1981) (finding that African-American women did not constitute a discrete class for the purposes of Title VII suit); *DeGraffenreid v. Gen. Motors Assembly Div.*, 413 F. Supp. 142, 143 (E.D. Mo. 1976) ('[T]his lawsuit must be examined to see if it states a cause of action for race discrimination, sex discrimination, or alternatively either, but not a combination of both').

4 I will discuss these challenges *infra* but it bears noting, at the outset, that the broader group of discrimination plaintiffs in the United States loses its claims at disproportionately high rates at both the trial and appellate levels (Clermont and Schwab 2004: 449–52). Employment discrimination plaintiffs who prevail at trial are reversed 42 per cent of the time; judgments for employer-defendants are reversed less than 8 per cent of the time (ibid.: 450). See also Clermont and Eisenberg (2002: 957–8). Contributing

In this chapter, I offer an account of why intersectionality theory has faced challenges both in theory and practice. More particularly, I isolate a set of factors that sheds light on the environment into which intersectional claims are made and the sources of resistance within that environment. Together, these factors reinforce what we see in the literature and case law – that simple categories exert a powerful gravitational pull notwithstanding our awareness of the complexity that lies within and around them. My claim is that when contemplating an intersectional or multidimensional vision of equality, we would do well to take these 'simplicity' factors into account in thinking about how to make that vision a reality.

The four simplicity factors range in their focus from cognitive constraints to broader social and institutional dynamics, presenting, in essence, a cross-sectional perspective on the relationship between identity and law. The first looks internally to the way in which our information-processing schema and other cognitive superstructures favour relatively simple categories. Second, through social networks and movements, we see that relatively simple categories have retained their salience as the foundation for large-scale social movement organizing, even as nuanced identity categories have become increasingly important within smaller communities. Third, shifting the focus to institutions, I examine the legal advocacy organizations that bring identity-based claims to courts and the ways in which these groups frequently buttress the simplistic formulation of identity-based legal claims through their unitary-identity focus. And finally, turning to the judiciary, we see that the institutional legitimacy and capacity constraints of courts tend towards simplification as well, and resist the more complex and holistic analysis demanded by intersectional and multidimensional identity theories.

To be clear, I do not intend, by highlighting these factors, to suggest that we give up on having the law be more responsive to the complex nature of identity. Instead, as with any effort to move the law in a particular direction, it is important to understand not only where we would like to be but also how we might get to our preferred destination.[5]

In that spirit, the remainder of the chapter proceeds in several steps. I first offer a caveat regarding the court-focused inquiry here. I then briefly describe the nature of anti-discrimination law and intersectionality theory's efforts to bring that law into closer relation with lived experience, and consider some of the scholarly and judicial resistance to those efforts. With this foundation, I turn to an extended discussion of the simplicity factors. All of this, again, is aimed to prompt further conversation about how best to understand, both theoretically and operationally, the challenges posed by complex identity claims and to lay the groundwork for overcoming them.

---

to this situation is the high bar set for proving discrimination. In the context of a hostile environment or harassment claim, the Supreme Court has held that Title VII is violated only upon a showing of 'severe or pervasive' conduct, adding that '[m]ere utterance of an ... epithet which engenders offensive feelings in an employee', does not sufficiently affect conditions of employment to implicate Title VII. *Harris v. Forklift Sys.*, 510 U.S. 17, 21 (1993) (quoting *Meritor Sav. Bank v. Vinson*, 477 U.S. 57, 67 (1986) (citation omitted)).

5   It might be striking to some that political opportunity structure is not listed as a distinct factor shaping the viability of complexly rendered identity claims (McAdam et al. 1996). After all, political opportunities and constraints inevitably shape the legal landscape, including legislative frameworks, advocates' choices, and courts' responses to both, in virtually all areas of law. This is certainly true for identity law, including in the employment arena where so much of the identity jurisprudence is focused. For this reason, I want to be clear that the absence of a standalone political opportunities factor does not signal the absence of politics from the discussion here but rather the pervasive presence of politics throughout the analysis.

A Caveat

Although my primary concern here is with the barriers to meaningful judicial embrace of multidimensional views of identity, with a special focus on United States courts,[6] it almost goes without saying that courts are just one part of the anti-discrimination framework. As a practical matter, anti-discrimination law enforcement, even when well done, cannot respond fully to the complex ways in which biases manifest and shape individuals' participation in and vulnerability to discrimination (Sturm 2001: 475–8).[7] Consequently, achievement of non-discriminatory workplaces and other environments does not depend solely, or even largely, on what happens in court. Instead, an interactive approach – in which courts catalyse but do not become the focal point for shifting dynamics in the workplace, and in which workplaces design structural mechanisms to deter discrimination at the outset rather than developing reporting systems to focus primarily on *post hoc* correction – may well be the most effective means of limiting discrimination.[8]

Law and society scholars reinforce this point about the limitations of the law as articulated by courts, reminding us that that version of law is but one among many and, in practice, may not ultimately be terribly influential. There are, instead, layers of translation and reinterpretation by the many actors whose lives are shaped by that law, either directly as enforcers and/or subjects or, more atmospherically, as individuals operating in environments affected by judicial pronouncements (Emens 2007: 823–7; Merry 2006: 55).[9] Others, too, have underscored the limits of the law altogether as a source for redressing identity discrimination, maintaining that cultural strategies are at least as important, if not more effective, for changing the ways in which people perceive and react to identity differences.[10]

Yet even while taking these limitations seriously, we should not understate the power of judicial rulings to shape the direction and scope of identity law as it permeates workplaces and society.[11]

---

6   My focus on US courts is intended, in the context of this volume, to offer the US experience for its comparative value as well as to suggest that the simplicity factors discussed here may have universal relevance even if they manifest differently across jurisdictions.

7   'The complex and dynamic problems inherent in … discrimination cases pose a serious challenge for a … system that relies solely on courts (or other external governmental institutions) to articulate and enforce specific, across-the-board rules' (Sturm 2001: 461). See also Green (2005: 665) arguing that 'discriminatory work cultures are too complex and too intertwined with valuable social relations to be easily regulated through judicial pronouncements and direct regulation of relational behavior'.

8   Some scholars have agreed with the value of focusing on structural changes while also expressing scepticism about how far structural approaches actually go to overcoming the difficulties faced by anti-discrimination law (Bagenstos 2006: 1).

9   Emens (2007: 823–7) discussing the effects of 'desk-clerk law', which is 'what the person at the desk tells you the law is'; Merry (2006: 55) discussing the role of 'intermediaries, or translators, between plural legal systems'.

10   As one commentator has written: 'The temptation for gay equality advocates may be to recreate in the domain of culture the kind of linear cause and effect relationship that once marked what is now widely recognized as a naïve faith in formal legal mechanisms to autonomously secure meaningful equality. … It is therefore important to assess the emancipatory possibilities of changing media representations of lesbians and gay men within a framework sensitive to the dynamic relationship between legal and cultural forces' (Schacter 1997: 726).

11   Law and culture can likewise be described as having this type of dialectical relationship, with cultural and legal understandings of identity categories in a mutually constitutive relationship. Schacter (1997: 720), noting that 'larger cultural discourses about sexuality and identity give texture and meaning to the legal category'.

While we may depend on non-judicial actors to 'convene and directly oversee the problem-solving process', courts 'establish ... the general norm' to be followed (Sturm 2001: 532), or at least to be reacted to by others. This norm-stating function remains influential and consequential at least for purposes of setting a baseline for employers and others concerned only with insulating themselves from liability, and as a point of information for those with broader anti-discrimination values and commitments.[12]

On the Tensions within Anti-Discrimination Law's Protected Categories

Anti-discrimination laws, on their face, seem to anticipate few of the problems that stymie courts and scholars regarding the complexity of identity categories. Instead, they typically present a sequenced list of identity traits designated for protections, with the implication being simply that the traits on the list receive protection, and all others do not, absent some separate provision.[13] In that sense, US Supreme Court Justice Antonin Scalia was quite right when he observed, with respect to a law prohibiting sexual orientation discrimination, that an employer could discriminate freely because an applicant 'is a Republican; because he is an adulterer; because he went to the wrong prep school or belongs to the wrong country club' yet not because the applicant is gay.[14] As the tone of his remarks suggests, the inclusion – or exclusion – of certain traits can be a significant point of contention.[15]

Superficially, however, the task the adjudicator faces seems to be straightforward – all that needs to be determined is whether the litigant was discriminated against based on one of the traits that has been deemed protected. Of course, discerning whether the challenged acts were actually motivated by the protected trait, rather than for some other reason, and whether the acts rise to the level of actionable discrimination, even if they are tied clearly to the protected trait, can be fraught with difficulty.[16]

---

12   Donohue III (1986: 1431) arguing that in an environment where employers make decisions based on profit and efficiency, 'legal intervention can also serve to facilitate or enhance the operation of the market, thereby furthering the objective of wealth maximization' and that 'antidiscrimination legislation may be thought of as a tool to perfect the market response to employer discrimination'.

13   See, e.g., California Fair Employment and Housing Act, codified in Government Code §12940 for a sequenced list of protected identity traits; cf. 42 U.S.C. §1983 (blanket provision prohibiting discrimination).

14   *Romer v. Evans*, 517 U.S. 620, 652–3 (1996) (Scalia, J., dissenting).

15   We see this as well, for example, in the dramatic voter initiative battles over whether to add sexual orientation to anti-discrimination measures in jurisdictions around the United States. See *Romer v. Evans*, 517 U.S. 620 (1996); *Equality Foundation of Greater Cincinnati, Inc. v. City of Cincinnati*, 128 F.3d 289 (6th Cir. 1997), *cert. denied*, 525 U.S. 943 (1998). Richard Epstein argues against anti-discrimination laws generally, asserting that they restrict freedom of choice, provoke racial conflict, encourage more devious forms of discrimination, and undermine standards of merit (Epstein 1992).

16   This question – whether the challenged acts were 'because of' a protected characteristic – is one of the central inquiries in an anti-discrimination case. Title VII of the Civil Rights Act of 1964 provides, for example, that '[i]t shall be an unlawful employment practice for an employer ... to fail or refuse to hire or discharge any individual, or otherwise to discriminate against any individual with respect to his compensation, terms, conditions, or privileges of employment, *because of such individual's race, color, religion, sex, or national origin*'. 42 U.S.C. § 2000e-2 (emphasis added). See Minow (1987: 11) finding that disparate treatment on the basis of race or gender is an obvious example of discrimination, but proceeding to analyse 'the guise of objectivity and neutrality' that afflicts legal reasoning in our society. See also *U.S. Postal Serv. Bd. of Governors v. Aikens*, 460 U.S. 711, 716 (1983), noting that '[t]he law often obliges finders of fact to inquire

But, even setting those issues aside, tremendous difficulty remains in conceptualizing the protected categories themselves, particularly when we focus on the interactions among the categories. Think of a kaleidoscope as roughly analogous, where the shapes within it are the components of identity. Even if we assume a limited number of objects in the kaleidoscope, those objects combine and recombine in a near-infinite number of ways. Each shake of the cylinder insures that the shape of things at one moment is almost certain to be different from the next. The same can be true for identity-based interactions in the workplace or in other environments. Deciding who is 'in' or 'out' of one or more protected categories for purposes of applying the anti-discrimination law in a particular case can seem nearly impossible.

Several distinct features of identity contribute to this difficulty in working with the protected categories. For one, even the seemingly simplest aspects of identity resist being sharply defined. As identity performance theory has elaborated, individuals often experience discrimination not strictly because of an observable and relatively fixed characteristic linked to their protected trait, such as skin colour, anatomy, or even marital status, but rather because of the way they either fit or fail to conform to stereotypes about behaviours or personal styles associated with their identity group.[17] That is, in most contexts, decisional rules that turn on an individual's status (such as rules about applicants for employment, university admissions or bank loans) are a thing of the past. Today, identity-related harms occur more often because an individual is, for example, 'too ethnic', a man is 'too effeminate', or a gay person is 'too flamboyant'. We can see this in the increasing number of cases where employers have penalized employees for having a Spanish-inflected accent or African hairstyle or other characteristics that are unquestionably related to their protected identity trait but not necessarily to a thin understanding of the trait as listed in an anti-discrimination law (Carbado and Gulati 2000: 1307).[18]

When we think multidimensionally about identity discrimination, the inquiry becomes even more complicated. Not only are the individual protected traits potentially unstable, in that their boundaries are subject to contestation, but also, as intersectionality theory reminds us, the traits themselves do not exist in isolation.[19] Consequently, they are not as easily separable for purposes of a discrimination claim as anti-discrimination law's sequential listing of identity traits implies. Indeed, returning to the kaleidoscope analogy, if we think about distinct traits as the small colour chips in the scope, we know that when a blue chip sits atop a red chip and we see a purple colour, it is not meaningful to separate the work of the blue chip from that of the red because the two

---

into a person's state of mind' and that '[it] is true that it is very difficult to prove what the state of a man's mind at a particular time is'.

17   See Rich (2004: 1199–230) arguing that interpretations of Title VII that 'fail to account for the role that volitional behavior or race/ethnicity performance plays in defining individual identity' leave courts unable to reach 'equitable resolution' of discrimination claims; Yuracko (2006: 369) seeking 'to begin the process of defining the ways in which employers use trait discrimination so as to begin a more useful normative discussion about when, if ever, antidiscrimination law should prohibit such discrimination'.

18   For additional literature addressing identity performance theory, see Ramachandran (2005: 300) observing that 'negotiating multiple identity performance demands simultaneously often places intersectionals in a uniquely restricted situation, one that has been referred to in other contexts as a "catch 22" or "double bind"'; Roberts and Roberts (2007: 378–86) discussing '[i]dentity [p]erformance as [s]trategic [r]esponse to [w]orkplace [c]ultural [p]rofiling'.

19   For early discussions of intersectionality theory, see, e.g., Crenshaw (1991: 1243–4) exploring 'how the experiences of women of color are frequently the product of intersecting patterns of racism and sexism, and how these experiences tend not to be represented within the discourses of either feminism or antiracism' (footnote omitted).

have blended, at least for the moment. Along these lines, others have addressed at length the way in which identities exist in multiple dimensions (Hutchinson 2002: 435–6), interact in synergistic ways (Hutchinson 2000: 1361–8; Kwan 1997: 1264)[20] and have multiple, context-contingent valences (Carbado and Harris 2008).[21]

Notably, although there was some resistance at first, this basic point of intersectionality theory has become increasingly well-understood and accepted by judges, at least with respect to the 'simple' intersections of two identity categories. As a US federal appeals court observed, for example, in an employment discrimination case brought by an Asian woman who had been rejected several times when seeking a job for which she had been well-qualified: 'Asian women are subject to a set of stereotypes and assumptions shared neither by Asian men nor by white women' so that the absence of evidence of discrimination against Asian men or white women would not disprove the plaintiff's claim.[22] The same set of judges recognized, as well, that 'the attempt to bisect a person's identity at the intersection of race and gender often distorts or ignores the particular nature of their experience'.[23] Others, too, have recognized the absurdity of a jurisprudential regime that would fail to recognize the distinct salience that identity characteristics may have when considered in combination with each other.[24]

Yet, as written, anti-discrimination measures do not expressly cover the discrimination experienced intersectionally by someone who is subordinated at work because of his or her combination of identity traits. And the outcomes of intersectional cases indicate that the law, in operation, does not provide much in the way of meaningful protection, even when courts express agreement with intersectionality's basic premise. Instead, individuals bringing these cases tend to get little traction for their claims. While individuals with single-trait discrimination cases often lose their cases, those who bring complex claims appear to lose at even higher rates. In one case involving a black female plaintiff who claimed race and sex discrimination, for example, the court, in rejecting her claim, noted that 'following the [sex-plus] rationale to its extreme, protected subgroups would exist for every possible combination of race, colour, sex, national origin and

---

20   See also Wing (2008: 2897) using the concept of 'global multiplicative identity', to illustrate 'the intersectionality of identities and its applicability to Muslim women'; Wing (2001: 833–62) also discussing 'global multiplicative identity' theory, and applying it to study polygamy.

21   Observing that one's 'determination that any given process is race neutral or a racial preference is unavoidably contingent on a mixed question of fact and normativity: our characterization of the social context in which the racial decision-making occurs' (Carbado and Harris 2008: 1210).

22   *Lam v. Univ. of Haw.*, 40 F.3d 1551, 1562 (9th Cir. 1994).

23   Ibid.

24   See, e.g., *Jefferies v. Harris County Cmty. Action Ass'n*, 615 F.2d 1025, 1032 (5th Cir. 1980) ('The essence of Jefferies' argument is that an employer should not escape from liability for discrimination against black females by a showing that it does not discriminate against blacks and that it does not discriminate against females'); *Vasquez v. City of Los Angeles*, 349 F.3d 634, 638, 643 (9th Cir. 2003) (finding that comments about the plaintiff having a 'typical Hispanic macho attitude' were insufficiently severe or pervasive to state a national origin discrimination claim); ibid. at 654 (Ferguson, J., dissenting) (stating that comments about the plaintiff having a 'typical Hispanic macho attitude' showed 'particularly offensive stereotypes about Hispanics as lazy, and about Hispanic males as aggressive and domineering' and finding that the remarks and other conduct stated a claim 'as to whether [the plaintiff] was subjected to an abusive workplace because of his race and his sex'); *Anthony v. City of Sacramento*, 898 F. Supp. 1435, 1445 (E.D. Cal. 1995) (stating that '[t]he epithet "black bitch" cannot be designated exclusively as either racist or sexist').

religion'.[25] In short, as one scholar observed, courts have 'basically given up on the complex plaintiff' (Kotkin 2009: 1462).[26]

Stumbling Blocks for Intersectionality

Much of the scholarship related to intersectionality theory in identity law has become stymied as well. In part, theorists have been troubled by the difficulty of defining identity categories that remain sensitive to intersectionality's premise regarding the multiple, shifting relations among identity characteristics in a given individual, yet also manage to encompass more than the single individual they describe. For some, this concern has heightened the difficulties associated with even the single categories we deploy in discrimination law, including race, ethnicity and disability, which often overshadow the important distinctions within those group designations (Hollinger 1995; Rivera 2007).[27] Others, taking the point further, have bemoaned the 'infinite regress problem: the tendency of all identity groups to split into ever-smaller subgroups, until there seems to be no hope of any coherent category other than the individual' (Ehrenreich 2002–3: 267). Following from this challenge, some who have studied identity law conclude that the categories should be eliminated, or at least diminished in importance, because they 'undermine the universalism that should guide equality theory … produce balkanization and backlash; and … promote group stereotyping' (Schacter 1997: 700),[28] all of which ultimately outweigh their possible benefits (Abrams 1994: 2496; Chang and Culp 2002: 485).

In this light, operationalizing these facially clear anti-discrimination laws reminds us, unavoidably, of the complex nature of the identities the laws are designed to protect. Moreover, as judges' and scholars' observations indicate, these complications are no secret. On the one hand, as just noted, abstract recognition that identity discrimination comes in complex forms has led many theorists to conclude that identity categories will necessarily be fatally inaccurate because they must oversimplify unduly if they are to fit more than the one subject being described. At the same time, courts seem to find the prospect of multidimensional identities – and indeed, at times, any more than one identity category – as impossibly complex in operation, if not conceptually.

Elsewhere, I have explored other options for stepping out of this bind (Goldberg 2009, 2011). These include, most significantly, a recommendation that we shift away from the view that discrimination can best be seen only by comparing the person discriminated against to someone similar in all respects but for the protected trait. While this comparator-based approach can sometimes work well in Taylor-esque workplaces where large numbers of workers have identical or closely comparable jobs (Taylor 1911), most workplaces simply do not have a close-to-identical counterpart for each person who has experienced discrimination. More to our point here, the

---

25   *Judge v. Marsh*, 649 F. Supp 770 (D.D.C. 1986).

26   See also *infra* notes 32–4 and accompanying text.

27   Hollinger (1995: 963) observing that the category Hispanic-American obscures significant differences between Mexican-Americans, Cuban-Americans and Puerto Ricans, and that Asian-American obscures differences between Filipino-Americans, Chinese-Americans, Japanese-Americans and Korean-Americans; Rivera (2007: 902) exploring 'how the homogenization of various subclassifications of Latinos under the "Latino" category at times masks inequities suffered unevenly among subclasses that differ racially, historically, and by national origin'.

28   In particular, such scholars worry 'that identity categories are born of inequality and thus can reinforce that inequality by their very usage, and that identity categories undermine equality by encouraging identity essentialism and erasure' (Schacter 1997: 705).

comparator-focused approach becomes increasingly difficult to work with when the individual seeking redress is a member of multiple protected classes. At this point, difficult conceptual questions arise about precisely who the comparators should be, including whether the comparison should be to someone who shares all but one, or none, of the plaintiff's characteristics, as well as how exactly one goes about discerning discrimination from whatever comparison is proffered.

Here, however, rather than explore the alternatives to a comparator-driven understanding of discrimination as a means of unstitching intersectionality from its current conceptual bind, my interest is in understanding why we have gotten into this bind in the first place. And it is to these points – and the factors I proposed at the outset – that I turn now.

Factor One: Cognitive Preferences

In recent years, legal scholars have looked increasingly to social science research to understand a variety of important features related to identity discrimination.[29] Researchers have examined, for example, how social groups and identities are formed; how 'in-groups' prefer their own members and are more likely to treat 'out-groups' with less nuance than their in-group peers; and the ways in which social stigmas shape implicit biases in individuals who overtly disavow those same biases. Further, extensive studies have shown the ways in which human beings use categories and 'schemas' as cognitive shortcuts to make sense of the otherwise overwhelming quantity of information we need to process (Blasi 2002; Chen and Hanson 2004; Jolls and Sunstein 2006; Krieger 1995).[30]

Even to the extent there are disagreements within the literature about how to measure bias and about how best to understand the operation of schemas, categories, social frameworks and other heuristics, there is widespread agreement that our brains crave simplicity and resist complication (Allport 1979; Blasi 2002; Krieger 1995; Mitnick 2007).[31] Consequently, a principal explanation for why intersectionality and identity performance theory and advocacy have not gained greater traction in court may be simply that we are not well-equipped intellectually to handle the arguments.

In the case law, for example, we can see that cognitive preferences for simplicity may have produced proof frameworks that accommodate unitary discrimination claims far better than

---

29   Some have argued that information related to these observations should be introduced in litigation, either through jury instructions, experts, or other means of 'debiasing' judges and jurors who are likely themselves to share the biases that are challenged by plaintiffs in a discrimination lawsuit (Bielby 2003a: 377; Jolls and Sunstein 2006: 996; Walker and Monahan 1987: 559).

30   See generally Blasi (2002: 1241) providing a 'brief overview of the rapidly developing science regarding stereotypes and prejudice' and 'sketch[ing] some of the implications for lawyers and other advocates'; Chen and Hanson (2004: 1110) examining 'stereotypes, categories, schemas, and knowledge structures ... and their potential relevance for law and legal scholarship'; Jolls and Sunstein (2006: 996) discussing implicit bias and 'how the law might better deal with that problem'; Krieger (1995: 1164) arguing that 'the way in which Title VII jurisprudence constructs discrimination, while sufficient to address the deliberate discrimination prevalent in an earlier age, is inadequate to address ... subtle, often unconscious forms of bias' that 'represent today's most prevalent type of discrimination'.

31   See Blasi (2002: 1253) discussing evidence of cognitive simplification strategies; Krieger (1995: 1188): 'Every person, and perhaps even every object that we encounter in the world, is unique, but to treat each as such would be disastrous. ... We would rapidly be inundated by an unmanageable complexity that would quickly overwhelm our cognitive processing and storage capabilities'. Mitnick (2007: 834): '[C]ognition theory shows that it simply is the case that our mental capacities, including especially our working memory, are subject to critical limitations in social perception. ... [T]he result ... is an inherent tendency toward generalization, and with it, categorization'.

complex ones. Under the comparator framework just discussed, it is relatively manageable for courts to measure a black employee's discrimination claim by comparison to the circumstances of a white employee. But when they try to assess two or more joint grounds for discrimination, the comparator process becomes more cognitively difficult to manage. Courts first have to decide upon the appropriate comparator, which they typically deem to be a person who does not share any of the protected characteristics that are the basis for the discrimination claim (Kotkin 2009: 1491–2).[32] At that point, the pool of comparable employees will necessarily be smaller than for the individual who claims only one trait as the basis for discrimination.

As one court explained, 'the more specific the composite class in which the plaintiff claims membership, the more onerous th[e] ultimate burden' of providing discrimination becomes.[33] This burden is twofold. In part, the difficulty is the empirical one of finding a comparable employee without the protected characteristics at issue. In addition, and more relevant here, is the conceptual difficulty – as the numbers of comparators become smaller, judges tend to become more sceptical that the protected trait, rather than a quirk of the plaintiff-employee, was the reason for the discrimination.[34] So, for example, when a black woman brought a race and sex discrimination case, the federal court reviewing her claim found that the 'generally small sample size' of other black women, as compared to individuals who were neither black nor female, 'undermined the evidentiary value of the statistics' showing that black women were underrepresented in senior-grade army positions.[35]

Current iterations of intersectionality theory suggest that this sort of scepticism about comparison's revelatory effects is well-founded for single-trait comparisons as well, in that all individuals have multidimensional aspects of their identities and positions in a workplace and that

---

32   Cf. *Philipsen v. Univ. of Mich. Bd. of Regents*, No. 06-CV-11977-DT, 2007 WL 907822, at *6 (E.D. Mich. 22 March 2007) (observing that '[c]ourts are split … over whether the proper comparator may include only a person outside of the protected class who has the same "plus characteristic" as the plaintiff (in this case, a male with young children) or whether the comparator may include any *person* (male or female) who lacks the "plus" characteristic (in this case, a female without young children)'.

33   *Jeffers v. Thompson*, 264 F. Supp. 2d 314, 327 (D. Md. 2003).

34   This presents a particular challenge for individuals who bring discrimination claims based on more than one protected characteristic as well as for those who tend to be unique, or in a small minority, in their workplaces. See *supra* notes 24–5 and accompanying text. Even in less complex, first-generation-type cases, sample-size issues can be impediments for individuals bringing discrimination claims. For example, in a case brought by black female students who argued that they were punished more harshly for hazing sorority pledges than were comparable white students, Judge Posner rejected the proffered comparators as inadequate. He observed, in addition, the difficulties with inferring discrimination absent identical comparators: 'In a large number of dissimilar cases, if there were reason to think the dissimilarities were randomly distributed and therefore canceled out, an inference of discrimination might be drawn. And likewise in a small sample if the cases were identical except for a racial difference. But in a very small sample of dissimilar cases, the presence of a racial difference does not permit an inference of discrimination; there are too many other differences, and in so small a sample no basis for thinking they cancel out.' *Williams v. Wendler*, 530 F.3d 584, 588–9 (7th Cir. 2008).

35   *Judge v. Marsh*, 649 F. Supp. 770 (D.C. Cir. 1986). See also *Morita v. S. Cal. Permanente Med. Group*, 541 F.2d 217, 220 (9th Cir. 1976), *cert. denied*, 429 U.S. 1050 (1977) ('[S]tatistical evidence derived from an extremely small universe … has little predictive value and must be disregarded'). The problem with a small sample size is that 'slight changes in data can drastically alter appearances'. *Sengupta v. Morrison-Knudsen Co.*, 804 F.2d 1072, 1076 (9th Cir. 1986). See also *Contreras v. City of L.A.*, 656 F.2d 1267, 1273 n.4 (Cal. Ct. App. 1981) ('Statistics are not trustworthy when minor numerical variations produce significant percentage fluctuations').

close comparisons are nearly always hard to come by. Yet the comparator proof structure currently in place in US courts, in particular, manages this difficulty by resisting complication. That is, courts applying this comparator analysis overlook the multidimensional aspects of identity for single-identity claims, and instead treat single-trait comparisons as meaningful and revelatory of discrimination. By contrast, comparisons involving two or more identity traits typically become the object of scepticism, even though they actually present little more complexity when viewed holistically through intersectionality theory's lens. Cognitive psychology suggests that this situation, where single-trait claims are viewed more sympathetically or favourably than intersectional claims, arises in part because our comparative skills are weaker for multifactor than for single factor comparisons.[36]

The point here is not that our cognitive limitations preclude us forever from achieving more textured legal identity categories in adjudication, or that complex discrimination does not occur. Indeed, to the contrary, anecdotal and social science evidence regularly documents the real experience of intersectional discrimination (Kotkin 2009: 1456–7, 1461). Instead, the takeaway is that we may be more likely to succeed in achieving protection for complexly rendered identities to the extent we frame claims in ways that take account of our seemingly innate, cognitively wired preference for simplicity.

Factor Two: Social Salience

Even if our cognitive preferences lead us to prefer clear and simple categories over complex ones, our brains neither dictate the content of those categories nor fix the categories in place forever. Instead, the surrounding culture, understood through individuals, social groups, and political, cultural and legal institutions, plays a critical role in shaping what these categories look like and how they are experienced.[37] Working within these social narratives, individuals regularly identify and align themselves with relatively simple identity categories, even as they understand themselves to have complex, intersectional identities. Even awareness of the socially constructed nature of identity has not displaced these simple categories' power. For example, although race was once thought to be a clear, natural distinction between people, it is widely understood today to be a social construct.[38] Yet it remains a powerful social identifier and basis for movement organizing. Likewise, sex is understood to be more malleable than it once was, and the differences between men and women that were once deemed natural[39] are increasingly treated as reflecting social stereotypes and being shaped by social norms.[40] Still, sex differences remain socially powerful, whether characterized along the Mars/Venus relationship axis or by the persistence of women's organizations or sex-segregated bathrooms.

---

36   See *supra* note 30.

37   For discussions of the interaction of law and society, see generally Post (2003: 485) and Minow (1997).

38   For a review of recent relevant findings from biology, anthropology, sociology and psychology, see Hoffman (2004: 1116–28).

39   See, e.g., *Bradwell v. Illinois*, 83 U.S. 130, 141 (1872) (noting that 'nature … has always recognized a wide difference in the respective spheres and destinies of man and woman' and that '[m]an is, or should be, woman's protector and defender').

40   See, e.g., *United States v. Virginia*, 518 U.S. 515, 550 (1996) (noting that 'generalizations about "the way women are," … no longer justify denying opportunity to women whose talent and capacity place them outside the average description').

Reinforcing the contingent nature of these categories is the fact that their salience also often varies geographically, so that identity categories that may seem fundamentally defining in one context are all but unremarkable in another. In the United States, we see this in the varied categories that are protected in local anti-discrimination ordinances so that, for example, individuals of Appalachian origin receive explicit protection in Cincinnati, which is near Appalachia,[41] but not in New York or Los Angeles.

Although unitary, socially-constructed identity categories such as race, sex and sexual orientation inevitably flatten innumerable other socially significant differences among group members, as intersectionality theory reminds us, they nonetheless exert great power in defining individual and group identity as well as social movement organizing. Seen in this light, the trend toward relatively simplistic identity categories in law is not surprising, as it arguably both reinforces and is reinforced by these categories' powerful social functions.

Factor Three: Identity-Based Legal Advocacy

In addition to cognitive limitations and social salience, institutional concerns also contribute to the sticking power of simple identity categories in adjudication. In particular, and ironically, the institutional structure of identity-based advocacy appears to reinforce the barriers to the achievement of more textured and nuanced treatments of identity in court. An array of incentives, from fundraising to winning cases and more, encourages law reform organizations as well as individual lawyers to prioritize the simplest and most straightforward identity claims, or at least to reduce complex claims to a simple form. As a result, the actors that we might expect would be most likely to find ways over or around the barriers just identified are themselves often not prepared to lead this charge (Goldberg 2009: 124).

Most immediately, we see that advocacy organizations, particularly in the United States, are structured along unitary rather than multidimensional lines. Notwithstanding all that we know about our complex selves, our large-scale identity law reform organizations structure themselves simplistically, focusing on, for example, race *or* ethnicity *or* sex *or* sexual orientation *or* gender identity[42] *or* disability. Even within these categories, organizations frequently focus on one particular strand within the identity group. Among the race- and ethnicity-focused organizations, for example, the NAACP Legal Defence and Educational Fund (LDF) concentrates heavily on the rights of African-Americans, while other organizations, such as the Mexican American Legal Defence and Education Fund, the Puerto Rican Legal Defence and Education Fund, the Asian American Legal Defence and Education Fund, and the Native American Rights Fund, concentrate on the groups for whom they are named. We do not have, by contrast, a women of colour or older disabled people's legal defence fund operating on a significant scale.

With missions focused on constituencies that are conceived along a single identity characteristic, it is not surprising that intersectional claims are not these organizations' priorities. Indeed, if an African-American lesbian were to bring her identity discrimination claim to the race, sex and sexual orientation groups, each organization would ask whether *its* core identity concern would be sufficiently central to justify dedicating resources to the case.

41　Cincinnati City Ordinance No. 79-1991; Cincinnati City Ordinance No. 490-1992.

42　Some large groups in the United States that originally focused exclusively on sexual orientation, such as Lambda Legal, have integrated a focus on gender identity as well, although separate gender identity groups, such as the Transgender Legal Defense and Education Fund, have also emerged.

For reasons of path dependency, this uni-identity structure is unlikely to change significantly. These organizations emerged along identity lines not randomly but rather as the legacy of their related social movements. Apart from LDF, which was founded in 1940, the other organizations just mentioned emerged in the 1970s and 1980s directly out of their constituencies' own social movements. By the time questions of internal diversity began to roil the 'single' identity social movements, organizations had been created, funding sources had been developed, and infrastructures had been built. This is not to say single-identity organizations were immune from change or destruction but rather that they already had firm footing by the time many social movements began to fray.

Funding concerns and interests reinforce this landscape's stability. In part, as a practical matter, it would be very difficult for a start-up intersectional organization to stake out a place on a large scale, given the plethora of longstanding organizations already in existence. Moreover, from an efficiency standpoint, organizations with a broader and simpler focus typically will have a larger natural constituency for purposes of both fundraising and outreach. This owes in part to the cognitive point discussed earlier, in that simpler messages are likely to be easier to convey, as well as to the continued social salience of the general identity categories. The social salience point dovetails with a simple mathematical point – an organization like LDF is likely to have a broader group of adherents if it focuses on race issues relevant to both men and women than focusing primarily on women of colour.[43] Moreover, given that men as a group earn more than women, and whites as a group earn more than people of colour, organizations with whites and/or men in their base have easier access to a wealthier base of potential donors.[44] To the extent anti-discrimination law is seen as a resource, it too reinforces a unitary focus because advocacy organizations invest in developing expertise related to claims in their individual categories.

Private lawyers also lack incentive to advance complex identity theories in litigation. To the extent simpler claims are easier to win, they have every reason, for themselves and their clients, to present their claims as simply as possible. Moreover, unlike advocacy organizations, for whom the primary aim of litigation is to develop good precedent, individual lawyers face economic constraints that make good settlements, rather than good case law, the usual priority. As a result, law-reform organizations are the most likely actors to bring complex identity theories. Yet, as we have just seen, their organizational structures do not facilitate such an approach.

Factor Four: Institutional Legitimacy

A final factor that may reinforce the gap between theory and practice lies within the adjudicating institutions themselves – the courts have a strong concern with protecting their legitimacy and, as I will suggest here, complexly conceived identity categories pose a threat to legitimacy that simple categories generally do not. Most basically, judicial legitimacy derives, in significant part, from courts appearing to function in a non-arbitrary fashion and from their not undertaking analyses that exceed their capacity.[45] To the extent that categories are perceived as malleable, the

---

43   There is a counter-argument, of course, that more narrowly focused organizations will attract more intensely committed constituents.

44   See US Department of Labor (2005).

45   As many critical theorists have observed, however, not all courts aspire to even-handedness, and even those that do cannot successfully resort to 'neutral' decision-making principles (Black 1960). Crenshaw (1988–90: 2): 'Dominant beliefs in the objectivity of legal discourse serve to suppress ... conflict by discounting the relevance of any particular perspective in legal analysis and by positing an analytical stance that has no specific cultural, political, or class characteristics'; Kennedy (1986: 518) challenging judicial claim

role of sorting between who is in or outside the protected category appears to turn more on the decision-maker's judgments than on the designations in the law.

While courts and other institutions carry out this sorting function regularly in all types of cases, the sorting becomes more tenuous from an institutional competency perspective when the decision-maker has to define a social category such as identity. This is because, as I have argued elsewhere, determining the indicia of a protected identity seems more like an anthropological or sociological function than a legal task (Goldberg 2002: 643). That is, identity is primarily a social construct and only secondarily a legal construct. As a result, defining the boundaries of protected identity categories implicates individual experiences and sensibilities to a far greater degree than, say, defining breach in contract doctrine or proximate cause in tort law.

Not surprisingly, an assortment of legitimacy challenges for courts stem from identity's status as an often unstable and indefinite social identifier. Amidst these challenges, the distinct difficulty posed by intersectionality relates back to the cognitive psychological issues associated with the comparator proof structure, as discussed at the outset. If intersectional claims are going to translate meaningfully in the adjudication process, courts must move away from the demand that litigants produce a comparator to show that 'but for' the protected characteristic, he or she would have been treated fairly in the workplace or other environment. Yet the closest substitute in discrimination law – a holistic assessment, much like the analytic framework for evaluating sexual harassment claims[46] – is fraught with institutional difficulties.

By contrast to the comparator approach, which is treated as a quasi-mechanical method of reducing the alternate explanatory variables so that discrimination is the 'obvious' explanation for an employer's challenged conduct, a holistic assessment relies more openly on the decision-maker's judgment about the situation before the court. This move toward a holistic assessment would enable decision-makers to consider an array of evidence that might indicate an employer's hostility or bias towards a subset of workers, such as Asian women or older people with disabilities, in workplaces where comparator proof does not exist or would be subject to scepticism because of the relatively small numbers of comparable employees who lack the litigant's protected traits.

Yet the problem is that without a comparator to 'prove' that discrimination has occurred, courts risk appearing undisciplined, unrestrained and/or stretched beyond their institutional capacity as they immerse themselves in discerning identity-related hostility or marginalization. In this sense, their embrace of a relatively unconstrained framework could be taken not as a valuable shift towards fuller enforcement of anti-discrimination law but instead as evidence of the judiciary's frayed legitimacy.

Conclusion

As we think about how to carry forward the insights offered by intersectionality theory, both in theoretical work and in court, we need, of course, to develop new affirmative theories and practices to build on the growing conceptual acceptance that identity-based discrimination can be, and often is, intersectional in nature. Yet we also need to have a clearer understanding of the reasons why intersectionality theory's insights, while accepted at a general level, have been stymied both as

---

to objectivity; Rubenfeld (2002: 1141) describing the Supreme Court's political agenda in anti-discrimination jurisprudence.

46   As the US Supreme Court has written, '[w]orkplace conduct is not measured in isolation'; instead, 'whether an environment is sufficiently hostile or abusive' must be judged 'by "looking at all the circumstances"'. *Clark Cty. Sch. Dist. v. Breeden*, 532 U.S. 268, 270–1 (2001) (citations omitted).

courts have decided complex claims and as theorists have sought to extend them in new directions. In that vein, the simplicity factors identified here – from cognitive limitations to social salience, and from institutionalized advocacy to judicial legitimacy – deserve consideration. By finding ways to render complex claims more simply and proposing proof structures that are sensitive to both the complex realities of individuals and the simplifying preferences of courts and advocates, we may open new possibilities for bringing anti-discrimination law into closer alignment with lived experience.

Chapter 12

The Assimilationist Anti-Discrimination Paradigm and the Immigrant Muslim Woman: Suggestions on How to Re-Conceptualize Discrimination Claims

Lynn Roseberry

Introduction

Since the terrorist attacks in the United States on 11 September 2001, schools and employers in Europe have been adopting dress codes that prohibit Muslim women and girls from wearing any kind of Muslim veiling, often at the urging of politicians and government officials.[1] Muslim women have increasingly been required to choose between accepting employment or wearing their Muslim headscarves. Muslim girls have increasingly been required to choose between wearing a Muslim veil or attending the school of their (or their parents') choice. The dress codes in these cases strike at the intersection of several discrimination grounds. The dress codes do not affect Muslims as a group, but only a sub-group of Muslims – *women*. Furthermore, not all Muslim women are affected by the dress codes. Most of those affected by the dress codes are immigrants or descendants of immigrants from non-Western countries, and thus they also possess a minority ethnic[2] identity as compared to the majority of the population in all Member States of the European Union (EU). Yet most of the litigation about these dress codes has been framed as either religious freedom or discrimination on grounds of religion. The courts have generally upheld these dress codes against both kinds of claims.

In this chapter I want to show how European judicial approaches to the dress codes seem to be developing on the basis of assumptions that establish what American legal scholar Kenji Yoshino has called the 'assimilationist' paradigm for anti-discrimination law, the essence of which is a requirement that persons claiming discrimination must show that they are physically unable to assimilate to the majority norm. I intend to show that the underlying assumptions of the assimilationist paradigm block judicial treatment of the potentially multiple grounds of discrimination that are often involved in the dress code cases.[3]

---

1   Abdo (2008) provides an overview of judicial decisions and other national practice in the EU.

2   I will be using the term 'ethnic identity' or 'ethnic origin' to refer to membership in a socially defined group based on cultural criteria, such as language, customs and shared history (Tatum 2002: 16). I will use the term 'racial identity' to refer to membership in a group that is socially defined but on the basis of physical criteria such as skin colour and facial features (Tatum 2002: 16).

3   I will use the term 'immigrant women' to refer to women who immigrated from non-Western countries, whose first language is not the language of a Western country, and whose parents are not citizens of a Western country. 'Western countries' include all EU Member States plus Andorra, Iceland, Liechtenstein, Monaco, Norway, San Marino, Switzerland, Canada, the United States, Australia and New Zealand. I will not be dealing with the important distinctions between and among the categories of documented and undocumented immigrants.

I begin by presenting the assimilationist paradigm, as described by Kenji Yoshino and its underlying assumptions about identity and the harm caused by discrimination. I then introduce the legal framework, established by EU anti-discrimination law and the European Convention on Human Rights that applies to European dress code cases. Next, I intend to show that current European legal approaches to dress code cases, as exemplified by two national court decisions, appear to follow the parameters established by the assimilationist paradigm and that by doing so they privilege the perspectives of dominant social groups in relation to Muslim women and legitimate discrimination against them. Following this, I question the appropriateness of the model of identity that defines the parameters of the assimilationist paradigm in light of modern psychological research on racism, prejudice and the formation of gender, racial and ethnic identities. I suggest that by incorporating the insights of current social psychological research into legal analysis of the dress code cases, courts may be better able to avoid privileging the perspectives of dominant groups and thus find it easier to recognize Muslim women's experience of discrimination. Finally, I intend to show how incorporating modern social psychological understandings of prejudice and identity into legal analysis of dress code cases can change the parameters of the analysis and cast light on the intersectional discrimination experienced by Muslim women. I conclude the chapter by proposing new parameters for the legal analysis of intersectional claims involving religion, gender and ethnicity or race that will bring the multiple identities of Muslim women more clearly into focus, thus increasing the likelihood that discrimination practised against Muslim women will be recognized and remedied.

The Assimilationist Paradigm

In the EU, anti-discrimination law has granted the most protection against discrimination based on race and sex while the other prohibited grounds of discrimination have received less protection (Schiek 2002a: 290–314; Bell and Waddington 2001: 587–611). This differentiation in protection resembles a pattern established in American anti-discrimination law. For example, the American Supreme Court has established different levels of scrutiny to be applied to claims of discrimination brought under the Equal Protection clause in the Constitution's fourteenth amendment, depending on which ground of discrimination is alleged. Race has been held to be a 'suspect classification' which requires the application of the strictest form of constitutional scrutiny.[4] Sex is also a suspect classification, but because biological sex is deemed to represent some 'real' differences between men and women, the Court applies an intermediate level of scrutiny.[5] Sexual orientation,[6] age[7] or disability,[8] are not considered suspect classifications and are thus given only the lowest level of scrutiny – rational basis review.[9]

---

4   See, e.g., *Johnson v. California*, 543 U.S. 499, 505–6 (2005); *Grutter v. Bollinger*, 539 U.S. 306, 326 (2003).

5   See, e.g., *United States v. Virginia*, 518 U.S. 515, 533 (1996) (subjecting a public college's gender-based admissions policy to intermediate scrutiny).

6   See, e.g., *Equality Foundation of Greater Cincinnati, Inc. v. City of Cincinnati*, 128 F.3d 289 (6th Cir. 1997)(denying gays heightened scrutiny, in part because of their invisibility).

7   *Massachusetts Board of Retirement v. Murgia*, 427 U.S. 307 (1976).

8   *Board of Trustees of the University of Alabama v. Garrett*, 531 U.S. 356 (2001). The majority in *Garrett* was following an earlier decision, *Cleburne v. Cleburne Living Center, Inc.*, 473 U.S. 432 (1985), in which the Court had refused to find the 'mentally retarded' to qualify as a suspect classification.

9   By ruling that age and disability are not suspect classifications, the Court merely held that the Constitution does not prevent the States from discriminating on the basis of age or disability as long as they

American legal scholar Kenji Yoshino (2002) points out that the schism in protection against discrimination on grounds of race and sex on the one hand and sexual orientation on the other has been justified in American law in part by the fact that race and sex are considered to be 'immutable' and 'visible' characteristics, over which the individual has no control, whereas sexual orientation is generally considered to be invisible as it is defined primarily by sexual behaviour performed in private. It is often assumed that characteristics that are *not* morphological and biologically fixed *can* be changed, and therefore discrimination claimants *must* change them. To fail to do so is viewed as tantamount to wilfulness: a refusal to do what is justifiably expected. Yoshino calls this approach towards discrimination the 'assimilationist paradigm'.

Yoshino (2002) developed his analysis of the assimilationist paradigm in American anti-discrimination law by showing how the reasons given for granting gays a far lower level of protection against discrimination than has been granted racial minorities and women corresponds to the perception that gays are able to assimilate to heterosexual norms in three ways: conversion, passing and covering. Conversion occurs when the homosexual changes his or her identity – either by changing their bodies through a sex change operation or by changing their sexual orientation through an exercise of will. A conversion demand operates to exclude gays completely from employment and other social institutions and corresponds to the concept of direct discrimination on the basis of sexual orientation. Passing occurs when the underlying identity is merely hidden, for example when a lesbian hides her sexual orientation from family, acquaintances, employers and co-workers. A passing demand consists of requiring the gays to act as if they were heterosexual and to represent themselves as such.

Covering occurs when the underlying identity is simply downplayed in order to help others ignore a person's sexual orientation, for example by not engaging in public displays of same-sex affection, in gender-atypical activity that could code as gay, or in gay activism. Yoshino (2002: 778) derives the term and concept of 'covering' from the work of sociologist Erving Goffman, who observed that even persons who are ready to identify themselves as possessing a stigmatizing characteristic may nonetheless make a great effort to keep that characteristic from looming large.

Yoshoni (2002: 773–4) argues that the distinctions drawn between conversion, passing and covering proceed from two important assumptions. First, it is assumed that these different kinds of assimilation demands do not overlap – 'that one can cover without passing and that one can pass without converting'. Second, the demands vary in severity. Conversion is always considered to be more burdensome than passing, and passing is always considered to be more burdensome than covering. These assumptions are in turn based on a particular model of identity, which Yoshino dubs 'the classical model'. Yoshino conceives of this model of identity as a set of concentric circles. At the centre is the individual's recognition of having a certain identity, like race. The next circle comprises explicit disclosures that one has that identity. The outer circle comprises behaviour that may be interpreted as signalling that one has a particular identity.

Yoshino (2002: 774) then explains that the amount of protection given by American anti-discrimination law traces this model by extending the most protection against conversion demands, which are recognized as constituting direct attacks at the centre of one's identity.[10] Covering demands, which are directed at the outer circle of identity – where one 'merely' signals that one has a certain status – are considered to be less harmful, both because they constitute less of an

---

have a rational basis for it. Title VII, the federal employment discrimination act, prohibits discrimination on the basis of age and disability in both public and private employment.

10   Yoshino explicitly points out only the relationship between the different kinds of assimilation demands and the level of animus associated with them. However, the idea that the seriousness of the attack on one's identity varies according to how far within the circle the demand reaches is implicit in his model.

intrusion on one's identity and because such demands signal a weaker level of animus on the part of the alleged discriminator. Both passing and converting demands amount to direct discrimination on protected grounds, for example when employment is made conditional on actually having the desired identity or the ability to keep up the appearance of having the desired identity.

Yoshino's (2002: 774) primary criticism of the assimilation model is that these three modes of assimilation are not always easily distinguishable from one another. Categorizing the mode of assimilation depends on the information available to the audience when the assimilation conduct is performed. Yoshino (2002: 772) gives the example of gays who refrain from public displays of affection may be simultaneously passing with respect to people who do not know that they are gay and covering with respect to those who do. The difficulty in distinguishing between the three kinds of assimilation demands might in turn suggest that, contrary to the prevailing assumption, these different assimilation demands may not be essentially different from each other.

The Legal Framework: Principles of Non-Discrimination and Freedom of Religion

Discrimination claims arising from employer and school dress codes are complicated by the fact that the dress codes can implicate several grounds of discrimination, and the protection provided against discrimination is regulated by diverse instruments with different approaches in both the EU legal system and the human rights regime established by the European Convention on Human Rights (ECHR). Both the EU and the ECHR prohibit discrimination on grounds of race, ethnicity, religion and gender, but the prohibitions do not have the same material scope. The material scope of EU legal protection against discrimination varies with the different grounds of discrimination, which makes it difficult to invoke EU legal protections against discrimination in cases where multiple grounds are implicated. Dress codes prohibiting the wearing of Muslim veils have been adopted by both employers and schools, but only discrimination on grounds of race, ethnic origin and sex is prohibited in both employment and education. Discrimination on grounds of religion is prohibited only in the employment sphere.[11]

The ECHR's Article 14 contains a prohibition against discrimination on grounds of religion but only with regards to securing 'The enjoyment of the rights and freedoms set forth' in the Convention. The Convention does not include a right to employment or a right to education, so Article 14 cannot be invoked against employment or school dress codes. Complaints about employer or school dress codes that prohibit the wearing of Muslim veils must then be framed as interference with the right to *manifest* religion or belief, which is protected by Article 9 ECHR. Article 9(1) ECHR recognizes that '[e]veryone has the right to freedom of thought, conscience and religion', and that this 'right includes freedom, either alone or in community with others and in public or private, to manifest his religion or belief, in worship, teaching, practice and observance'. However, the right to manifest one's religion or belief is not absolute, as Article 9(2) ECHR provides that this particular aspect of freedom of religion is subject to 'such limitations as are prescribed by law and are necessary in a democratic society in the interests of public safety, for the protection of public order, health

---

11   A proposal for a directive on implementing the principle of equal treatment between persons irrespective of religion or belief, disability, age or sexual orientation (COM (2008) 426 final), contains a provision, Article 2, that would prohibit discrimination based on the mentioned criteria in both the public and private sector in areas other than the labour market, specifically, social protection, including social security and health care; social advantages; education; access to and supply of goods and services which are available to the public, including housing.

or morals, or for the protection of the rights and freedoms of others'.[12] The European Court of Human Rights has emphasized in its case law that 'Article 9 does not protect every act motivated or inspired by a religion or belief. Moreover, in exercising his freedom to manifest his religion, an individual may need to take his specific situation into account'.[13] The European Commission and Court of Human Rights have accordingly allowed most restrictions on public manifestations of religion in employment[14] and educational settings.[15]

While of course the freedom of religion protected by Article 9 ECHR is not a prohibition against discrimination, the legal analysis of claims of infringement of this right is very similar to the legal analysis of claims of indirect discrimination on grounds of religion in EU law. First, Article 9 ECHR and the prohibition against indirect discrimination on grounds of religion in Directive 2000/78/EC establishing a general framework for equal treatment in employment and occupation (Employment Framework Directive) can apply simultaneously to dress code cases. Article 2(2)(b) of the Framework Directive prohibits indirect discrimination, which is understood as 'occur[ring] where an apparently neutral provision, criterion or practice would put persons having a particular religion or belief at a particular disadvantage compared with other persons, unless that provision, criterion or practice is objectively justified by a legitimate aim and the means of achieving that aim are appropriate and necessary'. Article 9 ECHR would also apply to situations where the disadvantage characterized as indirect discrimination consists of an interference in the right to manifest a certain religion or belief. Under Article 9, the next step is to determine whether the 'interference' is 'prescribed by law' and 'necessary in a democratic society in the interests of public safety, for the protection of public order, health or morals, or for the protection of the rights and freedoms of others'. Public safety, protection of public order, health or morals or the protection of rights and freedoms of others, may certainly be considered to be the 'legitimate aim' required by Article 2(2)(b) of the Employment Framework Directive to justify indirect discrimination. Likewise, Article 9's requirement that the interference be 'necessary' generally coincides with the Directive's additional requirement that the justification of indirect discrimination include a showing that the interference in the religious practice is 'appropriate and necessary' to achieve the 'legitimate aim' (e.g. public safety, public order, health, morals, etc.).

The Assimilationist Paradigm in Dress Code Cases

The two dress code cases presented below exemplify the prevailing European judicial approach to Muslim women's and girls' complaints about dress codes. In the case from Denmark, an employer's dress code was the subject of the complaint and was formulated as indirect discrimination on the grounds of religion. The case from the UK concerned a school's dress code. Thus the complaint was framed as an infringement of the claimant's rights under Article 9 ECHR.

Article 9 ECHR clearly makes a distinction between behaviour, putting limits on the freedom to manifest one's religion, and the internal state of holding a belief, which Article 9 does not limit. On the other hand, the prohibition against indirect discrimination does not make an obvious distinction between behaviour and belief, but as I intend to show in the following discussions

---

12   ECHR (European Convention of Human Rights), Article 9(2).

13   *Kalac v. Turkey*, 1 July 1997, § 27, *Reports* 1997-IV, 27 EHRR 552.

14   See, e.g., *Konttinen v. Finland*, no. 24949/94, (1996) 87 DR 68; *X v. United Kingdom* 8160/78, (1981) 22 DR 27, 4 EHRR 126.

15   See, e.g., *Sahin v. Turkey*, no. 44774/98, 10 November 2005; *Dahlab v. Switzerland*, no. 42393/98, ECHR 2001-V; *Karaduman v. Turkey*, no. 16278/90, (1993) 74 DR 93; *Valsamis v. Greece*, 18 December 1996, *Reports* 1996-VI, 24 EHRR 294, para. 38.

of the Danish indirect discrimination case and a British Article 9 ECHR case, the distinction between behaviour and the internal state of holding a belief tends to seep into the analysis of indirect discrimination, thus permitting the application of the assimilationist paradigm. Both these decisions may be understood as the result of applying the false assumption that the three modes of assimilation – conversion, passing and covering – are essentially different from each other. Furthermore, I will argue that upholding the dress codes in these cases is made possible by privileging the majority perspective from which the dress codes appear to be examples of covering demands, which the assimilationist paradigm represents as minimal, and thus acceptable, burdens on an individual's identity.

The Assimilationist Paradigm and Indirect Discrimination: The Føtex Case

In *Føtex*,[16] a young Moroccan woman was fired from her job in the bakery of a supermarket, Føtex, when she began to wear a *hijab* to work four years after she had been hired. Wearing a *hijab* was not permitted by the store dress code, which had been adopted by the employer after consultation with employee representatives. The dress code prescribed that employees that had direct customer contact must wear a uniform, which did not include hats or other head coverings, and they were not allowed to display religious and political symbols. The purpose of the dress code, according to the material distributed by the employer to the employees, was to ensure that the employees had a neutral and uniform appearance in order to avoid potential conflicts between members of the staff and customers. The employer offered to transfer the claimant to another a job, where she would not have any customer contact, so that she could wear the *hijab* while working. She refused to accept the change in her working conditions and was dismissed. She brought a claim of indirect discrimination on grounds of religion. Although no claim of ethnic discrimination had been brought, the employer presented evidence at trial showing that the employer's staff included a relatively large number of first- and second-generation immigrants from non-Western countries.

The case ultimately reached the Danish Supreme Court, which recognized that Muslim women would be disadvantaged by the policy as compared with both Muslim men and non-Muslim women, but held that the policy pursued a legitimate aim and that it fulfilled the requirements for justification as explained in the explanatory remarks in the preparatory works for the Danish employment discrimination act. The explanatory remarks to the anti-discrimination legislation had incorporated an earlier Supreme Court judgment, in which the Court held that a department store's dress code was disproportionate to the asserted legitimate aim (projecting a certain image to the public) because it was too vague (it did not require uniforms or any particular clothing, but only that the employees should be well-groomed) and it was not applied to all the employees. Accordingly, the Supreme Court held in *Føtex* that the supermarket's dress code was justified because it was sufficiently specific, it was intended to project a certain image to the public, and it applied to all the employees that worked in areas where they would have customer contact.

The supermarket's dress code in *Føtex* may be understood as a covering, passing or a conversion demand depending on the meaning ascribed to the *hijab* and the observer's knowledge of the employees' various identities. If the *hijab* is understood to be merely a manifestation of one's faith, which can be suppressed without denying the woman's status as a Muslim, then it may be viewed as a covering demand. This appears to be the perspective of the employer and employee representatives in this case, as they treat religious and political symbols as belonging to the same category: outward signs of particular religious and political convictions. Further, the employer

---

16   U 2005, 1265 H.

emphasized that it had no objections to Islam or any other religion; it was just the wearing of religious articles of clothing and other symbols that posed a problem. Indeed, the fact that the Danish court could treat the dress code as constituting only indirect discrimination, rather than direct discrimination, despite the employer's express desire to exclude employee manifestations of religious belief, stems from the conviction that restrictions on behaviour are viewed as distinct from restrictions on identity, i.e. Muslim women are not discriminated against, they are merely required to leave their religious garb at home. The dress code is not seen as intruding upon the inner circles of the employee's identity.

On the other hand, while the employer may know that the employee is Muslim, the dress code ensures that the customers will not discover the employee's 'true identity'. Thus, the employee may experience the dress code as a passing demand: she understands that she is being required to hide her identity from the customers. If the employee believes that she must wear the *hijab* in order to *be* a Muslim, then she may experience the requirement of removing the *hijab* as a conversion demand: she cannot be a Muslim woman, as she understands it, and keep her job. Further, if most of the women she encounters in her social circle are Moroccan women who wear the *hijab*, she may feel that she cannot fully *be* a Moroccan Muslim woman while at work.

The Assimilationist Paradigm and Article 9 ECHR: The Begum Case

In *Begum*,[17] Shabina Begum brought a claim based on Article 9 ECHR after she was prohibited from wearing the *jilbab* in school. The female pupils at Denbigh High School, where the headteacher was of Bengladeshi origin and Muslim and 80 per cent of the pupils are Muslim, could choose between three versions of the school uniform, which had been devised after consultation with parents, pupils, staff and the local mosques: (1) a v-neck jumper, school tie, plain white shirt, black shoes and navy blue trousers or (2) an A-line or pleated knee length navy skirt, or (3) a navy blue *salwar kameez*, which is a combination of a sleeveless smock-like dress with a square neckline revealing the wearer's shirt collar and tie and loose trousers tapering at the ankles. The girls are also permitted to wear blue headscarves. Shabina Begum was the daughter of Bangladeshi citizens who immigrated to the UK before she was born. Shabina wore the *salwar kameez* for two years, from the ages of 12 to 14, without complaint. When she was 14, she decided she wanted to wear a full-length *jilbab* to school, which is a long coat-like garment worn by some Muslim girls who believe they must wear it after they have started to menstruate in order to comply with their understanding of Koranic injunctions regarding women's dress.[18]

The majority opinion in *Begum* followed the Article 9 case law of the European Court of Human Rights and took the view that the prohibition on Shabina Begum's wearing a *jilbab* in school did not amount to an interference with her freedom of religion.[19] The court emphasized the various possibilities for Shabina and her family to choose differently so as to avoid coming into conflict with the school's uniform policy. The majority noted that the school lies outside the catchment area where Shabina's family lives, but they had chosen the school for her anyway, even after having been informed of the school's policy in regard to uniforms, and that there was no evidence to indicate that the claimant would have had any real difficulty in attending another school where pupils were permitted to wear the *jilbab*.[20] Furthermore, the majority noted that Shabina's older sister had worn

---

17 *R. (On the application of Begum) v. Headteacher and Governors of Denbigh High School* [2007] 1 AC 100 [Hereinafter referred to as '*Begum*'].

18 See Ward (2006: 315) for additional background on veiling practices.

19 *Begum*, paras 22–5.

20 *Begum*, para. 25.

the *salwar kameez* throughout her time at the school, as Shabina herself also had during her first two years at the school, without objection, and that '[i]t was of course open to the respondent, as she grew older, to modify her beliefs', which she did 'against a background of free and informed consent by her and her family'.[21] The majority's reasoning falls clearly within the assimilationist paradigm already established by the European Court of Human Rights in its case law on religious freedom: restrictions on religious behaviour in educational settings is generally permitted.

Baroness Hale found that there had been an interference with Shabina's religious freedom,[22] thus indicating she might see the dress code as entailing more than just a covering demand, but she found the refusal to let Shabina wear a *jilbab* was justified by resorting to the assimilationist paradigm's emphasis on freedom to choose. She analysed the proportionality of the dress code against the extent to which the uniform policy interfered with the girls' freedom to choose Islamic or secular dress.[23] Baroness Hale first states that she would assume that an adult Muslim woman who chooses to wear the Islamic headscarf does so freely, recognizing that '[t]hat there are many reasons why she might wish to do this'.[24] However, while Baroness Hale does not rule out that some Muslim women may freely choose to wear some form of veiling, she asserts that there are 'different views in different communities about what is required of a Muslim woman', one of which is that 'strict dress codes may be imposed upon women', thus denying Muslim women freedom to choose for themselves.[25] She also points out that some Islamic dress requirements require women to cover more than men, and are thus an expression of sex inequality in and of themselves.[26] Thus, while Baroness Hale is willing to believe that adult women may genuinely choose to subject themselves to veiling requirements, and 'it is not for others ... to criticize or prevent [them]', she does not believe that schools should apply such a hands-off approach to its students.[27] She explains:

> [The school's] task is to help all of their pupils achieve their full potential. This includes growing up to play whatever part they choose in the society in which they are living. The school's task is also to promote the ability of people of diverse races, religions and cultures to live together in harmony. Fostering a sense of community and cohesion within the school is an important part of that. A uniform dress code can play its role in smoothing over ethnic, religious and social divisions. But it does more than that. Like it or not, this is a society committed, in principle and in law, to equal freedom for men and women to choose how they will lead their lives within the law. Young girls from ethnic, cultural or religious minorities growing up here face particularly difficult choices: how far to adopt or to distance themselves from the dominant culture.[28]

---

21   *Begum*, para. 25.

22   Baroness Hale, *R (on the application of Begum) v. Headteacher and Governors of Denbigh High School* [2007] 1 AC 100, para. 92.

23   Note that this approach is not consistent with the EU discrimination directives' proportionality requirement, which entails a determination of whether the aim is legitimate and whether the means of achieving the aim are both appropriate and necessary. See Article 2(2)(b) in Directive 2000/43/EC on racial and ethnic discrimination and in Directive 2000/78/EC on occupation and employment. However, it is probably in line with the approach to freedom of religion cases in the Article 9 case law of the European Court of Human Rights as it is described in, e.g., Vickers (2006) and Langenfeld and Mohsen (2005).

24   *Begum*, para. 92.

25   *Begum*, para. 95.

26   *Begum*, para. 95.

27   *Begum*, para. 92.

28   *Begum*, para. 97.

In this passage, Baroness Hale clearly reveals that from her point of view the extent to which girls like Shabina choose to wear a Muslim veil is a matter of choice regarding how far to adapt to the dominant culture, not a matter of a right to manifest one's identity. Thus, the uniform policy can be characterized as a covering demand impinging only on the outer circle of identity, rather than a passing or conversion demand.

Baroness Hale then minimizes the seriousness of the intrusion into the outer circle of identity by questioning whether school-age girls even have the capacity to make genuine choices. She adopts a point of view articulated by Frances Raday (2003) which sees the wearing of veils by school-age girls as the result of 'patriarchal family control' and mandatory policies that reject veiling in state schools as providing 'a crucial opportunity for girls to choose' feminist freedom.[29]

For Baroness Hale it seems that school-age girls may either do as their patriarchal families tell them or as their school tells them. According to this point of view, they simply do not have the capacity to choose to veil themselves in any meaningful sense of the word. Young girls who veil themselves are therefore not even signalling their identity, but rather their family's identity. Thus, the uniform policy can hardly be said to interfere with even the outer circle of Shabina's identity.[30]

To the extent Shabina wears the *jilbab* because she feels it reflects her identity, she may experience the refusal to accommodate her decision to wear the *jilbab* as a conversion demand, i.e. that the school policy is intended to exclude Muslims holding more conservative views of Islam, or as a passing demand, if she understands that the school is willing to accept her to the extent she feels that she is merely being asked to act as if she has another identity.

Privileging the Majority's Understanding of Assimilation Demands

Whether the assimilation demands in *Føtex* and *Begum* constitute conversion, covering or passing demands cannot be determined according to any objective criteria. From the courts' perspective, the dress codes constituted only interference in the outer circle of the individual's protected identity status (religion, ethnic origin, gender). The inner circle remained intact. The claimants were not being asked to change their identity status; they were merely being asked to conform to the dress codes or go elsewhere. From the claimants' perspective they were being asked to 'pass' or 'convert': conservative Muslim young women were not welcome, unless they act as if they are not conservative Muslim young women. The choice between whose perspective should prevail is not dictated by any objective principle. The courts in these cases reached their decisions by privileging their own perspectives over that of the claimants. Indeed, little ink was spilled over the claimants' experience of their exclusion from work and school as a result of the clothing they were wearing. The end result is that majority religious, ethnic and gender norms are given a privileged status in evaluating school and employer policies that tend to exclude immigrant women with minority ethnic and religious identities.

---

29   *Begum*, para. 98.

30   Pre-adolescent girls probably do lack the capacity to choose based on their own sense of identity. Psychologists generally agree that younger children lack the physical and cognitive development needed to engage in the self-reflective process necessary to the formation of identity. However, according to Tatum (2002: 20) adolescents begin to reflect on questions about who they are, and choices about what to wear and how to behave are very much a reflection of this process of identity formation.

Changing the Paradigm: from Liberal Autonomy to Feminist Agency and Psycho-Social Theories of Identity, Racism and Prejudice

The 'classical model' of identity on which the assimilationist paradigm depends corresponds generally with liberal legal theories of the legal subject. Abrams (1999: 810–12) points out that liberal theories share the common assumption that there is 'a self' – the core of Yoshino's model of concentric circles – 'marked by strong boundaries that are theoretically possible to maintain against the claims and incursions of others'. According to such theories, social influence may be important in defining this self during childhood and adolescence, but once an individual reaches maturity, social influences are assumed to have only minimal influence on the individual. Abrams explains that liberal theories of the legal subject require that social influences must be carefully kept at a distance from the internal motivational structure of the actor in order to maintain the position that personal autonomy exists as more than merely an ideal. General adherence to this understanding of the legal subject is what makes it seem plausible that a covering demand does not threaten the core of an individual's identity. However, as the foregoing discussion of the two dress code cases demonstrates, whether an assimilationist demand is harmless or operates as a screening device to exclude immigrant women from educational and employment opportunities is a highly subjective determination that depends on the perspective from which the assimilationist demand is evaluated. If anti-discrimination law is to provide a remedy for the disadvantage that arises from applying discriminatory majority social norms, a different theory of the legal subject may be needed.

The most obvious alternative to liberal theories of the legal subject is post-structuralism, which Carle (2005: 319–20) describes as a collection of different theoretical projects that are engaged in 'denounc[ing] liberal individualism for its untenable notions of the individual as an autonomous agent free to shape his or her destiny'. Post-structural theories of identity are diametrically opposed to liberal theories, holding that all human knowledge and action are social constructs and therefore there is no 'self' outside a social context. Thus described, post-structuralist theories of identity hold obvious attractions for someone seeking to explain why covering demands are equally serious violations of personal dignity and freedom as conversion demands. According to these theories, signalling behaviour – such as public displays of affection between gays or the wearing of a *hijab* or a *jilbab* by immigrant women –would be constitutive of identity. Making distinctions between covering and conversion demands is unintelligible within a post-structuralist theory of identity.

However, while post-structuralism may solve the problem of eliminating distinctions between covering and conversion demands, its conflation of signalling behaviour with identity poses other problems. As Yoshino (2002: 893) discovers when he tries to adapt post-structuralist philosopher Judith Butler's theory of identity to anti-discrimination law, the question of which performances fundamentally constitute the identities protected by anti-discrimination law inevitably arises. Yoshino (2002: 937) asks: without a core self against which to measure assimilation demands, how are we 'to determine which traits will "count" as traits that ought to be protected against covering demands'?[31] Yoshino finds no solution to this problem. Instead he (2002: 937–8) promotes the idea of 'having [a] conversation' – through litigation or through public debate – 'about which kinds of performative traits … might constitute' identity. This approach holds little promise for change.

---

31   This is the 'slippery slope' problem that arises from the concern that if one covering demand is considered discrimination, all kinds of demands placed on cultural acts in the workplace will be considered discrimination. According to this view, if employers permit employees to wear the *hijab* as an expression of ethnic, religious and gender identity, then white racist employees should be allowed to wear symbols of racist ideology like the swastika.

Just as problematic as identifying which traits are worthy of anti-discrimination law's protection is the relative absence of human agency within post-structuralist theories. Post-structuralists' rejection of conceptions of the self as existing separate from or prior to social context makes it difficult for them to account for human agency in their theories. Carle (2005: 339) points out that a consequence of this rejection is that post-structuralist theories have difficulty accounting for any possibility for social change brought about through acts of will. Abrams (1995) and other feminist and progressive theorists engaged in framing legal and political strategies for combating oppression have been dissatisfied with post-structuralist theories of the constructed self for this very reason.

Abrams (1999) has attempted to resolve the conflict between liberal theory's concept of autonomy with the post-structuralist concept of socially constructed identities by developing a theory that allows for the possibility of self-definition and self-direction – which she calls agency, to distinguish it from liberal autonomy – while recognizing that the process of self-definition is powerfully shaped by the forces of social construction in a context of unequal power relations. Abrams (1999: 824) describes self-definition as 'determining how one conceives of oneself in terms of the goals one wants to achieve and the kind of person, with particular values and attributes, one considers oneself to be', but asserts that the possibility of self-definition arises first when the individual becomes aware of the extent to which one's conception of self is socially constituted. She observes (1999: 825–6):

> A woman may become aware, for example, that images or attitudes she has regarding her body, her competence to perform certain tasks, or her strength or vulnerability in relation to others, are shaped by norms that describe these matters at least partly as a function of gender. Developing this awareness does not permit her to transcend these socially conditioned visions of self, but it allows her greater room in which to affirm, reinterpret, resist, or partially replace them. ... Though she does not have recourse to some complete, pre-social self that can be uncovered, she may draw on moments of insight that arise from her reflection on her experience, or attitudes she holds that are shaped by other social influences. This process of reflection and comparison, which is facilitated by her awareness of certain self-conceptions as socially shaped, may allow her to identify more strongly with certain images and strive for greater distance from others.

Abrams (1999: 826) further asserts, as many feminists do, that the social or cultural norms that embody negative judgments about women's competence and bodies 'do not simply make it more difficult for women to develop independent self-conceptions'. Rather, these negative norms make it more difficult for women to develop *positive* self-conceptions that are a necessary condition for even imagining the possibility of choosing a path that does not conform to limiting gender stereotypes. However, Abrams (1999: 826–7) manages to find room for agency, despite the role played by social norms, in the observation that we are all subjects with a range of attributes that are assigned various positive or negative meanings in a particular culture, 'so that our ability to define ourselves in positive and authorizing ways may be assisted by some of these meanings, and undermined by others'. Abrams illustrates the point with the example of a hypothetical woman of colour, whose self-conception may be undermined by negative social meanings assigned to her race or gender, but she may feel herself authorized by positive social meanings attributed to her heterosexual orientation or by positive meanings assigned to her race and gender by her church or a circle of friends.

Whereas the liberal concept of autonomy located the process of self-definition within an individual pre-social self, Abrams' theory of agency acknowledges to a far greater degree that self-definition is not simply a matter of individual will but rather involves a collective element. Abrams (1999: 828) asserts that it is through social dialogue that a woman may become aware that 'her self-conception does not simply reflect her own shortcomings, but is a function of views and expectations that are instilled socially'.

While Abrams' theory seems to be able to combine a concept of the legal subject that preserves some possibility of agency with the recognition that identity is largely formed as a result of social processes, it does not provide a means of determining when a discrimination prohibition should apply to protect an individual from an assimilation demand. The liberal theory of the legal subject included a means of determining when employment and school policies were discriminatory by making a distinction between the protected identity and behaviour. Abrams' theory eschews that distinction and does not seem to provide a readily accessible alternative measure to take its place.

Psychological theories of identity-formation and studies of black Americans' experience of racism, elements of which are recognizable in Abrams' theory of agency, may indicate a way towards developing such an alternative measure. Like Abrams, psychologists working on understanding how racism and other forms of discrimination affect identity formation accept the importance of social relationships in the construction of individual identity. Erik Erikson, the psychoanalytic theorist who coined the term 'identity crisis', is generally credited with introducing this understanding of identity. Erikson (1968: 22) describes the process of identity formation as follows:

> In psychological terms, identity formation employs a process of simultaneous reflection and observation ... by which the individual judges himself in the light of what he perceives to be the way in which others judge him in comparison to themselves and to a typology significant to them; while he judges their way of judging him in the light of how he perceives himself in comparison to them and to types that have become relevant to him. This process is, luckily, and necessarily, for the most part unconscious except where inner conditions and outer circumstances combine to aggravate a painful, or elated, 'identity-consciousness'.

Tatum (2002) asserts that, in general, psychologists characterize the experience of racism in relation to Erikson's reference to 'outer circumstances' that create a 'painful identity-consciousness'. In other words, racism and other forms of prejudice do not allow those targeted by prejudice to remain unconscious about the social context in which the targeted aspects of their identity develop. For example, Tatum (2002) has observed that in reflecting on who we are, we identify those aspects of our identity that belong to a socially disadvantaged category as having more importance than others. In her teaching psychology to American college students, Tatum regularly gave her students a classroom exercise which consisted of completing the sentence, 'I am ...' using as many descriptors as they can think of in 60 seconds. Tatum (2002: 21) noticed that students of colour usually mention their racial or ethnic group, women usually mention being female, Jewish students often say they are Jews, and students who are comfortable about revealing it may mention being gay, lesbian or bisexual. White students rarely mention being white. Men do not usually mention their gender; mainline Protestant Christians rarely mention their religious identification; and it is very unusual for anyone to mention being heterosexual. In other words, in the areas where a person is a member of the dominant or advantaged social category, the category is not mentioned. Tatum (2002: 21) explains:

> That element of their identity ... is taken for granted by them because it is taken for granted by the dominant culture. ... [T]heir inner experience and outer circumstance are in harmony with one another, and the image reflected by others is similar to the image within. In the absence of

dissonance, this dimension of identity escapes conscious attention. ... The aspects of our identity that is the target of others' attention, and subsequently of our own, is often that which sets us apart ... as 'other' in their eyes.

Tatum (2002: 22) connects these observations with discrimination in American society. She notes that in the United States, otherness is commonly defined on the basis of race or ethnicity, gender, religion, sexual orientation, socio-economic status, age, and physical or mental ability, and that each of these categories has a form of oppression associated with it: racism, sexism, religious oppression, heterosexism, classism, ageism and ableism, respectively. Tatum asserts that it is no coincidence that these targeted categories, with the exception of class and sexual orientation, correspond to prohibitions against discrimination in American law. Each form of oppression involves a group considered dominant, which is systematically advantaged by their membership in the dominant group, and a group considered subordinate, which is systematically disadvantaged, but as Tatum (2002: 22), points out, most of us possess both dominant and targeted traits so that in some situations we may be targeted for domination while in others we may target others.

From these observations, we may conclude that whether one is dominant or targeted in any given situation depends on the dominant and targeted traits present in those around us and the extent to which they have power to express their dominance. The determination of whether a given policy or practice amounts to the kind of oppression that should be covered by prohibitions against discrimination is not so much a question of identifying traits that warrant protection as making an assessment of the relationships of dominance and subordination present in a given case.

In the dress code cases, the prohibited grounds of discrimination provide the basis for determining whether the claimants possess targeted traits. We can assume that race or ethnic origin, religion and gender all provide occasions for oppression of women who are members of racial, ethnic and religious minorities. Whether the dress codes being applied to them amount to oppression that should be characterized as illegal discrimination depends on whether they disadvantage them relative to persons who possess traits belonging to dominant categories: 'men', and racial ethnic and religious majorities of both sexes. However, determining the extent to which a policy disadvantages targeted persons depends very much on the perspective from which the policy is evaluated. There is a substantial risk that the perspective of those belonging to dominant categories will always win out, as members of dominant groups are generally unaware of their dominance. Here recent psychological and sociological research on how members of dominant groups understand their relationships to targeted categories provides some insight on how to address this problem.

First, American psychologists Samuel Gaertner and John Dovidio (1986: 62) have studied a phenomenon they call 'aversive racism', which has developed in the United States over the past 50 years. They have observed that, during this period, overt forms of prejudice have declined in frequency while a more subtle, often unintentional form of prejudice among white Americans has appeared. They note that white 'aversive racists' generally have strong egalitarian values and deny any personal prejudice but still harbour negative feelings or beliefs about minority groups that lead them to discriminate, often unintentionally, when their behaviour can be justified on the basis of some factor other than race (Gaertner and Dovidio 1986: 66). Tatum (2002: 23) elaborates on this insight by pointing out that '[d]ominant groups, by definition, set the parameters within which the subordinates operate ... [T]hey hold the power and authority in society relative to the subordinates'. As Tatum's class exercise illustrates, members of dominant groups can avoid awareness of their dominance, and explain the existence of inequality on the basis of norms that work to preserve their privileged status without referring to the prohibited grounds of discrimination.

Second, the work of sociologist Lawrence Bobo (1999) on group position theory supports the psychological explanation of dominance outlined above. Bobo (1999: 449–54) explains that according to this theory, racial prejudice is not just a collection of irrational feelings and stereotypes about race but rather '[is] best understood as a general attitude or orientation involving normative ideas about where one's own group should stand in the social order *vis-à-vis* an outgroup'. High-status group members are concerned about their group's relative status-group ranking as compared with perceived subordinate groups and will articulate their own values in such a way that the group maintains cohesion and excludes unwanted others. Bobo (1999: 454) explains that in order to maintain the group's status, members of the dominant group 'must make an affectively important distinction between themselves and [perceived] subordinate group members ... linked to ideas about the traits, capabilities and likely behaviours of subordinate group members'.

The social psychological research outlined above suggests that even people who profess egalitarian values remain acutely aware of group status issues and will seek to defend and justify their position of dominance by targeting behaviour they associate with targeted identity traits so as to avoid the appearance of discriminating on the basis of morphological characteristics, which is understood to be illegal and immoral. Thus, a distinction between behaviour and identity may, in many circumstances, be a false one, and may serve to entrench the kinds of oppression that anti-discrimination law is meant to eliminate. Instead of assuming that behaviour constitutes a neutral and legitimate target for restrictions, courts should subject such restrictions to heightened scrutiny when they serve to exclude people sharing targeted characteristics covered by the prohibited grounds of discrimination from educational and employment opportunities.

Rethinking *Føtex* and *Begum*

In *Føtex* the express purpose of the dress code was to avoid potential conflicts between members of the staff and customers. While the Danish courts did not question the legitimacy of this aim, it seems highly suspect when viewed in light of group position theory and the concept of aversive racism. The employer's express anxiety about conflicts between groups may be understood to be an expression of group status worries, indicating that we should determine whether the dress code articulates values held by higher status groups and whether the expression of those values serves to maintain cohesion of the higher status group and exclude members of lower status groups.

Tatum's explanation of the relationship between dominant and targeted characteristics tells us to look for manifestations of group status worries in connection with policies that tend to exclude groups possessing targeted characteristics in the categories of gender, religion, race and other prohibited discrimination grounds. In *Føtex* the dress code was adopted by the employer in cooperation with the employees in this case, who were said to include a substantial number of ethnic minorities, but the dress code does not impose any burdens on persons who possess dominant gender (male) and religious traits (the dominant religious norm in Denmark is Protestant Christianity). Women having dominant ethnic traits (white northern European) are less likely to be burdened by the policy than those having targeted (minority) ethnic traits, as they are less likely to be Muslims. According to this combination of social norms, religious belief is generally considered to be a private matter and women are not expected to wear headscarves or other kinds of veils.

Assuming that the employer and majority of the employees who participated in formulating the dress code possess the mentioned dominant traits, the concept of aversive racism suggests that their fears of conflict and desire to repress the targeted characteristics arise from their perception of their higher status in the social hierarchy. Thus, the aim of the dress code appears to be to maintain the higher social status of those having dominant traits in relation to Muslim immigrant women and should raise a presumption of direct discrimination, which is prohibited by the Employment Framework Directive.

In *Begum*, the dress code may not appear to involve oppression by the dominant racial, ethnic and religious groups in the UK as the policy was adopted by a school whose headteacher was also an immigrant from Bangladesh and whose students were 80 per cent Muslim. While the headteacher and majority of the students possess a targeted ethnic trait in relation to British society as a whole, group status theory raises the question of whether the school's dress code represented an attempt by a group sharing a dominant characteristic in relation to Shabina Begum – such as socio-economic status and moderate religious groupings within Islam – to dominate and marginalize a perceived subordinate group. As in *Føtex* the uniform code was adopted to avoid conflicts between ethnic groups within the school, suggesting that the code reflects the dominant group's effort to maintain cohesion and exclude a perceived subordinate group.

Baroness Hale's opinion represents the perspective of another dominant group in relation to Shabina Begum and her family: Western white women. Baroness Hale's opinion measures Muslim women's veiling practices against a background norm that equates such practices with a special kind of patriarchy that is foreign to the Western commitment to sex equality. The binary juxtaposition Baroness Hale makes between feminist freedom and foreign patriarchal cultural echoes the feminism versus multiculturalism discourse of Susan Moller Okin (1999), who portrays freedom and culture or ethnicity as mutually exclusive. The separation of gender and ethnicity in this way turns gender into women's essential identity, justifying the domination of minority ethnic groups and making it possible to claim that women of colour can – and therefore should – simply give up their ethnic identities.

As the work of Tatum and other psychologists points out, privileging gender over ethnicity in this way is enabled by the fact that persons possessing dominant characteristics are unaware of their dominance. Because they possess a dominant characteristic – which in this case is Baroness Hale's ethnicity (and socio-economic status as well) – they believe that they can objectively determine that foreign patriarchal cultures, which are perceived as subordinate, have nothing to offer the women that live within them.[32] Hence, Baroness Hale is able to disregard her own membership in a dominant ethnic group which allows her to focus on the perceived targeted characteristic she shares with Shabina: gender. By focusing on gender, and ignoring ethnicity, Baroness Hale is able to presume that all women share the same interests and that 'feminist freedom' means the same thing to all women and that it is desired or should be desired by all women.

Kathryn Abrams' theory of agency challenges this view, by emphasizing that gender and ethnicity are but two of many vectors of identity that are mutually constitutive of one another and cannot be analysed as isolated phenomena. Furthermore, the insistence that Muslim immigrant women who practice veiling are victims of especially patriarchal Eastern cultures denies the possibility of agency within patriarchy, and denies these women the possibility of acting on their own behalf. Shabina Begum and other young ethnic minority Muslim girls may find positive reflections of their identity in their cultural communities, which they may eventually be able to mobilize to bring about changes in their lives without have to cast aside family and community

---

32   Okin (1999: 22–3) has famously asserted that most Western liberal cultures 'have departed far further from [their patriarchal pasts] than others', and that '[f]emale members of a more patriarchal minority culture may be much better off if the culture into which they were born were either to become extinct (so that its members would become integrated into the less sexist surrounding culture)' or if the culture were 'encouraged to alter itself so as to reinforce the equality of women'. For criticism of this discourse, see, e.g., Volpp (2001).

ties. Finally, the psychological theories of identity formation that Tatum draws on suggest that Shabina's decision to wear a *jilbab* may have been an initial step in the process of self-reflection that begins in adolescence and initiates the formation of identity. Wearing a *jilbab* may have been her first answer to the question of who she is because she experienced her religious belief as more targeted than her gender or ethnicity. Excluding her because of her decision to wear the *jilbab* only confirms that understanding of herself.

Conclusion

As seen in the two dress code cases discussed above, judicial approaches to dress code cases appear to proceed on the basis of a liberal theory of the legal subject that makes a sharp distinction between identity and behaviour, which is one of the defining parameters of the assimilationist paradigm. However, modern psychological theories of identity formation and social psychological research on racism and prejudice challenge this understanding of the legal subject and indicate that making sharp distinctions between behaviour and identity tends to obscure discriminatory practices.

In order to avoid obscuring the discrimination practiced against Muslim women through dress codes, the sharp distinction between behaviour and identity must be replaced with an understanding that identity is formed through social interaction and that gender, ethnic, religious and other aspects of identity necessarily include behavioural components. Taking this understanding of identity as the starting point for determining whether a dress code is discriminatory eliminates the need to distinguish between different kinds of assimilation demands. Instead, determining whether a dress code is discriminatory requires an analysis of the claimant's dominant and targeted traits in relation to the dress code's author as well as the judge. By accounting for the claimant's dominant and targeted traits, the relationships of dominance among the parties and the judge(s) are revealed, and the court may be better able to avoid privileging the perspectives of those enjoying a dominant position in the context of the dress code at issue.

The analysis of a Muslim woman's discrimination claim arising from a dress code according to the approach suggested here could proceed as follows. First, the court must determine whether the claimant is invoking a right to engage in behaviour that signals her membership in a subordinate group. A positive answer indicates further inquiry is required. The next question is whether the defendant, and anyone else seeking to justify the dress code, has any dominant characteristics in relation to the claimant. With regards to immigrant women it would be especially important to consider group positions in relation to socio-economic status, gender, ethnicity or race, and national origin. One dominant characteristic in relationship to the claimant should be enough to require further inquiry. All the prohibited grounds of discrimination should be considered as possible arenas for domination. Finally, in examining the justification for the dress code, references to the prohibited grounds of discrimination, either by invoking the need to protect one targeted characteristic from domination while ignoring other targeted characteristics, e.g. claiming that the dress code is intended to protect women from the patriarchy of non-Western cultures, or by citing the need to avoid conflict between groups defined by identity categories covered by the prohibited grounds of discrimination should be regarded as attempts to coerce compliance with a dominant norm at the expense of other elements of the claimant's identity. In short, such justifications constitute evidence of direct discrimination.

Regardless of whether the complaint is based on one or several discrimination grounds, this alternative approach would require the court to recognize that in order to provide Muslim women effective protection against discrimination, it must take into account all the prohibited grounds of discrimination in order to determine whether the defendant's justification for the dress code can be accepted. All grounds of discrimination that can be identified with the claimant – sex, religion, ethnic origin and/or race – must be considered in order to account for relationships of dominance between the claimant and the defendant and between the claimant and the court. For example, if the justification offered for the dress code includes the aim of avoiding conflict between groups, as it did in both *Begum* and *Føtex*, the court must determine whether the groups are identifiable by race or ethnic origin, religion and/or sex. If so, then the presumption must be that the dress code is in fact intended to maintain dominant group positions, and the justification cannot be accepted. If the defendant is not able to provide evidence on this issue, then the EU directives' rules on burden of proof require that any doubt is resolved to the benefit of the claimant. Similarly, if the justification offered for the dress code refers to the need to protect the claimant's right to sex equality against the claimant's own religion or culture, the justification isolates the claimant's gender from her religion and culture – contrary to the understanding of identity outlined above – and targets her religion and culture for disadvantageous treatment. The claimant's own personal traits thus serve as additional grounds of discrimination (religion and ethnic origin) and the justification cannot be accepted.

Because Article 9 ECHR so explicitly applies an assimilationist approach to religious freedom and because the ECHR does not include any discrimination protection with regards to access to education or employment, the ECHR does not offer any obvious opening to using this approach in dress code cases litigated in the ECHR system.

The alternative approach could probably be applied under current EU anti-discrimination legislation, although in a school dress code case, the complaint must be framed as a sex and/or ethnic origin discrimination claim in order to fall within the scope of the current directives. Nothing in the directives or in the ECJ's case law suggests that courts may not consider all relevant grounds of discrimination, even when they are not invoked by the claimant. It may therefore be considered contrary to the general principle of non-discrimination to accept a justification for a dress code that clearly invokes additional discrimination grounds, particularly when they are associated with the claimant's ethnic, gender, religious, etc. identity. Similarly, a justification that refers to conflicts between groups identifiable by any of the discrimination grounds that are associated with the claimant's own identity must also be seen as contrary to the principle of non-discrimination. Discrimination on one prohibited ground of discrimination may not be justified by a need to discriminate on other prohibited grounds without making a travesty of anti-discrimination law.

Likewise, nothing in the directives or in the ECJ's case law suggests that courts may not adopt a different understanding of identity. The directives do not require or prohibit application of a particular understanding of identity. Courts have simply incorporated the familiar background norm of liberal individualism without any obvious reflection on its consequences or alternatives.

This approach to dress code cases satisfies the need to distinguish between legitimate and discriminatory restrictions on behaviours, but without relying on the distinction between identity and behaviour that characterizes the assimilation paradigm. It also focuses attention on the multiple identities of the claimant, so that all the relationships of dominance in the case – including those between the claimant and the court – can be dealt with instead of being allowed to operate under cover of protecting one identity against another, e.g. femaleness versus patriarchal religion or culture.

The main obstacle to changing judicial approaches to these cases is teaching judges and litigators to see the multiple identities of Muslim women and the relationships of dominance and subordination that lie at the root of discrimination. This is admittedly a formidable obstacle, and it may require a combination of training and legislation to clarify the legal basis for considering all grounds of discrimination in cases where only one ground has been alleged and to re-define discrimination so that it clearly includes considerations of relationships of dominance and subordination based on the prohibited grounds of discrimination.

Chapter 13

A Legal Remedy for Corpulent Women of Colour

Iyiola Solanke

Introduction

The increase in body size crosses nations, age, class, race and ethnicity (Jeffery and Linde 2005: 55). Over the last two to three decades 'overnutrition and obesity[1] have been transformed from relatively minor public health issues that primarily affect the most affluent societies to a major threat to public health that is being increasingly seen throughout the world' (Seidell 2005: 3). Sixty-one per cent of Americans are overweight, and 20 per cent are obese: about 25 per cent of all Americans under the age of 19 are overweight or obese (Critser 2003: 4). The Organization for Economic Cooperation and Development, ranked Britain's overweight and obesity rate (62 per cent) in 2006 as the worst in Europe and the third worst in the world, behind Mexico (69.5 per cent) and the United States (67.3 per cent).[2] The prevalence of obesity in the UK has trebled since the 1980s: 22 per cent of men and 23.5 per cent of women are now obese and well over half of all adults are either overweight or obese – almost 24 million adults. In addition, overweight and obesity are also increasing in children: according to the 2006 Health Survey for England, almost 31 per cent of boys and 29 per cent of girls aged 2–15 fall into these categories.[3] In the United States, around 20 per cent of 6–8 year olds and 30 per cent of 12–14 year olds are obese or overweight. The trend is similar throughout the European Union (EU), from Finland (47.7 per cent) in the north to Spain (51.1 per cent) in the south: children and adults are getting fatter (Seidell 2005: 15–16). Excess avoirdupois will be a long-term problem.

The purpose of this contribution is to examine the social consequences and legal implications of these trends. Empirical evidence increasingly shows that size matters beyond public health concerns: men and women who are overweight and obese are refused employment, training and promotion because of their weight. For example, Bonnie Cook, who was 5'3" and weighed 329lbs, was denied re-employment at a state agency because the employer believed that her weight meant that she would be unable to do her job properly, even though she had previously had an excellent employment record. The employer also claimed that her weight would lead to increased absenteeism and potentially higher compensation claims.[4] Likewise, Arazella Manuel, who was 5'7" and weighed 345lbs, was refused a job as an airport shuttle-bus driver due to the belief that her size would prevent her from helping passengers in an emergency.[5] Similarly, Catherine McDermott

---

1 Obesity is measured using the Body Mass Index (BMI), which has four categories – underweight (below 18.5), normal (18.5–24.9), overweight (25–29.9), obese (30 and over).

2 Available at: www.irdes.fr/EcoSante/DownLoad/OECDHealthData_FrequentlyRequestedData.xls [accessed: 12 June 2009].

3 *Volume Two: Obesity and Other Risk Factors in Children* [Online: Health Survey for England 2008] Available at: www.ic.nhs.uk/webfiles/publications/HSE06/HSE06_VOL2.pdf [accessed: 12 June 2009].

4 *Cook v. Rhode Island, Department of Health, Retardation, and Hospitals*, 10 F.3d 17, 23, 28 (1st Cir. 1993).

5 *EEOC v. Texas Bus Lines*, 923 F. Supp. 965 (S.D.TX 1996), 971.

was refused a job with the Xerox Corporation because it was assumed that she posed a financial risk to the company as a result of higher absenteeism, higher utilization of long-term and disability benefits, medical care plans and life insurance.[6] Also, Mary Nedder, who was 5'6" and weighed 375lbs was released from her teaching post at Rivier, a Catholic college in Nashua, New Hampshire because according to the college president her size reduced her ability to teach.[7] In these successful cases, disability discrimination legislation was used to challenge weight discrimination. However, this is a limited remedy and, in this chapter, I consider how a holistic (Fredman and Szyszczak 1992) redress could be designed.

The chapter begins with discussion of the differential consequences of being an above-average weight. In the next part, I show first that size matters; second, that size matters more for women than for men and, third, that size matters more to white women, but has far more significant consequences for black women. There is ample scientific evidence to support the first and second claims, but relatively little in relation to the third. Few studies have considered the interaction of race, gender and size but I present some evidence for the reader to consider. Having established this, I discuss the existing laws that address weight discrimination or 'fatphobia' and use of disability discrimination law in particular in the United States but also in Britain, Ireland and France. I question whether fat should be treated as a disability and highlight the disadvantages of this. Subsequently, I lay out a case for a holistic approach, promoting a re-education, re-conceptualization and re-contextualization. I highlight briefly the complex interaction between weight gain and stress, poverty, migration. Having shown that behaviouralism belies the 'obesogenic' environment in which we live, I then propose an alternative route to the creation of a legal remedy for corpulent women of colour (Lien et al. 2008) which focuses on stigma and context, an approach which would also be appropriate for use at the European level.

The Problem with Size

Size Matters

As far as the government and business is concerned, size matters because it reduces health and increases costs. For the public purse and employers, weight increases expenditure. According to medical experts, there are numerous health consequences to excess weight, including diabetes, angina, osteoarthritis, stroke, gout, gall bladder disease, breast cancer, cancer of the colon and ovarian cancer. To this list can be added disorders such as hypertension and disabling physical conditions: shortness of breath, reduced mobility, sleep apnea, lower back pain (Seidell 2005: 16). In short, overweight people are said to be more prone to heart disease, stroke, high blood pressure, diabetes, chronic depression and many other life-threatening conditions. A 2007 report predicted that if current trends continue, by 2050 60 per cent of men, 50 per cent of women and 26 per cent of children and young people will be obese; cases of type 2 diabetes will rise by 70 per cent; cases of stroke will rise by 30 per cent; and cases of coronary heart disease will rise by 20 per cent, all of which will ultimately cost the public purse nearly £46bn (BBC News 2007).

For individuals, however, size matters for a second reason – it reduces work opportunities and life chances. Being overweight is bad for job prospects and career: society in general and employers in particular are fatphobic. There is a general public disdain towards those who are fat

---

6   *McDermott v. Xerox Corp.*, 102 A.D.2d 543 (1984), 544.
7   These cases are further discussed below (215–16).

and such persons are often the target of overt discrimination, open ridicule and public humiliation – fat people are spat at on the street (Pelling 2005). In relation to employment, studies demonstrate that overweight candidates are less likely to be hired even if equally competent on job-related tests as non-fat candidates. In a recent poll, nearly 80 per cent of 300 senior managers and directors of major companies acknowledged that there was a prejudice against fat people in business: more than two-thirds agreed that 'fat people were seen as lacking in self-discipline and self-control, energy and drive' (Jackson 2007). Routine discrimination on the grounds of size was also discovered by *Personnel Today* during a survey conducted in 2005 (*Personnel Today* 2005). The survey reported that corporations openly and regularly discriminate against the overweight. Two thousand human resource personnel were asked to choose between two equally qualified job applicants, one fat and the other a 'normal weight': 93 per cent chose the latter, only 7 per cent the former; 12 per cent said they would not employ 'fat' people in client facing roles; 30 per cent agreed that 'obesity is a valid medical reason for not employing a person'; 47 per cent thought that obesity impeded employee output; and 11 per cent thought obesity a fair ground for dismissal.

Researchers have also found that 'if hired, persons who are obese are often assigned to non-visible jobs, receive more disciplinary actions, have their performance evaluated more negatively and earn less when compared to non-obese employees' (Bell and McLaughlin 2006). Furthermore, employers judge overweight job applicants more harshly than those with a conviction or a history of mental illness (Roehling 2002: 177). Overweight individuals are rated less desirable as subordinates, co-workers and bosses. Studies show that weight discrimination is indeed 'a widespread phenomenon that has a significant negative impact on the lives of untold individuals' (Roehling 2002: 187). It is evident at every phase of the employment cycle including: career counselling, selection, placement, compensation, promotion, discipline and discharge. Being 'slightly overweight, extremely overweight, or obese are all generally viewed in various employment contexts as less desirable than being average or thin' (Bell et al. 2003: 210).

Size Matters More for Women than for Men

'Disparate treatment of women in employment settings based on weight is not merely a theoretical possibility it is a practical likelihood' (Roehling 2002: 186). Weight matters more for women than men: 'overweight women receive less desirable job assignments than overweight men and while even mildly obese women earn significantly less than their non-obese counterparts there is not a similar wage penalty among mildly obese men' (Roehling 2002: 186). A 14-year analysis of schoolchildren and their eventual prospects found that obese girls were likely to be trapped in low-earning jobs by the time they reach age 30 (Dobson and Jones 2005: 13). Research has found that overweight and obese young adult women in the United States and UK earn significantly less than non-overweight women or those with other chronic health problems (Hill 2003: 68). Bell et al. (2003: 202) also found that young obese women earn 12 per cent less than non-obese women. Studies have concluded that: overweight women earn less than non-overweight women, but overweight men did not earn less than slim men; overweight women are more segregated into lower paying occupations but fat men are more dispersed in higher paying occupations; overweight women have less schooling, earn less annually, have 10 per cent higher rates of poverty and are 20 per cent less likely to be married than non-overweight women. Overweight men are 11 per cent less likely to be married than non-overweight men but experience none of the other negative consequences of size (Bell and McLaughlin 2006: 462). In brief, overweight women are evaluated more negatively than overweight men (Roehling 2002: 178). This weight discrimination is additionally problematic because women are more likely to be obese than men (Bell and McLaughlin 2006: 461).

Women are also subject to more stringent weight standards than men. This is especially apparent in the airline industry. In *Frank v. United Airlines*,[8] a group of female employees who had failed to comply with United's weight requirements for women, successfully challenged the airline's weight policy (Quindlen 1993). The weight policy for flight attendants discriminated on the basis of sex: the maximum weights for male flight attendants was based on weight tables for men with *large* body frames, while the maximum weights for female flight attendants was based on weight tables for females with *medium*-body frames. For example, the maximum weight for a 5'7", 30-year-old woman was 142 pounds, while a man of the same height and age could weigh up to 161 pounds. In *Gerdom v. Continental Airlines*[9] Continental argued that more stringent weight restrictions for females was a genuine occupational qualification (GOQ) because svelte, attractive stewardesses were part of its competitive strategy. These arguments were rejected by the court, which held that customer preference was unrelated to the ability to do the job and could not justify a weight policy that discriminated against females (Roehling 2002: 179). United dropped its weight policy in 1993, but airlines in other parts of the world continue to use them with impunity. For example, an Indian court recently sanctioned the decision of Air India to fire 10 air hostesses whom it decided were 'too fat to fly' (Blakely 2009: 35). The hostesses had failed to slim down to meet company weight restrictions, calculated according to height and age. Sheela Joshi, a 51-year-old hostess who had worked with Air India for 25 years, was grounded when a spot weigh-in found that she was 1.9kg over the prescribed limit for her height (Bartow 2006). She submitted a petition to the Indian High Court of Delhi but the Court declined to declare Air India's policy unconstitutional.[10]

Size Matters More to White Women, but has More Serious Consequences for Black Women

According to Critser (2003: 4) obesity 'disproportionately plagues the poor and the working poor': to this can be added the black and ethnic minority. The prevalence of obesity varies not only by income and class but also by race and ethnicity. Among African-Americans, 28.6 per cent are classified as obese, compared with 21 per cent of Hispanics and 18 per cent of whites (Bell et al. 2003). In the United States about 40 per cent of black Hispanic and Native American women are obese (Bell and McLaughlin 2006). In households with an annual income of less than $10,000, 33 per cent of blacks, 26 per cent of Hispanics and 20 per cent of whites were obese. In households with an annual income between $20–25,000, 27 per cent of blacks, 18 per cent of Hispanics and 20 per cent of whites were obese. Households with an income of $50,000 or more, 23 per cent of blacks, 22 per cent of Hispanics and 16 per cent of whites were obese (Critser 2003: 110). Black and single-parent – predominantly female – households tend to fall into the lower income brackets.

Despite these statistics, women of colour (Lien et al. 2008) have rarely been the focus of or included in studies on size and eating habits. It has long been assumed that they have a more positive approach to body size and do not have a problematic relationship with food. A study at the University of Arizona claimed that 70 per cent of black girls were satisfied with their bodies

---

8   *Leslie Frank et al. v. United Airlines, Inc.*, 216 F.3d 845 (9th Circuit 2000). It was finally settled in February 2004. Report is available at: www.lieffcabraser.com/pdf/20040211_united_order.pdf. Case available at: http://caselaw.lp.findlaw.com/scripts/getcase.pl?court=9th&navby=case&no=9815638 [accessed: 18 September 2009].

9   *Gerdom v. Continental Airlines, Inc.*, 692 F.2d 602, 605-06 (9th Cir. 1982).

10   *Sheela Joshi and Ors. v. Indian Airlines Ltd*, Writ Petition C Nos. 12875-83 (2006), May 31 2007. [Online]. Available at: http://courtnic.nic.in/dhcorder/dhcqrydisp_J.asp?pn=1912&yr=2007 [accessed: 18 September 2009].

compared to 90 per cent of white girls who were *dissatisfied* with their size (Ingrassia 1995). Likewise, overweight older black women are reportedly more satisfied with their weight than older white women (Bell and McLaughlin 2006: 463). Curiously, the very public battle fought by Oprah Winfrey to control her weight did not weaken these ideas: they continue to be used to chastise white women and girls who strive to reach size zero (Critser 2003: 119). Against these assumptions research on weight management and eating disorders can legitimately focus on white upper- and middle-class girls and women.

However, it is gradually being acknowledged that methodological bias has led to misunderstanding of the relationship between black women and their bodies. For example, research into eating disorders that relied on hospital admission data created a sample bias in favour of those who have the means to seek and receive professional help at the expense of those lacking such access. Alternative sample selection leads to dramatically different results: a recent study on bulimia, based on data from a 10-year survey of more than 2,300 young girls in schools in California, Ohio and Washington, D.C., came to the disturbing conclusion that black girls are more likely to be bulimic than white girls (*Medical News Today* 2009). A team of economists at the University of Southern California used the data to create a longitudinal picture of bulimia. Beginning at age nine or 10, participants were questioned annually about eating habits and associated psychological issues such as body image and depression. The results showed that, contrary to popular belief, black girls were 50 per cent more likely than white girls to exhibit bulimic behaviour, including both binging and purging: about 2.6 per cent of black girls were clinically bulimic, compared to 1.7 per cent of white girls. Beyond this, the level of bulimia in the black girls was found to be more severe. Also, girls from families in the lowest income bracket were significantly more likely to experience bulimia than their wealthier peers.

There is therefore little credence in the claim that girls and women of colour do not suffer from eating disorders per se. Even if anecdotal evidence demonstrates that corpulent women of colour find greater acceptance within their communities than their white counterparts within white communities, this does not lead to the conclusion that they are more comfortable being fat (Hsu 1988). Whilst this cohort may have a broader definition of attractiveness – incorporating factors such as style, personal grooming and posture – they remain vulnerable to eating disorders arising from the portrayal of the successful career woman as smart and thin – Oprah Winfrey is a perfect example of how pernicious this stereotype can be. Clinicians report that almost 8 per cent of their visitors are African-American women who 'are just as likely to abuse laxatives as white women are' (Fitzgibbon and Stolley 2009) to avoid weight gain. This trend may be related to acculturation and assimilation into dominant norms, with the level of acceptance of overweight declining as the level of education and income rises. Research into black college populations suggests that the more integrated and middle-class women of colour are, the more likely they are to display a problematic relationship to their body and food, and develop eating disorders (Shaw 2006: 78) Paradoxically, the more positive approach to size within their communities may mean that black and Hispanic women with food management problems are unable to turn to their friends or family for support: whilst white girls and women discuss these problems, communities of colour may not (Adesioye 2009).

The higher prevalence of overweight and obesity amongst women of colour has at least two implications. First, employer standards on size are likely to affect more women of colour. This was indeed the argument raised by an African-American woman who was denied a hostess-trainee position because her hip measurements exceeded the maximum allowed by the employer's neutral height and weight chart. She raised a complaint of indirect discrimination arguing that, due to genetic differences, the employer's hip measurement standard had a disproportionate impact on

African-American women (Roehling 2002). Secondly, employer prejudices on size are likely to affect more women of colour, who are more likely than white women to be overweight and less likely to be in hiring and firing positions (Bell and McLaughlin 2006: 463). Finally, the reduced level of stigma associated with weight for women of colour reduces their incentive to address weight problems, and ultimately leaves them more vulnerable to weight discrimination in the labour market.

Using Law to Tackle Fatphobia

There is little existing law that directly prevents weight discrimination. In many cases, disability law has been used. However, this is a limited option, possible only where obesity is related to a disabling condition or disability law covers imputed disability, as in the US Americans with Disabilities Act 1990. In this section, I will discuss weight discrimination statutes in the United States and cases where the disability route has been successfully used.

Few US states have statutes which specifically protect the overweight and obese. Michigan is the only state with laws that include height and weight as protected categories under anti-discrimination law: the Elliott-Larsen Civil Rights Act[11] bans discrimination in employment based on race, colour, religion, national origin, age, sex, height, weight or marital status. In addition, some sub-state authorities in California have enacted local laws barring weight and personal appearance discrimination: Santa Cruz has a law prohibiting unlawful discrimination on the basis of 'age, race, colour, creed, religion, national origin, ancestry, disability, marital status, sex, gender, sexual orientation, height, weight, or physical characteristic'[12] and San Francisco's city code bars discrimination on the grounds of ancestry, national origin, place of birth, sex, age, religion, creed, disability, sexual orientation, gender identity, weight or height.[13] Outside of California, Washington, DC has a statute prohibiting discrimination in employment based upon 'race, colour, religion, national origin, sex, age, marital status, personal appearance, sexual orientation, family responsibilities, physical handicap, matriculation, or political affiliation'.[14]

The use of these codes illustrates that they are not superfluous – in Michigan, the Elliott-Larsen Act dealt with nearly 200 weight discrimination complaints in its first 10 years (Bell and McLaughlin 2006). In California, Jennifer Portnick successfully used the San Francisco prohibition to challenge a decision by fitness organization Jazzercise Inc. She brought a case before the San Francisco Human Rights Commission when Jazzercise refused to provide her with the training necessary to open a franchise. Portnick, 5'8" tall and weighing 240lbs, had been doing high impact aerobics for 15 years. Her impressive stamina resulted in an invitation to audition to be a certified Jazzercise instructor. However, the management focused on her weight rather than her fitness and encouraged her to trim down, wanting her to look 'fit', i.e. thinner than the public. Portnick challenged the assumption that fitness equated to size. The case was settled in May 2002 when Jazzercise Inc. agreed to remove the need to look 'fit' from company policy (Gumbel 2002).

In the absence of such statutes, an alternative route to a remedy can be disability discrimination legislation. Claims have been successful where size has been turned into a disability rights issue

---

11   Elliot Larsen Civil Rights Act, Act 453 of 1976, Sec. 209.

12   Santa Cruz Municipal Code, Chapter 9.83. Available at: www.codepublishing.com/CA/SantaCruz/html/SantaCruz09/SantaCruz0983.html [accessed: 21 June 2009].

13   San Francisco Municipal/ Police Code Article 33. Available at: www.municode.com/content/4201/14140/HTML/index.html [accessed: 21 June 2009].

14   District of Columbia Code Subchapter II, S. 1-2501 (1987 & Supp. 1993).

(Kirkland 2008: 103). Weight per se is not a disability: overweight and obese people are not disabled but may sometimes be so. Difficulties which are related to weight either directly (such as excess weight restricting mobility, or causing joint strain and shortness of breath) or indirectly (as a consequence of reduced cardiac output, the risk of stroke or diabetes) can fall under disability legislation (Williams 2008: 93). For example, walking can become difficult because of knee strain due to long-term excess weight on the joint. This could fall under the definition provided in the UK Disability Discrimination Act 1995 (DDA), whereby 'a person has a disability ... if he has a physical or mental impairment which has a substantial and long-term adverse effect on his ability to carry out normal day to day activities'.[15] The employer must then make reasonable adjustments to accommodate their needs. This can mean re-organization of work duties, adjustment of the workspace (providing a more comfortable chair and desk) or an allowance for business rather than economy class travel. Likewise a person whose obesity has been caused by, or led to, conditions such as depression, diabetes or arthritis may find a remedy under the DDA. Thus although being fat or obese is not necessarily a disability, it may sometimes fall under the scope of the DDA.

The broader definition under the Americans with Disabilities Act (ADA) offers protection where a disability is assumed. Under the ADA, a disability is defined as '(A) a physical or mental impairment that substantially limits one or more of the major life activities[16] of such individual; (B) a record of such an impairment; or (C) being regarded as having such an impairment'.[17] Section C has proved crucial to claims concerning weight discrimination. As it includes presumptions of disability – an omission in the DDA – many persons who have been refused employment or lost employment on account of their weight have successfully sued using this sub-section. Arazella Manuel, Catherine McDermott and Mary Nedder all relied upon it to challenge assumptions made during pre-employment medical checks.

In the case of Arazella Manuel, the examining doctor stated in court that he observed Ms Manuel 'literally waddling down the hall' and estimated that it took her about five times as long as it took somebody else. He felt that he 'owed the public and other people the right to have a driver that could give them some protection in case of an accident or fire or something like that'. The doctor acknowledged that he had no special training in what it takes to be a bus driver. His uninformed assumption meant that Manuel won her case.[18] Xerox likewise refused to hire Catherine McDermott as a business systems consultant after the Director of Health Services advised that whilst her weight would not impact upon her job performance, it would endanger the financial health of the company – there would be higher absenteeism, higher utilization of long-term and disability benefits, medical care plans and life insurance.[19] Unlike in *PECO*, where the court defended the employers 'inherent

---

15   Disability Discrimination Act 1995, Part 1, Article 1(1).

16   'Major life activities' can include everything from 'caring for one's self, performing manual tasks, walking, seeing, hearing, speaking, breathing, learning, and [even] working' (*Bragdon v. Abbott*, 524 U.S. 624, 638–9 (1998) (citing 45 CFR § 84.3(j)(2)(ii); 28 CFR § 41.31(b)(2) (1997)). According to this definition, even if an obese person has difficulty performing the normal daily functions of living and working, he or she will not be considered disabled under the ADA unless the obesity 'substantially limits' a major life activity (see *Hazeldine v. Beverage Media, Inc.*, 954 F. Supp. 697 (S.D.N.Y. 1997: employee's weight did not limit major life activity)).

17   (42 U.S.C. § 12102(2); see also *Francis v. City of Meriden*, 129 F.3d 281, 286 (2d Cir. 1997) ('an impairment within the meaning of subsection (C) plainly refers to a "physical or mental impairment" within the meaning of subsection (A)').

18   *EEOC v. Texas Bus Lines*, 923 F. Supp. 965 (S.D.TX 1996), 971. Paras 976–8. The above cases are discussed in Kirkland (2003).

19   *McDermott v. Xerox Corp.*, 102 A.D.2d 543 (1984), 544.

right to discriminate among applicants for employment [based on risk of loss to the company] and to eliminate those who have a high potential for absenteeism and low productivity',[20] McDermott successfully challenged this unproven assumption. Rivier College was also sued by Nedder[21] because college officials assumed that a fat person was unhealthy and also disabled.

Such 'common sense' assumptions can also be challenged under Irish equality law. A similarly broad definition is contained in Section 6(1) of the Irish Employment Equality Act (EEA). The EEA also covers discrimination on the grounds of disability, including actual and potential difficulties. In particular, section 6(2)(e) defines disability as 'a condition, illness or disease which affects a person's thought processes, perception of reality, emotions or judgment or which results in disturbed behaviour, and shall be taken to include a disability which exists at present, or which previously existed but no longer exists, or which may exist in the future or which is imputed to a person'. A recent case under this statute concerned a Care Attendant who was denied a post as Staff Nurse with the Health Service Executive (HSE) because the employer presumed that her obesity was a disability, although it employed her to do the same job on a temporary basis.

The HSE initially refused to employ her because, as in the cases above, she failed the necessary medical assessment prior to appointment. The Director of Human Resources and the Occupational Health Physician agreed that her weight was predictive of work-related impairment and refused to give her the required health clearance. The Occupational Health Physician suggested that she would have difficulty in accessing patients because of her weight and she would be unable to run fast enough should there be an emergency. A later report stated that a person of her size would find it difficult to effectively perform chest compressions, although the applicant already performed these duties as a care attendant. When these facts were considered, the HSE was held to have discriminated against the complainant on the disability ground: at no point did the HSE actually carry out an assessment of the risks associated with her obesity or communicate them to her prior to its decision to defer health clearance. It also failed to provide any guidance on what the complainant needed to do to secure health clearance.[22]

However, weight per se is not a disability under the EEA, DDA or ADA. Protection is provided where the source of the weight is a genuine medical or psychological condition, such as depression or diabetes. A weight requirement is not unlawful under disability legislation if it is directly related to the essential requirements of the job as defined by the employer.[23] Fat people who are treated differently based upon their appearance alone will not enjoy the protection of disability discrimination law.[24] Weight discrimination can continue with impunity in cases where the cause of overweight or obesity is not an underlying condition. Thus Deborah Marks, who weighed 270lbs and had been named Telemarketer of the Year by her employer, was unable to seek a legal remedy when the same employer refused to promote her to a face-to-face sales job because of her size. When she complained, she was told to lose weight because presentation was extremely important. As being 'unpresentable' does not assume a disability, she could not use the

---

20   *PECO v. Pennsylvania Human Relations Commission and Joyce A English*, 68 Pa. Commw. 212 (1982), 228.

21   *Nedder v. Rivier College* 908 F. Supp 66 (D.N.H 1995), 944 F. Supp 1996.

22   See *Health Service Employee v. The Health Service Executive*, December E2006-013 (on file with author). I am grateful to Judy Walsh for bringing this case to my attention.

23   Although employers cannot just sack or dismiss employees because they are obese but must show the impact of the person's size on the business, as shown in a recent case where the Post Office lost an unfair dismissal claim brought by a 25-stone postman who had been dismissed on health grounds after his weight suddenly increased (Williams 2008: 96).

24   In relation to the ADA, see *Coleman v. Georgia Power Co.*, 81 F. Supp. 2d 1365 (ND Ga. 2000).

ADA.[25] Joyce English, an African-American woman who was 5'8" and weighed 341lbs, also lost her case against the Philadelphia Electric Company (PECO) when she was refused employment as a Customer Service Representative after failing the pre-employment medical check.[26] The Penn Human Relations Commission argued that her obesity was a disability protected by the ADA but this was rejected because she was not in any way limited by health problems.[27] Flight attendants at Delta Airways were likewise unable to use disability legislation to challenge the airline's weight and appearance requirements for flight crew because they could not provide evidence demonstrating that they failed Delta's weight requirements 'due to some cognizable medical condition'.[28]

Weight discrimination dressed up as a problem of presentation can be tackled by laws focusing on physical appearance. These laws can potentially cover fattism. In the EU, France introduced a law focusing on appearance: in 2001, the provisions of the Labour Code on employment discrimination were modified to include a prohibition on the grounds of 'physical appearance'. Article L122-45 of the Labour Code now reads: 'no person can be eliminated from a recruitment process, sanctioned or dismissed due to their age, sex, lifestyle, sexual orientation, family situation, non-membership, whether genuine or assumed, of an ethnic group, nation, race, political beliefs, trade union activities, religious beliefs, physical appearance, surname, state of health or disability'.[29]

This covers recruitment, access to a placement or in-company training programme, pay, training, redeployment within a company, posting, qualifications, job classification, promotion, transfer and contract renewal. Employers using 'presentability' as an excuse could therefore be challenged. Fat activists are increasingly pushing for protection in the form of anti-discrimination law (Khullar 2009) and the French approach might be a useful way to provide this.

It would be sensible for protection against weight discrimination in Europe to also be included within the European Union anti-discrimination framework. Article 13 TEC at present mentions neither weight nor appearance. However, Article 3(1) of the Lisbon Treaty places an obligation upon the EU to promote the 'wellbeing' of its peoples. This interest in wellbeing could arguably be used as a basis upon which to introduce protection against weight discrimination – according to the European Commission, health is integral to the growth and jobs agenda (Rankin 2009: 16). Should the Lisbon Treaty not enter into force, a statutory reform would require an agreement between the Heads of State and Government to amend the Treaty of Rome at an Intergovernmental Conference. This is a lengthy procedure with no guarantee of success.

Alternatively, the imputed disability approach could be incorporated into EU law. Disability is already prohibited under Article 13 TEC, thus the use of disability legislation would be a faster route to a European remedy (Korn 1997). It could be argued that such a remedy for fattism is implicit in the recent judgement of the European Court of Justice (ECJ) in *Coleman*[30] where the ECJ

---

25   *Marks v. National Communications Association, Inc.*, 72 F.Supp. 2d (S.D.N.Y. 1999), 322, 327.

26   She passed all pre-employment tests but the examining physician refused to certify her for employment because her obesity would create risk of medical problems leading to high absenteeism, low productivity and other costs to the company.

27   *PECO v. Pennysylvania Human Relations Commission and Joyce A English*, 68 Pa. Commw. 212 (1982), 228.

28   *Delta Air Lines v. New York State Div. of Human Rights*, 91 N.Y.2d 65, 73, 689 N.E.2d 898, 666 N.Y.S.2d 1004 (1997) Available at: www.epexperts.com/modules.php?op=modload&name=News&file=article&sid=1462.

29   Law 2001-1066 of Nov 16 2001.

30   Case C 303/06 [2008] ECR I-5603.

held that the prohibition of disability discrimination under the Employment Framework Directive 2000/78[31] protects those suffering from discrimination by association. Ms Coleman was primary carer to her disabled son and claimed that she had been subject to unfair constructive dismissal because of this. As she was not herself disabled, the British Employment Appeals Tribunal (EAT) asked the ECJ whether such a situation was covered by the Employment Framework Directive. The ECJ replied in the affirmative, stating that the protection of the Directive 'is not limited only to people who are themselves disabled'. Although discrimination by association is not the same as discrimination based upon a mistaken perception, this ruling could be interpreted to mean that imputed disability is also unlawful in the European sphere.[32] This, however, would need to be clarified by the ECJ, and recent case law from the UK indicates some opposition to such an interpretation.[33]

Yet entrenching protection from obesity in disability law would establish above-average weight as a departure from a 'normal' thin body. This is precisely the stereotype and stigma that courts need to address if fat people are to be protected from arbitrary fattism. Despite the medical definitions of overweight and obesity, it is unclear at what stage weight becomes excess according to the general public and employers: this can vary depending on culture, country and even commercial sector (O'Reilly 2008). Paradoxically, the healthier a fat person, the more vulnerable they will be. As they are more likely to be fat, this has more serious consequences for women of colour: women like Joyce English who are fat, healthy and capable. How can law help these women? The answer to this question depends on how we define the type of discrimination: is it multiple or intersectional? In other words, does weight compound racial and gender discrimination or do race, gender and weight discrimination *intersect*?

A Judicial Remedy for Corpulent Women of Colour

There is sadly little research and thus scant information on the relationship between race, gender and weight. An exception is the recent publication by Andrea Shaw, which suggests that the stigma attached to weight does not compound but *intersects* with the stigma attached to race and gender. In *The Embodiment of Disobedience* she argues that fatness and blackness share a similar and complex relationship with the female body: 'both characteristics require a degree of erasure in order to render women viable entities by Western aesthetic standards' (Shaw 2006: 1). In Anglo-American culture, where slenderness and whiteness are prized commodities, 'the fat black woman's body poses a dual challenge to the colonially inspired dominant aesthetic norms ... [the] fat black body resists both imperatives of whiteness and slenderness as an ideal state of embodiment'. Yet at the same time, her large size makes her presence imposing, undermining attempts to erase the black female presence (Shaw 2006: 9).

How, then, are fat black women incorporated into the public mind? Shaw argues that there are only two options: the domesticated 'Mammy' or the hypersexualized 'Hottentot Venus' The 'mammy' is confined to the domestic realm where her oversized body:

---

31   Council Directive 2000/78 on equal treatment in employment and occupation OJ L 18/22.

32   My thanks to Anna Lawson for highlighting this point.

33   Justice Slade recently held in *Aitken v. Commissioner of Police of the Metropolis* UKEAT/0226/09 [EAT] 21 June 2010 that treatment on the basis of a mistaken perception that an employee suffers from a disability does not fall within the definition in s.3 DDA of direct disability or disability-related discrimination. Available at: www.bailii.org/uk/cases/UKEAT/2010/0226_09_2106.html [accessed: 25 June 2010].

represents an overabundance of maternal resources … In the role of a domestic caretaker, she represents the ultimate state of black allegiance to whiteness: the ready availability of nurture despite her own economic oppression effected by those she must serve. Her fatness signals an infinite reserve of maternal dedication, suggesting an inability of black women to be oppressed since their supply of strength, love, and other emotional resources can never be depleted. Furthermore, the link between fat and motherhood implies an inclination, if not need, to serve as caretaker, which in turn implies a sadomasochistic element of desire and fulfilment in black women's experience of economic abuse and marginalisation, and mitigates moral responsibility on the part of her abusers. (Shaw 2006: 21)

But on the other hand, the fat black female body signifies the ultimate Venus – a 'triple fetishization' occurs: race, gender, fatness equates with 'the primal, the erotic and the exotic' (Shaw 2006: 49) – disorder, sexual abandon and easy access. Shaw suggests that these stereotypes explain the success of large black female chat show hosts (Oprah Winfrey, Star Jones) and singers (Aretha Franklin, Missy Elliott, Queen Latifah, Jennifer Hudson): in the public space fat black women are 'mammies' and vixens, distributing care and raw emotional expression.

Shaw therefore suggests that fat black women occupy specific spaces in the public consciousness which is qualitatively different to that occupied by non-fat black women (Solanke 2009b). This would mean that the discrimination experienced by these women is also qualitatively different. If so, single-issue legislation, including new statutes focusing on weight, would be unable to remedy this intersectional discrimination. Women like Joyce English – black, fat, capable, and perhaps even comfortable with their appearance – need more holistic legal protection from race, gender and weight discrimination that recognizes the injury inflicted upon them as fat black women, a combination of traits that do not easily lend themselves to conversion, passing or covering (Yoshino 2001).

How could more holistic protection be provided? I suggest that this needs to be preceded by a re-education to promote wider understanding, a re-conceptualization of discrimination law that targets underlying social meanings and assumptions, and a re-contextualization of judicial analysis that systematically considers environmental factors. I discuss these in turn below. Whilst education can change beliefs that fatness is a question of personal choice, law can challenge stereotypes that limit opportunity and success to a specific colour, gender and size – if the image of success remains linked to whiteness and slenderness, weight prejudice will be unquestioningly accepted. Just as Jennifer Portnick in San Francisco challenged the stereotype held by Jazzercise that fat people who exercise (but, like her, remain fat) could not represent health, the courts need to change common sense to recognize that blackness and fatness can be hallmarks of success.

Re-Education

'Anti-fat' attitudes are prevalent in society (Solovay 2000) yet anti-fattism laws have little political legitimacy. Weight discrimination is acceptable largely as a result of the widespread assumption that fat is mutable (Korn 1997) – fat is seen as voluntary therefore there is a low level of public sympathy for the overweight and obese (Oliver and Lee 2002). Children associate fatness with low intelligence, laziness, social alienation and unattractiveness; adults see the obese as undisciplined, inactive, unappealing and with emotional or psychological problems. The only positive stereotype imagines fat people to be funny and warm. This is ironic, as the social rejection encountered by many overweight people (Hill 2003) can lead to depression. Fattism is so entrenched that it is easier for legislators to pass bills protecting food manufacturers than their often ill-informed customers: by the end of 2004, few of the over 110 bills designed to tackle weight discrimination in the United States had become law; in contrast, as of March 2005, 15 US states had passed laws banning obesity lawsuits (Fried 2005: 270–9). Fattism has been described as the 'last great acceptable prejudice' (Pelling 2005: 24).

The more obesity is attributed to individual behaviour, the greater anti-fat prejudice (Hill 2003: 70). Behavioural understandings of weight are encouraged by official campaigns which stress healthy eating and lifestyles.[34] Such campaigns implicitly condone public vilification of the overweight and discrimination on the basis of size: if fat is a result of overeating and lack of exercise, then fat people are lazy and deserve neither public assistance nor sympathy. Yet, the behavioural focus must be questioned – it is 'hard to believe that the prevalence of obesity has tripled because people have deliberately decided to gain weight' (Hill 2003: 69). The current fat epidemic is a complex phenomenon caused by more than excess energy intake and low energy expenditure. Research suggests that obesity arises from a complex interaction of non-behavioural reasons including environmental, genetic, psychological, physiological, metabolic, socio-economic, lifestyle and cultural factors. Sleep deprivation can contribute to obesity – poorly rested bodies produce sub-optimal amounts of leptin, a hormone that regulates appetite, leading to increased cravings for sweets and salty carbohydrates like crisps and chips (Crawford and Jeffery 2005). Some people may have malfunctioning thyroid or pituitary glands, physical problems or be on medication that promotes weight gain.[35]

Fatness can be the result of genetic problems. An example is Prader-Willi syndrome, a rare genetic disorder where sufferers have a constant desire to eat. About 70 per cent inherit it from their father and 30 per cent from the mother. It can go undiagnosed and left untreated sufferers can eat themselves to death – a 13-year-old Californian girl who died in 1997 weighing 49 stone was thought to be an undiagnosed Prader-Willi case (Laurance 2004: 6). Alternatively, 'metabolic-environment' dissonance can lead to weight gain. Studies have found that a metabolism that is designed to cope with under-nutrition cannot quickly adapt to normal levels of nutrition: mothers who experienced starvation during pregnancy tend to have children metabolically predisposed to retain fat. Thus if the mother comes from a poor food community but the child grows up in a food-abundant culture, the food environment conflicts with the biological metabolism and results in weight gain. This may explain the predominance of obesity in some migrant communities. In addition, poor families suffer from what is known as 'shantytown syndrome' – over-eating as a response to uncertain patterns of labour and irregular income which make the source of tomorrow's meals unknown (Critser 2003: 130–1).

The 'pain of poverty' can also act as a driver towards obesity: in urban environments ravaged by drugs and violence, food acts as a safe shelter and the television a shield from gun-ridden streets (Critser 2003: 73, 111; Harnack and Schmitz 2005: 30). Over-eating is rampant amongst the poor and working poor who work under stressful conditions, live in neighbourhoods that are full of fast food restaurants but devoid of safe places to play and exercise, and send their children to schools where fitness classes are not provided. As Critser (2003: 2) says, on one level success with weight loss is not just a triumph of will but a triumph of a 'economic and social class' which enjoys access to medical care, safe spaces in which to exercise, healthy food and literature on health.

More generally, the 'nutrition transition' and the loss of 'nutritional self-determination' has contributed to the growing global waistlines. It is debateable whether people are eating more

---

34   See for example the British Health Department's new three-year 'Change4Life' healthy eating campaign. Available at: http://news.bbc.co.uk/1/hi/health/7791820.stm [accessed: 17 June 2009].

35   Weight gain is a side effect of some medication used to manage the menopause, for example.

(Fox 2003: 14) but accepted that the level of fats and sugars in the everyday diet has risen. The 'nutrition transition' has seen a reduction in the intake of fibre, complex carbohydrates, fruits and vegetables and an increase in the ingestion of fat, cholesterol, sugar and other refined carbohydrates. International food supplies now contain more fat[36] and added sweeteners, and we eat more animal-source foods (meat, fish and milk) than cereals and grains (Popkin 2005). The addition of saturated fats (Critser 2003: 11–12) and sugars to the food supply, especially cheap sweeteners derived from corn (high fructose corn syrup or HFCS), has been identified as a major contributor to the obesity epidemic (Jeffery and Linde 2005: 61). Its use in sweet drinks,[37] ready-made and long-life products has also been associated with type 2 diabetes (Critser 2003: 134–7; Wilkin 2003: 39)

HFCS is popular because it cheap to produce and six times sweeter than cane sugar. However, the financial advantages of HFCS – farmers had a market for their corn and consumers had cheap basic foodstuffs – need to be offset against the health costs. The true price of cheap 'value' meals is a dangerous nutritional transition and a loss of 'nutritional self-determination', or the ability to control the amount of non-nutritional substances (fats and sugar) that we ingest (Critser 2003: 33). Loss of nutritional control is an element of the 'obesogenic' environment in which we live – a world where fat- and sugar-laden foods together with labour-saving devices and sedentary work/ leisure activities make it hard to stay thin, and where obesity itself has, in the form of diet foods and health centres, become integral to economies (Bray 1996: 253).

It seems therefore that our approach to obesity needs to 'acknowledge properly the influence of an obesogenic environment and not be based on a misconceived notion of will power' (Hill 2003: 61). As argued by Jebb et al. (2007), 'the notion of obesity simply being a product of personal over-indulgence has to be abandoned for good'. In 2005, the US Surgeon General also spoke of a need to shift from the notion that obesity is the fault of the individual (Fried 2005: 267).

Governments have thus far done little to protect individuals from the nutritional transition and loss of nutritional autonomy: in Britain, £70m is spent on promoting foods that are high in fat, salt and sugar while the Department of Health has a total budget of £750,000 (Leather 2003: 56); in the United States the food industry spends about '$50 per person per year to publicise food products whilst the USDA spends about $1.50 per person per year for all types of nutritional education' (Jeffery and Linde 2005: 64). The EU, limited in its activity in relation to health due to its marginal competence, spent only 350 million euro in the last six years on public health, whilst devoting billions to the Common Agricultural Policy each year (Rankin 2009: 18).

Re-Conceptualization and Re-Contextualization

Re-education may achieve political legitimacy for anti-fat laws but does not determine how such laws should be designed. In order to be of use to the largest group of victims – corpulent women of colour – I suggest that it must be holistic. I have argued that a more holistic form of discrimination law can be reached by revising the traditional logic informing the creation of categories of protection and systematically incorporating a contextual analysis into judicial decision-making.

There is no inherent reason why legal protection from discrimination is organized upon the basis of categories, but these may have been inevitable given the nature of political campaigns for equality law (Solanke 2009b). The use of open-ended lists[38] addresses atomization but not

---

36   From 1991–6/7, global production of vegetable fats and oils (soybean, sunflower, rapeseed, palm, groundnut) rose from 60 to 71 million metric tons.

37   By the mid-1980s Coke and Pepsi were using 100 per cent HFCS instead of the 50:50 sucrose: fructose used previously (Critser 2003: 18).

38   As for example in the European Convention on Human Rights or the Canadian Constitution.

the identification of grounds. If the creation of categories were informed by the logic of stigma rather than the logic of immutability (Lenhardt 2004; Solanke 2009a), discrimination law could move beyond the limited protection it currently provides to a more holistic remedy. A stigma is an attribute which, even though not necessarily immutable, is denigrated (Dijker and Koomen 2007: 8) and 'deeply discrediting' (Goffman 1990: 12) in a way that 'tarnishes' the whole identity of an individual. All other traits, including abilities, 'are subordinated to or negated by this trait, which is immediately felt to be more central to the "actual" identity of the individual' (Page 1984: 10). Under this logic, discrimination law would be re-focused on stigmas to which the public response is always punitive (Page 1984: 3) rather than just negative (Nussbaum 2004: 176); which therefore make a significant difference in relation to access to and acquisition of resources in key areas, such as health, housing, education, training and employment; and which finally are difficult to escape (Levin and van Laar 2006: 4).

The stigma associated with overweight and obesity is outlined above (Hill 2003: 69). Many people have an intense fear of fat. In one reported study, 25 per cent of women and 17 per cent of men said they would sacrifice three or more years of their lives to be thin. Some women reportedly avoid pregnancy because they fear gaining weight and becoming fat. Others smoke cigarettes in an effort to remain thin or reject the advice that they quit smoking because they fear they will gain weight should they quit (Puhl and Brownell 2003). Using the logic of stigma anti-discrimination law could offer a remedy for single, multiple and intersectional forms of discrimination.

Stigmas are by definition contextual – they are socially determined and maintained (Goffman 1990: 14). If the spotlight of discrimination law is widened to respond to social meanings, then the judicial purview must likewise be broadened to consider social context. In order to adjudicate intersectional claims, courts need a way to consider social context in their decision-making when faced with intersectional claims. The need to consider context in determination of discrimination was suggested by Lord Griffith in his dissent in *James v. Eastleigh Borough Council*,[39] where he argued that the reason for differential treatment was not the difference in sex, but the difference in economic wellbeing. In his view, the context informing the disputed rule was determined by economic reality – those living on a pension were usually less well off than those who are working. Set against this social framework, there had been no sex discrimination even though Mr James remained a member of the protected group.

There are examples of the use of social context in judicial decision-making. In 1997, the Supreme Court of Canada upheld the original judgement of Judge Corrine Sparks[40] to acquit a black youth (R.D.S.)[41] of assault charges against a white police officer during the arrest of another youth. The case had been referred to the Supreme Court because after making her judgement, Judge Sparks had made general comments about strained relations between police and non-white groups, and the tendency for police to overreact when dealing with those groups. Her comments lead to accusations that she was biased and a petition for her decision to be reversed.[42]

In upholding the decision and conduct of Judge Sparks, the Supreme Court said:

> The requirement for neutrality does not require judges to discount their life experiences. Whether the use of references to social context is appropriate in the circumstances and whether a reasonable

---

39   *James v. Eastleigh Borough Council* [1990] 2 AC 751.

40   At that time the only black judge in Nova Scotia, Canada.

41   *R. v. S. (R.D.)*, [1997] 3 S.C.R. 484.

42   Sonia Sotomayor was likewise accused of bias and subjected to similar treatment when she discussed the value of her experience as a Latina in her role as judge. The text of her speech has been republished, see Sotomayor (2009).

apprehension of bias arises from particular statements depends on the facts. A very significant difference exists between cases in which social context is used to ensure that the law evolves in keeping with changes in social reality and cases, such as this one, where social context is apparently being used to assist in determining an issue of credibility.

A majority of 6-3[43] rejected the accusations and the request to overturn the decision. The Supreme Court held that a reasonable person would not think that Judge Sparks was biased and, further, that Judge Sparks had used her experience and knowledge of the community to understand the social context behind the case.

Social framework analysis (Monahan et al. 2008; Borgida and Kim 2007) has also been systematically used in cases of sexual discrimination in the United States. It can be described as a process for systematic consideration of the context surrounding a set of facts arising from a case. The use of such a contextual analysis was first suggested by Charles Lawrence. Lawrence, writing specifically on race, proposed that courts test the cultural meaning of a challenged act by gathering evidence from the social context in which the decision was made (Lawrence 1987). This process is usually conducted via the review of scientific studies presented in court by an expert witness. The role of the expert witness is not to establish a link for the court, but to educate it on the causes and consequences of the type of discrimination concerned, so that it has an empirically rich backdrop upon which to come to a decision.

In many cases,[44] social evidence offered by qualified social scientists has played a key role in employment discrimination litigation: 'by offering insight into the operation of stereotyping and bias in decision-making, social framework experts can help fact finders to assess other evidence more accurately' (Hart and Secunda 2009: 2). The expert assists the court in its decision-making by providing a detailed context against which to evaluate the acts complained of. For example, in Wal-Mart, details were gathered on its organizational history, structure and processes, culture, practices and correspondence, diversity and equal opportunity policies. These were then examined against the backdrop of social research on organizational inequalities to determine the likelihood that the discrimination complained of could occur (Bielby 2003b). The court is left to decide whether or not it did occur.

Conclusion

It could be argued that we should not be surprised by the upsurge in overweight and obesity: the more we earn, the more our pattern of consumption changes. It is not only lower food prices but also faster lifestyles that encourage us to pay less attention to what we eat. Combined with mass media pushing a new mode of consumption, and technological development which encourages reduced domestic (microwave ovens, cheap transportation) and leisure effort, the rise in general population size should have been expected (Popkin 2005: 92). Yet appearance still matters very much (Fowler-Hermes 2001: 32).

Obesity is not just a public health issue but also a matter which affects equality of opportunity. The general public, government and employers are fatphobic. Empirical evidence shows that excess

---

43   Lamer C.J. and Sopinka and Major J.J. dissenting.

44   For example, in the United States: *Price Waterhouse v. Hopkins*, 490 U.S. 228, 233-35 (1989), *Beck v. The Boeing Company*, case No.2:00-cv-00301-MJP (W.D. Wash. Nov. 10 2003, *Dukes v. Wal-Mart Stores, Inc.*, 474 F.3d 1214 (9th Circuit, Dec 11th 2007)).

avoirdupois is more damaging to the lives and careers of girls and women than boys and men, and most damaging to corpulent girls and women of colour. There is also good reason to be concerned about this. Size is not a general determinant of aptitude, ability or performance. This discrimination therefore needs to be addressed. However, before any legal measure can be politically legitimate, a mass re-education is necessary to highlight non-behavioural explanations of weight gain.

Law is also important. EU law does not formally prohibit fattism – like other public health issues, this remains within the competence of the Member States.[45] Kirkland (2008: 131) may be correct that the most likely form of rights expansion for fat people will come through a gradual expansion of already existing legal terms like disability. The extension of existing EU disability discrimination law may help to some extent, but is problematic: size is not a disability and if treated as such would be formally entrenched as an aberration rather than a norm. The creation of a new statute may be possible using the post-Lisbon focus on 'wellbeing' but this does not facilitate intersectionality hence corpulent women of colour would still be left without a remedy.

I suggested that stigma be used as a logic to develop an holistic approach in anti-discrimination law and also drew upon the suggestion made by Lord Griffiths in *James* that context be systematically included in the judicial determination of discrimination by using the social framework analysis. Taken together, these changes could strengthen the impact of equality law. The social framework analysis could be useful not only in intersectional cases, but also those involving institutional racism, bringing awareness into courtrooms that could enhance the effectiveness of anti discrimination law in general.

---

45   Although the Commission's has funded some public health projects, for example, the Ensemble Prévenons l'Obésité des Enfants ('let's work together to prevent childhood obesity'), a nutrition education programme in France.

PART IV
Intersections between Gender, 'Race' and Disability from EU Perspectives

Chapter 14

Gendered Experiences of Racial Discrimination: Comparative Socio-Legal Research

Isabelle Carles, Erica Howard and Eleonore Kofman

Introduction

Although multiple and intersectional discrimination is increasingly discussed by academics (Ashiagbor 1999; Makkonen 2002; Hannett 2003; Fredman 2005a; Smith 2005; Schiek 2005; Grabham 2006; Moon 2006b; Verloo 2006; Yuval-Davis 2006; Gerards 2007; McColgan 2007; Burri and Schiek 2009) and policy-makers in the European Union, interest in the topic, the understanding of key concepts, the most significant target groups, and the available evidence for discrimination and policy-making in this field, all differ enormously between countries. In some countries, there is a long history of academic debate and policy-making in relation to different strands of discrimination, and in particular gender and race. Several countries, such as Denmark, Ireland, Sweden and the UK have identified multiple discrimination as an issue and have moved to single equality bodies (European Commission 2007e). In other countries discrimination legislation is recent as, for example, in Spain. The measurement of racial discrimination may also be highly contested, as in France. As Vieten (this volume) has highlighted, there are specific genealogies of concepts and the incorporation of minorities, national and migrant, which have to be taken into account and have a bearing on how we operationalize multiple and intersectional discrimination.

Our aim in this chapter is to present some of the discussions arising from a comparative European project, *GendeRace – The Use of Racial Anti-discrimination Laws: Gender and Citizenship in a Multicultural Context*, which examined through empirical research some of the problems in moving beyond the national level in understanding and evaluating multiple discrimination. We first present the project, the diversity of the countries involved, their history of immigration and relationship with minority groups. In the subsequent section, we focus on the difficulties of comparison arising from the fact that race and ethnicity in particular are contested concepts and thus their interpretation and treatment vary markedly between countries. It may also be difficult to capture any evidence for racial discrimination, especially in countries where data on race or racial origin are considered sensitive, requiring high levels of data protection and ethical standards. In the third section we then examine the ways in which multiple discrimination is handled in legislation.

About GendeRace

Although the Eurobarometer Survey on discrimination in the European Union provides information on how people perceive themselves as discriminated against (European Commission 2008c), little is known about how individuals' reactions to the racial discrimination legal framework are shaped, particularly in relation to gender. As a result, there is scope to improve our understanding of the effectiveness of anti-discrimination legislation by examining it from the point of view of the subject and from a gender perspective.

The GendeRace project aims at improving our knowledge of multiple discrimination based on race and gender in order to propose practical recommendations to improve the protection of complainants. It focuses on the analysis of the use of racial anti-discrimination laws, primarily by women and men from an immigrant background in six European countries. The research was funded by the European Union under FP 7,[1] and brings together six European research teams from France, Bulgaria, Germany, Spain, Sweden and the UK.

The objective of the GendeRace project is firstly to improve our understanding of the phenomenon of multiple discrimination through the analysis of the experiences of women and men confronted with discrimination. The aim is to stimulate new and complementary actions to better assess the effectiveness of policies and practices in the field of anti-discrimination based on race and gender. The key questions are how to reach disadvantaged groups, especially foreign and minority women, and how to better frame policies, laws and practices in order to address multiple discrimination based on race and gender.

One of our hypotheses is that, because of the *single discrimination ground approach* to equality legislation in most European countries, the present legal framework does not address multiple discrimination based on race and gender properly. We also argue that social relations based on gender and race or ethnicity influence the perception and use of racial anti-discrimination laws. We postulate that men and women experience different kinds of discrimination and react in different ways to the phenomenon. Furthermore, the institutional framework provides different responses according to gender in term of action and conflict resolution.

In order to deepen our understanding of the impact of gender experiences of racial discrimination, it was decided to combine quantitative and qualitative approaches. The research methodology analyses the different levels in which social divisions operate, as institutional, interceptive and representative and in the subjective constructions of identities, as developed by Yuval-Davis. For her 'the point is to analyse the differential ways in which different social divisions are concretely enmeshed and constructed by each other and how they relate to political and subjective constructions of identities' (Yuval-Davis 2006: 205).

The different forms of discrimination are addressed through the analysis of legal frameworks, case law and complaints at the institutional and representative level. The review of complaint files held by national bodies and in NGOs responsible for giving advice to victims allows us to explore the reasons why a particular discrimination ground was chosen to file the legal complaint. The objective is also to analyse the files in a gender perspective.

Interviews with around 70 lawyers and stakeholders were conducted to analyse the interactive and representative levels. The aim was to gather the views of experts such as academics, lawyers dealing with complaints and stakeholders in the field of feminist and anti-racist NGOs on the impact of the ground-specific approach to equality legislation.

The subjective constructions of identities were explored through the study of around 200 semi-directive qualitative interviews of foreign nationals and members of ethnic minorities. The objective of these interviews is to identify representations of the law held by those experiencing racial discrimination and the influence of these representations on the use of the legal framework. The interview strategy takes account of both racial equality legislation from the point of view

---

1   The research for this project has received funding from the European Community's Seventh Framework Programme *FP7/2007-2011* under *grant agreement* n SSH7-CT-2007-217237. The content for this chapter does not necessarily reflect the opinion or position of the European Commission.

of gender and also gender equality legislation in terms of racial discrimination. This multiple perspective is present in each of the components of the research. Across the selected countries, a series of differences which impact on the conduct of the research have emerged.

Diversity of Countries and Contexts Involved in the GendeRace Project

The six countries selected for the project have a very different experience of the fight against discrimination. In Sweden and the UK, there is a long history of recognizing discrimination and legislation to tackle discrimination, especially sex and race discrimination, has been in place for many years. In contrast, Bulgaria has more recently established laws against discrimination. In between these two poles are France, Germany and Spain. But even if almost all the partner countries have put in place legislation against gender discrimination, some have sought to avoid implementing EU directives combating racism and racial discrimination.

This is the case for Germany, which was referred to the European Court of Justice[2] for failing to pass all necessary legislation to bring national law into line with the Racial Equality Directive 2000/43 of 29 June 2000. In addition, the anti-discrimination directives' implementation has led to very controversial discussions among political parties and employers' associations, who accuse the law of increasing bureaucracy, damaging the economy and of being a 'Jobkiller' (Wilpert 2003). As a result of the ECJ's decision, Germany finally adopted a comprehensive legal framework, including all the grounds of discrimination in the same law in the 2006 Act implementing Directives 2000/43, 2000/78, 2002/73 and 2004/113.[3] Nevertheless, discrimination and anti-discrimination is not a major issue in the current debate in Germany (Wilpert and Howe 2008).

Spain was also reluctant to implement the new directives and has not yet developed a coherent and coordinated national framework to fight against racism. There exists legislation dealing with discrimination such as the Law 62/2003, of 30 December, of fiscal administrative and social measures or the Legal Decree 5/2000, 4 August 2000 (Law on Infractions and Sanctions of Social Order) covering all grounds of both the Racial Equality Directive (2000/43/EC) and Employment Framework Directive (2000/78/EC). There is also a lack of clarity as to whether the framework is only for third country nationals or whether it should also address the problem of internal racism directed at the *Gitano* community and second generation and internal immigrants (Jubany Baucells 2008b). In addition, debate on multiple discrimination is only now emerging as part of the current debate on race and gender. A few sociologists and anthropologists are now introducing the key concept of multiple discrimination and intersectionality which had previously only been developed with reference to sexual orientation and disability (Jubany Baucells 2008a).

France only very recently developed a legal and institutional framework against racial discrimination due mainly to the 'colour blind' republican model of French integration (Carles 2008). For many years French policies and public discourse focused on integration (Lorcerie 2000; Fassin 2002). As a result it was admitted that discrimination against foreigners exists but it is supposed to disappear once individuals obtain French citizenship. The change came at the end of the 1990s under pressure from the EU and national debate through publication of research and reports on discrimination, especially in the employment field (Vourc'h et al. 2000; Poiret and De

---

2   Case ECJ C-329/04 *Commission v. Germany*, judgment of 28 April 2005, Official Journal 11.6.2005/C 143/13, not reported in ECR.

3   The General Equal Treatment Act (Allgemeines Gleichbehandlungsgesetz) 18 August 2006, BGBI 2006, 1897.

Rudder 1997; Noël 2000) and at different career stages such as recruitment (Bataille 1997). It became obvious that French young people from a migrant background faced discrimination in access to employment and goods and services (Simon et al. 2001; Barou et al. 2003; Boumaza 2003; Chignier Riboulon 2003; De Wenden and Body-Gendrot 2003; Faure 2000; Brenner 2002; Felouzis et al. 2002; Payet et al. 2002; Fassin et al. 2001; Assier-Andrieu and Gotman 2004). However it is now accepted that France provides the necessary prerequisites for combating discrimination even if it is still necessary to improve the fight against institutional discriminations (Fassin 2008).

This is also the case in Bulgaria where the Commission for Protection against Discrimination on all grounds has been in place for several years now and a general law against discrimination was adopted in 2004 (Bulgarian Protection against Discrimination Act 2004). However, equality and anti-discrimination is treated legislatively in general terms without special attention being paid to gender issues. In addition, a Draft Gender Equality Act has been subject to discussion for several years but its adoption has been delayed. It can be said that the debate on the Roma/gender discrimination remains restricted among social scientists and NGO activists, apart from whom there has not been a public debate on discrimination and discriminatory attitudes (Grekova et al. 2008).

In addition, all these countries have a diverse population in terms of ethnicity and religion. Britain and France both have a long experience of immigration due to their colonial past. In Sweden immigration increased after the Second World War and the immigrant population was mainly composed of people from Nordic countries and former Yugoslavia. In Germany, the recruitment of foreign workers began in the mid-1950s and concerned mainly individuals from Turkey. This was the result of an agreement between Germany and Turkey (1963) leading to a massive recruitment of foreign workers. In the other countries, immigration flows are more recent, as in Spain where the immigration process began only after Franco's death. In Bulgaria also, refugees and immigrant issues are relatively new and strongly linked to the entry of this country in the EU.

However, all these countries are experiencing new and more recent immigration flows which are more diverse, with increasing numbers of asylum seekers and refugees from Eastern Europe, the Middle East and Latin America. Migrant status and the reasons people come to Europe are also very diverse. In the UK, for instance, the recent flows of Eastern Europeans can be explained by the implementation of a policy which is more open to labour migration within the EU (Ruhs 2006).

This diversity in the history of immigration among countries has a strong influence on the project's target groups which differ from one country to another even if some common trends can be identified.

In the sample examined in the GendeRace project, the main victims of discrimination in all the countries are immigrants and citizens with ethnic origins different from that of the majority of the (indigenous) population. In many countries, migrants and ethnic minorities who are citizens are still not treated as equal members of society. They are still perceived as migrants and foreigners and, as a result, they experience various forms of discrimination irrespective of their citizenship status. This is the case of the Roma who represent the most disadvantaged victims of discrimination in Spain and in Bulgaria where, in both cases, they are citizens. In Bulgaria, for instance, according to the latest 2001 Census results, the Roma group numbers 370,908 persons or 5.57 per cent of the population (see: www.nsi.bg/Census/ethnos.htm). However as the ethnic and self-identification is voluntary and free, numerous experts believe that the actual number of the Roma population is significantly higher. At the same time, despite the freedom of self-identification, the rest of the Bulgarian population define the Roma as individuals belonging to the same group. A representative sociological survey called 'Ethnocultural situation in Bulgaria' conducted in 1992 displayed that the publicly accepted image of the Roma was extremely negative. In Spain, estimates of the Roma population range from 500,000 to 600,000 (Institut Nacional de Estadistica 2007). According to a CIS national survey (2006), the Roma who have been part of the Spanish social fabric for centuries, represent the most highly disadvantaged group of victims.

Another group of people often experiencing discrimination are Muslims who have been subjected increasingly to harassment and discrimination in the past decade. This is the case in Germany for people from Turkey, in France and Spain for people from North Africa and in the UK for people from the Indian subcontinent and the Middle East. A specific case are the Pomaks who are ethnic Bulgarians of Muslim religion. There is no official data about their number but expert estimates place it around 250,000 people (see www.nsi.bg/Census/Ethnos.htm). Within these Muslim communities, women are potentially subject to multiple discrimination. For example, in Sweden, the group that seems to be the least integrated into the labour market and in education are Muslim women from Asian and African countries, especially from Somalia and Iraq.

This diversity of experience in the fight against discrimination and target groups and history of immigration among countries could also lead to different interpretation of concepts related to multiple discrimination and to difficulties of comparison.

Difficulties of Comparison

Contested Concepts

The most contested terms in relation to the GendeRace project are those of race and racism in relation to discrimination. These terms are, first of all, historically and socially specific and must thus be seen in their historical and social context in each country. Their meanings have of course changed over time and the terms have been used in different ways at different times. Before the eighteenth century, the term race was hardly used, but when it was it denoted nothing more than a group of people with a common line of descent, a common ancestry. When people came into contact with other people, race was used as a term to relate to these other people and to define themselves in relation to these other people. Race thus denoted observed variations between people. Not until the eighteenth century did race become a biological term when the world was seen as populated by distinct races, each with different biological characteristics. This biological distinction became linked to a hierarchy between the races, with some races being considered superior to others. This inferiority/superiority was used to justify exclusion, subordination and even extermination of certain groups considered to be inferior (Benedict 1983; Miles 1989; Mason 1995; Furedi 1998; Bulmer and Solomos 1999; Banton 1992, 2002). Many people argue that race was used or 'reinvented' with this ranking attached to it to explain events in the eighteenth and nineteenth centuries like white domination, colonization, slavery and other forms of exploitation (Miles 1989; Furedi 1998).

The terms 'race' and 'racism' are, therefore, heavily negatively loaded in Europe and elsewhere. Memories of the Holocaust and the abuse of theories about race and racism are casting long shadows over the debates. So, in many EU countries, it is problematic to talk about race and racism without reference to the Holocaust. For example, during the negotiations about Council Directive 2000/43/EC, the EU Member States faced 'a conundrum: how to speak about "race" in a Directive which fights racism' (Tyson 2001: 201). As he reports, the negotiations show clearly that some Member States saw the use of the term race as 'tantamount to accepting racist theories that alleged the existence of separate human races'. Of the GendeRace partner countries, Sweden wanted to delete any reference to race, while France proposed replacing the words 'racial or ethnic origin' with 'the alleged membership or non-membership of a racial or ethnic group'.[4] However, other Member States wanted to use the word 'race' rather than solely relying on ethnic origin in order to make clear that the Directive was combating racism. The Commission, in answer to the wish to remove any reference to race, recalled Article 13 EC (Treaty of Rome, as amended now Article 19 Treaty on the Functions of the European Union (TFEU)) as the legal basis – Article 13 EC (now Article 19 TFEU) also mentions racial or ethnic origin – and drew attention to the fact that 'it is politically impossible to remove a reference to race, as it could be construed as an intention to exclude such discrimination from the scope of the Directive' (Council 2000a). Of the partner countries, Spain and Germany expressed a preference to stick to the wording of the Treaty. In the end, a compromise was reached in keeping the terms 'racial or ethnic origin' but adding Recital 6 to the Preamble stating that the EU rejects theories which attempt to determine the existence of separate human races; and, that the use of the term 'racial origin' in the Directive does not imply an acceptance of such theories. The use of the term 'race' in this chapter equally does not imply that the authors accept such theories.

In the Preamble of the International Convention for the Elimination of all Forms of Racial Discrimination (ICERD), a United Nations Instrument to which all partner countries are signatories, the States Parties also reject theories of racial superiority by expressing that they are 'convinced that any doctrine of superiority based on racial differentiation is scientifically false, morally condemnable, socially unjust and dangerous, and that there is no justification for racial discrimination, in theory or in practice, anywhere'. And, in General Recommendation 7 of the European Commission against Racism and Intolerance (ECRI), a body of the Council of Europe of which all partner countries are members, a footnote to Para 1(a), states: 'since all human beings belong to the same species, ECRI rejects theories based on the existence of different "races"'. (Note the use of 'race' in quotation marks) (European Commission against Racism and Intolerance 2002). While the ICERD dates from 1966, the Race Equality Directive and the Recommendation were both adopted since 2000, but the European States still found it necessary even then to state their rejection explicitly, which shows that the use of the term race is still very sensitive in Europe.

Scientists in the 1930s disproved the theories about biological differences and most writers, writing after the Second World War, acknowledge that there is no scientific evidence to support any theory that there are different, separate, biological races. However, biological notions of race do still appear to be present in political discourse and popular thinking. The term is still used in everyday language to label differences between people, especially differences in skin colour.

Therefore, the terms 'race' and 'racism' are problematic and there is strong resistance to using these terms in some of the European partner countries. Within the GendeRace project, many discussions have taken place as to the definition of these terms. For the moment all partners have agreed that race will be considered in the following way: race and ethnic groups, like nations, are imagined communities. They are ideological entities, made and changed in struggle. They are discursive formations, signalling a language through which differences may be named and explained (Bulmer and Solomos 1999). Where the terms 'race' or 'racial' are used together with the term 'discrimination', the GendeRace Partners use the definition of racial discrimination given in Article 1(1) of the ICERD:

---

4   Council of the European Union, *Outcome of Proceedings of the Social Questions Working Party*, 6435/00, Brussels, 1 March, footnote 7; Council of the European Union, *Outcome of Proceedings of the Social Questions Working Party*, 6942/00, Brussels, 31 March, footnote 12; Council of the European Union, *Outcome of Proceedings of the Social Questions Working Party*, 8454/00, Brussels, 16 May, footnote 12.

Any distinction, exclusion, restriction, or preference based on race, colour, descent or national or ethnic origin which has the purpose or effect of nullifying or impairing the recognition, enjoyment or exercise, on an equal footing, of human rights and fundamental freedoms in the political, economic, social, cultural or any other field of public life.

And, racism will be defined as it is in ECRI's General Policy Recommendation No. 7 (ECRI 2002): racism is:

the belief that a ground such as race, colour, language, religion, nationality or national or ethnic origin justifies contempt for a person or a group of persons, or the notion of superiority of a person or group of persons.

So when race is used as a ground for discrimination, it points to a distinction based on a person's assumed biological race, colour, descent or national or ethnic origin. In Europe, the terms 'ethnicity' or 'ethnic origin' are often used together with, or as an alternative to, race or racial origin, as in Council Directive 2000/43/EC. It is difficult to draw a boundary between the concepts of ethnicity and race as they overlap in many aspects. It is suggested that the terms 'ethnic' and 'ethnicity', when coupled with race, are used to clarify that not only distinctions based on assumed biological traits but also those based on cultural traits are included. When used instead of race, it is often as a euphemism, to avoid the negative implications that the word 'race' has. If you drop any reference to race from Council Directive 2000/43/EC as some countries advocated, the Directive would prohibit discrimination on the ground of ethnic origin. Ethnic and ethnicity are used as euphemisms because they are less negatively loaded. But they also have varying definitions. The principles and recommendations for population and housing censuses, Revision 2, Draft, United Nations, September 2006 (Simon 2007: 28) affirms that ethnicity is a social construct with fluid boundaries. The UN (cited in Simon 2007) defines it in the following way:

Ethnicity is based on a shared understanding of history and territorial origin (regional and national) of an ethnic group or community as well as on particular cultural characteristics such as language and religion … Ethnicity is multidimensional and is more a process than a static concept, and so ethnic classifications should be treated with moveable boundaries.

We therefore had to deal not only with different sentiments in relation to the terms 'race', 'racism' and 'ethnicity' within the GendeRace project, but we also had to be aware of the differences in coverage of different bodies of national legislation. Of the instruments already mentioned, the ICERD covers race, colour, descent or national or ethnic origin, while ECRI defines race as including colour, language, religion, nationality or national or ethnic origin. Council Directive 2000/43/EC covers racial (or in other language versions: race) and ethnic origin. In relation to the GendeRace project, this means that it is not clear what is included under race/racial discrimination in the national law of each partner country. Does this Directive protect against colour discrimination, as colour can be seen as an indicator of race? Does it cover discrimination based on descent? Then there is the problem with discrimination on the basis of nationality. This is not covered under this Directive – as is clear from Article 3(2) of the Directive and Article 12 EC (now Article 18 TFEU) – but is national origin discrimination covered? Discrimination on the ground of religion and belief is covered by another EU measure (Council Directive 2000/78/EC) and thus this is not covered by Council Directive 2000/43/EC. However, people who discriminate against others do not often make a difference between these grounds, a dark skin is linked to different race, nationality, national origin, religion, etc., and all these are often combined in the motive behind discriminatory behaviour.

If we look at the national legislation, the British Race Relations Act 1976 covers colour, race, nationality or ethnic or national origin. Of the GendeRace partner countries, France and Spain prohibit discrimination on the grounds of race or racial and ethnic origin and nationality. Germany prohibits discrimination on racist grounds or on those pertaining to ethnic background, while the Bulgarian law on the protection against discrimination contains an open-ended list of discrimination grounds which includes race, nationality, ethnic origin, citizenship and origin. The new Swedish single Anti Discrimination Act which came into force on 1 January 2009, covers, in its open list of grounds, ethnic origin. In a factsheet of the Swedish Government on the new anti-discrimination law it is stated (without any further explanation as to the reason for this):

> The concept of 'race' that was previously part of the definition of the 'ethnic origin' grounds of discrimination is to be removed. This change does not mean that protection against discrimination on grounds of ethnic origin is weakened.[5]

The GendeRace project therefore had to contend with a number of problems concerning the language of race, racism, race discrimination and ethnicity as well as different coverage of the national laws and differences in the groups subject to discrimination. On top of this, it encountered issues of the availability and access to different kinds of data which in part stem from the conceptual differences and attitudes to the existence of racial discrimination. This is the subject of the following section.

Availability and Access to Data

In the report in 2006 to the Council and European Parliament on the application of Directive 2000/43/EC (European Commission 2006b), the Commission noted the crucial role which could be played by statistics in activating anti-discrimination policies and referred to the misunderstandings in the relationship between data protection and the production of statistics on discrimination. There are substantial variations in data collection which are influenced by national conventions. The source of data, the purpose for which they were gathered, the criteria used and the method of collection may vary considerably from one country to another. The categories themselves may change over time, reflecting policy concerns and the changing population being studied. In turn this raises issues of how discrimination and equality of opportunity may be measured and monitored without statistical evidence (Simon 2004b). One of the main constraints to collecting data on discrimination comes from legislation and case law prohibiting intrusion into people's private lives and governing the conditions under which computerized data can be collected and disseminated. Different balances may have been struck between the need to identify a person's race or ethnic origin in order to document discrimination, on the one hand, and the ethical regulations and stringency applied to the protection of people's private lives, on the other hand.

In terms of data relating to individuals, legal provisions derive from Council Directive 95/46/EC which has been transposed into all EU countries and aims to guarantee citizens' privacy by enforcing respect for anonymity and to restrict the collection of 'sensitive' data (the list of these data will correspond to grounds of discrimination) to certain conditions. All EU states have transposed

---

5   See: www.regeringen.se/content/1/c6/11/80/10/4bb17aff.pdf.

the Directive on the processing and transmission of such information. Whilst Article 8 prohibits the processing of personal data revealing racial or ethnic origin, political opinions, religious or philosophical beliefs, trade-union membership, and the processing of data concerning health or sexual life, there are a number of principles which authorize exceptions under certain conditions to the collection of what is defined as sensitive data. In some countries interpretation is strict and only data explicitly referring to 'ethnic' or 'racial' origin are prohibited; in others it is broader and includes anything that may act as a proxy, for example nationality, country of birth and name.

All countries include a list of exemptions to the collection of sensitive data but the grounds of exemption are not the same in each state. It may exclude employment or health and vital interests and files kept by NGOs. The latter may be permitted to keep such data on condition that the processing relates solely to the members of the body and that the data are not disclosed to a third party without the consent of the data subjects (Article 8(2d)). On the other hand, there may be highly sensitive areas such as social welfare where proxies are prohibited even though information is collected in the census, for example on nationality and place of birth in France.[6] Finally states may lay down exemptions for reasons of public interest (Article 8(4)) as is the situation in the UK.

Only the UK has an established tradition of collecting and using data on ethnic minorities and identities (Howard et al. 2008). It is based on laws and regulations governing the production of sensitive statistics which were laid down in the Race Relations Acts (1976 and 2000) where it is argued that there is a need to collect data for the purposes of ethnic monitoring which can be used to highlight potential inequalities, investigate their underlying causes and remove unfairness and disadvantage (Simon 2007: 42). Promoting equal treatment is also mentioned in the list of exemptions from the Data Protection Act 1998. In France permission to collect personal data must be requested from the CNIL whose powers were established with one of the first data protection laws in Europe in 1978. In 2005 it acknowledged 'that the aims of combating discrimination in the matter of employment are legitimate in terms of public interest but considered that in the absence of ethno-racial typologies, on which it expressed strong reservations, there was no purpose to analysing names or nationality' (Simon 2007: 49–50). There has been a lively public debate on the collection of ethnic statistics but the decision not to collect data on race and ethnicity has been reaffirmed in France in the decision of the Constitutional Council in November 2007 to prohibit the use of racial and ethnic origin in studies which seek to measure diversity (Decision no. 2007-557 DC 15 November 2007). However, since its inception in 2005 the High Authority against Discrimination and for Equality has been analysing the complaints submitted to it as an indicator of the kinds and grounds of discrimination being experienced. Furthermore it has been possible in the past few years to study the situation of descendants of immigrants in France drawn from data on tests for job seekers and applicants for housing.

In Germany, the transposition of Council Directive 95/46/EC in 2003 stipulated that a key condition of the collection of statistics was ensuring that personal consent is obtained. Federal agencies and the public sector are subject to greater supervision than private sector organizations. However, case law on collection of ethnic statistics is very limited. It is only since 2005 that the migrant background of men and women has been collected in micro censuses. However data on discrimination are incomplete. Not only is there no official data on discrimination in employment but there is also little non-official data (Baer 2005 cited in Simon 2007). There is also little public debate on discrimination and anti-discrimination and on the collection of statistics except for some

---

6   The Commission Nationale Informatique et Libertés deemed in 1980 that data in this area could only be collected under three headings: French, EU alien and non-EU alien (Simon 2007: 19).

NGOs and researchers. However some larger cities, such as Berlin, Wiesbaden, Essen and Stuttgart, are beginning to set up systems to collect data on integration which includes discrimination. For example, Berlin produced an Anti-Discrimination Report 2005–7 (Wilpert and Howe 2008).

There is less systematic data available in some countries due to the recency of their immigration flows and/or the development of their anti-discrimination legislation. Collection of such data may be the subject of interest by academics and undertaken in small-scale studies or by NGOs, both of which only yield a very partial coverage, as is the case of Spain (Jubany Baucells 2008b).

Significant data for collection also changes over time. Thus familiar categories such as ethnic minority in the UK, which are embedded in legislation and have until recently determined who may benefit from protection against discrimination, may impede the way we understand more recent changes to bring in new groups to be covered by legislation. The categories of data collection on ethnicity need to be flexible and incorporate a subjective appreciation to take account of duration of settlement, mixed marriages and diversification of flows. For example, in the UK the original ethnic classification was developed in response to post-colonial migration but has in recent years been modified to take account of political representation by groups such as the Irish, who though 'white', were able to demonstrate considerable discrimination in terms of a number of economic and social indicators. Inter-marriages between ethnic groups have generated an increasing number of children in mixed categories. Discrimination against other 'white' groups such as the Eastern Europeans has become more common but it is difficult to assess due to their inclusion in the broad category of 'white'. Many Middle Eastern migrants also classify themselves as 'white' (Kofman et al. 2009). These developments require a much more sophisticated understanding of processes of racism and racialization beyond a simplistic 'black' and 'white' dichotomy. Gender statistics too use the broad ethnic categories rather than country of birth or nationality which would capture more accurately recent changes in immigration and groups subject to discrimination.

Another variation is the collection of data on religion which is included in official statistics in a number of countries such as Bulgaria, Germany and the UK (as from the 2001 census) but not on ethnic monitoring forms. As Muslims have been subjected increasingly to harassment and discrimination in the past decade, religious identity, including dress, and belief have become the object of exclusionary and discriminatory practices (Fundamental Rights Agency 2009). In this regard, discriminatory practices have a gender dimension, especially in relation to education and employment, and the wearing of distinctive clothing (Poulter 1997; Schiek 2004; Ben Mohamed 2001; Bribosia and Rorive 2004; Knights 2005; Mazher Idriss 2005; McGoldrick 2006; Gibson 2007; Institute of Race Relations 2008; Howard 2009; *Guardian* 2009).

Though only providing limited coverage, it is NGOs who are more likely to collect data on the newly recognized forms of discrimination. NGOs have an important role to play in raising awareness of different forms of discrimination and the interaction between them (Simon 2004b), particularly where there is constitutional opposition to the collection of data or simply lack of official data.

Application of Multiple and Intersectional Discrimination

The subject of multiple discrimination has come to the fore in the EU as well. Both the EU Race Equality and Employment Framework Directives adopted in 2000 explicitly recognize, in one of their recitals, the possibility of multiple discrimination and mention that women are often the victims of multiple discrimination (Recital 14 Race Equality Directive and 3 Employment Framework Directive). But the term 'multiple discrimination' does not appear anywhere else in either of these

Directives and no definition is given nor any indication as to how to deal with cases of multiple discrimination. In fact, one of the main criticisms of the EU anti-discrimination Directives has always been that there is a hierarchy between grounds, with better protection provided against discrimination on the grounds of race and sex than on the grounds of religion and belief, disability, age and sexual orientation. One of the often mentioned consequences of the hierarchy is that it makes it difficult to deal with cases of multiple discrimination.

The European Commission appears to have taken this criticism on board and has, recently, started to show an interest in the problem of 'multiple discrimination'. It commissioned a study for which the report came out in September 2007 (European Commission 2007e). The commissioning of research projects like the GendeRace one, are a sign of interest in this as well. However in the explanatory memorandum of the proposal issued in July 2008 for a new Directive extending the scope of the protection against discrimination on the grounds of religion or belief, disability, age and sexual orientation outside the employment sphere, the Commission reports that, in its consultation, attention was drawn to the need to tackle multiple discrimination, for example by defining it as discrimination and by providing effective remedies. It then states: 'These issues go beyond the scope of this directive but nothing prevents Member States taking action in these areas' (European Commission 2008b: 4). In other words, the EU will not provide for this, it is left to the Member States to do so. The European Parliament has made a number of amendments to the proposal, including that multiple discrimination should also be covered by the Directive.[7] Multiple discrimination occurs, according to the Parliament, when discrimination is based on any combination of the grounds of religion or belief, disability, age or sexual orientation or on any one or more of these grounds and also on the grounds of any one or more of sex, racial or ethnic origin or nationality. Therefore, the Parliament advocates that the EU legislates against multiple discrimination on two or more grounds.[8] It remains to be seen whether this amendment will be accepted by the Council, as unanimity is required.

Looking at the institutional framework available, we find that there does not appear to be any legislative provision to deal with multiple discrimination in the partner countries of the GendeRace project or in many of the other EU Member States with the possible exception of Germany where it is nonetheless only implicit (European Commission 2007e).[9] The exception in the GendeRace project is Bulgaria, where Article 11 of the Protection against Discrimination Act mentions multiple discrimination.[10] The so-called single-ground approach seems to be the most commonly used approach in the courts in most European countries. A good example of the single-ground approach is the British case of *Bahl v. the Law Society* [2004] IRLR 799. Ms Bahl claimed to have been discriminated against by the law society both on the grounds of her race or ethnic origin and of her gender. In this case, the Employment Tribunal found that Ms Bahl could be compared to

---

7   European Parliament Legislative Resolution of 2 April 2009 on the Proposal for a Council Directive on implementing the principle of equal treatment between persons irrespective of religion or belief, disability, age or sexual orientation (COM(2008)0426 – C6-0291/2008 – 2008/0140(CNS) - P6_TA(2009)0211).

8   Ibid., amendment 37.

9   Section 4 of the German Equal Treatment Act (above footnote 3) provides that where 'Discrimination is based on several of the grounds … [it] is only capable of being justified … if the justification applies to all the grounds liable for the difference of treatment'. This appears to assume that claims of multiple discrimination will be admissible, however, there are no further explicit provisions and it is still too early to assess how cases on this will develop.

10   Article 11(2) of the Bulgarian Protection against Discrimination Act 2004 determines: 'State and local government bodies, and public bodies shall take, as a priority, measures within the meaning of Art. 7 (1.13) and (1.15) in order to equalise opportunities for victims of multiple discrimination'.

a white man, so that the effect of both race and gender could be considered. However, both the Employment Appeal Tribunal and the Court of Appeal held that this was an incorrect interpretation of the law and that each ground must be considered and decided upon separately. Therefore, in a single-ground approach, each ground of discrimination needs to be proven separately and will be looked at by the court separately.

Examining the legislation in Britain, this does not make any specific mention of or provisions for cases where multiple grounds are involved, although it does not appear to explicitly prohibit claims on multiple grounds either. However, the Courts tend to consider each ground separately and to make a ruling on each ground separately as was confirmed in the *Bahl* case referred to above. At present, there does not appear to be an intersectional approach in UK law.[11] And, because the courts will only consider each ground of discrimination separately, equality bodies and other organizations providing legal advice and assistance will often deal with cases of intersectional discrimination by deciding which ground is the strongest and then proceeding on this ground only. Alleging more grounds might also lead to difficulties with proof and thus a strategic decision is made as to which ground to pursue.

However, the British Government issued a new Equality Bill at the end of April 2009, which brought together all equality legislation in a single act. The Bill did not contain any provision for multiple discrimination claims but the day after the new Bill was issued, the Government started another consultation on this.[12] It proposed to add a provision to the new Bill which would allow claims to be made on two grounds together, but not on more than two. However this is limited to direct discrimination claims. Using the *Bahl* case as an example, under the new proposals, Ms Bahl would be able to claim for sex discrimination, for race discrimination and for discrimination on the combination of both race and sex. Two reasons are given for allowing claims to be made on two grounds together, but not on more than two grounds and for limiting this provision to direct discrimination claims; first, allowing claims for discrimination on three or more grounds would complicate the legislation and make it more difficult for businesses and employers to know how to avoid discrimination; and, second, from the previous consultation it is clear that providing for a combination of two grounds together would be enough in the vast majority of cases. In our interviews with stakeholders in the UK, the general opinion appeared to be that the new Act should definitely contain a provision for multiple ground cases, although most stakeholders did not expect this to lead to a large number of extra discrimination claims. Unfortunately, the interviews took place before the new Bill and consultation document came out, so we do not have information as to whether the stakeholders interviewed agreed that providing for a combination of two grounds together would be enough in the vast majority of cases.

The single-ground approach appears to be the most common approach in most EU countries, certainly in the GendeRace partner countries.[13] However, there appears to be a tendency amongst

---

11   However, this could well be changing. Recently, an Employment Appeal Tribunal (EAT) upheld an Employment Tribunal decision which decided that there was indirect discrimination on the combined grounds of race and sex (*Ministry of Defence v. Debique* [2010] IRLR 471). Although an EAT decision does not establish precedent and, therefore, other tribunals and courts are not obliged to follow this case, they might well do so, especially in the light of the proposal to provide for multiple ground claims in the Equality Bill we mention in the following.

12   This consultation paper can be found at: www.equalities.gov.uk/pdf/090422%20Multiple%20 Discrimination%20Discussion%20Document%20Final%20Text.pdf [assessed: 20 January 2010].

13   The Romanian law regarding equality between men and women does define multiple discrimination as an act of discrimination and provides that discrimination on two or more grounds is to be treated as an 'aggravating circumstance'. In Ireland, claims of additive and intersectional discrimination can be investigated

EU Member States to move towards single equality acts and single equality bodies, covering all grounds of discrimination prohibited by national law. This does not exclude a single-ground approach, but it might make a multiple-ground approach easier, as we shall see below. Of the partner countries, Bulgaria and Germany have both a single equality body and a single equality act and France has a single equality body but several pieces of legislation. In January 2009, Sweden changed from a number of acts and bodies to a single act and a single body. Spain has a specialized body covering race and ethnic origin only. And, in Britain, in October 2007, the Equality and Human Rights Commission took over the tasks of the previous three British Equality Commissions (for race, gender and disability) and its remit was extended to include the other grounds on which discrimination is prohibited in British law as well as human rights. One of the arguments has always been that a single Equality Commission will be able to deal more efficiently with cases of multiple discrimination. This was repeated in the consultation on the single new Equality Bill. With the adoption of the new Equality Act, Britain will have a single equality act and a single equality body. So, of the partner countries, most have single acts and single bodies.

But, what is the importance of a single act and a single body? A single act, covering all grounds of discrimination prohibited by the national legislation, will contain the same definitions of key concepts like direct and indirect discrimination, harassment and victimization and will contain the same provisions on the shift in the burden of proof, legal standing in proceedings and other procedural rules. This makes it much easier to argue that discrimination on a combination of grounds covered by the act is also covered. This is further supported by a single equality body which can deal with all grounds of discrimination. Where there are separate acts for different grounds, as was the case of Britain, there are often differences in definitions, in areas covered, in procedural provisions, etc. This makes it much more difficult to allow a claim on more than one ground. Where there is more than one Commission, the victim has to decide which Commission to go to for help and advice, and this one Commission might not be able to advise on grounds they do not cover. One Commission provides a 'one-stop shop' for victims and employers to get advice on all grounds at the same time.

Conclusion

Whilst multiple discrimination is increasingly being discussed at different levels, it is also clear that there are enormous differences across a range of aspects between the different Member States of the European Union. There are not only differences in the stage of development of the national legislation against (race and gender) discrimination, in the understanding of the concepts of race, racism and ethnicity, and between the main groups targeted by racial discrimination in each country, but there are also great differences in the collection of ethnic data and the availability of such data for third parties. All this would suggest that it might be better if the EU took action to prescribe that the Member States should take legislative measures to provide for multiple discrimination. However, the Commission has simply left it to the individual states, some of which are not even taking discrimination very seriously or are not providing national coverage. This means that any implementation of legislation on multiple discrimination will take different forms and move at different speeds at each national level.

---

as a single case. The British Government bases its assessment of the financial impact of the proposal mentioned on figures from Ireland.

This is already the case as we discovered in the GendeRace project. First, looking at the institutional framework available, we find that there does not appear to be any legislative provision dealing with multiple discrimination in the partner countries of the GendeRace project, possibly with Germany being an exception where the reference is nonetheless only implicit (European Commission 2007e). The exception in the GendeRace project is Bulgaria, where Article 11 of the Protection against Discrimination Act mentions multiple discrimination. Second, we find that there is a different institutional framework among partner countries and a tendency towards the development of single acts and single equality bodies covering all prohibited grounds of discrimination prohibited by national law. This could be seen as a very positive step because it could provide a way towards the acceptance of claims of discrimination on intersectional grounds.

However, although the move towards single acts and single equality bodies should be seen as a positive step, it does not mean that multiple discrimination is or will be handled properly. In France, for example, the equality body (HALDE) is competent for all grounds of discrimination since its creation in 2004 but this does not mean cases have been brought on more than one ground. Furthermore, there is no legal rule addressing multiple grounds of discrimination such as race and gender. Complainants can claim to be victims of discrimination on a number of grounds, but there is no method developed for each case in order to apprehend the specificity of multiple grounds claims. In brief, a single equality body does not seem to be sufficient: it is necessary to provide for legislation and to actively implement adequate methodologies to be sure that multiple discrimination would be treated properly.

Chapter 15

EU Non-Discrimination Law and Policies in Reaction to Intersectional Discrimination against Roma Women in Central and Eastern Europe

Kristina Koldinská

Introduction

For many years it has been argued that Roma are one of the most excluded groups in Europe (UNDP 2003) and the most prominent group at risk of poverty in the region of Central and Eastern Europe (Ringold et al. 2005). In addition, Roma represent one of the most important minorities in this region. Around 70 per cent of the European Gypsy population (some 8 million people) live in Central and Eastern Europe.[1] In the Czech Republic circa 3 per cent of the population is Roma; Slovakia counts Roma as constituting some 7 per cent of its population (European Commission 2004b); and Hungary estimates that Roma make up 4–6 per cent of its population (Ministry of Foreign Affairs, Hungary 2004).

In these three countries Roma are one of the most frequently attacked groups. Recently, several individuals died or were severely injured as a result of violent attacks.[2] Moreover, far-right parties are gaining in popularity, being welcomed by the majority population.[3] The latest report of the European Commission against Racism and Intolerance (ECRI) Europe comments on this Europe-wide situation as follows: 'In 2008, anti-Gypsyism continued to be a worrying problem, with extreme forms of racism and discrimination being experienced by Roma and Travellers. … Public opinion continued to be openly hostile towards Roma … sometimes encouraged by political figures who incited racial hatred against this group often for electoral purposes' (ECRI 2009).

While Roma as an ethnic group suffer discrimination, this impacts especially severely on Roma women. As socio-demographic data indicates, Roma women are at even greater disadvantage than Roma men and women from the majority population. In this respect, multiple discrimination, mostly intersectional discrimination (see below: 234–44) against Roma women is at issue, some forms of which are alarming.

---

1 The terms Roma and Gypsy are often used interchangeably; a practice which is imprecise. 'Gypsy' refers to the whole ethnic group, including travellers, whereas 'Roma' constitutes one ethnicity, sometimes meaning simply those Gypsies from Central and Eastern Europe.

2 In Hungary, for example, one Roma man was shot in front of his house; a Roma couple were killed when their house was attacked with a hand grenade, although their children survived. In the Czech Republic, a two-year-old girl suffered 80 per cent burns to her body after her family was fire-bombed during the night.

3 At a rally in a Northern Bohemian town in November 2008, demonstrators linked to the far-right Czech Workers Party chanted anti-Roma slogans. News reports stated that after the rally the demonstrators attempted to reach the mainly Roma neighbourhood of the town armed with stones, firecrackers and petrol bombs intending to attack the Roma community.

This chapter focuses on policy and legislative responses to inequalities suffered by Roma women at national, European and international levels. It seeks to examine whether current legislation and policies and proposals for their amendments are in a position to address effectively the discrimination faced by Roma women and how such instruments could be better deployed to enhance their effectiveness.

The Czech Republic, Slovakia and Hungary have been selected for exemplary examination. This choice is intended to illustrate the experiences of similar countries which in comparative law terms are members of one 'family'. For that reason, neither Romania nor Italy has been included in this chapter, even if those countries deserve special attention.

This chapter will first briefly discuss the situation of Roma women in the countries concerned and the responses of national governments, international organizations and certain interest groups. Thereafter, recent proposals for reform of EU law and policy will be analysed and assessed. This is followed by a discussion on the potential use of existing EU and international law instruments to combat intersectional discrimination against Roma women. The chapter concludes with a more general assessment of the interaction between law and policy in combating intersectional discrimination faced by Roma women.

Situation of Roma Women in Europe, with a Focus on the Selected Countries

Roma continuously face many social problems and, in comparison with the majority society in all Central and Eastern European countries, are worse off. This is even more true for Roma women, who are often more seriously affected by general problems facing Roma than are Roma men. The general situation of Roma women in the 27 EU Member States is well discussed in a recent report for the European Commission (Corsi et al. 2008). Some of the discriminatory aspects of the situation faced by Roma women in selected Central and Eastern European countries have been discussed in earlier work by the present author (Koldinská 2009a, 2009b). That research identified housing, health conditions, access to education and employment as the most important fields in which Roma women are disadvantaged or experience discrimination.

More than one half of Roma households live in material poverty (some 70 per cent in Slovakia), often in segregated localities as a consequence of inequality and unequal treatment which, in turn, results in practical exclusion from the majority society. Difficult conditions in Roma settlements, which are often overcrowded and without electricity or running water, especially affect Roma women who spend most of their lives in such accommodation, with poor housing worsening their workload in relation to domestic work, their isolation and even their state of health.

In the field of education, Roma women attain a lower level of education than Roma men, although both groups experience discrimination in access to education. The majority of Roma pupils in the Czech Republic, Hungary and Slovakia go to 'special' schools which primarily exist for the education of children with learning difficulties. In relation to the Czech Republic, in an important judgment, the European Court of Human Rights held such practice to constitute discrimination against Roma children.[4] Difficulties experienced by many Roma children have their roots in sub-standard housing and in the extremely poor social situation of Roma families. Roma girls often receive even lower levels of education than Roma boys, not only because of the very low levels of educational attainment in special schools, but also because of the fact that Roma tend to give birth

---

4   *D.H. and Others v. the Czech Republic* No 57325/00. Judgment of 13 November 2007. For an analysis of this judgment see Arnardóttir (2009) or Degener (this volume: 29–46).

at a relatively young age and frequently discontinue their education following childbirth. Corsi et al. (2008) argue also that the low educational level of Roma women has particularly negative implications for future generations, because women whose mothers' education remains basic have been shown to give birth earlier in their life than women whose mothers have attained greater levels of education.

Low educational levels and family responsibilities also lead to discrimination against Roma women in the field of employment. Roma in general suffer from very high levels of unemployment, often of a long-term nature. This situation more often affects Roma women with lower levels of education than their male counterparts. Roma women are most often employed in unskilled work and as seasonal and occasional labour providing services in the black or grey economy; jobs which provide very low wages and no access to social security benefits (Corsi et al. 2008). Roma women are often also victims of prostitution and human trafficking. The high unemployment level of Roma women increases also their dependency on social benefits, which is again higher than that of men, who at least sometimes succeed in finding jobs in cities, often in the form of heavy manual labour.

Roma women face greater health risks than non-Roma women. These risks are connected with early and multiple pregnancies and abortions, heavy workload at home, poor housing, malnutrition and also with the fact that Roma women do not make adequate use of healthcare services, sometimes because they are hindered by their traditional rules of hygiene and modesty.

In all of the three countries under consideration, Roma women face coercive sterilizations, one of the most extreme forms of discrimination within the field of healthcare. The profile of cases involves the targeting of Roma women for invasive and mostly irreversible surgical procedures aimed at ending their ability to have children. The women concerned have often been excluded from any form of dignified involvement in the decision to sterilize.[5] Despite an awareness that such cases are still occurring, especially in Central and Eastern Europe, none of the countries concerned have adopted decisive and effective policy measures to prevent such conduct.

The disadvantaged situation of Roma women in relation to housing, employment, education and healthcare can be described, at least in part, as a consequence of discrimination. The following section examines this discrimination in more detail with a view to its identification.

Identification of Discrimination Against Roma Women

From the examples of disadvantage suffered by Roma women it is clear that as an ethnic group they suffer more intense social exclusion than do Roma men. This social exclusion plays a further highly significant role in the discrimination of Roma. For example, discrimination in education is a consequence of the social exclusion of Roma. Roma children are not able to follow lessons, not because they are less intelligent, but because they live in socially excluded families, lacking a culture of staying on at school. The fact that Roma girls study less further deepens the social exclusion, as mothers are almost solely responsible for the upbringing of children. If they do not have a more advanced level of education and their children live in a socially excluded environment, that social exclusion is more easily transmitted to the next generation.

Roma women suffer historically from prejudice and discriminatory behaviour exhibited by the majority society and from within the Roma ethnic group. An example of the first source of

---

5   For more detail on coercive sterilisations see Magyari-Vincze (2006) and Slovak NGO Coalition (2008).

prejudice may be found in the literary and artistic representation of Roma women as mysterious figures who may lure away a father or son from a respected family. As an example of the second form of prejudice, one could point to the humiliating procedures a Roma bride has to endure during a traditional wedding ceremony, when, for example, on the following morning the husband must demonstrate a blood-stained bed sheet to the whole family.

Historic discrimination against Roma women continues in modern forms, such as coercive sterilizations, which as a phenomenon occur exclusively in relation to Roma women (not to white women and not to Roma men), or human trafficking, in which the victims are often Roma women (sometimes even trafficked by their own relatives). In other fields, for example, employment or education, Roma women experience discrimination because they are Roma. However, the fact that they are women strengthens the intensity of the discrimination – it raises the level of their unemployment, and reduces the level of their education.

In many situations ethnic minority women, including Roma women, experience intersectional discrimination where it is difficult to say whether the discrimination arises on grounds of their gender or their ethnicity (Fredman 2009).[6] The inequalities mentioned above arise, in fact, as a combination of various oppressions, which together produce a very specific situation of Roma women that differs from the situation of majority women, or the situation of immigrant women, and also from the situation of Roma men.

To sum up, I argue that discrimination faced by Roma women is multifaceted – based on two discriminatory grounds – ethnicity and gender. Discrimination against Roma women in education, employment and healthcare is intersectional, as both grounds operate in combination and a unique situation arises. Within this discrimination, social exclusion plays a dual role: it is both one of the causes of discrimination against Roma women and, at the same time, one of the consequences of this discrimination. Social exclusion completes the vicious circle perpetuating and reinforcing intersectional discrimination against Roma women, thus making it even more difficult to break this cycle. In a way, social exclusion intersects with gender and ethnicity, although in itself not a ground of discrimination.

Searching for Solutions for Discrimination Against Roma Women

Having identified and labelled the discrimination experienced by Roma women as intersectional discrimination strongly influenced by social inclusion, the next issue is to identify what instruments are needed to improve the situation of Roma women. The instruments of law and policy selected should be capable of combating intersectional inequalities and also social inclusion.

Equality theory identifies two notions of equality: formal equality, which requires everyone to be treated in exactly the same manner, and substantive equality, which acknowledges differences in starting positions that might necessitate differential treatment in order to reach real, effective equality (Fredman 2005a; Henrard 2007: 13). This approach to equality aims to compensate for social or historical disadvantages suffered by certain groups.

As regards Roma women, formal equality is important and must be promoted. However, alone this is inadequate. Instead, different treatment is very much needed for Roma women, because both social and historical disadvantages are at issue. As the situation of Roma women in some countries is even deteriorating, effective equality achieved through instruments of substantive equality is urgently needed.

---

6   A rich literature on multiple discrimination exists which distinguishes between compounded and intersectional discrimination (Nielsen 2009; Verloo 2006; Fredman 2005c and 2008).

The notion of substantive equality can be further divided into equality of opportunity and equality of results. Howard (2008) argues that 'anti-discrimination measures intend to achieve the first, aim to equalise the starting point for everyone so that everyone can compete on the same level, while measures intending to achieve the second aim to equalise the outcome or result'. This means that in order to attain substantive equality, both anti-discrimination measures, as well as policies aimed at reaching equality should be established. In other words, if substantive equality for Roma women is to be enhanced, two pillars of minority protection must be established in law and policy: non-discrimination protection in combination with individual human rights and specific standards aimed at protecting and promoting the right to identity (Henrard 2007: 14). The first is more a question of law, the second of policy instruments, which could, under specific circumstances, be transformed into legal obligations on public authorities.

In order to achieve substantive equality for Roma women, solutions need to combine law and policy instruments. The challenge for the legislature is to amend current legislation such that it applies where intersectional discrimination occurs. Policy instruments, on the other hand, need to be customized to address the basic problems of Roma women described above.

Legislative and Policy Measures at National Level as a Response to Intersectional Discrimination Against Roma Women

In the countries under consideration, from the beginning of the 1990s there was little will to improve the situation of Roma in general. Public authorities only started to consider improvements to the situation of the Roma population after racially motivated violence against Roma was registered alongside increasing unemployment within Roma communities together with the continued dependency of Roma communities on social benefits, developments which aroused the antipathy of the majority of the electorate towards local politicians (for example in the Czech Republic).

As regards legislative measures, a prohibition on discrimination and the equality principle were introduced into national constitutions. In all three countries, extended anti-discrimination norms were adopted only in transposition of EC anti-discrimination directives. Despite these anti-discrimination statutes, none of the countries concerned has a legislative document that mentions or let alone defines multiple or intersectional discrimination. Nor is there any case law in which courts have had to deliver judgment in a case of intersectional discrimination and have named it as such (Burri and Schiek 2009).

Article 8 of the Hungarian Equality Act (Act CXXV of 2003 on Equal Treatment and the Promotion of Equality of Opportunities) prohibits discrimination on 19 grounds, and the last paragraph adds as a twentieth ground 'another situation, attribution or condition'. Multiple discrimination is, however, not specified. Nor in Slovakia does legislation explicitly define multiple discrimination. The Anti-discrimination Act (Act No 365/2004 Coll. on Equal Treatment in Certain Areas and on Protection against Discrimination) identifies different grounds of discrimination but does not include any definition for cases where grounds are cumulative. In that connection, Magurová (2009) indicates that in 2008 the inclusion of a definition of multiple discrimination was proposed in connection with an amendment to the Anti-discrimination Act. That proposal was, however, rejected by the government. Not even the most recent Czech legislation (Act No. 198/2009 Coll. on Equal Treatment and Protection against Discrimination) adopted in June 2009 includes any hint of the concept of multiple discrimination.

One way of introducing multiple discrimination at least into case law might be through the open-ended enumeration of discrimination grounds in legislation (Fredman 2005b). This is most certainly not the approach of the Czech anti-discrimination legislation which establishes an exhaustive list of discrimination grounds. The Slovak anti-discrimination law also lists the discrimination grounds in a closed manner, specifying each field where equality is protected. The only open-ended list of discrimination grounds is provided by Hungarian anti-discrimination law. However, Hungarian case law has not yet addressed multiple discrimination, even if it is probable that cases where more than one ground of discrimination is relevant frequently occur (Kollonay 2009).

Not only in the countries under consideration is legislation on multiple discrimination lacking, with a corresponding absence, even in Hungary, of case law, regrettably also there are not even any specific policy measures in the Czech Republic, Slovakia or Hungary intended to combat intersectional discrimination against Roma women. There are some policy and legal measures in favour of Roma in general, but none of these instruments considers the special situation of Roma women.

In all three countries, a policy paper or a strategy has been published: in the Czech Republic, the 'Policy for Roma Integration', in Slovakia, the 'Medium-term Strategy for the Development of the Roma National Minority', and in Hungary, the 'National Action Plan on Social Inclusion'.[7] None of the national action plans explicitly mention Roma women or instruments to improve their situation or address intersectional discrimination experienced by Roma women. This indicates that at a governmental level, the specific situation of Roma women has not yet been taken into account, a situation which needs urgent rectification.

Aside from government initiatives, in terms of policy aimed at the inclusion of Roma women there are certain individual success stories that may be described as 'good practice' (ECRI 2001):

- Roma advisers at the level of local administration have been introduced in the Czech Republic. Many Roma women are active as advisers in the public administration and related departments.[8]
- Roma assistants have been introduced into schools in the Czech Republic and also in some regions in Slovakia, mainly in areas with a high percentage of Roma. The majority of these assistants are Roma women.
- In Hungary, a pilot project has been launched including kindergarten-like services for Roma children and training for their parents focusing especially on Roma women (mothers).
- Motivational courses for unemployed Roma women and for Roma women on maternity leave are run in Prague in some problem areas.
- The Hungarian 'Public Health Programme for a Healthy Nation' devotes a separate chapter to address the health inequalities of social groups facing multiple disadvantages. The goal has been set of training 'health champions' from the Roma minority to be employed by local government. In addition, special training for district nurses to enable them to respond more effectively to the needs of the Roma population and the launch of special health improvement programmes is envisaged.

---

7   These strategy documents underline the relationship with majority society as the first step towards the inclusion of Roma. To achieve that goal they identify the need to reduce unemployment, improve housing and health provision, and counteract residential 'ghettoization'. In addition, they highlight the importance of reducing poverty and providing education and training. All the governments also support the maintenance and development of the identity of the Roma community through the support of cultural events, festivals, concerts, etc. (Corsi et al. 2008).

8   Roma women are also employed at Roma advice centres or Roma civic associations. Roma women are beginning to occupy positions as directors of nursery schools, and in a few cases also elementary schools.

These examples of good practice simply confirm that intersectional discrimination against Roma women is strongly connected to their social exclusion. In fact, all the current projects, including the government ones, aim to foster the social inclusion of Roma women, a practice which at the same time reduces the risk of discrimination.

The drawback to the good practices identified is the fact that they are single initiatives or projects not forming part of a systematic policy aimed at intersectional equality for Roma women. On analysing the socio-economic data and current policy (generally absent) towards Roma, or Roma women, the conclusion must be reached that much remains to be done to establish both kinds of substantive equality instruments in all the countries under discussion. In that regard, the recommendations of international organizations to Slovakia, Hungary and the Czech Republic in relation to Roma women may provide useful pointers.

Recommendations of International Organizations

The UN Committee on the Elimination of All Forms of Discrimination against Women ('the CEDAW Committee') and the UN Committee on the Elimination of All Forms of Racial Discrimination ('the CERD Committee') have issued recommendations to the countries concerned with a view to improving the situation of Roma women. These recommendations are of two types.

The first type of recommendation focuses on multiple discrimination (the term used by both organizations) experienced by Roma women in general. These include the recommendations of the CEDAW Committee urging the Czech Republic and Slovakia to take effective measures to eliminate multiple forms of discrimination against Roma women. The Czech Republic was further encouraged to enhance respect for the human rights of Roma women. For Slovakia, the CEDAW Committee had slightly more specific recommendations to strengthen the coordination among all agencies working on Roma, non-discrimination and gender equality issues, in particular in the areas of health, education, employment and participation in public life.[9] Even if this first type of recommendation is not very specific, it is nonetheless helpful that the recommendations identify discrimination against Roma women as multiple and urge States to consider it a serious problem which must be addressed.

Much more specific and extensive are recommendations of the second type, aimed at the issue of coercive sterilization. In the case of Hungary (but also in the case of the Czech Republic), the CERD Committee has called on governments to accept responsibility and to facilitate access to justice for involuntarily sterilized women. The Committee also called for an information campaign among doctors in order to avoid such cases in the future;[10] in the same vein were recommendations issued by the CEDAW Committee, which urged Hungary to pay damages to a coercively sterilized woman and to review domestic legislation.[11] After receipt of those recommendations, Hungary finally paid damages to the victim.

The CEDAW Committee is currently the most demanding body on this issue. In its reports, it recommended to Slovakia to monitor all healthcare centres that perform sterilizations and to ensure also that complaints filed by Roma women regarding coerced sterilization are duly acknowledged and that the victims of such practices are granted effective remedies. Also the Czech Republic was urged by the CEDAW Committee to take urgent action to implement the recommendation of the

---

9   CEDAW: Report on its forty-first session. General Assembly Official Records 63rd Session Supplement No 38 (A/63/38), pp. 96–7.

10   CERD seventieth session (2007): Concluding observations, Czech Republic, CERD/C/CZE/CO/7.

11   CEDAW thirty-ninth session (2007): Concluding observations, Hungary, CEDAW/C/HUN/CO/6.

national ombudsman with regard to coercive sterilization, to introduce mandatory training for the staff of health institutions and for social workers on patients' rights, and to compensate victims of sterilizations already carried out.[12]

Whereas the States are characterized by their absence of a systematic response to the situation of Roma women, in contrast, the documents of both committees are heavily oriented to substantive equality and in the case of coercive sterilization to equality of results. Both committees tend to promote a coherent policy which already has produced results, notwithstanding their lack of a direct influence on domestic policy and legislation.

The policy measures recommended by international organizations are supported also by awareness raising (for example ILGA annual conferences on the intersection between sexuality and other grounds) and other support activities (informal working group on multiple discrimination aimed at promoting effective responses to multiple discrimination at both the European and national levels) provided by (mainly international) interest groups. As a good example of such support activities, the European Roma Rights Centre (ERRC) should be mentioned. The Centre has a Women's Rights Officer whose work focuses directly on addressing the impact of race and gender on Roma women, producing publications on the issue. The Centre is involved also in relevant advocacy and litigation activities such as reporting to CEDAW and taking up cases concerning the coercive sterilization of Roma women in several European countries. In fact, in the abovementioned Hungarian coercive sterilization case, the ERRC played a decisive role representing the victim in communications with CEDAW. This informal support by interest groups constitutes a valuable additional input which may speed up the establishment and spreading of effective instruments to combat and prevent intersectional discrimination. As such instruments have not been found to exist at national level, the following parts of this chapter will scrutinize law and policy at EU and international level.

Proposed EU Legislative and Policy Reform

In the EU, proposals have been presented specifically aimed at the Roma, including a proposed Roma inclusion directive and a call for minimum standards to be adopted within the framework of the OMC (open method of coordination). Both proposed instruments will be analysed for their potential to respond effectively to intersectional discrimination.

Proposals for a Roma Inclusion Directive

A Roma inclusion directive was proposed some years ago. Among the arguments advanced for a specific directive was the view that the Race Equality Directive[13] had proved inadequate to address discrimination against Roma and was not specifically aimed at achieving the integration of groups that are traditionally excluded, such as the Roma. The possibility to use stronger language advocating the need for positive measures was also mentioned (Xanthaki 2005). Moreover, supporters of the proposal envisaged that a directive on Roma integration would provide an extra level of protection for Roma European citizens and leave no room for a possible reductionist interpretation by States.

---

12   CEDAW: Report on its thirty-sixth session. General Assembly Official Records 61st Session Supplement No. 38 (A/61/38), p. 200.

13   Council Directive 2000/43/EC of 29 June 2000 implementing the principle of equal treatment between persons irrespective of racial or ethnic origin [2000] OJ L 180/22.

Such a directive was intended to complement the Race Equality Directive in establishing a clear European policy on minorities (European Commission 2004b).

The EU Network of independent experts on fundamental rights supported the idea of a special directive and recommended to the European Commission to:

> consider proposing a directive based on Article 13 EC (Treaty of Rome, as amended now Article 19 Treaty of the Functions of the European Union (TFEU)) and specifically aimed at improving the situation of the Roma/Gypsies population. This directive should be based on the studies documenting the situation of the Roma/Gypsies population … It should take into account the need to effectuate the desegregation of the Romani/Gypsy communities, where this is required, especially in employment, housing and education. (European Commission 2005: 64)

Ultimately, a directive on Roma inclusion was not adopted. The potential advantages and disadvantages of such a measure may be stated briefly as follows. First, the directive would have been the only instrument of EC law to focus on simply one ethnic group. This might initially appear unusual, unless one accepts the view that Roma cannot be easily brought within the protection of the Race Equality Directive, as they do not constitute a race, not even an ethnic minority. The Council of Europe's Parliamentary Assembly Recommendation of 1993 'On Gypsies in Europe' argues that 'living scattered all over Europe, not having a country to call their own, they are a true European minority, but do not fit in the definitions of national or linguistic minorities'.[14] However, that approach is rejected by van Boven (2002) who argues that the Race Equality Directive deals also with groups and persons belonging to ethnic or national minorities who have been victimized by persistent and entrenched discrimination, such as Roma and Sinti. From this perspective, the argument can be made that the Race Equality Directive already provides sufficient protection against discrimination, even for Roma. However, the European Network Against Racism (ENAR), in its analysis (2005) of the Directive also from the point of view of Roma, concludes that 'the Directive fails to make a substantial difference to the experiences of the most vulnerable ethic minority communities in Europe, including Roma and traveller communities'. Similar uncertainties exist in relation to a potential directive on Roma inclusion, in particular, whether it would cover the specific experiences of Roma women and properly include the concept of intersectional equality.

Moreover, it is also doubtful whether Article 13 EC (now Article 19 TFEU) is an appropriate legal basis for the adoption of such a specialized measure. That article provides simply a legal basis for action to combat discrimination and allows for measures aimed at promoting equality. Currently, the issue of social inclusion is addressed through the open method of coordination. Not even the adoption of a general directive on social inclusion has been proposed. Hence, the chances for the adoption of a directive on Roma inclusion on the basis of that article are all the more remote. On the other hand, the second proposal concerning the Roma might have greater chances of success.

Policy Measure Proposals at EU Level

Influenced by the abovementioned documents and realizing that the adoption of a specific directive on Roma inclusion is unrealistic, a more appropriate mechanism, an EU Roma strategy, was proposed in 2008. There are three dimensions to the strategy: the accountability of

---

14   Cited in Clements (2004).

national authorities for their responsibility to protect Roma persons, equal access to education, healthcare and housing for Roma communities, and the empowerment of Roma communities through involvement and participation in the civic and economic life of the country (Mueller 2008). Its underlying idea is to ensure effective mainstreaming, define the obligations of EU Member States and provide a framework for addressing Roma exclusion (EU Roma Policy Coalition 2008).

The EU Roma Policy Coalition envisages that such a strategy would be accompanied by a gender mainstreaming approach. They suggest to include this in all policies targeting the social inclusion of disadvantaged ethnic minorities and specific policies addressing the differentiated needs of disadvantaged ethnic minority women facing intersectional discrimination. Addressing the living conditions of an ethnic minority and Roma women means considering their different needs and the multiple interactions between social and economic factors influencing their daily lives.

These requirements are quite likely based on previous documents of EC institutions aimed at Roma women. In 2005, the European Parliament issued a resolution on the situation of Roma women[15] in which it urged Member States to adopt minimum standards within the framework of the open method of coordination with the aim of taking a range of measures to ensure that women and girls have access on equal terms to quality education for all, including adopting positive laws requiring school desegregation and setting out the specifics of plans to end separation. Furthermore, some priority fields were identified in the resolution, for example, the improvement of housing conditions and possibly the establishment of a mixed housing system, access to adequate and timely provided healthcare especially for Roma women, employment and inclusion policies, and financial and other support for NGOs and their activities in favour of Roma women.

In 2007, the Advisory Committee on Equal Opportunities for Women and Men, recommended in its opinion to the European Commission (Advisory Committee on Equal Opportunities for Women and Men 2007) that the latter should include consideration of possible policy and legal responses at European level to the phenomena of multiple discrimination, with a special focus on the situation of ethnic minority women in general and, in particular, disadvantaged or socially excluded groups of each sex.

The abovementioned proposals for soft law instruments, using the OMC to develop a Roma Inclusion Strategy, appear to be considerably more realistic than the proposal for a specific directive. Notwithstanding the undisputed legal strength of a directive, the proposed directive on Roma inclusion would probably not constitute an instrument radically different to the existing Race Equality Directive and most likely would aim primarily at formal equality. It is questionable whether such a directive would immediately impose on public authorities any positive duties to achieve equality in fact, including those aimed at resolving intersectional discrimination. A strategy of that kind is much more readily established through the OMC and soft law instruments, in particular through mainstreaming. The only major danger to this second approach is that it is much easier for 'attractive' objectives, instruments, methods and mainstreaming procedures to remain simply a paper commitment and scarcely to enter practice, as they are non-binding (Szyszczak 2006). For that reason, it is important to consider also the possibilities provided by existing provisions of EC law and current policies.

---

15   European Parliament resolution on the situation of Roma women in the European Union. Resolution P6_TA(2006)0244.

Possible Reform of EU Legislation and Policies in the Light of Existing Instruments

EC Law as a Possible Instrument to Combat Multiple Discrimination

Although EC law provides the broadest possible range of anti-discrimination instruments, it does not include measures to combat multiple or intersectional discrimination. Article 13 EC (now Article 19 TFEU) paved the way for the adoption of further directives aimed at protection against discrimination on the grounds not of sex, but of racial or ethnic origin, religion or belief, disability, age or sexual orientation. That list is exhaustive and therefore no room exists for the ECJ to add to those grounds.

Some authors regard as an obstacle to using EC law to resolve multiple discrimination cases the fact that three different kinds of equality directive exist: on race and ethnic origin, gender equality, and discrimination based on other grounds (Fredman 2009: 85). Other authors go further and identify a hierarchy of grounds according to the different material and personal scope and scheme of the directives. Seemingly, there is a hierarchy of grounds, where race is at the top (by reason of the Race Equality Directive) and age is at the bottom of the scale (Howard 2006; Schiek 2002a). However, that apparent hierarchy should not be regarded as a feature which in all cases precludes the courts from addressing multiple or intersectional discrimination (Schiek 2005, 2006).

The principle of equality set out in Article 13 EC (now Article 19 TFEU) is interpreted as establishing the 'constitutional character of the principle of equal treatment', as recent ECJ case law confirms (Schiek 2006). The equality principle acquired an important position also within the EU Charter of Fundamental Rights, in which a whole chapter (III) is dedicated to equality. Article 21 of the Charter covers all of the six grounds listed in Article 13 EC (now Article 19 TFEU), as well as additional grounds such as social origin, genetic features, language, political or other opinion, membership of a national minority, property and birth. The list is open-ended, which would support the possibility to address also multiple discrimination cases. Article 51 of the Charter indicates that the principles set out by the Charter should guide the development of policy in the EU and the implementation of these policies by national authorities. In relation to equality, this could point the way to mainstreaming.

Although multiple discrimination is not mentioned in any primary law document, the secondary law instruments of the Race Equality Directive and the Employment Framework Directive[16] do at least mention the issue in their respective preambles. Recital 14 of the preamble to the Race Equality Directive and recital 3 of the preamble to the Employment Framework Directive recall that the Community should aim to eliminate inequality and to promote equality between men and women, especially since women are often the victims of multiple discrimination. However, neither directive includes any provision specifically addressing the issue of multiple discrimination.

It is unexceptional for an instrument of EC secondary law to mention an issue in its preamble without including such in the normative part. This habit of the EU legislature has been criticized on the grounds that this gives rise to non-legal statements, generally in a preamble, often without any indication of the legal value of such (Xanthaki 2001). Accordingly, it is uncertain whether the reference to multiple discrimination in the preambles of those directives has any legal consequence. Future ECJ case law on multiple discrimination may shed some light on the matter.

Evidently, the situation would be easier if multiple discrimination appeared in the main text of directives. Problematic in that regard, however, is the likely need to establish a definition of

---

16   Council Directive 2000/78/EC of 27 November 2000 establishing a general framework for equal treatment in employment and occupation, [2000] OJ L303/16.

multiple discrimination and thus introduce a new concept to EC law. Here we must reiterate the point that neither is there any ECJ case law (unlike the situation before the legislative introduction of the concept of indirect discrimination) nor does legal theory have a crystal-clear view on what constitutes multiple discrimination and how it should be categorized. It is therefore improbable that in the near future EC law is likely to incorporate a definition of multiple discrimination within existing equality directives.

On examining the existing directives for any indication pointing to their possible use in challenging discrimination on more than one ground, there is little to be found. The only possibility appears to be the interrelation between international human rights law and the directives which in many cases cite human rights documents in the preamble. CEDAW, CERD and the European Convention on Human Rights (ECHR) are cited in Directive 2002/73,[17] Directive 2004/113[18] and the Race Equality Directive. This might suggest that these directives must be interpreted in the light of both CERD and CEDAW and as a result the intersection of gender and race has to be considered (similarly Schiek 2002a).

Interestingly, the Employment Framework Directive includes in recital 4 of the preamble a reference to CEDAW, but not to CERD. The explanation may be found in recital 10 which indicates that the Race Equality Directive already provides protection against discrimination in employment based on race or ethnic origin. The combination of references to the abovementioned international human rights instruments and multiple discrimination in the preamble to the directives appears currently to be the only indication of an interpretation capable of offering protection against multiple discrimination.

As this approach is rather weak, further development of the current directives may be called for. Given that it would be very difficult to incorporate all the remaining grounds into each individual directive, a good starting point could be the intersection between gender and race, described as the most prominent type of intersectional discrimination (Fredman 2005a). In this connection, the three abovementioned directives, in particular, fall to be considered: accordingly, gender and race could be specially protected in the area of access to employment (Directive 2002/73) and goods and services (Directive 2004/113). Both areas are covered also by the Race Equality Directive, although its scope is more limited. In the area of employment, the material scope of both the gender and race directive is the same; the only important difference is Article 1(1a) of Directive 2002/73, which defines gender mainstreaming as a positive obligation on Member States, whereas no mainstreaming is envisaged in the Race Equality Directive. The Race Equality Directive and Directive 2004/113 simply permit positive action.

Therefore, if in relation to the intersection between gender and race discrimination the current wording of the directives is retained, provision for multiple discrimination most likely could be achieved (if at all) only in the area of employment and access to goods and services, offering protection only against discriminatory behaviour. Positive action is permitted in relation to gender and ethnic origin, but no positive duty on Member States can be derived from the current equality directives, except as regards gender mainstreaming in employment.

From the point of view of material scope, the Race Equality Directive remains the broadest, as its scope goes beyond labour market equality, prohibiting racial and ethnic discrimination as regards

---

17   Directive 2002/73/EC of the European Parliament and of the Council of 23 September 2002 amending Council Directive 76/207/EEC on the implementation of the principle of equal treatment for men and women as regards access to employment, vocational training and promotion, and working conditions, [2002] OJ L269/15.

18   Council Directive 2004/113/EC of 13 December 2004 implementing the principle of equal treatment between men and women in the access to and supply of goods and services [2004] OJ L373/37.

social advantages, education, access to and supply of goods and services.[19] That fact speaks for the incorporation of a gender element to the Race Equality Directive (by way of amendment), thereby retaining the directive's generous scope and ensuring protection of the intersection of gender and race also under the Race Equality Directive. However, this would result in some duplications. Therefore, not even an amendment to the Race Equality Directive constitutes a perfect solution to the problem of how to insert the issue of multiple discrimination into the normative element of EC secondary law.

Under the current regime of equality directives, EU legislation aims primarily to establish formal equality, although there are also certain tendencies towards a more substantive concept of equality (Howard 2008). Schiek (2005: 442) goes even further when she concludes that 'meeting the challenge of multidimensionality is a consequence of striving for substantive equality', the 'effective enforcement [of which] becomes a problem for equality law'. In fact, current EC legislation can be used only in a very specific manner to assert protection against intersectional discrimination on the grounds of gender and ethnic origin and supplementing the current layout of the equality directives would be highly difficult.

In any event, for the purposes of improving the situation of Roma women, EC law alone will never constitute an adequate instrument. Equality law exists simply to protect victims of discrimination who wish to take active measures to challenge the injustice they experienced personally in an individual situation. Of much greater relevance are effective policy measures, targeted at a particular group and intended to resolve its specific problems. In this context, positive action measures, an instrument falling between pure law and pure policy, need to be examined.

Positive Action Permitted Under the EC Directives

For the purposes of addressing multiple discrimination, the possibility of using positive action as permitted under the Race Equality Directive may also be considered. The equality directives simply permit positive action and do not make it mandatory; a situation probably resulting also from the view that positive action measures always contradict the principle of equal treatment and as such constitute a form of discrimination (Howard 2008).

Certain authors argue that in the specific field of ethnic origin and race equality it is inadequate simply to permit positive action, which in other contexts – no judgment of the ECJ exists interpreting the positive action provisions of the Race Equality Directive – has been subject to strict interpretation by the ECJ (Henrard 2007: 29–30). Such a strict interpretation of existing positive action provisions may limit the opportunity to take appropriate measures to protect against multiple discrimination. However, there is some speculation that the ECJ might possibly allow for a slightly broader interpretation of positive action in the light of the wording of Article 13 EC (now Article 19 TFEU) (Schiek 2002a; Howard 2008).[20]

If positive action is to become an effective instrument in the fight against multiple discrimination, it needs to be well thought out. That task currently lies in the competence of the Member States. In this context, Fredman makes an interesting suggestion on how to shape positive action capable of effectively addressing multiple discrimination. She proposes a targeted positive action, arguing that 'it is well known that the most advantaged of the disadvantaged

---

19   Schiek (2002a) observes that as a result of this broad material scope gender discrimination has been downgraded from its previously dominant position.

20   Others take the opposite view, considering the Race Equality Directive to be more restrictive. They anticipate that the ECJ will extend its previously established approach to positive action also to the other grounds covered by Article 13 EC (Bell and Waddington 2001 cited in Howard 2008: 176).

group may make best use or even capture the benefits of positive action measures. This problem could be mitigated by targeting positive action on groups defined on the basis of multiple discrimination which by definition comprise the least advantaged in each of the relevant groups' (Fredman 2009: 84).

As regards the group under consideration in this chapter, this would mean that positive action measures could be targeted directly at Roma women. For example, Member States could provide in legislation that a Roma woman who applies for a job should be given preference if she is assessed as equally competent as another candidate who is not a Roma woman. Some training projects could also be opened exclusively to Roma women. Such positive action measures could contribute to combat intersectional discrimination against Roma women. However they need to be well thought out and not over-used. Even if deployed properly, positive action constitutes only part of the solution. Alone, it is unlikely to eliminate the causes of the poor situation of Roma women. At most, some of the consequences of their unequal position, discrimination and social exclusion would be addressed.

As a result, assessments such as those of ENAR (2005) which conclude that in the absence of mandatory positive action the anti-discrimination model will never be effective, particularly for the most vulnerable groups in society, must be treated with considerable scepticism. On the other hand, some positive obligations are completely necessary if substantive equality for Roma women is to be reached. Simply to permit the adoption of measures without the introduction of mandatory obligations would temper the move towards substantive equality (Howard 2008). Therefore, the possibility to introduce positive obligations in relation to intersectional discrimination with a focus on Roma women needs to be examined.

Positive Obligations in Favour of Roma Women

The above discussion indicates that existing equality directives, including the possibility for positive action, constitute a starting point to address the specificities of Roma women, but remain inadequate to tackle effectively and at multiple levels intersectional inequalities. Accepting Fredman's view that policy measures need to be concentrated on groups defined on the basis of multiple discrimination, consideration should be given also to another aspect of her thesis, that is, positive obligations.

The advantage of positive obligations is that instead of waiting for ad hoc individual complaints about discrimination, actors have a duty to take the initiative, examining existing structures and removing barriers to equality (Fredman 2008b). This relieves individual victims of the burden and expense of litigation. The results are likely to be systematic and not merely ad hoc. The duty to bring about change lies with those who have the power and capacity to act. The right to equality is thus available to all, not just to those who complain. Positive obligations require steps to be taken which are forward-looking, structural and group-based (Fredman 2009: 80).

Positive duties can already be inferred from some EC Treaty provisions (for example, Articles 3 and 141 EC, now Articles 8 and 157 TFEU), and also from the EU Charter of Fundamental Rights (Article 23) (Fredman 2005a). However, positive duties are lacking, for example, in the Race Equality Directive (Henrard 2007: 31). The only field in which they have already been introduced through mainstreaming is gender equality. The added value of mainstreaming seems to be that it is anticipatory, as it prevents discriminatory effects through a prior assessment (Howard 2008). Correspondingly, in connection with intersectional discrimination, 'equality mainstreaming' is required. According to Verloo (2006), 'the fact that multiple inequalities are not independent means that "equality" mainstreaming cannot be a simple extrapolation of gender mainstreaming.

If intersectionality is at work in strategies against inequalities, then new and more comprehensive analytical methods are needed'.

One such complex area is that of equality for Roma women. Indeed, this very area has been used to illustrate the need to react to multiple discrimination through positive obligations (Fredman 2009: 76). In the case of Roma women, positive obligations are to be recommended for at least two reasons. First, there is an urgent need for systematic measures to mainstream equality for Roma women. Second, in the specific case of Roma women (disadvantaged in education, often isolated in poor housing), the individual claim-based possibilities provided by the equality directives are simply too meagre and ineffective (Koldinská 2009: 266). The logical conclusion is that in the absence of positive obligations the situation of Roma women in Europe will hardly improve at all.

For that reason, the proposed OMC strategy on Roma inclusion should be positively rated for its inclusion of gender mainstreaming, requiring policy formulation always to take account of the needs of Roma women. This should serve as inspiration for the further development of EC law and policy, which should in all cases include positive obligations.

Possibilities to Address Multiple Discrimination at International Level

In addition to instruments of EU law and policy, there are also international law sources which need to be considered for their potential to address intersectional discrimination, notwithstanding the absence of any specific mention of Roma women.

The United Nations recognized the necessity of combating intersectional discrimination in Beijing in 1995 at the World Conference on Women, where it was pointed out that some women face multiple forms of discrimination based on race, language, ethnicity, culture and religion.[21] The recognition of multiple discrimination became also a key part of the resulting Beijing Platform for Action (Fredman 2005c). Specific recommendations for the elimination of racially motivated violence against women were made and the conference urged the use of the existing instruments of UN law: CERD and CEDAW.

CERD is the most comprehensive international standard in legal mechanisms to combat racial discrimination. The Convention is a reflection of the high priority given in the United Nations to the eradication of racial discrimination and its core provisions form part of customary international law on human rights and *jus cogens* (van Boven 2002). CEDAW is to some extent connected with CERD. Its preamble states that elimination of all forms of racism, racial discrimination, etc. is indispensable for the full enjoyment of rights for women and men. Neither convention expressly mentions multiple discrimination. However, both allow space for their interpretation as a tool for combating multiple forms of discrimination against women or on grounds of race.

In fact, the CERD Committee has taken steps to address the gender dimensions of racial discrimination in its work. At its 55th session, the Committee adopted an amendment to its reporting procedure requesting States parties to provide information on the situation of women in the context of racial discrimination. At its following session in March 2000, the Committee adopted a general recommendation on the gender-related dimensions of racial discrimination. The recommendation not only emphasizes that racial discrimination does not always affect women and men in the same way, but also recognizes the specific impact that some forms of racial discrimination can have on women. The Committee has agreed to consider gender issues linked to racial discrimination in its work.

---

21   Information on the Beijing conference can be found on the UN's website. Available at: www.un.org/womenwatch/daw/beijing [accessed: 30 May 2009].

Similarly, CEDAW has begun to integrate race considerations into its review of State parties' reports, as a result of the fact that the UN Special Rapporteur against racism and the Special Rapporteur on violence against women have considered the intersection of gender and racial discrimination in their reports on certain countries. Indeed, the importance of CEDAW and CERD should not be underestimated. Recent reports and decisions urging various States parties to amend legislation or policy were in many cases heeded by the countries concerned.[22]

CEDAW and CERD reports have resulted in an increase in interest also from other UN institutions. For example, the UN Office of the High Commissioner for Human Rights (2001) in its report on the gender dimension of racial discrimination recommended:

> The intersection of gender and race must be considered when drafting and revising national legislation and policies. States should integrate a gender perspective into all programmes of action and policies aimed at combating racism, racial discrimination, xenophobia and related intolerance. Similarly, race considerations must be taken into account when adopting measures to eliminate gender discrimination. States must, furthermore, review and repeal all policies and laws that could negatively affect women from racially disadvantaged groups.

That recommendation constitutes nothing but an invitation to introduce positive obligations in the form of gender and race mainstreaming – let us say – intersectional equality mainstreaming. These steps taken by international organizations should inspire the EU to strengthen its efforts aimed at the inclusion of Roma and to consider the specific needs of Roma women.

Within Europe, given the importance to the legal and political order of the ECHR, the Council of Europe may be expected also to contribute to the efforts to eliminate multiple discrimination. Article 14 ECHR prohibits discrimination on any of the stated grounds, including sex and race which head the list. Some authors argue that the ECHR has been inadequate as an anti-discrimination device because of the narrow scope of its non-discrimination provision (van Boven 2002). Others, however, underline as an advantage of Article 14 ECHR the fact that it uses an open-ended list of discriminatory grounds, through use of the phrase 'any grounds such as'. This indicates that the list of grounds is not exhaustive and other grounds also may be considered (Howard 2006). The wording of Article 14 ECHR may therefore be interpreted as offering a greater possibility to the European Court of Human Rights to consider multiple discrimination in cases where grounds are combined. Arnardóttir (2009: 55) argues that 'this provision may be seen as aspiring to ensure multidimensional equality in the sense that a claimant wishing to bring a discrimination claim may do so based on a multitude of identities'.

The potential strength of the Council of Europe in the field of anti-discrimination has been increased also by the adoption of Protocol No 12 to the ECHR which provides for a general prohibition of discrimination and aims to remove the limitations of the existing provision. However, within the territory of the EU this protocol lacks efficacy, as only six of the Member States have ratified it (none of them countries considered in this chapter).

The influence of the ECHR, in particular Article 14, should not be overstated. The European Court of Human Rights has not delivered any judgment on multiple discrimination and the Council of Europe cannot be expected to resolve intersectional problems alone (Arnardóttir 2009: 67). Nonetheless, the Council of Europe contributed an important policy instrument, when it established ECRI, a monitoring body to combat racism, xenophobia, anti-Semitism and intolerance from the perspective of the protection of human rights. Its remit is to review Council of Europe Member

---

22   See the discussion in the first part of this chapter.

States' legislation and policy, propose further action and study international legal instruments in the field of combating racism and xenophobia. ECRI's action covers all necessary measures to combat violence, discrimination and prejudice faced by persons or groups of persons on the grounds of race, colour, language, religion, nationality and national or ethnic origin. The list of grounds is open-ended, therefore other grounds could be added (Howard 2005), including a gender dimension. ECRI is clearly one of the possible organizations that could be active in the field of intersectional equality mainstreaming by way of its recommendations addressed to the governments of Council of Europe Member States.[23]

The Council of Europe has without doubt great potential to combat both racial and multiple discrimination. Its activities may well be accompanied by more intensive consideration of multiple discrimination issues by the European Court of Human Rights. However, as regards substantive equality for Roma women, current policy-making activities and proposals for further measures emanating from the EU and its institutions appear more likely to achieve that goal. The Council of Europe only has instruments of potential use in combating multiple discrimination but has not issued any document, information or recommendation which would at least, in part, assist in addressing intersectional discrimination. For the purposes of equality for Roma women, the ECRI may have potential. At present, however, no steps have been taken in that direction.

Interaction of Law and Policy in Combating Intersectional Discrimination with a Particular Focus on Roma Women

Intersectional discrimination faced by Roma women has dramatic consequences for many members of this sub-group. The discussion above has examined possible instruments to combat the inequalities experienced by that group considering the potential to apply legislation already in force (and proposals for new legislation) and existing policy measures.

From that analysis an important question results: how can law and policy best interact in order to improve the position of Roma women? Before offering an answer to that question, let us state that interaction between law and policy is essential if the situation of Roma women is to be improved. Legal instruments alone are inadequate, as law is unable to respond to the specific problems of one section of an ethnic group. Nor are policy instruments alone sufficient, as these are unenforceable and do not guarantee active protection against intersectional discrimination in individual cases. Instead, both types of instrument are needed. Law is needed to define specific anti-discrimination rules which may be used to protect the rights of the victim before a court and to obtain a remedy. This should be possible on the basis of principles contained in the equality directives as implemented in national law. However, no courts in any of the countries under consideration in this chapter have delivered such a judgment. The same is true for the ECJ. Interpretation of directives is a matter for the ECJ and therefore it may be expected to determine whether the current instruments are capable of combating intersectional discrimination.

Law and policy are capable of interacting through positive action measures and positive obligations. Both are present in current EC law and policy and may be present also in national legislation and policy. Legal instruments may result in the incorporation of certain ideas in policy and, in turn, policies may provide the impulse for a process of legislation. In particular, mainstreaming is an instrument that appears at first sight to be a policy instrument, but which may have also legal consequences both in the drafting of legislation and decision-making. To improve

---

23   Current ECRI recommendations can be found on the Council of Europe's website. Available at: www.coe.int/t/dghl/monitoring/ecri/activities/GeneralThemes_en.asp [accessed: 31 May 2009].

the position of Roma women most effectively, mainstreaming should be practised at least in the most problematic areas: housing, education, employment and healthcare. This has implications primarily for social rights. Accordingly, when adopting (legislative) decisions in those fields, the possible consequences for Roma women should be considered. At the same time, active policy instruments in favour of Roma women ought to be established. For example, existing good practice could be extended to operate on a wider level. A positive obligation to establish Roma advisors and Roma assistants (maybe also by giving preference to Roma women) might be one possibility. In the same vein, a duty to provide educational opportunities, actively recruiting at national level, offered mainly or exclusively to Roma women might be established. Such obligations could easily be provided for in national legislation.

The interaction of law and policy is therefore one of the most appropriate ways to attain substantive equality for Roma women. The proposed OMC could contribute to the realization of that aim.

Conclusions

In this chapter the situation of Roma women has been outlined in connection with highly alarming cases of intersectional discrimination. Substantive equality has been identified as the correct goal in combating intersectional discrimination experienced Roma women, a situation worsened by social exclusion.

Current legislation – whether at national, international or EU level – does not include any express instruments to combat intersectional discrimination. However, it appears possible to invoke existing EC law to claim remedies in the case of intersectional discrimination where gender and ethnic origin overlap. This approach remains to be confirmed by the ECJ.

The form most frequently used at present to take account of intersectional discrimination is that of policy papers and recommendations by international bodies. Not only do these employ the term 'intersectional discrimination', but they also propose specific solutions, often aimed directly at improving the situation of Roma women. Many proposals include positive obligations, a feature identified in this chapter as a possible effective future solution to intersectional discrimination experienced by Roma women.

Finally, we can now answer the question posed at the start of the chapter: current legislation and policy are not yet fully in a position effectively to combat discrimination against Roma women, but if further developed and the necessary interaction between law and policy established, the situation of Roma women may start to improve. The solutions to such a complex and multifaceted problem must harness interactions between law and policy instruments, where although policy may be preferred, law must not be neglected, if long-lasting substantive equality for Roma women is to be secured.

Chapter 16

Intersectionality in EU Law: A Critical Re-appraisal

Dagmar Schiek and Jule Mulder

Introduction

In the sister-volume of this publication, Ruth Nielsen (Nielsen 2009) investigated the extent to which EU law is capable of addressing intersectional discrimination. She warned against neglecting intersectional cases, and encouraged a proactive reading of current Treaty and the secondary law. Since then, the EU has published studies on 'multiple discrimination' (Burri and Schiek 2009; European Commission 2007a), increased relevant soft law policies, planned some legislative developments (European Commission 2008b) and expressed its intention to use the 'new governance mechanisms to address the issue of multiple discrimination' (European Commission 2008a: 9).

This chapter critically assesses the extent to which these developments create new opportunities to respond adequately to discrimination at the intersection between race gender and disability, and investigates whether more can be done to achieve that goal. It will focus on legal and policy developments at EU level, but will also reflect on their possible implications for different legal cultures. First, the way in which EU law and policy have addressed the problems associated with this phenomenon will be summarized. This will be followed by an overview of ways in which national legal orders tackle the problem. Finally, a critical appraisal from a comparative socio-legal and social actor perspective will be offered.

EU Legislation and Policy in Relation to Intersectionality

EU law does not (yet) use the term intersectionality. The term 'multiple discrimination', however, has already found its way into the recitals of Directives 2000/43/EC and 2000/78/EC, which observe that women are often the victims of multiple discrimination.[1] Moreover, the directives oblige the Commission to include a reference to their impact on 'women and men' in their reports on the implementation of those directives (Article 17 Race Equality Directive and Article 19 Employment Framework Directive). These obligations however, have not been fully implemented. While the report on the implementation of the Racial Equality Directive contains some information under the heading 'Gender mainstreaming and multiple discrimination' (European Commission 2006b: 1, 7), the equivalent report on the implementation of the Employment Framework Directive does not even contain a similar heading (European Commission 2008e).

A proposal for a Council directive on implementing the principle of equal treatment between persons irrespective of religion and belief, disability, age or sexual orientation other than in the field of employment and occupation is currently being debated by the EU institutions. The original

---

1   Cf. recital 14 of Directive 2000/43/EC and recital 8 of Directive 2000/78/EC, the same formula is used in recital 13 of the draft directive equal treatment on all grounds except sex and race outside the employment context (European Commission 2008b).

Commission proposal (European Commission 2008b) merely repeated the approach of including a reference to multiple discrimination in a recital. The European Economic and Social Council has called upon the Commission to issue a recommendation on the subject[2] and the Committee of the Regions has stressed the need to introduce positive secondary EU law defining the concept of multiple discrimination.[3] Subsequently, the European Parliament's (EP) proposed amendments[4] *inter alia* relate to multiple discrimination. First, the EP proposed an explicit clarification of the fact that discrimination includes multiple discrimination (Article 1). Second, it suggested an obligation of the Commission to include information about multiple discrimination in its implementation reports. Finally, the EP proposed adding the following definition of multiple discrimination:

> Article 1
>
> 2. Multiple discrimination occurs when discrimination is based:
>   a. on any combination of the grounds of religion or belief, disability, age, or sexual orientation, or
>   b. on any one or more of the grounds set out in paragraph 1, and also on the ground of any one or more of
>   i. sex (in so far as the matter complained of is within the material scope of Directive 2004/113/EC as well as of this Directive),
>   ii. racial or ethnic origin (in so far as the matter complained of is within the material scope of Directive 2000/43/EC as well as of this Directive), or
>   iii. nationality (in so far as the matter complained of is within the scope of Article 12 of the EC Treaty).
> 3. In this Directive, multiple discrimination and multiple grounds shall be construed accordingly.

The definition seems to follow the traditional common law approach of precise and detailed statutory provisions, which leaves limited scope for judicial development by teleological interpretation. It does not cover employment cases nor intersections between gender and 'race' except where they intersect with one of the other grounds covered by the directive. It might therefore have negative repercussions on the reading of the other directives, especially at the hands of judges from jurisdictions prone to systemic interpretation – a style of interpretation according to which a body of law is considered in its entirety in the light of systemic considerations. Under a systemic approach, the fact that one of the non-discrimination directives explicitly acknowledges multiple discrimination would suggest that the issue was not meant to be covered by directives remaining silent on the matter.

It seems unlikely that the planned directive will be agreed for some time. In five successive sessions of the Employment and Social Affairs Council[5] ever more outstanding issues (concerning

---

2   Opinion of the European Economic and Social Committee on the 'Proposal for a Council directive on implementing the principle of equal treatment between persons irrespective of religion or belief, disability, age or sexual orientation' (OJ 182/19 of 4.8.2009, at 23).

3   Opinion of the Committee of the Regions on non-discrimination, equal opportunities and the implementation of the principle of equality between persons OJ C 211/90 of 4.9.2009, at 93–4.

4   European Parliament legislative resolution of 2 April 2009 on the proposal for a Council directive on implementing the principle of equal treatment between persons irrespective of religion or belief, disability, age or sexual orientation OJ C 137/68 of 27.5.2010.

5   See Report from the Presidency of 19 November 2010, Interinstitutional File 2008/0140 (CNS), Report from the Presidency of 17 May 2010, Interinstitutional File 2008/0140 (CNS), Report from the Presidency of 17 November 2009, Interinstitutional File 2008/0140, and Report from the Presidency of 2

legal certainty, material scope and cost connected to age and disability discrimination) have been identified, but the Council has not demanded additions regarding multiple or intersectional discrimination.

However, below the level of positive law, the concept of multidimensionality has been embraced by the Council. The issue was first mentioned in recital 4 of the 2000 Council Decision establishing a Community action programme to combat discrimination. This states that equality of women and men requires action on multiple discrimination. Further, recital 5 states that all forms of discrimination are equally intolerable, suggesting that new policies combating discrimination should address multiple discrimination.[6] The Council decision establishing a programme on gender equality also contained a recital and a substantive article stressing the relevance of multiple discrimination against women.[7] In its decision to establish the European Year of Equal Opportunities for All (2007),[8] the Council identified raising awareness of the problem of multiple discrimination as one of its objectives (Degener, in this volume: 38–42), in its resolution on the follow up to that Year,[9] Member States and the Commission are urged to take full account of the 'special issues arising from multiple discrimination'. Finally, the Council resolution on the situation of persons with disabilities[10] recognizes the cumulative effects of gender and disability, the logical consequence of which is that women with disabilities often face multiple discrimination (see also Lawson, in this volume: 47–61).

The Commission has prioritized a commitment to addressing multiple discrimination within its policies combating discrimination on grounds other than gender,[11] although it was within the gender equality discourse that the Commission used the term 'intersectionality' for the first time. Today, the perspective is clearly focused on using gender mainstreaming principles for making reference to multiple discrimination against women in legal and policy instruments concerning the other equalities.[12] To that end, the most current recommendation is for the EU to conduct analysis and for the Member States to (voluntarily) implement relevant legislation (European Commission 2010). Less attention is given to the need to mainstream 'other equalities' into gender equality law and policy and thus to address the situation of women suffering disadvantage at the intersections of gender with race and disability.

June 2009, Interinstitutional File 2008/0140 (CNS), and minutes from the respective Council sessions (for the first Council session in October 2008 there was no presidency report).

6   2000/750/EC: Council Decision of 27 November 2000 Official Journal L 303, 02/12/2000 pp. 23–28.

7   Decision 1554/2005/EC amending Council Decision 2001/51/EC establishing a programme relating to the Community framework strategy on gender equality [2005] OJ L255/9 and Council Decision 848/2004/EC establishing a Community action programme to promote organizations active at European level in the field of equality between men and women [2004] OJ L159/18, recital 3 and Article 3 (b).

8   Council Decision No. 771/2006/EC of the European Parliament and of the Council of 17 May 2006 establishing the European Year of Equal Opportunities for All (2007) – towards a just society [2006] OJ L146/1.

9   Council resolution of 5 December 2007 on the follow-up of the European Year of Equal Opportunities for All (2007) OJ C 308/1.

10   Council Resolution of 17 March 2008 on the situation of Persons with disabilities in the European Union (OJ C 75/1 of 26.3.2008).

11   The analysis of the Commission practice to separate gender equality and 'new equalities' into separate socio-legal fields is beyond this chapter, and has been more thoroughly covered elsewhere (Schiek 2010a).

12   For example, the Commission Opinion on The Future of Gender Equality Policy after 2010, states: 'The EC should ensure that a gender equality perspective is fully enacted in European anti-discrimination policies and legislation' (European Commission 2010).

ECJ Case Law on Intersectional Discrimination

The case law of the Court of Justice has been widely acknowledged as an influential political force in the development of European integration (Alter 2009); and it also shapes EU non-discrimination law. Due to its wide jurisdiction, the Court has undoubtedly had countless opportunities to consider intersectional disadvantage (Nielsen 2009: 37). For instance, many leading nationality discrimination cases concern migrant women whose migration may well have been linked to their gender role (e.g. as a partner in a heterosexual relationship).[13] Intersectional discrimination may well have been relevant in cases where the Court had to appraise Member States' restrictions of the free movement of sex workers.[14] However, the question of whether these restrictions also involved gender discrimination was not considered. The Court has also decided a number of cases where gender interacted with age[15] or sexual orientation[16] before EU law prohibited discrimination on these latter grounds.

Since the number of EU discrimination grounds has expanded, the Court has had more opportunities to address intersectional discrimination. However, so far, there has only been one case in which it has explicitly considered discrimination on two grounds. The Lindorfer case[17] concerned the pension rights of EU civil servants. These vary according to gender and age of entry into the service. Two AG opinions were issued – the second one explicitly covering age discrimination. The Court, however, did not consider any cumulative or intersectional effects of the discrimination. In a number of other cases, only one discrimination ground was debated although there was at least the potential for this ground to intersect with gender, 'race' or disability.

For example, in cases on age discrimination, additional issues of indirect gender or ethnic discrimination have not been considered at all. Compulsory retirement policies were at issue in the Age Concern litigation[18] and the more recent Peterson case.[19] Such policies presuppose a certain model of working life, according to which a worker accumulates sufficient pension rights to retire comfortably at the specified age. Those structurally excluded from traditional career patterns (e.g. women who take time out to care for children or other family members and others whose entry into or progress in working life is delayed due to gender or race discrimination) are often unable to accumulate sufficient entitlements and may therefore wish to continue working beyond that age. In *Bulicke*,[20] a woman challenged an employer's decision to offer a position only to persons of a certain age. The advertisement included the following line: 'Do you like talking on the phone? Then you are exactly the right person for us. We'll even give you the opportunity to earn money doing it. Are you between 18–35 years of age, with a good knowledge of German and looking for a full-time job?'. As telephone marketers are predominantly female, several issues of implicit discrimination arise here – including the exclusion of people (predominantly women) who might prefer to work part-time while taking on caring responsibilities, but these were not addressed.

---

13   Case C-259 et al./91 *Allué and Coonan* [1993] ECR I-4309, ECJ 33/88 [1989] ECR 1591; Case C-272/92 *Chiara Spotti* [1993] ECR I-5202; Case C-15/96 *Schöning-Kougebetopoulou* [1998] ECR I-47; Case C-419/92 *Scholz* [1994] ECR I-505.

14   Case 115/81 and 116/81 *Adoui* [1982] ECR 1665; Case C-268/99 *Jany* [2001] ECR I-8615.

15   Case 149/77 *Defrenne* [1978] ECR 1365; Case 152/84 *Marshall* [1986] ECR 723; Case C-77/02 *Steinicke* [2003] ECR I-9027; Case C-187/00 *Kutz-Bauer* [2003] ECR I-2741.

16   Case C-249/96 *Grant* [1998] ECR I-00621; Case C- 13/94 *P v. S* [1996] ECR I-02143.

17   Case C-227/04P *Lindorfer* [2007] ECR I-6767.

18   Case C-388/07 *Age Concern* [2009] ECR I-1569.

19   Case C-341/08 *Petersen* 12 January 2010.

20   Case C-246/09 *Bulicke* 8 July 2010.

Another example is *Kücükdeveci*,[21] where a woman of Turkish origin was denied transferral from a position in packaging to marketing (which would have secured her employment) partly because of her accented German. This claim was rejected by the national court without referring to the Court of Justice. The reference only concerned the statutory notice period, which had been shortened from seven to one month because *Kücükdeveci* acquired seven of her 10 years seniority before her 25th birthday. The statutory rule demanded to ignore these seven years, which constitutes direct age discrimination. The underlying ethnic discrimination, and the potentially indirect gender and ethnic discrimination by the notice period were not considered in the case (see on these aspects Schiek, in this volume: 16–17, Schiek 2010a).

Gender dimensions of discrimination have also been neglected in cases of sexual orientation discrimination, such as *Maruko*[22] and the pending case of *Römer*.[23] Both cases deal with different occupational pension rights granted to heterosexual married couples and same-sex couples living in a civil union. Although it remains to be seen whether the Court of Justice will address the gender dimension in *Römer*, AG Jääskinen refused to acknowledge any possible connection between the more favourable treatment of married couples and Article 141 EC (now Article 157 TFEU) which grants equal rights to men and women. He thus ignores the interconnection between gender and sexual orientation and the lack of static categories of sex (Schiek, in in this volume: 16).

Preceding chapters have mentioned the Coleman case [24] in which only the disability aspect and not the gender aspect of discrimination was considered (Degener, in this volume: 42, Schiek, in this volume: 17, Solanke, in this volume: 217–18). Similarly, in FERYN,[25] the Court had to decide whether the employer's public statement that he would not employ Moroccans as up-and-over door fitters (because customers would not feel comfortable allowing them into their houses) constituted race discrimination. If the assumption was that those at home during the daytime would be largely ethnic majority females and that they would be frightened by having an ethnic minority male around, there would clearly be a gendered dimension to the race discrimination but this was not addressed at all.

Overall, Court of Justice case law does not (yet) set a good example of tackling intersectionality. This is surprising because, after the adoption of Directives 2000/43 and 2000/78, the Court has had many more opportunities to address the problem of multiple discrimination (Nielsen 2009: 42). This neglect is in contrast to the dynamic interpretation of EU law applied by the Court in other fields (Alter 2009: 4).

National Law

In assessing the viability of EU strategies in combating intersectional disadvantage, it is helpful to contemplate why the EU judiciary has been slow to acknowledge the phenomenon. A comparative approach may enrich this investigation.[26] Accordingly, whether and how Member States addressed

---

21 Case C-555/07 *Kücükdeveci* of 19 January 2010.

22 Case C-267/06 *Maruko* [2008] ECR I-1757.

23 Case C-147/08 *Römer*, opinion AG Jääskinen of 15 July 2010.

24 Case C-303/06 *Coleman* [2008] ECR I-5603.

25 Case C-54/07 *FERYN* [2008] I-5187.

26 The following is based on the contributions of national legal experts from the Network of Legal Experts on Equality between Women and Men, which again are available in full in the report (Burri and Schiek 2009).

the issue in their legislation as well as the way in which it has been recognized in advocacy and case law will be considered below.

There are altogether seven Member States whose legislation refers to multiple or intersectional discrimination.[27] The German General Equal Treatment Act takes a timid approach. It states that, in cases of multiple discrimination, the requirements for each single ground must be fulfilled.[28] Austrian law goes a little further. Its four statutes on equality and non-discrimination provide for multiple discrimination to be taken into account in determining the compensation to be awarded in discrimination cases.[29] Similar rules are to be found in Italian and Romanian statutory instruments.[30] More ambitiously, Polish legislation expressly provides that direct and indirect discrimination may both be based on more than one ground.[31] Spanish[32] and Bulgarian[33] legislation place on public authorities a positive duty to address the problem of multiple discrimination, for example in devising policies and conducting surveys. Definitions of multiple discrimination can be found in Bulgarian and Romanian legislation. Article 11 of the Bulgarian Protection Against Discrimination Act (PADA) defines multiple discrimination as 'discrimination on the grounds of more than one of the characteristics under Article 4 (1)'. Article 4 of the revised Romanian Act on Equal Opportunities defines as multiple discrimination 'any discriminating action based on two or more discrimination criteria'. Most of this legislation is designed to implement EU non-discrimination directives which suggests that these Member States read the directives as implying a prohibition of multiple or intersectional discrimination. This would appear to be in line with the general requirements of interpreting EU law – whether primary or secondary – in a dynamic way (Schiek 2005: 462–3).

Even where national legislation does not explicitly acknowledge multiple or intersectional discrimination, it could be interpreted in a teleological way to do so. Accordingly, national experts from Cyprus, Denmark, France, Iceland, Ireland, Malta, the Netherlands, Norway, Portugal, Slovakia, Spain and Sweden consider that their national legislation allows claims of multiple discrimination. Even in Belgium, Finland, Greece and Hungary, where courts have often ignored a second or third dimension of discrimination, such an interpretation was regarded as possible or even necessary. Experts from Ireland, the UK, Slovakia and the Czech Republic have explicitly doubted whether their countries' statutes could be read as implicitly covering intersectional and multiple discrimination (Burri and Schiek 2009: 29, 47, 77, 114, 132).

Practical experiences in court, infrequent as yet, complete the picture. The Danish Supreme Court[34] has considered disadvantage at the intersection between ethnicity, religion and gender in a

---

27   The Commission working document on the proposed directive, only three Member States have been identified as mirroring multiple discrimination in their legislation (Communities 2008: 22, with footnote 82), whereas a thorough analysis in August 2009 demonstrated that there are no less than seven Member States (Burri and Schiek 2009).

28   § 4 General Equal Treatment Act. Additionally, Germany recognizes the special need of disabled women in several other provisions (Degener, in this volume: 43).

29   § 9 (4) Federal Disability Equality Act, § 7j Act on the Employment of People with Disabilities, §12 section 13 Equal Treatment Act (private sector) and § 19a Federal Equal Treatment Act (Federal Public Sector).

30   Italy: Article 1 of decree no. 215/2003, Romania: Governmental Ordinance 77 of 2003.

31   Article 18(3a) (3) Labour Code for direct discrimination and Article 18(3a) (4) Labour Code for indirect discrimination, amended 2003 and 2008.

32   Article 14.6 Act 3/2007.

33   Article 11 of the Act on Protection Against Discrimination 2004.

34   In the *Føtex* case (U 2005, 1265H.), for a critical appraisal of this see Lynn Roseberry (in this volume: 196–7).

case where the claimant had relied only on religious discrimination in challenging her dismissal as a salesperson in the cosmetic department of a large store because of wearing a hijab. Although the challenge did not succeed because of the bargaining process on which the department store's dress code had been decided upon, the Court's reasoning suggests a willingness in principle to recognize multiple discrimination claims. The Paris Court of Appeal[35] has also accepted, in principle, a claim for ethnic and sex discrimination related to career progression and access to training. The claimant (a black woman) identified, as relevant comparators, several white men and a white woman. The court accepted this choice of comparators and focused on whether there was an objective justification for the difference in treatment. The Dutch Equal Treatment Commission has indicated that it might acknowledge intersectional sexual and ethnic harassment by referring to sex/ethnic harassment.[36] In the particular case, however, the Commission held that there was insufficient proof of harassment. A more encouraging example comes from Norway: two Asian women were denied a room in an Oslo hotel on the grounds that no spontaneous bookings by Asian women would be accepted. The Tribunal recognized this as intersectional discrimination on grounds of ethnicity and gender, based on the stereotyping of Asian women as prostitutes.[37] However, as in the Dutch case, the Tribunal had no competence to award damages – the amount of which would probably have been the only tangible advantage of acknowledging such intersectionality. In *Network Rail Infrastructure Ltd v. Griffiths-Henry*,[38] the English Employment Appeal Tribunal accepted that in a claim of race and sex discrimination, for the purposes of shifting the burden of proof a black female claimant may name a group of white male comparators; and, in *Tilern de Bique*,[39] it explicitly referred to the 'double disadvantage' which was 'reflected in the factual reality' of a black female soldier who was also a single mother. These cases are only from a lower court, and the EAT respected the authority of the Court of Appeal decision reported below, in which intersectionality was not acknowledged, explicitly in *Network Rail* (Moon, in this volume: 166).

There are also examples of national courts failing to recognize intersectional disadvantage. In the frequently quoted case of *Bahl v. Law Society*,[40] the English Court of Appeal required an applicant to prove sex and race discrimination separately where these were interlinked (Moon, in this volume: 165–6). The Irish Equality Tribunal refused to acknowledge intersectional discrimination when it was presented with statistics demonstrating that older women were disproportionately excluded from a pension fund.[41] Similarly, a first instance German court rejected a claim of indirect ethnic and gender discrimination[42] based on combined statistics. Cases in which female employees are disadvantaged because they cover their heads in line with Muslim traditions are often dealt with on the basis of religious discrimination whilst the gender and ethnic dimensions are overlooked.[43]

---

35   Judgment of the Paris Court of Appeal, 29 January 2002, no° 2001/32582.

36   ETC Opinion 2007-40.

37   The Equality Tribunal, Case no. 1/2008, available at: www.diskrimineringsnemnda.no/sites/d/diskrimineringsnemnda.no/files/62958820.doc [accessed: 24 July 2010]. On case law of the Norwegian Equality Tribunal regarding the hijab see (Skjeie 2009: 303–5).

38   [2006] IRLR 865 EAT.

39   [2010] IRLR 471.

40   *Bahl v. Law Society* [2003] I.R.L.R. 640 and [2004] I.R.L.R. 799.

41   DEC- P2009 – 001 and available at: www.equalitytribunal.ie [accessed: 30 March 2009].

42   Wiesbaden Labour Court 5 Ca 46/08 of 18 December 2008, EzA – SD 2009, no. 2, 5–6. The case was settled in November .

43   Examples include the German Constitutional Court 24 September 2003 (2 BvR 1436/02) BVerfGE 108, 282 and the Dutch Equal Treatment Commission (e.g. opinion 1996-109 or opinion 2004-112, on similar cases see Burri, in this volume: 106–8).

The cases in which multiple discrimination has been acknowledged are mainly from jurisdictions where legislation does not explicitly mention the notion. By contrast, some of the cases where intersectional aspects have been ignored are from jurisdictions (such as Germany) where it is explicitly addressed in legislation. Thus, this short comparison of national case law demonstrates that a legislative reference to multiple or intersectional discrimination does not necessarily lead to judicial approval of the concept, and that the absence of such reference does not necessarily prevent courts from recognizing it.

The reasons quoted by national experts for the negative attitude of judges and advocates to intersectionality are diverse. Frequently mentioned factors include factual ignorance of the problems of intersectionality and the additional interest being attracted by younger non-discrimination grounds (such as age or ethnicity). In common law countries and newer Member States, the necessity to find a comparator was also identified as problematic. Most frequently, experts mentioned the difficulties caused by the different material scope of legislation covering different discrimination grounds, which results in advocates strategically choosing the ground with the widest scope. Problems associated with proving intersectional discrimination were regarded as similarly troublesome (Burri and Schiek 2009: 18–20; Goldberg, in this volume: 177–90), especially where there are no suitable statistics (Carles Howard and Kofman, in this volume: 227–40).

These observations call for a more thorough critical analysis of what EU law can sensibly contribute to tackling disadvantage at the intersections between disability, gender and 'race'. That analysis should consider whether intersectional cases are made actionable in court and also whether EU law and policy are capable of impacting on social reality and empowering social actors willing to combat intersectional disadvantage in other ways.

Critical Appraisal

Such a critical appraisal rests on assumptions about how the EU and its law impact on Member States and vice versa – a full examination of which is beyond the scope of this chapter. The EU is a multi-level polity which requires any examination of political or legal development to consider the interaction between levels of governance. [44] Additionally, we consider the development of any European social field to be the result of social interactions.[45] Consequently, socio-legal fields contain the relevant legal norms and the potential to shape relations of power. The socio-legal field is also a social space where legal norms are interpreted and applied, and in which social actors challenge or support power relations. In these challenges, they will sometimes strategically rely on legal institutions and norms (Fligstein 2008: 8; Nash 2009: 30–34). In a European socio-legal field, these spaces span different Member States. Therefore, for analysing any European socio-legal field, a comparative approach is crucial. Comparing non-discrimination law is not without difficulty, mainly due to its aspirations to change society (Schiek et al. 2007: 13–25). Evaluations of EU law and policy on intersectional disadvantage thus require consideration to be given to the style of the relevant legal orders as well as to the political, social and economic

---

44   This approach has much in common with political science approaches theorizing the EU under the label of multi-level governance (Jachtenfuchs and Kohler-Koch 2004).

45   This approach has much in common with social constructivism (for an overview see Risse 2009), which, in its sociological variant, also integrates aspects of multi-level governance and institutional theory, as *inter alia* exemplified by (Fligstein 2008).

backgrounds of their non-discrimination law.[46] Such evaluations would also be capable of offering guidance to those concerned with developing relevant EU law and policy. Some of the issues which should be considered in order to offer the critical appraisal promised above will now be briefly outlined.

Intersectionality in Comparative Perspectives

The starting point of any such analysis is the general character of EU non-discrimination law and policy. Besides its role of facilitating the internal market through avoiding nationality discrimination and of creating inroads for a European level social policy via the field of gender equality (Schiek, in this volume: 20), EU non-discrimination law has clearly been inspired by developments in the UK and the US;[47] and the younger directives partly result from lobbying activities by the Starting Line Group, a think tank dominated by Anglo-Dutch intellectuals (Geddes and Guiraudon 2004: 340–44). Accordingly, this is one of the few fields in EU law where common law influences are dominant.

Without overly stressing the divergence between common and civil law,[48] we can safely assume that there are differences in legal style. Smits has noted the contrast between an 'absence of systematisation or a desire thereof' (in the common law) and the 'systematisation and the programmatic desire thereof' in civil law (Smits 2002: 79, 88). While this is a rather rough categorization, it still offers some heuristic value.

It allows us to understand that, in a common law country, the piecemeal legislation which follows single interest movements is not generally seen as problematic. Parliamentary legislation is traditionally interpreted narrowly by the courts and rules developed in one field of law are not generally transposed to others. This legal style appears as averse to systematization from the perspective of a continental writer such as Smits. The basis of this approach lies in the traditional division of labour between common law judges and parliamentary legislators, according to which the former develops the common law incrementally whereas the latter responds to political programmatic demands through legislation (Zweigert and Kötz 1998: 265–8). Further, *inter alia* under European influences (both from the EU and the Council of Europe), the UK and Irish legal systems are developing legislation in code-like acts (such as the Equality Act 2010), using more teleological reasoning in case law and expressing some desire for more systemization (Smits 2002: 97). Nevertheless, the underlying approaches remain distinctive. In the field of discrimination law, this underlying style becomes apparent in a remaining tendency of literal interpretation of legislation. This tendency results in a reluctance to transfer principles derived from one single strand of non-discrimination law to others. Obviously, this also is a hindrance for embracing intersectional advantage. Consequently, it is not surprising that UK lawyers tend to welcome a clear and specific statutory definition of multiple discrimination (e.g. Moon, in this volume: 170–73).

Notwithstanding these difficulties, intersectionality is intensely debated in common law countries in general (including the UK and Ireland). This corresponds to the long tradition in outlawing discrimination in all social realms, a tradition that is not rooted in any jurisdictional style, but rather in a heightened awareness of diversity and intense appreciation for individuality in these countries.

---

46   With this, we are relying on critical approaches to comparative law in applied versions, drawing on the structural school as well as socio-legal approaches generally (Schiek 2010b: 207–10).

47   Accordingly, the EU has been accused of transplanting outdated modes of legislating against discrimination from the UK to other Member States (Hepple 2004: 3).

48   For a critique of such endeavours see Mattei and Robilant (2002).

Many European countries have a colonial past and/or experienced wave after wave of immigration over centuries. However, only few of them, such as the UK – as well as the Netherlands and partly Belgium, albeit for different historical reasons – have cultivated a policy style that tolerates, but does not assimilate difference. This has now developed towards a multicultural paradigm. According to this paradigm, society is seen as a multiplicity of communities, rather than as a single homogenous community. Resulting equality policies have generally tended to protect those individual communities by preserving their different identities. As community identity is dependent on people belonging to it, this may have repercussions on the social mobility of individuals (Schiek 2005: 451). Losing all its members would threaten any community, and losing all its communities would threaten a society that is based on multiculturalism. Even multiculturalism as a civic idea, as promoted by Tariq Modood, must thus insist on maintaining identity formations that have priority over other additional identity traits:

> While there is much of contemporary post-immigration ethnicity and religious formations in Western societies that is better understood in terms of hybridity, associational and multiple identities, some ethnic and religious identities are being manifested as having a primacy rather than sitting alongside any individuals other identities. (Modood 2007: 117)

For intersectional disadvantage, this means that such disadvantaged groups must be defined as new groups. In socio-political strategies this is mirrored in the development of new target groups (e.g. Romani women) for protection against discrimination (Koldinská, in this volume: 241–58). In legal discourse, this can result in proposals to add the 'other status' category to non-discrimination legislation (Arnardóttir 2009: 60–61, Moon, in this volume: 168–9), which can then be used to accommodate combined, multiple or intersectional identities. However, it seems difficult to use this logic to move beyond the group paradigm. As explained above, multiculturalism presupposes the existence of distinct communities upon which society is built. Discrimination law based on multiculturalism will always tend to protect the groups along with the individuals deemed as belonging to them, and has thus a limited potential to accommodate fluid and changing identities. Thus, the common law countries seem in a difficult position. On the one hand, their legal system complicates acknowledging intersectional cases. On the other hand, the disposition towards multiculturalism encourages development of discrimination law in line with social requirements. However, multiculturalism is only able to accommodate intersectionality in so far as it does not threaten the communities which constitute society.

The majority of the EU Member States (including many of the post-2004 Member States) are civil law countries. In these legal cultures, the trend to systematization leads to the rejection of pin-pointed and single-issue based legislation. As has been shown, in the field of intersectionality this results in fewer conceptual problems in interpreting non-discrimination law derived from single strand strategies as encompassing intersectional discrimination. Based on systemic traditions, the Continental Member States should generally be inclined to embrace non-discrimination law due to the long tradition of constitutional equality principles. This is, however, not the case. Being less pragmatic than the common law countries, these legal cultures support a strict division between private and public law. Constitutional principles of non-discrimination are located in the sphere of public law. Private law in its entirety is governed by the principle of private autonomy of individuals. Applying non-discrimination principles in private law thus appears as an illegitimate intrusion of public law principles into that realm, which also threatens autonomy of individuals. Accordingly, Western Continental countries have opposed the introduction of non-discrimination law much more fiercely than common law countries or the more pragmatic BENELUX countries.

At a cultural level, a fundamentally different approach to diversity and difference underlies this opposition. Migration research and racial and ethnic studies recount endless evidence of deep divisions in approach between the Anglo-American world and Continental Europe in this regard (see, for example, Geddes and Guiraudon 2004). Most Continental European countries have been subjected to recurrent migration waves and ethnic diversity. As a reaction to this, Western European countries established an ideology of national unity, which proved hostile to recognizing any claims to group diversity or specific group rights. French Republicanism is usually quoted as a prime example of this. It is said that the Republic is constituted of individuals, who relate 'to the state unmediated by other corporate bodies' (Stychin 2001: 352). This state finds itself 'intolerant of constituted groups and inclusive of their constituent members as individuals' (ibid.). Relating to intersectionality, the Republican approach to the equality principle defies the development of any groups. Consequently, persons suffering from intersectional disadvantage are not held back by any fictional group membership that should enjoy priority from being acknowledged in their individuality.[49] However, this may well be connected to disregarding any structural problems resulting from discrimination by ascription (Carles, Howard and Kofman, in this volume: 229–31). Interestingly, Eastern European countries have developed stronger principles of minority protection despite similar experiences (Nousiainen, in this volume: 141–55).

While the Scandinavian countries are often submerged in the civil law family, there are some noteworthy differences which may well impact on the development of anti-discrimination law (Pihlajamäki 2004: 469–70). In their legal tradition, these countries are considered as being less inclined towards highly abstract generalization than other civil law countries, relying on reasonableness and realism instead. They do not follow case law methodology either, but rather rely on usage and custom to a greater extent than other civil law countries. The approach to developing legal principles is still based on teleological argument, but systematization is less central to these more pragmatic legal orders. Law is seen as a social practice, often resulting from collective processes, and institutions such as ombudsmen have a long tradition in creating social practices outside formal court proceedings (Fahlbeck 2002). Due to their peripheral geographical position, the three Nordic EU Member States have not experienced large waves of migration until the 1980s. Apart from the minority of the Sami and the Roma, and Russophone parts of the population in Finland, there has traditionally not been much ethnic diversity. In all these countries, however, women's movements have been strong, and gender equality law and policy has a long tradition.

Possibly due to the pragmatic approach to legal developments, non-discrimination legislation has been implemented without many problems, except that in most countries gender equality remained a separate strand of legislation (Roseberry 2002: 252). Against this background, a pragmatic approach to intersectional disadvantage seems to be possible, although experiences are not very far developed yet, and a certain tendency towards 'assimilationalism' has been detected (Roseberry, in this volume).

In conclusion, the different legal cultures and socio-political traditions in the EU imply that Member States will have different strengths and weaknesses in addressing intersectional disadvantage. EU law and policy on intersectionality should respect this diversity.

---

49   See above, footnote 35, for an example from case law.

Ways Forward for the EU to Adequately Address Intersectional Disadvantage

The reluctance of social actors, legislators, advocates and the judiciary to acknowledge intersectional disadvantage is based on a multiplicity of reasons. This suggests that EU law and policy should tackle the problem through a multiplicity of strategies – an approach which would respect the diversity of legal cultures and socio-economic structures underlying non-discrimination law and practice. These strategies should aim to encourage legislators, advocates and the judiciary to recognize the problems of intersectional disadvantage and to empower social actors to address them. Above all, they should allow for spontaneous and incremental development in this field – a field which has only recently begun to be widely discussed in Europe.

EU legislation First, some encouragement to regulate and adjudicate on intersectional disadvantage at the national level might be provided by explicitly recognizing the phenomenon in EU law. This would ease the difficulties encountered so far by the English Court of Appeal and the Irish Equality Tribunal in accepting intersectional claims. In addition, such an acknowledgement would raise awareness of intersectional disadvantage. Accordingly, it has been suggested that the EU should make it clear that intersectional discrimination is covered by its non-discrimination system despite the fact that it is based on a closed list (McColgan 2007: 92–3). Retaining the closed list would mean that direct discrimination would not have to be subjected to an open-ended justification defence (Moon, in this volume: 163) – a defence which would have seriously damaging consequences in countries (such as the Continental European countries from East and West) which are reluctant to acknowledge non-discrimination law in the marketplace altogether. Accordingly, the legislative innovation that is needed is one which states that unlawful discrimination includes discrimination based on more than one ground or on an intersection of grounds.

The present demand of the EP and some academics (Bell 2008a: 9) to include such a clause in a directive which covers only four out of the six grounds covered by the existing non-discrimination directives, and which applies only to some non-employment spheres, appears problematic from the perspective of more systemic approaches to legal interpretation. From that perspective, such an initiative would not appear to be a cautious first step upon which to build, but would instead seem to be an acknowledgement that directives not mentioning multiple or intersectional discrimination do not apply to such cases. This would have devastating effects on the development of any adequate response to intersectional disadvantage by way of teleological interpretation. Accordingly, a separate directive covering all grounds would seem more appropriate.

Should intersectional disadvantage become acknowledged as a category of EU non-discrimination law, without providing a pin-pointed definition, this would also have the potential to spur the Court of Justice into developing the concept further if given the opportunity.

As EU non-discrimination law is presently modelled on UK law, it also suffers from some of the difficulties which common law jurisdictions often experience in acknowledging intersectional discrimination. In most of these countries, finding the appropriate comparator[50] proves a major difficulty in cases of intersectional disadvantage (Hannett 2003: 68). There may be other ways of establishing discrimination than on the basis of a comparator (on one such approach see Goldberg, in this volume: 183–9). For example, the ECJ has recognized that pregnancy is a uniquely female condition and has accordingly categorized discrimination on grounds of pregnancy as discrimination on grounds of sex without requiring the identification of a male comparator. Similar reasoning

---

50 On a general critique of the comparator concept from inner-common law perspectives see Bell (2007: 205–7).

can be applied to intersectional cases. For example, stereotypes imposed on Asian women[51] will affect neither non-Asian women nor Asian men. Thus, it would seem inappropriate to require a non-Asian man as a comparator, as the comparator logic would have it. Given free rein, judicial creativity could be allowed to find stereotyping[52] based on gendered racial prejudice as a causal link between disadvantages (Radacic 2008: 857) and intersecting discrimination grounds. The EU law definition of direct discrimination insists on a comparator, although the severity of this requirement is mitigated by the fact that hypothetical comparators are permitted. Making it clear that discrimination could also be established without reference to a comparator, would enhance the opportunities to find more flexible approaches in national and EU level case law.[53]

EU policy Clearly, legislation is not the only way for the EU to influence or even shape a European socio-legal field. Officially acknowledged since the turn of the century (European Commission 2001; Scott and Trubek 2002), new forms of governance (de Búrca and Scott 2006) are useful for achieving Europeanization, especially in fields where legislating is not possible because of lack of competence or where younger developments require flexibility of approach. Such new forms of governance are characterized by interaction between public and private actors and the establishment of processes enhancing learning and development, as they aim to respond to the increasing complexity of policy fields within the EU (Scott and Trubek 2002: 2). In the field of gender equality, the principle of gender mainstreaming has been used within a number of processes under the 'open method of coordination' (Beveridge and Velluti 2008) and mainstreaming ethnic equality is presently being developed as a new method (Bell 2008c: 43–67). The European policy in the field of race equality has been characterized as a hybrid between governance by binding legislation and through new methods (de Búrca 2006). On the one hand, the protection of human rights should not be entrusted to non-binding policy instruments (de Búrca 2006: 98). On the other hand, societies in 27 very diverse Member States and at European levels will only become convinced of subscribing to anti-racism if the binding instruments are supported by new governance (de Búrca 2006: 118–20). Accordingly, it is not surprising that the European Commission propagates new governance methods as a means of developing effective policies for addressing intersectional disadvantage (European Commission 2008a).

Existing EU Commission activities in the wider field of equality and non-discrimination include the establishment of expert networks, the initiation of capacity building activities such as training and publications, and the funding of non-governmental organizations at EU level. The problem of 'multiple discrimination' has received attention in all three fields. The Commission has funded action studies (European Commission 2007a) and research projects (Carles, Howard and Kofman, in this volume), it has commissioned its expert networks to discuss multiple and intersectional discrimination (Burri and Schiek 2009).

Especially in the field of intersectional disadvantage, the politics of creating enforceable rights should be accompanied by more discursive and reflective activity. As has been stressed above, appropriate legal strategies for combating intersectional disadvantage are yet to be developed. This necessitates capacity building strategies, as well as the mainstreaming of different equality policies into each other. New governance models could also be employed to develop appropriate

---

51   See above footnote 37.
52   Which is similar to stigmatizing, see also Solanke (2009b).
53   For example, in Directive 2000/43/EC, Article 2 2. a) could read: 'direct discrimination shall be taken to occur where one person is treated less favourably on grounds of racial or ethnic origin, for example if treated less favourably than another is, has been or would be treated in a comparable situation'.

modes of positive action to combat intersectional disadvantage (Fredman 2009: 81–5). At present, mainstreaming efforts in new governance policies is focused on mainstreaming gender into the other equalities. Even the youngest directive on gender equality, Directive 2010/41/ EU on equal treatment between men and women engaged in self-employed activity[54] nowhere mentions multiple or intersectional discrimination, despite the fact that women of ethnic minority background are often relegated to self-employed activities because they are not accepted in the employment market.

Which actors to promote legal developments?   We have stressed the need to encourage social actors to engage with intersectional disadvantage if such disadvantage is to be combated successfully. After all, participatory models of policy development have been acknowledged as most suitable for promoting social change (Lenoble and Maeschalck 2010). Accordingly, empowering social actors can be assumed to be an important element of establishing a successful policy combating intersectional disadvantage. The question is where to find such actors.

Admittedly, it is much easier to ask this question than to answer it. Those who have successfully campaigned for any single strand of equality policy will often be opposed to intersectional strategies (Holzleithner 2005: 945). Even before successful campaigning, a social actor's perspective seems to naturally demand 'strategic singularity' (Luft and Ward 2009: 11), which again leads to 'single strand approaches'.

The easiest option to overcome such single-stranded approach is to add specific multi-stranded social actors to the portfolio. In line with this, the Commission has started to support initiatives at certain intersections. Attention is currently focused primarily on Romani women, intersectional discrimination against whom is funded to such an extent as to elicit criticism within Roma organizations (Oprea 2009). In addition to this and to funding European Network Against Racism (ENAR) as the major European anti-racism NGO (Bell 2008c: 78), the Commission has promised to fund 'networks of NGOs representing intersectional groups' (European Commission 2008a: 9).

However, even if the problems associated with a publicly funded civil society (Bell 2008c: 79) are disregarded, the establishment of such specific groups does not seem unproblematic. While allowing for the recognition of some intersectional disadvantage, this approach still requires compartmentalization into different identities. Such compartmentalized strategies seem to reflect a multicultural approach, in that new specific group identities are promoted in order to provide new 'constituencies' as targets for EU equality politics. It raises the question of whether this might again result in acknowledging only certain forms of identity and neglecting others.

A tentative answer to the question; which actors should promote legal development, therefore, could entail the interaction between a policy creating rights and the dynamics that might be hoped to arise from supporting the initiation of combined interest groups in the field of equality and non-discrimination. By effectively lobbying for 'legal opportunity structures' (Evans Case and Givens 2010), the Starting Line Group seems to have succeeded in establishing structures facilitating strategic litigation, but arguably has also set in motion a self-energizing process to create ever more lobbying groups. Widening the perspective towards intersectional disadvantage may well support multi-ground groups or multi-ground coalitions capable of engendering intersectional equality policies in social reality.

---

54   (2010) OJ L 180/1 of 15 July 2010.

Conclusion

The question of whether and to what extent EU law and policy recognize disadvantage at the intersection between gender, race and disability, and provide sufficient support for combating it, can presently only be answered with a decisive 'not yet'. As the fact-finding section above has demonstrated, the EU has only recently started to consider the problem of 'multiple discrimination', and that recognition of this concept has only slowly started to trickle down into legislation and policy documents. Even Court of Justice case law, which has traditionally moved ahead of the legislature, has largely ignored intersectional disadvantage.

We can thus conclude, first, that the appraisal of intersectional discrimination in EU law is uneven, highlighting the relevance of gender-mainstreaming equality politics not focused on gender, but omitting to demand that gender politics adequately address the diversity of women. Second, we can conclude that a legislative appraisal of intersectional and multiple discrimination at EU level would have the potential of propelling the development of the field forward. This would, in our view, depend on this appraisal being normatively open. A premature closure of the debate on defining intersectional discrimination and appropriate remedies would inhibit the incremental development of appropriate principles. Third, some existing obstacles for such incremental development should be removed. These consist of different material scopes and strengths of protection for the three single-strand nodes on which this book focuses ('race', sex and disability), and in the comparator-based definition of discrimination in EU law. Finally, the problem of creating appropriate social actors to combat intersectional disadvantage is a challenge for the future development of this European socio-legal field.

Bibliography

Abdo, A. 2008. The legal status of hijab in the United States: A look at the sociopolitical influences on the legal right to wear the Muslim headscarf. *Hastings Race & Poverty Law Journal*, 5, 441–90.

Abrams, K. 1994. Title VII and the complex female subject. *Michigan Law Review*, 92(8), 2479–540.

Abrams, K. 1995. Sex wars redux: Agency and coercion in feminist legal theory. *Columbia Law Review*, 95, 304–76.

Abrams, K. 1999. From autonomy to agency: Feminist perspectives on self-direction. *William and Mary Law Review*, 40, 805–46.

Ader, W. (ed.) 2006. *Nées en France – Jeunes Musulmanes dans la Societé Laïque*. Stuttgart: Reclam.

Adesioye, L. 2009. Black girls have body issues too – not all of us like being bootylicious. *Guardian* [Online]. 7 April. Available at: www.guardian.co.uk/commentisfree/cifamerica/2009/apr/07/african-american-women-bulimia/print [accessed: 16 June 2009].

Advisory Board for Ethnic Relations. 2002. *Suomen venäjänkielisen väestönosan kysymyksiä*. Helsinki: Venäjän ja Itä-Euroopan instituutti.

Advisory Committee on Equal Opportunities for Women and Men. 2007. *Opinion on the Gender Dimension of the Inclusion of Ethnic Minorities* [Online]. Available at: www.frauen.bka.gv.at/DocView.axd?CobId=30036 [accessed: 31 May 2009].

Ahdar, R. and Leigh, I. 2005. *Religious Freedom in the Liberal State*. Oxford: Oxford University Press.

Ahmad, W.I.U. (ed.) 2000. *Ethnicity, Disability and Chronic Illness*. Buckingham: Open University Press.

Ahmad, W.I.U., Darr, A. and Jones, L. 2000. I send my child to school and he comes back an Englishman: Minority ethnic deaf people, identity politics and services, in *Ethnicity, Disability and Chronic Illness*, edited by W.I.U. Ahmad. Buckingham: Open University Press, 67–4.

Ahmed, S. 2008. The politics of good feeling. *Australian Critical Race and Whiteness Studies Association ejournal*, 4(1), 1–17 [Online]. Available at: www.acrawsa.org.au/ejournal.htm [accessed: 19 February 2010].

Aikio-Puoskari, U. and Pentikäinen, M. 2001. *The Language Rights of the Indigenous Saami in Finland: Under Domestic and International Law*. Rovaniemi: Northern Institute for Environmental and Minority Law.

Akandji-Kombé, J.-F. 2005. The material impact of the jurisprudence of the European Committee of Social Rights, in *Social Rights in Europe*, edited by G. de Búrca and B. de Witte. Oxford: Oxford University Press, 89–108.

Alba, R. 2005. Bright vs. blurred boundaries: Second generation assimilation and exclusion in France, Germany and the United States. *Ethnic and Racial Studies*, 28(1), 20–49.

Alexy, R. 2002. *A Theory of Constitutional Rights*. Oxford: Oxford University Press.

Allport, G.H. 1979. *The Nature of Prejudice*. 25th anniversary edition. Cambridge, MA: Perseus Books.

AlSayyad, N. and Castells, M. (eds) 2002. *Muslim Europe or Euro-Islam – Politics, Culture, and Citizenship in the Age of Globalisation*. Lanham, MD: Rowman & Littlefield.

Alston, P. 2005. Assessing the strengths and weaknesses of the European Social Charter's supervisory system, in *Social Rights in Europe*, edited by G. de Búrca and B. de Witte. Oxford: Oxford University Press, 45–68.

Alter, K. 2009. *The European Court's Political Power*. Oxford: Oxford University Press.

Anagnostou, D. and Psychogiopoulou, E. 2008. *Supranational Rights Litigation, Implementation and the Domestic Impact of Strasbourg Court Jurisprudence: A Case Study of Greece*, ELIAMEP [Online]. Available at: www.juristras.eliamep.gr/wp-content/uploads/2008/09/casestudygreece.pdf [accessed: 20 May 2009].

Anagnostou, D. and Triandafyllidou, A. 2007. Regions, minorities and European integration: A case study on the Muslims in Thrace. *Romanian Journal of Political Science*, 6(1), 101–26.

Angelopoulos, G. 1997. From the Greek as person to the person as Greek: An anthropological view of the construction of ethnic identities in rural Macedonia in the late 19th – early 20th centuries [in Greek]. *Elliniki Epitheorisi Politikis Epistimis*, 9, 42–61.

Anthias, F. 1990. Race and class revisited: Conceptualising race and racisms. *Sociological Review*, 38(3), 19–42.

Anthias, F. 2001. New hybridities, old concepts: The limits of 'culture'. *Ethnic and Racial Studies*, 24(4), 619–41.

Anthias, F. and Lloyd, C. (eds) 2002. *Rethinking Anti-racisms*. London: Routledge.

Anthias, F. and Yuval-Davis, N. 1983. Contextualizing feminism: Gender, ethnic and class divisions. *Feminist Review*, 15, 62–75.

Anthias, F. and Yuval-Davis, N., in association with Cain, H. 1993. *Racialised Boundaries*. London: Routledge.

Arabatzi, T. 2008. *Women and Men as Depicted in the Turkish Language School Textbooks of the Minority Education in Western Thrace* [in Greek], postgraduate thesis [Online: Aristotle University of Thessaloniki]. Available at: http://cds.lib.auth.gr/submit/archive/Griza/gri-2009-2232.pdf [accessed: 20 May 2009].

Aral, B. 2004. The idea of human rights as perceived in the Ottoman Empire. *Human Rights Quarterly*, 26, 454–82.

Arnade, S. and Häfner, S. 2005. Towards visibility of women with disabilities in the UN Convention. *International Rehabilitation Review*, 55(1), 16–9.

Arnadóttir, O.M. 2009. Multidimensional equality from within: Themes from the European Convention on Human Rights, in *European Union Non-Discrimination Law: Comparative Perspectives on Multidimensional Equality Law*, edited by D. Schiek and V. Chege. Abingdon: Routledge-Cavendish, 53–90.

Arnadóttir, O.M. and Quinn, G. (eds) 2009. *The UN Convention on the Rights of Persons with Disabilities: European and Scandinavian Perspectives*. Leiden and Boston, MA: Martinus Nijhoff.

Artinopoulou, V., Farsedakis, I., Papagiannopoulou, M., Zoulinaki, A., Katsiki, G., Ksydopoulou, E. and Papamihail, S. 2003. *Domestic Violence Against Women: First Pan-Hellenic Epidemiological Research* [in Greek]. Athens: Research Centre for Equality Issues (K.E.TH.I.).

Asch, A. 2001. Critical race theory, feminism, and disability: Reflections on social justice and personal identity. *Ohio State Law Journal*, 62, 391–415.

Ashiagbor, D. 1999. The intersection between gender and 'race' in the labour market: Lessons for anti-discrimination law, in *Feminist Perspectives in Employment Law*, edited by A. Morris and T. O'Donnell. London: Cavendish, 139–60.

Asimakopoulou, F. and Hristidou-Lionaraki, S. 2002. *The Muslim Minority of Thrace and Greek-Turkish Relations* [in Greek]. Athens: Livanis Publications.

Aspinall, P.J. 2007. Approaches to developing an improved cross-national understanding of concepts and terms relating to ethnicity and race. *International Sociology*, 22(1), 41–70.

Asscher-Vonk, I.P. 2007. De interactie tussen de Commissie Gelijke Behandeling en de rechter. *Sociaal Maandblad Arbeid*, 6, 225–9.

Asscher-Vonk, I.P. and Hendriks, A.C. 2005. *Gelijke behandeling en onderscheid bij de arbeid.* 2nd edition. Deventer: Kluwer.

Assier-Andrieu, L. and Gotman, A. 2004. *Immigration et accès aux droits sociaux: Enquête sur les logiques discirminatoires dans la mise en oeuvre de la CMU*. Paris: ADRI, Cepel, FASILD.

Attaőv, T. 1992. The ethnic Turkish minority in Western Thrace, Greece. *The Turkish Yearbook*, XII, 89–99.

Aybars, A.I. and Tsarouhas, D. 2010. Straddling two continents: Social policy and welfare politics in Turkey. *Social Policy and Administration, Special Issue on Welfare and Social Policy in the Middle East*, 44(6), 746–63.

Baer, S. 2008. Ungleichheit der Gleichheiten? Zur Hierarchisierung von Diskriminierungsverboten, in *Universalität – Schutzmechanismen – Diskriminierungsverbote. 15 Jahre Wiener Weltmenschenrechtskonferenz*, edited by E. Klein and C. Menke. Berlin: BWV Berliner Wissenschafts-Verlag, 421–50.

Bagenstos, S.R. 2006. The structural turn and limits of antidiscrimination law. *California Law Review*, 94(1), 1–47.

Bailleau, G. and Trespeux, F. 2008. Les bénéficiaires de l'aide sociale départementale en 2007. *Etudes et Résultats*, No. 656, September 2008.

Balibar, E. and Wallerstein, I. 1991. *Race, Nation, Class: Ambiguous Identities*. London: Verso.

Bano, S. 2007. Islamic family arbitration, justice and human rights in Britain. *Law, Social Justice & Global Development Journal*, 2007 (1) [Online]. Available at: www.go.warwick.ac.uk/elj/lgd/2007_1/bano [accessed: 29 January 2009].

Banton, M. 1992. The nature and causes of racism and racial discrimination. *International Sociology*, 17(1), 69–84.

Banton, M. 2002. *The International Politics of Race*. Cambridge: Polity Press.

Banton, M. and Hirsch, M. 2000. *Double Invisibility: A Study into the Needs of Black Disabled People in Warwickshire*. Leamington Spa: Council of Disabled People, Warwickshire.

Banton, M. and Singh, G. 2004. 'Race', disability and oppression, in *Disabling Barriers – Enabling Environments*, edited by J. Swain, S. French, C. Barnes and C. Thomas. 2nd edition. London: Sage, 111–17.

Barile, M. 2000. Understanding the personal and political role of multiple minority status. *Disability Studies Quarterly*, 20(2), 123.

Barnes, C. 1990. *The Cabbage Syndrome: The Social Construction of Dependence*. London, New York and Philadelphia, PA: Falmer Press.

Barnes, C. 2000. A working social model? Disability, work and disability politics in the 21st century. *Critical Social Policy*, 20(4), 441–57.

Barnes, C. and Mercer, G. 2003. *Disability*. Malden, MA: Polity Press.

Barou, J., Deroche, L., Maguer, A. and Viprey, M. 2003. *Les discriminations des jeunes d'origine étrangère dans l'accès à l'emploi et l'accès au logement.* Paris: La Documentation française (Études et recherche).

Bartow, A. 2006. *Thin Air* [Online: Feminist Law Professor]. Available at: http://feministlawprofs. law.sc.edu/?p=1208 [accessed: 18 September 2009].

Basdevant-Gaudemet, B. 2005. Staat und Kirche in Frankreich, in *Staat und Kirche in der Europäischen Union*, edited by G. Robbers. Baden-Baden: Nomos.

Bataille, P. 1997. *Le racisme au travail.* Paris: La Découverte.

Baubérot, J. 2004. Voile, école, femmes, laïcité, in *Le Voile, Que Cache-t-il?*, edited by J. Baubérot, D. Bouzar and J. Costa-Lascoux. Paris: Les Éditions de l'Atelier/Les Éditions Ouvrières, 49–78.

Baubérot, J. 2007. *Histoire de la Laïcité en France.* Paris: PUF.

Baubérot, J., Bouzar, D. and Costa-Lascoux, J. (eds) 2004. *Le Voile, Que Cache-t-il?* Paris: Les Éditions de l'Atelier/Les Éditions Ouvrières.

BBC Caribbean 2010. *BBC Caribbean News in Brief* [Online: BBC Caribbean]. Available at: www.bbc.co.uk/caribbean/news/story/2010/04/100422_april22am.shtml [accessed: 20 June 2010].

BBC News. 2007. Obesity 'not individuals fault'. *BBC News Online* [Online], 17 October. Available at: http://news.bbc.co.uk/1/hi/health/7047244.stm-[accessed: 17 June 2009].

Begum, N., Hill, M. and Stevens, A. (eds) 1994. *Reflections: Views of Black Disabled People on their Lives and Community Care.* London: Central Council for the Education and Training of Social Work.

Beleza, M.L. 2003. *Discrimination Against Women with Disabilities.* Strasbourg: Council of Europe Publishing.

Bell, M. 2002. *Anti-Discrimination Law and the European Union.* Oxford: Oxford University Press.

Bell, M. 2004. *Anti-Discrimination Law and the European Union.* 2nd edition. Oxford: Oxford University Press.

Bell, M. 2007. Direct discrimination, in *Cases, Materials and Text on International, Supranational and National Non-Discrimination Law*, edited by D. Schiek, L. Waddington and M. Bell. Oxford and Portland, OR: Hart, 185–322.

Bell, M. 2008a. Advancing EU Anti-Discrimination Law: The European Commission's 2008 proposal for a new directive. *The Equal Rights Review*, 3, 7–18.

Bell, M. 2008b. EU anti-racism policy – the leader of the pack?, in *Equality Law in an Enlarged European Union*, edited by H. Meenan. Cambridge: Cambridge University Press, 178–201.

Bell, M. 2008c. *Racism and Equality in the European Union.* Oxford: Oxford University Press.

Bell, M. and Waddington, L. 2001. More equal than others: Distinguishing European Union equality directives. *Common Market Law Review*, 38(3), 587–611.

Bell, M. and Waddington, L. 2003. Reflecting on inequalities in European equality law. *European Law Review*, 28(3), 349–69.

Bell, M.P. and McLaughlin, M.E. 2006. Outcomes of appearance and obesity in organizations, in *Handbook of Workplace Diversity*, edited by A.M. Konrad, P. Prasad and J.K. Pringle. London: Sage, 455–74.

Bell, M.P., McLaughlin, M.E. and Sequeira, J.M. 2003. Age, disability and obesity: Similarities, differences and common threads, in *The Psychology and Management of Workplace Diversity*, edited by M.S. Stockdale and F.J. Crosby. Malden, MA: Blackwell Publishing, 191–205.

Ben Mohamed, N. 2001. Les femmes musulmanes voilées d'origine marocaine sur le marché de l'emploi: Lettre d'information – TEF. *Centre de Sociologie du Travail et de la Formation*, n. 3–4, 1–23.

Benedict, R. 1983 [1942]. *Race and Racism*. London, Melbourne and Henley: Routledge & Kegan Paul.

Beng-Huat, C. 2005. When difference becomes an instrument of social regulation. *Ethnicities*, 5(3), 418–21.

Benhabib, S. (ed.) 2006. *Another Cosmopolitanism*. Oxford: Oxford University Press.

Berghahn, S. 2009. Deutschlands konfrontativer Umgang mit dem Kopftuch der Lehrerin, in *Der Stoff aus dem Konflikte sind – Debatten um das Kopftuch in Deutschland, Österreich und der Schweiz*, edited by S. Berghahn and P. Rostock. Bielefeld: transcript Verlag, 33–79.

Berghahn, S. and Rostock, P. (eds) 2009. *Der Stoff aus dem Konflikte sind – Debatten um das Kopftuch in Deutschland, Österreich und der Schweiz*. Bielefeld: transcript Verlag.

Berthoud, R. 2003. *Multiple Disadvantage in Employment: A Quantitative Analysis*. York: Joseph Rowntree Foundation.

Berthoud, R., Lakey, J. and McKay, S. 1993. *The Economic Problems of Disabled People*. London: Policy Studies Institute.

Bertrams, M. 2003. Lehrerin mit Kopftuch? Islamismus und Menschenbild des Grundgesetzes. *Deutsches Verwaltungsblatt*, 113, 1225–33.

Beveridge, F. and Velluti, S. 2008. *Gender and the Open Method of Coordination: Perspectives on Law, Governance and Equality in the EU*. Aldershot: Ashgate.

Bhabha, H.K. 1994. The other question: Stereotype, discrimination and the discourse of colonialism, in *The Location of Culture*, edited by H.K. Bhabha. London and New York: Routledge, 66–84.

Bhavnani, R. 1994. *Black Women in the Labour Market: A Research Review*. Manchester: Equal Opportunities Commission.

Bhavnani, R., Mirza, H.S. and Meetoo, V. 2005. *Tackling the Roots of Racism: Lessons for Success*. Bristol: Policy Press.

Bhopal, K. 1998. How gender and ethnicity intersect: The significance of education, employment and marital status. *Sociological Research Online*, 3(3), 1–14 [Online]. Available at: www.socresonline. org.uk [accessed: 19 February 2010].

Bielby, W.T. 2003a. Can I get a witness? Challenges of using expert testimony on cognitive bias in employment discrimination litigation. *Employee Rights & Employment Policy Journal*, 7(2), 377–400.

Bielby, W.T. 2003b. Expert Report of William T. Bielby, PhD in *Betty Dukes, et al. v. Wal-Mart Stores, Inc.* (on file with author).

Bignall, T. and Butt, J. 2000. *Between Ambition and Achievement, Young Black Disabled Peoples Experiences and Views of Independent and Independent Living*. Bristol: Policy Press/Joseph Rowntree Foundation.

Black, C.L. 1960. *The People and the Court: Judicial Review in a Democracy*. New York: Macmillan.

Blakely, R. 2009. Air hostesses fired as airlines plump for svelte staff. *The Times*, 6 January, 35.

Blasi, G. 2002. Advocacy against the stereotype: Lessons from cognition psychology. *University of California-Los Angeles Law Review*, 49(5), 1241–82.

Bobo, L. 1999. Prejudice as group position: Microfoundations of a sociological approach to racism and race relations. *Journal of Social Issues*, 55, 445–72.

Bodewig, C. and Sethi, A. 2005. *Poverty, Social Exclusion and Ethnicity in Serbia and Montenegro: the Case of the Roma*. Washington, DC: World Bank.

Borgida, E. and Kim, A. 2007. Reflections on being an expert witness, in *Sex Discrimination in the Workplace: Multidisciplinary Perspectives*, edited by F. Crosby, M. Stockdale and S. Ropp. Malden, MA: Blackwell Publishing, 117–29.

Boumaza, N. 2003. *Relations interethniques dans l'habitat et la ville: Agir contre la discrimination et promouvoir les cultures résidentielles*. Paris: L'Harmattan.

Bourdieu, P. 1998. *On Television*. Translated by P. Parkhurst Ferguson. New York: New Press.

Bowen, J.R. 2006. *Why the French Don't like Headscarves – Islam, the State and Public Space*. Princeton, NJ: Princeton University Press.

Bowen, J.R. 2007. A view from France on the internal complexity of national models. *Journal of Ethnic and Migration Studies*, 33(6), 1003–16.

Bowen, J.R. 2009. Recognising Islam in France after 9/11. *Journal of Ethnic and Migration Studies*, 35(3), 439–52.

Bowers QC, J. and Moran, E. 2002. Justification in direct sex discrimination law: Breaking the taboo. *Industrial Law Journal*, 31(4), 307–20.

Boylan, E. (ed.) 1991. *Women and Disability*. London: Zed Books.

Boyle, K. and Sheen, J. 1997. *Freedom of Religion and Belief – A World Report*. London: Routledge.

Brah, A. 1993. Race and culture in the gendering of labour markets: South Asian young Muslim women and the labour market. *New Community*, 19(3), 441–58.

Brah, A. 1996. *Cartographies of Diaspora – Contesting Identities*. London: Routledge.

Braithwaite, J. and Mont, D. 2008. *Disability and Poverty: A Survey of World Bank Poverty Assessments and Implications*. SP Discussion Paper No 0805. Washington, DC: World Bank.

Bray, G. 1996. Coherent, preventive and management strategies for obesity, in *The Origins and Consequences of Obesity*, edited by D. Chadwick and G. Cardew. Ciba Foundation Symposium 201. Chicester: John Wiley and Sons, 228–54.

Brenner, E. (ed.) 2002. *Les territoires perdus de la république: Antisémitisme, racisme et sexisme en milieu scolaire*. Paris: Mille et une mois.

Bribosia, E. and Rorive I. 2004. Le voile à l'école: Une Europe divisée. *Revue trimestrielle des droits de l'homme*, 941–73

Brillat, R. 2005. The supervisory machinery of the European Social Charter: Recent developments and their impact, in *Social Rights in Europe*, edited by G. de Búrca and B. de Witte. Oxford: Oxford University Press, 31–44.

Brion, F. and Manço, U. 1998. Exclusion and the job market: An empirical approach to Muslim women's situation in Belgium. *Muslim Voices*, European Commission, Brussels, 18–19.

Brittain, E., Dustin, H., Pearce, C., Rake, K., Siyunyi-Siluwe, M. and Sullivan, F. 2005. *Black and Minority Ethnic Women in the UK. 2005* [Online: Fawcett Society]. Available at: www.fawcettsociety.org.uk/index.asp?PageID=46 [accessed: 15 July 2010].

Britz, G. 2003. Das verfassungsrechtliche Dilemma doppelter Fremdheit: Islamische Bekleidungsvorschriften für Frauen und Grundgesetz. *Kritische Justiz*, 36(1), 95–102.

Bugra, A. and Keyder, C. 2006. Turkish welfare regime in transformation. *Journal of European Social Policy*, 16(3), 211–28.

Bulmer, M. and Solomos, J. (eds) 1999. *Racism*. Oxford: Oxford University Press.

Bunglawala, Z. 2008. *Valuing Family, Valuing Work – British Muslims, Women and the Labour Market*. London: Development Agency Report.

Burri, S. and Prechal, P. 2008. *EU Gender Equality Law* [Online: Luxembourg: Office for Official Publications of the European Communities]. Available at: http://ec.europa.eu/social/main.jsp?catId=641&langId=en and at: http://bookshop.europa.eu/eubookshop/advancedSearch!firstPage.action [accessed: 20 January 2010].

Burri, S. and Schiek, D. 2009. *Multiple Discrimination in EU Law: Opportunities for Legal Responses to Intersectional Gender Discrimination?* European Network of Legal Experts in the Field of Gender Equality [Online: European Commission]. Available at: http://ec.europa.eu/social/main.jsp?catld=641&langld=en&moreDocuments=yes [accessed: 25 November 2010].

Byrne, B. 2009. Not just class: Towards an understanding of the whiteness of middle-class schooling choice. *Ethnic and Racial Studies*, 32(3), 424–41.

Campbell, J. and Oliver, M. 1996. *Disability Politics: Understanding our Past, Changing our Future*. New York: Routledge.

Carbado, D.W. and Gulati, M. 2000. Working identity. *Cornell Law Review*, 85(5), 1259–308.

Carbado, D.W. and Harris, C.I. 2008. The new racial preferences. *California Law Review*, 96(5), 1139–214.

Carle, S. 2005. Theorizing agency. *American University Law Review*, 55, 307–93.

Carles, I. 2008. L'élaboration des politiques publiques de lutte contre les discriminations raciales: Trois exemples européens (Actes du 2° Congrès de l'Association Française de Sociologie, in *Revue en ligne Asylon(s)* n 5).

Castles, S. 2000. *Ethnicity and Globalisation: From Migrant Worker to Transnational Citizen*. London: Sage.

Cavanaugh, K. 2007. Islam and the European project. *Muslim World Journal of Human Rights*, 4(1), 1–20.

CEDAW. 1997. *Third Periodic Report of States Parties: Finland*. CEDAW/C/FIN/3. Geneva: United Nations.

CEDAW. 2002. *Report of the Committee on the Elimination of Discrimination against Women, Twenty-sixth session (14 January–1 February 2002), Twenty-seventh session (3–21 June 2002), Exceptional session (5–23 August 2002), General Assembly Official Records Fifty-seventh Session, Supplement No. 38 (A/57/38)*. New York: United Nations.

CEDAW. 2004. *Fifth Periodic Report of States Parties: Finland*. CEDAW/C/FIN/5. Geneva: United Nations.

CEDAW. 2007. *Summary Record of the 768th Meeting (Chamber A), Held at Headquarters, New York, on Wednesday, 24 January 2007*. CEDAW/C/SR.768 (A) [Online: UNHCHR]. Available at: www.unhchr.ch/tbs/doc.nsf/c12563e7005d936d4125611e00445ea9/09ac31e054c40587c12572d5004f8196/$FILE/N0721946.pdf [accessed: 1 March 2009].

CEDAW. 2008. *Report of the Committee on the Elimination of Discrimination against Women*. A/63/38. Geneva: United Nations.

Cesari, J. and McLoughlin, S. (eds) 2005. *European Muslims and the Secular State*. Aldershot: Ashgate.

Chalmers, D., Davies, G. and Monti, G. 2010. *European Union Law*. 2nd edition. Cambridge: Cambridge University Press.

Chamba, R., Hirst, M., Lawron, D., Ahmad, W. and Beresford, P. 1999. *Expert Voices: A National Survey of Minority Ethnic Parents Caring for a Disabled Child*. Bristol: The Policy Press.

Chang, R.S. and Culp, Jr. J.M. 2002. After intersectionality. *University of Missouri-Kansas City Law Review*, 71(2), 485–92.

Chen, R. and Hanson, J. 2004. Categorically biased: The influence of knowledge structures on law and legal theory. *Southern California Law Review*, 77(6), 1103–254.

Chignier Riboulon, F. (ed.) 2003. *Les discriminations quant à l'accès au logement locatif privé des catégories sociales moyennes étrangères ou perçues comme étrangères: Une étude réalisée à partir des quartiers lyonnais et parisiens*. Paris: FASILD.

Circulaire, *JORF No.118* du 22 mai 2004, .9033.

Clarke, L. 2007. Sexual harassment law in the United States, the United Kingdom and the European Union: Discriminatory wrongs and dignitary harms. *Common Law World Review*, 36(2), 79–105.

Clements, L. 2004. *Litigating Cases on Behalf of Roma Before the Court and Commission in Strasbourg* [Online]. Available at: www.errc.org/cikk.php?cikk=487 [accessed: 23 June 2009].

Clermont, K. and Eisenberg, T. 2002. Plaintiphobia in the appellate courts: Civil rights really do differ from negotiable instruments. *University of Illinois Law Review*, 2002(4), 947–78.

Clermont, K. and Schwab, S. 2004. How employment discrimination plaintiffs fare in federal court. *Journal of Empirical Legal Studies*, 1(2), 444–58.

Colley, L. 1994. *Britons – Forging the Nation 1707–1837*. London: Vintage.

Commissie Gelijke Behandeling. 2007. *Equal Treatment Commission. Annual Report 2007* [Online: Commissie Gelijke Behandeling]. Available at: www.cgb.nl/artikel/publications [accessed: 25 November 2010].

Commissie Gelijke Behandeling. 2008. *Equal Treatment Commission. Annual Report 2008* [Online: Commissie Gelijke Behandeling]. Available at: http://cgb.nl/node/14861 [accessed: 17 December 2009].

Committee of Ministers. 2006. Recommendation CM/Rec(2006)5 of the Committee of Ministers to member states on the Council of Europe Action Plan to promote the rights and full participation of people with disabilities in society: Improving the quality of life of people with disabilities in Europe 2006–2015.

Committee of Ministers. 2007a. Recommendation CM/Rec(2007)17 of the Committee of Ministers to member states on gender equality standards and mechanisms.

Committee of Ministers. 2007b. Explanatory Memorandum CM(2007)153 add to the draft Recommendation of the Committee of Ministers to member states on gender equality standards and mechanisms, paras 181 and 182.

Communities. 2008. SEC (2008) 2180 – Commission Staff Working Document accompanying the proposal for a Council Directive on implementing the principle of equal treatment between persons irrespective of religion or belief, disability, age or sexual orientation. Brussels: European Commission.

Conaghan, J. 2009. Intersectionality and the feminist project in law, in *Intersectionality and Beyond: Law Power and the Politics of Location*, edited by E. Grabham, D. Cooper, J. Krishnadas and D. Herman. London and New York: Routledge-Cavendish, 21–48.

Conference for Security and Cooperation in Europe. 1992. *Helsinki Document 1992: The Challenges of Change. Decision II: CSCE High Commissioner on National Minorities* [Online]. Available at: www.minelres.lv/osce/heldec1.htm [accessed: 4 July 2009].

Conniff Taber, K. *Isolation Awaits French Girls in Headscarves* [Online: Women's e-News, 3 March 2004]. Available at: www.womensenews.org/article.cfm/dyn/aid/1738 [accessed: 7 June 2009].

Corsi, M., Crepaldi, M., Samek Lodovici, M., Boccagni, R. and Vasilescu, C. 2008. *Ethnic Minority and Roma Women in Europe: A Case for Gender Equality?* [Online: European

Commission]. Available at: ec.europa.eu/social/BlobServlet?docId=4833&langId=en [accessed: 8 July 2009].

Costa-Lascoux, J. 2004. La loi nécessaire, in *Le Voile, Que Cache-t-il?*, edited by J. Baubérot, D. Bouzar and J. Costa-Lascoux. Paris: Les Éditions de l'Atelier/Les Éditions Ouvrières, 79–99.

Council. 2000a. Council of the European Union, *Outcome of Proceedings of the Social Questions Working Party*, 6435/00, Brussels, 1 March.

Council. 2000b. Council of the European Union, *Outcome of Proceedings of the Social Questions Working Party*, 6942/00, Brussels, 31 March.

Council. 2000c. Council of the European Union, *Outcome of Proceedings of the Social Questions Working Party*, 8454/00, Brussels, 16 May.

Council of Europe. 2000. *Opinion on Finland, Adopted on 22 September 2000 by the Advisory Committee on the Framework Convention for the Protection of National Minorities*. ACFC/INF/OP/I(2001)002. Strasbourg: Council of Europe.

Council of Europe. 2001a. *Committee of Experts Evaluation Report on the Application of the European Charter of Regional or Minority Languages in Finland*. ECRML (2001)3. Strasbourg: Council of Europe.

Council of Europe. 2001b. *Resolution ResCMN(2001)3 on the Implementation of the Framework Convention for the Protection of National Minorities by Finland*. Strasbourg: Council of Europe.

Council of Europe. 2006. *Second Opinion on Finland, Adopted on 2 March 2006 by the Advisory Committee on the Framework Convention for the Protection of National Minorities*. ACFC/OP/II(2006)003. Strasbourg: Council of Europe.

Council of Europe. 2007. *Resolution CM/ResCMN(2007)1 on the Implementation of the Framework Convention for the Protection of National Minorities by Finland*. Strasbourg: Council of Europe.

Council of Europe. 2009. *Spain Hosts Council of Europe Conference on Women and Disabilities*. Press Release 105(2009). Strasbourg: Council of Europe.

Crawford, D. and Jeffery, R. (eds) 2005. *Obesity Prevention and Public Health*. Oxford: Oxford University Press.

Cremers-Hartman, E. 2004. *Gelijke behandeling bij de arbeid in zes wetten. Een actueel overzicht van hoofdlijnen, overeenkomsten en verschillen*. PS Special 2004(5). Deventer: Kluwer.

Crenshaw, K. 1988–90. Foreword: Toward a race-conscious pedagogy in legal education. *National Black Law Journal*, 11(1), 1–14.

Crenshaw, K. 1989. Demarginalizing the intersection of race and sex: A black feminist critique of antidiscrimination doctrine, feminist theory and antiracial polities. *University of Chicago Legal Forum*, 139–67.

Crenshaw, K. 1991. Mapping the margins: Intersectionality, identity politics, and violence against women of color. *Stanford Law Review*, 43(6), 1241–99.

Crenshaw, K. 1991–2. Race, gender and sexual harassment. *Southern California Law Review*, 65, 1467–76.

Crenshaw, K. 2000. Demarginalizing the intersection of race and sex: A black feminist critique of antidiscrimination doctrine, feminist theory and antiracist politics, in *The Black Feminist Reader*, edited by J. James and T. Sharpley-Whiting. Oxford and Malden, MA: Blackwell, 208–38.

Critser, G. 2003. *Fat Land: How Americans Became the Fattest People in the World*. London: Penguin.

Crowley, H. and Hickman, M.J. 2008. Migration, postindustrialism and the globalized nation-state: Social capital and social cohesion re-examined. *Ethnic and Racial Studies*, 31(7), 1222–44.

CRPD. 2009. *Guidelines on Treaty-Specific Document to be Submitted by States Parties under Article 35, paragraph 1, of the Convention on the Rights of Persons with Disabilities 18 November 2009* [Online]. Available at: www.ohchr.org/Documents/HRBodies/CRPD/CRPD-C-2-3.pdf [accessed: 20 July 2010].

Czermak, G. 2004. Kopftuch, neutralität und ideologie. *Neue Zeitschrift für Verwaltungsrecht*, 23(8), 943–5.

Damjanovic, D. and De Witte, B. 2009. Welfare integration through EU law: The overall picture in the light of the Lisbon Treaty, in *Integrating Welfare Functions into EU Law: From Rome to Lisbon*, edited by U. Neergaard, R. Nielsen and L. Roseberry. Copenhagen: DJOF Publishing, 53–94.

DARES. 2003. L'emploi des personnes handicapées ou ayant des problèmes de santé de longue durée, *Premières Synthèses Informations*, No. 41.3, October. Paris: Ministère des affaires sociales, du travail et de la solidarité.

De Búrca, G. 2006. EU race discrimination law – a hybrid model?, in *Law and New Governance in the EU and the US*, edited by G. de Búrca and J. Scott. Oxford and Portland, OR: Hart, 97–119.

De Búrca, G. 2010. The European Union in the negotiation of the UN Disability Convention. *European Law Review*, 35(2), 174–96.

De Búrca, G. and Scott, S. 2006. Introduction, in *Law and New Governance in the EU and the US*, edited by G. de Búrca and J. Scott. Oxford and Portland, OR: Hart, 1–12.

De Schutter, O. 2005. *Social Affairs and Equal Opportunities, the Prohibition of Discrimination under European Human Rights Law – Relevance for EU Racial and Employment Equality Directives*. Luxembourg: European Commission, DG for Employment.

De Schutter, O. and Deakin, S. (eds) 2005. *Social Rights and Market Forces: Is the Open Co-ordination of Employment and Social Policies the Future of Social Europe?* Brussels: Bruylant.

De Varennes, F. 1996. *Language, Minorities and Human Rights*. The Hague: Martinus Nijhoff.

De Wenden, C. and Body-Gendrot, S. 2003. *Police et discriminations raciales: Le tabou français*. Paris: Editions de l'Atelier.

De Witte, B. 2009. The crumbling public/private divide: Horizontality in European anti-discrimination law. *Citizenship Studies*, 13(5), 515–25.

Debus, A. 2001. Machen Kleider wirklich Leute – Warum der 'Kopftuch-Streit' so spannend ist. *Neue Zeitschrift für Verwaltungsrecht*, 20, 1355–60.

Degener, T. 2001. Disabled women and international human rights, in *Women and International Human Rights Law*, edited by K.D. Askin and D.M. Koenig. New York: Transnational, 267–82.

Degener, T. 2005. Disability discrimination law: A global comparative approach, in *Disability Rights in Europe: From Theory to Practice*, edited by C. Gooding and A. Lawson. Oxford and Portland, OR: Hart, 87–106.

Degener, T. 2008. Zur Erforderlichkeit der Ausdifferenzierung des Diskriminierungsverbotes, in *Universalität – Schutzmechanismen – Diskriminierungsverbote. 15 Jahre Wiener Weltmenschenrechtskonferenz*, edited by E. Klein and C. Menke. Berlin: BWV Berliner Wissenschafts-Verlag, 373–95.

Degener, T. 2009. Welche legislativen Herausforderungen bestehen in Bezug auf die nationale Implementierung der UN-Behindertenrechtskonvention in Bund und Ländern? *Behindertenrecht*, (2), 34–52.

Degener, T., Dern, S., Dieball, H., Oberlies, D., Frings, D. and Zinsmeister, J. 2008. *Antidiskriminierungsrecht Handbuch für Lehre und Beratungspraxis mit Lösungsbeispielen für typische Fallgestaltungen*. Frankfurt: Fachhochschulverlag.

Delgado, R. (ed.) 1995. *Critical Race Theory: The Cutting Edge*. Philadelphia, PA: Temple University Press.

Department for Work and Pensions. 2006. *Households Below Average Income 1994/5–2004/5*. London: Department for Work and Pensions.

Despouy, L. 1992. *Human Rights and Disabled Persons*, Human Rights Studies Series No 6. Geneva: UN Publications.

Dijker, A. and Koomen, W. 2007. *Stigmatization, Tolerance and Repair*. Cambridge: Cambridge University Press.

Disability Rights Commission. 2004. *Our Rights, Our Choices: Meeting the Information Needs of Black and Minority Ethnic Disabled People – Laying the Foundations for Black and Minority Ethnic Disability Organisations* [Online: Disability Rights Commission]. Available at: http://www.leeds.ac.uk/disability-studies/archiveuk/DRC/DRC.html [accessed: 8 December 2010].

Discrimination Law Association. 2009. *Equality Bill: Assessing the Impact of a Multiple Discrimination Provision: Reply to Consultation* [Online]. Available at: www.discriminationlaw.org.uk/node/328#attachments [accessed: 15 July 2010].

Discrimination Law Review. 2007. *A Framework for Fairness: Proposals for a Single Equality Bill for Great Britain – A Consultation Paper* [Online]. Available at: www.communities.gov.uk/documents/corporate/pdf/325332.pdf [accessed: 20 June 2010].

Djavann, C. 2006. Bas les voiles!, in *Nées en France – Jeunes Musulmanes dans la Societé Laïque*, edited by W. Ader. Stuttgart: Reclam.

Dobson, R. and Jones, L. 2005. Overweight girls face a lifetime of discrimination and low pay. *Independent on Sunday* [Online], 18 September. Available at: www.independent.co.uk/news/uk/this-britain/overweight-girls-face-lifetime-of-discrimination-and-low-pay-507331.html [assessed: 20 July 2010].

Dodds, C., Keogh, P., Chime, O., Haruperi, T., Nabulya, B., Sersuma, W. and Weatherburn, P. 2004. *Outsider Status: Stigma and Discrimination Experienced by Gay Men and African People with HIV*. London: Sigma Research and NAT.

Donohue III, J.J. 1986. Is Title VII efficient? *University of Pennsylvania Law Review*, 134(6), 1411–31.

Doyle, B. 2008. *Disability Discrimination: Law and Practice*. London: Jordans.

Driedger, D. and Gray, S. (eds) 1992. *Imprinting our Image: An International Anthology by Women with Disabilities*. Charlottetown: Gynergy Books.

Duncan, B. and Berman-Bieler, R. 1998. *International Leadership Forum for Women with Disabilities: Final Report*. New York: Rehabilitation International.

Eaton, M. 1994. Patently confused, complex inequality and Canada v Mossop. *Rev. Cons. Stud.*, 1, 203–29.

ECRI. 1997. *Report on Finland*. CRI(97)51. Strasbourg: Council of Europe.

ECRI. 2001. *Practical Examples in Combating Racism and Intolerance Against Roma/Gypsies* [Online]. Available at: www.coe.int/t/dghl/monitoring/ecri/Good_practices/3-Roma_Gypsies/CRI(2001)28.pdf [accessed: 25 May 2009].

ECRI. 2002. *Second Report on Finland*. CRI(2002)20. Strasbourg: Council of Europe.

ECRI. 2007. *Third Report on Finland*. CRI(2007)23. Strasbourg: Council of Europe.

ECRI. 2009. *Annual Report on ECRI's Activities*. CRI(2009)21 [Online]. Available at: www.coe. int/t/dghl/monitoring/ecri/activities/annual report 2008.pdf [accessed: 31 May 2009].

Ehrenreich, N. 2002–3. Subordination and symbiosis: Mechanisms of mutual support between subordinating systems. *University of Missouri-Kansas City Law Review*, 71(2), 251–324.

Elwan, A. 1999. *Poverty and Disability: A Survey of the Literature*, Social Protection Discussion Paper No. 9932. Washington, DC: World Bank.

Emens, E.F. 2007. Changing name changing: Framing rules and the future of marital names. *University of Chicago Law Review*, 74(3), 761–863.

ENAR. 2002. *ENAR Shadow Report 2002: Racism and Race Relations in the UK* [Online: ENAR]. Available at: http://cms.horus.be/files/99935/MediaArchive/pdf/Report%20UK%202002.pdf [accessed: 18 February 2010].

ENAR. 2005. *Council Directive Implementing the Principle of Equal Treatment Between Persons Irrespective of Racial or Ethnic Origin, Five Year Report on the Application of the Directive: Overview of ENAR's Initial Assessment* [Online]. Available at: http://cms.horus.be/files/99935/ MediaArchive/pdf/OKT05_ENAR_RD_5yr_Report.pdf [accessed: 23 September 2009].

Epstein, R. 1992. *Forbidden Grounds: The Case Against Employment Discrimination Laws*. Cambridge, MA: Harvard University Press.

Equal Employment Opportunity Commission. 2006. *Compliance Manual. Section 15: Race and Color Discrimination* [Online]. Available at: www.eeoc.gov/policy/docs/race-color.html [accessed: 23 December 2009].

Equal Opportunities Commission. 2004. *Advising Ethnic Minority Women about Discrimination at Work* [Online]. Available at: http://webarchive.nationalarchives.gov.uk/20071104153841/ http://83.137.212.42/sitearchive/eoc/PDF/sex_and_race_advisor.pdf?page=19291 [accessed: 14 July 2010].

Equal Opportunities Commission. 2007. *Moving On Up?* [Online: Equal Opportunities Commission]. Available at: www.eoc.org.uk/Default.aspx?page=17693 [accessed: 20 June 2010].

Equalities Review. 2007. *Fairness and Freedom: The Final Report of the Equalities Review* [Online: Cabinet Office]. Available at: http://archive.cabinetoffice.gov.uk/equalitiesreview/ upload/assets/www.theequalitiesreview.org.uk/equalities_review_-_fairness_and_freedom. doc [accessed: 18 July 2010].

Equality and Diversity Forum. 2008. *Multiple Discrimination: Justice for the Whole Person* [Online: Equality and Diversity Forum, 2nd edition]. Available at: www.edf.org.uk/blog/ ?p=1482 [accessed: 20 June 2010].

Equality and Diversity Forum. 2009. Multiple discrimination consultation response [Online]. Available at: www.edf.org.uk/blog/?p=6228 [accessed: 15 July 2010].

Erikson, E. 1968. *Identity, Youth, and Crisis*. New York: W.W. Norton.

Esping-Andersen, G. 1990. *The Three Worlds of Welfare Capitalism*. Cambridge: Polity Press.

Esping-Andersen, G. 1999. *Social Foundations of Post-Industrial Economies*. Oxford: Oxford University Press.

Esposito, J.L. and Mogahed, D. 2007. *Who Speaks for Islam? What a Billion Muslims Really Think*. New York: Gallup Press.

Essed, P. 1990. *Everyday Racism: Reports of Women from Two Countries*. Claremont, CA: Hunter House.

Essed, P. 1991. *Understanding Everyday Racism – An Interdisciplinary Theory*. London: Sage.

Essed, P. and Trienekens, S. 2007. 'Who wants to feel white?' Race, Dutch culture and contested identities. *Ethnic and Racial Studies*, 31(1), 52–72.

EU Roma Policy Coalition. 2008. *Towards a European Policy on Roma Inclusion* [Online]. Available at: www.romadecade.org/portal/downloads/News/Towards%20an%20EU%20Roma%20Policy%20ERPC%20-%20Final.pdf [accessed: 23 June 2009].

European Commission. 1991. Recommendation 92/131/EEC of 27 November 1991 on the protection of the dignity of women and men at work [1992] OJ L49/1, including as an Annex a code of practice on measures to combat sexual harassment.

European Commission. 2001. White Paper European Governance COM(2001) 428 final. Brussels: European Commission.

European Commission. 2004a. Communication from the Commission to the Council and the European Parliament: Recommendation of the European Commission on Turkey's progress towards accession, COM (2004) 656 final, 6/10/2004 Brussels.

European Commission. 2004b. *The Situation of Roma in an Enlarged European Union* [Online]. Available at: ec.europa.eu/social/main.jsp?catId=518&langId=en&moreDocuments=yes [accessed: 8 July 2009].

European Commission. 2005. *The Protection of Minorities in the EU*. EU Network of Independent Experts on Fundamental Rights. Thematic Comment No. 3 [Online]. Available at: ec.europa.eu/justice_home/cfr_cdf/doc/thematic_comments_2005_en.pdf [accessed: 30 May 2009].

European Commission. 2006. The application of Directive 2000/43/EC of 29 June 2000 implementing the principle of equal treatment between persons irrespective of racial or ethnic origin. Document COM (2006) 643 final. Brussels: European Commission.

European Commission. 2006a. *A Roadmap for Equality Between Women and Men – 2006–2010 – Communication from the Commission to the Council, the European Parliament, the European Economic and Social Committee and the Committee of the Regions*. Document COM(2006) 92 final.

European Commission. 2006b. *Communication from the Commission to the Council and the European Parliament. The Application of Directive 2000/43/EC of 29 June 2000 Implementing the Principle of Equal Treatment Between Persons Irrespective of Racial or Ethnic Origin*. COM (2006) 643.

European Commission. 2007a. *Tackling Multiple Discrimination: Practices, Policies and Laws* [Online]. Available at: http://ec.europa.eu/social/main.jsp?catId=738&langId=en&pubId=51&type=2&furtherPubs=no [accessed: 15 July 2010].

European Commission. 2007b. *Communication from the Commission to the Council, the European Parliament, the European Economic and Social Committee and the Committee of the Regions: Situation of Disabled People in the European Union: The European Action Plan 2008–2009*. Document COM(2007) 738 final.

European Commission. 2007c. *Commission Staff Working Document – Accompanying Document to the Communication from the Commission to the Council, the European Parliament, the European Economic and Social Committee and the Committee of the Regions – Situation of Disabled People in the European Union: the European Action Plan 2008–2009*. Document SEC(2007) 1548 final.

European Commission. 2007d. *Conference Proceedings: Equal Opportunities for All – Multiple Discrimination Matters 6–7 December, Elsinore, Denmark* [Online]. Available at: www.nationalgypsytravellerfederation.org/download/files/Conference_Proceedings.doc [accessed: 27 June 2009].

European Commission. 2007e. DG Employment, Social Affairs and Equal Opportunities. 2007. *Tackling Multiple Discrimination Practices, Policies and Laws (Brussels)*. Available at: http://ec.europa.eu/social/main.jsp?catId=618&langId=fr&moreDocuments=yes [accessed: 3 November 2010].

European Commission. 2008a. Communication from the Commission to the European Parliament, the Council, the European Economic and Social Committee and the Committee of the Regions. *Non-discrimination and Equal Opportunities: A Renewed Commitment*. COM(2008) 420 final.

European Commission. 2008b. *Proposal for a Council Directive on Implementing the Principle of Equal Treatment Between Persons Irrespective of Religion or Belief, Disability, Age or Sexual Orientation*. COM(2008) 426 final.

European Commission. 2008c. *Discrimination in the European Union Perceptions, Experiences and Attitudes*. Special Eurobarometer 296. Brussels: European Commission.

European Commission. 2008d. *On-going Evaluation of the 2007 European Year of Equal Opportunities for All*. Copenhagen: Rambøll Management.

European Commission. 2008e. The application of Directive 2000/78/EC of 27 November 2000 establishing a general framework for equal treatment in employment and occupation COM (2008) 225 final. Brussels: European Commission.

European Commission. 2009. *Equality Between Women and Men – 2009 Report from the Commission to the Council, the European Parliament, the European Economic and Social Committee and the Committee of the Regions*. Document COM(2009) 77 final.

European Commission. 2010. Opinion on the Future of Gender Equality Policy [Online]. Available at: http://ec.europa.eu/social/main.jsp?catId=481 [accessed: 15 July 2010].

European Commission against Racism and Intolerance. 2002. General Policy Recommendation No 7, *On National Legislation to Combat Racism and Racial Discrimination*. CRI (2003) 8, in, *Compilation of ECRI's General Policy Recommendations* (2003). Strasbourg: Council of Europe.

European Commission against Racism and Intolerance. 2004. *Activities of the Council of Europe with Relevance to Combating Racism and Intolerance*. CRI (2004) 7. Strasbourg: Council of Europe.

European Parliament. 2006. *European Parliament Resolution on the Situation of Roma Women in the European Union*. 1 June 2006. P6_TA(2006)0244. Strasbourg: European Parliament.

European Platform for Roma Inclusion. 2009. *Common Basic Principles on Roma Inclusion: The First Meeting of the Integrated European Platform for Roma Inclusion. Annexed to the Conclusions of the Social Affairs Council Meeting of June 2009* [Online]. Available at: www.eu2009.cz/scripts/file.php?id=56513&down=yes [accessed: 12 July 2010].

European Roma Rights Centre. 2004. *Strategic Litigation of Race Discrimination in Europe: From Principles to Practice* [Online: INTERIGHTS and Minority Policy Group]. Available at: www.errc.org/db/00/C5/m000000C5.pdf [accessed: 29 May 2009].

European Women's Lobby. 2008. *Engendering the Lisbon Strategy for Growth, Jobs and Social Inclusion. Equality between Women and Men as a Central Component for Economic Development and Social Well-being* [Online]. Available at: www.womenlobby.org/SiteResources/data/MediaArchive/policies/Economic%20and%20social%20justice%20for%20women/EWL%20contribution%20to%20Spring%20Council_enjmarch08.pdf [accessed: 13 July 2010].

Eurostat. 2006. *A Statistical View of the Life of Women and Men in the EU25*, News Release, 6 March [Online]. Available at: epp.eurostat.ec.europa.eu/cache/ITY_PUBLIC/3-06032006-BP1/EN/3-06032006-BP1-EN.PDF [accessed: 30 June 2009].

Evans, C. 2008. Introduction, in *Law and Religion in Theoretical and Historical Context*, edited by P. Cane, C. Evans and Z. Robinson. Cambridge: Cambridge University Press, 1–15.

Evans Case, R. and Givens, T. 2010. Re-engineering legal opportunity structures in the European Union? The Starting Line Group and the politics of the Racial Equality Directive. *Journal of Common Market Studies*, 48(2), 221–41.

Fahlbeck, R. 2002. Industrial relations and collective labour law: Characteristics, principles and basic features, in *Stability and Changes in Nordic Labour Law*, edited by P. Wahlgren. Stockholm: Stockholm Institute for Scandinavian Law, 78–133.

Fassin, D. 2002. L'invention française de la discrimination. *Revue Française de science politique*, 52(4), 403–23.

Fassin, D., Carde, E., Ferre, N. and Musso-Dimitrijevic, S. 2001. *Un traitement inégal: Les discriminations dans l'accès aux soins*. Bobigny. Universtié de Paris Nord, 13.

Fassin, E. 2008. *Une brève histoire des discriminations: Discriminations: pratiques, savoirs, politiques*. Paris: La Documentation Française, 49–56.

Faure, M. 2000. L'universel républicain à l'épreuve: Discrimination, ethnicisation, segrégation. Catégorisation de la population pénale et discriminations. Montrouge *VEI* n°121.

Fedtke, J. and Oliver, D. 2007. *Human Rights and the Private Sphere*. New York: Routledge-Cavendish.

Felouzis, G., Liot, F. and Perroton, J. 2002. *Ecole, ville, ségrégation: La polarisation sociale et ethnique des collèges dans l'Académie de Bordeaux*. Bordeaux: Université Victor Segalen.

Filadelfiová, J., Gerbery, D. and Škobla, D. 2007. *Report on the Living Conditions of Roma in Slovakia* [Online: Bratislava, Bonn: UNDP, Friedrich Ebert Stiftung]. Available at: http://www.fes.de/gpol/inhalt/publikationen_mr2.php [accessed: 1 December 2010].

Fine, M. and Asch, A. 1981. Disabled women: Sexism without the pedestal. *Journal of Sociology and Social Welfare*, 8(2), 233–45.

Fine, M. and Asch, A. 1988. *Women with Disabilities: Essay in Psychology, Culture and Politics*. Philadelphia, PA: Temple University Press.

Fink, C. 2004. *Defending the Rights of Others: The Great Powers, the Jews, and International Minority Protection, 1878–1938*. Cambridge and New York: Cambridge University Press.

Finkelstein, V. 2004. Representing disability, in *Disabling Barriers – Enabling Environments*, edited by J. Swain, S. French, C. Barnes and C. Thomas. 2nd edition. London: Sage, 13–20.

Finnish Ministry of Social Affairs and Health. 2009. *The Proposal of the Working Group for a National Policy on Roma*. Working Group Report [Online]. Available at: www.stm.fi/c/document_library/get_file?folderId=39503&name=DLFE-11164.pdf [accessed: 12 July 2010].

Finnish National Board of Education. 2000. *Core Curriculum for Pre-school Education 2000* [Online]. Available at: www.oph.fi/download/123162_core_curriculum_for_pre_school_education_2000.pdf [accessed: 12 July 2010].

Finnish National Board of Education. 2008. *Immigrant Education: Statistics* [Online]. Available at: www.oph.fi/download/48000_maahanmuuttajat_suomessa_311207.pdf [accessed: 15 November 2009].

Fitzgibbon, M. and Stolley, M. 2009. *Minority Women: The Untold Story* [Online]. Available at: www.pbs.org/wgbh/nova/thin/minorities.html [accessed: 16 June 2009].

Fligstein, N. 2008. *Euroclash: The EU, European Identity, and the Future of Europe*. Oxford: Oxford University Press.

Forced Migration Review. 2010. Disability and Displacement, Special Issue, 35 [Online]. Available at: www.fmreview.org/disability/FMR35.pdf [accessed: 1 December 2010].

Foroutan, Y. 2008. Employment differentials of second-generation Muslim immigrants: Assimilation and discrimination hypothesis. *Immigrants & Minorities*, 26(3), 219–41.

Fouquet, A., Gauvin, A. and Letablier, M.T. 2000. Des contrats sociaux entre les sexes différents selon les pays de l'Union européenne, in *Egalité entre femmes et hommes: Aspects économiques*, edited by B. Majnoni d'Intignano. Paris: Conseil D'Analyse Economique, 105–46.

Fowler-Hermes, J. 2001. The beauty and the beast in the workplace: Appearance-based discrimination claims under EEO laws. *The Florida Bar Journal*, 75(4), 32 [Online]. Available at: www.floridabar.org/DIVCOM/JN/JNJournal01.nsf/128c8017467c98d385256ad20044c99b/3c84f1732a06780f85256b1100573d1b?OpenDocument [accessed: 18 September 2009].

Fox, K. 2003. Underactivity or overnutrition?, in *Adult Obesity: A Paediatric Challenge*, edited by L. Voss and T. Wilkin. London: Taylor & Francis, 13–21.

Franks, M. 2000. Crossing the borders of whiteness? Muslim women who wear the hijab in Britain today. *Ethnic and Racial Studies*, 23(5), 917–29.

Fraser, N. 1997. *Justice Interruptus: Critical Reflections on the 'Postsocialist' Condition*. New York: Routledge.

Fraser, N. 2003. Social justice in the age of identity politics: Redistribution, recognition, and participation, in *Redistribution or Recognition: A Political-Philosophical Exchange*, edited by N. Fraser and A. Honneth. London and New York: Verso, 7–107.

Fraser, N. and Honneth, A. 2003. *Redistribution or Recognition? A Political-Philosophical Exchange*. London: Verso.

Fredman, S. 2002. *Discrimination Law*. Oxford: Oxford University Press.

Fredman, S. 2003. The age of equality, in *Age as an Equality Issue: Legal and Policy Perspectives*, edited by S. Fredman and S. Spencer. Oxford and Portland, OR: Hart, 21–69.

Fredman, S. 2005a. Changing the norm: Positive duties in equal treatment legislation. *Maastricht Journal of European and Comparative Law*, 12(4), 369–97.

Fredman, S. 2005b. Double trouble: Multiple discrimination and EU law. *European Anti-discrimination Law Review*, 2005(2), 13–18 [Online]. Available at: www.migpolgroup.com/public/docs/32.EuropeanAnti-discriminationLawReview_Issue2_EN_10.05.pdf [accessed: 28 June 2009].

Fredman, S. 2005c. Providing equality: Substantive equality and the positive duty to provide. *South African Journal on Human Rights*, 21(2), 163–90.

Fredman, S. 2006. Transformation or dilution: Fundamental rights in the EU social space. *European Law Journal*, 12(1), 41–60.

Fredman, S. 2008a. *Human Rights Transformed: Positive Rights and Positive Duties*. Oxford and New York: Oxford University Press.

Fredman, S. 2008b. Making a difference: The promises and period of positive duties in the equality field. *European Anti-discrimination Law Review*, 2008(6–7), 43–52 [Online]. Available at: www.migpolgroup.com/public/docs/145.EuropeanAnti-discLawReview_6_7_en_11.08.pdf [accessed: 28 June 2009].

Fredman, S. 2009. Positive rights and positive duties: Addressing intersectionality, in *European Union Non-Discrimination Law: Comparative Perspectives on Multidimensional Equality Law*, edited by D. Schiek and V. Chege. Abingdon: Routledge-Cavendish, 73–89.

Fredman, S. and Szyszczak, E. 1992. The interaction of race and gender, in *Discrimination: The Limits of Law*, edited by B. Hepple and E. Szyszczak. London and New York: Mansell, 214–26.

Fried, E.J. 2005. The potential for policy initiatives to address the obesity epidemic: A legal perspective from the United States, in *Obesity Prevention and Public Health*, edited by D. Crawford and R. Jeffery. Oxford: Oxford University Press, 265–83.

Fundamental Rights Agency. 2009. *European Minorities and Discrimination Survey: Data in Focus Report*. Muslims. EU MIDIS.

Furedi, F. 1998. *The Silent War: Imperialism and the Changing Perception of Race*. London: Pluto Press.

Gabel, S., Curcic, S., Powell, J., Khader, K. and Albee, L. 2009. Migration and ethnic group disproportionality in special education: An exploratory study. *Disability & Society*, 24(5), 625–39.

Gaertner, S. and Dovidio, J. 1986. The aversive form of racism, in *Prejudice, Discrimination and Racism*, edited by S. Gaertner and J. Dovidio. Orlando, FL: Academic Press, 61–89.

García Villegas, M. 2004. On Pierre Bourdieu's legal thought. *Droit et Société*, 57–70.

Garner, S. 2006. The uses of whiteness: What sociologists working on Europe can draw from US research on whiteness. *Sociology*, 40(2), 257–75.

Gaspard, F. and Khosrokhavar, F. 1995. *Le Foulard et la République*. Paris: La Découverte.

Geddes, A. and Guiraudon, V. 2004. Britain, France and EU anti-discrimination policy: The emergence of an EU policy paradigm. *West European Politics*, 27(2), 334–53.

General Secretariat for Gender Equality. 2005. *6th National Report of Greece, Period 2001 – 2004, to the UN Committee on the Elimination of Discrimination Against Women*. Athens: GSGE.

General Secretariat for Gender Equality. 2008. *Report of Policies and Actions on Gender Equality (2004–2008)* [Online: General Secretariat for Gender Equality]. Available at: www.isotita.gr/en/index.php [accessed: 8 March 2009].

Gerards, J. 2007. Discrimination grounds, in *Cases: Materials and Text on National, Supranational and International Non-Discrimination Law*, edited by D. Schiek, L. Waddington and M. Bell. Oxford and Portland, OR: Hart, 170–84.

Gerards, J.H. and Heringa, A.W. 2003. *Wetgeving gelijke behandeling*. Studiepockets Staats-en Bestuursrecht 38. Deventer: Kluwer.

Gerstenberg, O. 2005. Germany: Freedom of conscience in public schools. *International Journal of Constitutional Law*, 3, 94–106.

Geschiere, P. 2009. Autochthony in Europe: The Dutch turn, in *The Perils of Belonging – Autochthony, Citizenship, and Exclusion in Africa and Europe*, edited by P. Geschiere. Chicago, IL: University of Chicago Press, 130–68.

Ghorashi, H. 2007. Who dares to experiment with culture?, in *Citizens and Subjects: The Netherlands, For Example*, edited by R. Bradiotti, C. Esche and M. Hlavajova. Amsterdam: Mondrian Stichting, 125–35.

Gibson, N. 2007. Faith in the courts: Religious dress and human rights. *Cambridge Law Journal*, 66(4), 657–97.

Gilbert, G. 2002. The burgeoning minority rights jurisprudence of the European Court of Human Rights. *Human Rights Quarterly*, 24(3), 736–80.

Gill, T. and Monaghan, K. 2003. Justification in direct sex discrimination law: Taboo upheld. *Industrial Law Journal*, 32(2), 115–22.

Goffman, G. 1990. *Stigma: Notes on the Management of Spoiled Identity*. London: Penguin.

Goldberg, D.T. 2002. *The Racial State*. Oxford and Malden, MA: Blackwell.

Goldberg, D.T. 2006. Racial Europeanization. *Ethnic and Racial Studies*, 29(2), 331–64.

Goldberg, S. 2009. Intersectionality in theory and practice, in *Intersectionality and Beyond: Law, Power and the Politics of Location*, edited by D. Cooper. New York: Routledge-Cavendish, 124–58.

Goldberg, S. 2011. Discrimination by comparison. *Yale Law Journal*, 120.

Goldberg, S.B. 2002. On making anti-essentialist and social constructionist arguments in court. *Oregon Law Review*, 81(3), 629–62.

Gonzalez, M.J., Jurado, T. and Naldini, M. 2000. Introduction: Interpreting the transformation of gender inequalities in Southern Europe, in *Gender Inequalities in Southern Europe: Women, Work and Welfare in the 1990s*, edited by M.J. Gonzalez, T. Jurado and M. Naldini. London and Portland, OR: Frank Cass, 4–34.

Goodwin, M. 2009. Multidimensional exclusion: Viewing Romani marginalisation through the nexus of race and poverty, in *European Union Nondiscrimination Law: Comparative Perspectives on Multi-Dimensional Equality Law*, edited by D. Schiek and V. Chege. Abingdon: Routledge-Cavendish, 137–62.

Gordon, D., Parker, R. and Loughran, F. with Heslop, P. 2000. *Disabled Children in Britain: A Re-Analysis of the OPCS Disability Surveys*. London: Stationery Office.

Gori, G. 2005. Domestic enforcement of the European Social Charter: the way forward, in *Social Rights in Europe*, edited by G. de Búrca and B. de Witte. Oxford: Oxford University Press, 69–88.

Government Equalities Office. 2009a. *Equality Bill: Assessing the Impact of a Multiple Discrimination Provision. Summary of Responses*. Available at: http://sta.geo.useconnect. co.uk/staimm6geo/pdf/Equality%20Bill%20Multiple%20Discrimination%20Summary%20of %20Response.pdf [accessed: 15 July 2010].

Government Equalities Office. 2009b. *Explaining the Equality Bill: Dual Discrimination* [Online]. Available at: www.equalities.gov.uk/pdf/peers%20breifing%201st.pdf [accessed: 15 July 2010].

Government Equalities Office. 2009c. *Equality Bill: Assessing the Impact of a Multiple Discrimination Provision* [Online]. Available at: www.equalities.gov.uk/pdf/ 090422%20Multiple%20Discrimination%20Discussion%20Document%20Final%20Text.pdf [accessed: 15 July 2010].

Grabham, E. 2002. Law v Canada: A new direction for equality under the Canadian Charter? *Oxford Journal of Legal Studies*, 22(4), 641–61.

Grabham, E. 2006. Taxonomies of inequality: Lawyers, maps, and the challenge of hybridity. *Social and Legal Studies*, 15(1), 5–23.

Grabham, E., Cooper, B., Krishnadas, J. and Herman, D. 2009. *Intersectionality and Beyond: Law, Power and the Politics of Location*. London and New York: Routledge-Cavendish.

Gray, J., Ford, K. and Kelly, L. 1988. The prevalence of bulimia in a black college population. *International Journal of Eating Disorders*, 7, 733–40.

Greek Helsinki Monitor and Minority Rights Group – Greece. 2006. *Parallel Report on Greece's Compliance with the UN Convention on the Elimination of All Forms of Discrimination against Women* [Online]. Available at: www.iwraw-ap.org/resources/pdf/Greece(1).pdf [accessed: 29 May 2009].

Greek Helsinki Monitor and the World Organisation Against Torture (OMCT). 2002. Violence Against Women in Greece – Report Submitted to the Committee on the Elimination of Discrimination against Women at its Exceptional Session 5–23 August 2002 [Online: OMCT]. Available at: www.omct.org/pdf/VAW/GreeceEng2002.pdf [accessed: 20 April 2009].

Greek Helsinki Monitor, Centre for Research and Action on Peace (KEDE), Coordinated Organization and Communities for Roma Human Rights in Greece, Minority Rights Group – Greece and The Support Center for Children and Family. 2004. *State Violence in Greece: An Alternative Report to the United Nations Committee Against Torture 33rd Session* [Online: OMCT]. Available at: www.omct.org/pdf/procedures/2004/joint/s_violence_greece_10_2004. pdf [accessed: 29 May 2009].

Greek Ombudsman. 2006. *Promoting Equal Treatment: The Greek Ombudsman as National Equality Body, Report 2006* [Online]. Available at: www.synigoros.gr/diakriseis/pdfs/12_10_ EqualTreatmentReport2006.pdf [accessed: 30 May 2009].

Greek Ombudsman. 2007. *Promoting Equal Treatment: The Greek Ombudsman as National Equality Body, Report 2007* [Online]. Available at: www.synigoros.gr/diakriseis/pdfs/isi-metax-engl-2007-teliko.pdf [accessed: 30 May 2009].

Greek Ombudsman. 2008. Quality of education, classification of degree and professional rights of minority teachers [in Greek]. *Theoria kai Praksi Dioikitikou Dikaiou*, 2/2009, 230–5.

Green, T.K. 2005. Work culture and discrimination. *California Law Review*, 93(3), 623–84.

Greer, S. 2006. *The European Convention on Human Rights. Achievements, Problems and Prospects*. Cambridge and New York: Cambridge University Press.

Grekova, M., Kosseva, M., Avramov, O. and Kjurkchieva, I. 2008. GendeRace – The use of racial anti-discrimination laws: Gender and citizenship in a multicultural context. *State of the Art Report*, ANNEX 6. Bulgaria report.

Grillo, T. 1995. Anti-essentialism and intersectionality: Tools to dismantle the master's house. *Berkeley Women's Law Journal*, 10, 16–30.

Guardian. 2009. Veiled threats: Row over Islamic dress opens bitter divisions in France, 27 June, 24–5.

Guardian. 2010. BBC does 'not value' older female newsreaders, says Harriet Harman [Online: *Guardian*]. Available at: www.guardian.co.uk/media/2010/jan/03/bbc-female-newsreaders-harriet-harman [accessed: 19 July 2007].

Guiraudon, V. 2009. Equality in the making: Implementing EU non-discrimination law. *Citizenship Studies*, 13, 527–41.

Gumbel, A. 2002. Gym instructor wins 'fit and fat' dispute. *Independent*, 9 May [Online]. Available at: www.independent.co.uk/news/world/americas/gym-instructor-wins-fit-and-fat-dispute-650620.html [accessed: 30 September 2009].

Gunn, T.J. 2004. Under God but not the scarf: The founding myths of religious freedom in the United States and laïcité in France. *Journal of Church and State*, 46(1), 7–24.

Haarscher, G. 2004. *La Laïcité*. Paris: PUF.

Hall, S. 1996. New ethnicities, in *Stuart Hall – Critical Dialogues in Cultural Studies*, edited by D. Moreley and K.-H. Chen. New York and London: Routledge.

Hamdan, A. 2007. The issue of hijab in France: Reflections and analysis. *Muslim World Journal of Human Rights*, 4(2), 1–27.

Hammarberg, T. 2009. *Report by Thomas Hammarberg, Commissioner for Human Rights of the Council of Europe following his Visit to Greece on 8–10 December 2008 – Issue Reviewed: Human Rights of Minorities*, CommDH(2009)9 [Online: Council of Europe]. Available at: wcd.coe.int/com.instranet.InstraServlet?Index=no&command=com.instranet.Cm dBlobGet&InstranetImage=1156816&SecMode=1&DocId=1368674&Usage=2 [accessed: 1 March 2009].

Hammarberg, T. 2010. *Report by Thomas Hammarberg, Commissioner for Human Rights of the Council of Europe following his Visit to Bulgaria – Comm. DH 1, 9 February 2010* [Online:

Council of Europe]. Available at: https://wcd.coe.int/ViewDoc.jsp?id=1581941&Site=Comm DH [accessed: July 2010].

Hancock, A.-M. 2007. When multiplication doesn't equal quick addition: Examining intersectionality as a research paradigm. *Pespectives on Politics*, 5(1), 63–78.

Hannett, S. 2003. Equality at the intersections: The legislative and judicial failure to tackle multiple discrimination. *Oxford Journal of Legal Studies*, 23(1), 65–86.

Hannikainen, L. 2003. *Suomen venäjänkielisen väestönosan kysymyksiä. Etnisten suhteiden neuvottelukunnan asettaman työryhmän raportti*. Helsinki: Venäjän ja Itä-Euroopan instituutti.

Haritaworn, J. 2009. Hybrid border-crossers? Towards a radical socialisation of 'mixed race'. *Journal of Ethnic and Migration Studies*, 35(1), 115–32.

Harnack, L. and Schmitz, K. 2005. The role of nutrition and physical activity in the obesity epidemic, in *Obesity Prevention and Public Health*, edited by D. Crawford and R. Jeffery. Oxford: Oxford University Press.

Hart, M. and Secunda, P. 2009. A matter of context: Social framework evidence in employment discrimination class actions. Colorado Law School, Legal Studies Research Paper Series, Working Paper Number 09–04. *Fordham Law Review*, 78(1), 37–70.

Helander, E. and Kailo, K. (eds) 1998. *No Beginning, No End: The Sami Speak Up*. Circumpolar Research Series No 5. Edmonton and Alta: Canadian Circumpolar Institute with the Nordic Sami Institute.

Hellenic Ministry of Foreign Affairs. 1999. *The Muslim Minority of Thrace* [in Greek] [Online: Hellenic Resources Network]. Available at: www.hri.org/MFA/foreign/musmingr.htm [accessed: 29 January 2009].

Hellenic Ministry of Foreign Affairs. 2007. *The Muslim Minority of Thrace* [Online: Ministry of Foreign Affairs]. Available at: www.mfa.gr/www.mfa.gr/en-US/Policy/Multilateral+Diplomacy/Global+Issues/Human+Rights/MUSLIM+MINORITY+OF+THRACE.htm [accessed: 29 January 2009].

Henkes, C. and Kneip, S. 2009. Die Plenardebatten um das Kopftuch in des Landesparlamenten, in *Der Stoff aus dem Konflikte sind – Debatten um das Kopftuch in Deutschland, Österreich und der Schweiz*, edited by S. Berghahn and P. Rostock. Bielefeld: transcript Verlag, 249–74.

Henrard, K. 2007. *Equal Rights Versus Special Rights?* [Online]. Available at: bookshop.europa.eu/eubookshop/bookmarks.action?target=EUB:NOTICE:KE7807246:EN:HTML&request_locale=EN [accessed: 8 July 2009].

Hepple, B. 2004. Race and law in fortress Europe. *Modern Law Review*, 67(1), 1–15.

Hepple QC, B., Coussey, M. and Choudhury, T. 2000. *Equality: A New Framework. Report of the Independent Review of the Enforcement of UK Anti-Discrimination Legislation*, University of Cambridge Centre for Public Law and Judge Institute of Management Studies. Oxford and Portland, OR: Hart.

Hesselink, M. 2003. The horizontal effects of social rights in European contract law. *Europa e Diritto Privato*, 1–18.

Hewitt, P. 2004. *Hewitt and Falconer Publish White Paper on the New Commission for Equality and Human Rights*, Department for Trade and Industry, press release 12/5/04 DTI News Release P/2004/187: 12 May 2004, source as reference to press release: O'Cinneide (2007).

Hickman, M.J. 1998. Reconstructing deconstructing 'race': British political discourses about the Irish in Britain. *Ethnic and Racial Studies*, 21(2), 288–307.

High Commissioner on National Minorities. 1996. *The Hague Recommendations Regarding the Education Rights of National Minorities and Explanatory Note* [Online]. Available at: www. osce.org/documents/hcnm/1996/10/2700_en.pdf [accessed: 4 July 2009].

Hiilamo, H. 2002. Perheiden taloudellinen tukeminen, in *Suomalainen hyvinvointi 2002*, edited by M. Heikkilä and M. Kautto. Helsinki: Stakes, 214–28.

Hiilamo, H. 2005. Subjektiivisen päivähoito-oikeuden toteutuminen Ruotsissa ja Suomessa 1990-luvulla, in *Onko meillä malttia sijoittaa lapsiin*, edited by P. Takala. Helsinki: Kelan tutkimusosasto, 58–79.

Hill, A. 2003. Self image and the stigma of obesity, in *Adult Obesity: A Paediatric Challenge*, edited by L. Voss and T. Wilkin. London: Taylor & Francis, 61–72.

Hoffman, S. 2004. Is there a place for 'race' as a legal concept? *Arizona State Law Journal*, 36(4), 1093–160.

Hogben, L. 1931. *Genetic Principles in Medical and Social Science*. London: Williams & Norgate.

Hollinger, D.A. 1995. *Postethnic America: Beyond Multiculturalism*. New York: Basic Books.

Holtmaat, R. 2003. Stop de inflatie von het discriminatiebegrip! Een herbezinning op het onderscheid tussen discriminatie en ongelijke behandeling. *Nederlandse Juristenbladed*, 78, 1266–74.

Holtmaat, R. 2006a. Discriminatie of onderscheid: Het kleine verschil met grote gevolgen of het grote verschil met kleine gevolgen?, in *Gelijke behandeling: Principes en praktijken; evaluatieonderzoek Algemene Wet Gelijke Behandeling*, edited by M.L.M. Hertogh and P.J.J. Zoontjes. Nijmegen: Wolf Legal Publishers, 3–113.

Holtmaat, R. 2006b. European Network of Legal Experts in the non-discrimination field, *Catalysts for Change? Equality Bodies According to Directive 2000/43/EC*, MPG, HEC [Online: European Commission]. Available at: www.stop-discrimination.info/fileadmin/pdfs/Reports/Catalysts_for_Change_en.pdf [accessed: 31 October 2009].

Holtmaat, R. and Tobler, C. 2005. Cedaw and the European Union's policy in the field of combating gender discrimination. *Maastricht Journal of European and Comparative Law*, 12(4), 399–425.

Holzleithner, E. 2005. Mainstreaming equality: Dis/entangling grounds of discrimination. *Transnational Law and Contemporary Problems*, 14, 927–50.

Honneth, A. 2003. Redistribution as recognition: A response to Nancy Fraser, in *Redistribution or Recognition: A Political-Philosophical Exchange*, edited by N. Fraser and A. Honneth. London and New York: Verso, 110–97.

hooks, b. 2000. Black women: Shaping feminist theory, in *The Black Feminist Reader*, edited by J. James and T. Sharpley-Whiting. Oxford and Malden, MA: Blackwell, 131–45.

Hountoumadi, A. 1998. *Research on the Potential of Intervention at the Area of Metaxourgio – Social Inclusion of Muslim Women* [in Greek]. Athens: Research Centre for Equality Issues (K.E.TH.I.).

House of Commons Communities and Local Government Committee. 2006/7. *Equality, Sixth Report of Session 2006–07* [Online]. Available at: www.publications.parliament.uk/pa/cm200607/cmselect/cmcomloc/468/46802.htm [accessed: 15 July 2010].

House of Commons Work and Pensions Committee. 2009. *The Equality Bill: How Disability Equality Fits Within a Single Equality Act, Third Report* [Online]. Available at: www.publications.parliament.uk/pa/cm200809/cmselect/cmworpen/158/15802.htm [accessed: 15 July 2010].

Houziaux, A. 2004. Un conflit de lois, in *Le Voile, Que Cache-t-il?* edited by J. Baubérot, D. Bouzar and J. Costa-Lascoux. Paris: Les Éditions de l'Atelier/Les Éditions Ouvrières, 11–24.

Howard, E. 2005. Anti race discrimination measures in Europe: An attack on two fronts. *European Law Journal*, 11(4), 468–86.

Howard, E. 2006. The case for a considered hierarchy of discrimination grounds in EU law. *Maastricht Journal of European and Comparative Law*, 13(4), 445–70.

Howard, E. 2008. The European year of equal opportunities for all – 2007: Is the EU moving away from a formal idea of equality? *European Law Journal*, 14(2), 168–85.

Howard, E. 2009. School bans on the wearing of religious symbols: Examining the implications of recent case law from the UK. *Religion and Human Rights*, 4, 7–24.

Howard, E., Kofman, E. and Wray, H. 2008. GendeRace – The use of racial anti-discrimination laws: Gender and citizenship in a multicultural context, State of the Art Report, ANNEX 3; UK Report.

Hristopoulos, D. 2002. *Otherness as a Relation of Power: Aspects of the Greek, Balkan and European Experience* [in Greek]. Athens: Ekdoseis Kritiki.

Hsu, G. 1988. Are eating disorders becoming more common among blacks? *International Journal of Eating Disorders*, 7, 113–24.

Hughes, G. 1998. A suitable case for treatment? Constructions of disability, in *Embodying the Social: Constructions of Difference*, edited by E. Saraga. London and New York: Routledge, 44–88.

Hughes, J. 2005. 'Exit' in deeply divided societies: Regimes of discrimination in Estonia and Latvia and the potential for Russophone migration. *Journal of Common Market Studies*, 43(4), 739–62.

Human Rights Commission. 2001. *An Intersectional Approach to Discrimination*. Ontario: Discussion Paper.

Human Rights Watch. 1999. *Greece: The Turks of Western Thrace*, 11(1) (D) [Online: Human Rights Watch]. Available at: www.hrw.org/legacy/reports/1999/greece/index.htm [accessed: 22 May 2009].

Human Rights Watch. 2009. *Diskriminierung im Namen der Neutralität* [Online]. Available at: www.hrw.org/en/node/80858/section/5 [accessed: 18 March 2009].

Hussain, Y. 2005. South Asian disabled women: Negotiating identities. *The Sociological Review*, 53(3), 522–38.

Hussain, Y. and Bagguley, P. 2005. Citizenship, ethnicity and identity: British Pakistanis after the 2001 'riots'. *Sociology*, 39(3), 407–25.

Hutchinson, D.L. 2000. 'Gay rights' for 'gay whites'? Race, sexual identity, and equal protection discourse. *Cornell Law Review*, 85(5), 1358–91.

Hutchinson, D.L. 2002. New complexity theories: From theoretical innovation to doctrinal reform. *University of Missouri-Kansas City Law Review*, 71(2), 431–46.

Inglot, T. 2008. *Welfare States in East Central Europe*. Cambridge: Cambridge University Press.

Ingrassia, M. 1995. The body of the beholder. *Newsweek*, 125(7), 24 April, 66–7.

Institut Nacional de Estatdistica. 2007. Encuesta nacional de immigrantes 2007. Available at: www.ine.es/inebmenu/mnu_migrac.htm.

Institute for Public Policy. 2010. *Benchmarks for Measuring Effectiveness of Social Services for Adults with Mental Disabilities in the Context of Social Inclusion Policies, Romania* (available only in Romanian).

Institute of Race Relations. 2008. Cultural cleansing. *European Race Bulletin*, 62, 18–25.

Inter-Parliamentary Union. 2009. *Women in National Parliaments*, updated 30 April 2009 [Online: IPU]. Available at: www.ipu.org/wmn-e/classif.htm [accessed: 29 May 2009].

Ipsen, J. 2003. Karlsruhe locuta, causa non finita. *Neue Zeitschrift für Verwaltungsrecht*, 22, 1210–13.

Jachtenfuchs, M. and Kohler-Koch, B. 2004. Multi-level governance, in *European Integration Theory*, edited by A. Wiener and T. Dietz. 1st edition. Oxford: Oxford University Press, 97–115.

Jackson Preece, J. 1998. *National Minorities and the European Nation-States*. Oxford: Clarendon Press.

Jackson, N. 2007. When bigger isn't always better. *Independent*, 1 February, 13.

Jäger, S. and Link, J. 1993. *Die vierte Gewalt: Rassismus und die Medien*. Duisburg: DISS.

Jasinskaja-Lahti, I., Liebkind, K. and Solheim, E. 2009. To identify or not to identify? National disidentification as an alternative reaction to perceived ethnic discrimination. *Applied Psychology: An International Review*, 58(1), 105–28.

Jasinskaja-Lahti, I., Liebkind, K., Jaakkola, M. and Reuter, A. 2006. Perceived discrimination, social support networks and psychological well-being among three immigrant groups. *Journal of Cross-Cultural Psychology*, 37(3), 1–19.

Jebb, S., Butland, B., Kopelman, P., McPherson, K., Thomas, S., Mardell, J. and Parry, V. 2007. *Tackling Obesities: Future Choices*, Foresight [Online: Foresight]. Available at: www.foresight. gov.uk/OurWork/ActiveProjects/Obesity/Obesity.asp [accessed: 17 June 2009].

Jeffery, R. and Linde, J. 2005. Evolving environmental factors in the obesity epidemic, in *Obesity Prevention and Public Health*, edited by D. Crawford and R. Jeffery. Oxford: Oxford University Press, 55–73.

Jolls, C. and Sunstein, C.R. 2006. The law of implicit bias. *California Law Review*, 94(4), 969–96.

Jubany Baucells, O. 2008a. *Gènere i racisme: Més enllà de la doble discriminació*. Àmbits de Politica i Societat. Num 38. COLPIS. Barcelona.

Jubany Baucells, O. 2008b. GendeRace – The use of racial anti-discrimination laws: Gender and citizenship in a multicultural context, State of the Art Report, ANNEX 2. Spain Report.

Julkunen, R. 1994. Suomalainen sukupuolimalli – 1960-luku käänteenä? in *Naisten hyvinvointivaltio*, edited by A. Anttonen, L. Henriksson and R. Nätkin. Tampere: Vastapaino.

Kajastie, K. 2000. Women and fixed-term employment, in *Perspectives of Equality: Work, Women and Family in the Nordic Countries and EU*, edited by L. Kalliomaa-Puha. Copenhagen: Nordic Council of Ministers, 143–64.

Kantola, J. and Nousiaien, K. 2009. Instituitonalising intersectionality in Europe. *International Feminist Journal of Politics*, 11(4), 459–77.

Karafyllis, A. 2006. *The Profile of the Greek Muslim Students of the Department of Primary Level Education of the Democritus University of Thrace* [in Greek]. Paper to the 4th International Conference on History of Education, Patras, 6–8 October [Online: University of Patras]. Available at: www.elemedu.upatras.gr/eriande/synedria/synedrio4/praktika1/karafyllis.htm [accessed: 29 May 2009].

Kearns, G. 2003. Nation, empire and cosmopolis: Ireland and the break with Britain, in *Geographies of British Modernity*, edited by D. Gilbert, D. Matless and B. Short. Oxford: Blackwell, 204–28.

Keith, L. and Morris, J. 1996. Easy targets: A disability rights perspective on the 'children as carers' debate, in *Encounters with Strangers: Feminism and Disability*, edited by J. Morris. London: The Women's Press, 89–114.

Kennedy, D. 1986. Freedom and constraint in adjudication: A critical phenomenology. *Journal of Legal Education*, 36(4), 518–62.

Khullar, M. 2009. 'Fat activists' seek law banning weight discrimination [Online: The WIP]. Available at: www.thewip.net/contributors/2009/07/fat_activists_seek_law_banning.html [accessed: 30 September 2009].

Kirkland, A. 2003. Representations of fatness and personhood: Pro-fat advocacy and the limits and uses of law. *Representations*, 82, 24–51.

Kirkland, A. 2008. *Fat Rights: Dilemmas of Difference and Personhood.* New York: New York University Press.

Kluger, R. 1975. *Simple Justice: The History of Brown v. Board of Education and Black America's Struggle for Equality.* New York: Knopf.

Knights, S. 2005. Religious symbols in the school: Freedom of religion, minorities and education. *European Human Rights Law Review*, 5, 499–516.

Knowles, C. 2008. The landscape of post-imperial whiteness in rural Britain. *Ethnic and Racial Studies*, 31(1), 167–84.

Knox, J. 2008. Horizontal human rights law. *American Journal of International Law*, 102(1), 1–47.

Koelman, S.M. 2005. *Algemene wet gelijke behandeling: Wet gelijke behandeling van mannen en vrouwen, Wet gelijke behandeling op grond van handicap en chronische ziekte, Wet gelijke behandeling op grond van leeftijd bij de arbeid.* Deventer: Kluwer.

Kofman, E., Lukes, S., D'Angelo, A. and Montagna, N. 2009. *The Equality Implications of being a Migrant in Britain: A Review.* London: Equality and Human Rights Commission.

Koldinská, K. 2009a. Multidimensional equality in the Czech and Slovak Republics: The case of Roma women, in *European Union Non-Discrimination Law: Comparative Perspectives on Multidimensional Equality Law*, edited by D. Schiek and V. Chege. Oxon and New York: Routledge-Cavendish, 249–77.

Koldinská, K. 2009b. Institutionalising intersectionality – a new path for equality for new Member States of the EU? *International Feminist Journal of Politics*, 11(4), 547–63.

Kollonay, C. 2009. National report on multiple discrimination in Hungary, in *Multiple Discrimination in EU Law*, edited by S. Burri and D. Schiek [Online]. Available at: http://ec.europa.eu/social/BlobServlet?docId=3808&langId=en [accessed: 8 October 2009].

Kontra, M., Skutnabb-Kangas, T., Phillipson, R. and Barady, T. 1999. *Language: A Right and a Resource.* Budapest: Central European University Press.

Korkut, L. 2003. *Report on Measures to Combat Discrimination in the 13 Candidate Countries: Country Report Turkey.* Utrecht: MEDE European Consultancy.

Korn, J. 1997. Fat. *Boston University Law Review*, 77, 25–67.

Korteweg, A. and Yurdakul, G. 2009. Islam, gender and immigrant integration: Boundary drawing in discourses on honour killing in the Netherlands and Germany. *Ethnic and Racial Studies*, 32(2), 218–38.

Kotkin, M. 2009. Diversity and discrimination: A look at complex bias. *William and Mary Law Review*, 50(5), 1439–500.

Kotzampasi, A. 2003. The scope of Islamic law in family law relations of Greek Muslims [in Greek]. *Elliniki Dikaiosyni*, 44, 57–72.

Koukoulis-Spiliotopoulos, S. 2005. The amended Equal Treatment Directive (2002/73): An expression of constitutional principles/fundamental rights. *Maastricht Journal of European and Comparative Law*, 12(4), 327–68.

Krieger, L.H. 1995. The content of our categories: A cognitive bias approach to discrimination and equal employment opportunity. *Stanford Law Review*, 47(6), 1161–248.

Krzyzanowski, M. and Wodak, R. 2008. *The Politics of Exclusion: Debating Migration in Austria*. New Brunswick, NJ: Transaction Press.

Ktistakis, Y. 2006. *Islamic Religious Law and Muslim Greek Citizens: Between Communitarianism and Liberalism* [in Greek]. Athens and Thessaloniki: Sakkoulas Publications.

Kumar, K. 2002. The nation-state, the European Union and transnational identities, in *Muslim Europe or Euro-Islam – Politics, Culture, and Citizenship in the Age of Globalisation*, edited by N. AlSayyad and M. Castells. Lanham: Rowman & Littlefield, 53–68.

Kurtovik, Y. 1997. Justice and minorities, in *The Minority Phenomenon in Greece: A Contribution of Social Sciences* [in Greek], edited by K. Tsitselikis and D. Hristopoulos. Athens: Kritiki, 245–80.

Kwan, P. 1997. Jeffrey Dahmer and the cosynthesis of categories. *Hastings Law Journal*, 48(6), 1257–92.

Kymlicka, W. 1995. *Multicultural Citizenship – A Liberal Theory of Minority Rights*. Oxford: Clarendon.

Kymlicka, W. and Patten, A. 2003. Language rights and political theory. *Annual Review of Applied Linguistics*, 23, 3–21.

Laborde, C. 2008. *Critical Republicanism: The Hijab Controversy and Political Philosophy*. Oxford: Oxford University Press.

Langenfeld, C. 1990. *Die Gleichbehandlung von Mann und Frau im Europäischen Gemeinschaftsrecht*. Baden-Baden: Nomos.

Langenfeld, C. and Mohsen, S. 2005. Germany: The teacher head scarf case. *International Journal of Constitutional Law*, 3, 86–94.

Latraverse, S. 2008. *Report on Measures to Combat Discrimination: Directives 2000/43/EC and 2000/78/EC. Country Report: France* [Online: European Commission]. Available at: www.non-discrimination.net/content/media/2007-FR-Country%20Report%20Final.pdf [accessed: 1 March 2010].

Laufer, J. 2005. L'égalité professionnelle, in *Femmes, Genre et Sociétés: L'état des Savoirs*, edited by M. Maruani. Paris: La Découverte, 237–46.

Laulom, S. 2009. French legal approaches to equality and discrimination for intersecting grounds in employment relations, in *European Union Non-discrimination Law: Comparative Perspectives on Multidimensional Equality Law*, edited by D. Schiek and V. Chege. Oxon: Routledge-Cavendish, 279–94.

Laurance, J. 2004. The boy who can't stop eating. *The Independent Review*, 19 October, 6.

Lawrence, C. 1987. The id, the ego, and equal protection: Reckoning with unconscious racism. *Stanford Law Review*, 39, 317–88.

Lawson, A. 2008. *Disability and Equality Law in Britain: The Role of Reasonable Adjustment*. Oxford: Hart.

Leather, S. 2003. Social inequalities, nutrition and obesity, in *Adult Obesity: A Paediatric Challenge*, edited by L. Voss and T. Wilkin. London: Taylor & Francis, 53–60.

Lenhardt, R. 2004. Understanding the mark: Race, stigma, and equality in context. *New York University Law Review*, 79, 803–931.

Lenoble, J. and Maeschalck, M. 2010. Renewing the theory of public interest: The quest for a reflexive and learning-based approach to governance, in *Reflexive Governance: Redefining the Public Interest in a Pluralistic World*, edited by O. de Schutter and J. Lenoble. Oxford and Portland: Hart, 3–21.

Lester, A. and Bindman, G. 1972. *Race and Law*. London: Penguin.

Levene, T. 2006. Fat chance for the overweight. *Saturday Guardian*, 7 October 2006, 5.

Levin, S. and van Laar, C. 2006. *Stigma and Group Inequality*. London: Lawrence Erlbaum Associates.

Lewis, G. 2009. Celebrating intersectionality? Debates on a multi-faced concept in gender studies: Themes from a conference. *European Journal of Women's Studies*, 16(3), 203–10.

Leyden, W. von. 1985. *Aristotle on Equality and Justice: His Political Argument*. Hampshire and London: Macmillan.

Lien, P., Hardy-Fanta, C., Pinderhughes, D. and Sierra, C. 2008. *Expanding Categorization at the Intersection of Race and Gender: 'Women of Color' as a Political Category for African American, Latina, Asian American, and American Indian Women*. Paper to the American Political Science Association: Annual Meeting, Hynes Convention Center, Boston, Massachusetts [Online]. Available at: www.allacademic.com//meta/p_mla_apa_research_citation/2/7/9/6/8/pages279689/p279689-1.php [accessed: 22 June 2009].

Linton, S. 1998. *Claiming Disability*. New York: New York University Press.

Loenen, M.L.P. and Goldschmidt, J. (eds) 2007. *Religious Pluralism and Human Rights in Europe: Where to Draw the Line?* Antwerp and Oxford: Intersentia.

Loenen, T. 2009. The headscarf debate – approaching the intersection of sex, religion and race under the European Convention of Human Rights and EC equality law, in *European Union Non-Discrimination Law – Comparative Perspectives on Multidimensional Equality Law*, edited by D. Schiek and V. Chege. London and New York: Routledge-Cavendish, 313–28.

Lombardo, E. 2003. EU gender policy: Trapped in the Wollstonecraft dilemma? *European Journal of Women's Studies*, 10(2), 159–80.

Lorcerie, F. 2000. La lutte contre les discriminations ou l'intégration requalifiée. *Revue VEI enjeux*. 121.

Losen, D.J. and Orfield, G. (eds) 2002. *Racial Inequality in Special Education*. Cambridge, MA: Harvard Education Press.

Louis, B. St. 2002. Post-race/post-politics? Activist-intellectualism and the reification of race. *Ethnic and Racial Studies*, 25(4), 652–75.

Luft, R. and Ward, J. 2009. Towards an intersectionality just out of reach: Confronting challenges to intersectional practice. *Advances in Gender Research*, 13, 9–37.

McAdam, D., McCarthy, J.D. and Zald, M. 1996. *Comparative Perspectives on Social Movements: Political Opportunities, Mobilizing Structures, and Cultural Framings*. Cambridge, MA: Harvard University Press.

McColgan, A. 2007. Reconfiguring discrimination law. *Public Law*, 74–94.

McColgan, A. 2009. Class wars? Religion and (in)equality in the workplace. *Industrial Law Journal*, 38(1), 1–29.

McColgan, A., Niessen, J. and Palmer, F. 2006. *Comparative Analyses on National Measures to Combat Discrimination Outside Employment and Occupation*. Utrecht and Brussels: Human European Consultancy and Migration Policy Group.

McCrone, D. and Bechhofer, F. 2008. National identity and social inclusion. *Ethnic and Racial Studies*, 31(7), 1245–66.

McGhee, D. 2003. Moving to 'our' common ground – a critical examination of community cohesion discourse in twenty-first century Britain. *The Sociological Review*, 51(3), 376–404.

McGoldrick, D. 2006. *Human Rights and Religion: the Islamic Headscarf Debate in Europe*. Oxford and Portland, OR: Hart.

McVeigh, R. 2009. Céad Míle Slán, in *Darkmatter* [Online]. Available at: www.darkmatter101. org/site/2009/08/05/cead-mile-slan [accessed: 22 February 2010].

McVeigh, R. and Rolston, B. 2009. Civilising the Irish. *Race & Class*, 51(1), 2–28.

Magurová, Z. 2009. National report on multiple discrimination in Slovakia, in *Multiple Discrimination in EU Law*, edited by S. Burri and D. Schiek [Online]. Available at: http:// ec.europa.eu/social/BlobServlet?docId=3808&langId=en [accessed: 8 October 2009].

Magyari-Vincze, E. 2006. *Social Exclusion at the Crossroads of Gender, Ethnicity and Race – a View of Romani Women's Reproductive Health* [Online]. Available at: pdc.ceu.hu/ archive/00003117/ [accessed: 8 July 2009].

Mahrenholz, E.G. 2009. Das Kopftuch und seine Verwirklichungen. in *Der Stoff aus dem Konflikte sind – Debatten um das Kopftuch in Deutschland, Österreich und der Schwei*, edited by S. Berghahn and P. Rostock. Bielefeld: transcript Verlag, 193–224.

Makkonen, T. 2002. *Multiple, Compound and Intersectional Discrimination: Bringing the Experiences of the Most Marginalized to the Fore* [Online: Åbo Akademi University]. Available at: web.abo.fi/instut/imr/norfa/timo.pdf [accessed: 20 March 2009].

Malik, M. 2007. Modernising discrimination law: Proposals for a single equality act for Britain. *International Journal of Discrimination and the Law*, 9(2), 73–94.

Manfredi, S. and Vickers, L. 2009. Retirement and age discrimination: Managing retirement in higher education. *Industrial Law Journal*, 38(4), 343–64.

Mansell, J., Knapp, M., Beadle-Brown, J. and Beecham, J. 2007. *Deinstitutionalisation and Community Living – Outcomes and Costs: Report of a European Study, Volume 2: Main Report*. Canterbury: Tizard Centre, University of Kent.

Mantzoufas, P. 2000. The ethnic and religious identity as an element of the free development of the personality: The case of minorities [in Greek]. *Armenopoulos*, 54(8), 1037–67.

Mason, D. 1995. *Race and Ethnicity in Modern Britain*. Oxford: Oxford University Press.

Mattei, U. and Robilant, A. 2002. The art and science of critical scholarship, post-modernism and international style in the legal architecture of Europe. *European Review of Private Law*, 10(1), 29–59.

Maydell, B.v., Borchardt, K., Henke, K.-D. and Leitner, R. 2006. *Enabling Social Europe*. Berlin and Heidelberg: Springer.

Maylor, U. 2009. What is the meaning of 'black'? Researching 'black' respondents. *Ethnic and Racial Studies*, 32(2), 369–87.

Mazher Idriss, M. 2005. Laicité and the banning of the 'hijab' in France. *Legal Studies*, 25(2), 260–95.

Meço, H.C. 2007. *The Position of Women in Islamic Law and Our Response to the Attacks Against Islamic Law* [Online: Mufti of Komotini]. Available at: www.muftikomotini.com/ index.php?m=art&c=3&n=12 [accessed: 29 January 2009].

Medical News Today. 2009. Black girls are 50 percent more likely to be bulimic than white girls. *Medical News Today* [Online]. Available at: www.medicalnewstoday.com/articles/142820.php [accessed: 16 June 2009].

Meenan, H. (ed.) 2007. *Equality Law in an Enlarged European Union – Understanding the Article 13 Directives*. Cambridge: Cambridge University Press.

Mernissi, F. 2003. *Beyond the Veil – Male-Female Dynamics in Muslim Society*. London: Saqi Books.

Merry, S.E. 1988. Legal pluralism. *Law and Society Review*, 22, 869–96.

Merry, S.E. 2006. Human rights and transnational culture: Regulating gender violence through global law. *Osgoode Hall Law Journal*, 44(1), 53–75.

Miles, R. 1989. *Racism*. London and New York: Routledge.

Milios, G. 1997. The formation of the neo-Greek nation and state as a process of economic and population homogenization, in *The Minority Phenomenon in Greece: A Contribution of Social Sciences* [in Greek], edited by K. Tsitselikis and D. Hristopoulos. Athens: Kritiki, 281–314.

Ministry of Foreign Affairs, Hungary. 2004. *Fact Sheets on Hungary* [Online]. Available at: www.kulugyminiszterium.hu/NR/rdonlyres/05DF7A51-99A5-4BFE-B8A5-210344C02B1A/0/Roma_en.pdf [accessed: 8 July 2009].

Minow, M. 1987. Justice engendered. *Harvard Law Review*, 101(1), 11–95.

Minow, M. 1997. *Not Only for Myself: Identity Politics and the Law*. New York: New Press.

Mirza, H.S. 1992. *Young, Female and Black*. London: Routledge.

Mitnick, E.J. 2007. Law, cognition, and identity. *Louisiana Law Review*, 67(3), 823–70.

Modood, T. 1992. Cultural diversity and racial discrimination in employment selection, in *Discrimination: The Limits of Law*, edited by B. Hepple and E.M. Szyszczak. New York: Mansell, 227–39.

Modood, T. 2007. *Multiculturalism as a Civic Idea*. Cambridge, MA: Malden.

Modood, T., Berthoud, R., Lakey, J., Nazroo, J., Smith, P., Virdee, S. and Beishon, S. 2007. *Ethnic Minorities in Britain – Diversity and Disadvantage – Fourth National Survey of Ethnic Minorities*. London: Policy Studies Institute.

Modood, T., Triandafyllidou, A. and Zapata-Barrero, R. (eds) 2006. *Multiculturalism, Muslims and Citizenship – A European Approach*. Abingdon: Routledge.

Modood, T., Berthoud, R., Lakey, J., Nazroo, J., Smith, P., Virdee, S. and Beishon, S. 1997. *Ethnic Minorities in Britain: Diversity and Disadvantage*. Fourth PSI Survey. London: Policy Studies Institute.

Monaghan, K. 2009. The Equality Bill: A sheep in wolf's clothing or something more? *European Human Rights Law Review*, 4, 512–37.

Monahan, J., Walker, L. and Mitchell, G. 2008. Contextual evidence of gender discrimination: The ascendance of 'social frameworks'. *Virginia Law Review*, 94, 1715.

Moon, G. 2006a. From equal treatment to appropriate treatment: What lessons can Canadian equality law on dignity and on reasonable accommodation teach the UK? *European Human Rights Law Review*, 6, 695–721.

Moon, G. 2006b. Multiple discrimination – problems compounded or solutions found? [Online]. Available at: www.justice.org.uk/images/pdfs/multiplediscrimination.pdf [assessed: 29 July 2010].

Moon, G. 2007. Enforcement bodies, in *Cases, Materials and Text on National, Supranational and International Non-Discrimination Law*, edited by D. Schiek, L. Waddington and M. Bell. Oxford and Portland, OR: Hart, 915–21.

Morlok, M. and Krüper, J. 2003. Auf dem Weg zum 'forum neutrum'? – Die Kopftuch-Entscheidung des BVerwG. *Neue Juristische Wochenschrift*, 56, 1020–22.

Morris, J. 1993. Gender and disability, in *Disabling Barriers Enabling Environments*, edited by J. Swain, V. Finkelstein, S. French and M. Oliver. London: Sage, 85–92.

Morris, J. (ed.) 1996. *Encounters with Strangers: Feminism and Disability*. London: The Women's Press.

Morris, R. and Clements, L. 2001. *Disability, Social Care, Health and Travelling People*. Cardiff: Traveller Law Research Unit.

Mossuz-Lavau, J. 2003. Une Loi? Non, *Le Monde*, 17 December.

Muckel, S. 1999. Religionsfreiheit für Muslime in Deutschland, in *Dem Staate, was des Staates – der Kirche, was der Kirche ist – Festschrift für J Listl zum 70. Geburtstag*, edited by J. Isensee, W. Rees and W. Rüfner. Berlin: Duncker & Humblot, 239–57.

Mueller, S. 2008. *Analysis of Anti-Segregation Policy in Countries Participating in the Decade of Roma Inclusion* [Online]. Available at: www.szmm.gov.hu/download.php?ctag=download&do cID=20411 [accessed: 8 July 2009].

Munir, L.Z. n.d. *General Introduction to Islamic Law* [Online: Law and Finance International Partnership course materials]. Available at: www.lfip.org/laws718/docs/lily-pdf/Introduction_ to_Islamic_Law.pdf [accessed: 7 March 2009].

Näkkäläjärvi, K. 2006. *Saamen kielilain toteutuminen vuosina 2004–2006. Kertomus saamen kielilain toteutumisesta.* Saamen kielineuvosto: Saamen kielen toimisto.

Nash, K. 2009. *The Cultural Politics of Human Rights – Comparing the US and the UK.* Cambridge: Cambridge University Press.

National Equality Panel Report. 2010. *An Anatomy of Economic Inequality in the UK* [Online: Government Equalities Office]. Available at: www.equalities.gov.uk/national_equality_panel/ publications.aspx [accessed: 14 July 2010].

Nielsen, R. 2009. Is European Union equality law capable of addressing multiple and intersectional discrimination yet? Precautions against neglecting intersectional cases, in *European Union Non-Discrimination Law – Comparative Perspectives on Multidimensional Equality Law*, edited by D. Schiek and V. Chege. London: Routledge-Cavendish, 31–51.

Niemi, R. 2006. Kuka pelkää kotiäitiä?, in *Vääryyskirja*, edited by T. Helne and M. Laatu. Helsinki: Kelan tutkimusosasto.

Noël, O. 2000. L'universel républicain à l'épreuve. Discrimination, ethnicisation, ségrégation. La face cachée de l'intégration: Les discriminations institutionnelles à l'embauche. *VEI* n°126, Montrouge, CNDP.

Nussbaum, M. 2004. *Hiding From Humanity.* Princeton, NJ: Princeton University Press.

Nylund-Oja, M. and Pentikäinen, J. 1997. *Suomen kulttuurivähemmistöt.* Helsinki: Suomen Unesco-toimikunnan julkaisuja.

O'Cinneide, C. 2007. *Report on Measures to Combat Discrimination Directives 2000/43/ EC and 2000/78/EC Country Report 2007* [Online: European Network of legal experts in the non-discrimination field]. Available at: www.non-discrimination.net/en/law/ National%20legislation/country-reportsEN.jsp [accessed: 25 July 2010].

O'Cinneide, C. 2008. *Report on Measures to Combat Discrimination Directives 2000/43/EC and 2000/78/EC Country Report 2008* [Online: European Network of legal experts in the non-discrimination field]. Available at: www.migpolgroup.com/public/docs/169.2008_ Countryreportonmeasurestocombatdiscrimination_UK_EN.pdf [accessed: 20 June 2010].

Okin, S. 1999. Is multiculturalism bad for women?, in *Is Multiculturalism Bad for Women?*, edited by J. Cohen, M. Howard and M. Nussbaum. Princeton, NJ: Princeton University Press, 7–24.

Oliver, J. and Lee, T. 2002. Public opinion and the politics of America's obesity epidemic. *KSG Working Paper No. RWP02-017.*

Oliver, M. 1990. *The Politics of Disablement.* Basingstoke: Macmillan.

Oliver, M. 1996. *Understanding Disability: From Theory to Practice.* Basingstoke: Macmillan.

Ombudsman for Minorities. 2009. *Annual Report of the Ombudsman for Minorities 2008* [Online]. Available at: www.vahemmistovaltuutettu.fi/intermin/vvt/home.nsf/files/VV2008_englanti/ $file/VV2008_englanti.pdf [accessed: 7 July 2009].

OMCT. 2002. *Violence Against Women in Greece – Report Submitted to the Committee on the Elimination of Discrimination against Women at its Exceptional Session 5–23 August 2002* [Online: Greek Helsinki Monitor and the World Organisation Against Torture]. Available at: www.omct.org/pdf/VAW/GreeceEng2002.pdf [accessed: 20 April 2009].

OMCT. 2004. *State Violence in Greece: An Alternative Report to the United Nations Committee Against Torture 33rd Session* [Online: Greek Helsinki Monitor et al.]. Available at: www.omct. org/pdf/procedures/2004/joint/s_violence_greece_10_2004.pdf [accessed: 29 May 2009].

Omi, M. and Winant, H. 1994. *Racial Formation in the United States.* 2nd edition. New York: Routledge.

Ontario Human Rights Commission. 2001a. *Discussion Paper – An Intersectional Approach to Discrimination: Addressing Multiple Grounds in Human Rights Claims* [Online]. Available at: www.ohrc.on.ca/en/resources/discussion_consultation/DissIntersectionalityFtnts/pdf [accessed: 11 June 2010].

Oprea, A. 2009. Intersectionality backlash: A Romani's feminist response. *Roma Rights*, 2 [Online]. Available at: www.errc.org/cikk.php?page=3&cikk=3564 [accessed: 29 October 2010].

O'Reilly, A. 2008. Too fat to work. *The F Word – Contemporary UK Feminism* [Online]. Available at: www.thefword.org.uk/blog/2008/06/too_fat_to_work [accessed: 22 June 2009].

Örücü, E. 2007. Developing comparative law, in *Comparative Law – A Handbook*, edited by E. Örücü and D. Nelken. Oxford and Portland, OR: Hart, 43–65.

Örücü, E. and Nelken, D. (eds) 2007. *Comparative Law – A Handbook.* Oxford and Portland, OR: Hart.

Ostrander, R. 2008. When identities collide: Masculinity, disability and race. *Disability and Society*, 23(6), 585–97.

Owen, D. 1994. *Ethnic Minority Women and the Labour Market: Analysis of the 1991 Census.* Manchester: EOC.

Page, R. 1984. *Stigma.* London: Routledge and Kegan Paul.

Pannick, D. 1985. *Sex Discrimination Law.* Oxford: Clarendon Press and Oxford University Press.

Pantelidou-Malouta, M. 2007. State feminism, gender equality policies and social sentiments [in Greek]. *Elliniki Epitheorisi Politikis Epistimis*, 29, 5–39.

Parens, E. and Asch, A. 2000. *Prenatal Testing and Disability Rights.* Washington, DC: Georgetown University Press.

Parker, C. with Bulic, I. 2010. *Wasted Time, Wasted Money, Wasted Lives ... A Wasted Opportunity?* London: European Coalition for Community Living.

Paskalia, V. 2007. *Free Movement, Social Security and Gender in the EU.* Oxford: Hart.

Paskalia, V. 2009. Co-ordination of social security in the European Union: An overview of recent case law. *Common Market Law Review*, 46, 1177–218.

Patten, A. 2001. Political theory and language policy. *Political Theory*, 29(5), 691–715.

Payet, J.P., Geoffroy, G., Laforgue, D. and Vissac, G. 2002. *Monde et territoires de la ségregation scolaire.* FASILD. Bron: ARIESE.

Pelling, R. 2005. Of course it's ok to call another woman a Hobnob-guzzling, lazy lard arse. *Independent on Sunday*, 30 October [Online]. Available at: www.independent.co.uk/opinion/columnists/rowan-pelling-of-course-its-ok-to-call-another-woman-a-hobnobguzzling-lazy-lardarse-507300.html [accessed: 20 July 2010].

Personnel Today. 2005. Obesity research: Fattism is the last bastion of employee discrimination [Online]. Available at: www.personneltoday.com/Articles/2005/10/25/32213/Fattism+is+the +last+bastion+of+employee+discrimination.htm#ArticleBody [accessed: 20 July 2010].

Phillipson, R., Nannut, M. and Skutnabb-Kangas, T. 1995. Introduction, in *Linguistic Human Rights: Overcoming Linguistic Discrimination*, edited by T. Skutnabb-Kangas and R. Philipson. Berlin: Mouton de Gruyter, 1–18.

Pierce, M. 2003a. *Minority Ethnic People with Disabilities in Northern Ireland*. Dublin: Equality Authority.

Pierce, M. 2003b. Disabled ethnic minority people in Ireland: The need for recognition, in *Re-thinking Identity: The Challenge of Diversity*, edited by K. Zappone, Joint Equality and Human Rights Forum, 7–23 [Online]. Available at: www.ihrc.ie/download/pdf/rethinking_identity_ the_challenge_of_diversity.pdf [accessed: 15 July 2010].

Pihlajamäki, H. 2004. Against metaphysics in law: The historical background of American and Scandinavian legal realism compared. *American Journal of Comparative Law*, 52(2), 469–87.

Pitt, G. 2007. Religion or belief: Aiming at the right target?, in *Equality Law in an Enlarged European Union*, edited by H. Meenan. Cambridge: Cambridge University Press, 202–30.

Platero Mendez, R. 2007. Intersecting gender and sexual orientation: An analysis of sexuality and citizenship in gender equality policies in Spain. *Critical Review of International Social and Political Philosophy*, 10(4), 575–97.

Pofalla, R. 2004. Kopftuch ja-Kruzifix nein? *Neue Juristische Wochenschrift*, 57, 1218–20.

Poiret, C. and De Rudder, V. 1997. *La prévention de la discrimination raciale, de la xénophobie et la promotion de l'égalité de traitement dans l'entreprise: Une étude de cas en France*. Fondation Européenne pour l'amélioration des conditions de vie et de travail/URMIS.

Pool, R. 2001. *Fat: Fighting the Obesity Epidemic*. Oxford: Oxford University Press.

Popkin, B. 2005. The implications of the nutrition transition for obesity in the developing world, in *Obesity Prevention and Public Health*, edited by D. Crawford and R. Jeffery. Oxford: Oxford University Press.

Post, R. 2003. Law and cultural conflict. *Chicago-Kent Law Review*, 78, 485–508.

Poulter, S. 1997. Muslim headscarves in school: Contrasting legal approaches in England and France. *Oxford Journal of Legal Studies*, 17(1), 43–74.

Priestley, M. 1998. Constructions and creations: Idealism, materialism and disability theory. *Disability and Society*, 13(1), 75–94.

Primon, J.-L. 2004. L'insertion professionnelle après des études supérieures des femmes issues des familles d'immigrés des pays du Maghreb: Une inégalité redoublée. *Marché du travail et genre Maghreb Europe*, Coll. Brussels Economic Series, Ed. du Dulbea asbl.

Psychogiopoulou, E. 2008. *Strasbourg Court Jurisprudence and Human Rights in Greece: An Overview of Litigation, Implementation and Domestic Reform* [Online: ELIAMEP]. Available at: www.juristras.eliamep.gr/wp-content/uploads/2008/09/greece.pdf [accessed: 20 May 2009].

Puhl, R.M. and Brownell, K.D. 2003. Psychosocial origins of obesity stigma: Toward changing a powerful and pervasive bias. *Obesity Reviews*, 4(4), 213–27.

Purporka, L. and Zádori, Z. 1999. *The Health Status of Roma in Hungary*. Budapest: World Bank Regional Office Hungary.

Quindlen, A. 1993. Public and private: In thin air. *New York Times* [Online]. Available at: www. nytimes.com/1993/05/16/opinion/public-private-in-thin-air.html?sec=health [accessed: 18 September 2009].

Quinn, G. 1999. The human rights of people with disabilities under EU law, in *The EU and Human Rights*, edited by P. Alston, M. Bustelo and J. Heenan. Oxford: Oxford University Press, 281–326.

Quinn, G. 2008. Disability discrimination law in the European Union, in *Equality Law in an Enlarged European Union*, edited by H. Meenan. Cambridge: Cambridge University Press, 231–77.

Quinn, G. and Degener, T. 2002. *Human Rights and Disability: The Current Use and Future Potential of United Nations Human Rights Instruments in the Context of Disability*, OHCHR, New York and Geneva: United Nations (U.N. Sales No: E.02.XIV.6).

Radacic, I. 2008. Gender equality jurisprudence of the European Court of Human Rights. *European Journal of International Law*, 19(4), 841–57.

Raday, F. 2003. Culture, religion and gender. *International Journal of Constitutional Law*, 1, 663–715.

Raittila, P. 2004. *Venäläiset ja virolaiset Toisina. Tapaustutkimuksia ja analyysimenetelmien kehittelyä*. Tampere: Tampere University Press.

Ramachandran, G. 2005. Intersectionality as a 'catch 22': Why identity performance demands are neither harmless nor reasonable. *Albany Law Review*, 69(1), 299–342.

Ramirez, D. 1995. Multicultural empowerment: It's not just black and white anymore. *Stanford Law Review*, 47(5), 957–92.

Rankin, J. 2009. Ambitious goals with limited funds. *European Voice*, 14(36), 18–19.

Razack, S.H. 2004. Imperilled Muslim women, dangerous Muslim men and civilised Europeans: Legal and social responses to forced marriages. *Feminist Legal Studies*, 12(2), 129–74.

Reay, D., Hollingworth, S., Williams, K., Crozier, G., Jamieson, F., James, D. and Beedell, P. 2007. 'A darker shade of pale?' Whiteness, the middle classes and multi-ethnic inner city schooling. *Sociology*, 41(6), 1041–60.

Reid, M.K. and Knight, M.G. 2006. Disability justifies exclusion of minority students: A critical history grounded in disability studies. *Educational Researcher*, 35(6), 18–23.

Reuter, S. and Mazur, A.G. 2003. Paradoxes of gender-biased universalism: The dynamics of French equality discourse, in *Gendering Europeanisation*, edited by U. Liebert. Brussels: P.I.E.- Peter Lang, 47–82.

Rex, J. 1986. *Race and Ethnicity*. Milton Keynes: Open University Press.

Rey Martinez, F. 2008. La discriminacion multiple: Una realidad antigua, und concepto nueavo. *Revista Espanola de Derecho Constitutional*, 84, I–XIII.

Ribas Mateos, N. 2000. Old communities, excluded women and change in Western Thrace (Thracian Greece, the Provinces of Xanthi, Rhodopi and Evros). *Papers: Revista de Sociologia*, 60, 119–50.

Rich, C.G. 2004. Performing racial and ethnic identity: Discrimination by proxy and the future of Title VII. *New York University Law Review*, 79(4), 1134–270.

Ringold, D., Orenstein, M.A. and Wilkens, E. 2005. *Roma in an Expanding Europe: Breaking the Poverty Cycle*, Washington, DC [Online]. Available at: www.wds.worldbank.org/external/default/WDSContentServer/WDSP/IB/2004/11/17/000090341_20041117141419/Rendered/PDF/301560PAPER0Ro1Sum01see0also0301761.pdf [accessed: 8 July 2009].

Risse, T. 2009. Social constructivism and European integration, in *European Integration Theory*, edited by A. Wiener and T. Diez. 2nd edition. Oxford: Oxford University Press, 144–60.

Rist, R. 1970. Social class and teacher expectations: The self-fulfilling prophecy in ghetto education. *Harvard Educational Review*, 40, 411–51.

Rivera, J. 2007. An equal protection standard for national origin subclassifications: The context that matters. *Washington Law Review*, 82(4), 897–966.

Robbers, G. (ed) 2005. *Staat und Kirche in der Europäischen Union*. Baden-Baden: Nomos.

Robert, J. 2003. Religious liberty and French secularism. *Brigham Young University Law Review*, 28(2), 637–60.

Roberts, L.M. and Roberts, D.D. 2007. Testing the limits of antidiscrimination law: The business, legal and ethical ramifications of cultural profiling at work. *Duke Journal of Gender Law and Policy*, 14(1), 369–406.

Robertson, S. 2004. Men and disability, in *Disabling Barriers – Enabling Environments*, edited by J. Swain, S. French, C. Barnes and C. Thomas. 2nd edition. London: Sage, 75–80.

Roehling, M. 2002. Weight discrimination in the workplace: Ethical issues and analysis. *Journal of Business Ethics*, 40, 177–89.

Roggeband, C. and Verloo, M. 2007. Dutch women are liberated, migrant women are a problem: The evolution of policy frames on gender and migration in the Netherlands 1995–2005. *Social Policy and Administration*, 41(3), 271–88.

Rorive, I. 2009. A comparative and European examination of national institutions in the field of racism and discrimination, in *New Institutions for Human Rights Protection*, edited by K. Boyle. Oxford: Oxford University Press, 137–73.

Roseberry, L. 2002. Equality rights and discrimination law in Scandinavia, in *Stability and Changes in Nordic Labour Law*, edited by P. Wahlgreen. Scandinavian Studies in Law, 43, 215–56.

Roseberry, L. 2009. Religion, ethnicity and gender in the Danish headscarf case, in *European Union Non-Discrimination Law: Comparative Perspectives on Multidimensional Equality Law*, edited by D. Schiek and V. Chege. Abingdon and New York: Routledge-Cavendish, 329–51.

Rousso, H. 2001. *Strong Proud Sisters: Girls and Young Women with Disabilities*. Washington, DC: Center for Women Policy Studies.

Rubenfeld, J. 2002. The anti-antidiscrimination agenda. *Yale Law Journal*, 111(5), 1141–78.

Ruhs, M. 2006. *Greasing the Wheels of the Flexible Labour Market: Eastern European Labour Migration in the UK*. Oxford: COMPAS Working Paper No. 38.

Ruwanpura, K. 2008. Multiple identities, multiple discrimination: A critical review. *Feminist Economics*, 14(3), 77–105.

Ryan, C. 2002. The difference between difference and otherness, in *Who, Exactly, is the Other? Western and Transcultural Perspectives*, edited by S. Shankman and M. Lollini. Portland, OR: University of Oregon Press.

Sacksofsky, U. 2009a. Religion and equality in Germany: The headscarf debate from a constitutional perspective, in *European Union Non-Discrimination Law: Comparative Perspectives on Multidimensional Equality Law*, edited by D. Schiek and V. Chege. Abingdon and New York: Routledge-Cavendish, 353–70.

Sacksofsky, U. 2009b. Kopftuchverbot in den Ländern – Am Beispiel des Landes Hessen, in *Der Stoff aus dem Konflikte sind – Debatten um das Kopftuch in Deutschland, Österreich und der Schweiz*, edited by S. Berghahn and P. Rostock. Bielefeld: transcript Verlag, 275–93.

Safran, W. 2008. Names, labels, and identities: Sociopolitical contexts and the question of ethnic categorization. *Identities: Global Studies in Culture and Power*, 15(4), 437–61.

Said, E. 1978. *Orientalism: Western Conceptions of the Orient*. London: Routledge.

Salway, S. 2008. Labour market experiences of young UK Bangladeshi men: Identity, inclusion and exclusion in inner-city London. *Ethnic and Racial Studies*, 31(6), 1126–52.

Sami Parliamentarian Conference. 1995. *Declaration From the First Sami Parliamentarian Conference* [Online]. Available at: www.sametinget.se/1433 [accessed: 12 July 2010].

Sanchez, J. 2008. *Study on the Specific Risks of Discrimination Against Persons in Situation of Major Dependence or with Complex Needs – Country Report: France* [Online: European Commission]. Available at: www.non-discrimination.eu [accessed: 1 March 2010].

Sauli, H., Bardy, M. and Salmi, M. 2002. Elinolojen koventuminen pikkulapsiperheissä, in *Suomalainen hyvinvointi 2002*, edited by M. Heikkilä and M. Kautto. Helsinki: Stakes, 32–61.

Schacter, J.S. 1997. Skepticism, culture, and the gay civil rights debate in a post-civil-rights era. *Harvard Law Review*, 110(3), 648–731.

Schavan, A. 2004. Das Kopftuch ist ein Politisches Symbol. *Zeitschrift für Ausländerrecht und Ausländerpolitik*, 24(1), 5.

Schiek, D. 2002a. A new framework on equal treatment of persons in EC law? Directives 2000/43/EC, 2000/78/EC and 2002/???/EC changing Directive 76/207/EEC in context. *European Law Journal*, 8(2), 290–314.

Schiek, D. 2002b. Torn between arithmetic and substantive equality? Perspectives on equality in German labour law. *International Journal of Comparative Labour Law and Industrial Relations*, 18(2), 149–67.

Schiek, D. 2004. Just a piece of cloth? German courts and employees with headscarves. *Industrial Law Journal*, 33(1), 68–73.

Schiek, D. 2005. Broadening the scope and the norms of EU gender equality law: Towards a multidimensional conception of equality law. *Maastricht Journal of European and Comparative Law*, 12(4), 427–66.

Schiek, D. 2006. The ECJ decision in Mangold: A further twist on the effects of directives and constitutional relevance of Community equality legislation. *Industrial Law Journal*, 35(3), 329–41.

Schiek, D. 2007a. Indirect discrimination, in *Cases, Materials and Text on International, Supranational and National Non-Discrimination Law*, edited by D. Schiek, L. Waddington and M. Bell. Oxford and Portland, OR: Hart, 323–476.

Schiek, D. 2007b. *Allgemeines Gleichbehandlungsgesetz*. Munich: Sellier Publishers.

Schiek, D. 2009. From European Union non-discrimination law towards multidimensional equality law for Europe, in *European Union Non-discrimination Law: Comparative Perspectives on Multidimensional Equality Law*, edited by D. Schiek and V. Chege. Oxon: Routledge-Cavendish, 3–27.

Schiek, D. 2010a. EU non-discrimination law and policy: Gender in the maze of multidimensional equalities, in *Liber Amicorum Heide Pfarr*, edited by M. Koerner, M. and R. Zimmer. Baden-Baden: Nomos.

Schiek, D. 2010b. Comparative law and European harmonisation – a match made in heaven or uneasy bedfellows? *European Business Law Review*, 21(2), 203–55.

Schiek, D. and Chege, V. (eds) 2009. *European Union Non-Discrimination Law: Comparative Perspectives on Multidimensional Equality Law*. London and New York: Routledge-Cavendish.

Schiek, D., Waddington, L. and Bell, M. (eds) 2007. *Cases, Materials and Text on National, Supranational and International Non-Discrimination Law*. Oxford and Portland, OR: Hart.

Schofield, H. 2003. *Jewish Dad Backs Headscarf Daughters* [Online: BBC 10 January 2003]. Available at: http://news.bbc.co.uk/1/hi/world/europe/3149588.stm [accessed: 20 May 2010].

Scott, J. and Trubek, D.M. 2002. Mind the gap: Law and new approaches to governance in the European Union. *European Law Journal*, 8(1), 1–28.

Seidell, C. 2005. The epidemiology of obesity: A global perspective, in *Obesity Prevention and Public Health*, edited by D. Crawford and R. Jeffery. Oxford: Oxford University Press, 3–19.

Shakespeare, T. 1996. Power and prejudice: Issues of gender, sexuality and disability, in *Disability and Society: Emerging Issues and Insights*, edited by L. Barton. Essex: Longman, 191–213.

Shapiro, J.P. 1993. *No Pity: People with Disabilities Forging a New Civil Rights Movement*. New York: Times Books.

Shaw, A. 2006. *The Embodiment of Disobedience: Fat Black Women's Unruly Political Bodies*. Lanham: Lexington Books.

Sheldon, A. 2004. Women and disability, in *Disabling Barriers – Enabling Environments*, edited by J. Swain, S. French, C. Barnes and C. Thomas. 2nd edition. London: Sage, 69–74.

Siim, B. 2000. *Gender and Citizenship: Politics and Agency in France, Britain and Denmark*. Cambridge: Cambridge University Press.

Silvers, A. 1999. Triple difference: Disability, race, gender and the politics of recognition, in *Disability, Divers-ability and Legal Change*, edited by L.A. Basser Marks and M. Jones. The Hague, Boston and London: Martinus Nijhoff, 75–100.

Silvers, A., Wassermann, D. and Mahowold, M.B. 1998. *Disability, Difference, Discrimination Perspectives in Bioethics and Public Policy*. Lanham, MD: Rowman & Littlefield.

Silvestri, S. 2009. Islam and religion in the EU political system. *West European Politics*, 32(6), 1212–39.

Simon, P. 2004a. L'encombrante visibilité, in *La Laïcité Dévoilée – Quinze Années de Débat en Quarante Rebonds*, edited by J.-M. Helvig, F. Pouillon, F. Khosrokhavar and F. Gaspard. Paris: Libération Ed. De l'Aube.

Simon, P. 2004b. *Towards a Set of Common Rules for the Measurement of Discrimination*. European Conference on Data to Promote Equality, Helsinki, 9–10 December.

Simon, P. 2007. *Ethnic Statistics and Data Protection in the Council of Europe Countries*. Strasbourg: Council of Europe.

Simon, P., Kirszbaum T., Chafi, M. and Tissot, S. 2001. *Les discriminations raciales et ethniques dans l'accès au logement social*. Paris: Groupe d'Etude et de Lutte contre les Discriminations.

Singh Chowdhary, M. 2004. France: Religious freedom in the land of Voltaire. *Sikh Spektrum*, 16 [Online]. Available at: www.sikhspectrum.com/052004/manbir_france_9.htm [accessed 1 June 2009].

Sintomer, Y. 2009. Kopftuch und 'foulard': Ein vergleichender Blick aus Frankreich auf die deutsche Debatte, in *Der Stoff aus dem Konflikte sind – Debatten um das Kopftuch in Deutschland, Österreich und der Schweiz*, edited by S. Berghahn and P. Rostock. Bielefeld: transcript Verlag, 131–48.

Skjeie, H. 2007. Headscarves in schools: European comparisons, in *Religious Pluralism and Human Rights in Europe: Where to Draw the Line?* edited by M.L.P. Loenen and J. Goldschmidt. Antwerp and Oxford: Intersentia, 129–45.

Skjeie, H. 2009. Multiple equality claims in the practice of the Norwegian anti-discrimination agencies, in *European Union Non-Discrimination Law: Comparative Perspectives on Multidimensional Equality Law*, edited by D. Schiek and V. Chege. Abingdon and New York: Routledge-Cavendish, 295–309.

Slovak NGO Coalition. 2008. *Joint Submission: Shadow Report to CEDAW for the Slovak Republic* [Online]. Available at: www2.ohchr.org/english/bodies/cedaw/docs/ngos/IWRAW_Asia_Pacific_Slovak41.pdf [accessed: 9 September 2009].

Small, J.G. and Grant, E. 2005. Dignity, discrimination and context: New directions in South African and Canadian human rights law. *Human Rights Review*, 6(2), 25–63.

Smith, B.G. and Hutchison, B. (eds) 2004. *Gendering Disability*. New Jersey: Rutgers.

Smith, O. 2005. Ireland's multiple ground anti-discrimination framework – extending the limitations? *International Journal of Discrimination and the Law*, 8, 7–31.

Smith, R.K. 2007. Unveiling a role for the EU? The 'headscarf controversy' in European schools. *Education and the Law*, 19(2), 111–30.

Smits, J. 2002. *The Making of European Private Law Towards a Ius Commune Europaeum as a Mixed Legal System*. Antwerp, Oxford and New York: Intersentia.Solanke, I. 2009a. Stigma: A limiting principle allowing multiple-consciousness in anti-discrimination law?, in *European Union Nondiscrimination Law: Comparative Perspectives on Multi-Dimensional Equality Law*, edited by D. Schiek and V. Chege. Abingdon: Routledge-Cavendish, 115–36.

Solanke, I. 2009b. Putting race and gender together: A new approach to intersectionality. *Modern Law Review*, 72(5), 723–46.

Solovay, S. 2000. *Tipping the Scales of Justice*. Amherst: Prometheus Books.

Soltaridis, S. 2006. The election of the pseudo-Mufti divides the minority [in Greek]. *Eleftherotypia*, 28 December 2006.

Sotomayor, S. 2009. *A Latina Judge's Voice* [Online: *New York Times*] Available at: www.nytimes.com/2009/05/15/us/politics/15judge.text.html [accessed: 25 September 2009].

Spinner-Halev, J. 2008. Legal pluralism, privatization of law and multiculturalism. *Theoretical Enquiries in Law*, 9(2), 553–72.

Squires, J. 2008. Intersecting inequalities: Reflecting on the subjects and objects of equality. *Political Quarterly*, 79, 53–61.

Stasi Report. 2003. *Rapport sur la Laïcité dans la République*, 11 December 2003.

Statistics Finland. 2007. The largest foreign-language groups 1997 and 2007, based on population and cause of death statistics. Available at: www.stat.fi/til/vaerak/2007/vaerak_2007_2008-03-28_kuv_004_en.html [accessed: 6 July 2010].

Stein, S. and Berthou, K. 2005. France, in *EU and International Employment Law*, edited by V. Du Feu, V. Edmunds, E. Gillow and M. Hopkins. Bristol: Jordans, looseleaf.

Stienstra, D., Fricke, Y. and D'Aubin, A. 2002. *Baseline Assessment: Inclusion and Disability in World Bank Activities*. Winnipeg: Canadian Centre on Disability Studies.

Stolcke, V. 1995. Talking culture: New boundaries, new rhetorics of exclusion in Europe. *Current Anthropology*, 26(1), 1–24.

Stolcke, V. 2003. Comment on R.D. Grillo, 'Cultural essentialism and cultural anxiety'. *Anthropological Theory*, 3(2), 175–7.

Stolleis, M. 2003. Historische und ideengeschichtliche Entwicklung des Gleichheitssatzes, in *Gleichheit und Nichtdiskriminierung im nationalen und internationalen Menschenrechtsschutz*, edited by R. Wolfrum. Berlin, Heidelberg and New York: Springer, 7–24.

Stoller, R.J. 1968. *Sex and Gender: On the Development of Masculinity and Femininity*. New York: Science House.

Stratigaki, M. 2007. *The Gender of Welfare Policy* [in Greek]. Athens: Metaichmio Publications.

Street, H., Howe, G.Q.C. and Bindman, G. 1967. *The Street Report on Anti-Discrimination Legislation*. London: Political and Economic Planning.

Stuart, O. 1993. Double oppression: An appropriate starting point?, in *Disabling Barriers – Enabling Environments*, edited by J. Swain, V. Finkelstein, S. French and M. Oliver. London: Sage/Open University, 93–9.

Study Group on Social Justice in European Private Law. 2004. Social justice in European contract law: A manifesto. *European Law Journal*, 10(6), 653–74.

Sturm, S. 2001. Second-generation employment discrimination: A structural approach. *Columbia Law Review*, 101(3), 461–568.

Stychin, C.F. 2001. Civil solidarity of fragmented identities? The politics of sexualities and citizenship in France. *Social & Legal Studies*, 10(3), 347–75.

Suomen romanit. 2004. Sosiaali- ja terveysministeriö, esitteitä 2004, 2.

Sur, M. 2009. General framework and historical development of labor law in Turkey. *Comparative Labor Law and Policy Journal*, 30(2), 183–98.

Sural, N. 2009. Anti-discrimination rules and policies in Turkey. *Comparative Labor Law and Policy Journal*, 30(2), 245–72.

Syrigos, A. 2007. New dynamics in the Muslim minority of Thrace [in Greek]. *Fileleftheri Emfasi*, 31, 34–43.

Szyszczak, E. 2006. Experimental governance: The open method of coordination. *European Law Journal*, 12(4), 486–95.

Tanttu, J. 2008. Venäjänkielisenä Suomessa 2008: Selvitys vähemmistövaltuutetulle. Helsinki: Edita.

Tatum, B. 2002. *Why Are All the Black Kids Sitting Together in the Cafeteria?* New York: Basic Books.

Tavares da Silva, M.R. 2002. *Twenty-five Years of Council of Europe Action in the Field of Equality Between Women and Men*. EG (2002) 5. Strasbourg: Council of Europe.

Taylor, C. 1992. The politics of recognition, in *Multiculturalism and the Politics of Recognition*, edited by A. Gutman. Princeton, NJ: Princeton University Press, 25–73.

Taylor, F.W. 1911. *The Principles of Scientific Management*. Norwood, MA: Plimpton Press.

Thorson Plesner, I. 2005a. Legal limitations to freedom of religion or belief in school education. *Emory International Law Review*, 19(2), 557–86.

Thorson Plesner, I. 2005b. *The Islamic Headscarf Controversy and the Future of Freedom of Religion and Belief*. Paper to the Seminar: The European Court on Human Rights between Fundamentalist and Liberal Secularism, Strasbourg, 28–30 July.

Thynne, J. 2007. Moira: Furore over national treasure [Online: *Independent*]. Available at: www.independent.co.uk/news/media/moira-furore-over-a-national-treasure-443727.html [accessed: 19 July 2007].

Tilly, C. 1998. *Durable Inequality*. Berkeley, CA: University of California Press.

Traustadóttir, R. and Johnson, K. (eds) 2000. *Women with Intellectual Disabilities: Finding a Place in the World*. London: Jessica Kingsley Publishers.

Troumpeta, S. 2001. *Constructing Identities for the Muslims of Thrace – the Example of Pomaks and Roma* [in Greek]. Athens: Ekdoseis Kritiki.

Tsitselikis, K. 2004a. Personal status of Greece's Muslims: A legal anachronism or an example of applied multiculturalism?, in *The Legal Treatment of Islamic Minorities in Europe*, edited by R. Aluffi and G. Zincone. Leuven and Paris: Peeters, 109–32.

Tsitselikis, K. 2004b. The historical structure of the protection of minorities in Greece, in *1953–2003: The Rights in Greece from the End of the Civil War to the End of Metapolitefsi* [in Greek], edited by M. Tsapogas and D. Hristopoulos. Athens: Ekdoseis Kastanioti, 110–23.

Tsitselikis, K. 2007. The pending modernisation of Islam in Greece: From *millet* to minority status. *Südosteuropa*, 55(4), 354–73.

Tyson, A. 2001. The negotiation of the European Community directive on racial discrimination. *European Journal of Migration and Law*, 3, 199–221.

UN. 1995. Beijing Declaration. Available at: www.un-documents.net/beijingd.htm [accessed: 30 July 2010].

UN. 2000. Racial Discrimination, Xenophobia and Related Intolerance, Durban. Declaration 2 [Online: UN General Assembly Report of the World Conference against Racism]. Available at: www.un.org/WCAR/durban.pdf [accessed: 18 July 2010].

UNDP. 2003. *Roma in Central and Eastern Europe: Avoiding the Dependency Trap* [Online]. Available at: http://roma.undp.sk [accessed: 8 October 2009].

UN Economic and Social Council. 2008. Mainstreaming Disability in the Development Agenda, Report for the Commission for Social Development. 46th session, 6–15 February.

UN Office of the High Commissioner for Human Rights. 2001. *Gender Dimensions of Racial Discrimination* [Online]. Available at: http://www.unhchr.ch/pdf/wcargender.pdf [accessed: 8 July 2009].

United Nations. 2002. Report of the Committee on the Elimination of Discrimination against Women [Online: United Nations]. Available at: daccess-ods.un.org/access.nsf/Get?Open&DS=A/57/38(SUPP)&Lang=E [accessed: 30 June 2009].

US Department of Labor. US Bureau of Labor Statistics. 2005. *Women in the Labor Force: A Databook* [Online]. Available at: www.bls.gov/cps/wlf-databook-2005.pdf [accessed: 1 November 2010].

Vakulenko, A. 2007. 'Islamic headscarves' and the European Convention on Human Rights: An intersectional perspective. *Social & Legal Studies*, 16(2), 183–99.

Välimäki, A.L. 1999. *Lasten hoitoapu: Lasten päivähoitojärjestelmä Suomessa 1800– ja 1900–luvulla*. Helsinki: Suomen Kuntaliitto.

Van Bijsterveld, S.C. 2001. Freedom of religion: Legal perspectives, in *Law and Religion*, edited by R. O'Dair and A. Lewis. Oxford: Oxford University Press, 299–309.

Van Boven, T. 2002. *The Committee on the Elimination of Racial Discrimination: Trends and Developments* [Online]. Available at: www.errc.org/cikk.php?cikk=1432 [accessed: 8 July 2009].

Van den Berhe, F. 2001. *'Race' in European Law – an Analysis of Council Directive 2000/43/EC* [Online]. Available at: www.eumap.org/journal/features/2001/oct/racelaw [accessed: 8 July 2009].

van den Brink, M., Jongsma, D. and Luiken, O. 2006. *The (Im)possibilities of an Intersectional Approach under Dutch Equal Treatment Legislation*. Paper to the Conference: Equal is Not Enough. Dealing with Opportunities in a Diverse Society, Antwerp, 13–15 September 2006, unpublished.

Vandenhole, W. 2005. *Non-Discrimination and Equality in the View of the UN Human Rights Treaty Bodies*. Antwerp: Intersentia.

Veldman, A. 2001. Het zwarte gat: Gelijke behandelingswetgeving in de 21e eeuw. *Nemesis*, 33–6.

Verloo, M. 2006. Multiple inequalities, intersectionality and the European Union. *European Journal of Women's Studies*, 13(3), 211–28.

Vernon, A. 1996. A stranger in many camps: The experience of disabled black and ethnic minority women, in *Encounters with Strangers: Feminism and Disability*, edited by Jenny Morris. London: The Women's Press, 48–68.

Vernon, A. 1998. Multiple oppression and the disabled people's movement, in *The Disability Reader. Social Science Perspectives*, edited by T. Shakespeare. London and New York: Cassell, 201–10.

Vernon, A. 1999. The dialectics of multiple identities and the disabled people's movement. *Disability and Society*, 14(3), 385–98.

Vernon, A. 2002. *User-Defined Outcomes of Community Care for Asian Disabled People*. Bristol: The Policy Press.

Vernon, A. and Swain, J. 2002. Theorizing divisions and hierarchies towards a commonality or diversity?, in *Disability Studies Today*, edited by C. Barnes, L. Barton and M. Oliver. Cambridge: Polity Press, 77–97.

Vickers, L. 2006. Is all harassment equal? The case of religious harassment. *Cambridge Law Journal*, 65(3), 579–605.

Vickers, L. 2008. *Religious Freedom, Religious Discrimination and the Workplace*. Oxford and Portland, OR: Hart.

Vieten, U.M. 2007. *Situated Cosmopolitanisms; The Notion of the Other in Contemporary Discourses on Cosmopolitanism in Britain and Germany*. PhD Thesis. University of East London.

Vieten, U.M. 2009. Intersectionality scope and multidimensional equality within the European Union: Traversing national boundaries of inequality? in *European Union Non-Discrimination Law*, edited by D. Schiek and V. Chege. London and New York: Routledge-Cavendish, 91–113.

Vieten, U.M. 2011 (forthcoming). Situating contemporary discourses on cosmopolitanism in Britain and Germany: Who is the Other, anyway?, in *The Cause of Cosmopolitanism: Dispositions, Models and Transformations*, edited by P. O'Donovan and L. Rascaroli. Oxford: Peter Lang.

Volpp, L. 2001. Feminism versus multiculturalism. *Columbia Law Review*, 101, 1181–218.

Vosniadou, S. and Vaiou, L. 2006. *The Position of Women in the Academic Staff of the University of Athens* [in Greek]. Paper to the 4th International Conference on History of Education, Patras, 6–8 October 2006 [Online: University of Patras]. Available at: www.elemedu.upatras.gr/eriande/synedria/synedrio4/praktika1/Baiou_bosniadou.htm [accessed: 29 May 2009].

Vourc'h, F., de Rudder, V. and Tripier, M. 2000. *L'inégalité raciste*. Paris: PUF.

Voulgaris, G., Dodos, D., Kafetzis, P., Lyrintzis, C., Michalopoulou, K., Nikolakopoulos, I., Spourdalakis, M. and Tsoukalas, K. 1995. The perception and encounter with the 'Other' in modern Greece. *Elliniki Epitheorisi Politikis Epistimis: Greek Review of Political Science*, 5, 81–100.

Waddington, L. 2007a. Reasonable accommodation, in *Cases, Materials and Text on National, Supranational and International Non-Discrimination Law*, edited by D. Schiek, L. Waddington and M. Bell. Oxford and Portland, OR: Hart, 629–756.

Waddington, L. 2007b. Case C-13/05, Chacón Navas v. Eurest Colectividades SA, judgment of the Grand Chamber of 11 July 2006. *Common Market Law Review*, 44(2), 487–99.

Waddington, L. 2009. Breaking new ground: The implications of ratification of the UN Convention on the Rights of Persons with Disabilities for the European Community, in *The UN Convention on the Rights of Persons with Disabilities – European and Scandinavian Perspectives*, edited by O.M. Arnardóttir and G. Quinn. Leiden: Martinus Nijhoff, 111–40.

Waddington, L. and Lawson, A. 2009. *Disability and Non Discrimination Law in the European Union: An Analysis of Discrimination Law Within and Beyond the Employment Field* [Online:

European Commission]. Available at: www.migpolgroup.com/public/docs/Disabilitynon-discriminationlawEU.pdf [accessed: 17 June 2010].

Walby, S., Armstrong, J. and Humphreys, L. 2008. *Review of Equality Statistics*. Manchester: Equality and Human Rights Commission.

Walker, L. and Monahan, J. 1987. Social frameworks: A new use of social science in law. *Virginia Law Review*, 73(3), 559–98.

Ward, I. 2006. Headscarf stories. *Hastings Int'l & Comparative Law Review*, 29, 315–41.

Warner, M. 1991. Introduction: Fear of a queer planet. *Social Text*, 9(4), 3–17.

Weber, M.C. 2007. *Disability Harassment*. New York and London: New York University Press.

Weil, P. 2005. *La République et sa Diversité*. Paris: Seuil.

Weller, M. (ed.) 2005. *The Rights of Minorities: A Commentary on the European Framework Convention for the Protection of National Minorities*. Oxford: Oxford University Press.

Whittle, R. 2002. The framework directive for equal treatment in employment and occupation: An analysis from a disability rights perspective. *European Law Review*, 27(3), 303–26.

Wieviorka, M. 2002. Race, culture, and society: The French experience with Muslims, in *Muslim Europe or Euro-Islam – Politics, Culture, and Citizenship in the Age of Globalisation*, edited by N. AlSayyad and M. Castells. Lanham: Rowman & Littlefield, 131–45.

Wiles, E. 2007. Headscarves, human rights, and harmonious multicultural society: Implications of the French ban for interpretations of equality. *Law & Society Review*, 41(3), 699–736.

Wilkin, T. 2003. The seeds are sown in childhood, in *Adult Obesity: A Paediatric Challenge*, edited by L. Voss and T. Wilkin. London: Taylor & Francis, 39–49.

Williams, N. 2008. *Managing Obesity in the Workplace*. Abingdon: Radcliffe Publishing.

Wilpert, C. 2003. Racism, discrimination and citizenship: The need for anti-discrimination legislation in the Federal Republic of Germany, in *Challenging Racism and Discrimination in Britain and Germany*, edited by Zig Layton-Henry and Czarina Wilpert. Basingstoke: Palgrave Macmillan.

Wilpert, C. and Howe, C. 2008. GendeRace – The use of racial anti-discrimination laws: Gender and citizenship in a multicultural context, State of the Art Report, ANNEX 4, Germany Country Report.

Wimmer, A. 2008. Elementary strategies of ethnic boundary making. *Ethnic and Racial Studies*, 31(6), 1025–55.

Wing, A.K. 2001. Polygamy from southern Africa to black Britannia to black America: Global critical race feminism as legal reform for the twenty-first century. *Journal of Contemporary Legal Issues*, 11(2), 811–80.

Wing, A.K. 2008. Twenty-first century loving: Nationality, gender, and religion in the Muslim world. *Fordham Law Review*, 76(6), 2895–906.

Witt, D. 1999. *Black Hunger: Food and the Politics of US Identity*. New York: Oxford University Press.

Witte, J. 2006. Facts and fictions about the history of separation of church and state. *Journal of Church and State*, 48, 15–46.

Xanthaki, A. 2005. Hope dies last: An EU Directive on Roma integration. *European Public Law*, 11(4), 515–26.

Xanthaki, H. 2001. The problem of duality in EU legislation: What on earth is really wrong? *Common Market Law Review*, 38, 651–76.

Yazbeck Haddad, Y. (ed) 2002. *Muslims in the West – From Sojourners to Citizens*. Oxford: Oxford University Press.

Yoshino, K. 2002. Covering. *Yale Law Journal*, 111, 769–938.

Yotopoulou-Marangopoulou, A. 1998. The historical turn of the Council of State towards factual equality. Comment on the decisions 1933/98 and 1917–1929/1998 of the Council of State [in Greek]. *To Syntagma*, 4, 773–92.

Young, I.M. 2009. Structural injustice and the politics of difference, in *Intersectionality and Beyond*, edited by E. Grabham, D. Cooper, J. Krishnadas and D. Herman. Abingdon and New York: Routledge-Cavendish, 273–98.

Yuracko, K.A. 2006. Trait discrimination as race discrimination: An argument about assimilation. *George Washington Law Review*, 74(3), 365–438.

Yuval-Davis, N. 1997. *Gender and Nation*. London: Sage.

Yuval-Davis, N. 2004. Borders, boundaries and the politics of belonging, in *Ethnicity, Nationalism and Minority Rights*, edited by S. May, T. Modood and J. Squires. Cambridge: Cambridge University Press, 214–30.

Yuval-Davis, N. 2006. Intersectionality and feminist politics. *European Journal of Women's Studies*, 13(3), 193–209.

Yuval-Davis, N. 2007. Intersectionality, citizenship and contemporary politics of belonging. *Critical Review of International Social and Political Philosophy*, 10(3), 561–74.

Yuval-Davis, N. and Anthias, F. (eds) 1989. *Woman – Nation – State*. London: Macmillan.

Yuval-Davis, N., Anthias, R. and Kofman, E. 2005. Secure borders and safe haven and the gendered politics of belonging: Beyond social cohesion. *Ethnic and Racial Studies*, 28(3), 513–53.

Zappone, K. (ed.) 2003. *Re-thinking Identity – the Challenge of Diversity* [Online: Joint Equality and Human Rights Forum]. Available at: www.ihrc.ie/download/pdf/rethinking_identity_the_challenge_of_diversity.pdf [accessed: 15 July 2010].

Zine, J. 2003. *Staying on the 'Straight Path': A Critical Ethnography of Islamic Schooling in Ontario*, unpublished PhD thesis (quoted by Hamdan 2007).

Zinsmeister, J. 2007. *Mehrdimensionale Diskriminierung Das Recht behinderter Frauen auf Gleichberechtigung und seine Gewährleistung durch Art. 3 GG und das einfache Recht*. Baden-Baden: Nomos.

Zweigert, K. and Kötz, H. 1998. *An Introduction to Comparative Law*. 3rd edition. Oxford: Clarendon Press.

Index